## MURDEROUS ALLIANCE

"Go out," the Frenchman told them. "Spread yourselves through the whole country as far as you can go. Take scalps. Kill the English, all of them. Kill them in any way you like—with club or gun, knife or tomahawk. Torture them with fire and coals. Burn their houses, destroy their livestock, destroy all they own. Drive them back to the sea-cities, and there our armies will come and finish the destruction. Kill them!"

The French command. The Iroquois obey.

## WILDERNESS EMPIRE

Bantam Books by Allan W. Eckert
Ask your bookseller for the books you have missed

**THE FRONTIERSMEN
WILDERNESS EMPIRE
THE CONQUERORS**

# Wilderness Empire

## A Narrative

ALLAN W. ECKERT

BANTAM BOOKS
TORONTO · NEW YORK · LONDON · SYDNEY

WILDERNESS EMPIRE

*A Bantam Book / published by arrangement with
Little, Brown and Company*

### PRINTING HISTORY

*Little, Brown edition published July 1969*
*Bantam edition / October 1971*

| | |
|---|---|
| 2nd printing . September 1974 | 5th printing .. September 1980 |
| 3rd printing .... March 1975 | 6th printing .. September 1980 |
| 4th printing .. February 1979 | 7th printing .. December 1980 |
| 8th printing ... December 1981 | |

*Bantam Books are published by Bantam Books, Inc. Its trade-
mark, consisting of the words "Bantam Books" and the por-
trayal of a rooster, is Registered in U.S. Patent and Trademark
Office and in other countries. Marca Registrada. Bantam
Books, Inc., 666 Fifth Avenue, New York, New York 10103.*

PRINTED IN THE UNITED STATES OF AMERICA

17 16 15 14 13 12 11 10 9

*True and lasting friendship is always a rare commodity, a great blessing, a priceless gift. For the unquestioning and unwavering friendship he has given to me, this book is dedicated with sincere warmth, appreciation and affection to*

HOMER S. RHODE

"*Something in his natural temper responds to Indian ways. The man holding up a spear he has just thrown, upon which a fish is now impaled; the man who runs, with his toes turned safely inward, through a forest where a greenhorn could not walk; the man sitting silent, gun on knee, in a towering black glade, watching by candle flame for the movement of antlers toward a tree whose bark has already been streaked by the tongues of deer; the man who can read a bent twig like an historical volume—this man is William Johnson, and he has learned all these skills from the Mohawks . . .*"

—from the pen of a friend of William Johnson

*Documents Relative to the Colonial History of the State of New York,* Volume VI, p. 741.

# AUTHOR'S NOTE

*Wilderness Empire* is fact, not fiction. Every incident herein described actually occurred; every date is historically accurate; every character, regardless of how major or how minor, actually lived the role in which he is portrayed.

This book is meant to provide an accurate and comprehensive, yet swiftly paced and dramatic picture of the events and people of the time period it covers. It is the result of years of intensive research through a great multitude of original documents, including many hundreds of personal letters, notes and memoranda, diaries, legal papers, military records, journals, depositions, tribal records where they exist, governmental reports, logbooks, newspapers and magazines of the time, and other sources. Nor have modern books of history been excluded for reference.

Within the text there are occasional numbered notes keyed to a Chapter Notes section at the back of the book. These are amplification notes which provide material that is essentially tangential to the subject under discussion but nevertheless of added interest and value in providing the reader with a greater understanding of the events portrayed, and a stronger sense of orientation where geographic locales are concerned.

By far the greater majority of Indians written about in history are referred to by nicknames or clumsy translations of the actual meaning of the Indian name. As a result, there are virtually hundreds of Indians who were known as Billy or Joe, Captain Jack or Delaware George, Colonel Bull or other such nicknames. The great Mohawk chief Tiyanoga, for example, is unfortunately far more familiarly known in history by the somewhat deprecating nickname of Hendrik, and the famous Chief Joseph Brant was actually named Thayendanegea. The Wampanoag chief Metacomet was called King Philip and his brother, Wamsutta, was dubbed Alexander. Catahecassa became known as Black Hoof and his predecessor as principal chief of the Shawnees, Hokolesqua, is more familiar as Chief Cornstalk.

It is my feeling that there is a much greater dignity, in addition to a certain charm and musical ring, to the actual Indian names. Therefore I have endeavored, wherever possible in this volume, to refer to the Indians by their own true names. Admittedly, many of these names appear unpronounceable at first glance, but such is not really the case. To aid the reader in this respect, at the back of the book is a listing by tribe of all the Indian characters who appear herein and, where necessary, these names are also spelled phonetically for correct pronunciation. Included, as well, is each Indian's rank or status in the tribe and, in some instances, his family relationships.

More dialogue will be found in this narrative than is normally found in a book depicting actual history. It is self-evident that no one can know for certain what any person of the past was thinking or what he said unless his conversation was taken down or he personally wrote or dictated what he said and thought. Nonetheless, all of the dialogue of this narrative is very closely traced and, in large measure, represents what the actual principal, then or later, wrote that he said or thought at the time. Much of this material was not initially recorded as dialogue and is, in a manner of speaking, a form of hidden dialogue. For example, when the trader George Croghan writes in his journal:

*Chief Scarroyaddy is angry and tells me that General Braddock, while professing friendship for the Indians, does not like them and cannot hide this fact from them . . .*

—then I felt fully justified, when depicting the meeting between Scarroyaddy and Croghan, to have the chief approach the trader with a sour expression and say disgustedly, "Your chief of the soldiers tells us with his mouth that he is our friend, but his eyes tell us that this is not true." Similarly, when William Johnson writes to Governor George Clinton and says:

*As soon as I saw Nichus coming, I knew something was very wrong and wished I was home in bed instead of again having to hear him complain about whatever was bothering him now . . .*

—then I again felt justified, as I presented this scene of the chief approaching Johnson, to say that at this moment Johnson thought how nice it would be if he could just be in bed right now instead of having to face whatever was coming.

By all means, certain techniques normally associated with the novel form have been utilized in this book in order to help provide continuity and maintain a high degree of reader interest, but in no case has this been at the expense of historical accuracy. Where dialogue takes place in this book, it is actual quoted conversation from another source, or dialogue reconstructed from the "hidden dialogue" in the manner above described, or—in a few scattered instances— historical fact utilized in the form of conversation to maintain the dramatic narrative pace. There has been no instance of whole-cloth creation of dialogue or fanciful fictionalization.

Even in the case of Indian conversation this is true. The Indian dialogue recorded here has come from the pages or reports by Johnson, Croghan, Weiser, Colden or other individuals closely associated with them and who spoke their language, as well as from the minutes of the many Indian-white councils, and from such unpublished manuscript sources as John E. Coogan's well-researched and valuable work, *"The Eloquence of Our American Indians"*—a dissertation he submitted in partial fulfillment of his Ph. D. degree at Fordham University in 1933.

As further aid to the reader there is, at the back of the book, a chapter-by-chapter listing of the principal sources for the facts, dialogue and possibly controversial information contained in the text. There is also the complete index which will hopefully prove useful.

*Wilderness Empire* is the second volume in the author's projected series entitled *The Winning of America*, of which *The Frontiersmen* was the first volume. The individual books are not dependent upon one another, yet they strongly complement each other, and all contribute to the series' principal theme, which is a presentation of precisely how the white man took North America from the Indians.

Step-by-step this series will move across the continent, showing clearly and in the most fundamentally human terms, how the land was won—through encroachment, warfare, trickery, grant, treachery, alliance, deceit, theft, and treaty.

Too often with such a theme the cause is overshadowed by the act and the act thereupon overemphasized. It is the purpose of this series to penetrate to the initial and most basic causes: the simple meetings between individuals, along with their thoughts and goals and speech as these have been ferreted out from the original documents; the things—often little and, at the time, seemingly insignificant—that were said and done which resulted in events of great historic import.

Many of the characters in *The Frontiersmen* appear, again, here in *Wilderness Empire*—men such as Daniel Boone, Pucksinwah, George Croghan, She-me-ne-to, Simon Girty, and others—just as many characters in both of these books are apt to appear in subsequent volumes of *The Winning of America* series. This is because it is a story that began at the first white contact with the Indians of this continent, and which continued through the centuries until subjugation or extinction of the tribes was total.

It is neither the intention nor the desire of the author to champion the cause of the Indians or that of the whites; there were heroes and rascals on both sides, rights and wrongs on both sides. The facts are presented chronologically, just as they occurred, and with the greatest possible accuracy. There has been no author intrusion, no editorializing. It has not been necessary. The facts speak amply for themselves, and whatever conclusions are drawn must be drawn by the reader himself.

*Englewood, Florida*                                ALLAN W. ECKERT
*February, 1969*

# ILLUSTRATIONS

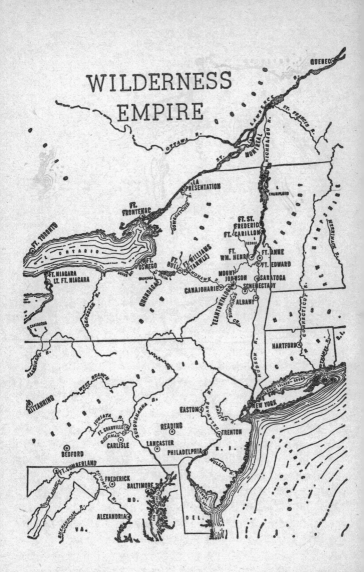

# WILDERNESS
# EMPIRE

QUEBEC

MONTREAL

LA PRESENTATION

FT. FRONTENAC

FT. TORONTO

FT. NIAGARA
LT. FT. NIAGARA

OSWEGO

FT. BULL

FT. WILLIAMS
FT. STANWIX

ONONDAGA

CANAJOHARIE

FT. ST. FREDERIC
FT. CARILLON

FT. WM. HENRY

FT. ANNE

FT. EDWARD

MOUNT JOHNSON

SARATOGA

SCHENECTADY

ALBANY

HARTFORD

KITTANNING

BEDFORD

FT. GRANVILLE

CARLISLE

EASTON

READING

LANCASTER

TRENTON

PHILADELPHIA

NEW YORK

FT. CUMBERLAND

FREDERICK

BALTIMORE

MD.

ALEXANDRIA

VA.

DEL.

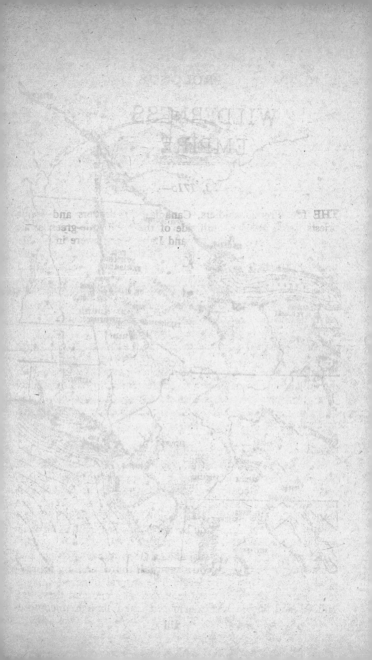

# PROLOGUE

**[ July 23, 1715—Saturday ]**

THE few French soldiers, Canadian fur traders and Jesuit priests living on the south side of the great blue-green strait which joined Lake Michigan and Lake Huron were in a state of excitement. They were overjoyed; happier now than at any time since their enterprises had been thoroughly undermined sixteen years ago. Now, at long last, government officials in Versailles and Paris as well as in Quebec and Montreal were beginning to recognize the commercial importance and military significance of this site called Michilimackinac.[1]

Only a handful of white men were here now. In fact, only a handful had *ever* been here since the Jesuit father Jacques Marquette had established his mission called St. Ignace[2] on the north side of the strait, across from Michilimackinac. That year—1671—had been a proud one for France. It was on June 14 that Sieur de St. Lusson had stood on the banks of the Sault Sainte Marie some fifty miles north of here with his arms upraised in rather grandiose gesture and made his impressive declaration in a loud voice.

"I hereby take possession for France," he had said, "of lakes Superior and Huron and of all other countries, streams, lakes and rivers contiguous and adjacent—those already discovered as well as those yet to be discovered—which are bounded on one side by the seas of the North and of the West, and on the other side by the South Sea, and in all their length and breadth!"

The three Jesuit priests and sixteen other French and Canadians behind him nodded and murmured smiling approval at the well-rehearsed speech. The several hundred Indians in a semicircle behind them took this as a cue and they, too, nodded and smiled and murmured, even though uncompre-

1

hending of what was occurring here. It was well for the white men that these assembled Ottawas, Chippewas and Hurons did not understand. The claim was highly audacious in several respects—mainly in that it ignored the fact that not only did Spain and Great Britain have similar claims on this same vast territory, but that it was in reality a territory owned and occupied by a large number of Indians of native Great Lakes tribes, along with the remnants of other tribes defeated, dispossessed and dispersed by the fierce Iroquois warrior far to the east of here decades ago.

Such was the reason the Jesuits had come originally; that the savages so disrupted might be gathered together and converted to Christianity. The fact that by far the greater majority of those allegedly converted had not the foggiest notion—and cared less—of what they had been converted to, so long as they received gifts from the missionaries, did not daunt the Jesuits in the least.

To strengthen their mission and the growing fur-trading post at St. Ignace, Fort de Buade was erected about 1690 and a smaller fur-trading outpost called Fort St. Joseph[3] was erected the following year on the St. Joseph River, some thirty miles upstream from its mouth near the southeastern edge of Lake Michigan.

All had gone well for the gradually growing French and Canadian settlement around Fort de Buade until a French captain showed up as the new commander of the fort in 1694. At thirty-three he was an aggressive, intelligent and able officer. He was also a great admirer of the governor of Canada, Louis de Buade—the Count Frontenac[4]—who had sent him to take command of this post. He adhered to Frontenac's policies and shared Frontenac's prejudices.

His name was Antoine de la Mothe-Cadillac.

Religion had not fared well at St. Ignace, even though the Jesuits in residence promoted it more stringently than ever. Mainly this was so because the mission had taken something of a back seat to the fur-trading interests. On the whole, the fur traders were Canadians—the rough, uncouth and greatly promiscuous lot often called *coureurs de bois*, meaning bush lopers. Though they permitted the Jesuits to minister to them when they felt they needed it, such feeling was more the exception than the rule. These were men who, though of French forebears, had been born in this wild land. Here they lived, traded and interbred with the Indians to such extent that they were hardly more than Indians themselves.

While Cadillac was not an especially religious man, he

2

nonetheless went out of his way to offer his friendship to the two resident priests, Father Superior Carheil and Father Marest. These two begowned missionaries, however, spurned his offers and instead made him the object of their antipathy. In characteristic manner, Cadillac shrugged at their treatment and responded in kind. The two men of the cloth had picked a formidable adversary.

The beginning of their dislike for him centered about his providing the Indians with liquor—a procedure he had been ordered by his superiors to follow in accordance with the recommendations of authorities of the French court. Any liquor was known to have considerable value in attracting Indians, thereby keeping them allied to the French and preventing the English from securing a toehold in the fur trade. Despite its value, the Jesuits considered the practice immoral. Cadillac, for persisting in the practice in spite of their objections, they considered as a special kind of sinner worthy only of contempt. For drinking it himself with considerable relish and in considerable quantities, they condemned him.

For his own part, Cadillac first tried to ease the matter by establishing an argument for the liquor on dietary grounds. He listened with outward seriousness to the complaints of the Jesuits and then smiled at them disarmingly.

"A little brandy after the meal," he told Father Carheil, upon finishing the usual Fort de Buade meal of fish and smoked meats, "seems necessary to cook the bilious meats and crudities they leave in the stomach."

Carheil was neither convinced nor amused. Living up to Cadillac's private description of him as the most passionate and domineering man he ever knew, the father superior set about actively trying to provoke Cadillac into acts of physical violence against him and thereby have grounds by which to have him removed from command.

"You deserve to be condemned!" Carheil stormed at him one day. "And certainly you should be ashamed of the trade in brandy which you encourage with the Indians."

Cadillac sighed and fell back on his most telling argument: "I only obey the orders of the court."

"You ought to obey God, not man!"

The commander's eyes narrowed and he now addressed Carheil coldly. "Your talk smells of sedition a hundred yards off. I suggest you retract that statement."

It was more than a suggestion; it was an order.

Carheil, now in a blinding rage, shook his bony fist only an

3

inch or so in front of the officer's nose and cried, "You, sir, give yourself airs that do not belong to you!"

Cadillac nearly lost control then. He clenched his own fist and stepped close to Carheil. For a moment he nearly forgot the man was a priest and was on the point of striking him, but then he controlled himself and merely gripped the missionary's arm and propelled him ungently toward the door.

"Get out!" he said tightly, pushing Carheil outside with such force that the father superior's feet became entangled in his flowing robe and he very nearly fell on his face. "And don't come back in here again."

Cadillac told of this incident and others in his report to Frontenac and added, with more than a touch of sarcasm:

*I do what I can to make them my friends, but, impiety apart, one had better sin against God than against them; for in that case one gets one's pardon, whereas in the other the offense is never forgiven in this world, and perhaps never would be in the other, if their credit were as great there as it is here.*

But the animosity they soon shared over the brandy was as nothing compared to that which erupted when it became known that Cadillac was advocating to his superiors the abandonment of Fort de Buade in favor of the erection of a new fort far more strategically placed. By this time the Count Frontenac had died and it was to the Count de Maurepas that Cadillac directed his recommendation. The location he suggested was along the strait—or *detroit*, as it was termed—which separated Lake Huron from Lake Erie. Convinced of the imperative need for France to build a fort at this *detroit*, he wrote to Maurepas:

*It is the most important of all the Western passes and the key to the upper great lakes, with the vast countries watered by their tributaries, and it gives Canada her readiest access to the valley of the Mississippi. If we hold it, the English will be shut out from the Northwest and if, as seems likely, the English should seize it, the Canadian fur trade will be ruined. In addition, our possession of it will be a constant curb and menace to the Five Nations, as well as a barrier between those formidable tribes and the Western Indians, our allies. Think you as well, if the intended French establishment at the mouth of the Mississippi is made, this detroit fort would*

4

*be an indispensable link of communication between Canada and Louisiana.*

There was strong opposition, not only at Fort de Buade and Michilimackinac, but at Montreal as well. The Canadians and their families at Michilimackinac lived wholly or in part by their home trade and were naturally against the establishment of any other post which would necessarily draw away some of their own established business. Even the construction of Fort St. Joseph, small as it was, had had an effect on their economy and they felt that the prosperity of a large new post on the *detroit* of lakes Huron and Erie would be the ruin of Michilimackinac.

Montreal, too, wanted to see no such change, preferring to continue the practice of having the tribes come from the north and west every summer to congregate in the capital, during which time an exciting carnival atmosphere prevailed and a regular fair was held under the palisades of the city. This annual event, it was believed, would cease with the construction of the proposed *detroit* fort, and so they were against it.

Most especially, the Jesuits were against the plan. This was because Cadillac envisioned not only a strong and well-garrisoned fort, but a church as well; one which would be served not only by the Jesuit, but by Récollet friars and priests of the Missions Etrangères. Even the thought of such a partnership was distasteful to the Jesuits, who felt the northwest was their own private domain for converts. They also intensely disliked Cadillac's suggestion that provisions be made at the *detroit* fort to civilize and educate the Indians and especially to teach them to speak the French language. Cadillac wrote:

*It is essential that in this matter of teaching the Indians our language the missionaries should act in good faith, and that His Majesty should have the goodness to impose his strictest orders upon them; for which there are several good reasons. The first and most stringent is that when members of religious orders or other ecclesiastics undertake anything, they never let it go. The second is that by not teaching French to the Indians they make themselves necessary [as interpreters] to the King and Governor. The third is that if all Indians spoke French, all kinds of ecclesiastics would be able to instruct them. This might cause them [the Jesuits] to lose some of the presents they get; for though these Reverend*

5

*Fathers come here only for the glory of God, yet the one thing does not prevent the other. Nobody can deny that the priests own three-quarters of Canada. From St. Paul's Bay to Quebec, there is nothing but the seigneury of Beauport that belongs to a private person. All the rest, which is the greater part, belongs to the Jesuits or other ecclesiastics. The Upper Town of Quebec is composed of six or seven superb palaces belonging to Hospital Nuns, Ursulines, Jesuits, Récollets, Seminary priests, and the bishop. There may be some forty private houses, and even these pay rent to the ecclesiastics, which shows that* the one thing does not prevent the other. *One may as well knock one's head against a wall as hope to convert the Indians in any other way* [than that of civilizing them]; *for thus far all the fruits of the mission consist in the baptism of infants who die before reaching the age of reason.*

This latter remark was not exactly accurate, but there could be no argument that as far as the western Jesuit missions were concerned, the apostolic results had been scant and highly impermanent.

But with the pressure brought upon officials in Montreal and Quebec by the Jesuits and fur traders, it seemed for a time that they would win the battle. Count de Maurepas had relayed Cadillac's plan on to the new governor, Callières, who did not receive it with favor. And the Canadian intendant, Champigny, whose office was the supervision of commerce and finance, was strongly opposed to it, since he was a fast friend of the Jesuits.

Despite this opposition, Cadillac persevered. When a meeting between himself, Champigny and Callières at the Château St. Louis in Quebec proved unsatisfactory, he journeyed to Versailles, France, in the autumn of 1699. There he had a personal interview with the French Colonial Minister, Pontchartrain. He expounded at length on his plan and Pontchartrain saw the wisdom in it, agreed to it at once and commissioned Cadillac to execute it.

Cadillac had won.

Fort de Buade at St. Ignace was quickly abandoned and Fort Pontchartrain was built on the northwest bank of the *detroit* between Lakes Huron and Erie and just below the mouth of smaller Lake St. Clair in July, 1701. Very soon, instead of it being referred to by the fort's proper name, it became known simply as Detroit.

Cadillac found considerable satisfaction in the fact that the dissolution of Fort de Buade and construction of Detroit had almost precisely the effect that the traders and Jesuits of Michilimackinac and St. Ignace had feared. The more northern trading post and mission only barely managed to hang on to a meager existence. The Canadian traders lost their business to Detroit and the Ottawas and Hurons, who made up the bulk of the converts of the Jesuit fathers Carheil and Marest, simply picked up and moved to a new village site close to Detroit. Only two years after the establishment of the place, Cadillac wrote to Pontchartrain:

*Only twenty-five Hurons are left at Michilimackinac for the Reverend Father Carheil and I hope in the autumn I shall pluck this last feather from his wings; and I am convinced that this obstinate priest will die in his parish without one parishioner to bury him.*

But while successful in these endeavors, Cadillac had some significant Indian troubles which presaged further troubles for all Frenchmen with the Indians in times to come. The relationships of the Indians who flocked to Detroit were not always cordial. Resident bands of Hurons, Ottawas and Chippewas[5] established camps or villages in close conjunction to those of the Miami and Potawatomi tribes who had come here from the St. Joseph River area and that of the upper Maumee River. There were also Foxes, Sacs and Mascoutens, along with a few Menominees, who had moved here from the Green Bay area to the west of Lake Michigan. While all these Indian bands got along reasonably well together at first, a rumor suddenly arose and reached the Ottawas that the Hurons and Miamis were concocting a plan to join forces and ambush them. The Ottawas acted first, attacking both Huron and Miami tribesmen. Cadillac, who might possibly have prevented it, since his influence with the Indians was strong, was away at the time. Before he returned, a great deal of blood had been spilled, including that of a Récollet missionary.

When the commander did come back, he immediately made the serious mistake of promising the head of the Ottawa chief to the Miami chief, then did an abrupt turnabout and pardoned the Ottawas. Retaliating in their anger, the Miamis killed three Frenchmen, forcing Cadillac to lead his men against them and make them submit. But the fires of resentment continued to burn in the Miamis and they soon moved south again to their previous villages on the upper

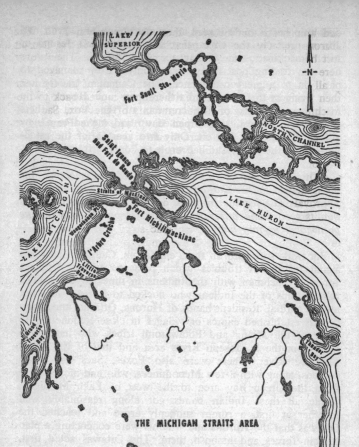

THE MICHIGAN STRAITS AREA

Maumee and the headwaters of the Wabash. One faction even continued down the Wabash to near its mouth at the Ohio River before establishing a new village. Here they openly invited English traders to visit them.

Jesuits and fur traders alike breathed a collective sigh of relief in 1710 when Antoine de la Mothe-Cadillac was sent to govern in Louisiana. It was a premature sigh. The Detroit troubles were not over. The Menominees, angry over the whole business, packed up and went back across Lake Michigan. The Foxes, Sacs and Mascoutens remained, but they were not especially liked by the other tribes around Detroit and war broke out between them in November, 1712. The Hurons and Ottawas were permitted sanctuary in the Detroit fort by the new commandant, Captain Dubuisson, and from here they carried out forays which resulted in the slaughter of all the Green Bay warriors. More than half of the Ottawas then living in the Detroit area thereupon moved back to the Michilimackinac region. The remnants of the Fox, Sac and Mascouten tribes still at Green Bay blamed the French for the carnage and vowed there would come a day of reckoning—another omen for the French enterprises. Now only the Hurons, Potawatomies, part of the Chippewas and about half the Ottawas remained in the vicinity of Detroit.

As they had been doing ever since Cadillac had won approval of his plan and Fort de Buade was dissolved, the Jesuits continued petitioning the government for the reestablishment of a fort at the Mackinac strait. And now, at last, they had been heard and the small French populace still there was overjoyed. A strong picket fortification was being constructed on the south side of the strait, directly across from St. Ignace. It would have a permanent garrison and it would be known by the name of Fort Michilimackinac.

At just about this same time, far to the east across the North Atlantic on the island of Ireland, a child was being born. The first shrill wails filled the air in the Manor of Killeen at Warrenstown, County Meath. The babe was a boy; strong, healthy and, for his size, very loud.

His father was Christopher Johnson, a relative nonentity who was a tenant miller of the Earl of Fingal. Yet, Christopher Johnson had somehow managed to reach far above his mean station to woo, win and wed a lovely girl named Anne Warren, daughter of the owner of this fine stone manor. Now they had a son—their first, after three daughters—and they proudly named him William.

William Johnson.


[ *December 31, 1720—Saturday* ]

Conditions hadn't changed much over the years for the French, the Canadians and the Indians in the upper Great Lakes area since the construction of Fort Michilimackinac. True, strained relations with the various Indian tribes did ease some and the trade in furs was brisk. But there remained a certain reticence among the Indians where these white men were concerned. It was not exactly fear, not exactly distrust, not exactly dislike; yet, it was a peculiar sort

9

of undercurrent melding all of these things which somehow never quite manifested itself. As long as no open hostility was displayed, however, the French were quite willing to maintain cordial relations.

In truth, it went far beyond that. There were many young white men at these nine western forts and a distinct scarcity of young marriageable white women. It was therefore not surprising that a fair number of the Frenchmen took their cue from the Canadian *coureurs de bois* and cohabited with Indian women. Of this number, in fact, there were a good many who took squaws as wives. These marriages in themselves tended to have a cementing effect on French-Indian relations and the immediate concern which prevailed when Fort Michilimackinac was being built that the Indians would ally themselves to the English had gradually diminished over the years.

This was not to say that the French were any less concerned over the territorial aims of Great Britain on this continent. And so, while ostensibly extending their fur-trading posts, the French continued with their program of constructing new forts. They were ever mindful of Cadillac's sensible plan to establish a strong connecting linkage between France's Great Lakes empire and her colony in Louisiana.

Such a linkage would, at the same time, effectively build a fence around the English claims—such as that of Virginia which, by Royal charter, extended all the way from the Atlantic to the Mississippi. A chain of French forts was to make up this linkage and the first to the southwestward of Detroit was one that had been constructed in 1712 among the Miami Indians at the junction of the St. Joseph and St. Mary's rivers, where the Maumee River was formed. This post, named in deference to the Indians of the area, became Fort Miamis.

It was followed in 1713 by the rebuilding and manning of LaSalle's old abandoned Fort St. Louis, which was located on the Illinois River just above the mouth of the Vermilion River. On the west side of Lake Michigan, Fort La Baye was constructed at the southern tip of Green Bay in 1717. The next year another fort was erected—this one far to the north in Lake Superior's Chequamegon Bay. Located on Madeline Island, it was named Fort La Pointe.

Fort Ouiatenon went up the next year almost midway down the length of the Wabash River; and now, this year, another new and highly important fort was built on the east side of the Mississippi almost exactly halfway between the

10

mouths of the Missouri and Ohio rivers and not more than a dozen miles north of where the Kaskaskia River emptied into the muddy Mississippi. It was named Fort de Chartres.[6]

Other forts were planned, but with these nine in existence —Detroit and Forts St. Joseph, Michilimackinac, La Pointe, La Baye, Miamis, Ouiatenon, St. Louis and de Chartres— along with those farther to the east at Niagara and along the St. Lawrence River, France felt content in her belief that her claim to the Great Lakes was well secured.

Though there were some faint rumblings among the Indians about these forts, no definite complaint was made and there was scarcely an Indian in the territory who could truthfully deny that his standard of living had not improved with the coming of these white men. For the furs they gathered during their winters' hunting and trapping, the French gladly traded them items of considerable usefulness and great value in this wilderness—steel knives and tomahawks to replace those of stone; blankets to replace crudely woven reed mats and hides; fine brass kettles instead of heavy, easily broken clay pots; steel needles in place of bone; far superior fabrics to those woven by the Indians themselves; beads for use in wampum belts instead of laboriously drilled bits of stone and mussel shell; and, most importantly, guns and horses. An Indian armed with a gun could hunt far more easily and with better results than with a bow, and mounted on a horse he could travel great distances with relative ease.

Little wonder that the Indians were not only greatly attracted to, but actually became considerably dependent upon, the new French posts. Nor was it any wonder that the biggest, best and most centrally located of these forts—Detroit —continued to be the focal point for so many tribes and the hub of a whole string of new Indian villages thrown up nearby.

One of these, an Ottawa town, was on the same side of the river as Detroit and not more than a mile upstream. It was a curious town in that while it boasted a population of some two hundred men, women and children, there were only ten buildings. In each of these lived anywhere from eighteen to twenty-six Ottawas.

The buildings were placed to form generally straight streetlike areas between them and, though constructed of seemingly frail materials, they were quite sturdy and weatherproof. Decidedly large quonset-type structures, each was upwards of one hundred thirty feet long, twenty feet high and twenty-four feet wide. The erection of one rarely took more than a day or two, with almost the whole population working on it. Very long, straight and limber tree trunks divested of branches and about as thick at the base as a man's lower leg, were sunk in the ground about a dozen feet apart in parallel lines; these uprights were then bent toward one another until they met and lashed together in great arches with tough strips of basswood bark. From arch to arch were then fastened, about a foot apart, poles as thick as a man's wrist. To form a sort of second floor, cross-members were also fixed straight across the span about eight feet off the ground. The whole structure—with the exception of a ventilation slit two feet wide at the top of the arch and running the length of the roof—was covered with interlaced bark and hides to form an amazingly comfortable multiple dwelling with three apartments to each side, and each apartment having sleeping quarters along the wall similar to a line of double bunks. At each end of this "longhouse," as it was called, was a doorway covered with a buffalo hide flap.

It was on the ground floor of one of these apartments this year that a nude Chippewa woman had lain on her back on a spongy, blanket-covered reed matting. Several other women hovered nearby. The fact that she was a Chippewa squaw in an Ottawa dwelling was not too remarkable, since her husband was an Ottawa and she was in the process of delivering his son.

She was happy that the birth time was at hand. When her pregnancy was beyond doubt, her husband had moved her to these quarters and had not bedded with her or even come near her since then. This was Ottawa custom, for it was held that sexual intercourse ruined the nourishment an unborn child received from its mother, causing it to waste away. Further, it was believed that the male fluids might even displace the nourishment and cause the infant's death.

Her face was lightly beaded with perspiration and her body hunched with the spasms of labor, but she made no other sound than something of a whispered grunt at each spasm. Not even when the baby actually came did she cry out, though the squaws attending her, upon seeing that the newborn was a boy, gave vent to a pleased, collective "Ahhhh!" The father would be very proud. Carefully the attending squaws bathed and greased the baby and ministered further to the mother.

For thirty days after her delivery, the mother remained confined and did not see her husband, nor he the infant. On the thirty-first day, however, she returned to their shared quarters, built a fire and was thereby, according to custom, purified.

For three months after that she resumed her normal chores of cooking, gathering firewood and chewing heavy raw buckskin to make it pliable so it could be fashioned into moccasins for her husband's winter wear. Through all this she carried the baby boy with her. At times he was snugly wrapped in cloth strips and tied to a cradleboard to which the father had affixed a miniature bow and arrow. The mother could then, with the aid of a headband, take her baby with her on her back and yet have her hands free for work. At other times she simply carried him without the board inside her robe or waistband.

Not until the end of those four months after the birth of the child was a special ceremony held to name him. It was a family affair, attended by all the relatives and friends of the parents who could be summoned and crowded into one of the spacious rooms. All brought small gifts—cloths or little blankets, soft furry hides of raccoon or skunk, bobcat, fox or lynx. The mother had prepared a feast of raw, half-cooked and fully cooked meats and fish mixed with vegetables in a sort of gruel and as she served each of those present, the baby boy lay naked on a bobcat skin in the center of the room and gurgled. On this day his infancy would officially end. Until now he had been merely a baby, but now he would become a *person*, and there was a great difference.

After serving, the Chippewa mother took a seat and placed the child on her knees. From a wooden bowl she selected a choice bit of meat, chewed it well and then put her mouth over the baby's and forced it in. He sputtered a bit at first at this introduction to solid food, but managed to get some of it swallowed. The assemblage nodded and clapped their hands in approval. The process continued until the small quantity of food in the bowl was gone; and after each bit swallowed by the baby boy, both mother and father raised their voices in unison to a special Ottawa *manitou*—or god—recommending this *person* to him and imploring that god's special protection and guidance throughout this *person's* life.

The meal finished, the Chippewa woman cleaned the child and then held him firmly while, with swift, sure movements, his father perforated the tiny earlobes with a flat bone needle and then inserted little tubes of rolled bark which not only helped stop any bleeding, but which would hold the slit open until it could heal and ornamental beads could replace the

13

sticks. Through all of this the baby only whimpered a little, but the sound became a sharp squealing cry when the Ottawa punctured his son's nasal septum with an awl and then shoved a porcupine quill in the hole, to be left there until the wound healed. After healing, an almost circular stone ornament would be stuck in the gap so that it would hang permanently over the baby's lip. Such an ornament, the Ottawas believed, would ward off any spells future enemies might try to cast over him.

The mother sang soothingly to the babe to quiet him and, amazingly, considering the amount of pain he had undergone and the quantity of blood still running down his face, the child ceased his wailing almost at once and again the approving nods of heads followed.

"*Obwon*," said the father proudly. The prefix "*O*" being an Ottawa pronoun meaning "he is" and the "*bwon*" meaning "stopping it"—"He is stopping it"—referring to the cries. The letters "*bw*" in the word had the same sound as the letter "p," so that phonetically, the word had the sound of "*Oh-pahn*."

"*Obwon*," agreed the mother, and this same word was repeated numerous times among the onlookers.

An aged man to one side, toothless and frail, raised his hand and then got slowly to his feet. This was the grandfather of the child's father, and a greatly respected man. His name was Diyag, but since the letter "D" in the Ottawa tongue has the same sound as the letter "T," these two consonants are considered to be identical and his name was therefore pronounced "Tee-yag."

The old man waited as the murmur of the crowd stilled and then he looked down at his tiny great-grandson. He tapped his own bony chest with a skeletal finger and said, "*Diyag*," then pointed at the babe and said, "*Obwon—Obwon Diyag!*"

The father of the child placed his hands on the old man's shoulders and smiled with pleasure that his son should be so honored as to be offered the name of his respected great-grandfather. It was a good name for his son and he repeated it aloud several times: "*Obwondiyag . . . Obwondiyag . . . Obwondiyag.*" He ran the two words together and it came out with the sound of "*Oh-pahn-tee-yag.*"

And so was born and named the Ottawa Indian henceforth to be known as Pontiac.[7]

# CHAPTER I

[June 2, 1730—Tuesday]

CLOSE to the impressive stone Killeen Manor at Warrenstown, Ireland, fifteen-year-old William Johnson had few illusions about his place in the world. He knew it was unlikey that he would ever get very far from County Meath but, with the independent nature of the young, he wasn't particularly concerned about it. His life here in the crude tenant farmhouse within sight of his grandfather's great house was quite comfortable; certainly not as fine and luxurious and exciting as the life led by the youngsters of the manor house—children whose name was Warren or something equally respectable—but unquestionably better than the son of a tenant miller might normally have expected, especially in these times.

Christopher Johnson, his father, was by no means an ambitious or even very energetic individual. He never quite got over his sense of awe at being a part, even though a patently unwelcome part, of the Warren family through his marriage to Anne Warren. But he was thankful for it more than anyone really knew for, had not the opportune wedding taken place, he might now himself be counted among the rapidly rising numbers of beggars roaming Erin's countryside —men who desperately wanted to work the land but who had been forced out by landlords through a queer form of injustice.

Christopher Johnson was, as were so many of his tenant contemporaries, a Catholic. As such, he was forbidden by English law to purchase land and forced to be content at eking out a living as tenant of one of the rich Irish landlords. As if that were not enough, the law also forbade Catholics to rent any land on a lease longer than thirty-one years.

Though Johnson's grist mill was located at Killeen Manor, it was not a good enough business to support his family of

15

seven children—including the first three daughters and William, plus three more sons born after William—and so he rented from the Earl of Fingal a plot of one hundred ninety-nine acres. The lease had run out last year after the thirty-one year period and, probably because his in-laws were wealthy Warrens, he had been able to renew the lease without difficulty.

The lease limit was an effective, if cruel, damper on any form of tenant ambition. Few, if any, Irish landlords would do anything to help or encourage their tenants. Should the tenant himself display the ambition to improve his leased property, these improvements would automatically revert to the landlord when the lease expired. To get it renewed, the unfortunately ambitious tenant would find that the rent had risen considerably. After all, the landlord would claim, wasn't the property a better one now than when you first rented it? And so the homes of the tenants were ramshackle at best and commonly built to last, with luck, for just thirty-one years.

Few, indeed, were the landowners who still maintained their residence here; they left their manors under the care of overseers and spent their months and years enjoying the opulent life in London as hangers-on to the coattails of George II, who had risen to his seat on the imperial throne at the death in June, three years past, of King George I.

Such a life, while undeniably pleasant, was also costly for the absentee landlords and so their overseers found themselves in receipt of ever-increasing demands for cash to be sent. To economize at home, the overseers themselves began evicting tenant farmers and installing huge flocks of sheep where farms had been. So the dusty, narrow, rock-walled roads of Ireland grew ever more crowded with gaunt beggars who managed to live, but just barely.

Therefore, while Christopher Johnson's lot was not good, as no Catholic's was in Ireland, neither was it anywhere near as bad as it could have been. He was reasonably successful at overlooking the matter-of-course favors bestowed on the Warren children which somehow never materialized for the Johnson youngsters. While the Warren children, with their parents, frequently lived high with relatives in England, the Johnsons wandered about their poor farm and badly deteriorating mill, not quite sure what to do with themselves and, as far as young William was concerned not much caring.

It took no great power of deduction for William Johnson to see that the only people who could stay in the British Empire and remain Catholics were peasants, priests, and martyrs. And since the laws denied any kind of advancement to Catholics, the youth cheerfully abandoned the Catholic religion. He had never been especially devout anyway, and so he simply retained a vague belief in God and outwardly adopted the precepts of the Church of England.

He applied himself in a desultory manner to his studies and learned to read and write in a fashion that might have appalled a grammarian but which nonetheless informed him and put across to others the points he wished to make. After a brief stint at the mill helping his father, he gradually drifted away from such labors and mingled with people anywhere who would put up with him.

His failing—if failing it was at all—was just now making itself known: he loved girls, anywhere, any time. Already it was coming to be said that: "The chaste girl chased by William Johnson is soon not chaste at all!"

By and large, it was true. He was developing an enormous appetite for sex and, since he was big for his age and quite handsome, the girls were attracted to him almost as much as he to them. He was close to six feet tall already and had thick dark hair and a swarthy complexion. His mood could change in an instant and his eyes, which would appear a warm, dark hazel when he was romping in a haystack with a maiden, could very swiftly drain of color when anger struck him and seem to become a cold and smoky gray.

As he grew older his personality made him a standout in any crowd and both men and women gathered around him wherever he was and followed his lead in whatever he did. And whatever he did—riding, running, hunting, fighting—he did uncommonly well. His imagination was prodigious and his capacity for liquor matched his capacity for women whose voices were husky with desire.

He was something of a paradox, a young man of sharply defined contrasts. His affection and tenderness were matched by an explosive and often unbridled temper; his innate generosity and kindness matched, when called for, by bursts of disruptive violence. His companions, both male and female, had they attempted to foresee his future, might have been unanimous in their agreement that he was going somewhere.

At the moment, however, young William Johnson had no place to go.

[ *December 31, 1730—Thursday* ]

To his own parents and perhaps to others of his tribe, the

ten-year-old Ottawa boy, Pontiac, might have been considered attractive, but this was a feeling hardly shared by the Frenchmen of Detroit who occasionally saw him, or those Canadians on outlying farm plots who saw him more frequently.

He was of average height for his age and his somewhat slight build was only what might have been expected, since neither of his parents were especially large. His body had been garishly tattooed in designs of squares and diamond shapes on his chest, arms and legs. Where not tattooed, much of his flesh had been painted in odd whorls, zig-zags, diagonals and straight lines of yellow, red, blue and white. Now, as usual, much of this paint was worn away and he would soon need redecorating.

A loop of white porcelain beads hung from each earlobe. In his nose was a crescent-shaped stone worked to a smooth whiteness, its points just reaching the corners of his mouth. His hair was already being trimmed in standard Ottawa warrior style: a brushlike cut so that the hair above the forehead stood straight on end, perhaps an inch high, and then tapering in height toward the rear until at the back of the crown it was trimmed almost to the skin.

"This," his father had told him when it was first being trimmed with a knife honed to razor sharpness, "is so an enemy you may encounter cannot reach out to grip your hair and hold you while he plunges knife or tomahawk into your chest or breaks your head with his war club."

Pontiac was, of course, completely naked in the summer, as were all the boys and men. Only the women and girls regularly wore a sort of breechcloth which hung down in front from just below the navel to mid-thigh and was no more than six or seven inches wide. In winter all of them, men, women and children, wore whatever was necessary and whatever they could find to ward off the cold. In the men this usually amounted to a long coat of fur, buckskin pants and moccasins, but just as often it was an odd assortment of trade clothing: old shirts, nondescript trousers and the like, procured from the French traders. The women and children bundled up mainly in blankets and furs.

Pontiac was, in all respects but one, just about like any other Ottawa boy. The single exception was his eyes. They were deep, penetrating, extremely alert and gave the appearance of mirroring a keen mind. He missed little that went on and was already, among the youths of his age group, a leader in their games and hunts.

At the age of three he had been given a tiny bow which shot stiff straws and he had played with it and practiced with it for weeks and months. From this he graduated at age six to a stronger bow and arrows of light wood and his practice at marksmanship continued. Now he had a strong bow of osage wood and good arrows with flint and bone tips, and his aim with them was deadly. He could stop a rabbit in full run, impale a scampering squirrel to the trunk of a tree and even shoot occasional birds on the wing—mostly ducks and pigeons.

An avid student of woodcraft, Pontiac was already well enough versed in nature lore to sustain himself in the wilderness, if necessary, with or without any weapons. And, while the bow was for the moment his principal weapon in hunting, he was also becoming remarkably skilled in the use of the tools and weapons of both his people and the white men: guns and steel tomahawks, hunting knives, steel traps, fish nets, snares, deadfalls and the like. He was quick to see how far superior the French material objects were to those so laboriously and crudely crafted by his people.

It was with his bow, the French tomahawk and the knife that he would, next spring, accompany an Ottawa war party far to the south, to the other side of the great watercourse called *Spay-lay-wi-theepi* by the Indians and Ohio River by the English. There, if the proper gods had recognized and approved of their offerings and sacrifices, they might encounter individuals or parties from southern tribes—Cherokees or Choctaws, Natchez or even Upper Creeks—engage them in combat and return home victorious with scalps and equipment and perhaps some new slaves.

His education in matters pertaining to the Ottawa tribe was a family concern and his instruction was constant, given at any waking hour and so deeply implanted that the history of his race, tribal politics and warfare, economics, religion and medicine were memorized faultlessly and adhered to without deviation.

And now, for the first time, Pontiac was being permitted to sit in silent attendance at tribal council meetings and listen, with excitement and a tinge of fear, to news of his village, his tribe, other tribes and white men; to hear serious discussions of hunting and fishing and intertribal warfare; to listen while the men of his village or those of his entire tribe—including villages at Michilimackinac and elsewhere—discussed and pondered the benefits and problems that were

19

created by the encroaching whites. Already he could see that the problems far outweighed the benefits.

Off to the east and south, a speaker related, the Delawares were on the move again. Disunited and pushed out of their native coastal lands by the whites, they had been forced to resettle in the valleys of the Lehigh and Delaware rivers. Here they had been easily conquered by the fierce Iroquois and were subject to the will and whim of that confederation in all matters. Now, though some were remaining there in continued subjection, others were beginning to migrate still farther to the west to settle along the Allegheny and Monongahela rivers or even the upper Ohio, striving to get themselves out of the reach of both the Iroquois League and the ever-expanding English settlement. Some Delaware villages had already moved as far as the heartland of the Ohio country, in the valleys of the Muskingum and Tuscaroras and Walhonding rivers. At the same time the Shawnees from the western Pennsylvania and Virginia lands were moving into the same Ohio country, farther down along the great *Spaylay-wi-theepi* and up into the valleys of the Scioto River and its tributaries.

These matters and more the Ottawa councils discussed at length. It was rumored as well that in the lower Great Lakes country, especially from the Niagara River eastward through Lake Ontario and into the St. Lawrence valley, something of a showdown was forming between the French and English. While no person at the council was quite sure what this might mean to the Ottawa tribe, none had any doubt that they would be in some way affected.

To the north, it was reported, members of their own tribe at Michilimackinac, who had for years been contemplating a move of their village to some new site, had still reached no decision. More and more Chippewa were moving into the area, they too having been attracted by the trading post there. Their own village nearby was permanent and steadily growing larger and, though relations were good between the two tribes, the Ottawas were beginning to feel too crowded.

Just this year two new villages had been constructed by the Potawatomies here close to Detroit with a total population of nearly five hundred, and several other permanent Potawatomi villages had formed near the trading post at Fort St. Joseph.

Pontiac listened raptly, amazed at how quickly things seemed to be changing, how this world was not the same as it had been even as short a time as two or three years ago. He frowned slightly and, in a habit of long standing, flicked his tongue out to touch in turn the tips of the stone crescent hanging from his nose. The lad was already recognizing the strong influence of the whites and the changes they wrought as they increased in numbers.

Just as a matter of course, the English had always looked upon the French as intruders in North America. More and more they were becoming alarmed at the realization of a French empire fencing off the back doors of their colonies to such extent that the Frenchmen had even erected cedar crosses as boundary markers, and one colonial governor in classic understatement remarked that, "The French are on our lakes and their claims there might be very inconvenient to us."

Governor Keith of the Pennsylvania Colony was openly urging that the French be interrupted in their designs. Not long after that—just three years ago, in fact—the English outpost at the mouth of the Onondaga River on Lake Ontario was greatly refurbished, greatly strengthened and named Fort Oswego.[8] To the French, who considered all the Great Lakes theirs, this was an act of provocation and the two powers were abruptly on what seemed to be an inevitable collision course over who should have control of the lower Great Lakes and, for that matter, all of the Great Lakes territory.

Pontiac, of course, knew nothing of this. Even the warriors and chiefs of his tribe could not yet comprehend the enormity of the situation as it now stood. But to the French and English strategists, the whole picture was becoming only too clear: France held the chief anchors of defense against British pressure and the key to the entire Great Lakes system with such forts as those at Niagara and Detroit and Michilimackinac.

[ *August 4, 1733—Saturday* ]

Though French and English relations became ever more strained, by some miracle open warfare was still avoided. But each side was continuing to prepare for the conflict they felt must eventually come. The French were erecting yet another fort on the Wabash River, far downstream from Fort Ouiatenon. It was located roughly one hundred miles upstream from where that river emptied into the Ohio and only a short distance above where the Embarrass River joined the Wabash. In honor of its builder and first commanding officer, it

21

was named Vincennes, though frequently called Port St. Vincent. From here, hopefully, the lower Miamis could be encouraged to forget the injury handed them by Cadillac three decades ago and renew their friendship with France.

Now more than ever the French were being generous to the Indians, showering them with a multitude of promises and a substantial number of gifts. It was becoming patently clear that in the conflict looming, the side with Indian support would have an obvious advantage. Such Indian support was readily available to the French in the areas of the St. Lawrence River and the upper Great Lakes: the Abnakis, Algonkins, Caughnawaga Mohawks, Micmacs, Etechemins and Nipissings were all solid French allies; the Hurons, Ottawas, Chippewas, some of the Miamis, the Kaskaskias, Cahokias, Kickapoos, Menominees and others leaned directly toward the French.

Where the tribes more accessible to the English were concerned, however, the French were having troubles, particularly with the Iroquis League which was familiarly known as the Six Nations[9]—made up of the Oneidas, Senecas, Cayugas, Onondagas and Mohawks, plus a relatively new addition to the League, the Tuscaroras.

Both French and British were doing all they could to get this powerful league allied to them and, at the moment, neither were having any real measure of success. The idea of being used by one white force against another was repugnant to the Six Nations and they preferred to maintain a neutrality and let the whites settle their own problems. Nevertheless, both white parties redoubled their efforts in this important matter and the Iroquois welcomed their emissaries, not at all loath to take the gifts showered upon them in the efforts to win support.

In New York Colony, however, there were a number of men who were far more interested in the Iroquois for what they could get out of them for private gain than for striking up an alliance. One of these was no less a notable than New York's royal governor, William Crosby, in Albany.

With a group of associates he conceived an incredible plan and then set about putting it into effect. Unwilling to jeopardize his position with the scheme, he cast about with a practiced eye until he detected what he was sure was more than just a tinge of larceny in one Captain Walter Butler. Happily for Crosby, Butler just happened to be commandant of His Majesty's remote military outpost, Fort Hunter,[10] located at the mouth of Schoharie Creek where it joined the Mohawk River. He sent for Butler at once.

When Butler presented himself at the Governor's quarters. Crosby welcomed him inside and introduced him to Arie, the dark, silent Mohegan Indian who had some time ago attached himself to the governor. Crosby poured himself and Butler a drink, motioned the officer to a chair and then wasted no time getting down to business.

"Captain," he said, "the land surrounding Fort Hunter to the south of the Mohawk and east of Schoharie Creek is good land, is it not?"

"Yes sir," Butler replied, "some of it is better than good. A fair portion is already cleared and the soil is excellent. Much of it, though, is hilly and covered with forest."

Crosby, a victim of tuberculosis, nodded. He paused a moment to cough dreadfully and stain a fresh silken handkerchief. He then continued casually: "How would you like to own some of it; a great deal of it?"

Walter Butler's brow furrowed slightly. "It is already owned, sir. By the Corporation of Albany." He appeared surprised that the governor did not know of the treaty made by that private land company some years previously with the Iroquois for that area.

"Have you ever seen their deed to it, Captain?"

A light of comprehension dawned in the eyes of the officer and he shook his head. Crosby smiled and continued, "Neither have I. Now, are you interested in becoming a landowner?"

Still not speaking, Butler nodded and Crosby's smile became a grin. He had, indeed, picked the right man. From his desk he withdrew a large sheet of parchment, obviously a legal document, and for the next hour or so went over it in detail with Butler.

One week later, astride a fine horse and leading two heavily laden packhorses, Butler reached Fort Hunter. It was a disreputable, crumbling, rectangular structure with walls of sagging horizontal logs rather than upright pickets. It was so low and decrepit that in many places a strong running leap might carry a man entirely over it. Blockhouses marked either end and from its platform atop one wall, a single small cannon was positioned with its barrel set in the general direction of another wooden fortlike enclosure quite close-by. This palisade of sorts surrounded a number of long, low, rickety structures made of bark and, in general shape, not unlike those multiple residences built by the Ottawas near

Detroit. This was Teantontalogo,[11] the lower Mohawk town or "castle," as such a stockaded Indian village was called.

Immediately upon entering Fort Hunter, Captain Butler dispatched a messenger to Teantontalogo, inviting the chiefs and their followers to a big party. Smelling gifts in the wind, the Indians accepted with alacrity and that evening great quantities of rum flowed, the majority of it being deposited inside the Indians, especially the chiefs. With great friendliness and magnanimity, Butler presented the chiefs and warriors with many fine knives and excellent blankets. About the time that the chiefs were drunkenly proclaiming him their greatest friend among the white men, Butler produced the parchment that had been given to him by Crosby.

He huddled with the chiefs and explained with remarkable nebulosity what the pen scratchings meant, emphasizing that it was a document of lasting peace between the English and the Mohawks. One by one he handed the three principal chiefs of this village the document, along with a quill pen; and one by one, their hands clumsied by the effects of rum, the three sketched on the bottom the symbols of three of the clans of which the Mohawk nation was composed—the Turtle, the Bear, and the Wolf.

Then Butler himself took the pen and wrote beside each symbol, as best he could translate it into English letters, the name of the signer, followed by the legal terminology: "His mark."

With incredible ease, Captain Walter Butler had just secured a Mohawk deed for a staggering eighty-six thousand acres of mostly timbered land on the south side of the river bearing the tribe's name.

When, a few weeks later, the transaction became publicly known, the Corporation of Albany was distressed. Logically, they appealed to the governor, declaring that they owned the land in question, having received a previous deed from the Mohawks for it, and that Captain Butler had no right to it. Crosby was prepared for the protestations. When he exhibited doubt that such a deed existed in favor of the Corporation of Albany, it was delivered to his quarters as proof.

That was a blunder.

Crosby, without looking at it, handed it to Arie and bade him throw it into the fire, which Arie did. The parchment curled and burned to a blackened crisp. Crosby could now take oath to the fact that he had never seen any deed giving the Corporation of Albany title to the lands in question.

The governor smiled at the successful consummation of his

plan. His associates and Butler now owned the eighty-six thousand acres of land and Crosby's own share in the matter was the cream of the lot—fourteen thousand acres right where Schoharie Creek joined the Mohawk River.

One of the governor's associates in this matter happened to be James Delancey, member of one of New York's richest and most influential merchant families. Delancey was not only a friend, he was also Governor Crosby's chief justice. Furthermore, his sister, Susannah, had just celebrated her second wedding anniversary to a thirty-year-old captain of a major English warship. The naval officer's name was Peter Warren and when, in only a short time, the consumption carried the governor off to his grave, it was without difficulty that young Captain Warren picked up ownership of Crosby's fourteen thousand acres for the moderate price of a hundred and ten pounds.

And Peter Warren just happened to be the uncle of an eighteen-year-old lad in Ireland whom he had never even seen. It was a fascinating set of circumstances, since the lad in question lived in County Meath and his name was William Johnson.

### [ March 3, 1735—Sunday ]

Despite the potential threat of the crescent-shaped French empire solidifying at their backs, many of the English colonial leaders could not envision any real peril to come. So long had the supposed war threat with France hung over them that they were becoming inured to its presence, accepting it with blandness or apathy. But there were those few who continued to shrill their warnings at the expense of being branded war-seekers.

Colonel William Byrd of Westover, in Massachusetts Colony, was among the latter. An extremely successful merchant trader and planter, he was possessed of a foresight gravely lacking in many of the bewigged colonial authorities.

"I perceive," he warned bleakly, "that the French designs are soon to include the whole of this continent to the west of the Alleghenies, including those territories already in the charters of Connecticut and Virginia and others of our colonies. There is no doubt in my mind that the French will endeavor to control the mountain passes and, of greatest concern to us, to establish an active alliance with the Indians of that vast region.

"These inducements to the French," he added, "make it

prudent for a British ministry to be watchful and prevent their seizing this important barrier. In order, wherewith, it may be proper to employ some fit person to reconnoiter these mountains very diligently in order to discover what mines may be found there, as likewise to observe what nations of Indians dwell near them and where lie the most considerable passes, in order to their being secured by proper fortifications."

It was a statement inbued with considerable foresight but, unfortunately, few listened to Byrd and even fewer yet believed what he had to say.

## [ *April 9, 1737—Saturday* ]

The deed to some of the Pennsylvania lands which William Penn had acquired nearly five decades ago from the chiefs of the Delaware tribe was an ambiguous one to say the least. It was a deed hastily and somewhat fearfully drawn. Though the Delawares were occupying part of the land they were selling, their possession of it was only through the grace of the Iroquois, their conquerors, who permitted them to stay there. Thus, considerable care was taken by the Delaware chiefs to insure that knowledge of the sale did not reach the Six Nations.

According to the deed, the Proprietary of Pennsylvania had been given title to lands to the west of the Delaware River with the words: ". . . as far as a man can go in a day and a half." By this the Delawares had actually meant a brisk march of perhaps thirty miles as a maximum figure. The Proprietaries, however—the Penn family, whom the Indians called *Onas*—preferred to interpret it their own way.

Now, with diligent care, they prepared a trail which was straight and clear and then, at a minute after midnight on the appointed day, started a highly trained runner off on it. For thirty-six hours he ran and when at the end of that time he finally collapsed with his heart seemingly ready to burst from his chest, he had covered the respectable distance of one hundred fifty miles. This, then, was the western boundary the Proprietaries claimed for their deed.

The Delawares screamed with rage and at once, without thinking ahead very well, appealed for help to their overlords, the Iroquois.

Results came fast and representatives of both the Proprietaries and the Delawares were ordered by the Iroquois council to set forth their claims. Since the whites had not shown especial interest in the area before, this was the first intimation the Iroquois received that this land in question was deeded to Penn a half century ago by the Delawares in a secret deal. Their resultant rage as they studied the evidence was fearful to behold. A closed council of chiefs was called at Onondaga,[12] the capital village of the Iroquois League, at the southern tip of Lake Onondaga. When at last a decision was reached, a general council was called, attended by the Delaware chiefs and the Proprietaries and presided over by Canassatego and Red Head, the Onondaga chiefs.

A tall, unusually well-built man with broad chest and very muscular arms and legs, Canassatego stood before the assemblage with two belts of wampum in his grasp. These belts—or strings, as they were often called—had been made specifically for this talk and would serve as permanent records to what would transpire here.

The Delaware chiefs and their followers, grouped to one side of the great company of Iroquois on hand, stood silently and a trifle fearfully as Canassatego turned toward them and handed them one of the belts. It was about four feet long and seven or eight inches wide, its background color a deep purplish-gray and a whole series of designs and figures woven into it which were incomprehensible to the white men in attendance.

Having handed them this wampum belt, Canassatego resumed his previous stance and then in a moment the entire audience stilled to hear his speech. He looked toward the Delawares with an expression of open contempt and anger.

"Cousins, let this belt of wampum serve to chastise you! You ought to be taken by the hair of the head and shaken severely till you recover your senses and become sober. You don't know what ground you stand on or what you are doing!"

He stretched out his right arm and pointed toward the Proprietaries, but kept his stern gaze on the Delawares. "Our brother *Onas's* cause is very just and plain and his intentions are to preserve friendship." The extended arm swung and an accusing finger now pointed at the Delawares. "On the other hand, your cause is bad, your heart far from being upright, and you are maliciously bent to break the Chain of Friendship with our brother *Onas* and his people."

He moved his pointing finger toward his own face and continued, "We have seen with our eyes a deed signed by nine of your ancestors about fifty summers ago, for this very

27

land, and a release signed not many summers past by some of yourselves and chiefs now living, to the number of fifteen or upwards."

Canassatego slapped his hand down to his side and shook his head angrily. "But how came you," he asked the Delawares, "to take it upon you to sell land at all? We conquered you! We made women of you! You *know* you are women and can no more sell land than women. Nor is it fit you should have the power of selling lands, since you would abuse it.

"This land that you now claim has already gone through your guts! You were furnished with many clothes, with meat and with drink and with tools by the goods paid you for it, and now you want the land again, like children—" he paused and then added savagely, "—*as you are!*"

The Delawares had paled under the attack and now stirred uneasily. Things were not at all going as they had anticipated. But Canassatego was not yet finished with them. Contempt virtually dripped from the lips of the Onondaga chief as he continued:

"But what," he asked, "makes you sell land in the dark? Did you ever tell us that you had sold this land? Did we—" he thrust out his arm in a great sweep to take in all the assembled Iroquois, "—did we ever receive any part, even the value of a pipe-shank, from you for it? No, we did not! You have told us a blind story: that you sent a messenger to us to inform us of the sale, but that for some reason he never came amongst us, nor have we ever heard anything about it."

There was no doubt in the mind of anyone present that Canassatego was thoroughly disgusted at such a flimsy story. "This," he told the Delawares, "is acting in the dark, and very different from the conduct our Six Nations always observe in the sales of land. On such occasions they give public notice and invite all the Indians of their united nations and give them all a share of the presents they receive for their lands. This is the behavior of the wise united nations. But we find that you are none of our blood. You act a dishonest part, not only in this but in other matters. Your ears are ever open to evil and lying reports about our brethren; you receive them with as much greediness as lewd women receive the embraces of bad men!"

He paused again and now several members of the Delaware group were visibly shaking, greatly fearful of what punishment might now come from the Iroquois League, who could wipe them out to the last man with but little effort, should they so desire.

"And for all these reasons," Canassatego broke the long silence, his voice cold, implacable, "we charge you to remove instantly! We don't give you the liberty to think about it; you are women. Take the advice of a wise man and remove instantly. You may return to the eastward of the Delaware River where you first came from, but we do not know whether, considering how you have behaved yourselves, you will be permitted to live there. Or," he added meaningfully, "whether you have not also swallowed *that* down your throats as well as the land on this side. We therefore assign you two places to go—either to Wyoming or Shamokin.[13]

"You may," Canassatego reiterated, "go to either of these places—and then we shall have you more under our eye and shall see how you behave. Don't deliberate," he warned, handing them the second belt of wampum, which was shorter and narrower than the first but similarly colored and patterned, "but remove away immediately and take this belt of wampum.

"After our just reproof and absolute order to depart from the land," he said with finality, "you are now to take notice of what we have further to say to you. This string of wampum serves to forbid you, your children and grandchildren—to the latest posterity, forever!—from meddling in land affairs. Neither you nor any who descend from you, are ever hereafter to presume to sell any land, for which purpose you are to preserve this string in memory of what your uncles have this day given you in charge."

He dismissed them now with a gesture he might have used to shoo away a bothersome insect. "We have some other business to transact with our brethren, and therefore depart the council and consider what has been said to you."

Crestfallen, fearful, without having uttered a single word either in denial or protest, the Delawares left the council chambers. Within a week their villages in the disputed area had vanished and were rebuilt in part in the valleys of the Wyoming and the Shamokin by those who remained, while those who left the country for good traveled far to the west, hopefully out of reach of the Iroquois, and settled with their brothers on the Muskingum River to the north and west of the Ohio River, and some went even deeper into the Northwest Territory to build villages at the headwaters of the

Great Miami River and Auglaize River and Mad River. Even here they feared for their lives at the hand of the Iroquois.

Such was the power of the Iroquois League.

## [ *June 10, 1737—Friday* ]

All day long, virtually bursting with the greatest enthusiasm and excitement that had ever smitten him, William Johnson had gone from house to house here in County Meath, Ireland. The inhabitants of each residence listened in awe as the words tumbled from his lips. With his limited vocabulary, it was difficult for him to articulate the most wonderful thing that had ever happened to a young man who had just passed his twenty-second birthday.

Inside the mud walls of the crude tenant huts young Johnson expounded as best he could on the glories and wonders and opportunities to be found in America in general and in the Mohawk Valley of New York Colony in particular. Though he had never seen them, never even heard them accurately described by anyone who *had* seen them, yet he spoke with remarkable eloquence of the great forests and fields, the wild rivers and the creatures that flew or ran or swam there.

The fire of his enthusiasm spread to his listeners and they sat spellbound as he offered them a chance of a lifetime; in fact, a whole new life. It was all there—in the letter now safe in his breast pocket; a letter which he had received three days ago and which, since then, he had read a hundred times or more; a letter which said:

*My Dear Nephew William—*

*Although we have never met, I have heard from my beloved sister Anne—your mother—that you have grown to be a fine, strong, intelligent young man with great imagination and distinct qualities of leadership. I am pleased to learn this, for it has become my lot to seek the services of just such an individual, to manage for me a bountiful section of land I have become possessor of in the valley of the River Mohawk here in America. This title encompasses an area of 14,000 acres of fine ground.*

*Should you care to accept the offer I am about to make, I should like you to recruit a goodly number of peasants in your neighborhood (or elsewhere in Ireland), men of no more than twoscore years of age, married, honest and hale of health, and both fit and willing to work as tenant farmers on*

*the said land in New York Colony in return for their passage
to America, such passage to include wife and not more than
two children. You may offer them tenant parcels of 200
acres each and an indenture of five years, after which time,
should they so desire, they may stay on and draw wages and
also receive at nominal cost, up to ten acres of their own, or,
if they desire it, to leave and go where they will as freemen.*

*You, in turn, would manage them on this land, which, in
fairness I must add, is essentially wilderness. You would see
to the management of all affairs there as my agent. This
would include the establishment of a plantation which would
be yours to operate, accountable to none but me.*

*I would imagine you should have little difficulty in finding
such men as are required, and I urge that you recruit with
selection and make such offer only to those who are good
men and able to sign their indenture bills in their own hand. I
would not care to see among this number that you may
recruit, any men in whose background there is evidence of
mutinous nature, or men who have, for any reason whatsoever, served a period of time in prison. From such come the
seeds of discontent.*

*Provision will be made for your passage first and theirs
later. I would be on hand to greet you on your arrival in
Boston, at which time we could, in greater detail, discuss
what must be done.*

*I look forward to your quick reply and trust that it shall be
in the affirmative.*

> *With affection and Sin-
> cere good wishes for
> your continued health,
> I am,*

*New York*                                  *Your Uncle,*
*Apri 29, 1737*                    PETER WARREN

### [ March 16, 1738—Thursday ]

If ever two men were opposites, those two were William
Johnson and Peter Warren.

Johnson was tall—just a shade over six feet now—and
well built; Warren was almost a foot shorter and quite
thick-bodied, almost fat. Warren had bright blue eyes; Johnson's were a hazel-gray. Johnson had dark hair and swarthy
complexion; Warren was red-headed and had an almost sickly white skin liberally peppered with freckles. Warren was
extremely vain and talked about himself or his possessions or

accomplishments constantly; Johnson rarely did so. Warren was a dandy in his mode of dress; Johnson's clothing seldom fit and was never in style. Warren was well educated, and self-assured in the presence of nobility; Johnson was not a great deal more than literate and decidedly uncomfortable when in the presence of those above the station in which he had been reared.

Yet, despite these differences, the pair hit it off well enough at first, when Captain Warren met Johnson at Boston Harbor. As the officer rattled on easily about himself, his ship, his land, his wife, his friends, the things he had done and other matters concerning himself, William Johnson listened carefully and vaguely envied the position, wealth and status of his young uncle, wondering how it must feel to be so well endowed in practically all respects.

His interest sharpened considerably when, over a fine meal at the King's Inn, Warren got down to business and told what was expected of William on the Mohawk Valley land. Though the captain expressed satisfaction at the twelve County Meath families his nephew had recruited, Johnson got the distinct impression that he was disappointed and had expected more people than that. The naval officer could not seem to comprehend the reluctance of the destitute Irish to leave the land they loved and which they dreamed would one day be their own free land.

For several hours they remained at the table and discussed what lay ahead. Johnson learned where the property was and that to get there he must go to New York City and from there follow the Hudson River north to the predominantly Dutch city of Albany, which had long ago been called Fort Orange. Just above that was where the Mohawk met the Hudson and he would go up that watercourse to Schenectady, another town with an almost exclusively Dutch population.

"It's the last major town," Warren said. "Just a bit over twenty miles upstream from there you'll find Warrensburg."

"Warrensburg?"

"Yes, Warrensburg." There was just a trace of irritation in Warren's voice at the seeming obtuseness of his nephew. "That's what my fourteen thousand acres are called now—Warrensburg." The words rolled off his tongue as if caressed on the way out.

"It borders the south bank of the Mohawk for three and a half miles," Warren continued, "but it doesn't include the point of land—government land and Indian land—where

Schoharie Creek meets the river. The west side of Warrensburg then borders Schoharie Creek for another five miles. Twenty-two square miles in all."

Johnson was duly impressed. It was a far cry from the meager one hundred ninety-nine acre farm of his father, and his anxiety to see this new land was growing. But he was also disturbed that it was so far away from the nearest town. Somehow he had gotten the idea that there were several towns close-by and he asked his uncle about this.

Warren shook his head. "Nothing substantial. Farther upstream there are two villages populated with German immigrants, built on land granted by Albany landlords about fifteen years ago. These towns are called Stone Arabia and German Flats. But there are many outlying farms and cabins in the whole river valley between them and Schenectady.

"Your duties, William," Warren told him, getting back to the point of their discussion, "will be to establish a plantation—a farm, if you will—and cultivate this place using servants and slaves I will provide. I have already secured eight German families as tenants at other portions of the land, to go along with the twelve you recruited in County Meath. Part of your duty will be to rent other two-hundred-acre plots to settlers as they arrive in the area. Further, with a thousand pounds' worth in merchandise I will supply, you are to establish a store which will be primarily for the tenants of Warrensburg. Throughout all of Warrensburg—on the farm, over the tenant farms, at the store—you are to have full authority."

This was all like a dream to Johnson, but the impression he somehow got that the farm—its lands, buildings, servants and slaves—was to belong to him in exchange for his labors in establishing a store and managing the rest of Warrensburg as his uncle's agent, was a completely wrong conception. Warren was merely giving his sister's son a job, nothing more. He was, in effect, tossing a poor relative a bone.

But the mutual misunderstanding remained undetected for now.

[ *December 31, 1738—Saturday* ]

At eighteen years of age, Pontiac was not very attractive in physical appearance. He was slightly taller than medium height and, though his body was well formed and free of congenital defects or those caused by injury, his physique was not better than just average. Though not actually ugly, his

33

features could not have been termed handsome by European standards. Yet, this was perhaps unfair, for it was difficult to determine how he really looked behind the odd decorations he wore. There were few broad areas of skin still left unmarked. Wide tattooed bands encircled his lower arms, neck, chest, waist, stomach, buttocks, legs and feet. These were patterned in diamond shapes, circles and blocks and the only nongeometrical figures of any consequence were a large representation of the sun with heat rays emananting from it, which had been tattooed in the center of his chest—a sun which had eyes and mouth but no ears or nose—and the head of a bird of prey, presumably an eagle, in the center of his back.

Where tattooing had not left its permanent mark, as often as not he would be garishly painted in bright lines and curves of vermilion, blue or pasty white. Often, on ceremonial occasions, he would have half his body painted solidly one color—usually vermilion—with the color line beginning in the center of his brow at the hairline and running straight down to the crotch.

But where neither painted nor tattooed, his skin appeared somewhat lighter than the usual Ottawa skin coloring. His straight black hair was still cropped in that narrow, upright brush style, extremely short at the back of his skull and gradually increasing in length until it stood high and thick over his forehead. In a pouch dangling from a rawhide cord over one shoulder, he carried a small mirror he had gotten in trade from a Frenchman, and he inspected himself a dozen times a day with it—or even more—to make certain his paint was not smudged.

As was common to his people, as well as to many other Indian tribes, he was devoid of facial and body hair. His legs, arms and chest were smooth and even the underarms and pubic region were hairless. Almost always his entire body gleamed with a liberal application of clear bear oil. In his ears were still the circlets of white porcelain beads and the crescent-shaped stone still dangled pendulously from his nose.

His clothing—or lack of it—depended upon the season. In summer, with the bear oil acting as something of a protection against sun and wind, he mostly went naked, wearing only wide silver bands on his arms just above the elbows. Occasionally he wore a necklace of white plumes and, less often, a string of porcelain or brass beads around his throat. The soles of his feet were horny with calluses from having gone so long without shoes; even in cold weather he rarely wore more than ankle-high buckskin moccasins over his feet. Now and then in summer, when the mood struck him, he would wear a breechcloth, or perhaps just a gaudy calico shirt obtained from a Detroit trader. His dress—or undress—was reasonably representative of the Ottawa tribesmen as a whole. Even the women rarely wore more than a simple short breechcloth.

Pontiac's winter apparel was more protective. Besides the moccasins and breechcloth, he would sometimes wear soft doeskin leggins which covered only his legs from ankle to thigh. When it was exceptionally cold he might wear a French longcoat or a blanket draped over his shoulders and belted about his waist.

Gradually the tribal nudity was fading as more and more frequently he and his fellows were coming to wear items of white man's apparel, donning whatever took the eye at any given time. A warrior might, for example, feel in a shirt-wearing mood and don as many as four or five calico shirts, one atop another.

In his bearing Pontiac was proud and inclined to be arrogant, domineering. He was swift to anger and decidedly vindictive. Though obviously preparing for chieftainship, he was not yet a chief. Nevertheless, he had about him the air of a commander of men and already a rather large number of the young Ottawas followed him and looked to him for leadership and counsel. They felt this way, in part, because of his fighting abilities, for the regular forays to the south in war parties directed against the southern tribes had shown him to be an outstanding warrior, both clever and fearless. Already he had slain a dozen or more men and it was told about the council fires that one or two of these had been English traders seeking new fields of profit down the Ohio River or journeying the trackless forests en route to the Miami villages located on the upper, middle and lower Wabash River.

That he was keenly interested in tribal affairs there could be no doubt. Rarely was any Ottawa council held in which Pontiac did not take an active part, and often his opinions— well formed and confidently given—swayed the chiefs. Likewise, he frequently traveled to other villages to sit in on councils there when permitted to do so, especially among his mother's people, the Chippewas. Here too, on occasion, his words were listened to respectfully and his ideas frequently applauded and acted upon.

Up at Michilimackinac, which he visited often, about nine hundred of the Ottawas still maintained their village and regularly discussed moving elsewhere. The proposed sites most favored were on the Muskegon River, the Grand River, at the Grand Traverse and at L'Arbre Croche.[14] Even more Chippewas were moving into the Michilimackinac vicinity and, while the relations between the two tribes remained very good, the Ottawas just didn't want to live so close to them. But the deliberations over a new site, as they had been doing for years, broke down in long harangues and petty arguments as one or another faction favored different sites. They knew they would reach a decision eventually but, as always, it would take time.

There were now, in Pontiac's own Detroit area, a total of some thirty-three hundred and fifty Indians, about one in five of which was an adult man—a warrior. Of that total number, a thousand were Ottawas, another thousand were Hurons, eight hundred fifty were Chippewas—including three hundred Mississaugi Chippewas at nearby Lake St. Clair—and five hundred were Potawatomies.

In midsummer, however, this figure was changed when the Detroit Hurons not only grew suspicious and fearful of their neighboring Chippewas and Ottawas, but also became incensed at the bad deal the French traders were giving them. Led by Chief Orontony, whom the French called Nicolas, these Hurons abruptly pulled up one night and moved southward and then eastward, following the shoreline of the western end of Lake Erie. Not until they reached Sandusky Bay did they establish another village.[15]

On the surface, this move of Orontony's Hurons appeared to be of little moment, but it quickly had some grave ramifications. Before the year was out they were doing business with some enterprising and daring English traders and they were astounded at how much more the English paid them for their pelts, and at the lower cost to them of goods manufactured across the sea.

These were the same traders who had been regularly making the perilous trip to trade with the Miamis on the Wabash and Maumee rivers ever since those Indians had moved south following their difficulty with Cadillac at Detroit.

The difference in the prices was not so strange under the existing circumstances. It was the French government's own policy which was their undoing here in the matter of trade. The western fur posts were leased to the highest bidder and often the bids became astronomical as competition among the French and Canadian traders was keen and the government badly corrupt. In order to recoup his loss, the high-bidding trader was then forced to lower the price he paid the Indians for their pelts, while at the same time jacking up the cost to them of such items as blankets, guns, knives, axes and other manufactured goods. The English, with their industrialized homeland a better source of material items and no greatly involved or corrupt trading-license requirements, understandably undersold the French with ease. It provided a deadly wedge for the English to drive into the French-dominated wilderness.

But the English themselves were running into difficulties. All along the frontier, from the head of the Ohio River to the hills of western New York, a whole series of violent clashes with the Indians suddenly erupted. Numerous traders and settlers were being slain, their cabins burned, their cattle slaughtered, their possessions taken. And the reason was land.

The resentment of the Indians for white encroachers, especially the English, was a swelling tide, threatening to engulf the country.

### [ July 24, 1739—Tuesday ]

William Johnson may have been grossly inexperienced to be so suddenly thrust into the job he was called upon to perform at Warrensburg, but he was not a fool. In the year and more that he had spent here, he had learned a very great deal.

His initial journey up the Hudson and Mohawk rivers had been an exciting adventure. With spring in full glow to give it added emerald luster, it was a new and wonderful world wholly unlike anything he had envisioned. The beauty of the scenery as they moved up the Hudson overwhelmed him and Albany turned out to be a small city seemingly picked up intact in Holland and positioned here on these banks; quaint, brightly tiled houses with elaborate gingerbread workmanship, neatly swept streets, generally gay residents, well-tended fields and gardens, and picture-book apple orchards. Still, it was no little shock to see here and there a semi-naked, blanket-wrapped Indian or scraggly bearded, buckskin-clad frontiersman roaming the streets.

Johnson bought a horse in Albany from one of the city's leading citizens—Jeremias Van Rensellaer, who deftly cheated him in the process—and then rode a pleasant trail road to Schenectady. It was another Dutch town, but here there was not the aura of lightness felt in Albany; here the citizens seemed haunted by the specter of Indian attack.

West of the town he rode past farmers at work in their fields bordering the Mohawk, and his pulse quickened as he noted how the earth looked black and rich. In the distance ahead, however, there were rather large hills which gradually seemed to be pressing in on the river, as if reluctant to let it pass. And, with his spirits sagging somewhat, Johnson noted that these hills were steeper and more forbidding on the south side of the river, the side on which he was riding, the side on which Warrensburg was located.

The land continued to grow rougher and more barren of farms the farther he progressed. Those cabins which existed here now were no more than ugly log boxes, most of them devoid of windows and with only scant scratchings of cultivation close to them. As the hills rose beneath him, so the trees became ever more dense and, but for the narrowing river path, travel would have been close to impossible.

And then he had reached Warrensburg and found not open fields and delightful farms and people, but instead, woods denser than before—a tangled timberland which loomed off to west and south and east. Only when he reached the mouth of Schoharie Creek was there a clearing and an incredible sight met his eyes. Here were crowds of people lazily moving about at the two fortifications, Fort Hunter and Teantontalogo. Indian men, some clad in leggins, some in blankets, some in simple breechcloths, mingled unconcernedly with slovenly soldiers who were being attended by Mohawk women; squaws who considered themselves soldiers' wives but who were, in fact, merely carnal relief for the individual soldiers. Certainly if there was a fear of Indians alive in this country, it was not in evidence here.

Fort Hunter's garrison was only twenty soldiers and what little English language the three hundred sixty Mohawks here at Teantontalogo had picked up had come from them and it was a startling and distasteful thing to hear a warrior abruptly rattle off a string of the most vile profanities with the ease of a veteran trooper.

There was little of dignity or beauty about either of the structures, despite the tiny church inside Fort Hunter; a chapel presided over by the Reverend Henry Barclay, who was on the point of giving up the struggle to cope with the iniquities so much in evidence. Over the doorway of the church was the royal coat-of-arms and inside, at the altar, a tarnished silver communion plate was enriched with a grandiose inscription:

THE GIFT OF HER MAJESTY,
ANNE,
BY THE GRACE OF GOD OF BRITAIN,
FRANCE, IRELAND, AND HER
PLANTATIONS IN NORTH AMERICA,
QUEEN,
TO HER INDIAN CHAPEL OF THE MOHAWKS

Johnson wasted little time gawking. He had a big job to do and he set about doing it without delay; building farmhouse, barn, stables and barracks for servants and slaves with vigor and considerable care. After all, he believed, was not the farm itself one day to become his? Construction of the store followed and he located it on the winding road leading from Fort Hunter to the east. Soon after that he was actively seeking—and finding—settlers interested in the two-hundred-acre plots he had been commissioned to lease.

But there were problems of a serious nature and one of the worst of these was the very density of the trees and brush covering the hills which made up much of Warrensburg; hills which cloaked the land altogether too much with cool shadows. Clearing was done only at the expense of great amounts of time and labor and it became a major effort merely to transform a single acre to an open area where a cabin could be built and the land brought under cultivation. During the very height of this energy-sapping preoccupation came a letter to Johnson from his uncle, which said in part:

*. . . and in your management of affairs at Warrensburg, bear in mind that I would like you to change the forest into square fields, leaving hedgerows at each side, which will keep the land warm, be very beautiful, and subject you to no more expense than doing it in a slovenly, irregular manner . . .*

William Johnson, though not discouraged with his own efforts at reshaping Warrensburg, was thoroughly disgusted with the letter and his own reply was one of thinly veiled anger in which he countered by not mentioning the woods clearing at all but rather confining himself to another subject entirely and requesting that the Warrensburg store be provided with goods more suitable to the available customer.

It had not taken long at all, after the store was in operation, for him to realize that the goods Peter Warren had supplied initially to stock the store might have been useful to a citizen on the outskirts of Boston or New York City, but here they were not only not needed, they were unwanted and they remained unsold. The land-tilling German immigrants were uninterested in such luxuries as Irish linens, fancy inkpots, letter seals and the like. And the same held true of the other potential customers—Indians and traders. Delighted to hear of the new store, these people came in droves at first, laden with bundles of prime fur pelts to trade for goods suited to their needs. Not finding such goods in stock, they left in disgust and headed downriver for Schenectady or Albany.

Again Johnson learned fast and the order he sent east for supplies on Warren's credit very nearly caused his uncle to discharge him. How long can a store exist, Peter Warren grumbled from Boston, which stocked the items he had been billed a hundred and sixty pounds for: knives, scissors, bullet molds, lead bars, swords, coarse woolen shawls of black or crimson, gaudy calicoes of all colors, rifles with barrels four feet in length and pistols with barrels so long they looked more like walking canes than firearms, plain and ruffled pullover shirts, brilliant blue, green and scarlet stockings for women and children, axes and tomahawks, blankets, fish spears, spools of brass wire, flint-and-steel sets for firemaking, beads and trinkets, ribbons and garters of all colors, awls, combs and mirrors and hair cockades, tobacco and pipes and snuff boxes, pots and pans and kettles and, to top it off, such powder dyes as vermilion, blue, green, yellow, purple and deep wine-red. Why, the only thing his nephew had ordered that a civilized man would use was the liquor—and even that which he ordered was a cheap rum sold only by the barrel. Warren wrote testily to Johnson:

*... Of what possible use can the majority of these items be to those who come to shop? I fear you have been given bad advice and, worse, have acted rashly on it. I had hoped your judgment would have been better and I implore you to act with greater circumspection in the future ordering of supplies ...*

But the "useless" goods sold with fantastic speed and when they were gone and a most satisfactory profit shown, the original goods supplied by Warren still gathered dust on the shelves. Grudgingly, Peter Warren then suggested that Johnson continue to order those goods he felt would be *"of interest to the peculiar taste of your customers."*

Throughout the remainder of the year Johnson had cast longing eyes at the delightfully level ground directly across the Mohawk River from his farm. Here there was a level road quite heavily used, stretching from Schenectady to German Flats and Stone Arabia and into the wilderness beyond. Here were only scattered patches of trees and, with the hills not rising for some distance from the river, ground that was ripe for farming and building. All winter long, few were the travelers who disturbed the blanket of snow on the narrow, hill-winding road passing the Warrensburg store; but on the main thoroughfare, if such it could be called, on the other side of the river there passed in both directions a regular stream of travelers—Indians, traders, grizzled frontiersmen, settlers, and well-bundled German merchants in sleighs laden with goods.

The more he considered it, the more the land appealed to him. When the summer traffic again showed itself to be every bit as heavy as was that of winter—if not heavier—he made his decision. With customary directness he rode to Albany not quite a month ago—on June 30—and for a hundred and eighty pounds, which was virtually his entire savings of his share of the store's profit for the year, he bought the tract in question. The plot ran a quarter mile along the river's edge and was one mile in depth to the north. He bought the land in his own name and then, while still in Albany, wrote to Uncle Peter and proudly explained what he had done.

Warren was stunned, not only because he had never considered that Johnson had business acumen enough to even contemplate a land purchase of his own, but because he felt that Johnson had no real right to act in any manner except as the agent of Peter Warren. In his resultant letter of reply, however, he did not bring up these points, considering them beneath his dignity. He merely contented himself with verbally castigating his nephew and telling him bluntly that *as my dependent, I feel it proper to tell you that you have undoubtedly made a stupid investment.*

Now, with that letter of Warren's before him, confused and hurt by its tenor and implication, Johnson sat in his house and penned his reply in a distinctly cramped and awkward hand:

*My Dear Uncle*

*I find you are displeased at my purchasing the land, which, in everybody's opinion, is a good bargain. I can, any time I please, sell it for the money and more; so that I hope, Dear Uncle, you will not continue your opinion when you see it and know my design (which is this:) to have a careful, honest man there who will manage the farm which will at least clear, I am sure, £30 per annum. Moreover, the chief thing is a fine creek to build a saw mill on, having logs enough at hand, half of which creek belongs to me. So therefore I intend after a little time, please God, to build a mill there which may clear £40 per annum, and that without much trouble, so that the income of that may enable me the better to go out in the world; though I must acknowledge, Dear Uncle, that what great favors you were pleased to do me was a sufficient beginning, and I am with all gratitude imaginable contented with it and for the future shall be no way expensive nor troublesome to you ... As to my moving over where I made the purchase, to live there, I never had the least notion in the world of it ...*

### [ August 1, 1742—Sunday ]

It was a strange sight to see the Ottawas go.

For so many years they and their village had been a permanent part of the Michilimackinac area, and now it was ended. After long years of deliberation, the council of chiefs had finally reached a decision on where to establish their new village.

Their population here numbered now over a thousand, of which more than one hundred traveled to the new village site by canoe, each craft loaded high with bundles and sacks of equipment and supplies. The others walked, their large collection of nondescript dogs yipping and yapping and frisking about their heels as the journey began. Many of the larger dogs had had packs attached to them with rawhide straps and most, after a few minutes of futile attempt to rid themselves of their load, trudged along with somewhat dampened spirits among the crowd.

The twenty or thirty horses belonging to the tribe had also been heavily loaded and were apparently no happier than the dogs about it. What guns, axes, packs and other equipment remained were divided equally for the squaws to carry, and they complained least of all. Unfettered, the children raced and frolicked about, excited at this great event.

The trip by land was about twelve or fifteen miles shorter than by canoe and since the paddlers were in no especial hurry and took their time, they reached the new village site about the same time as the walkers. Those who walked had taken the trail which first went almost due west along the southern shore of the Strait, and then cut southwest along a much fainter trail which eventually led them to their destination, about twenty miles from Fort Michilimackinac.

The canoes also had gone west along the shoreline in the Strait, but Waugoshance was encountered near where the walkers had tuned south-westward. Waugoshance was a long, narrow neck of land which continued generally toward the west for six miles out into Lake Michigan and at the start of it there was a well-worn portage path for canoeists. This time, however, the Ottawas elected to continue paddling; it would take longer to unload, carry boats and contents to the other side and reload than it would to paddle all the way around.

At the end of the six miles they reached the tip of Waugoshance and turned sharply south, cutting carefully through the tricky currents of the small gap between the peninsula and an island hardly more than a stone's throw away. Then they began following the other side of the long, sandy neck back eastward toward the main bulk of the land.

The breeze was slight this day and they had no difficulty reaching the new village site just two or three miles south of Waugoshance. They drove their canoes several hundred yards up the small stream which emptied into Lake Michigan at this place and beached them at just about the same time the walkers were throwing down their loads in the same area.

The short journey was over. This was L'Arbre Croche—the place of the Crooked Tree.[16]

It was a beautiful location for a permanent seat of the Ottawa nation. The beaches were smooth with little surf, protected from prevailing winds and, with the little stream at hand, ideal for landing or launching canoes. The waters of lake and stream had an abundance of fish and the fields and woods adjoining were well populated with game and fowl. Most importantly, there were no other people around; Indian or white.

The Chippewa Indians at Michilimackinac were not too sorry to see the Ottawas go. That tribe had been on a choice location here and their departure left it open for the Chippewas to claim and build another village upon for their swelling population. By now their own numbers here had increased to about nine hundred.

Resentment was growing among these Indians and others of this far northwest area against the French and Canadian traders. Word had filtered north of the bountiful "presents" the Miami Indians on the Wabash and the Hurons at Sandusky Bay were getting from English traders for their pelts. So far the resentment was confined to grumbling, but it might easily flare into violence at any time. And, though they were far removed from it, the Frenchmen of Fort Michilimackinac and Detroit knew only too well of the bloodthirsty marauding being done by the Indians against the whites—irrespective of whether they were French or English—from the upper reaches of the Ohio to the valleys of the Shenandoah and Susquehanna and even to the headwaters of the Mohawk.

Most of the dead or vanished were English, but there were French losses, too, and each side became ever more convinced that the other was fomenting Indian unrest and actually instigating attacks. There was a degree of truth to it; both sides were deeply concerned with having the Indians allied to them and opposed to their white foe, but the fact of the matter was that certain Indians—Delawares, Shawnees, Chenussio Senecas, possibly even some Miamis, Hurons and Ottawas—were finding the time ripe for the killing of those whites who had come uninvited into their territories, especially those who put down roots. If the two white factions should fly at each other's throats over it, so much the better. Perhaps then they would so weaken themselves that both could be pushed out of these lands with ease.

The Six Nations held the key. Whichever side they allied themselves to, if any, could not help but win any war which might come. But the Iroquois remained a big question mark. Those in the southern portion of their territory and those farthest east—the Mohawks in particular—were obviously on very friendly terms with the English and were benefitting considerably in their trade with them. Those in the northern and far western section—most especially the Senecas and Onondagas—were presently being wooed to the extreme by the French, who lavishly gave them presents, and there could be no doubt that they, perhaps the Chenussio Senecas most of all, were leaning strongly toward French sympathy; but they, too, had not committed themselves and were bound by the ruling of the entire League. Those Iroquois nations in the middle maintained a strict neutrality and seemed intent on adhering to it. Matters of such gravity were for the Iroquois council to settle and since the League's decision would be, as it always had in its history, the course the Six Nations would follow, it became a matter of utmost concern to everyone.

And just at this moment a crisis had developed with ominous undertones. With unauthorized English settlement increasing to the west of the Susquehanna River, the Onondaga's chief speaker, Canassatego, had journeyed with a large Iroquois party all the way to Philadelphia for a grand council with the Pennsylvania Proprietaries again. Now he stood before them and spoke slowly, but with dignity and forcefulness:

"Brother *Onas*, we know our lands are now become more valuable. The white people think we do not know their value, but we are sensible that the land is everlasting and the few goods we receive for it are soon worn out and gone.

"We have further to observe, with respect to the lands lying on the west side of Susquehanna that, though Brother *Onas* had paid us for what portion of it that his own people possess, yet some parts of that country have been taken up by persons whose place of residence is to the south of this province, in the lands you call Virginia and Maryland, and from whom we have never received any consideration.

"This affair was recommended to you by our chiefs at our last treaty and you then, at our earnest desire, promised to write a letter to that person who has authority over those people and to procure his answer. As we have never heard from you on this, hear: we want to know what you have done in it.

"If you have not done anything, we now renew our request and desire you will inform the person whose people are seated on our lands that that country belongs to us in the right of conquest—we having bought it with our blood and taken it from our enemies in fair war."

Canassatego paused significantly and his gaze, directed at the Englishmen in attendance, narrowed as he continued:

"And we expect, as owners of that land, to receive such consideration for it as the land is worth. We desire you to press him to send a positive answer. Let him say 'Yes' or 'No'! If he says 'Yes,' we will treat with him; if 'No,'" and now the chief's voice hardened, "we are able to do ourselves justice. And we *will* do it, by going to take payment for ourselves!"

There was much more talk, by both Indians and whites, but little concrete action taken. How could the Pennsylvania Proprietaries put across the point that while they might to some degree control settlers from eastern Pennsylvania from staking out claims west of the Susquehanna, they had no authority whatever against those coming northwest from Virginia and Maryland to settle in the valleys of the Allegheny, Juniata, Monongahela, Youghiogheny and other streams?

What the whites needed desperately was a white man who knew the Iroquois and their language intimately, to put these and other points across. What the Indians needed was a white man who knew their language and their problems intimately, who sympathized with them and who could represent them among the whites with more authority than any Indian himself could.

And maybe such a man was in the area right now, within the reach of all.

## [ September 9, 1742—Thursday ]

As neatly as if he had planned it expressly for that purpose, William Johnson's new store on the north side of the Mohawk River took away from the Albany merchants a fantastic amount of business, and for this he incurred their undying wrath. Both commercially and strategically, his store's location was incredibly important.

For the English, the Appalachian chain of mountains acted as a barrier to easy entry into the heartland of North America. Running parallel with the Atlantic coast, this range was broken by streams in only two locations which gave access to the north-central territory. One was the mighty St. Lawrence River, which provided French access to the whole center of the continent via the Great Lakes. The other river, which did somewhat the same for the English but on a considerably lesser scale, was the Mohawk.

Sloops sailed upriver on the Hudson from New York City to Albany and from that point numerous smaller boats traveled the Mohawk up to near its headwaters where the westward course of the stream turned to the north and became largely unnavigable. At this turning point there was a portage which was known as the Great Carrying Place. Here, separated by only four or five miles, the waters flowed in two directions—southeastward to the ocean at New York City and northwestward to Lake Ontario. The portage from the Mohawk was not a difficult one and then the current of

Wood Creek carried the boats to Oneida Lake. The lake emptied by way of the Onondaga River, which joined Lake Ontario at a place the Iroquois had long called Oswego.[17] And it was here at the mouth of the Onondaga that the English had built Fort Oswego, thus making the Mohawk River a military supply route to the Great Lakes.

Since William Johnson talked with great numbers of traders, settlers, soldiers and Indians who came by, in a short time he had gained a respectable knowledge of the history and geography of this area and, with it, the determined knowledge that the fur business would be his key to wealth and power.

The Dutch, who had opened this area with the exploration of Henry Hudson in his ship, the *Half Moon,* in 1609, came not for territory but for trade. A peaceful and happy trade system was established with the Iroquois who were delighted to have the Holland merchandise in exchange for their furs. Fearful that settlement on this frontier by pioneers would cause friction and interrupt this vital and highly profitable trade, the Dutch West Indian Company had opposed any settlement in the valley of the Mohawk and gave Albany a trading monopoly.

When the Dutch interests fell to the English in 1664, the monopoly was recognized as being of great value and continued, but with some changes. Knowing the Iroquois could not trade with the French, who were the staunch allies of their enemies, the Hurons, the English thereupon took advantage of their monopoly by lowering prices paid for furs. They profited handsomely for a while, but the ultimate result might have been foreseen: the Iroquois signed a peace and trade treaty with the French. The resultant competition between France and England caused both to raise their prices paid for furs and to press extravagant gifts on the Indians to hold their trade steady.

Unable to be sure any longer that the Iroquois would remain allied to them, the English built Fort Hunter. The French countered by building a fort and trading post at the mouth of the Niagara River. The English, not to be outdone, followed up by building Fort Oswego and thereby opened the route to the Great Lakes and, against considerable opposition from the merchants, ended the Albany monopoly. German immigrants were then permitted freeholds in the Mohawk Valley.

Unwilling to lose in the deal, even though their monopoly was destroyed, the merchants in Albany began to deal direct-

47

ly with the French through smuggling. It was, of course, violation of both French and English laws. But France was still an agricultural country and the products she traded to the Indians were manufactured at much greater cost than the same products in industrial England. Therefore it became highly profitable for the English smugglers to ship goods straight north from Albany to Lake Champlain and there, where customs laws were unenforceable, to deal with Canadian smugglers who became, in essence, the middlemen. In this exchange the English got the furs they wanted and the French and Canadians got goods which they could sell at lower cost than the goods received through legal channels. Most of the furs were those which the French traders had gotten much farther to the west in the sprawling wilderness empire from the Hurons, Ottawas, Chippewas and other tribes; and these were the tribes who benefitted from the reduced cost of goods.

The Iroquois warmed quickly to Johnson's sympathy. They told him that the fur smuggling was depriving them of their own traditional commission as middlemen and that English guns—part of the material the English smugglers provided—were now going in a steady stream via French traders to arm tribes who were mortal enemies of the Iroquois. Further, the Albany merchants could now afford to be indifferent to the welfare of the Iroquois and the prices they paid them for their furs became even lower.

"They have cheated us," more than one Mohawk told Johnson. "They treat us like slaves." The young Irishman couldn't help feeling sorry for them and was himself angered on their behalf.

The German immigrants who had settled in the Mohawk Valley were small-time traders and farmers, existing mostly by competing with the Iroquois as middlemen for the Great Lakes furs or else growing wheat for market. To sell, they had to journey downriver to Albany where the merchants, too, had them over a barrel. That is, they had to go to Albany before, but now, with far less traveling and a much better deal, they could do business with this enterprising young man who had just opened his store along the main trail. Little wonder the Albany merchants were furious with Johnson.

They were not the only ones. Peter Warren controlled his anger well, but considered that his nephew had been highly insubordinate, if not downright traitorous. The fact that

Johnson still did a good job for him meant little to Warren in view of the young man's disruptive ambitiousness.

Johnson did not see it this way and had no idea his uncle felt so strongly about it. After all, he went out of his way to protect Warren's interests: he refused to seek tenants for himself, though he could have gotten them easily, because he knew Peter Warren's dream was to establish a populated manor; he continued to seek tenants for Warren and secured an impressive additional total of twenty-three families; he used his own servants and slaves, not Warren's, to till his farm; he had been faithful in all matters where Warren's interests were concerned, except that he had ambition and refused to envision a life ahead of total servitude to the officer.

Undoubtedly one of the things which galled Warren most was that in addition to the store across the river, his nephew had almost immediately begun construction of a large and impressive stone house. Though Johnson assured him that this was for an overseer, Warren had his doubts and, as matters further degenerated between them, doubt became reality. With galling nonchalance, Johnson named his new mansion *Mount Johnson* and on Saturday, February 9, 1740, he wrote his uncle a letter normal in every respect but one; instead of heading it *Warrensburg*, across the top were the words, *Mount Johnson*.

It was a declaration of independence.

Though in an essentially frontier area, Johnson still engaged to surprising measure in one of his greatest pursuits—women. Neither color nor race were of much concern to him in this respect and he was as apt to accept with pleasure the favors of a Dutch or English girl in Schenectady or Albany or New York City—which he visited annually for conferences with Warren—as he was to accept them from a Mohawk maiden in Teantontalogo or a fraulein from one of the rude houses in German Flats or Stone Arabia. In a time and place where everyone knew everyone, the never-ending search-find-and-conquer missions of William Johnson were choice items of gossip.

One such conquest was more important than most to William. He found her on the estate of two brothers named Phillips, whose property lay adjacent to Warrensburg. She was the Phillips' indentured servant girl—blond, buxom and beautiful!—whom one of them had purchased at a wharf in New York. Her name was Catherine Weisenberg and oddly, though she was German, she had come from Madagascar.

Almost at once she attracted William's roving eye. The attraction was decidedly mutual and William decided he must have her.

Without any attempt at guile, he went directly to the one Phillips brother who was home at the moment. He bargained rather forcefully with him and when he left, it was with Catherine in tow. When Phillips' brother returned a few days later, the one who had bargained with the manager of Warrensburg lamented:

"Johnson—that damned Irishman!—came the other day and offered me five pounds for her, threatening to horsewhip me and steal her if I wouldn't sell her. I thought five pounds better than a flogging and took it."

That William loved her was undeniable, but that he should even consider marriage to her was unthinkable. Catty, which was her nickname, knew this well and was quite content in her role of housekeeper and mistress. To have married her could have thwarted all his ambitions and closed doors to him that were now opening. Catty didn't mind; her man was big, strong, good-looking, an excellent provider and a superlative lover who was both passionate and tender. It was understood by both of them that when and if William brought home a bride, Catty would move on, free of any indenture or claim.

For now, however, she provided him warmth and companionship in addition to her regular household duties. And there was another thing she provided him which, under the circumstances, was not altogether surprising—children. On June 8, 1740, she bore him a daughter who, perhaps through his suggestion, perhaps not, was significantly named Ann, his own mother's name. Twenty months later, on February 7 this year, she bore him a son whom she named John.

The infants were baptized at the Fort Hunter chapel by the Reverend Henry Barclay[18] who discreetly, if not quite honestly, recorded the events in the Indian Chapel Register Book by naming the mother but omitting the name of the father. The minister, in elastic frontier fashion, knew that young English gentlemen—or Irish, for that matter—could not expect high-born ladies to share their frontier hardships, but neither should these young men be embarrassed by official records of the fruit of their conquests.

It was to Catty's credit that she accepted this in good grace. Even though someday she would have to leave, William, she was sure, would certainly continue to favor these children and to provide generously for her. In the meanwhile, she was sharing William's bedroom in Mount Johnson and, for a servant girl, she was living in luxury.

With the exception of the Dutch burghers in Albany, everyone in this country admired William Johnson. For the poor Germans in the area he had become something of a protector. Most were unable to read or write in English—in fact many not even in their own native tongue—and had heretofore been at the mercy of those in power. But William's dealings with them were very fair and his prices better than they had ever encountered. His flour mill ground incessantly with their wheat. He was welcomed into their poor homes, drank ale with them, smoked pipes with them, listened to their stories and laughed at their humor, danced with them before great roaring fireplaces and, when the dancing was done, stripped to the waist with the other men to flop in a communal pile—which included women—in front of the glowing embers. He would eat beside them and not take offense at the German fraus suckling their babes at the same table. Time and again he set up neighbors in the fur-trading business, backing them strongly enough that they could outbid the Albany profiteers in fur-buying at Oswego.

His business prospered phenomenally.

All of this appalled and angered the Albany merchants. To them these peasants were such dirt that even after brief business talks the merchants often paused to bathe. But above and beyond that, there was another practice in which Johnson was engaging that frightened them.

By building a remarkably fast friendship, he was binding himself to the Mohawks.

### [ October 2, 1742—Saturday ]

Tiyanoga, son of a Mohegan father and Mohawk mother, was one of the most powerful and influential chiefs of the Iroquois League. Among the Mohawks themselves he was principal chief and his word was law. Among the members of the confederacy he was a great figure and respected almost to the point of reverence.

Over the past decade his black hair had begun turning white, and now was a salt-and-pepper mixture which imparted a peculiar dignity to his appearance. From the left corner of his mouth and running almost to his ear stretched a great scar which had been carved upon his features in some bygone battle by the tomahawk of an enemy. The fact that he was still alive was almost conclusive proof that that particular enemy was not.

His nose was prominent and quite hooked and his skin was a deep, ruddy bronze. Though tall, he was growing heavy with his age and stooped ever so slightly. From all outward appearances, he must have been over sixty years of age, which was considerably past the normal life expectancy of an Iroquois warrior. His step was a little less sprightly than it was when he was in his prime, his eye a little less perceiving, his hearing slightly dulled. But Tiyanoga was yet a chief among chiefs, a warrior among warriors, a man among men.

That he had acquired this standing in the Iroquois League even though his father was a Mohegan was not surprising. The Iroquois system of government, tribal leadership succession and family was based on maternal lines rather than paternal. A child belonged to its mother's tribe and clan and its nearest male relatives, aside from brothers, were the maternal uncles.

Tiyanoga was one of the four so-called "kings" who had been escorted to London in that famous embassy of 1710, at which time Queen Anne had personally presented him with a huge feathered hat and a lace-fringed coat of royal blue. This journey alone had given him great tribal standing but, in addition, he had been and would continue to be, a great chief in his tribe and in the League.

In their characteristic manner of disrespect for Indians, the Albany Dutch, though recognizing him as a powerful chief, refused to call him by his proper name and instead dubbed him King Hendrik. This did not concern Tiyanoga in the least.

For well over two years now, the Mohawk chief had been watching a white man very closely, studying his every move, his every act, his every facial expression. Much of this observation had been done surreptitiously in the past but, in recent months it had become more open.

The white man in question was William Johnson who, from the very beginning of his residency here in the Mohawk country, had shown a sincere and lively interest in the Indians. The young man, Tiyanoga knew from personal observation, went out of his way to trade with them and to treat them fairly in every respect. This in itself was so unusual for a white man to do that when he heard of it, Tiyanoga had begun his surveillance in earnest.

Johnson was mentally and emotionally well adapted for trading with the Indians. For him it was more by far than just a bartering and exchange of goods. He felt an empathy toward the red man and was totally and unabashedly free of the feelings of guilt such an empathy tended to stir within the white individual with "Indian-lover" tendencies. He saw no reason whatever that he couldn't be as loyal and honest to them as he was to his fellow Englishmen.

Though initially a language barrier existed between them, William did not let this stand in his way. Through sign language of a sort he made himself understood reasonably well and he devoured what they showed and told him with amazing speed and retention: their methods of hunting and fishing, tracking, stalking, their games, all these and more became to him a challenge and he learned them well. Soon large numbers of Indians were coming regularly to see him and to trade at his store.

The Indians could scarcely believe what happened when William dealt with them. As was usual in trading deals, liquor flowed in abundance, but it was there that common custom ended. It was normal, after imbibing to excess, for the braves to fall into drunken stupor and then awaken to find their pelts mostly gone as payment for the rum that had been drunk, and not enough skins left with which to buy clothes and blankets and ammunition for them and their families in the months ahead.

Not so when William Johnson dealt with them.

This is what astounded them: when they came groggily erect the next morning, they found that the rum they had drunk was not charged against them, that their pelt bundles were intact, and that an excellent deal awaited them in the trade. And when the pleasant trading was finished, Johnson presented each man with a jew's-harp, showed them how to play it and then joined them in the gales of laughter which swept them all as they attempted to play.

Though the Reverend Barclay felt the Indians should never be given liquor and had for some time tried to establish prohibition for them at Fort Hunter and Teantontalogo, he had been unsuccessful, largely due to William's intervention. The young trader-miller-merchant felt the Indians had every right to get as drunk as they pleased on such occasions.

Even the whites in the Mohawk Valley were amazed at William's interest in Indian ways and how quickly he seemed to become one of them whenever in their presence. One man in the valley penned his opinion of Johnson in his diary:

*Something in his natural temper responds to Indian ways.*

*The man holding up a spear he has just thrown, upon which a fish is now impaled; the man who runs, with his toes turned safely inward, through a forest where a greenhorn could not walk; the man sitting silent, gun on knee, in a towering black glade, watching by candle flame for the movement of antlers toward a tree whose bark has already been streaked by the tongues of deer; the man who can read a bent twig like an historical volume—this man is William Johnson, and he has learned all these skills from the Mohawks. How can an admirer of ability fail to revere their control of their forest environment how can a lover of liberty fail to adore their denial of all exterior restraint?*

There was no doubt that Johnson did indeed admire them and after a long period of studying—with much approval—Johnson's treatment of the Mohawks, after watching him go out of his way to help them in any manner possible, after watching his clumsy efforts to learn the Mohawk tongue so that he could, in his own words, "more fairly deal with them and help them," Tiyanoga stepped in.

The chief took to visiting Johnson frequently and, pretending he had just discovered the white man's efforts at learning the Mohawk tongue, instructed him in it to the best of his ability. William had met Tiyanoga several times in passing, but until now had no idea that the chief could speak English. Few were the white men who did know. Though he found the ability useful, Tiyanoga was not especially proud of it and managed to maintain his secret. Besides, it was good not to have the white men know. Often he discovered things he was not intended by the whites to understand, simply because they considered him a red man who only spoke gibberish. In addition to English, Tiyanoga also spoke French with some degree of fluency.

The Mohawk tongue was a language extremely difficult to learn; so much so, in fact, that even the commissioners of Indian affairs had rarely attempted to learn it, and those few who tried almost always failed miserably. The wide variety of verbs, seemingly without rule, and the terrible compounded words made learning the language a nightmare. The word for wine, for example, was *oneharadesehoengtseragherie,* which meant "a liquor made of the juice of grapes."

As his familiarity with the language expanded under Tiyanoga's tutelage and he learned to converse with ever greater ease, even in abstract matters, the casual questions put to William by the Mohawk chief began to assume greater direction and importance. For his own part, William was so busy grasping the intricacies of replying that he had neither desire nor ability to answer any way but openly, with no attempt at guile.

The questions dealt often with the policies of the white men toward the Indians: why New York Colony's Indian commissioners were insincere and had no interest in the Indians save in the respect that it filled their own pockets; what could be done about the French-English problem, since it would likely be the Iroquois who would suffer, as they were in the middle, whether the English just wanted to use the Indians for their own purposes and then later, when the need was gone, cast them off.

Though by now Tiyanoga knew this young white man well, yet William's candid answers astonished and warmed him. No white man before had ever had such feeling for the Mohawk people, such interest in them, such admiration for them, such desire to help them. And so, since it was a matter concerning the entire Six Nations, Tiyanoga journeyed to Onondaga where a council was held to discuss the proposition he put before the entire body of chiefs.

What the Iroquois needed desperately now, the Mohawk chief told them, was a white champion who could, with ease, penetrate the motives of the whites and advise them in all honesty as to what should be their course. Today in this country, Tiyanoga told them, there is such a man and his name is William Johnson. He recommended that William be adopted into the Mohawk tribe as a full member and a member, as well, of the Iroquois League.

For once the deliberations were brief and though there was ample opportunity for their voices to be heard, no Iroquois lifted his voice in any way derogatory to William Johnson. It was, in fact, the other way around. Tiyanoga, deeply satisfied, left the council with its full accord in the matter of inviting the white man to become a Mohawk and an Iroquois.

This was no offer lightly made. In adopting him, the Mohawks—and to certain extent the other five nations of the League—were pledging to him their faith and their loyalty, just as he would be pledging his to them. He would have as much right in tribal affairs as any tribesman and he would be expected always to act to his best ability in behalf of both tribe and confederation.

When Tiyanoga approached him and offered him adoption into the tribe, Johnson was overwhelmed. He had never even considered it, for this was something the Iroquois only very rarely offered to white men. To be so honored touched him deeply and he did not know what to say except that he would be more than proud to call Tiyanoga his brother and the chief's people his people.

A special day was set for the ceremony at the principal Mohawk village of Canajoharie—called the Upper Mohawk Castle by the English—which was located thirty miles up the Mohawk from Teantontalogo. This was where Tiyanoga resided. For three days prior to the ceremony, braves arrived from throughout the Six Nations until the Lower Castle of the Mohawks, Teantontalogo, was practically empty and Canajoharie bursting at the seams. Numerous representatives from the Cayugas, Onondagas, Oneidas, Tuscaroras and Senecas were there, too. No white men from Fort Hunter or German Flats or elsewhere, however, were permitted to attend; none but William Johnson himself.

Inside of one of the long communal buildings he was stripped of his clothing and a breechcloth was fastened around him. His face and body were painted in a series of designs with a variety of colors until the man himself was hardly recognizable. A large belt of white wampum was placed around his shoulders and both ends hung nearly to the floor in front of him. Bands of pure beaten silver were fastened about his wrists and right upper arm.

The Indians had been milling about in and out of the building while this was going on, but now Chief Tiyanoga stood at the doorway, cupped his mouth and shouted in a peculiarly far-carrying tone:

*"Coo-weegh! Coo-weegh! Coo-weegh!"*

Those braves outside entered at a run and sat close together on the floor until the entire building except for a space twenty feet in diameter around the chief and William Johnson was a solid carpet of people. When they had settled themselves and quieted, pipes were lighted and smoked, with Tiyanoga and William sharing the same one. No word was spoken by anyone during this time and the blue haze of burning tobacco drifted lazily up and out the long slit which ran the length of the building in the arched roof above them.

When they had finished, Tiyanoga got to his feet and began to speak. Though it was material that every Indian in the room knew and it was being uttered for the benefit of William, yet they all listened as if it was the first time they had heard it. William was enthralled with what was being said.

In a resonant baritone voice, Tiyanoga spoke of how the Iroquois were a proud people, but that before the League was formed, the Five Nations had been separate, unallied tribes which were constantly fighting one another. So terrible was the carnage that they wrought upon one another for so many years that it was necessary to erect strong palisades around each village, to fortify it against onslaught. The remnants of these fortifications still remained among their chief villages and these were the fortifications that had been called Castles by the first white men who saw them.

At least, some two-and-a-half centuries ago, there came a remarkable happening. A being from the skies came to the earth and spoke to them, telling them to cease their fighting and unite themselves in a League for both defense and attack. Another being was there, too, and this one was a man who was already a great chief of the Onondagas—a man who was known to his people as Atotarho. A mighty warrior and magician as well, he was bound in some indefinable way to the being from above. Finally, there was a third being, again a man and again a chief, yet somehow supernatural, who appeared to various Mohawks, Oneidas, Onondagas, Senecas and Cayugas in their dreams and bade them form this League.

This man's name was Taounyawatha, who was also known to his people as Hiawatha. For a long time he traveled up and down the length of the Mohawk River, explaining the idea of the League to the various tribes. It was not, he told them, a League which would keep them from being warriors and waging war, but merely one which would prevent them from destroying themselves. And should they be attacked, they would rise as one to beat off and destroy the attackers.

The initial reluctance of the tribes, proud of their individuality, wore off at last and the five tribes agreed to the federation. The government thereby established was a good one; so strong and so indestructible that it had lasted until this day and would, everyone believed, last many times that much longer.

And then, twenty-seven summers ago, the Tuscaroras from the south had been adopted by the Oneidas and accepted into the League as members without vote in the League councils, and the Five Nations thereby became the Six Nations.

"When our five tribes joined as one at Hiawatha's bidding," Tiyanoga continued, "our tribes were in a line from the rising sun to the setting sun. The Mohawks were the farthest east, and then came the Oneidas. The Onondagas were in the middle. Next in line were the Cayugas and farthest west were the Senecas.[19]

"To us," he explained, "the League is one of our longhouses, with a door at each end. The Senecas are the guardians of the western door, while the Mohawks are the guardians of the eastern door and also the receivers of tribute. The Onondagas, because they are in the middle, are the keepers of the council fires and the keepers of wampum.[20] The village of Onondaga is the seat of government, where all official councils of the League are held.

"Our way of government," Tiyanoga said, "is this: our law says that the tribes will elect their representatives and there are also rules for calling these chiefs into council. On all matters of importance to the League as a whole, the representatives of the tribes must vote. If war is to be declared, the vote must be all one, with none opposed. Disputes between ourselves must be arbitrated before the council and never, under any provocation, be settled through violence. The number of chiefs who sit in this council as representatives of their people varies from tribe to tribe and village to village. Some have as few as eight, some as many as fourteen. In all, there are fifty principal chiefs of the Five Nations who sit in council and all are equals.[21]

"This," the graying chief told William Johnson, "is the League of which you are soon to be a member. These are your people and you are their brother as long as you shall live. And now," he raised his right hand high, "it is come."

At the signal, three young squaws who had been standing in the east doorway, each clad only in a breechcloth, threaded their way through the crowd and approached William. As one of them led the way, the other two each grasped one of his hands and, one before him and one behind, guided him outside and down the bank of the Mohawk River. Here they led him into the water until it was chest deep and then they leaped upon him and pulled him under. When they came up their hands were full of sand and pebbles and bottom grit and with this they scrubbed him vigorously until all trace of the paint that had been on his face and body was gone.

The three, giggling almost uncontrollably, then led him, dripping and with his skin atingle, back to the council house, which was now empty except for several Mohawk braves who were waiting with a new set of buckskin leggins and breechcloth for him, along with a ruffled shirt. These he donned at once and noted with admiration how the leggins, as well as the pair of moccasins and garters they gave him, were decorated with ribbons, beads, porcupine quills and scalp-locks of brilliant red hair—not the red of a carrot-topped individual, but blood red, as if dyed.

Again they painted his face, this time very carefully, in lines and circles of several colors. They seated him upon the sacred, ceremonial skin of an albino black bear and presented him with a pipe tomahawk decorated with eagle feathers and a pouch made of the whole skin of a skunk with the fur still on it. Inside the pouch was a mixture of tobacco and *killeg-nico*, which was shredded and cured sumac leaves. They also handed him a flint and steel for firemaking and even some special tinder.

Then they left him to sit by himself.

A feeling of eerie unreality came over him now as he sat all alone in this great chamber. It was strangely as if there was no past behind him, as if he were being born this very moment. He was awed and humbled by the feeling.

After perhaps fifteen or twenty minutes of quiet sitting, again there came the thrice-repeated call of Tiyanoga from just outside and at once the great room began to fill again with the men of the Iroquois League, this time all of them dressed in their finest garb. Once more the pipes were filled and lighted and smoked in utter silence—and this time William smoked his own new pipe.

Finally, Tiyanoga set his pipe aside, stood and beckoned William to stand beside him, and then spoke solemnly, his eyes locked on William's.

"My son," he said, "you are now flesh of our flesh and bone of our bone. By the ceremony which was performed this day, you are taken into the Mohawk nation and adopted into a great League of Nations. You are now received with great seriousness and solemnity in the room and presence and place of a great man. After what has passed this day, you are now one of us by an old strong law and custom. My son, we are now under the same obligations to love, support and defend you, that we are to love and defend one another; therefore, you are to consider yourself as one of our people and as one with our people, and forever more you will be known and respected in this tribe and in this League as Warraghiyagey—The-Man-Who-Undertakes-Great-Things."[22]

And William Johnson could not have been more honored had been knighted by the King of England.

59

# CHAPTER II

[ *April 22, 1745—Monday* ]

THROUGHOUT the frontier there was a sense of foreboding among the Indians and among many of the whites. It was as if something dreadful was coming, yet no one could place his finger on exactly what it was or why he felt this way. Even relatively minor events which would have been overlooked before seemed now to have a greater meaning, a more ominous import.

In the western Pennsylvania territory, where a great many Shawnees and Delawares were still living, incidents of white encroachment were increasing. Here and there fortified cabins were going up. Settlers who came to the country in small groups built their houses close together and looked to one another for mutual defense in times of crisis.

Traders from New England, from New York and Pennsylvania; from New Jersey, Maryland and Virginia were literally streaming into the Appalachian country east of the Susquehanna and a large number of the more daring were even crossing that stream to stake their claims on the land to the west of it. Almost without exception they were interested in but two things: to obtain land of their own, and to achieve personal gain ... and the two were so closely intertwined as to be one. To acquire these gains they dealt with the Indians privately and they cheated them outrageously. Appeals by Shawnee and Delaware delegates to the Pennsylvania colonial government resulted in nothing. Officials were wholly indifferent to their pleas for justice and fair trade.

Thoroughly disgusted, the Shawnees turned to the French and found the Canadian traders more considerate, even if their prices were higher, and thereupon pledged their allegiance to France. Immediately they removed almost entirely from the Pennsylvania country and resettled with the rest of

61

their tribe in the wild and remote Ohio country, along the banks of the Scioto and Little Miami rivers.

Some of the Delawares went with them to join their own brethren already on the Muskingum River, but the majority stayed behind, fearful that the Iroquois, who generally hated the French and were still bound to the English through ties of trade, would consider this as treachery and swoop down upon them to destroy them utterly.

Up at Sandusky Bay in the same Ohio country, a similar rift was occurring over this same problem of allegiance. With English traders coming to them more and more frequently, the hostility of the French at Detroit and that of the surrounding tribes became an almost tangible thing. When the English traders requested permission to build a trading post at Sandusky Bay, council was held and Huron opinion split. Since the split was deep, about half of the Hurons moved meekly back to the Detroit area and resumed residence there, while the other half—under Chief Orontony—remained at Sandusky Bay and granted the traders their request to erect the station on the north shore of the bay. It was just one more English wedge into the pro-French Indian country of the northwest.

The English took a step beyond this and proclaimed that because the Iroquois were their allies and had asked protection of the English—which they were not and had not—the Crown was now reaffirming in the strongest possible terms its "protectorate claim" to the lands west of the Alleghenies and down the Ohio River Valley.

As if to prove the lie, a party of Iroquois on the warpath against the Cherokees, passed through the Shenandoah Valley and were abruptly attacked by a Virginia militia detachment under command of Captains John McDowell and John Buchanan at Balcony Falls.[1] The fighting was brief but savage, with losses on each side about equal. McDowell and a number of his men were killed and the Indians scattered, but now a virtual state of war existed. Hastily, Lieutenant Governor William Gooch of Virginia made amends to the Iroquois through the payment of an indemnity, but the damage was done.

The entire Indian situation was growing ever more precarious.

[ *December 31, 1745—Tuesday* ]

War with France!

The dreaded news had flashed across the English colonies

earlier in the year with fearful impact. In May last year, before the colonies had even been notified by England that they were at war with their neighbors across the English Channel, the French captured an English island off the northern coast of America.

This was the Grand Banks area, where French and English both claimed fishing rights and the unexpected attack from France's fortress of Louisbourg on Cape Breton, Nova Scotia—or Acadia, as the French called it—was entirely successful. This was the beginning of King George's War, the North American segment of the War of the Austrian Succession.

Thus far it was a sea war, but throughout the frontier both Indians and whites remained poised for either fight or flight. In a brilliant campaign laid out by Governor William Shirley of Massachusetts, the Louisbourg fortress was taken. The New England militia led by the merchant general, William Pepperell, and the English fleet commanded by none other than Peter Warren, put the bastion under siege on May 5 this year and it surrendered to them on June 17. Both of the commanders received significant rewards for their efforts: Pepperell was knighted and became America's first baronet; Peter Warren was promoted to the rank of Admiral and given an award of twenty thousand pounds.

While this was going on, both the English and the French strove to get from their neighboring Indians unswerving pledges of allegiance. France was by far the more successful. Almost without exception the Indians she regularly dealt with pledged loyalty and support to the Canadian governor in any battles which might come against the English. Even the Caughnawagas—a northern branch of the Mohawks who had set themselves apart from the Iroquois League and lived along the St. Lawrence River—firmly allied themselves to the French.

The English were not so fortunate. Their hopes to ally to themselves the Iroquois League were dashed when, after lengthy counciling, that League declared its complete neutrality. It was a severe blow and the English set about doing whatever they could to rectify it. First they looked for a man who knew the Indians well and who could be trusted to be a sort of liaison between the Crown and them. None was so fitted for the job as William Johnson. Governor George Clinton of New York Colony, who had taken office in 1743, immediately appointed William to the post of Superintendent of Affairs of the Six Nations. He also made him a justice of the peace.

William, bouncing on his knee his third illegitimate child by Catherine Weisenberg—a girl named Mary, born a year ago last October 14—heard the news with great pleasure. In it he saw his big chance for power and glory and he leaped to the challenge.

Clinton knew of Johnson only through reputation, but he knew James Delancey personally and well. So impressed was he at the political ability and energy of the chief justice and so disposed himself not to be bothered with problems—preferring to concentrate on such matters as wining and dining himself—that he authorized Delancey to handle all governmental affairs. Occasionally, though, rousing himself enough to view with winefogged vision what was occurring, Clinton would express to Delancey his fear that the New York frontier might erupt in violence.

"After all," he remarked, "France's Indians have not declared neutrality as our Iroquois have."

Delancey brushed aside the governor's qualms. "Don't worry," he said, "even if the Six Nations won't fight, they certainly love their old Dutch allies too much to let any enemy brave ruffle a single hair on any New Yorker's head."

Such statements, both private and public, from Delancey—who was politically allied to the Albany faction in the colony's Assembly—caused Albany to feel quite safe. The merchants and townspeople settled back in an easy complacency.

William Johnson—Warraghiyagey—didn't share the feeling. Having by now taken part in many a Mohawk council and even several of the League councils at Onondaga, he was far from convinced that the Iroquois would stop any party of French Indians coming through. Not only were they determined to remain neutral, but the Mohawks—who were most inclined to espouse the English cause and had argued in its favor—were now themselves growing fearful of these whites.

For months they had been hearing rumors of intended action against themselves and Tiyanoga had told Johnson soberly, "With my own ears I have heard that the Albany people have agreed to kill us and drive us away from our lands, which they want. We have been warned to be alert at the time of the first snow, for that is when an attack will come against Teantontalogo, and this will be followed by another against my own village, Canajoharie, which is the heart of the Mohawk nation."

William had shaken his head and told the chief this was

ridiculous, that the English wished to have the Mohawks and the whole Iroquois League as allies, not as enemies. "You have been listening too closely to the chirping of bad birds, my friend," he told Tiyanoga.

The Mohawk wasn't convinced. He and Wascaugh, the chief of Teantontalogo, posted guards to watch. The first heavy snow had fallen when a procession of several sleighs loaded with supplies and ammunition slid neatly behind their horses in the dusk into Fort Hunter.

A runner sped into Teantontalogo shouting, "The white people of Albany are coming with drums and trumpets and several hundred soldiers to kill the Mohawks!"

At once Wascaugh ordered the place abandoned. Tiyanoga, who was on hand, quickly sent runners on their way to Onondaga and the capitals of the other Iroquois nations to alert them and then both chiefs had a brief, angry meeting with the Reverend Henry Barclay who was there.

"You," Tiyanoga accused savagely, "are the chief contriver of the destruction intended against us!"

Barclay's denials in a voice quaking with fear did not convince the chief. Tiyanoga turned and, with Wascaugh, strode toward the warriors and quickly organized an ambush for the supposedly advancing army from Albany. The Indians left the Lower Mohawk Castle uttering shrill cries of *"Quee! Quee! Quee!"*

Across the river at Mount Johnson, Warraghiyagey heard the cries as he lay in bed beside Catty. He felt the hairs at his nape prickle and leaped to his feet to dress. This sound the Mohawks had given vent to was the death cry, which is uttered only at times of imminent mortal peril. Within minutes he arrived on the run at Teantontalogo, only to find it barren of life except for the Reverend Barclay, who was now teetering on the edge of hysteria. The man of the cloth caught sight of him and rushed over.

"Oh, William, William," he cried, "they're gone, all of them. They accused me of setting some destruction against them. I thought they were going to kill me."

William Johnson squeezed his shoulder to reassure him, told him to go to the fort nearby and stay there until things settled down some and then set out himself to find Tiyanoga or Wascaugh. It was Tiyanoga who found him instead. The chief's face was set in tight, stern lines which gradually faded to a faint smile as Johnson told him earnestly that it just wasn't possible such an attack was planned and that the

65

ammunition and supplies that had arrived aboard the sleighs were only Fort Hunter's normal requisition.

"I know, Warraghiyagey," the chief said calmly, all trace of anger gone from him now. He motioned to a couple of his warriors to pass the word for the Mohawks to file back to Teantontalogo. Then he returned his attention to Johnson. "Perhaps now," he said, "your English will stop their games with us. The word is spread. Let us see what happens now."

It had all been an elaborate hoax to emphasize the danger of the situation prevailing on the frontier and the need for the English to treat with greater respect and deference the Indians of the Mohawk Valley and for them to adopt an Indian policy more favorable to all the Iroquois nations. It was the sort of game that tickled William's fancy and by the time he returned to Catty in Mount Johnson, he was chuckling. He could just visualize what effect tonight's action might have upon the complacent Albany residents.

As expected, the alarm swept across the entire frontier with chilling impact. Everyone knew that the Mohawks were the most pro-English of the entire Six Nations and the reports of their hysteria over an attack which failed to materialize was terrifying information. The same thought was in everyone's mind: if the Mohawks, apparently so fearful of the English, asked the French for protection, it would be given with alacrity and chances were that the entire Iroquois League, with all its strength and savagery, would ally itself to the enemy.

Cries of rage, alarm and accusation echoed in every quarter, the majority of them directed at Albany. The confused officials there could only insist that all this had probably been the work of outside agitators, most likely Jean Coeur—which was the collective name applied to French or Canadian agents infiltrating the countryside. Only Conrad Weiser, the shrewd Indian agent of Pennsylvania, saw through the scheme and laid the blame at Tiyanoga's feet, but few believed him. Policy changes were put into effect almost everywhere, stressing that the Indians were to be treated with care and respect and, "if possible, their confidence won back to their British friends." Even the French, after hearing the news, invited the Mohawk chiefs to Montreal to receive, without commitment, an abundance of presents and offers of immediate assistance if needed.

But the fun and games came to a sudden and fearful halt when just last month an army of four hundred French soldiers and two hundred twenty of the Caughnawagas and

Abnakis from St. Francis, Montreal and St. Frederic came unmolested through Mohawk territory to Saratoga,[2] thirty miles north of Albany. To have stopped them was, to the Mohawks, unthinkable. The Caughnawagas *were* Mohawks; they were still their brothers, even if they had disconnected themselves from the League many years ago.

Without serious opposition, this force attacked the town at dawn and burned it so completely that the only structure left standing when they departed was a sawmill somewhat apart from the main section of town. They killed or captured in the process one hundred and one individuals, including the Negro slaves of the residents. All the town's possessions were also taken away with them. The destruction was complete and helped, in part, by the terrified citizenry who burned their own fort and fled down the Hudson.

Now terror walked the streets of Albany and frenzied activity took place. Women, children and precious goods were shipped downriver to New York and the remaining residents girded themselves for defense. Residents along the Mohawk, too, fled to safer locales downriver. William Johnson himself was warned that the French had put a price on his head because he was a nephew of Admiral Peter Warren and was agitating within the Iroquois League. They invited him to abandon Mount Johnson and come to spend the winter in Albany.

William responded by sending some of his servants down, but he had no intention himself of leaving Mount Johnson. From Peter Warren he received a brass cannon and some swivels and he prepared for defense as best he could, making of his home a veritable fort.

Now Tiyanoga had come, deeply troubled, with the report that news had come to him of Frenchmen, Canadians and Caughnawagas advancing into the Mohawk Valley.

"They are coming, it is said," he told his adopted white brother, "in a great invading cloud. I will lead my people off into the woods that they may be safe and not forced to fight their own brothers."

William Johnson shook his head. He motioned at Catty and the children, at some of the servants who had remained with him and then swept his arm out to take in the entire house and all his possessions.

"Tiyanoga, you see here my home and my people. I have not sent away any of my possessions or effects, yet I, Warraghiyagey, have here as much value as perhaps the whole river. Since I, with my weak defense, intend to stay, how is it

67

that my brother shows fear and a desire to leave? You say the Caughnawagas are Mohawks, your brothers. Am I not also your brother? And if they are your brothers, are they not also my brothers? I do not fear them, nor do I want to do them injury, but I will not see them destroy my house and possessions, or harm my family. I will face them when and if the time comes. Can you, a great chief and a great warrior, do less?"

And Tiyanoga, swayed by the argument which touched his pride, could not. He returned to Canajoharie and remained there with his people. But the attack did not materialize and the stature of Warraghiyagey increased among the Mohawks.

### [ January 30, 1746—Thursday ]

The mounted warriors returning to the Ottawa village near Detroit numbered twenty-two—eleven less than the journey had begun with. For five months they had been gone, led by their war chief, Winniwok, who was also chief of the village. They had gone southward along a familiar warpath against the Cherokees and now they were returning with the cape of victory over their shoulders.

Although eleven of them had not returned, thirty-seven scalps had been brought back, along with much plunder, and the expedition can only have been termed successful.

But along with the cape of victory there was a cloak of sadness. One of those who had fallen beneath the war club of a Cherokee defender was Winniwok.

The loss of the chief was mourned, but the gap he left with his passing was quickly filled by the warrior who had been most outstanding in the battle; the warrior who alone had accounted for seven of the scalps that had been taken; the warrior who had ridden back at the head of the victorious party.

His name was Pontiac.

### [ March 12, 1746—Wednesday ]

The humpbacked Marquis de la Galissonière may have been deformed in body, but his mind was sharp and his foresight admirable. He was aware that to depend solely on alliance with the Indians to protect French interest in North America was foolhardy in the extreme. Undeniably, such alliance was very desirable, even urgent, but there was more to it than that. With their apparent inability to fully understand or adopt for themselves the European systems of commerce,

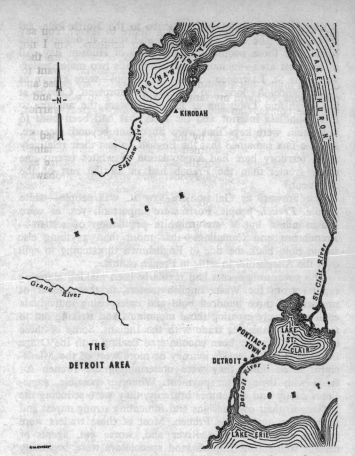

industry, politics and warfare, they were a doomed race. Eventually they must either merge with the whites or become extinct, there was no other way.

It would not happen in his lifetime, the governor knew, and perhaps not for a century or so, but the pattern was clear: wherever, the whites, especially the English, established themselves, the Indians were driven back. And so, however necessary French-Indian relations were now, it was in white strength that the real power lay.

Galissonière was painfully aware of the queer imbalance of territory and population among the whites here. France claimed all of North America from the Alleghenies to the

Rocky Mountains and from Mexico to the North Pole, excepting only the English Colonies and some ill-defined possessions of those people on the borders of Hudson Bay. All of this vast area—including the continent's two major waterways, the St. Lawrence and the Mississippi—were known as New France. As long ago Cadillac had foreseen, Canada at the north and Louisiana at the south were the anchors to this boundless interior and the forts that had been built to link them were keys that were important beyond measure. But the fact remained that the English, in just their relatively small territory here had a population of whites twenty-one times greater than the French had in all the rest of the continent.[8]

The answer, as Galissonière saw it, was people—white people, *French* people. Forts were important, yes, as were Indian allies, but it was a white population of settlers—Frenchmen and Canadians—that more than anything else would hold back the tide of Englishmen threatening to spill over the Alleghenies to settle in French claims.

The governor's agents had regularly been making alarming reports from the West. English traders, to the number of upwards of three hundred bold and enterprising individuals each year, were crossing those mountains and striking out to tap the profitable fur trade with the Indians. Some of these traders had already been encountered dealing with the Osage tribe, as far as a week's journey or more west of the Mississippi. In so doing they were undermining the French fur trade with their better payment. Wherever possible, sometimes subtly and sometimes brazenly, they were seducing the Indians to their own designs and fomenting strong unrest and aggravation against the French. Most of these traders were coming down the Ohio River and, worse yet, agents of certain well-known English land speculators were beginning to follow.

What was needed here in America was settlers, but not more traders and not more priests. Especially not more priests. In trying to make New France an exclusive bastion of Roman Catholic orthodoxy and in effect keeping a priest on guard at the gate to let none in but those he approved, France was closing the door on empire.

Nor was it a matter of settlers not being available and willing. Right at this moment in France, in a fervor of religious fanaticism, agents of the Crown were destroying scores of thousands in the Huguenot congregations; hanging the ministers, killing the men or imprisoning them for life in the galleys, kidnapping the children, penning the women in the filthy dungeons of Aigues Mortes where survival for over a year was little short of a miracle. With a wave of his hand the King could send to America the type of French settlers needed—Frenchmen of every station; peasants as well as nobles, farmers as well as soldiers, Huguenots as well as Catholics. Need was desperate for the most educated, the most industrious, those most tempered by adversity, the most competent and capable of self-rule that France could boast. One simple order from the King could send a quarter million such people to populate the valleys of the Mississippi and the Ohio and the St. Lawrence all the way from Quebec to Louisiana.

To request so large a party at once, the governor knew, would be to invite dismissal of the entire plan, for even transportation for such a mass migration would not come cheaply. But if a smaller number were petitioned at first, there was a possibility that the government might give in. Later, perhaps, more might be successfully requisitioned.

And so, with this sure knowledge of what needed to be done burning in his brain, Galissonière wrote to both the French colonial minister and the King in impassioned letters:

... As chief representative of the American policy of France, I feel that, cost what it might, we must hold fast to Canada and link her to Louisiana not only with forts, as we have been endeavoring to do, but, even more importantly, with no less than ten thousand settlers from the mother country.

These people, from all stations in our society, should be spread to settle and multiply in the broad valleys of the interior, to hold back the British Colonies and cramp their growth by confinement within narrow limits.

Already an ominous flow of British traders, against whom our forts have little control, moves westward from the mountains, even to beyond the Mississippi River. They are alienating the natives to our cause and close on their heels are coming land speculators with an eye to future English settlement.

It is true that Canada and her dependencies have always been a burden; but they are necessary as a barrier against English ambition; and to abandon them is to abandon ourselves; for if we suffer our enemies to become masters in America, their trade and naval power will grow to vast

71

*proportions and they will draw from their colonies a wealth
that will make them preponderant in Europe . . .*

### [ *August 11, 1746—Monday* ]

The attack by Indians under French and Canadian leadership, so dreaded all winter and spring throughout the Mohawk Valley, never became a reality. Now and again rumors of approaching forces flashed terrifyingly across the countryside, but all had proven groundless.

Governor George Clinton, because of James Delancey's tragic miscalculation in saying there was no possibility of French and Indian attack, only to have Saratoga wiped out almost on the heels of this reassurance, had a serious break with the chief justice. Though certain personal matters were also involved, not the least of which was Delancey's apparent contempt for the governor, it was the Saratoga attack which finally severed the cord that had so long been their tie.

At a dinner party attended by both men, a hot argument broke out between them. Faces flushed with anger, their voices grew louder until at last, with the whole assemblage staring at them, Delancey jumped to his feet and sent his chair crashing backward to the floor behind him. He pointed a trembling finger at the governor and his voice was thick with ill-controlled fury.

"Damn you, Clinton! If it's the last thing I ever do, I'll get you!"

Clinton was not much impressed by the threat. He watched calmly and quietly as Delancey stormed out, followed by some of his friends, and then casually continued his meal. But now, needing someone to work closely with him—especially someone who was knowledgeable about the Indians—he selected as his special adviser an Irish-Scot named Cadwallader Colden.

Not only was Colden author of a half dozen or more rather pedantic volumes on a variety of subjects, he had also written the only published works on the Iroquois League. They were authoritative books, too, since Colden was an adopted Mohawk. If he was somewhat lacking in imagination, as his enemies claimed, this was offset by a thorough background in New York politics, a strong allegiance to the King of England and a keen desire to fight the French.

Delancey, with his ties to Clinton broken, was more strongly than ever backed by the New York Assembly and now he convinced Albany again that it had no need to worry over possible attack from French or Indians or both. Albany's trade was so valuable, he declared, not only to the Indians but to the French in their continued smuggling, that no matter who else was attacked, Albany wouldn't be touched. As far as the Mohawk Valley was concerned, William Johnson was the only one now profiting from the furs coming downriver, so why worry about it? Acting on this point of view, the Assembly thereupon refused to send any of New York's militia there, claiming the Mohawk Valley settlers had all deserted their homes.

The result was that Fort Oswego was left isolated and unsupplied. The Albany merchants who had the commission to keep it supplied flatly refused to do so unless the government supplied military escorts for their supply trains. As if he had been waiting for just this knock of opportunity, William Johnson made his move. Others might have abandoned their Mohawk Valley homes, but he had no intention of leaving his and now he contacted Governor Clinton, offering to take on the job of shipping government supplies to the outpost on the old basis. For the first time, the Dutch merchants in Albany came over to his side and urged that he be given the contract. They were dead certain, when the contract was subsequently awarded to Johnson, that this Mohawk Valley upstart would soon be bankrupt.

William knew it wouldn't be easy and hadn't expected it to be. His supply boats would have to move upstream on the Mohawk, in and out of the river past numerous mean little portages around rapids, until they could go no farther. Then would come the miserable carry to the headwaters of Wood Creek for the float down to Oneida Lake. Bad storms were frequent on that large lake and the rest of the trip downriver to Fort Oswego would not be much easier. But this was precisely the type of challenge which intrigued William. He rose to meet it at once, stopping only briefly to write a note to Governor Clinton:

*I thank you, sir, for the kind favor of your appointment to this trust. I intend to have the first shipment on its way the latter end of this present week, which is very expeditious considering the little notice I have had . . .*

It was not the only challenge William Johnson met head-on. A growing war fervor was in the air. Explicit orders had recently come from the Crown that New York was to join the other colonies—Massachusetts in particular—in an attack against the French from the south and for this measure to approve a militia levy. Since this meant attacking through the Iroquois country, the orders further stated that the Six Nations were to be enlisted as allies if at all possible.

"Our Indian commissioners say that the Iroquois are very unwilling to enter the war," the Assembly replied, shaking its collective head in disgust, "and it is much better for us that the Indians should not intermeddle."

But the orders were positive and so, reluctantly in the extreme, funds were voted for a full-scale conference with the chiefs. Clinton and Colden summoned William Johnson. Because of his strong influence with the Mohawks, they wanted him to try to convert these Indians to a firmer British alliance.

All the tribes of the Iroquois League were invited to attend a grand council to be held in Albany beginning on August 19. The Indian commissioners of New York would send their agents among the more western tribes of the League. But William was requested to invite the Mohawks and, if he could manage it, to convince them to ally themselves with the English even before the council should begin, in the hope that they might sway the other nations to do likewise at the council. William agreed and immediately upon his return to Mount Johnson he sent runners out, calling for a preliminary council at Teantontalogo.

It was on a muggy evening in July that the Mohawks gathered in a great crowd at the village across the river from Mount Johnson. Their eyes widened as they saw in front of the council longhouse the black post that William Johnson had had erected, into which he had sunk his own tomahawk.

It was a call for war.

Surrounded with warriors who were his personal friends. William himself was on hand as Warraghiyagey—a Mohawk, not a white man. His buckskin breeches and moccasins were lavishly decorated with porcupine quills and atop his head was a black skullcap edged with beaten silver. From that silver band protruded one huge eagle feather. His bare chest, arms, back and face had been painted in the traditional gaudy designs and dried deerhoof rattles were strung around his wrists, knees and ankles. He looked far more Indian than white.

He had ordered a fine, five-year-old bull spitted to roast and, while it cooked, he crouched with the Indians in preliminary ceremony to eat his share of cooked dog meat from a communal platter. When the beef was almost black on the outside but still very rare inside, he fell to it with the others, hacked his chunk of meat off with his knife and gnawed it as they were gnawing theirs. The bread he had provided went well with it and even more so did the kegs of rum. Time and again as he and his young band of followers ate in his lodge, Tiyanoga and Wascaugh and a number of the older chiefs entered and tried to draw away the younger men, showing them that Warraghiyagey's tomahawk had been pulled from the post and buried ceremoniously, but they paid no heed.

At last Warraghiyagey threw back his head and a blood-chilling screech erupted from his throat. In an instant the same call left the mouths of a dozen or more others and from all over the village the men at once moved toward the grand council house. Since he had called the council, it was Warraghiyagey's right and privilege that he and his followers should be last to enter the great room. There was a great crowd present when they filed in.

All but Warraghiyagey sat and, as they did so, a drum beat began. At once his legs rose and fell in cadence and his heels thumped against the earthen floor with muted impact. For long minutes he stamped thus, now and then bending deeply at the waist and more frequently jerking his body spastically.

The Indians watched him intently, saw the concentration on his face, saw the sweat which soon made his body glisten in the firelight, heard him at last open his mouth again in that fearsome cry which for centuries had preceded slaughter in the wilderness, heard him at last begin his chant.

With each beat of the drums, with each pounding of his heels, with each flailing of his arms and jerking of his dripping body, he chanted a phrase.

"My brothers . . . my brothers . . . I call for war . . . Oh, hear me now . . . I call for war! . . . Your great good father . . . across the sea . . . your mighty King . . . has power great . . . has iron fist . . . has heart of panther . . . strength of bear . . . breath of otter . . . eye of eagle . . . mind of wolf . . . King George, your father . . . across the sea . . . has army great . . . of many guns . . . and many men . . . to help you drive . . . away your foe . . . your foe the French . . . into the sea . . . The Frenchman woos you . . . to your faces . . . but plans to strip you . . . of all you have . . . of all your forests . . . all your streams . . . all your game . . . all your furs . . . all your fish . . . all your land! . . . See him now . . . across your land . . . see him now in all his forts . . . from there to fight you . . . to wage great war . . . on my Mohawk brothers . . . on our Iroquois League!"

A strange transformation was taking place in the man who had been William Johnson but was now the Mohawk Warraghiyagey. At first his phrases had come in a gasped manner, jerky and almost incoherent; but then a wildness seemed to come over him, his eyes rolled and the spittle ran from his mouth corners and there was a measured tautness to every fiber of his being which communicated itself to the onlookers. His words droned on, surer now, rising and falling in tone, full of fire and feeling, angry, appealing, wild, beseeching, convincing. It was more as if he was being controlled then controlling.

". . . But will you here . . . my Mohawk brothers . . . see Great King George . . . your battles fight? . . . will you my brothers . . . prove yourselves . . . against this foe . . . your ancestral foe . . . this great French tree . . . whose branches spread . . . throughout the land . . . until the sun . . . is shut away? . . . Will you come join him . . . join great King George . . . take his hand . . . aid him in battle . . . as he helps you? . . . Forever win his praise and love? . . . . Forever know his thanks and kindness? . . . Join with him . . . my Mohawk brothers . . . in heart and hand . . . in mind and spirit . . . against the Frenchman . . . against your foe . . . against the one who robs you!"

On he chanted, while tendons in neck and back and chest strained against the skin which bound them, while beads of perspiration flew from him and twinkled briefly in the firelight as they fell. And when he finally stopped and held out his arms to them, there was a roar of approval and the screaming cry of war reverberated through the longhouse.

Now others rose to speak and as they spoke, Warraghiyagey danced in time to their words, again stamping his feet, jerking, jumping wildly in great bounds. Some of the speakers urged that the tomahawk be dug up and replanted in the war post; others begged for coolness and the need for wisdom, the need to let the white man fight his own fight and to remain neutral, aloof.

Still Warraghiyagey danced on, his vision fogged, hardly hearing, hardly caring, gripped by the force which moved him. Nor did he stop when suddenly Wascaugh, chief of this village and second principal chief of the Mohawk, leaped to his feet and gave his own chant and dance, calling not for peace and neutrality but for war as allies beside the Great

English army under the mantle of the great father across the sea, King George, and boasting of his own prowess which he claimed was known wherever the eagle flew.

Warraghiyagey danced on, pantomiming a leap upon an enemy, the cleaving of his head with a tomahawk, the taking of his scalp with knife. And one after another the older chiefs joined him and the room rocked with the chants they uttered and shuddered with the stamping of their feet. Warraghiyagey could not stop. Though others who had been dancing much less time than he were falling in exhaustion, yet he kept on as if possessed and the spirit that gripped him bred a contagion which settled over all until at last even old Tiyanoga, one of the few still seated, also leaped up and cast his blanket aside and echoed the stirring scream.

Tiyanoga and Wascaugh and then the others leaped to and around Warraghiyagey and the words they gave him were alike. "We are of one mind ... we are of one heart ... we are of one hand . . . with Warraghiyagey! . . . We will join ... as one man ... heart and hand ... to fight with the army ... the army of King George ... against the Frenchman ... against our common enemy ... It is our word ... It is our bond ... We have given it ... We will fight ... beside Warraghiyagey!"

And then at last consciousness left the white man, and he fell to the floor where he became almost indistinguishable from the many others crumpled there in exhaustion while other warriors danced on and screamed fearfully above them.

The battle was only partially won, though, and no one knew it better than William Johnson when he finally returned to Mount Johnson. Apparently he had the Mohawks, yet that tribe was only a part of the Iroquois League. If Tiyanoga and Wascaugh were not able to convince the League council at Onondaga, there could be serious trouble. Approval must be unanimous; one single dissenting vote would mean that neutrality would be maintained. And the fear that such a thing might occur abruptly became reality when, four weeks after he had filled Teantontalogo with the war fever, William was visited by Tiyanoga.

"Warraghiyagey," the chief said, "my news is not good. Many in the council were greatly displeased and they will not point their faces down this river. Some of them have agreed that they will attend the council in Albany to give their decision, but I will tell you now what it is: Canassatego and Red Head and Old Belt and almost all the other great chiefs not of the Mohawk tribe feel that it is to their common interest to remain neutral and that is their decision. They have further bound the Mohawks to inaction by council vote and there is some anger directed toward you that you would attempt to undermine the structure of our League."

Johnson grunted and then remained quiet for a moment as he studied the heavyset, rapidly graying chief. What he saw in the old man's eyes rekindled his flickering hopes. He grunted again and spoke.

"Is it not true, Tiyanoga," he said, "that some of the Mohawks have allied themselves to the French and are now known as Caughnawagas?"

"It is true, Warraghiyagey."

"Is it not possible then that Tiyanoga and his Mohawks have also the right to choose who they wish to fight beside, in order to protect themselves?"

"It is possible, Warraghiyagey."

"Then I ask you now as my brother, Tiyanoga, will you and your tribe not stand beside me at the Albany Council? Will not you and your tribe honor your conviction of the war dance at Teantontalogo? Will not you and your tribe help the English to fight the enemy who is as much yours as ours? Is not your heart as much English as the heart of Warraghiyagey is Mohawk?"

For a long moment Tiyanoga pondered silently, but then he reached out to place both his hands on Johnson's shoulders and he smiled.

"According to Iroquois tradition," he said, "all neighbors not in alliance with us are and must be enemies and warfare is the only path to glory. Neutrality while a war is waged in our country is not possible. Therefore, the council has declared unwisely and incorrectly in this matter. The Mohawks are strong and they are proud. I will stand beside my brother. The Mohawks will stand beside the English against the French."

A feeling of exultation surged through William Johnson. He had done it! Now it remained to be seen what would happen when the Iroquois Council discovered that the Mohawks had cemented themselves to the English. For Tiyanoga to have done this took great courage. He was knowingly and openly breaking a convenant well over two centuries old and his action might well shatter the entire League.

Already, far to the west, along the banks of the Allegheny River headwaters, the Seneca chiefs had begun the trek eastward to Albany. As they journeyed on the trail which connected their principal chain of villages, they were joined at each town by other chiefs and warriors. But when they reached Canajoharie, the heart of the Mohawk tribe, they saw with shock and anger that the Mohawks were painted for war.

With dour expression a delegation of five of the most important chiefs—Canassatego and Red Head of the Onondagas, Old Belt of the Senecas, Shikellimus[4] of the Cayugas and Torach of the Oneidas—left their large party and approached Tiyanoga. They did not greet one another. Canassatego was spokesman for the group and his eyes smoldered with rage. When he spoke, his words were cold and full of threat.

"The Mohawks," he told Tiyanoga, "ought to have remembered, before breaking League orders, that they are the smallest in number of any of the Six Nations."[5]

Tiyanoga drew himself up rather than quailing before the wrath of the Onondaga chief. His own dark eyes flickered with anger and his reply was no less threatening.

"It is true," he said slowly, "we are less considerable as to number than any of the other nations of our League—" as he spoke his hand moved up to curl around the haft of the knife at his waistband and he continued, "—but our hearts are truly English and all of us are *men!* If force be put to the trial here and now, perhaps our numbers will be found greater than you imagine."

For the space of a dozen heartbeats the only sound was a rustling and clicking as hands reached for tomahawks or war clubs or knives and as muskets were raised. Never since it had been formed had the Iroquois League approached so close to brutal rupture. But Canassatego made no move toward his own knife and in another moment he shook his head slightly. There was still anger in his voice when he spoke, but with it there was also a great depth of sadness.

"It is a matter which the council must discuss, Tiyanoga," he said slowly, "but there is no agreement in my heart for one who would do this. If I can be convinced that it is to the good of the League to aid the English, I will do so at this Albany Council, for I have been given authority to speak for the League. But for your rash move in thus preparing for war, I will not suffer those of the other nations to journey with you."

On this he directed his swarm of followers across the fording place here on the Mohawk River and the march toward Albany was continued. Along the way settlers rushed to their doors to witness one of the strangest sights ever seen on the Mohawk. Marching along the road bordering the southern side of the river was a great straggling cluster of Indians—Senecas, Tuscaroras, Oneidas, Cayugas and Onondagas—all of them, wearing simple buckskin breeches, sometimes with the accompanying shirt or blanket of everyday wear. Along the northern road in spaced single file, nude except for breechcloths, strode the Mohawks, their bodies painted garishly and one, two or three eagle feathers attached to their short hair at the crown. As they marched past Mount Johnson a sudden chorus of delighted screeches arose from them as the door opened and from it stepped a similarly dressed and painted white man whom they had named Warraghiyagey.

He took his place at the van with the chiefs Tiyanoga and Wascaugh and he was still there when, at 2 P.M. today, August 11, 1746, he led them past astonished residents through the very center of town. Toward the old Albany fort William Johnson paced them and when he looked up he saw, leaning over the ramparts, the figure of Governor George Clinton, a great smile wreathing his face. Following William's lead, each Mohawk as he passed directly beneath the governor, fired his musket into the ground as a salute. The governor turned and issued an order to someone behind him and in a moment the ground shuddered and the air reverberated as the fort's cannon spouted a deep-voiced return salute.

All of England, the well-pleased Clinton decided, would hear from him of this surprising and capable young William Johnson whom the Indians called Warraghiyagey—the man who had done what dozens of Indian commissioners before him had failed to do.

A part of the Iroquis League, at least, was England's!

### [ October 24, 1746—Friday ]

It had become standard practice through all the inland New Hampshire area for isolated farmers and their families to band together in times of danger under one roof for mutual protection. For over a year now the Abnakis, Pennacooks and Caughnawagas had been harassing the New England frontier and, while the Merrimack Valley had thus far been frightened but not badly harmed, it was wise to take precautions.

The New Hampshire farmers were forced to work in cooperation with one another; perhaps a dozen or more of

them moving from farm to farm in order to plant, to cultivate, to harvest. Throughout all of the past winter alarms
had been frequent but then, as warmer weather came and
crops were planted and tended without sight or sign of the
marauding Indians, tension relaxed and so did safety measures. Many of the farmers who had forted up together at
Rumford moved back to their individual farms and it seemed
that the danger was past.

The blow fell with brutal unexpectedness on August 15. A
war party made up of the three pro-French tribes left their
villages at St. Francis on the St. Lawrence River and near
Fort St. Frederic at Crown Point on Lake Champlain and
crept unseen into the Merrimack Valley, accompanied by a
handful of Canadian bush fighters, the *coureurs de bois*. A
detachment of eight militiamen from Captain Daniel Ladd's
company were out on a patrol in the woods perhaps no more
than half a mile distant, when a volley of shots sounded and
in a short time the screams of the men of that detachment
could be heard faintly. Ladd's remaining party was not large
and so he and his men advanced cautiously toward where the
sound had originated, fearful of ambush. The Indians and
bush lopers, however, were gone.

What they found at the scene was not pleasant. A single
survivor from the detachment tumbled out of the undercover, half out of his wits with terror, his story made largely
incoherent with hysteria. But it wasn't necessary to hear his
account to determine what had taken place. Five of the party
had been killed on the spot. The bodies had swiftly been
stripped and then systematically chopped up. Their scalps
were gone, as were their hearts. Their entrails had been
ripped out and now hung in disgusting strings from surrounding trees. Their genitals had been hacked away, and here
and there in the small clearing lay severed a bare hand, a
foot, a section of arm, a knee, a head.

Two of the men had disappeared and the single survivor
blubbered about the Indians having loaded them down with
the detachment's guns, clothing and equipment and then
forced them away with them. No one in Ladd's party needed
any explanation of what was virtually certain to follow for
those two; better they had died like these on the ground.

The Indian party, according to the survivor, was not especially large, but Ladd prudently led his force back to Rumford to get replacements for the company. One of the
volunteers he got there was a tall, stockily built youth who
looked older than his fourteen years. Glad for a chance to

shoulder arms with a company of men instead of remaining in the overcrowded shelter filled with women and old men, howling children and crying babies, he trudged with Ladd's company through the forest in search of the marauders.

Here and there the party found Indian sign, but the days stretched into weeks and then the weeks into months without an encounter. And now, with October drawing to a close, the rooftops of Rumford were once again in sight. Though the company would now be disbanded, the youth was sure of one thing: he would never again stay behind when there were Indians to be chased. Rather frighteningly for one so young, there was in his breast a burning hatred for the savages; a lust to spill their blood, to watch them suffer. While this time no Indians had been taken, in times to come they would be. And he intended to be on hand when such time came to aid in the slaughter.

He was the only member of Ladd's company who was not glad to see the long patrol come to a close. He had hoped with a fierce passion that he could have killed an Indian while he was still fourteen—had, in fact, vowed that he would—but it was a vow that no longer had any real likelihood of fulfillment.

In another three weeks, Robert Rogers would be fifteen years old.

### [ December 31, 1746—Wednesday ]

The Albany Indian Congress was more successful than William Johnson had dared hope. The great exhilaration of his arrival on August 11 leading the war-painted Mohawks and followed in a little while by the other League delegations was not diminished by subsequent events. The impact of these Indians marching into Albany was a picture that no resident of that city would ever forget. The savage congregation camped outside the walls of the Albany fort, and daily more of them arrived until, by the time the Congress convened on August 19, over seven hundred Indians were on hand, including a number of squaws and youngsters.

Clearly smarting at the coup pulled off by William Johnson, two men were in a bad mood. They were Philip Livingston and Conrad Weiser, the Indian agents of New York and Pennsylvania respectively. Johnson, they felt, with some justification, was infringing in their field and making them look bad. Livingston didn't get along well with the Indians in any case, but Weiser had long been acknowledged as the most influential white man among the Indians. Both men, hearing how Johnson had openly flaunted the edict of the Iroquois League in getting the Mohawks to declare for war, suspected that Johnson would quickly be murdered by one of the other League members.

Both agents considered this a splendid idea.

In addition to the Iroquois on hand, there was also a delegation of two representatives from the Mississaugi Chippewas who had been visiting Onondaga when the announcements of the Albany Congress had been made and who were invited by their hosts to attend.

All of the Indians were extremely anxious to hear what the New York governor would have to say but, as luck would have it, George Clinton came down with a fever on the morning of the opening council. He appointed Cadwallader Colden to represent him in the talks and Colden did an admirable job.

As in all such councils, he who called it had the right and privilege of speaking first. And, as always, he would speak at whatever length he desired without interruption, contradiction or question from anyone else as he made his points and passed out the belts of wampum to emphasize each point. Colden knew well the proper procedure to follow in making his speech; courtesy called first for an expression of sympathy, followed by a brief restatement of the past relationship of the two races before actually getting into the business at hand.

"Brothers," he began, "my heart is glad in your presence here and my wish is that you are all well and that you and your families will have full stomachs and long lives."

He paused while the official interpreter changed this to the Iroquois tongue and then continued:

"Brothers, my heart is also sad at the news of those among your families and friends who have died since our last congress; but let us know together that this meeting of our hearts and tongues serves to wipe off the sorrowful tears from your eyes and by this act your throats are become unstopped so that the words may pass. With this congress the bloody bed is washed clean and our minds and hearts left free of the sorrow for those who died.

"Brothers, our first friendship began with the arrival of the white man's first great canoe at Albany. At our arrival you were very much surprised, but seeing that what we had to offer you brought you pleasure and filled your need—as you were convinced when showed how to use what we brought—

all of you then resolved to take great care of this large canoe, that nothing should bring it harm. It was agreed between us to tie it fast with a great rope to one of the largest oaks on the river bank. But then, on considering this further at a later meeting, it was thought safest, lest a wind should blow down that tree, to make a long rope to bind us fast all the way to Onondaga. This was done and our friendship was great. You put the rope under your feet so that if anything hurt or touched this great canoe, you would know of it by the shaking of the rope. And if such came to pass, you agreed then to rise all as one and see what the matter was, and whoever hurt the great canoe was to suffer at your hands."

He paused and as the interpreter finished, one of the chiefs shouted out, *"Yo-hay?"*—Do you hear? At once from the assemblage came the resounding reply, *"Hay-gagh cohweh heglohmekah!"*—We hear and we understand!

"Your father down the great river," continued Colden, "the Governor of New York, was so pleased at this that in place of the great rope which tied us together, he made that bond a silver chain—a covenant chain—which was as shiny and bright as our hearts and would bind us forever in Brotherhood so that your warriors and ours should be one heart, one hand, one flesh, one blood; so that whatsoever happened to the one, happened to the other as well."

*"Yohay?"* came the question at his pause, and the immediate answer, *"Hay-gagh cohweh heglohmekah!"*

Colden smiled in approval and went on. "Our forefathers, finding this chain was good, ordered that if ever that silver chain should begin to stain, if ever it should begin to rust, if ever it should offer to crack, or if ever it should offer to break, that it should immediately be brightened and strengthened and not let to become dull or weak or broken on any account, for then you and we were both dead. Brothers, these are the words of our wise forefathers, white and Indian, which you know well."

Again the pause and the chorused reply to the question before Colden plunged into the matter at hand. His voice now became more intense, solemn and compelling:

"Brothers, the governor congratulates the Six Nations on being the great League of united nations that it is and he opens wide the door of eternal friendship. He congratulates you, too, on having reached that happy time when, with the English, you may have the opportunity to reestablish your fame as warriors over all the Indian nations and revenge all the injuries your country has received from our mutual enemies, the French. Already the great Mohawks have struck the war post with their hatchets and have painted themselves in preparation to fight beside the English. Will not the other great tribes of the Iroquois do the same? Will not the Onondagas and the Senecas, the Cayugas and the Oneidas and their children, the Tuscaroras, also raise on high the war whoop and march beside the English soldiers to strike down and destroy the Frenchmen?"

William Johnson, squatting on the ground with the Mohawks, was listening intently and with approval, but at the next words of Colden his face became hard, for the words were a lie; a cold, bald-faced, dangerous lie.

"Brothers," Colden continued, "already many thousands of soldiers from England have arrived in New York and are gathering there to march against the French. Tens of thousands more will be coming soon from the King to join them; they are probably already on their way. Already the Colonies have raised a great cloud of their own soldiers to join them. Already the French tremble as does the aspen with the first cool breezes of autumn, for it knows hard times are at hand, just as the French know it. How greatly the ancestors of the Iroquois here today would rejoice at such a chance to revenge themselves in full upon the lying Frenchmen! Brothers, I ask you now, is the covenant chain still bright? Will the Iroquois clasp hands with the English now and come with their armies as one body, one heart, one flesh and with but one goal—to destroy the French?"

"Yo-hay?" shouted the spokesman chief, and the answer this time was given individually by the chief representative of each tribe present.

"Hay-gagh cohweh heglohmekah!" shouted Tiyanoga from beside William Johnson and, in turn, came the same phrase from the chiefs of the other five tribes, and then even from one of the two Mississaugi Chippewa delegates, Chief Kaiwahnee.

The reply was not an affirmation of what the speaker had said. It was merely an indication from each delegate that the proposal had been heard and fully understood and that now the tribes themselves would go into council to discuss the matter and, in due time, give their reply.

At the moment, William Johnson was wrestling with a grave problem of his own. As an adopted Mohawk and an English subject, wherein did his loyalty lie? Was it upon his shoulders to tell the chiefs in the council in which he would

85

have a seat that thousands of English soldiers had *not* arrived at New York, that tens of thousand more were *not* coming, that the "great cloud of soldiers" from the Colonies was a mere handful of inexperienced militia who would probably run, witless with fear, at the first onslaught of an enemy? By the same token could he, at such a critical stage for his own interests and those of his countrymen, undermine the new confidence instilled in the Iroquois for the English? Could he now, when his own star was on the ascension with the colonial government and even the Crown, jeopardize that?

He rationalized in the matter. He had it in his power now, he felt, to become a powerful force for the whites among the Indians and for the Indians among the English. Would it not be better to foster this influence he was gaining, in the realization that later he might be able to do great things for both, and for himself at the same time?

For four days, as the Iroquois council went on in private and speaker after speaker expressed himself, William Johnson wrestled with the problem. When, at the end of the fourth day the council terminated and he had still said nothing, William knew he would remain silent and he prayed that what he was doing was best—for the English, for the Indians, for himself.

The general congress was reconvened and now it was Canassatego, the great orator chief of the Onondagas who spoke for the Iroquois League. The large audience stilled expectantly and the chief, his expression unreadable, faced Colden who was sitting to one side.

"Brother," Canassatego began, "the chain of friendship between us reflects the sun as do the ripples on the water of this river. We are now heartily entered into the war with you and will become one with the English army which is about to march.

"Brother, we will come. We will bring with us as many of our allies as we can draw together and all of us will wait for your great and strong army and join it to wipe away from our country the black shadow from the French cloud."

It was an incredible statement which caused Colden's eyes to widen. He had expected vacillation, dissent and a noncommittal answer, as had always before happened. But now, here it was: England had exactly what it had so long wanted and so desperately needed, and now it was in no position to accept. The talk of the army on hand, the greater army coming, the militia in readiness—all these had been only a stratagem. It was not anticipated that the Iroquois would

86

fully ally themselves but, rather, that they would go back to their own home councils for deliberation. Even then it was not expected that the result would be alliance but a continuance of the long neutrality. The idea of the army and militia was planted simply to help prevent Frenchmen from persuading the Iroquois to join them against the English. With the supposed knowledge that the English had this army in readiness, the Iroquois would not be apt to ally themselves to the French.

This was a potentially dangerous problem, aggravated by the fact that now the Indians did not go back to their villages at once as anticipated, but remained here to meet the mythical oncoming army. Perhaps the militia might be used, but beyond any doubt they would need the sturdiness and experience of British regulars to give them backbone and guidance. And even while the congress was in session, the awful news came to Clinton and Colden that a French naval action had blockaded the arrival of some legitimately expected British regulars. There was simply no army to provide. The whole situation dripped with irony.

Clinton had his hands full trying to feed and provide presents—as was expected—for these seven hundred Indians. Perhaps the whole secret would have been found out had not nature taken a hand. With devastating suddenness there was an outbreak of smallpox which swept relentlessly across the Indian encampment. Dozens, then scores of Indians sickened and died. Among them was Kaiwahnee of the Mississaugi Chippewa delegation.

He was buried by his companion, a young chief named Cooh, who covered the grave over with birch mats. Then Chief Cooh himself also came down with the pox. Dying, he asked Warraghiyagey to bring Clinton to him. With extreme reluctance and only at William Johnson's strong insistence that he do so, the governor came; holding his breath as long as he could and breathing shallowly when he could hold it no longer, fearful of sucking into his own lungs the dreaded infection.

"I beg the great father," the Mississaugi whispered hoarsely and haltingly, "that when the . . . the first French scalp is taken . . . it be sent to Nokalokis . . . my mother . . ."

Cooh closed his eyes and after a moment opened them again. His mouth moved as he tried to speak more, but he could not. In another minute or so his eyes closed again and his breath wheezed out a final time.

Clinton, not having understood a word of what the man

had said, nor even very curious about it, stepped back and then turned and swiftly retraced his steps to the fort, waving Johnson to follow him. In his own room he turned to face the big Mohawk Valley trader. Even while the Mississaugi chief was dying, the governor had thought of a way out of this predicament: dump it into the lap of William Johnson.

"William," said Clinton, sitting down behind a desk and quickly writing out an order, "I hereby appoint you to the office of colonel of the forces to be raised out of the Six Nations. From Mount Johnson or from Schenectady, whichever you choose, I want you to send out as many raiding parties of Indians as you can against the French and their Indians. It would be a good idea to appoint some white men to act as rangers with each party. There is," he glanced up at William, "no army coming for the Indians to join. A few companies of regulars, yes, but no army."

"I know that," William replied quietly.

"Well, dammit man, don't let the Indians know. Tell 'em the French have blockaded their entry into port. They have, as a matter of fact. That'll satisfy them for a while. In the meantime, you'll act as your own commissary. I can't assure you of any repayment for disbursements you might make, except that the colony will pay bounties—twenty pounds for a male prisoner, ten pounds for a male scalp, ten pounds for male children, dead or alive. No bounty on females. Move the Indians out right away. They may infect all of Albany."

Well aware that Clinton was merely getting himself out from under, William Johnson was nevertheless glad to get the commission. The title, which wouldn't greatly impress the whites here, was nontheless official sanction to deal with the Indians on government behalf and lead them. It would also raise his influence among the Iroquois considerably.

The news quickly spread throughout Albany and within a few hours the Indians were beginning to head away from the town. At Johnson's invitation, all those still ailing with smallpox were brought to his own home where both he and Catty nursed them until they died or recovered. All around Mount Johnson were mounds of freshly turned earth, beneath which, mostly in sitting positions according to tribal custom, were buried those who had not survived.

The great crowd around Mount Johnson gradually thinned as party after party of Indians was dispatched into the wilderness to the north on raiding missions. Even Tiyanoga, old though he was, had prepared himself to lead such a party when an Indian came to him with a personal invitation from the governor of Canada—the Marquis de la Galissonière—to come to Montreal "for talks."

When William attempted to discourage him from going, Tiyanoga shook his head. "I listened to the English, Warraghiyagey," he said, "and now I will listen to the French. Perhaps, unlike the English, they will talk with their hearts instead of just with their mouths."

He shook his head at Johnson's surprise. "Do not think I did not know there was no English army coming. Others may be content to accept tales about the great sea canoe being kept away by the French, but I am not. And do not think that the Iroquois are people of so little thought that they will fight the battles of the English for them without those promised armies.

"The Iroquois," he added, "have become allies of the English only with the understanding that there will be this great army of soldiers to fight with them. As soon as it becomes known to them that there is no such army, another council will be held at Onondaga and the alliance will end. Then the Iroquois will again be neutral—or else they may even go to the French side in anger over the lies and trickery of the Englishmen."

Without speaking further, without a parting handshake, and with only the barest nod of his head, Tiyanoga left for Montreal.

Johnson, reflecting on the colossal irony of it all, heaved a great, frustrated sigh and retired to his own house to lose his troubles momentarily in the heat-filled nearness of Catty.

Gradually the departure of the Indians continued until, by the second week in November, hardly any were left at Mount Johnson. Even those still unwell were helped away and taken back to their villages by their own people.

William went down to Albany again, there to be greeted by a smirking populace delighting in the fact that of all the Indian parties sent out by the upstart "Colonel of the Indians," not one had reported back in. Were they using the equipment which Johnson said he had given them to shoot partridges rather than Frenchmen? Or had Johnson in fact not distributed anything but merely pocketed the money those supplies were supposed to have cost?

But then, on November 25, the smirks and disparaging remarks were silenced when ten of William Johnson's frontier scouts and a dozen Mohawk warriors marched proudly into the town. They had with them eight white prisoners. They also had four scalps which they waved aloft on the ends of sticks—the scalps of a man, two women, and a young boy. The captives were a French militia captain, two Canadians, a pair of women and three French girls. William looked at the latter trio approvingly.

They were the sisters Vitry, and all three of them—despite a disheveled appearance and fatigue—were strikingly beautiful. The eldest was Catrine, twenty-two, who had brown hair and deep blue eyes and a pleasing figure. The youngest was Catiche who, at thirteen, showed promise of becoming almost a carbon copy of Catrine. But the loveliest of the three was Angélique Vitry. Though only fifteen, she was undoubtedly one of the most breathtaking females ever to set foot in Albany, and perhaps even in New York.

Her eyes locked on the tall, rugged form of William Johnson and, unbidden, she walked to him. Her wrists were tied together and in a gesture that seemed perfectly normal and natural, she pressed her hands against his arm. They looked at one another silently for a long while and then William turned her around and gently handed her back to her captor.

At the moment he had other plans, but William carefully filed away in his mind an idea for later with regard to her.

Now he took a place at the head of the procession and they paraded to the fort where, for a few hours, they were objects of great curiosity, before William led them aboard a sloop and embarked downstream with them for New York.

The excitement caused by their arrival in that great metropolis completely overshadowed what had been experienced in Albany. In Manhattan George Clinton had been as much mocked as Johnson had been in Albany and now he gloated in this savory vindication. He ordered a special military escort and the entire party was led through the streets to the fort where the cannon belched smoke and fire in noisy salute. There, in a fitting ceremony, Governor Clinton accepted with profuse thanks the scalps from the Indian leader of the party and gave him his note for the bounty payment—eighty pounds.

Later, in more private session, Willam Johnson presented to Clinton on behalf of the Iroquois, a petition signed at Mount Johnson by numerous chiefs against the New York Indian agent, Philip Livingston. It proved that though Livingston was charged, as Secretary of Indian Affairs, with the protection of the tribes, he had in fact been trying to steal their very lands.

Clinton studied the petition carefully, along with other

documents submitted to substantiate the charges, and then he became furious. At once he forwarded the papers to London with a terse recommendation:

*I think it necessary for retaining the affections of the Indians that Philip Livingston be removed from the office of Secretary of Indian Affairs. I have previously written you in regard to one William Johnson, to whom New York and the other Colonies are indebted for conversion of the Iroquois from neutrality to at least vocal alliance with England against France. He has run great hazards of losing his life in this endeavor and I recommend him the most highly for His Majesty's favor as an eminent leader in the common cause . . .*

The governor was especially interested in questioning the white men who were captives. Two of these he kept and one was sent on to Governor Shirley in Massachusetts for similar questioning, as he appeared to have important information regarding the strongholds and routes taken by the Abnaki Indians of St. Francis, who were terrorizing the New England frontier.

The female captives were returned to the Indians and Clinton now gave to William Johnson what he considered an urgent mission: to journey personally to Onondaga and there address the Iroquois Council in an effort to extract from them a solemn, unqualified declaration of war against the French, rather than just the alliance they had agreed to at Albany, which was contingent upon the arrival of English troops. William returned home at once.

He was just in time to meet the returning Tiyanoga and a gladness filled him, not only at seeing his old friend again, but at the fact that the Mohawk chief had with him a French prisoner and a scalp. They squatted together before the fireplace in Mount Johnson and Tiyanoga related what had happened.

He had been received in Montreal by Governor Galissonière with great honor and feasting. He had unabashedly led the governor to believe he was renewing the convenant of peace with him and for this, to Tiyanoga and his whole party, gifts of new clothing, guns, knives, ammunition and tomahawks were presented. The governor even gave him a note which instructed French commanders at all posts to supply Tiyanoga's delegation with anything it needed.

"Men who are not brothers to the Indians," Tiyanoga told

William, grinning wickedly, "and yet believe blindly what the Indians say—such men are fools and deserve whatever they receive. That Frenchman is such a fool. He would have us give our lives, life for life, to wipe out the English, but this is not the Indian way. The white general, no matter whether he is English or French, thinks little of sacrificing his men to win his goal, but to an Iroquois chief, no warrior of his is worth any other life in trade. It is our aim to take scalps without losing our own as part of the bargain. Such is the type of war we make."

He then went on to tell William that after leaving Montreal he went to visit the Caughnawagas and there found his cousin Mohawks somewhat disgruntled because the French were not taking very good care of them. The chief of these Caughnawagas, eyeing the new clothes and goods in the possession of Tiyanoga and his men, listened as the principal chief of the Mohawks suggested that while he was in this country he might lift a few French scalps.

The Caughnawaga chief had nodded and replied, "It is time that the French in Canada ought to be alarmed over us."

Tiyanoga had used the paper the governor of Canada had given him to borrow a French canoe from a military outpost and then paddled with his party up Lake Champlain. It was near Fort St. Frederic at Crown Point that they spotted the two French soldiers, ambushed them, killed and scalped one and captured the other.

It was with a twinge of remorse that William Johnson recalled now that he had tried to talk Tiyanoga out of going for fear he would be swayed by the French. He felt ashamed for having so little regard for his friend.

Now the owner of Mount Johnson told his own story to Tiyanoga; of the parades through Albany and New York—at which the chief laughed heartily—and at the presentation, with such dramatic results, of the Iroquois petition against Philip Livingston. Tiyanoga nodded gravely at this. That the report had been sent at once across the sea to King George II proved to Tiyanoga's satisfaction that his initial estimate of William's worth to the Mohawks and the Iroquois could be great.

He was also pleased and touched when he learned that William had taken the Frenchman's scalp that had been given to Clinton and had sent it on by Iroquois runners to Nokalokis, the mother of Cooh, at the Lake Huron village of the Mississaugis. Clearly Warraghiyagey was a man whose sympathies and interests were tied to the Indians and he felt for them deeply.

But when William told him of the mission he had been given by Clinton to go to Onondaga to address the council and ask from them a positive declaration of war against the French, the chief shook his head violently.

"No, Warraghiyagey, do not do it! Not until the English actually do have this great army they speak of should you face the council with such a request. To do so before then would cause you to lose much of the honor and respect that is yours, and your influence among the League members, which daily grows stronger, would certainly shrivel like the grape left too long upon the vine."

William considered this and decided Tiyanoga was right. He nodded. "Tiyanoga is a wise chief and an even better brother. I will do as he says and remain here."

They parted then, more closely joined than ever, both pleased with the friendship and respect of the other. William stood at the window and watched as Tiyanoga struck off upriver toward his own village of Canajoharie. He remembered how many times Catty had stood in this same spot and watched as he himself left on some journey. He thought briefly of the fact that no longer would Catty be here to greet him when he returned from such trips. He had given her money for herself and the children and sent her to New York, with the tacit understanding between them that she was not to return until summoned, but that in the meantime she would be well taken care of.

Now William turned from the window, blew out the candles and headed upstairs where, in a large room with a large bed for this large man there lay waiting an absolutely gorgeous fifteen-year-old French girl.

For fourteen pounds, William Johnson had bought from the Mohawks the lovely prisoner, Angélique Vitry.

### [ April 22, 1747—Wednesday ]

An hour before they arrived, news of the approach of the Mohawk delegation swept through the Mississaugi Chippewa village of Kinodah on the shore of Lake Huron's Saginaw Bay. By the time the party arrived the whole village was waiting and a feast was being prepared. Never before had the village been honored by a delegation from the Six Nations and it was with both eagerness and some trepidation that they waited to learn what great message it was that brought them here.

"Who among you," the leader of the Mohawks asked, "is known as Nokalokis, mother of Chief Cooh?"

"I am the one you ask for," said a huge squaw, rising from her blanket with surprising agility for one so gross. Her hair was long and unbraided, beginning to gray. Her arms were darkly stained nearly to the elbows from making dyes by boiling roots and bark and nuts. She was clad only in a breechcloth and a bright red strip of cloth tied around her neck. Her body was nearly formless and her mammoth udderlike breasts hung pendulously to her waist.

The Mohawk spokesman approached her and removed a scalp from his pouch. He handed it to her and then stepped back a pace or two.

"Mother of Cooh," he said, "you hold in your hand the enemy of your son. As your son lay dying, having only shortly before buried his companion from this same village, Chief Kaiwahnee—both men having died from the pimple-sickness of the white man—he asked the great father of New York that the first enemy scalp be sent to you. And Warraghiyagey, agent of that father, sent us to you with it and with his sorrow and with these gifts which we have placed before your fire.

"The Iroquois League has given its word to the English at a great Congress at Albany that they will march with the white army to be raised against the French. The Mississaugis are not great in number, boasting but eight times one hundred warriors, but they are brave and strong and it would be well if they, too, raised their tomahawks against the French who are swelling in their country in the guise of friendship but with the desire only to take what they have."

When he had finished, a great mourning filled the village for their dead chiefs and an anger against the French, against whom they laid the deaths. When the lamentation had subsided, toward evening, and the Mohawks had eaten and taken their leave, the French scalp was hung from a post in the center of Kinodah and nearly a hundred painted warriors danced around it with gradually increasing frenzy. Far into the night the dance lasted, until the young men dropped from exhaustion. They rose with the dawn and set out to avenge their chiefs by collecting French scalps of their own.

The Mohawk delegation had turned south and in two days had circled widely around Detroit, aware that Chief Pontiac and the Indians who were there under his general control were strongly pro-French. The Iroquois had little use for their ancient enemy, the Ottawas, and they knew that the snub of their passing through without stopping would insult and infuriate the war chief, perhaps even cause him to lose face.

Around the western end of Lake Erie the Mohawks traveled, stopping only for rest, until they had reached the Huron Village of Chief Orontony at Sandusky Bay. The Hurons, too, were ancient enemies of the Iroquois, but it was well known how Orontony had separated himself from both the Detroit Ottawas and the French, and how they were regularly entertaining English traders, even to the point of having let them build a small trading post here.

The Mohawks were met with the respect deserving of their stature as great warriors and the council fire was lighted. Again the Mohawks told what had occurred at Albany, presented their host with a war belt and asked that Orontony and his warriors raise their tomahawks against the French. Even as they talked an English trader arrived and confirmed most of what the Iroquois delegation had already said. And before the Mohawks left, a tomahawk painted red had been sunk into the blackened war post and warriors were already daubing themselves with paint.

By the time the party returned to the Mohawk Valley, a score or more fresh French scalps were being stretched on willow hoops at the two villages they had visited. At home they found more of the same. Warraghiyagey had not been idle.

In him, Tiyanoga and his warriors had placed their plans for getting greater favor and more justice from the English. Since a chief's prestige increased proportionately with the number of successful war parties he sent out, it only stood to reason for them that Warraghiyagey's influence among his white people would increase on the same basis. Parties of Mohawks had spread out in the wilderness from Mount Johnson and they had met with varying degrees of success. Though Tiyanoga now lay recuperating from wounds in his chest and arm, the victory he had won was impressive.

Prior to that raid, William had given a feast at Mount Johnson in which, as before, he led the war dance, clad only in a breechcloth which he discarded at the height of his dance-inspired passion. His three assistants, the Butler brothers—John, Thomas and Walter, Jr.[6]—watched with amazement as the affair reached its peak and they declared to one another that Johnson was "the damndest Indian of them all."

But even they became inspired and Walter, Jr. volunteered to go along with Tiyanoga's war party to represent the English.

The next morning the party had marched to a great elm nearby and stripped off a wide section of its bark. Then, on the bare wood, Tiyanoga had drawn symbols designating the intent of their mission. He had included twenty-three standing stick figures in black and one in green to represent the twenty-three Indians and one white man embarking on the mission. And when they returned, carrying Tiyanoga and another warrior who had been injured, they stopped first at the elm and sketched in eight more green figures and one in black, all of them lying down and their heads slightly detached from the stick-like bodies.

Tiyanoga was carried to Mount Johnson and there he was cared for with skill and concern by William, aided by Angélique Vitry, who was now William's ever-present shadow. It was from the Mohawk chief that Johnson learned the details of the skirmish and he wrote at once a report of the matter to Clinton: how the party had moved to the vicinity of Crown Point and surprised a party of twenty-three French soldiers and three Indians; how a fierce fight developed during which the French, with seven dead and seven wounded, plus one of their Indians killed, were forced back to within Fort St. Frederic; and how Tiyanoga himself was shot in arm and chest. William left no doubt that he considered this *"...the gallantest action performed by the Indians since the commencement of the present war ..."*

The bounties for the scalps brought in by Tiyanoga's party were paid by William out of his own pocket, and then he had the greatest of difficulty collecting in return from the government. At this time there were still nine war parties out, with one hundred nineteen warriors in the two largest parties. If they returned with many scalps, William would be hard put to pay the demanded bounties. Not only the bounty monies, but the gifts he presented to the Indians, along with the supplies, the guns and ammunition, the food—all these ate deeply into his profits. Again and again he appealed to Clinton for funds, but the governor, having problems of his own in getting operating funds from the New York Assembly, was so disenchanted with the whole business that he simply threw up his hands, packed up Johnson's reports and letters after only barely glancing at the first few lines and sent them with a note to Colden:

*Cadwallader: I have just received some letters from Colonel*

*Johnson, but my head aches so much I am not able to read them.*

There was nothing else for William to do but continue to make the bounty payments and supply the Indians and their families out of his own pocket and hope that eventually he would be reimbursed.

The hope died when he finally heard from Clinton.

The governor, himself alarmed by William's reports as related to him by Colden, had gone to the lengths of forwarding them to his superiors in London, but for now there could be no monetary or mercantile assistance. The Assembly had now balked him by even vetoing the governor's former right to pay bounty money for scalps and placing this function with the Assembly's commissioners in Albany. If the Indians wanted their scalp money, they would have to ask for it in Albany, and William Johnson knew they'd rather forget about scalping at all then to appeal to the hated Albany commissioners.

But the fact that William was continuing to pay the bounties out of his own pocket worked in his favor. His influence had become much greater among the Indians than any other white man's and was still growing daily. In fact, so great was his power becoming that the French were now offering the Caughnawagas or any other Indians who would undertake the mission, a reward:

Two hundred pounds for the head of William Johnson.

### [ *August 4, 1747—Tuesday* ]

The continuous waves of fear which lapped at the hearts of the English on the frontier from New England to western Virginia, were now echoed by a similar fear among the French in the West. A handful, a dozen, a score, half a hundred Frenchmen and Canadians—traders, *coureurs de bois*, settlers, soldiers—had been killed or plundered since the visit of the Mohawk delegation. Especially around Detroit and Fort Michilimackinac the situation had become grave.

After a party of five French traders returning to Detroit were slain by some of the Hurons, the squaw mistress of one of the French officers at Detroit told her lover that the Hurons were planning to attack the fort. The officer told the fort commandant, Captain Longueuil, who immediately called the nearby settlers into the fort for protection and then sent for Pontiac and several other chiefs of neighboring

Ottawa, Chippewa and Potawatomi villages, as well as some of the Hurons still in this area and not in agreement with Chief Orontony. All denied any intent to harm the fort or the Frenchmen in or around it.

Pontiac was perhaps the strongest in his denials and he continued to assure the commandant that the Ottawas and Chippewas were not responsible.

"I have heard," Longueuil replied, shaking his head and still not satisfied, "that Chief Nicolas—the Huron you call Orontony—is planning a major attack against us. My commander at Michilimackinac, Lieutenant Noyelle, informs me that several of our soldiers and many traders and settlers have been slain by one of your own parties from L'Arbre Croche, along with some Chippewa warriors. This must stop! If you are friendly to the French, as you claim to be, then it would be to your benefit to prove it by having Nicolas come here and disavow any such plan."

Pontiac nodded, his expression sour. He had heard the same news and, angered at Orontony's effrontery, was already gathering a party to pay the Huron chief a visit. He left Longueuil and the same evening set out in a fleet of twenty-seven canoes for Orontony's village. The party's reception there was strained but cordial. In a long council, Orontony admitted to the plan against Detroit but claimed it was fruit of a bad seed planted in him by the Iroquois delegation who had been here. Cowed by the menacing nature of the forces behind Pontiac, Orontony meekly returned to Detroit and told Longueuil in person that no attack would be led by him against Detroit. In fact, his village was going to move back to the Detroit area . . . at Pontiac's order.

But it did not happen.

Two nights later Orontony was gone and his village remained rooted at Sandusky Bay. What was worse, the English trading post there continued to prosper and consistently more Indians—and English traders—were coming there to transact their business. Captain Longueuil was very angry.

So was Pontiac.

## [ October 10, 1747—Saturday ]

Of one thing concerning the character of William Johnson there could be no doubt: he was a man who got things done—sometimes with official sanction, sometimes without it, and occasionally even in spite of it.

Such was the case now.

Where England and the colonial government continued to vacillate in the matter of sending an expedition against the French strongholds—becoming fearful and recommending it when border attacks grew severe and then refusing to allot funds for it when they slackened—William Johnson acted.

In a way, it was a form of self-preservation. Word reached him that soon an Iroquois army would present itself to him to be led to Albany in order to join the large English army they still believed would be waiting for them when they arrived. If they came and found no such army there or, worse yet, none even scheduled to be there, their anger would be directed at Warraghiyagey and William had little confidence that he would be able to come out of it with his life.

At the same time, seven of his Mohawk scouts came in to report that for two days they had spied unseen on a new French encampment at the mouth of Lac St. Sacrement,[7] a long crooked lake which connected with the upper portion of Lake Champlain.

With customary directness, William set about building an army of his own. He sent runners to every occupied house or cabin in the Mohawk valley and three hundred thirty-one white men armed with a variety of weapons soon arrived at Mount Johnson. At the same time he drew together a band of three hundred eighteen warriors, with representatives of each of the Six Nations included.

With this army of six hundred fifty men, including himself, he set off on August 28 for Lac St. Sacrement. He hoped that now, when the larger Iroquois force reached Mount Johnson, they would be mollified to some extent to find that an army more than half white had already gone to attack the enemy.

Arriving at the lake, Johnson and his men advanced cautiously toward the island upon which the French camp had been located. There was no sign of life but for some hours they kept the island under close surveillance. At length it was determined that no one was there. A close investigation then showed that the ashes were many days' cold and there was no way to determine where the enemy had gone; although the camp was so completely abandoned that William was sure they must have gone back up to Fort St. Frederic at Crown Point.

He ordered the bark stripped from a large tree on the lakeshore and upon the bare wood painted the figure of a large man with a rifle. Then he called the leading members of the Six Nations, who were with the army, to come to this spot.

"We should let the enemy know that we have been here," he told them, "so that they will not be so eager to send out further raiding parties. You will see I have already made a symbol which represents the white men who are here. I now request each of you, for your own particular nation, to make a symbol that they may know you were here as well."

Taken with the idea, the chiefs one by one stepped to the tree and marked on it a symbol by which the Indians who were with the French would recognize what tribes had been here. The Cayuga chief sketched a pipe with its bowl upside down and the Onondaga chief drew a great mountain. The Mohawks showed a steel, such as that used with flint to strike fire. For his own tribe and the Tuscaroras, the Oneida chief indicated a large stone and a small one, both painted red. The Senecas were the most populous and distant of the Iroquois nations and so the chief representing them sketched a whole series of symbols for individual towns with which William Johnson himself was only vaguely familiar.

On the off-chance that the French who had been here had gone down toward Albany, Johnson led his army straight south to the headwaters of Lake Champlain, then to the falls of the Hudson River and downstream to the city without incident.

Once again the residents became pale and alarmed at such a savage and moblike army stepping through their streets and now, for the first time, a real fear of William Johnson himself smote them. A man who could, by himself, call up such an army could have this city at his mercy at any time he chose. It was not a pleasant thought.

With William, as second-in-command, was one John L. Lydius, a great bull of a German immigrant with a tomahawk scar across his face and an empty eye socket which imparted to him a hellishly savage countenance. A good-humored bully, he would fight anyone, or even a group, at the blink of an eye and without provocation. When seeing someone he thought might make a worthy opponent, he would approach and with a malevolent glare, plant himself spraddle-legged and with his huge fists on his hips directly in front of the individual.

"You vant vit me to make fight?" he woud growl.

If the challenge was accepted, which occasionally happened, he fought with brutality; hitting, gouging, crushing, kicking, stomping, kneeing and generally wreaking havoc until his opponent was a bloody mass at his feet. If, however, the challenge was wisely unaccepted, he would roar with hawkish laughter, make great knotted fists and then demand that the man feel the huge twin balls of his biceps.

"Dey iss so big," he would brag, "because nuttink I eat bot aigs vot iss hart-boilt!" And it was true: his diet consisted almost solely of hard-boiled eggs washed down by vast quantities of hard liquor.

Now Johnson left Lydius behind, along with some minor Mohawk chiefs, to disband the army while he and Tiyanoga, along with chiefs of all the other five tribes—a group of about thirty Indians—continued down the Hudson to New York to demand the monies due. It was an unseasonably sweltering day when they arrived.

"By damn, Governor," William exploded when they reached Clinton's house, "the colony has *got* to help me with the goods and money owed to the Six Nations."

Even before he finished Clinton was shaking his head. "Now even less than before, William," he said sorrowfully. "I guess you haven't heard yet. The Assembly just passed what they called a 'remonstrance' which states that Indian affairs have bogged down to a disaster since I—and you—superseded the authority of the commissioners in Albany. Their arguments were that all the accounts of the Iroquois raids for scalps and prisoner-taking among the French are just amusements that the Indians would be doing anyway and that you and I have given our support to them simply so we could bill the colony for presents and supplies that never got to the Indians.

"They even called a witness," the governor continued mildly. "It was Joe Clement."

"Clement!" The name left William's mouth as if it were some great profanity. For months Joseph Clement had been a thorn in Johnson's side. On property of his own just twenty yards from Johnson's, he had set up a filthy, ramshackle tavern which offered the poorest rum imaginable. Whenever the Indians were paid their bounties for scalps or prisoners—bounties paid in goods by Johnson from his store—Clement would immediately trade his rot-gun rum for what they had been given and the Indians would wind up with only a miserable hangover and nothing to show for their deadly labors in the war parties. William's complaints about it to Clinton had become so strong that Clinton had finally put Clement out of business; at which Clement had sworn revenge and had apparently just gotten it with his false testimony delivered to the Assembly.

101

"You mean they actually *believed* him?" William was incredulous.

Clinton shrugged. "Why not? They wanted to. They'd have believed Satan himself if it meant they could save money by it. Anyway, the Assembly has flatly refused to allocate any money to reimburse you for the supplies you've been sending to Oswego, or for payment to the Indians, or for other services to the colony. Either that or they've used legal tricks to get around paying them."

It was a blow that winded William Johnson. Clinton was genuinely sorry and said he would continue to petition the Crown to pay him. In the meanwhile, however, he gave William a personal loan—without interest—of £1,400, to tide him over. With that, his store, mill, and fur trade, he might be able to keep his head above water.

Now Tiyanoga entered the discussion as spokesman for the Iroquois League and the fact that he was angry was instantly apparent. His tone was imperious, his demeanor haughty, his words clipped and demanding. For a while Clinton was even a little afraid that he meant to do him physical violence and he breathed a silent prayer of thanks that William Johnson was on hand to restrain the tomahawk-scarred savage.

Nothing was accomplished in this talk and the Indians, in a state of high anger, left with William. But then, later in the evening, Tiyanoga returned alone and met privately with the governor and this time when they parted it was with more pleasant feelings existing between them. Clinton was so fatigued by the interviews that he retired without even writing the day's events in his journal—an omission that rarely occurred and which he rectified first thing in the morning:

*Hendrik*, he wrote, calling Tiyanoga by his Dutch-given name, *and about thirty of his Indians, along with Colonel Johnson, today cornered me in my little parlor just over the kitchen, and a monstrous hot day. The chief, notwithstanding his promise to the Colonel not to be very loud and speak very plainly, was exceedingly angry indeed, and very impertinent, that I was hardly able to bear him. He called upon the Mohawks, and told them I had drawn them into the war, and that he was come down to see the army. Instead of seeing it, he found they were betrayed; that the French no sooner proposed anything but they set about it; and then hit me in the teeth of Saratoga.[8] As for his part, he would leave his castle and take all his people with him—and so we parted in a sort of pet.*

*In the evening, however, Hendrik sent word by Johnson that he wanted to see me in private. At first I would have nothing to say to him, but at last I thought it was well to hear what he had to say, but the scene was greatly changed, for he was all goodness, and we parted the best of friends that ever was, and did everything but hug and kiss, and he was quite sober, as, to do them justice, they every one was. I was forced to fill the dog's pockets. They leave me, God be praised, this afternoon ...*

What Governor George Clinton failed to note in his journal was what passed between himself and Tiyanoga to change the old Mohawk's mood. Tiyanoga had secured from the governor a solemn promise that he would place William Johnson in absolute charge over Indian affairs in New York Colony and also that he would terminate the Indian Commissioner's office of the New York Assembly. The principal chief of the Mohawks also exacted a promise of the governor that scalp bounties would be paid out of the royal treasury and that the governor would reinforce the army William Johnson had already raised by ordering the militia to join it under Johnson's command.

Tiyanoga told Warraghiyagey all about the private meeting as their party returned up the Hudson and Mohawk rivers. It was good news to Johnson, but the pleasure of it was quickly blunted. Shortly after his arrival home, he learned by special messenger that the Albany militia, in a body, had refused to obey the order to mobilize under command of himself. Now he wrote to Clinton despairingly:

*... My disappointment is made doubly miserable in view of the readiness of the Indians to fight for our cause. I will engage to bring 1,000 warriors into the field in six weeks' time, provided I have clothes, arms and ammunition for them, or forfeit £1,000 to them. But it is now not so much whether they will come at my call as it is whether they will come without being requested, as I have learned they are prepared to do. The Six Nations have sent war belts to all their allies and I am far short of a proper amount of supply for the numbers that may be expected. Should the Indians who rule such a huge area of wilderness arrive and find me empty-handed, it might affect the whole continent ...*

103

Robert Rogers was frustrated.

The lad's fifteenth year had passed and now almost half of his sixteenth and still he hadn't killed an Indian. Last year when the spring thaws came he had labored in the communal tilling and planting of the farms and then, in midsummer, he had enlisted in a company under Captain Ebenezer Eastman. Months were spent fruitlessly patrolling the woods and river basins without a single Indian sighting.

All winter they had forted up again and when by mid-March there had still been no threat, the settlers—independent by nature and now sated with such communal living—broke up and returned to their farms to till and plant their own lands.

Rogers was among those who went home. For going on two years now there had been no attacks and it was a welcome change for the Rogers family to lead their cows and workhorses back to their Mountalona Farm along the Merrimack River in Great Meadows, ten miles from Rumford. Under the circumstances it was a very logical move.

It was also a mistake.

On the first of April the Abnaki and Caughnawaga marauders appeared in droves and with the speed bred of terror, the settlers abandoned their cattle and goods and grouped together once again in fortified houses.

No war parties approached Rumford but today, when the Rogers family fearfully returned to Mountalona, they found their farm an utter ruin. Virtually every cabin, shed and barn had been burned to the ground after first being plundered of anything of value. All cattle and workhorses had been butchered and left lying on the ground where they had fallen.

With more than his share of bitterness, young Robert Rogers stared at the smoldering gray ashes of what had once been his home and, with a vehemence shocking in one so young, he reaffirmed his vow of eighteen months ago—to devote all his energies to the merciless slaughter of Indians.

The pall of blue-white smoke overhanging the Merrimack River Valley in New Hampshire was not unlike that which now rose over the Huron village of Chief Orontony at Sandusky Bay in the Ohio country. He and his people stood in a knot on a rise several miles away and watched while their village and all its possessions disappeared in the smoke which drifted lazily toward Lake Erie in the early spring air.

They could, all of them, be thankful that they had gotten off with their lives, but it was not much consolation now. They were ruined and had nothing. A deep bitterness for the French in general and the Ottawas in particular swelled in Orontony's breast.

There had been no warning that Chief Mackinac of L'Arbre Croche, principal chief of the Ottawa tribe, and Chief Pontiac, war chief of the same tribe, were coming against them. Though these two chiefs were often opposed in Ottawa tribal policies, this time they had ridden together, along with a number of Potawatomies and Chippewas which Pontiac had induced to accompany them from near his own village by Detroit.

For too long Pontiac and Mackinac had smarted under the abusive and accusatory tongues of Captain Longueuil and Lieutenant Noyelle—being blamed for murders and plundering they had not done. They were not overly concerned with the acts themselves, but since they had not shared in the plunder or scalps, they were outraged to bear the brunt of blame, when most of the attacks had originated with Orontony or his warriors.

Yesterday they had arrived, a French lieutenant from Detroit with them, at the Sandusky Bay Huron village. A hasty council was called and an ultimatum given to Orontony: either he would now observe his pledge given at Detroit last August of friendship to the French, or he must fight these allied forces of Ottawa, Chippewa and Potawatomi.

"If you accept the former alternative," the French officer said, disappointment edging his voice that an alternative had been offered at all, "then you will, to show your good faith and your dependency upon the French and our Indian allies, break off all relations with the English, beginning here." He picked up a flaming stick from the fire and carried it to the English trading post and set it afire.

Chiefs Mackinac and Pontiac nodded in approval. It would be just punishment for Orontony to have this same thing happen to his entire village. With village and possessions lost he would undoubtedly repair at once to the Detroit area, tail between legs, to take up humbled residence with the pro-French faction of his tribe there.

They declared their decision and gave Orontony only one course to follow: he could burn his own village and all that was in it, or they would do it for him.

105

Orontony deliberated all night and this morning, as the sun arose, he personally went from structure to structure, igniting every one. Not until the flames were at their peak did the party under Chiefs Pontiac and Mackinac move out and become quickly lost from sight without another word.

But Orontony, while not especially brave, was decidedly stubborn. He gathered his villagers behind him and struck out afoot—not to the northwestward as Pontiac had expected, but instead to the southwest toward the White River tributary of the Wabash River. Here, as he had been invited to do long ago by Chief Unemakemi,[9] he intended to join the Miami tribe and continue—with them and protected by them—to trade with the English.

### [ April 26, 1748—Tuesday ]

Everything—absolutely everything!—that happened these days seemed to William Johnson to get him into a tighter squeeze between the Six Nations and the English. Tiyanoga expressed it succinctly as he rode beside Warraghiyagey and the village of Onondaga was lost from sight behind them.

"Warraghiyagey," he said, "I would not be where you stand now. It is not a stand upon which a man can hope to live for long."

Johnson nodded gloomily but did not reply, thinking back over the whole chain of events that had put him into such an untenable position. It had all begun in early March while he was in New York conferring with Governor Clinton. At the same moment a party of six Mohawks were engaged in a routine scout a short distance north of Mount Johnson when they encountered a large party of Caughnawagas and Abnakis accompanied by a few *coureurs de bois*. At once the leader of the pro-French Indians pointed at them and shouted to his warriors, "Get them! We are men. We will have them all!"

Johnson's Mohawks had turned and were beginning to flee but at this shout one of them ducked behind a slender tree trunk and raised his rifle. He shouted back, "I am Gingego— a Mohawk and a man. I am one who will never fly from you or from any man!"

It was brave, but not at all wise.

Almost instantly a bullet tore through his brain and he flopped lifelessly on the ground. Another volley downed one of his companions. Three others were captured—including Chief Nichus[10]—and the final warrior escaped.

The one who escaped fled to Teantontalogo with the news

106

but not enough warriors were on hand there to go to the rescue. Two days later, when William Johnson returned, he immediately sent out a party of a hundred men, half of them Indians, half whites. At the scene of the attack they found a grisly sight. With legs pointing up into the air, the beheaded body of Gingego was stuck in a snowdrift. Both his body and that of the other dead Mohawk had been severely mutilated. Over a pile of cold ashes they found the remains of Gingego's head impaled on a stick. The scalp, lips, nose and ears had been sliced away and the head itself badly burned.

Within a month it was learned that the three captured Indians were imprisoned in a Montreal cell with chains that held them practically motionless. This, to the Iroquois way of thinking, was a fate infinitely worse than death and the entire League seethed with renewed anger at the news. Word also came, however, that if the Iroquois chiefs would come to Montreal to talk with Governor Galissonière, the three prisoners would be released to them.

"I will lead the party of chiefs there," Tiyanoga declared at once.

"No!" William Johnson shook his head hastily and held up his hand. "Don't do it, Tiyanoga. If you go, all our other endeavors are in vain!"

There was no doubt in Johnson's mind that the French governor would convince the Indians that their growing fears that the English were leading them into a trap were only too true. Already a whisper was sweeping through the League that the English had never meant to raise an army to go forth into battle with the Iroquois, and that their sole purpose in having said so was to expose the Six Nations to attack from Canada. So fraught with dreadful possibilities did William consider the invitation that he determined to go personally and at once to all the nations and stop them from going to Montreal. Tiyanoga volunteered to go with him to the various villages and William welcomed him.

Beginning April 11, he and Tiyanoga, five other Mohawk chiefs, fifty volunteers from Johnson's lately disbanded army, and his personal bodyguard of eight loyal Mohawks left Mount Johnson for a grand swing through Iroquois country, striking out directly westward first to the Seneca country on the Genesee River and then looping back through the other nations for a final grand council at Onondaga. It was a journey of over two hundred miles.

In every Iroquois village along the way, William—who came as the Mohawk chief, Warraghiyagey, rather than as an

Englishman—met with the local chiefs, whom he tried to influence to his way of thinking for when they should all get together again soon at Onondaga. There was a very good reason for this: the Onondaga Council was not, nor had it ever been, a platform for debate. In actuality, it was more of a vocal newspaper wherein Warraghiyagey would be permitted to express his ideas and offer suggestions. Later would follow the closed sessions of the tribal representatives in which the conclusions of those chiefs—unanimous, as they always had to be—would be reached and announced.

At each of these villages Warraghiyagey was met and treated with the utmost of respect and provided with the best of quarters and food, if not always with a sympathetic ear. And unfailingly he would be visited in his quarters by the loveliest of freshly washed and prettied maidens from whom he could choose a companion to while away the night. There were no tribal barriers or sexual taboos against this sort of thing. Indeed, offense might be taken if at least one maiden was not chosen, regardless of how weary the traveler might be. Johnson preferred not to give offense.

The women were bold and aggressive in his quarters, hungry for solid male closeness—and with good reason. As a matter of custom and virtually without exception, Iroquois men neither married nor engaged in sexual intercourse until the age of thirty. To do so they strongly believed, could stunt a young man's growth, weaken him, drain him, make him feeble and unable to function with the muscular stamina and coordination that intertribal warfare demanded. It was for this reason as well that for some time prior to going off to war, most Iroquois warriors abstained from sexual contact with their wives or any other woman. This was, William Johnson knew, one of the most perplexing things of all to the white men: that when Iroquois warriors defeated whites, they never raped the women as white soldiers had always done almost as surely as night followed day.

The possibility that the maid of the moment might become pregnant was not of the least concern to either Warraghiyagey or the woman. As a matter of fact, the entire village would be pleased at such an occurrence. They would feel that Warraghiyagey had honored them in that he had aided the tribe and the League toward the prime objective of population growth. Illegitimacy was no matter of consequence, since the Six Nations were of matrilineal structure: a child belonged to its mother's tribe, not it's father's. So far as the Iroquois were concerned, the many children sired by

Johnson were as purebred Iroquois as any other of the League.[11]

Thus, the weariness of the long journey and the fatiguing sessions with the numerous chiefs to incline them to his way of thinking was for Warraghiyagey in part compensated for by the always pleasant nighttime hours which followed. And on April 24—thirteen days, thirteen meetings and at least thirteen women after the trip had begun—Warraghiyagey and his party arrived at Onondaga. Surprisingly, he was little the worse for wear.

At the edge of the village area the party was met by a great line of warriors and chiefs with their guns cradled on one arm. At a signal from the Onondaga principal chief, Red Head, the guns were raised simultaneously and fired in a ragged burst of sound. Warraghiyagey stopped his party and had them return the salute in kind. Then they advanced in a group to the village proper—a great cluster of longhouses and individual bark huts, with here and there a crude log cabin or tepee.

While Tiyanoga and the other members of his party were taken care of, Warraghiyagey was ushered by Chief Red Head personally to a large dwelling which had been cleaned and newly matted for his comfort. On one of these mats he lay for an hour to rest—alone.

It was Canassatego who awakened him from his deep slumber by gently touching his arm.

"The chiefs of all our nations have gathered at the council house, Warraghiyagey. It is time to come."

Refreshed, Warraghiyagey nodded and followed the Onondaga orator to the long low building in which certainly close to a thousand warriors and chiefs had gathered. Each chief sat with a delegation of men from his own particular village, yet spaced so that all were in good hearing range and not too very far from the centrally located speaking platform—a dais about eighteen inches over the earthen floor, made of split logs pegged together with the rounded sides down and flat sections up, close together and covered over with deer hides tanned with the hair still on them.

Red Head was on the dais when Warraghiyagey and Canassatego entered and at once a silence fell. Red Head held out his arms toward William Johnson and said, "Welcome, Warraghiyagey, to our fire, to our hearts, to our council."

It was a pleasant start, but didn't last long that way. In fact, at once Red Head became colder and, as he began

109

addressing the white man, gave him a hard stare. Warraghiyagey met it unfalteringly.

"Brother Warraghiyagey," the chief said, "you have kept us at our village in readiness to march on Canada for too long. You have prevented our warriors from going about their hunting now almost two years, and all for nothing, as we can see no sign of your doing anything with your army as we were led to believe and expected.

"Brother Warraghiyagey, the war has made goods very expensive to trade for at Oswego and we have almost nothing to trade, since our men have not been able to hunt meat or trap fur for onward of two years. In our present condition we are to be pitied. Brother Warraghiyagey, what shall we do now to live, being in a miserable, poor condition?"

Chief Red Head stepped down and Warraghiyagey—William Johnson—immediately took his place.

"My Brothers," he began, "the questions of Chief Red Head are in all your hearts and I ask that you grant me the weary traveler's privilege of saying tomorrow what I am too tired now to put to words. I will, however, this night provide a feast for your chiefs and another for all warriors and dancers, who I hope will be merry, which is my greatest pleasure to make and see them be."

It was the anticipated response and it was met with grunts of affirmation and the nodding of heads. And so began a long and pleasant evening which was garnished for William Johnson at its close by a fine, soft, full-breasted squaw who—temporarily, at least—encouraged him to forget his weariness. But long after she breathed deeply in sleep beside him, Johnson lay awake mulling over what response he might make on the morrow. There was really only one thing to do, and that was to take the offensive, but it was a chancy business at best. Nevertheless, having made his decision, he rolled over on his side and immediately fell asleep.

If anything, the council house was even more crowded in the morning and Warraghiyagey launched without preamble into his reply.

"Brother Iroquois," he said, "the troubles and delays we have suffered for so long lie not in me nor in the English, but rather in our Brother Senecas here today in attendance. It was they who specifically asked me to set aside any major expedition against Canada until they had tried to win the Caughnawagas to the English cause, for it would not be right for brother to go against brother. On behalf of the English I agreed, for my heart was with them in this matter.

But while our hands were thus tied here by you, those of the French and the Abnakis and the Caughnawagas were not and we have since got the Frenchman's axe sticking fast in our heads day after day, and the Six Nations also.

"Brother Iroquois, although you here have brought honor to yourselves as individual nations and a League of Nations by as yet not hurting the Caughnawagas, still those onetime Mohawks, blackly inspired by French deceit, have murdered the well-loved Gingego in his own fields, and have given to the French to chain in unspeakable agony worse than any torture, three of your brothers, among who is Chief Nichus, son of the great Sagayeanquarashtow."

His voice took on a ringing hardness now as he raised one arm ending in a balled fist and said, "Brother Iroquois, I now desire you, if there remains the last spark of the noble spirit in you which your brave ancestors were noted to have throughout the world, that you may follow your brother Warraghiyagey's desire, and use the axe against them, which you have so long held unused in your hands."

With these words he removed from over his other arm where it was draped a wide and long belt of wampum—war wampum—and threw it to the floor of the dais.

"And should my Brothers not wish to pick it up," he added, "perhaps they will another."

At this he held out another belt of wampum, smaller and more lightly colored than the war belt. He swiveled back and forth so that all in attendance in the great room could see it clearly.

"Brother Iroquois, hear me now, with your ears and with your hearts: our brothers are chained in dark rooms and you are asked to come thither and your presence shall set them free. But I say to you that these are the whispers of a false bird and that a treachery awaits in Montreal. Do not go! We have many French prisoners of our own and I say to you that your great father, Clinton, will gladly trade them for your three brothers. I desire you now, by this belt of wampum, not to try any more, but leave it entirely to your Brother Warraghiyagey."

He threw the second belt to the dais and then turned and stepped lightly down and took a seat on the ground near the Mohawks. A thing beading of perspiration dampened his temples and the palms of his hands were moist. He had a desire to cough or clear his throat loudly, but stifled the impulse.

He had, with those words, taken a desperate but calculated

111

risk and, though he appeared outwardly calm, his heart was pounding with excitement and trepidation. The very last thing he wanted at this moment was to have the fifty council chiefs of the six tribes accept his challenge, pick up the war belt and break into a war dance. It would mean, beyond any doubt, that they would demand major English military assistance immediately, and none knew better than William Johnson himself that in the foreseeable future, no such aid was forthcoming. What he hoped to accomplish instead was the creation of an emotional state which would cause the chiefs to agree not to go to Canada for their prisoners.

Already Chief Red Head had returned to the dais and, as Warraghiyagey was sure would happen, replied that the council of chiefs would now meet to deliberate on this matter and that their answer would be given on the morrow.

For the remainder of the day William Johnson kept to himself in his quarters, undisturbed by anyone until, in the evening, a different Iroquois maiden than the one he had last night entered carrying under each arm a bulging beechwood bowl of steaming food. Slim and lithe and probably no more than fourteen or fifteen years old, her young body was clad only in a blanket tied around her waist and nearly touching the floor. She set the bowls on the floor beside Warraghiyagey's mat and he reached out ... though not immediately for the food.

In the forenoon of the next day—yesterday—the grand council was convened again. This time it was the Onondaga orator, Chief Canassatego, who stepped up onto the dais and directed the reply to Warraghiyagey.

"Brother Warraghiyagey," he said in a mellifluent tone, "we, the Six Nations now assembled here, must tell you that we cannot accept your war belt against our brothers, the Caughnawagas. And, further, we think it very hard and cruel to be hindered from fetching our own flesh and blood from Canada, who lie rotting and dying in irons, when we are offered them only to go for them. Yet, we say to you now that we will not go to Canada for this purpose before you make a trial for the redemption of our people. And, as you say you have so many French prisoners, we think you may easily do it if you have a love for us. That is all we have to say at this time."

With that the Onondaga Council had ended and now, with Tiyanoga and the Mohawks and his little army with him, William was on his way once more to Mount Johnson, fatigued, troubled, and not at all relieved that he had ostensibly won his aim in the council. The simple fact of the matter was that by merely refusing Governor Clinton's request to exchange prisoners, the governor of New France could arouse tremendous ill feeling among all the Iroquois for the English and William Johnson's own scalp was almost sure to be lifted. The worst part of the whole business was his promise that Clinton would offer the French captives in trade for three Indians.

It was a promise that Warraghiyagey had made without Governor George Clinton's permission or knowledge.

### [ *August 10, 1748—Wednesday* ]

Even though now well familiar with Iroquois behavior, there were times when William Johnson felt he did not know the Indians at all; times when they acted in a manner wholly different from that expected.

Such as now.

Immediately after returning from the Onondaga Council, William had successfully communicated his concern to Governor Clinton that unless steps were taken at once by the government to hold a full-scale council with the Six Nations and assure them that every possible effort was being made to secure the release of the imprisoned Mohawks, the whole League might fall under French influence. Clinton agreed to the council but arbitrarily brushed aside William's request that it be held at Mount Johnson "to thus increase what prestige I may have among the tribes." The council, Clinton had told him flatly, would be held where such councils were always held, in Albany.

Somewhat miffed at first, William was soon glad that it turned out that way. While the Indians were already en route to attend this grand council with the English, a messenger from Clinton brought news to the master of Mount Johnson which stunned him as if he had been struck with a sledge-hammer.

England and France had just signed an armistice and peace negotiations were under way at Aix-la-Chapelle, France. The King of England was therefore, in effect, abandoning his hard-won Indian allies as no longer being essential to the English cause. It was precisely what the French had told the Indians would happen one way or another and now Clinton, terrified of the Iroquois reaction to this news, wanted very much to cancel the council, but it was too late for that.

For once William Johnson stayed discreetly in the background, contributing to the Albany Congress nothing but his presence and thankful that it was Governors George Clinton and William Shirley who would have to make the explanatory speeches and bear the brunt of the Iroquois reaction. And that was where the Indians' reactions became so incomprehensible to the Irishman.

As both Clinton and Shirley spoke to them and circulated among them, the Six Nations showed a remarkable reserve and mildness. They listened carefully to the speeches of the officials—during which no mention whatever was made of the French-imprisoned Mohawks or the fitful negotiations under way to set them free—and when it came their own turn to speak, they not only voiced no complaints but actually reaffirmed their loyalty to the Crown.

Even when the Massachusetts governor made an entirely uncalled-for veiled threat to them—warning them that if they wavered in their loyalty they would be rooted out by the French, in whose power the English would leave such ungrateful Indians—they accepted his words with incredible meekness.

Well as he knew them, William Johnson now concluded that he would never be able to understand the Indian mentality well enough. Surprises like this only served to prove to him how little he—or any white man—really knew about the race of red men.

When the Congress was terminated, the Indians stopped off at Mount Johnson while en route to their villages, there to hold a council of their own. Without much choice in the matter, Warraghiyagey was beholden to entertain them rather lavishly and at his own expense. When it was concluded he questioned Tiyanoga at length about the odd and unexpected reaction of the League, but received no satisfactory answer. The Indians gradually drifted off to prepare for their next major council meeting at Onondaga.

Now, with all but one Indian gone from Mount Johnson, William sat down wearily and penned a report to Clinton in which he once again expressed his inability to comprehend the Indian reaction. In completing the report, he added:

... *Though I have been prodigiously tormented with the Indians here these past weeks and have questioned them diligently, I have received little satisfactory explanation. I believe we are underestimating their reasoning powers and that they have some long term planning afoot that is bound to affect us. Be that as it may, I have just now got rid of all the Indians from my house except the Seneca called the Grota Younga, who stays to be cured of an ulcer he has in his leg . . .*

*Thank God, the greatest hurry is now over for the time!*

*Wm. Johnson*

## [ November 1, 1748—Tuesday ]

Virtually every chief and sub-chief of the entire Iroquois League attended the grand council called at Onondaga shortly after the Albany Congress ended. They discussed the present situation at great length and the opinion William Johnson had voiced that the Iroquois had some "long term planning afoot" proved wrong only in degree. The remarkable understanding that these Indians had of their own position and that of the English and French, the grasp they had of the entire situation was both comprehensive and advantageous. Their seemingly unique advantage lay in the fact that not only was their own planning detailed, complex and decidedly long-range, but in that they apparently had a much better understanding of the whole scope of events—past, present and projected future—than even the most astute white man suspected or shared.

Old Belt, Canassatego, Red Head and Tiyanoga were the chiefs who spoke at greatest length in this council and their uncanny understanding of the whites and wherein the best interests of the Six Nations apparently lay was clearly evident in what they had to say.

They discussed the French and the English in general and such individuals as William Johnson, George Clinton, William Shirley, James Delancey, the Marquis de la Galissonière and others in particular. Events that had occurred during and since the Albany Congress were discussed in detail— dissected, studied, evaluated and assigned to their proper niche in the whole scheme of things. Events already occurred or presently occurring in Paris or Versailles, in Boston or New York or Albany, in Williamsburg or Philadelphia, in Quebec or Montreal, in the areas of the western Great Lakes and Ohio River Valley, and even among the Cherokees and Catawbas, Creeks and Choctaws to the south each had their place in the discussions and each contributed to the understanding of the whole.

"We know," they said, "that both the Englishmen and the Frenchmen wish to use us to their own ends and that whatever friendship or benefits they offer us are offered only through necessity and would not be given otherwise. We are thought to be ignorant and not understanding of what is happening around us, and it is well that they should think thus of us; we must let them continue to think this way, for in this very underestimating of us, they are weakened and we are strengthened. We know what they know, but they do not know what we know. It is good.

"They have now made a peace between them, which they call the Peace of Aix-la-Chapelle, the place where their ambassadors signed treaties. As if they were women, the English have meekly given back to the French the great fort of Louisbourg, which they won with their blood and so should be theirs forever by right of conquest, and this is a great weakness in them and will cause them trouble again.

"We are not much surprised that this peace should come between them. Was it not obvious it was coming by the fact that this past summer Warraghiyagey made no real effort to gather and send out scalping parties as before? Was this not the reason that the great army promised by the English never came to this land?

"What we must decide among ourselves is where now we stand. Do we remain pledged to the English, when it is obvious they have not kept faith with us, since they made peace with the French on the one hand while still encouraging us to make war on them unsupported, on the other? Do we remove our alliance from them and place it instead with the French who, for reasons dating back to our ancestors, we despise? Do we once again assume the mantle of complete neutrality, or do we speak only a mouth neutrality while leaning toward the English who, because of their numbers if for no other reason, are the stronger?

"Warraghiyagey, as agent of the English, does his work as none other has before him. As agent of the Iroquois, however, it would appear at first look that he has not done well by us. But is this really so? The answer must be no. The things he told us, those he promised us, were told and promised in good faith and he carried to us and from us only what he believed to be the truth. We knew among us, if not right away then later on, that the great English army promised by Governor Clinton would never march with us, nor have we really wished it to. Though it would have been wise for us to have united with a strong English campaign against Canada if such a campaign had become a reality, yet it is to our advantage that it did not. Any damage there which would upset the almost equally balanced power between these

116

whites would be less to our advantage than the present condition, in which we are able to use them against each other for our own benefit. The frequent calls we have made for the army promised by the English and the frights inspired by us in the heart of Warraghiyagey have kept them out of balance and have given us a better position from which to bargain than could otherwise have been achieved. Warraghiyagey has told Tiyanoga that he fears he has failed both his people and ours because he was not able to keep promises.

"But the promises of Warraghiyagey, where they have been in his personal power to keep, he has faithfully kept, and the fighting he led us to was to our taste and to our advantage in most respects. That our Mohawk warrior Gingego should have been killed and the League itself insulted by the mutilation of his body in his own land has been unfortunate and it is a matter we must settle among ourselves; and that the Mohawk prisoners are still chained in Montreal remains a great problem which we must soon see to if they are not quickly released. But in all, our warriors have enjoyed engaging in much warfare and have brought honor to themselves and their families and their tribe as well as to the League with the scalps they have taken; to which must be added that they have earned good pay from it without themselves suffering greatly from casualties. Perhaps most of all we are fortunate in having prevented a war among ourselves, which could have destroyed our League. Such a thing must never occur.

"The Senecas among us, who now lean themselves strongly toward the French, say that the English have now shown themselves to be liars and cowards, and to some extent this is true. It is not pleasant to have to deal in friendliness with such people. Yet, the Mohawks among us must live side by side with them and there is a serious problem here. If we try to protect ourselves with tomahawk and gun against evil traders who would cheat us and those who come by night to take our lands, though such killings be justified under our laws, there would then be retaliation mounted against us by their brothers and warfare would come between us. It is told us by Warraghiyagey and even by his governor that if white injustice comes to us we can appeal to the white man's laws, but their courts are far from the forest and favor the white man and their judges do not believe the words of any Indians.

"The only way, then, that the Mohawks—and thus the Six Nations—can prevent their own ruin, slavery and death is through a white protector, and the type of man we need is the type of man we have in Warraghiyagey. Although he is living on the border which separates us from the English, he exerts influence on the centers of government, even across the great sea as well as in this land. He is rich enough now to meet the needs of those of our people who come to him ill or hungry and he does not get these riches by cheating Indians.

"Among us here gathered, Warraghiyagey has earned great respect for his strength and courage and the fact that he has learned enough of our ways to be no longer a fool in the forest; yet still he knows how to act when in the great rooms of his leaders, which we do not. Above all, our Warraghiyagey has shown that he can help us without forcing us to lose our pride, which also none before him could do; he does not make us feel he is lowering himself to deal with us but instead shows a strong ability to feel what we ourselves feel, to understand our tribal and League customs by instinct as well as by memory. At the same time, he is able to do this without losing his vital contacts with the most powerful white men of his other world which, on our behalf, it is his mission to handle.

"We cannot expect Warraghiyagey to rise up to fight every battle only on the Indians' behalf, for to do so would cause him to betray his white interests and he would quickly be put out of power by them and be therefore rendered useless to serve us. Yet, as he has shown himself capable of in the past, he must wish to serve us to the utmost of his ability and never, in word or deed or even thought, betray us."

It was Tiyanoga who summed up the feeling of the council. His hair was now nearly all white and it starkly framed the darkness of his scarred face as he spoke.

"We know among us," he said slowly, "that such a man as we have need for is hard to find and that in Warraghiyagey we have found him. We must therefore support him as we wish him to support us. This will be difficult all the more in time to come. There is now a peace between English and French and since white men are always more concerned with money than with glory, there will soon come men swarming like the white man's honey bees, to take up land and live where their soldiers now tremble to stay. Great problems are sure to come for us and in order to face them without total war, we must rely on Warraghiyagey.

"Should he fail us through deceit or treachery," Tiyanoga added, his voice becoming sad, "which I do not believe will happen, then I will be the one who will kill him; but the

118

blade which pierces his heart will pierce mine as well, for he is my friend and my brother and I love him. But this I do not believe can happen, for I know him too well and can see into his heart.

"Should he fail us through reasons that are not of his making, then there will always be time to take him to us or send him away and then take up the war club.

"In the meanwhile, it is to the benefit of our League and the individual tribes in it that from this time forward, until conditions might indicate we should change, that we adopt again an unshakable neutrality. When the English and the French come again at one another's throats, as eventually they will, then let them come to us with their worry and their gifts and their entreaties for alliance. We will listen to their worry and we will take their gifts, and their entreaties for alliance. We will listen to their worry and we will take their gifts, but through it all we will be neutral."

No, the Indians on the whole were grossly underrated when considered by both French and English officials as "ignorant savages." Their perception was amazing, their analysis swift, and their understanding keen.

It was obvious that the white men had little conception of Indian intelligence depth, because almost at this same time King George II was giving to the newly formed Ohio Company[12]—made up principally of planters from the Dominion of Virginia and the Province of Maryland—a charter for half a million acres of land *west* of the Alleghenies. There were only three conditions to the grant: namely, that no less than one hundred families should be established upon it within seven years, that a fort be built upon it, and that a garrison be maintained at the fort.

Now all that the Ohio Company had to do was find a good man to explore the area, pinpoint the best possible land for the company to claim, and then lay out a trail from the east to these holdings.

England's subtle invasion of the west had just begun.

[ *December 31, 1748—Saturday* ]

The Treaty of Aix-la-Chapelle, ending King George's War, resulted in a restoration of amity between France and England . . . in Europe. In America it was another matter.

Bitter hatreds and severe competition do not wither away at once with the signing of a paper some three thousand miles away. The enmity held by the American factions of

English and French for one another remained; changed only in that it became covert. There were whisperings that the English were even more thoroughly undermining the French trade among the Indians, and this was true. And there were whisperings that the Indians were taking great delight in this situation which enabled them to maintain an enviable bargaining position between the Europeans, and this was true.

Pennsylvania, Virginia and Maryland continued to look westward and saw, with a certain degree of nervousness, that relations were not all they should be between them and the Iroquois, Delawares, Hurons, Shawnees and Miamis and they set about rectifying the situation.

An influential trader named George Croghan was empowered by Governor James Hamilton of Pennsylvania to improve these relations; to renew the chain of friendship and to offer these Indians trade deals even better than the ones before. And so Croghan packed up and traveled far to the west with his half-breed interpreter Andrew Montour—past the head of the Ohio River and into the Ohio country to the fertile river valleys of the Muskingum and Walhonding, the Scioto and Olentangy, the Great Miami and the Little Miami, the Wabash and the Sandusky, the Mad and the Auglaize and the Maumee.

His mission was a success. Many of the Delawares and Shawnees returned to the English fold; more of the Hurons did, too, divorcing themselves from their pro-French brethren and taking on the new tribal name of Wyandot and resettling on the Mad and Muskingum rivers. Alliance with the Miamis was much strengthened and a large new trading post built on a tributary[13] of the upper reaches of the Great Miami River.

Chiefs from all these tribes concerned were escorted to Lancaster, Pennsylvania, for a council with the English and there given the assurance of protection against French reprisal and the promise that ever more traders would be sent among them with the items they wanted and needed. In a short while the whole French fur-trading empire in the west was in considerable jeopardy.

The principal chief of the Miami tribe, Unemakemi, was warmly praised for his adherence to the English while living under the shadow of the French on the Wabash River head waters, and both he and the second principal chief of the tribe—a strong young man named Michikiniqua[14]—were presented with large bronze medallions to hang about their necks with wide scarlet ribbons. Unemakemi was given the

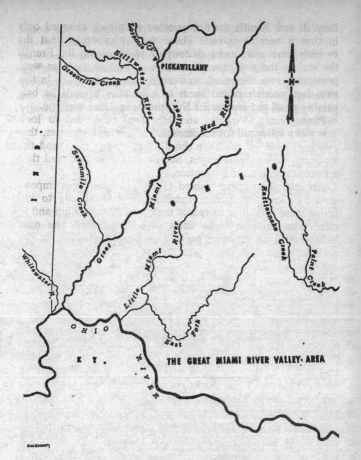

THE GREAT MIAMI RIVER VALLEY AREA

English name of Old Britain, which he took to be a great honor.

Upon Unemakemi's return to his village he gathered up all his people, along with those of Chief Orontony of the Hurons and moved away to establish, close to that new English trading post on the Great Miami River tributary, a new village—the largest and strongest individual Indian village between the Alleghenies and the Mississippi. Only one small faction of his tribe did not accompany him; a band living in a small village under Chief Cold Foot practically in the shadow of the French Fort Miamis.

Unemakemi named this sprawling new village Pickawil-

121

lany. It was a village of four hundred lodges at the outset and more were being built every week as new Indian groups or individuals attracted to it took up residence there. Now, at the end of the year, the population of Pickawillany was approaching two thousand, and even though they were only two days' march from the French at Fort Miamis on the headwater of the Maumee River, their allegiance was strongly English.

It was a bitter pill for the French.

# CHAPTER III

*[ April 28, 1749—Friday ]*

WILLIAM JOHNSON had just returned home—to his new and more spacious Mount Johnson, which he had begun building a mile away from the old Mount Johnson residence last fall. It was a fine, huge house, all of stone, and a place that would serve admirably as a place of sanctuary if attacked, as well as a place of residence.

Now, arriving there, he threw off his personality of Warraghiyagey as easily as he took off his coat, and resumed his identity as William Johnson, employee of the Colony of New York. For close to five weeks he had been traveling through Iroquois country, speaking in turn to the Mohawks and Oneidas, Onondagas, Cayugas, Tuscaroras and Senecas, assuring them of the continued friendship of the English and of himself.

At first it had gone well, but only at first. As he moved to the west and farther and farther away from English influence, his words were accepted with ever less enthusiasm until, in the western Iroquois lands along the headwaters of the Allegheny River, he ran into disturbingly strong proFrench feelings. This was particularly true among the Senecas under Chief Old Belt.

Here, at the figurative back door of the Iroquois Long House, as the line of confederated villages termed themselves, a pair of half-breed brothers, Daniel and Chabert Joncaire, had been just about as busy and convincing at winning the Indians to the French point of view as William himself had been among the Mohawks at the front door of the long house. In fact, so strongly opposed were the Senecas to any English notions that when William arrived among them he felt satisfied in his own mind that he would probably have been killed had he not come among them as Warraghiyagey rather than William Johnson.

At council after council among them he had talked and danced and talked some more until his voice was hoarse and his legs failing and now, having returned home at last, he was met by Angélique Vitry. The eighteen-year-old girl threw herself into his arms and kissed him passionately, hoping to stir in him some of the old fire that she sensed was diminished of late.

For a change, William was glad to see her and he returned the embrace abundantly. Nevertheless, even as the heat began to rise in him, he shook his head and gently set her aside, telling her to fetch paper, inkpot and quill. His report to Governor Clinton had to take precedence.

In moments the French girl had returned with them to his desk and then sat quietly on the floor at his feet, her head resting against his knee while for more than an hour he wrote. Even though he said nothing to her during this period, she could sense the anger in him as the words flowed from his pen.

Not until after he had filled several pages did William pause momentarily to reach down and stroke her hair and tell her that he would soon be finished and that in the meantime she should summon a messenger. And when she had gone away at once, he put the finishing touches to his report and his complaint of the:

*. . . confounded wicked things the French had infused into the Indians' heads; among the rest, that the English were determined, the first opportunity, to destroy them all. I assure your Excellency I had hard work to beat these and other cursed villainous things, told them by the French, out of their heads . . .*

He wrote another half page after that, signed it with a flourish and then folded and sealed the pages. By that time Angélique had returned with a German youth of about sixteen, to whom William handed the packet, along with a coin and a murmured word.

The lad nodded and disappeared into the darkness outside. Johnson closed the door slowly, thoughtfully, bolted it securely and then turned and found Angélique staring at him, her eyes deep with desire. In many ways she had become wearisome, yes. And demanding. And jealous. Soon, perhaps, he would have to get rid of her; judiciously, of course, and without hurting her too badly, if possible. But for now . . .

124

As she came to him and locked her small hands around his neck, he scooped her up and began carrying her up the steps.

[ *June 2, 1749—Friday* ]

The Marquis de la Galissonière sat at his desk, intent upon the letter he was writing. The grotesque hump on his back from his misshapen spine was most apparent at such times as this, when his body was leaning forward, his head and eyes turned downward, his thoughts inward. No one knew how he suffered from it—this great lump of flesh and twisted bone which perched between his shoulder blades like some devilish parasite he could never dislodge.

Most men who dealt with him, in fact, rarely thought of the hump at all, for when the governor's gaze was turned on them and boring into them, these eyes seemed to thrust aside all extraneous matters. Now, however, he paused in his writing and reached in back of him as far as possible and rubbed the aching deformity—an act in which he indulged himself only when alone.

The papers he was writing, the instructions he was penning, the orders, the reports—all of these would soon be behind him. Too often he had locked horns in correspondence with Louis XV and now the order from the colonial minister was there on his desk and he was being recalled to France, with the Marquis de la Jonquière to take his place here in Montreal. He knew Jonquière reasonably well; knew him as a tall, imposing, former naval officer with the capacity to become great and the courage of his convictions. But Jonquière was getting old and his avariciousness was a matter of regular gossip in the King's Court. Galissonière had little hope that his own plans for the French conquest of North America would be carried out by Jonquière, who was strong for devising plans exclusively his own.

But it would be a good while yet before Galissonière would be relieved and until then he determined to augment those plans already in motion and continue, despite that fatuous lout who ruled France, to make every effort to preserve and protect and improve the holding of France here in America.

Toward that end, early in January, Galissonière had induced twelve families from Montreal—totaling forty-six people—to settle at Detroit. It had taken money from his own pocket for supplies and transportation and other inducements to get them to go, but the governor knew with a passion that

125

it was ordinary people, simple, everyday Frenchmen, more than small knots of soldiers, who could do most in securing this land for France through the elemental expedient of sinking roots in the American soil. They had sunk them well, and this had all been explained in the reports Galissonière was completing at this time in his quiet office.

There came a light knocking on the governor's door and he swiftly removed his hand from his back and, in an unconscious gesture, straightened somewhat. He bade the visitor enter, saw it was the officer he had been expecting—a handsome young man in the uniform of a Chevalier de St. Louis—and, without a word, nodded him to a chair for the moment.

Almost as if there had been no interruption, he continued with his train of thought. Another threat to the French holdings here was the infernal English military and trading post at Oswego on Lake Ontario. Indians from all over were going there to trade for the better deals available. Even many of the Indians of the Sault Sainte Marie and Michilimackinac areas were going there instead of trading at Detroit —traveling by canoe through the waters of the North Channel and Georgian Bay of Lake Huron and then overland from the foot of Georgian Bay southward to the village of Toronto.[1] From here, on the north shore of Lake Ontario, they moved in hastily built canoes across the lake to trade their bales of beaver, otter, marten, ermine and mink pelts for goods the French budget could not provide.

In late April Galissonière had sent his aide, Captain Portneuf, with a large party of soldiers and workmen to build a well-stockaded trading house at Toronto in an effort to intercept the Indians en route to Oswego. They were not to stop them by force, which would have been disastrous to the French interest, but by tempting them with a great stockpile of as many as possible of the goods that they needed—most of which Galissonière had bought out of his own pocket— and, as even more insurance for stopping the Indians, an abundant supply of brandy.

But Oswego continued to be a thorn in the side of the French and Galissonière, for once with the warm approval of the colonial minister, gave instructions to one of the Sulpician priests of Montreal, the Abbé Francois Piquet, to establish a mission on the south side of the upper St. Lawrence River for the overt purpose of converting the Iroquois to Christianity. The mission was to be built at the mouth of the Oswegatchie River about one hundred miles upstream from Montreal.[2] Its convert purpose, however, was to win over as many Iroquois as possible to the French, much as the Caughnawagas had been won over. Only instead of Caughnawaga Mohawks, this time they would be aiming for a mixture of Cayugas, Onondagas and Senecas.

Even from his faraway seat in Versailles, the French colonial minister could see the danger of making a French attack—or even a French-supported attack—against Oswego, since France and England were now ostensibly at peace; but the English post was most troublesome and simply had to be wiped out. Discretion was the key word. That post would have to be attacked vicariously, through the Indians. As the colonial minister expressed this in a communiqué to the governor:

*If Abbé Piquet succeeds in his mission, we can easily persuade these savages to destroy Oswego. This is of the utmost importance; but act with great caution . . .*

And in another directive to Jonquière, still at this time in France, the colonial minister said:

*The only means that can be used for such an operation in time of peace are those of the Iroquois. If by making these savages regard such an establishment as opposed to their liberty, and, so to speak, a usurpation by which the English mean to get possession of their lands, they could be induced to undertake its destruction, an operation of the sort is not to be neglected; but M. le Marquis de la Jonquière should feel with what circumspection such an affair would be conducted, and he should labor to accomplish it in a manner not to commit himself . . .*

Now, in his office, Galissonière smiled to himself. This plan in attempting to establish the mission at Oswegatchie, already being carried out by Father Piquet, was one operation Monsieur Jonquière could not abandon; not with the colonial minister strongly supporting it. If his own evaluation of the character of Jonquière was correct, it would not be long after that officer took the reins of this office that he would be claiming as his own the idea for the establishment of the mission.

Galissonière shook his head slightly and chuckled. If that was the way it would happen, then so be it. Now, with his own time as governor running short, there was one more operation to set in motion which could be exceedingly important to France in the future. The treaty of Aix-la-Chapelle had done nothing to settle the American boundaries' question which so vexed the two European powers. In fact Galissonière was sure that all it had done was delay the eventual confrontation they must have in this matter. And with English traders crossing the Alleghenies and poaching on land France claimed as her own, ruining the French fur trade, seducing the Indians and stirring them up against the Frenchmen and even the Canadians, something had to be done quickly to vindicate French territorial rights to the valley of the Ohio River and the country which lay on both sides of it. And so, Galissonière had devised his plan.

To carry it out he had selected a young aggressive and capable officer whom only last month he had promoted to the rank of captain. The man's name was Pierre Joseph de Céloron de Bienville. And it was this very officer who had presented himself to the governor as ordered and now waited patiently in the fine leather chair beside the desk. Galissonière turned his head and fastened his eyes on the young man and immediately the officer sat a little straighter and became attentive. The governor smiled.

"Captain," he said, "I have selected you to undertake a mission of critical importance to France and to our empire here in America. Implant that point firmly in your mind. You must not fail in it."

Without waiting for Céloron to reply, Galissonière pointed to two bundles along the far wall close to the door through which the officer had entered.

"In those parcels," he said, "are tin sheets that have been impressed with the French coat-of-arms, along with seven leaden plates inscribed in a manner to claim in tangible means certain territories as French. In this packet," he arose, took a thick hide pouch from the polished desktop and handed it to the captain, "are explicit orders you are to follow.

"Your company has already been named and the men are at this time being outfitted for the expedition. Their canoes are also being readied. Since you are already familiar with the essentials of the mission, I needn't linger on the actual steps at this time. Except to say this: *under no circumstances* are you or your men to initiate attack upon any Englishmen or Indians. All Indians encountered will be treated with respect, their chiefs with honor. You will vocally encourage any English traders or settlers you may encounter to depart the area under threat of pain, imprisonment or death if they should return to French territory; but absolutely no physical action will be taken against them by you or your men—or against the Indians—except as might conceivably become necessary for self-preservation."

Through all of this the officer had been sitting quietly, the faintest trace of a smile beneath his thin moustache. Now, in a fluid motion conveying the impression of great reserve strength and speed, he got to his feet and stood at attention. He dipped his head slightly and his voice was firm when he spoke.

"Sir, I want you to know that I appreciate your naming me to this command. I will do all in my power to justify your faith in me."

"I'm sure you will, Captain Céloron; but just so we understand one another, I have been told that while a courageous officer, you are also a rash young man and inclined toward insubordination. This was partly the reason I chose you. A little rashness can be a powerful weapon, when tempered with common sense. But in the matter of insubordination, deviation from the letter of these orders you have received will not be countenanced. Is that fully understood?"

"Yes, sir." A faint flush tinged Céloron's cheeks.

"Very well. You have two weeks to prepare yourself and your men for this venture. Make good use of this time in finding out from those who have been in that country and dealt with the inhabitants, what you may expect to face en route in the matter of people and hardships of terrain. You can send a detail to remove these parcels and see to their safekeeping. Your departure is set for sunrise, June fifteen."

And Captain Pierre Joseph de Céloron de Bienville left the office of the governor of New France with the air of a man who clenched, in his own hand, his destiny.

[ *July 25, 1749—Saturday* ]

The sun had been just clearing the eastern horizon in a sky swept clear of clouds on June 15 when Captain Céloron gave a hand signal and his large party of men stepped into their canoes some three miles upstream from Montreal. A significant segment of the city's population had turned out for the event and the crowd broke into a rousing cheer at the move.

It was music to Céloron's ears.

He smiled. It *was* an impressive moment and he was thoroughly pleased to be the center of attention. Even when the Marquis de la Gallisonière had given him his hand in

129

final farewell and they had stepped apart, it was the young captain whom the eyes of the crowd followed, not the governor.

The Jesuit chaplain of the expedition, Father Bonnecamp, paused to ask solemn blessing on their endeavor and then was helped into one of the boats, his movements hampered somewhat by his heavy, flowing habit which reached to his shoes.

In addition to himself, Céloron had a total of two hundred thirty-four men in his party. Fourteen of these were nattily dressed officers and cadets, supported by twenty common soldiers picked from the governor's own guard. There were, as well, under the secondary command of the Canadian trader Chabert Joncaire, one hundred eighty Canadians—most of them young adventurers eager to do new things and see new lands and possibly even make their fortunes in the process. Finally, there was a band of twenty Indians, mostly Algonkins and Abnakis.

With dramatic flair, Captain Céloron signaled his fourteen subordinate officers and cadets who, in well-rehearsed manner, raised their muskets and fired a nearly simultaneous salute, practically tipping over one of the canoes in the process and frightening a large flock of ducks into a quacking, wing-flapping scramble over the water surface a hundred yards away.

The men were in twenty-three of the big canoes, each upwards of thirty feet in length and carrying eight or nine men per craft. Another ten canoes—smaller boats, laden with bundles of supplies—were each manned by two well-experienced Canadian *voyageurs*. Within minutes despite the strong St. Lawrence current against them, they had pushed out of sight of the Montreal throng and into the treacherous LaChine Rapids, which took every bit of their skill and daring to negotiate.

Captain Céloron had expected this first portion of the trip to be difficult, but hardly the trial it turned out to be. The rapids became progressively worse and on the third day, shortly after camp was broken and progress resumed, they encountered a particularly severe section of white water.

One of the boats carrying Canadians was swept momentarily into a turbulent eddy behind a great flat jutting rock. The craft seemed in imminent danger of being swamped and, in an effort to save himself, one of the young adventurers leaped from boat to rock, lost his footing on the slick moss which coated it, and fell. His head struck the rock and split open, briefly staining the water with a bright ribbon of red before he disappeared beneath the surface. It was a tragic occurrence but the young commander ordered his men on, not permitting them time for second thoughts. Father Bonnecamp said a brief prayer as they continued.

It was hours before they completed their negotiation of this single mile-long stretch of harsh water and in a relatively calm section above it pulled to shore to rest and take stock. It had not been a very auspicious beginning: one man lost and at least a half dozen of the canoes damaged enough to require immediate repairs.

These repairs were undertaken at once and in three hours they were afloat again. Soon, however, the rapids became so bad that they were portaging over land even more than paddling through the treacherous, foamy water. It was slow and disheartening travel, involving back-breaking labors both on the water and during the multitude of portages.

Not until June 25 did they finally reach the head of this extensive rapids and coast smoothly to shore at the mouth of the Oswegatchie River. Here, ensconced in a bark lean-to, they found the Sulpician, Francois Piquet, and two Iroquois Indians resting from their labors of building the mission, which looked suspiciously like a fort. The structure was about two thirds completed.

With a zeal befitting a political agent more than a gentle missionary, Father Piquet waxed eloquent about the great number of converts to French allegiance he would soon have, saying that his two Iroquois companions had reported seeing many of their Cayuga and Onondaga brethren hovering about nearby. Soon, he boasted, these very Indians would be raising their tomahawks and guns in a smashingly unexpected attack against Fort Oswego, which would utterly destroy the English outpost.

Céloron listened politely and even directed a good-sized work party of his own men to help raise the final timbers of the mission, which Piquet had already named La Présentation and which Jonclaire's Canadians immediately began calling Fort Présentation.

The captain had a grudging respect for the foresight Father Piquet had exhibited in choosing the site. It commanded the main body of the St. Lawrence River and could easily act as a barrier to hostile war parties or smugglers. An abundance of fish in the waters and game in the rich meadows and dense forest surrounding the site made it attractive to the Indians, who could come to it easily from their interior villages simply by floating down the Oswegatchie.

But Céloron was really not greatly interested in the Sulpician priest's enterprise and set off with his party early the next morning, his own force increased by the two Iroquois Indians, who had been given to him by Piquet. With the mouth of the river Oswegatchie marking the end of the rapids, the way was now smooth and navigation clear all the rest of the way up to Lake Ontario.

Hardly two hours after they embarked, members of Céloron's expedition, had they looked behind them, might have seen a rising pall of smoke. Their attention, however, was directed to what lay ahead and they did not even suspect that Fort Présentation was already turning into a pile of ashes as the result of an Iroquois attack. Abbé Piquet was still there, unhurt, sitting on a log and weeping. His job here was to be more difficult than he had anticipated.

Upon reaching the mouth of Lake Ontario, Céloron allowed his men two days' rest at Fort Frontenac,[3] located on the river's northern shore at the mouth of a small bay. Here the commandant relayed to his men the same written order that Galissonière had given him: that Fort Oswego should be passed in the midst of night and far enough offshore that their paddling would not be heard and their passage remain unsuspected.

Certain that the English garrison there was already aware of his mission, Céloron nonetheless obeyed the order and his flotilla, cautioned to absolute silence, glided past on a calm lake at two o'clock in the morning without incident.

They reached the small French post at the mouth of the Niagara River on July 6 without incident, but wasted no time there. All efforts now were utilized toward making the long and difficult portage around the cataract along the well-established portage path. In something near record time they had relaunched their canoes and entered Lake Erie at the mouth of Buffalo Creek.[4] The going was easy then, but it didn't last for long. Where a cairnlike Seneca marker on the southern shore of the lake indicated the start of a portage path his instructions had told him to watch for, the commander ordered his flotilla ashore and another tough portage was begun.[5]

It took seven days of rugged march through dense forests and over steep hills—during which time, hampered by almost daily rains, they rarely covered more than a mile a day—to reach the headwaters of the long, fingerlike body of water shown on Céloron's rough map as Lac Chautauqua.[6] After only a brief stop here for rest and food, they shoved off, once again in their canoes, and paddled to the southern end of the lake where the water became extremely shallow and the going was sometimes rocky, sometimes mucky, and always very difficult.[7]

They followed the little creek emptying out of its southern tip, which was soon joined by Cassadaga Creek entering from the north. In another three or four miles they reached the somewhat deeper Kanaquagon Creek.[8] Here the going became a bit easier, though even here they encountered frequent shallow riffles which necessitated much hard labor.

Father Bonnecamp, who had done more than his share of the work since the start of the expedition and considerably less than his share of the complaining, found even his patience sorely tried. It was with evident relief at noon today that he sat beneath a huge beech tree for a well-earned rest. Before the party was a large river which the creek they were following joined and, down that river, the great wild western lands. Bonnecamp took advantage of the respite to jot a few lines in his journal:

*In some places—and they have been but too frequent— the water was only two or three inches deep; and we were reduced to the sad necessity of dragging our canoes over the sharp pebbles, which, with all our care and precaution, stripped off large slivers of the bark. At last, tired and worn, and almost in despair of ever seeing La Belle Rivière,[9] we entered it at noon this day, the 29th . . .*

Although most of his company was exhausted, Céloron showed little sign of fatigue and immediately opened the parcels given to him by the Marquis de la Galissonière. One contained the square tin sheets stamped with the coat-of-arms of France and in the other were the seven lead plates. Finding the correct one for this location, he directed one of his men to complete the engraving—in the gap provided for it—by adding this day's date. While this was being done, he directed another man to nail to the beech tree beneath which Father Bonnecamp was sitting one of the big tin sheets. Finally, a third man was ordered to dig a hole four feet deep at the base of that tree.

As soon as these three jobs were completed to his satisfaction, the commander called his party into formation before the

133

tree and made a grand formal declaration, which was recorded by the notary of the expedition.

"In the name of France and to her benefit," Céloron intoned, "I, Pierre Joseph de Céloron de Bienville, do this day and time take possession of all this country, and proclaim King Louis the Fifteenth undisputed lord and protector over all these territories. Beneath this great tree to which I have attached the insignia of France, I now direct the burial of this leaden plate which substantiates this claim for all time and for all men."

With something akin to reverence, Céloron held the plate high for all to see and then knelt to place it face down in the hole; face down so that anyone in the future who might dig for it, would not deface it with the digging tools. The clearly legible engraving read:

*Year 1749*
*This in the Reign of Louis Fifteenth*
*King of France*
*We, Céloron, commanding the detachment sent by the Marquis de la Galissonière, Commander-General of New France, to restore tranquillity in certain villages of these cantons, have buried this plate at the confluence of La Belle Rivière and the Kanaougon, this 29th July, as a token of renewal of possession heretofore taken of the aforesaid Rivière La Belle, of all streams that fall into it, and all lands on both sides to the source of the aforesaid streams, as the preceding Kings of France have or ought to have enjoyed it, and which they have upheld by force of arms and by treaties, notably by those of Ryswick, Utrecht, and Aix-La-Chapelle.*

Although none of the Indians standing in a curious group to one side of Céloron's regular formation of troops and Canadians understood the French words, the ceremony sobered and somewhat frightened them. Without a word to anyone, the two Iroquois warriors given to the commander by Abbé Piquet backed silently into the brush and then disappeared.

Shortly after the formal proceedings, Captain Céloron again ordered the expedition into motion, but though they came to several Indian villages along the river bank before darkness forced them to halt, all had been abandoned—though in some the fires were still burning—and the very breadth of the forest bracketing the river seemed to the Frenchmen to carry a deadly foreboding.

Strangely enough, almost concurrently with the burial of this first lead plate, a similar grandiose land claim was being made at Williamsburg, Virginia. Thomas Lee, as president of the Virginia Council and governor of the Dominion of Virginia, was posting a public proclamation. It said:

*The Boundaries of Virginia are the Atlantic on the east, North Carolina on the south, the Potomac on the north, and, on the west, the Great South Sea, including California.*[10]

And all around this whole territory there were literally scores of Indian tribes containing many thousands of residents who, despite the lead plates of the Frenchmen and proclamations of the Englishmen, not only claimed all the land in question, but *knew* it belonged to them, and they had no intention of giving it up.

## [July 31, 1749—Monday]

Matters of his own private fur-trading and wheat-milling business occupied William Johnson during these months since the treaty with France was signed and it was the first respite from being in the middle between the Iroquois and whites that he had enjoyed for ages. He spent more time at home now and there he entertained a considerable variety of women, primarily Indian.

Because Angélique Vitry could not help but be in the way for such *tête-à-têtes*, William finally made the break with her and, under the solicitous guise of looking out for her future, provided her with money and, against her tearful protests, sent her with an Indian escort back to Canada to be reunited with her father and earlier-liberated sisters at Fort Frontenac.

His three children by Catherine Weisenberg—Ann, John and Mary—were now well settled in New York with their mother at his expense. Ann, now nine, and John, seven, were attending school and little five-year-old Mary would be starting in the autumn. And now, with both Catty and Angélique out from underfoot, William's only dependent remaining at Mount Johnson was Tagchuento, his son by a taciturn Mohawk woman from Canajoharie, far up the river, whom he had hired as a housekeeper. Though William never acknowledged fathership of those children he sired in the

135

Iroquois villages, he seemed to take delight in the little half-breed under his own roof and even went so far as to dub him little Will.[11]

For the English officers occasionally in the Mohawk Valley, it became quite the thing to do to go with Willliam to visit Teantontalogo or Canajoharie and sport with the young maidens there. William enjoyed taking the officers, but only so long as they treated the women with courtly manners. He considered them every bit as deserving of respect as white girls and was, in fact, himself coming to prefer them as agreeable companions, whether in or out of bed.

"The young Indian ladies," he commented, "are just as polite a set as the Albany ladies here and must be treated just as properly."

That they could make a lasting effect on the officers was evident in the repeated visits William had and the many letters he received from those men who had partaken of the delights that he had led them to—such as the one young militia lieutenant who sent *My compliments to little Miss Michael at the Mohawk's Teantontalogo and Mme. Curl'd Locks at Canajoharie.*

In addition to his business and his women, William found much of his time taken up with his imposing new Mount Johnson. The mansion, which was thirty-two feet wide and sixty feet long and had two main floors, had become a significant landmark. The kitchen was located in a daylit cellar and in the attic the gambrel roof was so high that two tiers of servants' sleeping quarters had been made by nailing planks across the rafters to form a loft within the attic itself.

From London, William had ordered sheet lead for the roof, a huge booming door-knocker, paint, nails, bolts, hinges, locks, latches and even a mammoth squared beam with his name and the year engraved upon it. His wall paneling, banisters, mantels, and other wood construction were finished from fine American cherry and black walnut and were beautifully engraved in semiclassical figures. There was in the main hall a great globe light, and in the built-in shelves of the study fine books on English history and natural philosophy. Engravings of various kinds, including Titian's *Love of the Gods* hung on his walls and in a glass-fronted cabinet lay on dark blue velvet a fine French horn, a trumpet and an ordinary hunting horn.

Fifty feet from the house a huge flour mill of his own design groaned deeply as it worked, and nearby were smaller houses for the tenant miller and cooper and blacksmith, as well as for servants and for slaves. There were barns and stables, a bakehouse, a pigeon house and even a good council house, along with sheds, tents and cabins for when the Iroquois should come here to meet.

There were always dozens upon dozens of people milling about the place—his own employees and slaves as well as an unending stream of visitors. Mount Johnson had become the talk of civilized North America and its fame had even brought visitors from England specifically to see it.

William Johnson's interests had spread to take in mills and shops in Schenectady and Albany and elsewhere and he was now, beyond doubt, one of the richest men in the whole territory. His broadened interests, fame and affluence, however, had not caused him to turn his back on Indian affairs. In fact, as he continued his efforts to keep the Six Nations from ransoming the Mohawk prisoners from Montreal with a separate peace, he was forced to support the cause of the Crown at almost entirely his own expense. The legislature had few funds it was willing to allocate for Indian affairs. His constant calls to Governor Clinton for help in this respect were essentially useless.

"William," Clinton complained, shaking his head, "my Assembly would rather give up the Indians to the French than yield any of their claims or expectations of power."

William Johnson expected such a comment and was ready for it. The shocking news had just been brought to him that an army of Frenchmen were at this very moment penetrating the western Iroquois lands for some unknown purpose, having been surreptitiously watched by the Iroquois since shortly before reaching the mouth of Lake Ontario. At last report they had turned southward and were traveling overland. Their ultimate destination was unknown, but it was apparently the Ohio River Valley. No matter what their business, William concluded, it couldn't possibly be to England's benefit. He now spelled out to Clinton—and through him to the English cabinet in London—a plan he had been formulating for a long while. He wrote:

*Indian Affairs are of much more importance to His Majesty's government than the whole act of ruling the colonists. On the whole, the Indians are reluctant to take the Crown's orders and cannot be relied upon to fight British battles. But this you must know: the Indians can be made into loyal allies and are, as a military force, stronger than English regular troops here. They are also more valuable economically. Does not the fur trade offer the Crown a a surer revenue than all the scheming activities and smuggling of the settlers?*

*To permit the narrow minds of the American Assembly to interfere in matters as important as Indian relations is madness. I myself have suffered great economic loss because I have been forced to rely for my just dues on New York's Colonial Government, and they of the Assembly have constantly denied me help. In these last two years alone I have had to try to match from my own purse what the French are expending, and though in this endeavor I have used over £600, yet the British interest continually loses ground. If I am to remain dependent upon such authority as the New York Assembly, I will have to resign. However, I will be happy to continue to manage England's Indian alliances if I am given an appointment that, by basing my office directly on the Crown, will make me independent of Colonial opposition.*

It was another calculated risk, but Johnson was not bothered with a false modesty. He was well aware that no white man on the frontier had as much influence over the Indians as he and the loss of his services to the Crown would be something on the nature of a disaster.

And now, with all done that he could do where politics was concerned, he turned his attention to the west and immediately sent out a dozen or more Indian messengers carrying purple war belts and a brief message calculated to stir nervousness and fear to the villagers:

*A French Army is moving through your western lands. Keep your warriors close to home, lest your villages be surprised and destroyed!*

### [ August 30, 1749—Wednesday ]

Chabert Joncaire spoke the Iroquois tongue as if he had been born to it. As a matter af fact, he had. Though his father was a French officer, his mother was a Seneca squaw and under the tutelage of both he had become an important intermediary for both nations. It was the basis for having him along on this expedition, Captain Céloron knew, but thus far the halfbreed's contribution had been little. He was a good guide, but even the Senecas were suspicious of him and the other Iroquois nations considered him double-tongued and not to be trusted.

This became evident to Céloron when, as his expedition progressed down the Allegheny and found ever more deserted villages, he sent Joncaire ahead to act as a messenger of peace to them. For the most part the half-breed was consistently unsuccessful in convincing them and they continued to flee in advance of the little army.

Finally, however, at the mouth of French Creek, they encountered Indians at the village known as La Paille Coupée.[12] Waiting for them here with Joncaire was the subchief Yellow Eyes, along with perhaps thirty warriors. The principal chief of the village, Keneghtaugh, was away. "Visiting Onondaga on business," Joncaire told the captain wryly as the French party landed.

Yellow Eyes, decidedly nervous and making a great effort not to show it, as were the warriors in the small group standing a dozen paces behind him, wanted to know at once why the Frenchmen were invading their country.

"Tell them," Céloron instructed Joncaire, "that we are not here to harm them in any way, but that we have come in peace and we are here to help them. Tell them that I have a message for them from the Marquis de la Galissonière."

The subchief heard Joncaire out without comment while Céloron extracted from his pouch a message in the governor's own hand. When Joncaire had finished and turned back to him with an unreadable expression, the commander said, "Translate, Chabert," and began reading the message phrase by phrase.

*My Children, since I was at war with the English, I have learned that they have seduced you; and not content with corrupting your hearts, have taken advantage of my absence to invade lands which are not theirs, but mine; and therefore I have resolved to send you Monsieur de Céloron to tell you my intentions, which are that I will not endure the English on my land. Listen to me, Children; mark well the word that I send you; follow my advice and the sky will always be calm and clear over your villages. I expect from you an answer worthy of true Children. I urge you to stop all trade with these English intruders, and send them back whence they came.*

For some time after Chabert Joncaire finished translating,

139

the chieftain remained silent. Céloron's eyes had already begun to narrow with anger when Yellow Eyes spoke.

"We have heard what you have said and our hearts are open to you and we will do as you say. We will order the English traders from our lands and do trade with them no more and do trade only with you, as our father in Montreal asks."

The captain nodded somewhat less than enthusiastically and then presented him with a good knife, a tomahawk and several other gifts. Then he gave the order to embark downstream again. Despite the compliance of Yellow Eyes, the commander was not pleased. Everyone felt it and Father Bonnecamp put it to words in his journal as they moved downstream, *We should all have been satisfied if we had thought them sincere; but nobody among us doubted that fear had extorted their answer.*

Eight miles below that village, the expedition paused at the mouth of a creek which Chabert Joncaire called Rivière Est Sable.[13] Here there was a huge rock inscribed with Indian markings which not even Joncaire could translate. On a nearby oak tree, Céloron had another tin plate attached and a lead plate buried at the base, its inscription identical to the first except for the name of the stream joining the Allegheny, and the date—which was now August 4.

The night was passed peacefully and on the third day following they reached the Delaware Indian village which Joncaire called Attiqué, but which the Delawares themselves referred to as Kittanning.[14] Not unexpectedly, all twenty-two lodges were empty, though the ashes of their cooking fires still glowed. Angrily, the captain kicked one such glowing pile of embers and sent the coals sailing into a pile of dried grasses used for bedding. They began smoldering at once and Céloron watched the wispy smoke for a long moment before reluctantly bidding his men to extinguish it.

Only a few miles farther downstream they reached an old Shawnee village that had been abandoned for some time, not just as a result of the French army's approach. But here there was a difference. Six English traders—rough, filthy, bearded men who seemed incessantly to be scratching their lice—were in one of the square wegiwas. There was a rising fear in their eyes as they saw the officer's force, but a peculiar insolence as well. Their apparent leader was a huge, dark-haired man in greasy leathers. His name was Hawker. A dark scar ran from alongside his nose, across

140

his right cheek and directly through his right ear, which was now in two sections.

In surprisingly good English, Céloron said, "You are English traders on French territory. I have authority from the French government to order you to leave this country at once and return no more, at your peril. This time you will be permitted to take your goods with you. If you are found here again, you will be imprisoned and your goods confiscated." He motioned to Hawker. "I will give you a message to take to your governor of the Pennsylvania."

The captain called for a scribe and then dictated a short message aloud:

"To Governor of the Pennsylvania from Captain Pierre Joseph de Céloron de Bienville. Sir, in a mission of inspection of lands in the valley of La Belle Rivière, which you call the Ohio River, I am greatly surprised to find Englishmen trespassing on the domain of France. This is an act which cannot be tolerated if peace is to remain between our nations. The trespassers have been warned and sent thither with this message to be delivered to your hand. I know that our commandant-general would be very sorry to be forced to use violence; but his orders are precise—to leave no foreign traders within the limits of his government. Much tribulation will surely be averted if you will instruct those traders within your realm to heed this regulation."

Being quite helpless to resist, Hawker watched as the officer signed the completed document and then he accepted it from him without relish.

"Reckon we'll go like you say," he muttered.

Without any further communication between them other than a wave of Hawker's hand to his own men, the traders collected their belongings and soon disappeared into the woods toward the east. None of the Frenchmen had any doubt that these traders would be back as soon as the canoe fleet pushed off again. Céloron shook his head, ordered the wegiwa they had been staying in burned and the expedition set off again, while the billowing smoke smudged the sky behind them.

The next day—August 9—they had reached the Seneca village named Alequippa Town, after the squaw who was chief. She was called Queen Alequippa by the English and, devoted to them, she and her people had fled the village before the French arrived. Once again, however, Céloron's men discovered six more English traders and the warning of the day before to Hawker and his men was repeated. And, as Hawker's men had done, they pretended to obey the evacuation order. In a neighboring village within sight of Alequippa Town, Céloron found only an ancient warrior and his squaw, whom Father Bonnecamp judged to be over a century old each.

Surprisingly, though it seemed an obvious place to bury one of the plates, no stop at all was made by the party the next day when, close to noon, they passed the point where the Allegheny and Monongahela rivers join to form the Ohio. Instead, they continued downriver some seventeen or eighteen miles until they reached a large Indian town named Chiningué, which Joncaire said the English traders were using as their prime wilderness headquarters and which they called Logstown.[15] That the news of their approach had preceded them was obvious. The late afternoon sun showed the river bank lined with natives and both the French and the English flags flying over the town on long wooden poles.

As Céloron's flotilla neared, a hundred guns or more were raised in supposed salute, but instead of being only powder-loaded the guns were charged with lead balls. The bullets whistled menacingly as they passed low over the canoes, causing the Frenchmen to curse and duck apprehensively. Only their commander remained standing upright in the bow of the lead craft.

"Stop!" he shouted. "If you do not stop firing at once I will order my men to return the fire!" Joncaire repeated the words in the Iroquois tongue.

The shooting petered out and it was not without nervousness that the French party alighted on the shore, drew up the canoes and climbed the steep bank to the village site. Though there were only a few over fifty dwelling places, there were far more people on hand than such a village could have accommodated—largely Shawnees, Delawares, Senecas and Cayugas—and Joncaire gave his commander the sotto voce opinion that this had become the gathering place of many of the Indians that had abandoned their towns upstream.

No immediate attempts were made to talk with the chiefs or the ten English traders presently here, nor did the chiefs or traders approach the area where Céloron indicated his own men should make camp. Joncaire disappeared in the twilight and when he returned, after full dark, it was with the disturbing information that some squaws had told him an attack was planned against the camp this night.

The captain at once ordered the camp encircled by a ring of sentries and both the guards and their officers walked rounds all night while the rest of the party slept in their clothing with their guns beside them. This preparedness evidently made the Indians think again and no attack took place. Early in the morning Céloron sent a messenger to ask the chiefs to a council and, before the sun was very high, they appeared. There was an extreme edginess on both sides, but this diminished as the commander, through Joncaire, read them another message from the French governor which was considerably more conciliatory than the first had been:

*Through the love I bear you, my Children, I send you Monsieur de Céloron to open your eyes to the designs of the English against your lands. The establishments they mean to make, and of which you are completely ignorant, tend to your complete ruin. They hide from you their plans, which are to settle here and drive you away, if I let them. As a good father who tenderly loves his Children, and though far away from them bears them always in his heart, I must warn you of the danger that threatens you. The English intend to rob you of your country; and that they may succeed, they begin by corrupting your minds. As they mean to seize the Ohio, which belongs to me, I send to warn them to retire.*

When Céloron and Joncaire were finished, the spokesman of the assembled chiefs, a Seneca known by the name of Monakaduto—Half King—got to his feet. He was a short, heavyset man who looked weak until one looked closely at his eyes.

"You who come to us under the name of friendship, hear me," he said, his voice deliberate and strong. "The Indians of this country—a country that *no one* can own, any more than a man can own the air he breathes or the water he drinks, but which is there for all to use wisely and well— these Indians need trade goods. They have accepted the English goods over the French only because they are better, cheaper and more abundant.

"It is not our wish," he added, "to hurt the heart of the French father in Montreal, just as he tells us that it is not in him to hurt us. But if we are to hunt our game and provide for our families, we must have powder and lead, blankets and whatever other goods are necessary for our livelihood. Our father in Montreal must provide for us the same

143

benefit as our English friends do. Will he do this? If so, then we will drive the English from among us and have nothing further to do with them."

Under the circumstances it was as good a response as he could have hoped for and the Indians, after gravely accepting a large quantity of gifts from Céloron, sent messengers to bring the ten traders before the French. As he had with the others, Céloron warned them off the grounds upon which they were now allegedly trespassing and, as before, the traders agreed to all that was demanded of them but, as Father Bonnecamp put it in his journal, *well resolved, no doubt, to do the contrary as soon as our backs are turned.*

Immediately after the council, Céloron's party shoved off again, now escorted by a half-dozen canoes with two Indians in each. With the powerful thrust of the Ohio River current behind them, the entire party was soon far downstream from Logstown. Not until they reached the mouth of Wheeling Creek,[16] however, did they put ashore to bury another lead plate similar to the other two.

This was on August 12 and when they shoved off from here, it was with evident worry that Chabert Joncaire reported to Céloron that eight of the Indians had vanished. The commander shrugged off the report without much concern and thought no more about it until they reached the mouth of the Muskingum River, where another plate was to be buried. Then, for the first time, it was discovered that one of the plates was missing—a plate designed for burial at the mouth of the Scioto River, still some days downstream. It was a cause for great anger on Céloron's part, but since there was no one against whom to direct the anger, the matter was merely recorded in the journals, and due ceremony held for the burial of the Muskingum River plate.[17]

The fifth plate was buried on August 18 at the mouth of the big river running into the Ohio from the south, which Céloron called Rivière Chinodahichetha.[18]

With the plate for the Scioto River stolen, there was no real need to stop at that river's mouth. But it would be dangerous for them if they did not stop, since at this point was located the large Shawnee town which the Indians called Sinioto, which the English called Shawnee Town, and which was termed St. Yotoc in Céloron's orders.[19] That the town was hostile to the French was a known fact, but Céloron had strong hopes of convincing these Shawnees that their best interests lay with the French. The party put to shore a short

144

distance above the river's mouth and then Céloron sent Joncaire ahead with a flag of truce to ask peace with them.

Joncaire took with him an Iroquois companion—à Seneca named Sequahe—and it was fortunate that he did so. Even as he held the flag aloft, the Shawnees shot through it and surrounded the pair in a yelling throng, brandishing knives, tomahawks and war clubs. Some of the warriors were for immediately burning the white man at the stake, but Sequahe interposed with a sternness that subdued them.

"Strike down this man, whose mother is Seneca, though his skin be white, and you strike down an Iroquois," he said. "Burn him and it is the flesh of an Iroquois which splits and blackens with the flames. Destroy him and the wrath of the Six Nations will fall upon you and you will likewise be destroyed."

So unnerved were the Shawnees at this powerful threat that they turned Joncaire loose, telling him that the French boats could come through unharmed and would even be given a warm welcome. Joncaire was not so sure there wasn't a double meaning in the promise. He related to Céloron upon his return what had happened and again Céloron considered the wisdom of merely passing the town by without stopping. Now it was Joncaire who urged him not to do so.

"If you do not stop now, they will believe you are afraid and be encouraged to follow and attack us."

The commander nodded and announced that they would stop for talks. Before leaving this safe spot, however, he ordered that all guns be primed and ready. If a fight came, he intended to give them their money's worth.

"No gun of ours," he nevertheless warned his men grimly, "is to be fired except by my command; but if such command is given, aim well and shoot rapidly."

While his men were preparing, Céloron took the opportunity to write a few lines in his journal:

*I know the weakness of my party, two-thirds of which are young men who have never left home before, and will all run at the sight of ten Indians. Still, there is nothing for me but to keep on; for I am short of provisions, my canoes are badly damaged, and I have no pitch or bark to mend them. So I embark again, ready for whatever might happen. I have good officers and about fifty men who can be trusted.*

A state of apprehension rode high in each man as they

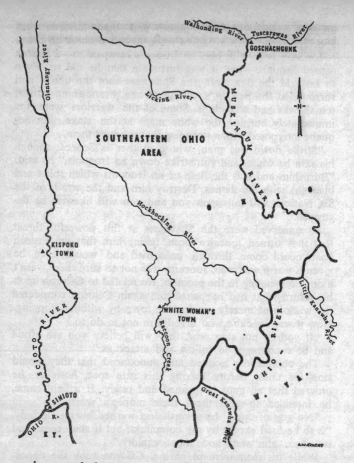

again moved downstream and it increased rather than diminished when they saw hundreds of armed Indians awaiting them on the shore. As had the Indians at Logstown, these Shawnees began to fire a "salute" which amounted to easily a thousand different shots, and Céloron prudently ordered his boatmen to land on the opposite side of the river, some three hundred yards across at this point.

Camp was pitched and guards posted to keep a close watch and finally, after many debates and some threatening gestures on the parts of both parties, a council meeting was agreed upon and held in Céloron's tent. A delegation of

146

half-a-dozen chiefs, a squaw who was the largest woman any man there had ever seen, and perhaps seventy warriors came across.

Six of the chiefs—including the huge woman—entered the tent for talks with the French commander, while the remaining Shawnees, alert and ready for anything that might happen, stood twenty or thirty yards away eyeing the nervous body of soldiers and Canadians who were a similar distance from the tent but separated from the Shawnee warriors by a hundred feet.

Inside, the chief first to speak was Hokolesqua, known to the English traders as Cornstalk. He was not only chief of this village called Sinioto across the river, he was chief of the Chalahgawtha sept of the Shawnees—one of the five clans which made up the Shawnee nation—and also principal chief of the entire Shawnee tribe.

The big female chief, who because of her size and bearing was called the Grenadier Squaw by the traders, went by the Shawnee name of Non-hel-e-ma. She was not unattractive, but amazingly large. She stood perhaps six-and-a-half feet tall and her well-formed body was in good proportion to her height, neither thin nor obese. She was chief of her own village some distance up the Scioto River and she was the sister of Hokolesqua.

Ki-kusgow-lowa was another of the chiefs and a powerful figure in the Shawnee nation. He was principal chief of the Thawegila sept. Red Hawk, a young man standing beside him, was second village chief of Sinioto under Hokolesqua. Next in line was Black Snake, a member of the Kispokotha sept of the Shawnees and second war chief of the entire tribe; a short, ugly man whose Shawnee name was She-me-ne-to. Finally, a minor chief of Sinioto village, known only by the name of Silverheels was here. He was the brother of both Hokolesqua and Non-hel-e-ma.

Chief Hokolesqua nodded briefly to Céloron and his voice was flat and emotionless as he spoke.

"We are sorry," he said, "for the treatment first given to your man, for we took him to be an enemy. But when we learned who he was, we sent him back to you in good health with an invitation for you to approach in peace. Now we would know what you are doing here; why have you come, what do you want and where are you going?"

Céloron was prepared to read them another message from the Marquis de la Galissonière, but instinctively realized there might be considerable danger in doing so. These Shawnees were fearsome warriors and they might not take kindly to the French claiming this very land upon which they lived. Instead, he spoke extemporaneously and to what he hoped was the best effect:

"Our and your great father across the sea, King Louis of France, fears for your safety. He sees plans afoot to steal your lands and hears whispers that men from the English colonies are already moving against you. He has sent me to give you warning that the Englishmen have great designs upon your country and are certainly preparing to take it from you."

Hokolesqua shook his head in disagreement. "My own eyes have seen the English and my own ears have heard them and my heart cannot believe that what you have said is true. In our village across the river there are now four English traders who have been with us for a long time. They come back and forth with goods we need and they treat us well and fairly and we see no threat in them. They know that should it become necessary, we could crush them as though they were fat caterpillars. And who is this father of yours— *not ours!*—across the sea that he should send *you* to warn *us?* Does he think we are children who are not able to detect the snarl of a dog before he bites? Go back and tell this King that we are able to protect ourselves very well, and we will do so if it becomes necessary, against Frenchmen or Englishmen or against both at once if the need should come."

Céloron felt the rush of anger flood through him and brought himself under control, though there was a slight sharpness in his voice when he replied.

"Our King wields a great sword," he said, "and his numbers are a thousand times yours, as you must know. Yet, he acts in your behalf and seeks only peace and friendship with you. More, he offers you his arm to help against those who might seek to injure you. Is this the way such an offer is to be received—with threats?"

Hokolesqua paused for a long while and when he spoke again his words and tone had softened. "If you have come with your open palms toward the sky and your hearts filled with friendship and peace, then there is no difficulty between us. I will this time close my eyes to the many men you have with you who wait your word with loaded guns in their hands. Though it does not seem to me that this is much of a way for you and your King to demonstrate your peaceful

148

and friendly intentions, yet I will this time close my eyes to them. I tell you now that you have leave to pass through our lands and you will not be hurt so long as hurt does not issue from you upon us, or upon our friends. I give you leave to pass, but I do not give you leave to stay or to put down roots anywhere for more than one night's camp."

There was really nothing Céloron could say in reply to that and so he merely thanked Hokolesqua and the other chiefs for their friendship and offer of safe passage, promised that he and his men would not camp for longer than one night anywhere while in Shawnee territory and then gave each of them a cup of brandy, which appeared to be the only part of this meeting which pleased them. Then, without further delay, he ordered his party afloat again and quickly the Scioto River village was lost in the distance behind them. In his journal he wrote:

*My instructions enjoin me to summon the English traders in Sinioto and instruct them to withdraw on pain of what might ensue, and even to pillage the English should their response be antagonistic; but I am not strong enough; and as these traders are established in a village and well supported by the Indians, the attempt would have failed and put the French to shame. I have therefore withdrawn with what pride such encounter as we suffered has permitted us to retain.*

The journey downriver was continued until noon today, August 30, when they reached the mouth of Rivière à la Roche—Rock River—better known to the English as the Great Miami River,[20] named after the Miami tribe which inhabited its valley.

Here the sixth and final lead plate was buried and a strong camp made for the rest of the day and night. The men were instructed to get a good night's rest, but sleep with their loaded weapons beside them. Beginning on the morrow, the journey would be upstream and rougher going by far than it had been since they first reached the downstream pull of the Allegheny.

What lay ahead of them, however, was the decidedly pro-English Miami tribe under Chief Demoiselle—Unemakemi—and it was not a prospect calculated to promote a very peaceful rest.

After all these many months of fruitless appeal and arbitration through messengers, William Johnson's and George Clinton's efforts bore fruit. The three Mohawk captives in Montreal, including Chief Nichus, had been abruptly and, for the moment, inexplicably released by the French governor.

For more than a year and a half they had been held and during all this time William had labored to gain their release while at the same time preventing the Iroquois from signing a separate peace with the French for this purpose. And now the big question was why? William was greatly pleased at the news but now filled with a new worry over what motive could have caused such a reversal on the part of the French governor.

He was not long in finding out.

The news of the captives' release reached Mount Johnson only a few days before the three themselves, pale and thin and weakened by the long imprisonment in a dark, windowless dungeon, returned to the Mohawk valley. In honor of their return, William sent runners to Teantontalogo and Canajoharie, inviting every Mohawk Indian—man, woman, or child—to a great party and feast at his place. But there was an ulterior motive to the invitation; he had a surprise in store for them which might weld them so firmly to the English that no further French appeal could win them away.

Only yesterday a Cayuga chief, Sacanghtradeya, had come to him bearing the lead plate that had been stolen from the Céloron expedition. A French-speaking neighbor had translated it for him and, though the import of it upset him badly, it would prove, he hoped, to be a powerful wedge for him to drive between the French and the Iroquois. He had planned to send the plate to Clinton at once, but now that the Mohawks were coming he decided to wait, and invited Sacanghtradeya to be his personal guest at the festivities.

The feast was spread on tables erected before the huge mansion. Three fine young bulls were butchered and spitted to roast and numerous kegs of rum were placed strategically about the grounds. William even called in an Irish band to play a noisy, if not too melodious, fanfare for the Indians when they should appear.

Appear they did, but only three hundred of them and all of them warriors. They were being led by Tiyanoga, Wascaugh and Nichus and every face was ugly with anger, They marched past the food and rum without pause and the ragged fanfare died aborning as the players saw the expressions of the Indians, lowered their instruments and began to back away.

Perplexed, William moved away from Sacanghtradeya, who still held the lead plate wrapped in buckskin. He advanced to meet them, smiling, and extended his hand in greeting. The three chiefs came to a halt a short distance in front of him and neither Wascaugh nor Tiyanoga even looked at William's extended hand nor offered their own. Nichus was even more insulting; he folded his arms across his chest and turned his back to William. The remainder of the Indians also stopped, their manner cold and menacing.

"Tiyanoga, what's wrong?" William asked. "What could cause you and your warriors to act this way to me?"

The old chief's look of sternness was replaced by an expression of bitterness and accusation, tinged with sorrow. His reply shocked William deeply.

"We have good reason for our feelings, Warraghiyagey," he said. "We have learned that you and the Governor Clinton are all French in your hearts and are planning with them to destroy us."

"French! Destroy you! Tiyanoga, you know that isn't true, can't possibly be true. You, my brother, you among all others of the Six Nations know that my heart and thoughts and blood are divided between the Iroquois and the English and that I hold only great love for both."

Tiyanoga shook his head and now Chief Nichus spun around and shot an accusing finger at William.

"You lie, Warraghiyagey! The truth that your heart is French and that of the Governor Clinton is French also is known to all in Canada. With my own eyes I have seen what was showed to me by the French governor himself—a very large belt of wampum, a purple war belt, which he said had been sent to him by you through Clinton to urge that the French and English join and cooperate to wipe us out. Yes! With my own ears I have heard him say that your plan was for the French and English to fall upon the Six Nations from both sides at once and destroy them every man and then, to settle the land difficulty that has existed between you, to divide up our land among yourselves. And the only reason that the Iroquois are not now under attack by you is because the French governor, who is a man of honor, would by no means

151

agree to any such thing, having too great a regard for all Indians whatsoever."

The charge was so preposterous that it was almost laughable. William studied Tiyanoga's face to see if in it he could read that this was another involved subterfuge designed to keep him on his toes and cause him to demand even greater concessions from the English government for the Iroquois.

And he was sure that he saw it!

Tiyanoga's next words confirmed it beyond any doubt to William Johnson and the burst of fear that had surged through him at the words of Nichus now abated.

"Warraghiyagey," Tiyanoga said, "my heart does not want to believe what my ears have heard from Nichus. When you begged of us in Onondaga to be permitted to arrange the release of these prisoners to keep us from committing ourselves to the French, we agreed, and now we have given you your wish. The prisoners have been released and we are not bound in word to the French. Yet, the Iroquois Council sends word to you through me that unless you can bring about a real improvement of the Indian policy of the English, we will no longer support you."

William nodded. Back on familiar ground now and with a clearer picture of what was happening, he relaxed some. He had no doubt whatever that Tiyanoga did not believe the story of a French-English conspiracy against the Iroquois. But it was equally obvious that Nichus most certainly believed it and it was up to William to dispel such feelings in the chief.

"Brother Aroghyidecker," he said, addressing Nichus by his more formal family name, "the French governor has pulled a heavy blanket over your eyes and plugged your ears so that you have not been able to see or hear the truth. I strip away that blanket and unplug your ears and now speak the truth: the war belts were sent out by me, it is true, but not to the governor of France. They were sent to the great leaders of the Six Nations and to the chiefs of all their villages to warn them of a French army which was moving through their western lands and of great threat to them. This you need not believe on my word alone."

He turned and motioned Sacanghtradeya to him and when the Cayuga joined them and had gravely shaken the hands of all three chiefs, William explained what had taken place.

"Warraghiyagey has spoken the truth," Sacanghtradeya said, nodding. "I myself was one of those who received such

152

a belt from him and a warning to keep my warriors at home lest the French army surprise us. Nor was this just the word of a false bird. One of my warriors became a member of the French party and watched as they moved downriver on the arm of that river which becomes half of the *Spay-lay-wi-theepi* and he watched as the leader of that party attached pieces of metal to trees and buried beneath them plates such as this."

He ripped off the buckskin covering from the lead plate and held it up for them to see.

"This plate my warrior took from them without they knew of it and he came with it to me. But we could not understand the meaning of these lines and so I brought it to Warraghiyagey and was with him when one who knows this language read it to us. And it is a matter of grave importance to all Iroquois and other Indian nations, saying as it does that the French governor, acting for the French King, claims all the land on both sides of the *Spay-lay-wi-theepi* as his own."

William Johnson now turned to Nichus with an edge of anger in his own voice. "Here you can see and hear the truth of this matter. I do not know how the French governor came in possession of one of the belts I sent out, which went only to Iroquois chiefs—a matter which the council should see into—but such a belt was not sent to him by me or by Governor Clinton. Through some trick, or the help of some chief among our League, he acquired it and he used it to blind your eyes and fill your ears with false tales. My heart is sad that you should have believed the words of a man who so loves Indians that he has kept you and your two brothers chained away from the sun and the moon for so long a time."

Nichus nodded and now stepped forward to hold out his hand to William, his manner now completely changed to one of contriteness.

"I am sorry that I spoke so quickly without first hearing your words, Warraghiyagey. I have been wrong. I see it. I have heard false words. I should not have listened to them. You are my brother; my heart and blood are with you again and will become separated no more."

Johnson shook hands with him and then with Wascaugh and Tiyanoga. The latter's old face cracked into a wide smile and he hugged William to him, delighted as always with the way this incredible white man could manage to extricate

153

himself from bad situations. And as the Irish band abruptly broke into a discordant musical piece, the rum kegs were opened and the celebration begun, William excused himself momentarily to return to his house.

He had a letter to write to Clinton ... and a lead plate to send him.

### [ November 20, 1749—Monday ]

The journey up the Great Miami River had been a strenuous one for the expedition under Captain Pierre Joseph de Céloron de Bienville. Time after time the river shallowed to such extent that it ran only an inch or two deep over rocks and gravel and the canoes had to be laboriously dragged across such riffles. They sprang leaks, becoming constantly wet and decidedly unsafe. And the riffles became even more numerous after they passed a place where within one mile two major rivers and a smaller creek joined the Great Miami.[21] Without the water those three streams had provided, passage became even harder.

It took thirteen days for them to reach Chief Unemakemi's principally Miami village of Pickawillany, near the mouth of that muddy little creek which joined the Great Miami. The morning of September 12 was bright and warm as they finally hove into sight of the village. Though they had heard that it was a large town, they were not at all prepared for one of this size. Only a year ago there had been but four hundred Indian homes here, surrounding the sturdy English trading post, and perhaps a population of two thousand, of which the majority were Miamis.

That had changed significantly. Now the trading station had itself become almost a fort in appearance, and rare were the times when fewer than a dozen English traders were not on hand. Moving by boat along the route followed by Céloron or overland in packhorse trains with bounteous supplies along winding, narrow trails, traders arrived and left in almost continuous procession. And the goods they brought so attracted the Indians that the fame of Pickawillany spread far and the village grew even more, dwarfing even Detroit with its numerous Indian villages scattered around it.

There were at least a thousand abodes here now and certainly no less than four thousand Indians, including women and children. Miami Indians were here in their largest concentration, but there were also strong representations of

154

Delawares under Chiefs Pipe and Pimoacan, Hurons under Chief Orontony, and Shawnees under Chief Moluntha. There were even some Kickapoos, Sac and Fox, Mascoutens, Kaskaskias, Peorias, Muncies, and a few smaller groups of Sioux, Cahokias, Osages, and Winnebagoes. But since it had begun as a Miami village established by Unemakemi and the largest single tribal representation was still Miami, Unemakemi remained as its principal chief.

Since they were of mixed tribes, however, they could not call Pickawillany truly a Miami village or a Shawnee or Delaware village or any other specific tribe. Therefore, so that they could be known as Indians from this melting-pot village of tribes, they adopted the name for themselves from the cry of the cranes which often screeched from the nearby river shallows. They called themselves Twigtwees.

Although some of the tribes who were congregated here were enemies, or at least not on friendly terms, Pickawillany was considered a neutral ground where all observed peace and could come and go for trade purposes without fear of attack. And right at this moment there were at least fifteen English traders at the post when word came of the approach of Céloron's little army. Not knowing quite what to expect, the traders left at once, leaving two volunteers to stay behind to guard their interests and protect their property when assured by Unemakemi that he would allow no harm to come to them.

While no hostility was shown to Céloron and his party as they beached their canoes before the village, neither was the welcome by Unemakemi, Orontony, and Moluntha—chief of the Shawnees' Maykujay sept—an especially cordial one. Céloron wasted no time getting down to business. He asked that a council of the various tribal chiefs be called for him to address and, when this was done, told them what he had told all the others except for the Shawnees at Sinioto: that these English traders were encroaching on lands claimed by France and would soon become a threat to the Indians and steal their country from them; that already land speculators were following the traders and that settlers were following the speculators; that soon the land would be gobbled up and unless the assembled chiefs acted now to drive the English back—with the help of the French King, of course—they would lose all they had and themselves be driven away.

Céloron presented the assembled chiefs with many gifts, but it was to Unemakemi that he most pointedly directed his remarks, doing everything in his power to convince the great chief of this Miami confederacy that the Twigtwees should be disbanded, Pickawillany abandoned, the English trading post destroyed and that the various tribes should return to their own areas.

"The governor has instructed me to tell you," he said, "that it would be to your own benefit and the safety of your people to remove at once from this place and return to French influence from whichever French fort is nearest your lands."

Unemakemi heard him out, thanked him politely for the gifts and for the warning of the danger the Twigtwees were in. "I am sure, Brother," he said, "that it is good advice you are giving me. Be assured that I will follow it ... but at a more convenient time than now. In the meanwhile, because there might be danger to you and your followers in this place, it is *my* advice to you that you see to your *own* safety and leave here at once. And that, too, is good advice."

There could be no mistaking the veiled threat in the words. Céloron knew Unemakemi had no intention of doing the things he suggested, but there was nothing he could do about it. To press the matter further would be placing himself and his men in distinct jeopardy. The fact was not lost on him that even the customary courtesy of being invited to stay and eat and rest here had been denied them.

He ordered his party to push on at once.

Still following the rough map provided for him by the governor, they left the larger river and now paddled up the muddy creek until they could go no farther. Here they unloaded the canoes a final time, stacked them all in a great pile and burned them.[22] The remaining supplies were divided among them into shoulder packs and they set off afoot along the portage trail which led to the headwaters of the St. Mary's River. When they came to that stream they followed the Indian path which paralleled it and moved downstream until they came to where this stream met the St. Joseph River to form the Maumee River or, as the Indians called it, the *Omee*.

Located here was Fort Miamis, which was presently under the command of Lieutenant de Raimond, but the welcome Céloron and his men had anticipated did not quite materialize. The entire garrison of twenty-two soldiers was under a severe influenza epidemic and rather than expose his own

156

force to it, Céloron ordered his men to pitch camp outside the fort.

Raimond, miserable in his own illness, could not generate much enthusiasm for Céloron's visit and showed even less interest in the details of the long expedition. He did, however, have a large collection of bark and wooden dug-out type canoes to which Céloron and his party were welcome. He had no supplies to give them, being on short rations himself and could only wish them good fortune on their return to Montreal, wistfully saying he wished he were going along and could be relieved of such a godforsaken command as this.

Another contingent of Miami Indians, these under Chief Cold Foot, were still inhabiting their little village not far from the fort, but Chabert Joncaire learned that their intention now was to stay there only a short while longer before moving on to join the majority of their tribe at Pickawillany under Unemakemi.

Céloron, with several of his officers, paid the chief a visit and once again went through the same harangue from the French governor, ending with the advice that Cold Foot and his people remain here or, better still, take up residence near Detroit, rather than leave the French influence to join Unemakemi. Cold Foot was noncommittal and in the morning Céloron bade farewell to Lieutenant Raimond, thanked him for the boats and started his party on the float down the Maumee River to Lake Erie.

On October 2 they had reached the mouth of the Maumee.[23] Feeling that they had served Céloron well enough and long enough, the Indians who had remained part of the expedition now helped themselves to what remained of the store of rum and in a short time had become gloriously drunk.

With the boats needing considerable refurbishing before they would be ready for travel on the lake, Céloron decided to camp here until every craft had been put into good shape.

By the fourth day the men were just finishing the work on the boats. The soldiers and Canadians seemed to be working with a renewed eagerness, now that their destination was Montreal and home. It had been a long and grueling trip which was drawing to a close and they were anticipating its end.

Only two places remained yet to be visited for any particular purpose—Fort Frontenac and La Présentation. The first of these they reached on November 3 and, for the first time since leaving this very fort on June 29, slept with a roof over their heads. The next day they embarked down the St. Lawrence River to La Présentation. Céloron, as eager as the rest to get home, would have preferred not stopping, but the Marquis de la Galissonière's orders were for him to see and report what progress Abbé François Piquet had made in his absence.

The indomitable Sulpician priest welcomed them heartily and they were surprised to see not the bulky mission they had helped him to finish, but a new and even bigger and more fortlike structure some distance from where the charred remains of the first still scarred the ground. Abbé Piquet told them of how it had been destroyed soon after their departure and how he had begun at once to build another. And, surprisingly, he had already collected a score or more of Indians—mainly Onondagas and Cayugas—who were well on the road to conversion and whose allegiance was now firmly with the French. Even the priest, in his expectation at the strife he planned to unleash against Fort Oswego, several times referred to his own mission here as *Fort* Présentation.

They left him the next morning and on November 10, after an absence of one hundred forty-eight days, set foot again in Montreal. Several of the young Canadians were so overwhelmed that they fell to their knees and kissed the ground.

Céloron found that Galissoniére had gone back to France and that the Marquis de la Jonquière was the new governor and it was to him that he made his report. And here, too, Céloron found waiting for him from France, a commission to become the new commanding officer of Detroit.

The Marquis de la Jonquière read Céloron's final report carefully. He had thought the expedition a wasted effort and expressed himself in this respect to Galissonière when he took over this office, but now he began looking at it in a new light. It had done no harm, perhaps, to have had Céloron plant the lead plates, warn the English traders away and try, if unsuccessfully, to turn the Indians back to the French, but to him the most revealing portion of the captain's report came at the very end where he wrote:

*. . . Father Bonnecamp, who is a Jesuit and a great mathematician, reckons that we have traveled twelve hundred leagues; I and my officers think we have traveled more.*[24] *All I can*

*say is, that the nations of these countries are very ill-disposed*
*towards the French, and devoted entirely to the English.*

It was this last line which so caught Jonquière's attention. If Céloron's expedition had done no more, it had at last, clearly and indisputably, revealed the deplorable condition of the French interests in the West and the grave need to redouble all efforts to win the Indians to French allegiance and, equally important, to build new and better forts to strengthen and increase the French toehold in this western wilderness.

And in this respect he went out again to the Indian encampment just outside the city to meet one of the most powerful of all the Iroquois leaders, the chief of the Onondagas—Red Head.

### [ February 1, 1750—Thursday ]

The governing committee of the Ohio Company was acting at last on its need to know more about the western lands and what particular lands they wished to select for the grant of five hundred thousand acres given to them by King George. They hired a particularly able Maryland frontiersman—Christopher Gist—for the job.

Gist, a tall, lanky individual had been in and out of the Indian territories for years, trading, exploring and sometimes fighting against—or with—Indians. He was a loner for the most part; now and then joining in for a specific objective with one or another of a small number of particularly able men he knew and trusted—men such as John Fraser and John Finley and even young David Duncan—but more often than not going his way alone. He was affable and essentially a gentle-natured person, but a fierce fighter who commanded respect from even the most uncouth and loutish of the largely criminal-type border men who lived a precarious existence on the fringe of colonial civilization. He had little sympathy for any brutish frontier bully who would, as for example Jacob Greathouse did, kill any Indian simply for the perverse enjoyment of doing it.

Himself never having knowingly or willfully cheated an Indian in all his years of trading with them, Christopher Gist was well liked by most of the natives and rarely had any difficulty with them. He could speak half-a-dozen Indian dialects with fluency and knew enough of Indian customs not to offend, either consciously or unconsciously, those he dealt with. He was an ideal choice for the job the Ohio Company wanted done and they laid out his instructions in a letter which said, in part:

*We must rely on your knowledge of the lands west of the mountains and, particularly, down the Ohio River Valley, to know where best to go to select the land most ideally suited to our needs, with which you are familiar. Such selected lands should be well described so that there will be no doubt now or later as to their exact locations. Bear in mind, sir, that this must be good, level land; we had rather go quite down to the Mississippi than take mean, broken land ...*

Not the slightest mention was made that this land in question was more than likely to be inhabited by Indians who loved it and had no doubt that it was theirs and who might not take lightly to the knowledge that at the gesture of some man across the sea who had never even seen it, it had suddenly become the property of an English colonial land company.

Even while Gist was being given his instructions, the company selected another Maryland frontiersman for a related but different job. He was to lay out the best possible trail from Philadelphia to the western lands—or at least from Philadelphia to the Ohio River or the Monongahela just above the Ohio, from which point settlers would be able to penetrate the wilderness by boat or raft.

The individual selected for this latter job was a bantam-sized Indian fighter named Thomas Cresap, who had so much courage that it seemed to seep out of his very pores. To help him in the job, Cresap took along a minor Delaware chief who was familiar with every stream, pass, valley and mountain between the Susquehanna and Monongahela. He was a long-faced Indian by the name of Nemacolin, who presented a generally sour disposition to the world but who, to his friends, was the pinnacle of warmth and good nature. Cresap had become friends with him years before and could not have selected a better man to help him. And Nemacolin made only one demand of Cresap: that when the trail was all laid out and improved, it should be known by his name.

Cresap was quick to agree.

The threats made by Céloron to the English traders had had absolutely no effect on them. They continued to come and go throughout the western lands, providing goods for whatever Indians would trade with them and, wherever possible, instigating the Indians to lift French scalps. It was time, the Marquis de la Jonquière decided, to take some more drastic steps than mere warnings.

The first such step materialized in respect to a party of five English traders led by John Patton, who was agent of one of the most prominent traders of the area, George Croghan. Two of the traders were agents of Croghan's friendly—and sometimes not so friendly—competitor, Hugh Lowry, who was not along this time.

The trading party was en route to Pickawillany with eight packhorse loads of goods, mainly tomahawks, knives, lead, gunpowder, vermilion and blankets. With shocking suddenness they found themselves surrounded by several dozen Ottawa Indians accompanied by two French officers and eight of their soldiers. Resistance was impossible in the face of such odds and the traders disgustedly surrendered their weapons and goods.

Pontiac was strongly in favor of butchering all five men on the spot. He was dissuaded by the French officer in charge only because that captain agreed that Pontiac and his warriors could have all the goods that had been confiscated. The threat still hung in the air over the captives, however, as camp was made for the night and the prisoners bound individually to trees.

During the night one of the Englishmen—Edgar Bangen—worked his way loose and escaped. The French captain, discovering this in the dawn's light, suggested that Pontiac send some of his men to track Bangen down and bring him back. Pontiac shook his head.

"Last night when we would have opened their bellies and strung out their bowels on the branches, you would not hear of it. Instead, you begged us to take these goods, and so we agreed. Now they are your prisoners and what you do with them—or what they do—is your concern. My warriors and I leave now to return to our village."

Without another word the Indians left, leading their plunder-laden horses. And within another half hour, the Frenchmen were leading the captives toward Niagara, from whence they would depart by boat for Montreal.

Christopher Gist's exploratory tour for the Ohio Company had thus far gone very well. Much of the land he traveled through he was already familiar with, but there was much yet that he planned to see, of which he had only heard about from the Indians.

When he reached Logstown—Céloron's Chininqué—not far down the Ohio from the junction of the Allegheny and Monongahela, he found the disreputable trading post currently inhabited by a handful of reprobate Indian traders. There were eight of them here—filthy, dangerous, evil-tempered men, every one of them wanted by the authorities for crimes committed against the Crown.

All eight looked on Gist's arrival with suspicion. They knew him by reputation and they didn't want him here. All they needed was some fool like this to come in and give the Indians what he considered as being fair prices for their furs and it would upset their whole system. Why give an Injin a pound's worth of good merchandise for a certain amount of furs when you could give him a pound's worth of inferior goods, which cost only a fraction as much, for ten times as many pelts? Hell, that was only good business. Besides, Gist was out of his territory here. He was a Marylander and these were Pennsylvanians, chiefly Irish and Scot, who considered Logstown their own private domain. There was enough competition among themselves without him coming in.

Only one of the men, a weasel-faced individual whom everyone called Doggie, knew Gist personally and had, in fact, accompanied him once on a trading expedition to the Cherokees with John Finley. He liked him well enough, but didn't want him here any more than did the others.

"Git yerself gone, Gist," he muttered, after they had moved aside from the rest of the group a little. "I ain't one to see you git hurt none, but you ain't apt to git home safe atall iffen you stay roun' here very long."

Gist shook his head and turned back to the whole group.

"I'm not here to trade," he said. "I'm on the King's business and merely passing through. But," he added, his voice now taking on a steely hardness, "if I *was* planning

162

to trade here, I'd do it . . . and I'd cut the throat of any man who tried to interfere."

He remained at Logstown only overnight, but did little sleeping. Even as the first gray light of dawn began silhouetting the trees, he was on his way westward. Not until he was a half a day beyond Logstown, however, did he consider himself safe from the traders who, in his estimation, constituted a greater threat to his life than did the Indians.

His reception at the Wyandot village of Muskingum, deep in the Ohio country, was somewhat better. At the tiny trading post here he met George Croghan and Andrew Montour, Croghan's assistant. Both agreed to go with him on his explorations, during which Croghan could continue the mission of friendship making he had been sent on by Governor James Hamilton.

Gist was disturbed but not especially surprised to hear of the capture by the French by the five traders to the northwest of here. He shook his head and commented glumly, "They keep pickin' at us and we keep pickin' at them and each time it gets a little worse. One of these days it'll bust out into war, you watch."

Croghan nodded. "Just why Hamilton sent me out. Word is that the French're gettin' more'n more Indians on their side. Bangen tol' me when he come in that it was Pontiac hisself leadin' that bunch what took 'em. An' I hear tell a right smart number of Iroquois ben switchin' sides to 'em. Mostly Cayugas an' Senecas an' a few Onondagas, I hear. Hamilton, he wants ever' Indian possible with us. An' don't you think we ain't a-gonna need 'em if war does bust out!"

From Muskingum, Croghan, Gist and Montour went to the village on White Woman's Creek and visited for a day with Mary Harris. She was a woman nearing fifty years of age, but who looked closer to seventy. Her hair was ivory-colored and her skin wrinkled. Her permanently bent back and pendulous breasts attested to a long hard life of drudgery and childbearing. Yet, she seemed content enough. She had been captured by the Indians in New England as a small child forty years ago and had lived with them ever since, twice being sold to different tribes. Now she was far more Indian than white, though she was still able to speak English to some degree.

"You look as to be good men," she told them, "but not most. Most is wicket. I 'member where at I was borned they was very religious. Now I wonder how white men kin be so wicket as they what I has saw in these woods. Awful wicket men."

Her voice trailed off into an unintelligible mumble of combined Indian and English words and Gist felt genuinely sorry for her. As the three men headed southwestward toward Shawneetown—the same village at the mouth of the Scioto that Céloron had called St. Yotoc—Croghan commiserated about her.

"She's got a good heart, that Mary Harris. Her ol' brain's kinda addlepated now, but she looks forward to me stoppin' by whenever I can an' I always try to bring her somethin' that might help her out. She's been taught, and still believes, no matter how hard I try to tell her different, that Christ was a Frenchman crucified by the English. Course, Andrew here," he dipped his head at Montour, "I think he believes it, too!"

They all laughed at this. Montour was an intelligent, if uneducated, man and always wore a queer admixture of white and Indian dress. His features were more European than Indian, but he had long ago formed the habit of almost daily drawing completely around his face a ring of bright red, made by mixing vermilion powder with bear grease. He wore a coat the color of bright rust, a ruffled shirt which was never tucked into his trousers, and a black cravat decorated with silver spangles. His hat was broad-brimmed and his ankle-high moccasins were worn over knee-length white stockings. In his ears were ornaments which looked like basket handles. He claimed to be the grandson of a French governor and an Indian squaw. His half-breed mother, Catherine Montour, was a native of Canada but was carried off by the Senecas in her youth and adopted by them, and it was with them that Andrew had spent his childhood.

At Shawneetown—Sinioto—the three men received a welcome far different than Céloron had gotten. A feast was prepared for them and Chief Hokolesqua seemed genuinely pleased to have them there, in spite of the fact that many of the Shawnee chiefs were at odds among themselves about the encroachment of the whites—English as well as French.

"The English," Hokolesqua told the three, "have treated us well; better than the French who come here trying to claim our lands."

Gist was relieved that Hokolesqua considered him only a trader and did not know that his mission was to claim land for the Ohio Company. They stayed the night in Shawneetown, presented Hokolesqua with a number of gifts and departed first thing in the morning to the northwestward along a trail which led to Pickawillany.

The farther they traveled, the more delighted Gist became with the land. Not long after leaving Shawneetown the men left the tree-cloaked hills and poor, rocky earth behind them, passing instead through great prairies and fertile lands ideal for farming. Shortly before reaching the sprawling village, Gist took advantage of a rest stop to write briefly to his employers:

*. . . This is good country, ideal for settlement. It is fine, rich, level land, well timbered with large walnut, ash, sugar maple trees and cherry trees; well watered with a great number of little streams and rivulets; full of beautiful natural meadows, with wild rye, blue-grass, and clover, and abounding with turkeys, elks, deer, and most sorts of game, particularly buffaloes, thirty or forty of which are frequently seen in one meadow . . .*

They approached Pickawillany on the opposite side of the river and swam their horses over. A large crowd of Indians greeted them and escorted them over. Chief Unemakemi was greatly pleased to see them and invited them into his house to eat and talk of small matters, with a formal council to be held the next morning in the *Msi-kah-mi-qui*—or council house.

With seven or eight hundred Indians in attendance, the council was opened shortly after sunrise and began with Croghan giving the Indians presents from the governor of Pennsylvania. Then he and Gist both made speeches professing strong friendship and thanking their host and all the Indians assembled here for remaining faithful to the English while so many of their neighbors were being swayed to French alliance.

"Know this, Brothers," said Unemakemi when they had finished, "that the French have come here and exerted themselves in various ways to make us leave here and come live again beneath their flag, but this is not our wish. We have no agreement with them, but with the English we have our treaty of peace and now, with your coming, that friendship is even more strengthened. We will not desert you if you need our help, and we know you will not desert us in such conditions."

165

At this moment there was something of a disturbance from outside. Dogs barked and voices were raised in excitement. As the eyes of all within the council house turned to the doorway, four Ottawa braves entered. They carried a French flag, two kegs of brandy and a large pouch filled with tobacco, all of which they placed at Unemakemi's feet.

"We bring greetings to Chief Unemakemi and his Twigtwees," said their spokesman, "from Captain Céloron at Detroit, who expresses his continued friendship with these gifts and reminds Unemakemi of his visit here last year and of the chief's promise to soon break up this village, send the Twigtwees back to live with their own tribes and himself and his Miamis to come again to live under the protection of the King of France. Our own chief, Pontiac, has told us further to say that this would be a wise thing to do, for it would be a bad thing to have Indians be forced to spill the blood of other Indians, which is what may happen in the spring if your dealing with the English is not then ended."

No one could miss the threat and a deep scowl grooved Unemakemi's face. From an assistant seated on the ground behind him, to whom he muttered a few words, he took four small strands of wampum the man removed from his pouch. Then he turned and addressed the Ottawas in a tone so harsh it rang of hostility.

"Brothers the Ottawas, we let you know by these four strings of wampum"—he handed these strings to the spokesman—"that we will not hear anything the French say, nor do anything they bid us do. They are not our friends as are the English here in attendance, who have come invited and not thrust themselves upon us as have you!"

He turned slightly to face northward toward Detroit and spoke again, this time as if actually addressing the Frenchmen:

"Fathers, we have made a road to the sunrising, and have been taken by the hand by our brothers, the English, the Six Nations, the Delawares, the Shawnees and the Hurons called Wyandots. We assure you, in that road we will go; and as you threaten us with war in the spring, we tell you that we are ready to receive you."

The stillness which followed his words was almost tangible and he let it settle over the crowd for fully a minute before turning back to the four Ottawas and continuing his address to them:

"Brothers the Ottawas, you hear what I say. Tell that to

your fathers, the French, for we speak it from our hearts!" He picked up the French flag draped over the brandy kegs and handed it to the spokesman. "Take this back to where it belongs, along with your gifts. It has no place here and we do not want your gifts. Go from here now, but do not return again, lest your bones remain here to whiten unburied on the ground."

After the party had departed grimly with the brandy, tobacco and flag, the council continued as if it had not been interrupted. No further mention was made by Unemakemi or the white men that now Pickawillany was committed beyond recall to the English. A lavish feast was held in the evening and the next morning Gist, Croghan and Montour were entertained with what Gist recorded in his journal as it progressed as a feather dance:

> ... It was performed by three dancing-masters, who were painted all over of various colors, with long sticks in their hands, upon the ends of which were fastened long feathers of swans and other birds, neatly woven in the shape of a fowl's wing; in this disguise they performed many antic tricks, waving their sticks and feathers about with great skill, to imitate the flying and fluttering of birds, keeping exact time with their music, which issued from rattles and strings and an Indian drum. From time to time a warrior would leap up, and the drum and the dancers would cease as he struck a post with his tomahawk, and in a loud voice recounted his exploits. Then the music and dance began anew, till another warrior caught the martial fire, and bounded into the circle to brandish his tomahawk and vaunt his prowess ...

The feather dance was actually a war dance which put the exclamation point to the declaration of Chief Unemakemi. Those Indians living in this village were now fully committed to the chief's declaration, as were any who might yet come to take up residence here. It would be good news for Croghan to take back to Governor James Hamilton and for Gist to relay to the Ohio Company members.

And once again Gist was relieved that the Indians had no inkling of the true reason for his being among them.

[ *May 10, 1750—Thursday* ]

William Johnson was furious, as well as a bit worried. Bad

167

enough that George Croghan's traders allowed themselves to be captured by the French and taken to Montreal, but for one of them—John Patton—to give in under questioning by Jonquière, regardless of how ungentle such questioning might have been, and admit that Croghan and Lowry had been instigating the Indians to kill Frenchmen, was unthinkable.

The fact that they had was common knowledge all over the frontier now and, with it, the fact that Jonquière had immediately authorized the commanding officers of all his frontier posts to offer the Indians a substantial reward for the heads of George Croghan and Hugh Lowry. The reward was impressive enough that even the friendly Indians might pause to seriously consider taking the risks involved to win it.

Now Johnson fired off a heated letter to Governor Clinton, damning the scheming French and demanding that Clinton take some sort of action to put an end to this reward business. He wrote:

*If the French go on so, there is no man can be safe in his own house; for I can at any time get an Indian to kill any man for a small matter. Their going on in that manner is worse than open war!*

And he was far from wrong.

### [ *June 18, 1750—Monday* ]

The Marquis de la Jonquière was tired and not well. He had lost considerable weight lately and had trouble dragging himself out of bed in the mornings. He frequently felt dizzy, and was becoming so irascible to those about him that he was forced to make a constant conscious effort to meet them civilly.

Problems seemed to come at him from all directions, unceasingly, and he was tired, very tired of it all. Today was no exception. The only enjoyable job he had been able to perform was the writing of an order which would send a company of soldiers to the Sault Sainte Marie and change the mission and trading station there, fifty miles north of Fort Michilimackinac, into something of a military outpost. But it was only a crumb to a man who needed a meal.

For an hour now he had been sitting behind his desk reading reports and letters and at last he took up pen to begin the job of writing to the French colonial minister in Versailles. Occasionally he paused to rub his aching temples as he reported that the step to garrison the Sault Sainte Marie had been taken. In past correspondence he had strongly urged that the post should not only be turned into one of war as well as one for the fur trade, but that the colonial minister should authorize him funds to establish several new forts along the shores of Lake Erie. The advice had at first been ignored and, when he would not let the matter die, he had been answered with a blunt refusal which came in today's dispatch. In part, the colonial minister had said:

*... Niagara and Detroit will secure forever our communications with Louisiana, so there is no necessity for additional forts expensive to build and maintain. M. de la Jonquière, we here are not pleased. His Majesty thought that expenses would diminish after the peace, but, on the contrary, they have increased. There must be great abuses. You and the Intendant must look to it. I have strong evidence of certain malpractices arising in Montreal and that of the money sent to Canada for the service of the King, the larger part is finding its way into the pockets of certain peculators and individuals in responsible positions ...*

For his own part, the governor of New France was sure that what misuses or abuses of governmental funds there might be could well be laid at the feet of the intendant, Francois Bigot, who was living in palatial luxury in Quebec. That Bigot was hopelessly corrupt, Jonquière had no doubt, but sensing it and proving it were two entirely different matters. Now it seemed to him that there was implication which included himself in this dispatch from the colonial minister. It hurt him deeply and his brow was furrowed as he strove to find the right words for his answer. At last, with painful slowness, his quill again began to write:

*Excellency, I have reached the age of sixty-six years and there is not a drop of blood in my veins that does not thrill for the service of my King. I will not conceal from you that the slightest suspicion on your part against me would cut the thread of my days ...*

After another half hour he finished his writing, wiped clean the tip of his quill and lay it aside to pick up another letter and, for the third time today, read it through. It was from George Clinton, the English governor of New York Colony, and it was not at all friendly:

*I write you, sir, to express in the strongest possible terms the concern and complaint of His Majesty, King George, for the illegal and reprehensible acts being committed at your instigation and with your approval. Foremost among these is your establishment of a new post—allegedly a fur-trading post but, in fact, a military establishment—on the portage leading around the Niagara cataract. Also, I must protest in terms equally strong, the arrest and imprisonment of four English traders in the country of the Miamis while in the pursuit of their business. Further, it has been reported to me by unimpeachable sources that you personally have caused to be placed a price upon the heads of two of our leading traders, George Croghan and Hugh Lowry and that this reward offer has been broadcast to the Indians. I cannot conceive of a man in your position as having proceeded with such a rash and foolhardy act, knowing full well that it places the entire frontier in jeopardy to any white man, French as well as English.*

*All of this, sir, forces His Majesty to assume that the French embassies of Louis XV have signed fraudulently not only the recent Treaty of Aix-la-Chapelle, but even that of Utrecht. As you must know, the erection of the post at the Niagara portage is an invasion of English territory. Just as is Oswego, Niagara and the Miami country where our traders were taken, is country of the Six Nations. The Treaty of Utrecht, signed by French plenipotentiaries and binding upon France as well as ourselves, places these locations in areas which are subject to the Dominion of Great Britain, as they are, indeed, within the country of the Six Nations.*

*Further, your excellency must be aware that the said treaty also provides that the subjects of both the French and English Crowns shall enjoy full liberty of coming and going on account of trade.*

*In the name of His Majesty, King George, I therefore demand that the post at the Niagara portage be abandoned at once and that the liberty of the four traders in question, and the goods confiscated from them, be restored at once; further, that you disavow the arrest of the four traders and punish its authors ...*

Jonquière shook his head. What kind of fool did Clinton take him for? What a pompous ass the man must be. English territory indeed! Free trade! Could he really, by the grandest stretch of the imagination, believe the French would withdraw from Niagara now that they were established there, or that the traders would be released and their goods given back to them?

A sardonic smile turned up the corners of his mouth. The screws had hardly begun to tighten and already the English were squealing like pigs. Well, they had not yet even *begun* to feel the sting of French irritation over British encroachment. But they would, oh yes.

And if the peace was ruptured, then so be it!

### [ *December 31, 1750—Monday* ]

The year spiraled to its close on a sour note for just about everybody.

Thomas Cresap worked long and hard to lay out the best possible trail between Philadelphia and the Monongahela River on the frontier, more than ever thankful for the help of the Delaware chief, Nemacolin. Without that Indian's aid, the job would have taken a great deal longer and the ultimate trail would probably have been nowhere near as direct or as good. But when this Nemacolin Trail was completed, Cresap was roundly criticized by practically everyone for naming it after a savage. After all, weren't there many brilliant colonial statesmen after whom it could have better been named?

Christopher Gist, preparing to leave Pickawillany to continue his explorations for the Ohio Company, announced that he was going to explore some land he had heard of but never seen to the south of the Falls of the Ohio.[25] Chief Unemakemi, however, came to him with a warning shortly before he left.

"I am told," the Miami chief said, "that in the area you plan to visit there is now camped a party of western Iroquois under French influence, who would gladly kill a lone Englishman. If you must go to see the *Can-tuc-kee* lands, then enter them across from the mouth of this Great Miami River and go toward the rising sun from there."

Thankful for the warning, Gist did as suggested and roamed curiously through a strange territory, bringing home even stranger stories of having found a place where the great bones of gigantic animals jutted from the earth in some sort of peculiar animal graveyard.[26] From this point, still following Chief Unemakemi's advice, he had turned eastward and made his way overland to the upper reaches of the Kanawha River and thence to his frontier home on the Yadkin River. After a brief rest here he traveled the remainder of the way to Roanoke with the report of his discoveries for the Ohio Company. And after all that effort of seven months, the Ohio Company did exactly nothing and virtually discarded Gist's report.

In a way, even though George Croghan's trip was more successful, its end result was an even greater disappointment. In accordance with James Hamilton's wishes, he had returned, after parting with Gist at Pickawillany, to Logstown. Here, under Chief Monakaduto, he had found an Indian council in progress. And here he publicly requested permission for the English to build a fortified trading post at the junction of the Monongahela and Allegheny rivers. Fully expecting the request to be denied, he was stunned and delighted when Monakaduto made his reply.

"The French want to cheat us of our country," the chief said, "but we still stop them and, Brothers the English, you must help us. We expect that you will build a very strong house on the *Spay-lay-wi-theepi,* which you call Ohio River, that in case of war we may have a place to secure our wives and children, likewise our brothers who come to trade with us."

But when Croghan returned to Governor Hamilton with this exciting news and his entire report was placed before the Pennsylvania Assembly, he was condemned for bringing expenses upon the government and the Indians were thereupon blandly neglected. The Assembly viewed with distaste the personal and formal request of Monakaduto, brought to them by Croghan, that the "strong house" be built at the confluence of the Monongahela and Allegheny. With scarcely any debate, the Assembly rejected the request and then further condemned Croghan for bringing it.

Disgusted and tired, George Croghan looked forward now to nothing more strenuous than a nice long rest at home, but even this was denied him. Hamilton ordered him back immediately to the Delawares to spend the winter with them and do all in his power to cement English relations with them.

That a strong post at the forks of the Ohio was vital to the English interests was clearly evident. Even the Penn family, proprietaries of Pennsylvania and always tightfisted with money, saw the value of an English post at this highly strategic site and offered four hundred pounds per year toward the cost of maintaining one, but still the Assembly would not even listen.

In Montreal, Jonquière was also well aware of the strategic value of that same triangular spit of land, having studied Céloron's report in depth. To Monakaduto he sent emissaries with lavish presents and the request to build a French fort at that spot; but the request was denied, the gifts not accepted and the embassy threatened with death if they did not remove from the area at once. Monakaduto was decidedly pro-English and, in fact, thoroughly convinced—unlike many others of the Seneca chiefs—that an English post here would greatly add to his people's safety and comfort. When Croghan showed up to report to him of the Pennsylvania Assembly's rejection of the plan, the chief immediately sent the proposal to Virginia.

It was just as poorly received there.

This was an incredible situation. Literally for years the English had been doing everything possible to gain a toehold in the frontier country in order to balk French claims and permit greater inroads of settlement from the colonies. And now that just such a possibility was offered, it was rejected out of hand. The shortsightedness of these two provincial assemblies was based solely on economics: both Pennsylvania and Virginia claimed the forks of the Ohio as being within their own territory, yet each felt that the other's claim might be the stronger. Neither wanted to sink money into improvements which might subsequently benefit or profit the other, so it was the entire British colonial cause which suffered.

The disputed boundaries caused other troubles which showed promise of being even worse in the future. Governor Robert Dinwiddie of Virginia complained:

"Till the line is run between the two provinces, I cannot appoint magistrates to keep the traders in good order."

The unscrupulous traders were well aware of just that fact and, relatively safe from any form of prosecution, treated the Indians abominably. When the Indians complained to Pennsylvania, they were told to see Virginia for redress, and vice versa.

Governor George Clinton of New York was one of the few who saw the growing danger and he was made aware of it through the reports made to him by William Johnson. He appealed to the New York Assembly for means to assist Pennsylvania in securing the much needed fidelity of the Indians on the Ohio, but the Assembly, always eager to balk Clinton personally in any way possible, promptly refused in an indignant reply to the effect that: "We will take care of our Indians, and they may take care of theirs."

Dismayed but not discouraged, Clinton wrote to all the other provinces and invited them to send commissioners to meet the tribes at Albany. He said in his letters to them, "In this way we may defeat the designs and intrigues of the French."

But of all the provinces, only Massachusetts, Connecticut and South Carolina sent commissioners. Even these came without the important presents upon which the Indians always set such store at councils with the white men and which were considered by them as required. In a letter to a friend of his, Clinton bewailed the incredibly lackadaisical attitude of the other colonial assemblies in general and the New York Assembly in particular:

*The Assembly of this Province had not given one farthing for Indian Affairs, nor for a year past have they provided for the subsistence of the garrison at Oswego, which is the key for the commerce between the colonies and the inland nations of Indians ...*

The same sour note of the year took in, above all, William Johnson. More and more frequently he was receiving reports from his Indians of individuals, groups, sometimes whole villages of Iroquois being won over to French allegiance. Abbé Francois Piquet in his so-called Fort Présentation at Oswegatchie had accumulated so many Iroquois that a substantial village had been formed around his mission post. That Sulpician priest was now boasting loudly of his successes and was particularly delighted with the fact that over a hundred warriors from Onondaga alone, the very capital of the Iroquois nation, had been converted to Christ, Catholicism and Canada—and to defend any of these three they were quite willing to kill. That the information taught them by Piquet was warped, to stay the least, was obvious. The warriors not only were being fed by Father Piquet the old sacrilegious political gambit that Christ was a Frenchman crucified by the English, but that the King of France was the eldest son of the wife of Jesus Christ!

174

It was an appalling situation threatening to undermine everything that William Johnson had worked toward. Nor had the brothers Joncaire—Daniel and Chabert—been idle. For weeks and months they had been moving about the Iroquois nations, doing all in their power to convince the Iroquois to reopen with vigor their long-dormant ancestral war with the Catawba tribe of South Carolina. When William heard of this, he nearly had apoplexy. If that war was renewed, as the Joncaires well knew, the entire English frontier would be kept in turmoil, with war parties of Iroquois going back and forth between New York and South Carolina. Unfortunate incidents with whites en route were bound to occur and the situation could swiftly degenerate into an English-Iroquois war. With frantic haste, William had interceded and managed to arrange a temporary truce until a Catawba delegation could come north to formally request from the Iroquois a peace treaty.

Through these past months William had become ever more angry and frustrated at the lack of support he received. At times he felt that of all the Englishmen, only Clinton really had faith in him and the governor, without the Assembly to back him up, was himself hamstrung. And no sooner had the Catawba-Iroquois threat been delayed than a new and dreadful one arose to take its place.

Chief Tiyanoga came in excitement to Mount Johnson with the news that so successful had Abbé Piquet been in his work that Chief Red Head of the Onondagas, titular chief of the entire Iroquois League, was showing ever-increasing French sympathies.

"It is a bad time, Warraghiyagey," Tiyanoga told William. "I have learned that Red Head has been arranging in secret to sell land very close to Onondaga itself to the French for a trading house. You know, as I do, that such a house will soon become a fort and if that happens the Onondagas will be tied to the French by their very nearness, even as we Mohawks are tied by our nearness to the English. How then, if such takes place, Warraghiyagey, can the Iroquois League keep from being broken apart if, as it seems must one day happen, the French and English raise the war hatchet against one another again?"

The situation was critical in the extreme and at once both William and Tiyanoga had summoned as many chiefs as possible to Mount Johnson, where both expounded at great length on the danger—not the danger to the French or

175

English cause, but to the fundamental unity of the Six Nations. The chiefs in attendance were also deeply alarmed and hastily approved the germ of a plan which William proposed. The whole body of chiefs then left at once for Onondaga.

The upshot of the matter was that another crisis was passed and Johnson was put into such a position of potential power and wealth that, had he been dishonest, it could have resulted in trouble beyond imagining. In an astounding move, the Iroquois League, in order to balk Red Head, had given to William a deed in his own name to the entire area around Lake Onondaga, extending outwards in all directions from the lake and conveniently taking in the area the French had wanted for their trading post. For this deed William paid them three hundred and fifty pounds. It was signed by all the chiefs, including even Red Head, who had not dared to dissent lest his secret dealings with the French come to public light. With its fresh water, fertile soil and salt springs, the land was enormously valuable.[27] William Johnson could have made much of it, but he had bought it with his word given as Warraghiyagey, the Mohawk, that he would keep it unimproved or else offer it to the English Crown with the same stipulation. He did the latter, adding his request that he be reimbursed by the Crown what the land cost him, at no profit to himself. The Crown refused.

The year was now rapidly drawing to a close and William Johnson's disillusionment grew. Only two weeks ago it had become too much for him to bear any longer—this business of exerting himself to great effort and expense on behalf of the King and the Colony without any form of reimbursement from either. Therefore, with his characteristic directness, he had written a letter to George Clinton:

*This is perhaps the last piece of Indian news I shall ever have occasion to trouble your Excellency with; the French are planning to build trading houses, which will actually be garrisoned forts, at all passes between Oswego and the Ohio. With this news, I hereby resign my duties in Indian Affairs and no longer represent the Colony of New York to the Indians, nor the Indians to the Colony of New York.*

If this unexpected resignation struck Clinton like a thunderbolt, it hit the Indians even harder. From village to village, council fire to council fire, the word passed. Warraghiyagey has put out his council fire forever! And not an Indian could help but realize that this was the incredible white Mohawk's way of protesting his own white people's refusal to keep and promote their trust with the Iroquois nations and other tribes.

That the white men were deceitful and rarely, if ever, kept their trust was nothing new to the Indians; but that there was a white man now who felt so strongly the injustice of it that he would discard his own influential position in protest was unique. If any of them had harbored doubts before about Warraghiyagey, such doubts were now wiped away. In Warraghiyagey they had had a white man they could trust above all others, a true and honest champion to themselves and their cause.

And now they had lost him.

This final night of the year was bitterly cold and a biting wind howled about the longhouse at Canajoharie. All during the day the chiefs of the Six Nations had come, blanket-wrapped and with feet incased in triple moccasins which left behind great bearlike tracks on the new snow covering the frozen face of the Mohawk River. And the tracks had all led to the main council chambers of this Upper Mohawk Castle. Even the fires lighted at intervals about the long interior of the room failed to dispel the chill which seemed to envelop each man of them, emanating as much from within as from without.

It was Tiyanoga who stood before them now and addressed them, his old voice still strong, but deeply sad:

"My Brothers, our hearts within us ache at the loss of our friend and brother Warraghiyagey to us. Even those among you who have scorned him in the past, now know of your foolishness in believing ill of him and are now, as are the rest of us, struck with the arrow of grief.

"Brothers, what are we to do now? Where are we to turn? Warraghiyagey has large ears and hears a great deal. He has been the ears of the Six Nations and what he has heard he has told us. How now shall we hear, when our ears have been cut away?

"Brothers, Warraghiyagey also has large eyes and he sees a great deal, not only of men's actions, both Indians and white, but of their meanings and what this may bring for the future. He has been the eyes of the Six Nations and what he has seen he has passed on to us. How now shall we see, when our eyes have been blinded?

"Brothers, hear me: Warraghiyagey was our tongue and

177

his mouth spoke our words and our thoughts where we ourselves could not speak them, and his words were wise and strong for us. How now shall we speak when our tongue has been severed?

"Warraghiyagey was our ears and our eyes and our tongue. He was our thoughts and our hopes. He was our strength and our wisdom and he concealed nothing from us. We had him in wartime, when he was like a tree that grew for our use. Now this tree seems to be falling down, though it had many roots, and should it fall we are ruined. His knowledge of us and our affairs made us think of him as one of us, and now he is no longer theirs or ours, and, Brothers, we are greatly afraid."

Even for the Indians, the year was ending on a sour note.

# CHAPTER IV

[ *June 28, 1751—Friday* ]

A HUGE blond man with pale blue eyes and the assured stride of a man who is confident in his own abilities, John Fraser stopped near the confluence of the two streams and inspected the Seneca village of Venango from cover.

It was not a large village; no more than a dozen or so lodges and a single longhouse for council meetings. It had been erected here by the village chief named Fron-goth less than a year ago. Here, in a sort of natural pass, it was importantly located for Fraser's purposes and it was here that he stood a good ᵇance of creating a small fur-trading empire of his own.

The streams were French Creek, entering from the northwest, and the Allegheny River, coming from the northeast.[1] From this ideal situation he could trade with the western Iroquois tribes—the Senecas and Cayugas especially—who could come downstream to a post located here far more conveniently than it was for them to reach Oswego or Mount Johnson. And from the northwest, the west and the southwest, he could draw the Delawares and Wyandots, the Shawnees and the Miamis and possibly even take some of the Huron and Ottawa trade from the French.

Again, as he had done before, Fraser blessed the lucky day that had seen him encounter Chief Fron-goth, who had just suffered a broken arm in a fall. With care and skill he had set and splinted the chief's arm and helped him back to his village. And, in gratitude, Fron-goth had invited him to set up his own personal trading post here in Venango.

Fraser knew vaguely that the French captain, Céloron de Bienville, had passed through here with his army a couple of years ago, but it concerned him not at all. There had been no

Frenchmen here since and with Fron-goth strongly supporting him, he would be in little real danger if any did come.

The nearest English trading post to him would be Logstown and that was over a hundred miles downstream. The traders there were too lazy and valued their own skins too much to come this far into the disputed territory very often. With luck, he would also be able to channel to his own use many of the furs that would have gone to Logstown.

It was an excellent opportunity on the whole, the trader John Fraser was not a man who let opportunity pass him by.

### [ *July 21, 1751—Sunday* ]

The journey just completed by Abbé François Piquet— who of late was coming to be called the Apostle to the Iroquois—had taken him over a month and he was distinctly pleased to be back again with his ever-growing flock of converts at La Présentation. And it was fitting and proper, to his way of thinking, that he should have returned here on the Sabbath in time to hold a sort of primitive Mass for the hundreds of Indians gathered.

La Présentation had changed considerably since the second mission had risen from the ashes of the first. Céloron's men had jokingly dubbed it Fort Présentation, but now it really did have far more the appearance of a fort than of a house of God. Palisaded and flanked by blockhouses, it loomed as an impregnable giant amidst the three villages of Iroquois that had sprung up in its shadow. Within the heavy palisades were, in addition to the chapel from which it all began, a storehouse, a barn, stables, a bakehouse and a sawmill. On the parapets now were five small cannon sent by Governor Jonquière and a permanent, if small, garrison of soldiers. That the place could easily withstand a concerted attack was obvious.

Piquet himself was a strange little man who burned with the fires of fanaticism in his efforts to convert the savages to the precepts of Catholicism, yet at the same time almost wholly disregarding the most basic commandments of Christianity and teaching the concepts of the religion in a manner that could only be termed as being warped.

To himself he justified his distortions on the grounds that they were much easier for the savage mind to grasp. At the same time, however, he thought it no sin to do all in his power to make the Indians rise in wholly unexpected fashion and butcher the English settlers and traders wherever they found them.

An extremely egotistical man, Father Piquet considered his own efforts at combatting the English menace as far surpassing those of the French government, either politically or militarily, and did not hesitate to say so in his letters. Keenly proud of his accomplishments here, Piquet retired to his own quarters after saying the Sunday Mass. He was very tired from his trip, but there were things to do before he rested. First he must write to both the governor and intendant of the great plan he had conceived and then make his regular entry in the voluminous journal which he kept of his own activities and impressions. He sat at a rude little desk in his own room. Though midday, it was dim in here and he lighted three candles. Then he wrote first to Governor Jonquière:

*Excellency—*

*It is a miracle that, in spite of envy, contradiction, and opposition from nearly all the Indian villages, I have formed in less than three years one of the most flourishing missions in Canada. I find myself in a position to extend the empire of my good masters, Jesus Christ and the King, even to the extremities of this new world; and, with some little help from you, to do more than France and England have been able to do with millions of money and all their troops.*

*I have now only just returned, with many new converts, to La Présentation, and hasten to report to you the points of my journey just completed which will be of especial interest to you. With six Canadians to paddle me and five of my most trusted Iroquois converts following in the canoe behind, we left La Présentation on June 15. We traveled up the St. Lawrence River for a stop at Fort Frontenac and were met by M. de Verchères and, later, by M. de Valtry and M. Belêtre. Conditions here are much worse than I remembered them. Though this place was once the resort of a great many Indians, whom I had hoped to convert and draw to La Présentation, now none were here, they having abandoned this place in favor of the English post of Oswego on the other side of the lake, which has greater attractions for them. We found the pork and bacon at Fort Frontenac very bad, and there was not brandy enough in the fort to wash a wound.*

*We crossed to the neighboring island² and there we were soon visited by the chaplain of the fort, the storekeeper, his wife, and three young ladies, all glad of an excursion to relieve the monotony of the garrison. My hunters had supplied me with means of giving them a pretty good entertainment. We drank, with all our hearts, the health of the authorities, temporal and ecclesiastical, to the sound of musketry, which was very well fired, and delighted the islanders. I also provided a feast for this band of Indians living here and discoursed of religion to them and, by the grace of God, persuaded them to move on the next day to La Présentation. I found them here when I returned today.*

*For eight days thereafter we continued westward along the north shore of Lake Ontario, encountering a multitude of incidents such as the fight between my dog, Cerberus, and a wolf, to the disadvantage of the latter, and the meeting with a very fine Negro of twenty-two years, a fugitive from Virginia. There were other incidents of this genre.*

*On June 26 we reached the new fort of Toronto, which presented a striking contrast to Fort Frontenac. The wine here is of the best; there is nothing wanting in this fort; everything is abundant, fine and good. Captain Portneuf is doing a good job in intercepting fur-laden Indians of the Northern tribes en route to Oswego to trade, providing them with sufficient quantities of goods and brandy to dispell these notions of theirs so disadvantageous to the French cause. Here, for example, while we visited, came a body of Mississagas[3] who would otherwise, no doubt, have carried their furs to the English. I was strongly impelled to persuade them to migrate to La Présentation, but remembering your admonition that I confine my efforts to other tribes, and lest the ardor of my zeal betray me to disobedience, I reembarked, and encamped six leagues from temptation.*

*On June 27 we arrived at your new fort at Niagara, our party now being followed by a large group of converts. We were warmly welcomed here by your commandant at this post, M. de Becancour, and by his chaplain and the storekeeper. Here I said my first Mass since leaving La Présentation and, after resting a day, set out for the trading house at the portage of the cataract. At this place I found M. Chabert Joncaire in the company of a large band of Senecas, though being all drunk—men, women and children—they were in no condition to receive the Faith, or appreciate the temporal advantages that attended it. On the next morning, however, I found them partially sober and invited them to remove to La*

Présentation; but as they still had something left in their bottles, I could get no answer till the following day.

I pass in silence an infinity of talks on this occasion. Monsieur de Joncaire forgot nothing that could help me, and behaved like a great servant of God and the King. My recruits increased every moment. I went to say my breviary while my Indians and Senecas, without loss of time, assembled to hold a council with Monsieur de Joncaire. The result of this was an entreaty directed to me that I promise not to stop at Oswego on the return, lest evil should befall me at the hands of the English. I promised to do as they wished, and presently set out on my return to Fort Niagara, accompanied by Monsieur de Joncaire and a satisfactorily large new group of followers. Our journey was a triumphal one, for whenever we passed a camp or wigwam, the Indians saluted me by firing their guns, which happened so often that I thought all the trees along the way were charged with gunpowder; and when we reached the fort, Monsieur de Becancour received us with great ceremony and the firing of a cannon, by which my savages were infinitely flattered. I gathered the new converts into the chapel for the first time in their lives, and there rewarded them with a few presents.

Having left La Présentation without a shepherd, I now deemed it time to return there and on July 6 embarked, followed by a great swarm of canoes. On the twelfth we stopped at the Genesee and went to visit the falls.[4] On the way there my Indians found a populous resort of rattlesnakes, and attacked these gregarious reptiles with great animation, but to my own great consternation, for all of them to a man were bare-legged and I feared for their safety. But already God was with them and forty-two dead snakes requited their efforts with not one of the sportsmen bitten.

When, in the afternoon, we returned to our camp on the lake shore, we found there a canoe loaded with kegs of brandy. The English had sent it to meet us, well knowing that this was the best way to cause disorder among my new recruits and make them desert me. The Indian in charge of the canoe, who had the look of a great rascal, offered some to me first, and then to my Canadians and Indians. I gave out that it was very probably poisoned, and immediately embarked again; to my joy, followed by all but a small handful who were willing to chance the danger for the opportunity to warm their insides.

183

On July 14 we encamped at Sodus Bay[5] and it is at this strategic point that I recommend strongly the building of a new fort. There can be no doubt that to do so would greatly strengthen the French cause on the south shore of Lake Ontario. Nevertheless, it would still be better to destroy Oswego, and on no account let the English build it again.

On the sixteenth we came in sight of this dreaded post. Several times in the days preceding we had met fleets of canoes going hither or thither, in spite of the rival attractions at Niagara and Toronto. Believe me, Excellency, no English establishment on the continent is of such ill omen to the French. It not only robs us of our fur trade, by which our people live, but threatens us with military and political, no less commercial, ruin. We must be in constant dread, as well, lest ships of war should be built here, strong enough to command Lake Ontario, thus separating Canada from Louisiana, and cutting New France asunder.

I kept my promise of some days hence that I would not land at the English post; but this did not keep me from approaching closely and observing it from my canoe. The shores are a desolation of bare hills and fields, with only a multitude of stumps of felled trees projecting above the ground. The fort is hedged around by a border of dense forest. Near the strand, by the mouth of the Onondaga, are the houses of some traders; and on the higher ground behind them stands a huge blockhouse with a projecting upper story. This building is surrounded by a rough wall of stone, with flankers at the angles, forming what is called the fort. It is commanded on almost every side; two batteries of three twelve-pounders each, would be more than enough to reduce it to ashes. Excellency, the post is a great and evil menace to us. It not only spoils our trade, but puts the English into communication with a vast number of our Indians, far and near. It is true that they like our brandy better than English rum; but they prefer English goods to ours, and can buy for two beaver-skins at Oswego a better silver bracelet than we sell at Niagara for ten.

Having left Oswego behind us, we subsequently came again to Fort Frontenac. Never was reception more solemn. The Nipissings and Algonkins, who were going on a war party with Monsieur Belêtre, formed a line of their own accord, and saluted us with musketry and cries of joy without end. All our little bark vessels replied in the same way. Monsieur de Verchères and Monsieur de Valtry ordered the cannon *of the fort to be fired; and my Indians, transported with joy at the honor done them, shot off their guns incessantly, with cries and acclamations that delighted everybody.*

*At this place now a goodly band of recruits joined us and I pursued my voyage to La Présentation with the canoes of my proselytes following in a swarm behind to their new home; that establishment which I began over two years ago, in the midst of opposition; that establishment which may be regarded as a key of the colony; that establishment which officers and interpreters and traders thought a chimaera— that establishment, I say, forms already a mission of Iroquois savages whom I assembled at first to the number of six, increased last year to eighty-seven, and this year to three hundred and ninety-six without counting more than a hundred and fifty whom Monsieur Chabert de Joncaire is to bring me this autumn. And I certify that thus far I have received from His Majesty—for all favor, grace and assistance—no more than a half a pound of bacon and two pounds of bread for daily rations; and that he has not yet given a pin to the chapel, which I have maintained out of my own pocket, for the greater glory of my masters, God and the King.*

*In closing, Excellency, I present a plan which I feel, if carried out, will be only to the greater glory of France on this continent. I propose to raise a war-party of thirty-eight hundred Indians, eighteen hundred of whom are to be drawn from the Canadian missions, the Six Nations, and the tribes of the Ohio, while the remaining two thousand are to be furnished by the Flatheads,[6] who are at the same time to be furnished with missionaries. This united force can first, in the guise of friendship and trade, penetrate the bastions of Oswego and, at a given signal, fall upon the English therein and destroy them one and all. Then the fort may be taken over by us and improved, or put to utter ruin. After this the Indian force can drive all the English, both traders and settlers, out of the area between Oswego and the Ohio and down the length of the Beautiful River. Finally, they may next attack the Dog Tribe,[7] who live near the borders of Virginia, with the people of which they are on friendly terms. If the English of Virginia give any help to this last-named tribe—which will not fail to happen—they (the war-party) will do their utmost against them, through a grudge they bear by reason of some old quarrels. Since they are masters at butchery, these savages can be convinced by me to do this and will assay it with eagerness, I assure you. And we need not concern ourselves with the recognizance that France at this time is at an alleged state of peace with the English. It will be the Indians who will be attacking them, not the French, and we can be held blameless.*

*With sincere prayers to your health, Excellency.*

*Abbé François Piquet*

### [ July 31, 1751—Wednesday ]

There were many, both Indian and white, who had thought at first that William Johnson's resignation was merely a gambit brought on by pique and that he would soon tuck his tail between his legs and resume his former duties. It didn't happen that way. Though he was bombarded with pleas and inducements on all sides, he refused to have anything more to do with an Indian post that was controlled by the New York Assembly.

Never before had the Indians been so devoted to him, so willing to uphold him in every respect, so proud of him. His influence among them, which before had been stronger than any other white man's, now increased a hundredfold. The entire Indian-English relationship had become snagged and no one had any idea what to do.

At first, in an attempt to mollify William, Governor Clinton had personally urged him to reconsider and, as an added inducement, sent him a monkey and a parrot as pets and pulled such strings in London as to result in having him appointed to the Provincial Council, the upper house of the New York legislature, which was a lifetime post greatly coveted by politicians. William Johnson was not especially impressed. Not only would he not resume his Indian Affairs duties, he even refused to leave Mount Johnson to take the oath of office required of his new appointment.

Nor would he attend the grand council now being held at Albany between the delegates of the Six Nations, led by Tiyanoga, and the English representatives from New York, Massachusetts, Connecticut, Pennsylvania and South Carolina. It was Tiyanoga who led off the talks and it didn't take any warming up for him to come to the point. He directed his remarks to Clinton himself:

"We desire his Excellency will be pleased to reinstate Colonel Johnson, or else we expect to be ruined. And our being ruined cannot help but badly affect the English and benefit the French."

Clinton flushed, cleared his throat and replied uneasily.

"Colonel Johnson absolutely refuses to continue in the management of your affairs, or ours. As you can see, though he has been invited to this congress, he has not presented himself."

Tiyanoga brushed the remark aside with a wave of his hand. "If Colonel Johnson will not come here at your request, perhaps Warraghiyagey will come here at the request of the Iroquois."

Clinton's features took on a scowl. "It is not necessary and can only occasion great delays," he complained. "This congress can proceed without him."

Tiyanoga shook his head. "His Excellency is wrong in all ways. It is necessary and the congress cannot well proceed without him here, for he is our ears and our eyes and our tongue. Nor will there be great delay, for any messenger will reach him sooner than a horse."

He turned to one of his young men and issued a rapid-fire string of commands in the Mohawk tongue. The youth nodded and instantly raced away and Clinton slapped his hands to his sides in exasperation, knowing the congress could not continue now until Johnson showed up. For the first time he was becoming greatly agitated at the man who had so long been in charge of Indian Affairs. How did he dare to treat the governor and the colony in such an offhand manner? His anger grew, supported by his aide, Cadwallader Colden, who had no great love for William Johnson. And by the time William arrived, dressed in the regalia of the Mohawk Warraghiyagey rather than in white apparel, both Clinton and Colden were muttering imprecations against him and thoroughly convincing themselves that he was nothing but a damned profiteer who was more interested in making a fortune through his fur trade than in establishing an intelligent Indian policy; overlooking the fact that William had long advocated one.

Now, even though William Johnson had arrived as Warraghiyagey and took his place with the Mohawks, pausing only momentarily to take his oath from Governor Clinton as a Provincial Council member, he said nothing else and the congress continued to limp along, accomplishing little. In fact, the only matter of real action that occurred was when a Catawba tribe peace embassy was nervously introduced by

187

first two singers, carrying banners of feathers and shaking pebble-filled gourds. Their voices rose eerily in the quiet.

In a short time they were followed by the main Catawba delegate—a thin, bespangled Indian with his hair unbraided and falling to the center of his back. His close-set dark eyes were bright with something akin to fear. Behind him in single file came four minor chiefs. His name was Chief Chik-o-gee.

The enmity of the Iroquois for him and his men was like a tangible thing in the air between them. William Johnson watched, feigning disinterest but actually very concerned. Now, at long last, he would see whose will would prevail in the matter—his own or that of Chalbert Joncaire.

When, on their final notes, the advance Catawba singers halted and pointed to Chik-o-gee with their feathered staffs, the chief in turn halted and lighted the calumet he had been carrying in his hand, along with a piece of smoldering punk. He smoked for a minute or more while the assemblage watched him in silence. Then he handed the pipe to one of his subchiefs who did the same and passed it on. When it returned to the chief he took several puffs more, blowing the smoke deliberately toward the Iroquois chiefs as a sign of peace, and then handed the pipe to one of his men to hold while he spoke.

"The Catawba," Chik-o-gee began, "have never wished a war with the Iroquois League, for this is like a sparrow wishing to do battle with an eagle. But the war was brought upon us by our fathers and yours, and it has been our heritage to continue it. And even though of late we have not actively battled one another, yet the war feeling remains between us and it is not a good thing. We wish to see it ended, that we may go our way in peace and that our families will need no longer feel fear when they roam the forest and field, lest a warrior throng of the Iroquois rise from behind bushes and grasses to strike them down.

"We are here," he continued, removing a tomahawk from his belt and holding it high, "to end for all time the war between us, and we do so for our parts with this act." He threw the weapon to the ground with such force that nearly the entire head of it was buried when it struck. "Now it is done. We ask the Iroquois to do the same and that for all time to come these weapons will remain buried and there will be peace between our people."

When he stopped there was a murmuring among the Iroquois until at length Canassatego of the Onondagas got to his

188

feet and took the place vacated by the Catawba chief. His eyes were locked on the Catawba delegation and there was no friendliness in his gaze. There was, instead, a deep contempt which was reflected in his first words.

"Men of the Catawba, it is an easy thing for you to ask peace when you have no horns left with which to fight. The Iroquois cut the horns from the heads of all your warriors until now they are timid, like the deer who in spring has shed his horns and flees at the slightest sound since he has no way to defend himself. Yet, it is not our wish to continue a war with those who come in honor to ask for peace.

"But have the men of the Catawba come in honor? In part they have, but in part they have not. We do not doubt that you wish peace, but if you so much desire it, why then are there still in your villages no fewer than three Iroquois prisoners—warriors taken by you five years ago and held ever since? Were you completely honorable in your wish for peace, you would have brought them back to their homes and returned them to unite with us. Perhaps you believed that in holding them you would be protected from our wrath, but better should you have shown your good faith by returning them with you."

Canassatego now took an unusually small string of wampum—no longer than eight or ten inches and only an inch wide—and handed it to Chik-o-gee. The very size of it was a terrible insult and the entire Catawba delegation blanched at the sight of it.

"This belt," Canassatego said, "serves to show that we have accepted your words for now and believe you acted in error more than in an attempt at trickery. This will be a belt to make you more powerful and give you small horns. If, four seasons from now, at this time of the next summer, you will return here with the prisoners, the peace will be completed and your horns lengthened. But do not make the mistake of thinking your small horns restored this day give you enough strength to defy us or that this belt signifies that we are at peace. There can be no peace between us until our warriors are returned. Until then, there can only be a truce— but if you then return again without them, or fail to return at all, the war will continue and the Catawbas will soon cease to be. Go now, for we wish to speak to the English."

When Chief Chik-o-gee and the rest of the Catawba delegation had silently gone away, Canassatego stepped aside in favor of the Mohawk chief, Tiyanoga, who now directed his own remarks to the Englishmen in attendance.

"Brothers, you have urged us constantly to protect and throw back French penetration of the western lands and the valley of the *Spay-lay-wi-theepi*. It may be that we will do this thing you desire, but it may be that we will not. Our brothers to the north, who live more closely to them, feel that the Frenchmen are not as you have told us they are.

"Do not think we cannot see with our own eyes and hear with our own ears. Your stories against them are not always true, while what they have said has more often come to pass. You tell us that the French mean to take over our lands and they tell us that you mean to do the same. But it is only the English, not the French, who are building log homes in the deep woods that have never before heard the cry of a tree bitten by an axe. If, as you say, your motives are just and honest, why then should this be so? Those French who have come, stay only for a little while. They build stores at which we can trade, but then they leave, or else only a few stay. But the English build homes and stick blades into the ground and expose the heart of the mother who is the earth, and you do not leave even then.

"Our ears and eyes are Iroquois ears and eyes and often they do not understand what they see and what they hear of what white men are doing and saying. Not so long ago we had good eyes and good ears when we had Warraghiyagey, but now we have him not and in the ways of the white man we are suffered to be blind and unable to hear. And we are afraid because we are not able anymore to understand what is happening around us. We are afraid that what you are saying and doing will ruin us.

"You ask us, Brothers the English, to have faith in you. You ask us to trust you and believe your words that you speak to us at such meetings as this. But how can we have faith in you and believe you when by the very actions you have taken you have plugged up our ears and thrown sand in our eyes and sewn our lips together?

"When Warraghiyagey is again our ears and eyes and tongue among the English, then will we believe what you have to say for us, for only then will we be able to understand your meaning. But not until then. Until that time, we will have to go to the French and talk with them to hear what they have to say to us and to see if their words and actions are any clearer to us than are yours."

It was on that note that the Albany Congress broke up, leaving behind for all concerned only an aura of the darkest foreboding. For the first time the English governors and commissioners felt that they were actually beginning to lose the Iroquois to the French.

And they, too, were afraid.

[ *November 4, 1751—Monday* ]

Pierre Joseph de Céloron de Bienville, commandant of Detroit, listened to the words of Chief Pontiac without pleasure. Since becoming commander of this fort he had acquired a good working relationship with most of the Indians who lived near it or came to it for trading purposes. The Hurons and Chippewas, the Potawatomies, even the Ottawas who lived under Chief Mackinac at L'Arbre Croche, all were basically easy to deal with—not especially demanding and fundamentally friendly to the French. But the Ottawas around the Detroit area under Pontiac, the largest single group of Indians in the vicinity, were haughty to the extreme and a constant aggravation to him.

This of itself would have been bearable, but Céloron was not entirely sure in his own mind that they were guiltless where French deaths were concerned. True, there hadn't been many such deaths—not more than a dozen since Céloron had taken this post, but the very fact that *any* had occurred was decidedly alarming. As long as it was possible for a Frenchman to be ambushed, killed and scalped only a short distance from his home and fort, then the situation must be considered critical.

On the occasions when he had spoken with Pontiac before, Céloron had found the chief a rather dynamic personality with original ideas and the evident courage of his convictions. The commander himself had never really had evidence enough to place the French deaths at Pontiac's feet, but he was certain that the Ottawa knew much more about them than he admitted to. In fact, it was altogether possible that he was responsible for them. It was no secret that he held no abiding love for the French. Various sources had reported to Céloron that Pontiac not infrequently voiced the desire to have the day come again when there would be no white men at all, English *or* French, in this country. But that alone was not grounds enough to accuse him of the murders.

The captain was not at all happy when orders dated

191

October 1 had come from the Marquis de la Jonquière directing him to attack the Twigtwees at Pickawillany. His own force here at Detroit was far too small to do so by itself. Any attempt to do it alone was suicidal. That it was desirable to have Pickawillany destroyed he had no doubt. More than once he had sent small French parties there to reiterate the demand that the village be broken up and the pro-English Indians under Chief Unemakemi go back to their home areas or else move back to the Detroit area and reassert French allegiance. And more than once they had failed to return at all.

But for his small force at Detroit—even with the help of a few from the garrison at Fort Miamis—to attempt to attack so large an assemblage of Indians without some sort of substantial outside help was simply ridiculous. Which, in essence, was why he had summoned Pontiac. If the Ottawa war chief could be won over to the belief that this had to be done and would join him with a supporting force, he might be able to do it.

As best he could, Céloron explained to Pontiac what a detrimental thing it was to have the pro-English village so close to them; that while the English goods were more abundant and of better quality and better priced than the French could presently provide for the Indians, this was a calculated move by the English to win the Indians to their side so that with their help the French could be run out of the country.

"You complain that our prices are poor as compared to theirs," Céloron said, "and I am forced to agree. But it is only because we are here that this is so. If we left here and there was no one for the English to bid against, you would receive for your furs much less from them than you now receive from us. It is their strategy only to gain a toehold here, to gradually make themselves ever stronger here until suddenly they have the power to hold the upper hand. Then it will be too late for the Indians to do anything about it. You are as aware as am I, Pontiac, that not many months ago Unemakemi permitted the English traders to strengthen their trading house at Pickawillany to such extent that it is now no longer a station of goods, but rather a fort. This is why I ask you now, before they become too strong there, to gather your warriors to join my men and march against them and destroy them. Will you do this?"

For a long time Pontiac stood silently and then he shook his head.

"It is not good, what you ask," he said. "It may not be good that the English are there and that many Indians, even part of our Hurons under Chief Orontony, remain there to be influenced by them. But what you ask is wrong, too. You ask for brother to go against brother, father against son. This is even worse."

It was not a good beginning, but Céloron had not expected immediate acceptance by Pontiac. He did, however, expect to be able to win him over gradually with promises of gifts and plunder and a chance to go into battle. But the more he tried to talk the Ottawa war chief into leading his Indians in the venture, the more Pontiac balked. Soon it become obvious that there was no use to go on.

In bad humor, Céloron broke off the interview and, after Pontiac had stalked away, wrote a brief message to Jonquière which in no way expressed the difficulty he was faced with here, but only reported that he was unable to follow the governor's orders.

It might have been to his advantage to be a bit more circumspect.

[ *November 8, 1751—Friday* ]

The Canadian-Ottawa half-breed, Charles Michel de Langlade, was a dark, aquiline young man of twenty-two, quite intelligent and well respected by both races. His brilliant white teeth glittered with startling brightness against his dark complexion when he laughed, which was often. He was the type of man who made strong friends almost instantly and never gave them cause to regret the friendship.

Within his effervescent personality he combined all the best characteristics of both sides of his parentage; a smooth, easygoing manner and inherent astuteness in trading matters from his father, along with a deep Ottawa pride and determination and courage from his mother. He entered into all things with flair and passion, loving and hating with every fiber of his being. He was an incredibly good friend to those who accepted his friendship, and an implacable foe to those whom he mistrusted or who mistreated him.

For his age, he had an enormous influence with all the tribes of the upper Great Lakes region.

Although most of his years had been spent in the Michilimackinac area where he was born, he had lived for a short while in Pontiac's village near Detroit and for an even longer time with Chief Mackinac's people at L'Arbre Croche. He rarely met any Indian who did not know him well and respect him. In his travels for the purpose of trading, he had met and married an Ottawa maiden named Oolatha. For the past two years they had lived at Green Bay west of Lake Michigan, but at the moment he was in Pickawillany and things were not going too well for him.

While he slept in the lodge of a friend, preparatory to trading the next day, the majority of his goods were stolen. Such a theft from him by the Indians here was unthinkable, so he promptly blamed the English traders. Though guilty, they denied any knowledge of it and then poured salt in the wounds by jeering at him to the effect that even if they did take the goods, what did a stripling half-breed like himself think he could do about it?

Furious, Langlade went to see Chief Unemakemi, who listened to him halfheartedly and then brushed away his complaints with a deprecating gesture.

"If you are not able to take care of your own goods," he told Langlade, "then you are not much of a man. You have come here uninvited, knowing that we wish nothing to do with those who are French or who have French interests. The Frenchmen not long ago ejected the English from the trading post on Sandusky Bay, thinking that then we would have to come to them, but we will not.

"We allow Frenchmen to come here if they wish to, but only if they understand that if they interfere with us, as some have done, we will kill them. The French lie to us, but the English do as they say they will do."

Chief Unemakemi had now worked himself into a temper and he continued heatedly, "I do not have your things; they are nothing to me. The trader Croghan, who just left here, brought us many gifts given in good heart. He and the other English traders have been good to us and supply our needs, which is more than the French have ever done. Cry to them and see how much comfort you receive. You are free to leave here now, but you are not welcome to return. Consider yourself fortunate that it is only your goods which have been lost."

That Unemakemi would speak to him in such an insulting way was incredible and young Langlade's face tightened.

"You will then," he said softly, "do nothing to help me recover my goods from the Englishmen?"

Unemakemi himself scowled. "Are your ears plugged with mud? I have said. I will not say again. You speak to Chief Unemakemi, not to a sparrow-hearted Frenchman. Leave here now, lest I pluck the heart from your breast and feed it to my dogs."

Without another word, Charles Michel de Langlade spun about and left the chief's quarters. He mounted his horse and rode out of the village of Pickawillany with never a turn of his head, the fury within him so blinding that he was miles away before he even realized it.

The theft had been bad enough of itself, but the humiliation suffered from Unemakemi was unforgivable. It was an offense which he would never forgive, never forget. When he met Unemakemi again—and he promised himself that he would, very soon—only one of them would live to see the next day's sun.

There was no other way.

[ *November 21, 1751—Thursday* ]

It was through the perpetual Clinton-Delancey feud that William Johnson decided he might help the Indian cause and overcame his distaste for white politics enough to take his seat in the Provincial Council at New York City. Rough and crude, no matter how dandied in the refinements of dress, he became immediately the object of smirks and snide remarks. This didn't bother him, for what people thought of him personally had never meant a great deal.

He had hoped to promote a sharp conflict within the Delancey-controlled Assembly, since there were a few members—a very few—in it who supported his own beliefs. The wedge he hoped to drive was a small one, but it could set a strong precedent. He strove to get five hundred pounds appropriated for Indian presents and much-needed repairs to Fort Oswego. But now he was in his opponents' arena and as ineffective there as they would have been before a Mohawk council fire.

He failed miserably and the reassurance he received from Tiyanoga on his arrival home that the Iroquois chiefs would continue to support him with all their heart was little consolation.

The Marquis de la Jonquière looked terrible. That his health was most seriously failing him now was a fact which he could no longer hide. Most of the time he remained in bed, listless, unable to get up the drive to move about any more than necessary to take care of vital physical functions.

To his chambers his secretaries brought a continuing stream of reports and letters and communications of other sorts—from France, from Louisiana, from Fort de Chartres on the Mississippi, from Detroit, and from the scattered French posts in the Great Lakes area. Little of the news was cheering, most of it downright bad.

While in the Western New York area the French interests were making surprising headway, largely through the efforts of Abbé Francois Piquet and Chabert Joncaire, in the far west they were degenerating. A case in point was the letter from Captain de Raimond at Fort Miamis:

*My people are leaving me for Detroit. Nobody wants to stay here and have his throat cut. All the tribes who go to the English at Pickawillany come back loaded with gifts. I am too weak to meet the danger. Instead of twenty men, I need five hundred. We have made peace with the English, yet they try continually to make war on us by means of the Indians; they intend to be masters of all this upper country. The tribes here are leaguing together to kill all the French, that they may have nobody on their lands but their English brothers. This I am told by Coldfoot, a great Miami chief, who I think is an honest man, if there is such a thing among Indians. If the English stay in this country we are lost. We must attack, and drive them out. War belts are being sent from tribe to tribe, and I hear rumors of plots and conspiracies from far and near.*

Chabert Joncaire, just returned from a trip into the Ohio country with his brother, Daniel, sent in a report to Jonquière which was equally disturbing:

*Though we seem to be holding our own, or even gaining, in the immediate Iroquois country, such is not the case on the Ohio. Because of pressure we have brought to bear, the Delawares have now moved away from our immediate reach and deep into the Ohio country, close to their brother tribes, the Shawnees and Miamis. Almost all of the Ohio Indians are* showing strong affection for the English who sell them goods at low rates, make ample gifts and give them gunpowder for just the asking.

Captain St. Ange, commanding at Vincennes on the Wabash, was dispirited in his report:

*Would that I could send you good news, Excellency, but I cannot. The country is in a turmoil and antagonism in the Indians against us appears to grow daily. Our guard posts have been doubled and the same situation is said to prevail at Forts Miamis, Ouiatenon and even de Chartres. It seems that a storm must soon burst on our heads.*

The communiqué from the Baron de Longueuil was perhaps the most depressing of them all. He had been sent by Governor Jonquière some months ago to tour all of the western country, from fort to fort, village to village, to assess the situation on a broad scale. And now his report confirmed the worst fears of the ailing governor:

*Your Excellency,*
*Little I have to report will bring you cheer. The Miamis have scalped two soldiers and the Piankeshaws have killed seven French settlers. Even more distressing is evidence received that I wish to disbelieve, but I am afraid is true; that ten French traders and two of their servants have been killed and then their bodies roasted over an open fire and devoured. A squaw I talked with, who had lived with one of the murdered settlers, declared to me that the tribes of the Wabash and Illinois Rivers—the Miamis, Piankeshaws, Kaskaskias, Cahokias, Peorias and others—are now joining in a league with the powerful Osages from the west shore of the Mississippi for the purpose of a combined insurrection. We are menaced with a general outbreak, and even Toronto is in danger. Before long the English on the Miami will gain over all the surrounding tribes, get possession of Fort de Chartres and cut our communications with Louisiana. To add to these grave problems, smallpox has broken out at Detroit. It is to be wished that it would spread among our rebels; it would be fully as good as an army. All of our troubles seem to originate with the trading post the English have at Pickawillany. Sometimes they are there to the number of fifty at once, perhaps more. It is they who are the instigators of revolt and the source of all our woes.*

The letter from the colonial minister in Versailles was the one Jonquière had been looking for more than any other; the one in which he prayed there would be relief for him. He had written to explain how out of hand the situation was growing, what great inroads were being made by the English, especially among the Miamis, Delawares and Shawnees. He had explained how he, in accordance with the colonial minister's orders, had himself ordered Céloron to destroy the seat of unrest, Pickawillany, and complained bitterly over that commander's failure to obey the order. He had told the minister how greatly this business troubled him, how it robbed him of sleep and was now robbing him of his health; and he had begged to be recalled to France. But the anticipated reply from the colonial minister was the biggest disappointment of all. No mention was made of Jonquière's health nor of his request to be recalled. The letter was, in fact, more in the nature of a rebuke:

*Last year you wrote that you would soon drive the English from the Ohio; but reports from you and private letters I have received say that you have done nothing. This is deplorable. If not expelled, they will seem to acquire a right against us. I order you to send force enough at once to drive them off, and cure them of all wish to return. Plunder them unmercifully, which I think will effectually disgust them and bring all trouble to an end.*

And so once again, in a voice croaky with emotion and frustration and sickness, the Marquis de la Jonquière reissued orders to Pierre Joseph de Céloron de Bienville to mount an attack against Pickawillany and sent him, along with the orders, an additional force of thirty-eight men from Montreal.

Then, his secretary gone and his chambers quiet, Jonquière abruptly sat up in his bed and in a rage swept the letters and reports onto the floor. And, with the crushing responsibilities and frustrations of his office suddenly overwhelming him, he fell back onto his pillow and wept.

### [ *December 29, 1751—Sunday* ]

At ten years of age, Simon Girty possessed no really deep and abiding love for his father.

In addition to being a man who frequently disappeared for

long periods of time, ostensibly on trading missions with the Indians, the elder Girty was a disreputable, dirty, foul-mouthed individual inclined to drunken sprees. Simon Girty, Sr., was simply not a very loveable man. He bore all of the ill traits of the lowbred Irishman and little of the good. Yet he did, in his own peculiar way, possess a deep love for his wife, Mary, and he never abandoned her permanently, as so many of his cohorts had their own wives.

He and Mary Newton, a pleasant but not outstanding English girl, had been married in 1737 not long after his emigration from Ireland, and they had their first son eighteen months later in 1739. They named him Thomas and followed him up in late 1741 with a second son named after his father. Another son, James, came along in 1743 and a fourth, George, was born in 1745. They had no daughters.

All four of the boys had been born in the same squalid cabin they still lived in here at Chambers' Mill at the mouth of Fishing Creek on the east bank of the Susquehanna. The Delaware Indians who lived nearby called the area Paxtang and so the little settlement that sprang up around the grist mill erected here by the Chambers family quickly became known as Chambers-in-Paxtang.[8] In the whole province of Pennsylvania it would have been difficult to find any commu-nity more suited to the epithet "wicked." Morality of any form was practically unknown.

Slatternly women drifted in and out with great regularity, and Fishing Creek had not been named for its angling at-tributes but rather for the bodies which the Chambers boys were kept busy fishing out of their millpond. For some reason the deep pool above the log dam had become a favored place for the disposing of bodies of white men killed in fights, white women killed in passion and Indians killed for fun.

Despite the fundamental iniquity of the settlement, reason-ably good relationships had been maintained with the Indi-ans. Trade was, after all, practically the sole source of income and no one wanted to kill the golden geese who brought prime beaver pelts in exchange for essentially worth-less doodads which cost only pennies.

Indians came and went with great regularity, though of late there had been a considerable frigidity developing be-tween the races. This had been caused by the fact that the Indians wished to see no white men settle west of the river Susquehanna and their wishes were being ignored. Already along such of the Susquehanna's western tributaries as Sherman's Creek and the Juniata River, land had been claimed, cabins had sprung up and now over fifty families were west of this watery divide.

A flimsy stockade of sorts had been erected around Chambers' Mill to make it a place of refuge should the Indians get out of hand—which they hadn't yet but, everyone agreed, were apt to—and the place was dubbed Fort Hunter,[9] though apparently no one was sure exactly why.

The Girty cabin was only a hundred yards or so from the stockade and though it had only one room in it for the parents and all four boys, yet the elder Girty had invited his quasi-partner in the trading business—a younger man named John Turner—to lodge with them, and Turner had accepted. It was a cozy arrangement, especially with the elder Girty away so much of the time, and if it violated the precepts of morality, no one seemed to care much, particularly Turner.

Just this afternoon Turner and the elder Girty had returned from a week's trading jaunt west toward the Allegheny River. They had brought back with them a middle-aged Delaware named No-me-tha—meaning the Fish—who was the brother of a chief in the tribe. No-me-tha had furs the white partners wanted to buy but they had nothing left with which to buy them. They told the Indian that they had trade goods and rum at their cabin and he came along to consummate the deal.

They did have the rum but not the goods, but this was of little consequence. From past experience they knew that after a quart or less of rum had worked its way down his throat and set his belly and brain afire, they could give him a hunting knife of theirs or something else worth only a dollar or two and he would gladly hand over his furs, worth the better part of a hundred dollars.

From their pallets in the half attic, the four Girty boys watched with interest as the three men took seats on the log-section stools around the crude table and Girty, Sr., called for Mary to bring the jug of rum. She did so wordlessly, then retired back to her corner where she continued to work on stitching two hides together and paying no attention whatever to the men.

No-me-tha was one of those Indians whose reaction to alcohol in any form was very swift. At the end of one cup of the rum he was giddy and snickering. At the end of the second cup he was decidedly drunk and weaving in his seat. He never got beyond the middle of the third cup.

At that point the elder Girty, who was trying to make the Delaware agree to the trade and having difficulty even getting his attention, reached across the table and patted the Indian softly on the cheek. No-me-tha, taking it as a game, reached out and patted Girty's cheek in return, but a little harder. Girty responded with a fairly hard slap on the Indian's cheek and No-me-tha retaliated with a round-house open-palm swing that struck the trader's face with the sound of a beaver's tail swatting the water. It knocked Girty off his seat and onto the hard-packed earthern floor. The gaiety was all gone now and Girty clawed for his knife, but No-me-tha was faster. With one fluid movement, despite his drunken state, he whipped his tomahawk from his belt and flung it. Girty had his knife half cleared of its sheath when the hatchet struck him in the forehead and buried itself to the haft.

Girty fell and never moved voluntarily again.

John Turner had seen it all coming and even as the tomahawk was thrown he had reached out and scooped up his rifle leaning against the wall nearby. When No-me-tha instinctively turned to face him, Turner calmly and precisely put a lead ball the size of an acorn into the center of his throat. The ball passed through the Indian's neck and out the other side, disintegrating a fair-sized chunk of vertebrae and doing its best to decapitate him.

There were screams and tears which did not last an extraordinarily long time and then the elder Girty was carried out and buried a few feet deep behind the cabin.[10] No-me-tha was dragged by the feet to nearby Fishing Creek by ten-year-old Simon and twelve-year-old Tom and consigned to the millpond.

Later, with Turner at the table again and conditions in the single room almost identical to what they had been before, with the exception of the absence of two adult males, Mary Newton Girty placed her hand on Turner's shoulder.

"Figgerin' t'stay on here, John?" she asked.

He looked at her for a long appraising moment and then sighed and nodded. "I reckon," he said.

And so, for the widow Girty and her four young sons there would still be a man around the house.

### [March 6, 1752—Friday]

Four men were in the Canadian governor's quarters.

At the governor's desk, his face a model of unemotional

patience, sat the Baron de Longueuil. At the head of the governor's bed was the governor's private secretary, abysmally uneasy and pretending not to be by standing with his hands clenched tightly behind him and his eyes fixed unseeingly on the religious painting hung on the wall across the room. At the foot of the bed was a rotund Jesuit priest, black-robed and silent, rosary and prayer book in his lap. And in the bed was the governor himself, the Marquis de la Jonquière, his raspy breathing the only significant sound in the gloom of the big room.

The single guttering candle on a table was nearly burned out and, as if he had divined this through some sixth sense, a servant entered quietly with two candle holders, each bearing a fresh, white, wax taper. He set these on the table and carefully lit them with the stub of the one burning, then blew that one out with a puff of wind that sounded abnormally loud in the chamber.

The governor's head turned slightly and his eyes opened. His colorless lips barely moved as he spoke:

"Wax candles, Jude? They were expensive. Ordinary tallow candles are good enough to die by. Bring them."

He closed his eyes, sighed faintly and died.11

Great silent tears rolled down the cheeks of his secretary and his chin quivered, but still he made no sound. The lips of the Jesuit priest moved, but his words were a sibilant, incomprehensible whispering. And at the desk, the Baron de Longueuil dipped the governor's quill pen into the heavy glass inkpot and wrote swiftly on a blank sheet of paper:

*The Colonial Minister at Versailles*

*Sir, the Marquis de la Jonquière, having this day died, I have, as second in command, assumed temporary duties as Governor of New France until such time as, at His Majesty's command, the office can be made permanent or another appointment made.*

### [ June 12, 1752—Friday ]

It was by design, not happenstance, that young Charles Michel de Langlade stopped at Detroit on his way north to L'Arbre Croche and Michilimackinac. It was common knowledge to all in these parts that the French commandant here at Detroit, Céloron, was very anxious to have Pickawillany destroyed but was himself too weak to do so. The young half-breed entered the fort and made his way to the captain's quarters without pause.

Céloron knew Langlade personally only through occasional vague contact, but he knew him by reputation quite well and had longed for an occasion to make their relationship a closer one so that the young man, on behalf of his French blood, might help tighten the alliance between the French and Indians in this country. Therefore, though he had instinctively looked up in anger at the unannounced person entering, he had smiled instead and shook hands with Langlade warmly.

Charles Langlade wasted no time getting down to the point of his intrusion and he made no apologies. With oddly harsh directness he spoke in a voice no longer choked with the anger that had initially blinded him upon his ejection from Pickawillany, but rather with a frighteningly implacable hatred.

"Captain, you wish Pickawillany destroyed. I will destroy it."

Taken by surprise, Céloron could only ask why, and Langlade told him briefly of his trade goods being stolen, but not of his encounter with the principal chief of the Miamis. Céloron frowned and shook his head.

"Not enough," he said. "You are not the first man to lose his goods to the English. This alone could not make you wish to destroy the village. What else is there that you have kept from me?"

Langlade paused momentarily and then said, "It is no longer possible for both Unemakemi and myself to stay alive. He has given me the insult too great to accept if I am to live with self-respect. I will kill him. Or he will kill me. We cannot both stay alive. He had said he will throw my heart to his dogs, but it is I who will tear his heart from him and devour it myself. I have promised this to myself. I will do it. My mother's people will help me."

In spite of himself, Captain Céloron felt a shiver race down his back at the dreadful intensity of the young man. There was no doubt in his mind that Charles Langlade would attempt what he said.

"Why do you come here then, Monsieur Langlade?" he asked. "What do you wish of me?"

"You wish Pickawillany destroyed," the half-breed repeated patiently, "as greatly as I wish Unemakemi dead. I want support from you. Men, supplies, powder."

Céloron considered this a moment, remembering his own treatment three years ago at Unemakemi's hands, and then he nodded. He removed from his desk two wide strands of dark wampum and extended them toward Langlade.

"These war belts are from the governor in Montreal, who has ordered the destruction of Pickawillany, and through these belts commissions what Indians I request to do so. They may help you to convince your mother's people. As for the other you ask, supplies and powder I can give you; men, I have not many. I can give you perhaps eight or ten, but that is all."

Now it was Langlade who nodded as he took the wampum. "It is enough. I will soon return."

With that he had gone away and, in the month that followed, Céloron had begun to convince himself that it had merely been empty talk from the young half-breed. But then, six days ago, all doubt had been dispelled. In a fleet of twenty-two canoes came Langlade leading over two hundred Ottawas and Chippewas fully painted and prepared for war— the cream of the warriors from both L'Arbre Croche and Michilimackinac. They stopped at Detroit for a day to pick up the promised supplies and gunpowder and to confer with both Céloron and Pontiac.

The Ottawa war chief was at first opposed to the move against Pickawillany, but he had known Langlade for many years and both respected and admired him. When he heard from Langlade in private of the theft and insult the young trader had undergone from the Englishmen and Unemakemi, he became as incensed as if it had been delivered to himself. He painted his own cheeks and tattooed breast and, accompanied by almost fifty of his own warriors, joined the half-breed's force. Céloron provided not eight or ten soldiers, but a dozen of them, telling them to follow the orders of Langlade as faithfully as if he were their superior officer.

The next morning at dawn the party embarked again in their canoes. They were over two hundred fifty strong now, against a village with a total population of close to eight thousand, at least a quarter of which would be able-bodied warriors. The odds did not dismay them. With the element of surprise on their side and led by Langlade and the war chief Pontiac himself, they would sweep across Pickawillany in a destroying flood.

Down the Detroit River they paddled and along the western shore of Lake Erie to the mouth of the Maumee.

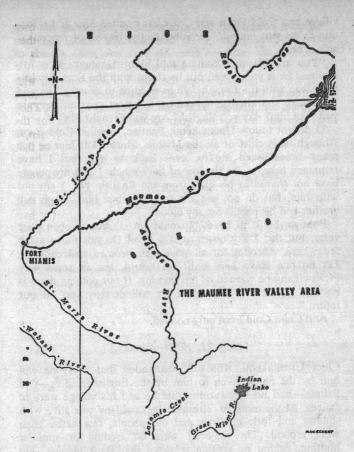

THE MAUMEE RIVER VALLEY AREA

They moved upstream at once and today, June 12, they reached the point where the Maumee was formed by the confluence of the St. Joseph and St. Mary's rivers. Here, at Fort Miamis, they stopped again to rest. The Indians began to redecorate themselves, rubbing away the gaudy, ceremonial war paint and replacing it with the somber blacks and browns, deep blues and pasty whites of battle paint. As they did this, the soldiers with the party repaired to the fort to deliver to Captain de Raimond a parcel of dispatches and letters from Detroit and Montreal.

Pontiac summoned Chief Cold Foot of the nearby Miami

village and Cold Foot, wary of what awaited him and reluctant to present himself, came hesitantly, fearful of reprisal if he did not.

"You are Miami," Pontiac told him. "Unemakemi is Miami and he is your chief, but he sleeps with the English while you sleep with the French. We have come to destroy him and his village and all who oppose us. Say now your answer, are you with him? Are you English? Are you French? Say!"

"I do not follow Unemakemi, Pontiac," replied Cold Foot, "though he is chief of all the Miamis. Since I left him he has many times asked me to come back to him, but I have remained here, in the shadow of the French. I and my people have not shared in his gifts from the English. No, I am not with him, but do not ask me to go against him. He is my brother and his people are my blood."

Pontiac shook his head. "I would not ask you to open your veins, but this I say now: remain here! Do not move away from here. Account for all your men, women and children. Let no one leave here until we return, lest in some way Pickawillany be warned of our coming. If our coming there is known, it is my promise that we will destroy you on our return."

And Chief Cold Foot only nodded.

### [ *June 21, 1752—Sunday* ]

Chief Unemakemi, who now demanded that everyone call him by the name given to him by the English traders—Old Britain—had no forewarning that he and his village were in danger. At the moment, although Pickawillany was alive with squaws and little children and old people, few active men were around. The majority were off trading or summer hunting, fishing or visiting relatives in distant villages. No more than a hundred warriors were left here.

Over the past two years as his power had increased and he had become not only the principal chief of the Miamis, but chief of a loose confederacy of a dozen or more tribes, Unemakemi had become arrogant and ever more convinced of his being a favorite of Manito.

Though he had been born along the midreaches of the Wabash River as a Piankeshaw, his father had been killed by a bear and when, three years later, his mother had accepted a Miami warrior as her husband, he was taken to the Miami village and brought up as a member of that tribe.

His ill treatment of Charles Langlade earlier in the year was much out of character for him. In times past he had been warm and kind and ever thoughtful of those with whom he came into contact. But in the past four years, since he had established Pickawillany, a peculiar change had come over him.

Partly, he was incensed that both the French and the Ottawas should try to tell him who he could or could not have as friends. In his irritation over this he condoned the letting of French blood when it could be done in secrecy, and even applauded the large party of his own men who, only a week or so ago, had ambushed ten French traders, killed them and their Negro servants, and then ate all of their victims. But the fact that he wanted neither French nor Ottawa to tell him what to do was not entirely the basis for the personality change in him. His actions were those of a man who felt he had become a God; and though the word of a principal chief always had been absolute law, now there was little benevolence with it. He had, in effect, become something of a tyrant.

On this bright and beautiful first day of summer, the sun was only a few hours high when the first indication of trouble reached him. From several hundred yards away in an adjoining cornfield, he heard the screaming of squaws. Instantly he snatched up his musket and plunged out of the doorway of his lodge. From a lodge close by sprinted his second principal chief, Michikiniqua—Little Turtle—a noted warrior.

The squaws, some with babies gripped tightly under their arms like little pigs, were racing in frantic haste out of the field where they had been working, their features contorted with terror and the only intelligible word to be heard from them was "Attack!"

Other warriors and chiefs of the Miami were rushing from their own lodges, as were some of Chief Orontony's Hurons, though Orontony himself did not appear. In moments the village was alive with Delawares, Weas, Miamis, Shawnees, Piankeshaws, Hurons and other Indians rushing back and forth like so many ants from a ruptured anthill, mostly uncertain what to do. Among them were eight English traders and one of them—Andrew Burney—knew exactly what to do.

"To the fort!" he shouted. "Everyone!"

Unemakemi heard him and repeated the command, as did Michikiniqua and Orontony, the latter having stumbled sleepily from his dwelling place. The aimless movement of

207

the runners now took direction as there was a general stampede toward the fortified trading house nearby. The shouting of the men, screaming of the women and crying of the children was suddenly overridden by a fantastic barrage of gunfire which cut down half a dozen warriors in the first moment.

One of these was Unemakemi.

The chief was still a hundred yards from the trading station when a sledgehammer blow smashed into his shoulder and tumbled him in a heap, sending his gun sailing a dozen yards or more from him. Instantly from the semicircle of shrieking attackers emerging from the cornfield, one lean figure detached itself and raced toward the fallen chief. It was Charles Michel de Langlade.

Twice, the young half-breed heard the sinister whirring of acorn-sized lead balls as they passed close to his head, and a third ball ripped though his buckskin shirtsleeve and gouged a shallow trench in his upper arm. He hardly noticed and, even as he ran, he jerked from his belt the thick-bladed hunting knife that was his trademark.

Unemakemi saw him coming and tried to reach his own gun, his right arm flopping loosely from the mangled shoulder. The two reached the weapon at the same time and though Unemakemi's left hand closed over it, a savage kick by Langlade broke the chief's wrist and sent the weapon spinning away. In an instant the young half-breed was astraddle the Miami chief's stomach, holding the injured arms down with his knees.

Langlade's face was wild, frightening, and for an instant their gazes locked and Unemakemi knew he was staring at death. Without a word, Langlade plunged his knife deep into the Miami's left side just below the rib cage and then jerked the keen blade clear across to the other side. He dropped the knife then and, while Unemakemi squirmed and jerked beneath him, thrust both hands into the widely gaping wound and then upward, pushing through fibers and membranes and shoving stomach, liver and other organs out of the way until the frantically palpitating heart was between his hands.

A strangled gasp came from Unemakemi as Langlade ripped the heart out and clear of the body cavity, and then the half-breed snatched up his knife from the ground and severed the strained aorta still attaching it to the body. Both men were abruptly bathed in the brilliant red blood and, incredibly, even though his heart was now detached from his

208

body and still pulsing unevenly in Langlade's hands, Unemakemi remained alive, his gaze still locked unbelievingly on the younger man. But not for long. Almost immediately the chief's eyes became glassy, then sightless and his head turned limply to one side in death.

Langlade screamed with inarticulate triumph, again dropped his knife and brought the weakening heart to his mouth. His strong teeth bit into it and, with difficulty, he tore a great chunk of the red muscle tissue away, feeling the meat quiver beneath his bite as he chewed it. Still the heart throbbed in his grasp and not until he had swallowed the first bite and fastened his teeth for another did it cease to function.

His face, hands and body dreadfully splashed with blood, Langlade appeared to be some nightmarish devil straight out of hell and for long minutes he remained totally oblivious to the battle raging around him.

Most of the Pickawillany warriors and all but three of the English traders had made it into the sanctuary of the fortified trading post, but their return fire at the attackers was skimpy and misdirected at best. Scattered about on the ground were the bodies which attested to the severity of the attack: thirteen other Miamis, one Shawnee and a Tuscarora.

The attackers themselves had not come off entirely unscathed. Three Ottawas and two Chippewas also lay dead among them and at least a dozen others were wounded in one way or another. A good percentage of those inhabitants of Pickawillany that had taken refuge in the trading station were also wounded and now the battle became more of a sniping action than an all-out fight.

The three traders who had been unable to reach the trading house—Edgar Bloom, Hugh Strand and Andrew Blaisdell—had taken refuge in one of the lodges, but quickly seeing they had no chance whatever, called to a French officer and surrendered themselves to him.

Pontiac directed his Indians intelligently and well, cautioning them to keep from exposing themselves, while all the while directing a withering fire into the portholes of the structure. In his left hand he held a knife and in his right a tomahawk and both were dripping with blood. Four scalps were already tucked into his waistband and now he ordered his warriors to round up all the squaws and children.

Inside the trading post there was a great wailing from the Indians, who milled about in the principal storeroom and tried to avoid the lead balls which buzzed wickedly through the ports and buried themselves in the log walls or ricocheted frighteningly inside. Of the five remaining traders—Thomas Burney, Andrew McBryer, James Dodge, James Kennedy and William Alder—the latter two were wounded, Alder slightly in the hip, Kenneth very seriously in the right side.

Burney and McBryer, who had been partners for years, were to one side of the big room, white-faced and talking in whispers that only they could hear. In a moment they began milling with the Indians and gradually moving toward the other side of the big room where a narrow door leading to a room hardly larger than a big closet was slightly ajar.

They slipped into it unnoticed by the others and closed it behind them. Burney fumbled in the darkness around them and suddenly was opening a cleverly concealed panel in the back wall of it. Beyond was another room, even smaller, and the pair crowded into it and resealed the panel so that it could no longer be opened from the closet side.

"Now, Andy," Burney whispered, "we keep quiet an' wait. Long as they don't take a notion t'burn 'er down, we got us a chance t'make it."

Desultory shooting continued from the Indians in the main room while the three remaining traders crouched against some whiskey kegs. Kennedy was in a very bad way, but the dulling effect of shock was still upon him and the pain was not yet unbearable. Alder had covered his own wound with a kerchief held in place by a long strand of rawhide wound around his upper leg and waist.

Dodge had begun to bandage Kennedy, but after a few trials simply shook his head and stuffed a torn wadding of trade blanket against it to staunch the flow of blood and, as Alder had done with his own wound, tied it in place with a strip of rawhide. Kennedy looked at him with surprising placidness.

"Am I done in, Jimmy?"

Dodge paused and then nodded. "Reckon mebbe so, boy. Might be you c'd make it with some good doctorin'," he shook his head, "but they ain't much chance fer that."

Kennedy showed no surprise or fear and merely closed his eyes. Dodge patted his knee awkwardly in sympathy and then turned to Alder.

"How you makin' out, Bill?"

Alder grimaced. "Hurts like hell, but ain't fatal. Never figgered on gittin' shot in the ass. What about the others?"

Both men looked around the room for a good while and

Dodge abruptly got up and opened three different doors, including the big closet, and looked inside each room carefully. When he came back to Alder he wore a puzzled expression and shook his head.

"Andy an' Tom was with us," he said, "but danged if they ain't gone now. You reckon they might'a snuck out an' got clear?"

Alder shook his head. "Don't see how, but I hope so. Ain't much chance we'll make it."

Dodge had no reply for this and the pair lapsed into silence. It was incredible how swiftly time had passed since the attack began. Already the sun was well past the meridian and now, from outside, came a deep, booming voice.

"Warriors inside the fort, hear me!" It was Pontiac. "Your chief is dead. Your best warriors lie on the ground before me. You, too, will die soon unless you do as bidden. We have your women here, and your children. But they wish you alive and we have no desire to kill you, as we could easily do. Our anger was against Unemakemi and those who would continue to uphold him even though he be dead, and also against the English traders who have caused all this to be brought upon you. We have three of them, but there are others inside with you. Give them to us and you will no longer feel our anger. You will be freed if you will promise to take your families and return to your villages and no longer be so foolish as to make friends with the English or harm the French. But if you do not do this, then we will kill you all, here, now, today! We give you no time to consider further but demand your answer now."

There was no choice. It was Chief Orontony himself who ordered several of his warriors to make prisoners of Kennedy, Dodge and Alder and then called out to Pontiac that the Englishmen were in his hands and that they would come out with them in peace and fight no more.

In five minutes the trading post had been vacated except for a handful of Pontiac's men who searched it thoroughly, looking behind bales and kegs and stores and into all rooms and hiding places. All but one. Then, satisfied that no one was left inside, they went back out and reported this to Pontiac.

Langlade stood before the clustered Indians who had emerged from the trading house. In his left hand, with the long black hair wound around his fingers, he held the head of Unemakemi. He raised it high so all could see.

"This is your chief!" he shouted. "This is he who thought it wise to call himself Old Britain and turn his back on us. This is you, if you do not separate yourselves from the English and return to the French!"

Expertly, then, he scalped the head, dropped it to the dirt and kicked it toward them. The head bounced and rolled to a stop only inches from Orontony, who backed up a few steps from it. Langlade smiled viciously.

"I have eaten the heart of him who would have thrown mine to the dogs. His strength is added to mine. Be warned!"

Pontiac himself now walked up to the three traders. Kennedy, only semiconscious, was being supported between Alder and Dodge. Pontiac tore the makeshift blanket-bandage away and looked closely at the man's wound. Before either flanking trader knew what he was doing, the war chief plunged his knife deeply into Kennedy's chest and the Englishman crumpled soundlessly to the ground. While warriors grasped Alder and Dodge and held them a short distance away, Pontiac slashed open Kennedy's chest and, as Langlade had done with Unemakemi, ripped out his heart and tore a chunk from it with his teeth. He threw the heart to one of his warriors who repeated the action. From one to another the dwindling muscle passed until at length only a gruesome chunk of membranous matter remained, which was unconcernedly tossed aside. And while all eyes were hypnotically fastened to this grisly tableau, no one saw the two remaining traders—Burney and McBryer—slip out of the door of the trading post, around the building and into the woods nearby.

In front of the building, white with fear, Dodge and Alder waited their turn, but as Pontiac turned back to them, Langlade stopped him.

"No," he said calmly, "these two and the other three are to be taken to Montreal. On this I have given my word to Captain Céloron."

Pontiac considered this briefly and then nodded, resheathing his knife. "Take the five of them out of my sight," he said. "They fill the air here with their stink and stir my appetite for blood."

Langlade, with a group of the Michilimackinac and L'Arbre Croche Indians, led the pair to where the other three were being guarded by the French soldiers, securely bound their wrists behind them and ordered them to sit.

"You will live only as long as you obey me," he said. "I

leave you here for now with French guards. Do not move. If you move, they will kill you instantly."

He left then to join the remainder of the war party who were now looting the village and stacking their plunder in a great pile. Every lodge was closely searched and then set afire and soon a pall of smoke such as had never before been seen in this country rose to form a great pillar in the clear, calm air.

The trading post was last to go, after all the goods worth taking had been removed from it. It was with deep pleasure that the dozen Frenchmen saw the detested structure being devoured by the flames. From this storehouse alone the plunder on hand mounted to over three thousand pounds worth of goods. This figure was nearly doubled by the items taken from the various lodges before they were burned.

Among the goods was a huge iron kettle which, with a very stout pole under the handle, it took two strong men to lift and place on a set of deeply forked upright limbs so that it hung some eighteen inches off the ground. A line of Indians formed and carried bucketful after bucketful of water to dump into the kettle until it was half full. Then, under directions from Pontiac, the bodies of Unemakemi, Kennedy and two of the defending Indians who had been killed outside, were hacked into great chunks and thrown into the pot. A fire was kindled beneath it and, when it was going well, pieces of hickory and oak were fed to it and the heat grew so intense that it forced the onlookers to step back.

When the meat was hardly more than half-cooked, it was speared with pointed sticks and tossed into a blanket spread out on the ground nearby. Then each of the attackers stepped up to cut off a chunk with his own knife and eat it. In this way, more of the strength of their enemies would pass into their own bodies. All this while the captive Indians watched fearfully and, when the orgy was done, Pontiac came to them and spoke again.

"From this day on you must be French Indians. There is no other way. The Miamis who are left among you and those who may return later will go to live with their wiser brother, Cold Foot, at the Miami-of-the-Lake.[12] The Hurons who are left here will return to Detroit to remain there where I may watch them and guide them. Their chief," and now his stern gaze fell on Orontony, "will now give me his word for himself and his people that he will come back and remain faithful to us and the French. If he does not do so, he will die this moment."

Orontony did not hesitate. "I will do as Pontiac says."

"The others among you who are of different tribes," Pontiac continued, "will return to your homes and will hereafter turn away or kill any English who come to you or any Indian who tries to turn you away from us or the French. It is Pontiac who tells you this. There is no choice for you. You are given this chance and no more. Go now, with your families and do not again tempt the hand of Pontiac, which does not often show mercy once and never twice!"

They began to move, hesitantly at first, but then the exodus turned into a galloping flight and within minutes every one of them had disappeared. Within another hour the packhorses the attackers had found here had been loaded with their plundered goods and the Indians under Pontiac themselves moved off toward the northwest.

Although the Pickawillany dead still sprawled on the ground, the attackers had buried their own fallen warriors. Langlade and four of the French soldiers quickly detached themselves from the procession and, leading their five tethered captives, set out overland in a northeastward direction.

For at least two hours after the attackers were gone there was no sound at the village site except the occasional popping of the many dwindling fires. But then there came a movement from the woods and out of the dusk came the remnant Miami Indians. They moved silently through the ruins and then the mournful death song of the squaws filled the air as the bodies and parts of bodies and bones of their dead were gathered and a hole dug for a common burial.

Directing the activity was the ugly warrior who had been second principal chief under Unemakemi. Now a sadness filled Michikiniqua such as he had never known before. With it was a great anger and a hatred that he knew could never leave him. He had longed for the day when he would take his place as principal chief of the Miamis, but he had not wished it in this manner. He knew as well that some of his tribe, in their fear, would go back to the Maumee to rejoin Cold Foot's band, but he and his strong core of followers would not. Before this his alliance with the English was merely one of trade and his contact with the French and Ottawas and Chippewas had been cold, but not belligerent. Now they were enemies and so they would remain until he no longer lived.

When all had been done that could be done here at the site

of Pickawillany, Michikiniqua led his people into the woods once more. Almost immediately they were intercepted by the two escaped traders who had been friends of Chief Little Turtle, as they called Michikiniqua.

The new principal chief greeted Burney and McBryer warmly and ordered his own men to disguise them as Indians in case some of Pontiac's men should still be nearby. Then the whole party moved downstream along the west bank of the Great Miami River for a few miles before turning westward to a point where two substantial streams joined.[13] Here a camp was made and here Thomas Burney and Andrew McBryer shucked off their Indian garb and talked at length with Michikiniqua. They told him they would leave for the east at once to report what had happened, and Michikiniqua nodded.

"It is well that you do this. Will you as well carry a message for me to the father of the Virginia, and another to the father of the Pennsylvania?"

Burney agreed to do so and Michikiniqua gave him some wampum, the scalp of an Ottawa and a calumet[14] to present to the governors. Then, as he dictated slowly, Burney wrote the messages on tanned skin, using a trimmed crow quill as a pen and the juice of hastily crushed berries as ink. The letter to Governor Robert Dinwiddie of Virginia was the first to be dictated by the new chief of the Miamis:

*Elder Brother!*
*This string of wampum assures you that the French King's servants have spilled our blood and eaten the flesh of three of our men and one of yours. Look upon us and pity us for we are in great distress. Our chiefs have taken up the hatchet of war. We have killed and eaten ten of the French and two of their Negroes. We are your Brothers.*

Michikiniqua's letter to James Hamilton of Pennsylvania was even longer and more detailed:

*Elder Brother!*
*We, your Brothers, the Miamis, have sent you by our Brother, Thomas Burney, a scalp and five strings of wampum in token of our late unhappy affair at Pickawillany; and whereas our Brother the Governor has always been kind to us, we hope he will now put to us a method to act against the French, being more discouraged for the loss of our Brothers,*

215

*the Englishman who was killed and the five who were taken
prisoners, than for the loss of ourselves; and, notwithstanding,
the two belts of wampum which were sent from the Governor of Canada as a commission to destroy us, we shall still
hold our faithfulness with our brothers and are willing to
die for them. We saw our great Piankeshaw King, who was
commonly called Old Britain by us, taken, killed and eaten
within a hundred yards of the fort, before our faces. We now
look upon ourselves as a lost people, fearing our Brothers
will leave us; but before we will be subject to the French, or
call them our Fathers, we will perish here.*

*From Michikiniqua who
is also Little Turtle*

### [July 17, 1752—Friday]

The grand council being held between the colonial ambassadors and Iroquois chiefs at Albany this month was showing
no more progress and considerably less amity than had that
of last year. The dominant thought in everyone's mind—
white and Indian alike—was the destruction of Pickawillany
and what it portended.

The Iroquois were worried. Runners had brought word of
the defeat and the fact that the previously nonallied tribes
and those not of the Iroquois who had been vacillating between French and English allegiance were now swinging
heavily toward the French. Some, in fact, had uprooted their
villages and moved them to the very shadow of French forts,
hoping in this way to show their fidelity to the French and
their desire that the French arm, obviously so strong, should
rest around their shoulders and protect them. Even some of
the Iroquois leaders who themselves had heretofore advocated strict neutrality were now inclining toward the
French.

The English were just as worried. Thomas Burney, after
leaving Chief Michikiniqua, had traveled first to Shawneetown
at the mouth of the Scioto River to spread the news of the
French victory—even though it was far more an Ottawa-
Chippewa victory than French—and the fact that one of
those who died at Pickawillany had been a Shawnee warrior.
From there he had gone directly to Carlisle, Pennsylvania, and
delivered the principal chief's message to James Hamilton.
The governor was just getting ready to go to Philadelphia to
meet with Robert Dinwiddie, and from there the two gover-

nors planned to travel to New York to confer with Governor George Clinton. Burney went with Hamilton to Philadelphia and delivered Michikiniqua's second message. The newspapers spread the story of the massacre and almost overnight the topic was on everyone's tongue. There was little concern for the Indians of Pickawillany, but the loss of the trading station and valuable goods, along with the life of at least one trader and possibly five more, was greeted with trepidation. This was an act of war!

Clinton, in a rather perplexing effort to assuage the feelings of the Iroquois who were still angered over the resignation of William Johnson, appointed fourteen Indian commissioners for New York Colony. They were, even Clinton had to admit, inveterate opposers of Johnson's policies. But when the governor tried to introduce them to the very Indians they were supposed to represent, the Iroquois chiefs turned their backs and told Clinton they would continue to support Warraghiyagey with all their might and be represented by none other.

For days a monotonous haggling went on between the parties, with essentially nothing accomplished except perhaps a widening of the rift between the two races. It was a council filled with ill feelings and into this atmosphere suddenly arrived the delegation of Catawbas from South Carolina, as ordered by the Iroquois at last year's council.

They were greatly frightened men, these four, and this time no singers preceded them into the speaking area and no pipes were lighted. At their head again was Chief Chik-o-gee, whom so many of the English liked to call Colonel Bull. On each of his cheeks had been painted a broad, greasy black streak. His men wore the same markings. It was the mark of death.

Chik-o-gee's actions were jerky, his eyes hollow with fear and he acted as if he expected to be slain on the spot. When he spoke, the words quavered in his throat and there was a distinct pleading tone in what he said.

"Chiefs of the Iroquois, hear me with your hearts! Though we are prepared and expect to die here at your hand, believe in your hearts that we have come in peace. You last year gave us a truce until now and directed us to bring back with us those few Iroquois who were our prisoners. You told us then that only when this was done could there be peace between us. As you can see, Chiefs of the Iroquois, your

217

warriors are not with us. They could not return. They are dead."

There was a sudden intake of breath from the assemblage and the mild hostility of the Iroquois became suddenly intense. With only the briefest of pauses, Chief Chik-o-gee continued:

"We did not kill them! In fact, we treated them well, and better treatment no prisoner has ever had. But a bad sickness was visited upon us and with it came death. One out of four of our people have died and our hearts are heavy with grief. The prisoners were touched with this sickness, too, Chiefs of the Iroquois, and though we did all we could for them, and those who cared for them were themselves taken sick, they died and we buried them honorably and have brought back to you their pouches and their cloths and their bracelets. More we cannot do. Now you may kill us. We are ready to die."

He stepped back to where his men stood and hardly watched as the Onondaga's orator chief, Canassatego, arose to speak. The Iroquois's expression was bleak and his words cold. He pointed a steady finger at Chik-o-gee and his party.

"Strangers and enemies: our warriors are dead and you ask us to understand. There is but one thing we understand; if they had been where they ought to be, if you had shown your good faith by freeing them upon your return to your own country last year after leaving here, they would be alive now. We understand why this was not done; that you kept them to bring them here with you when you came back, that their bodies might shield your own until from our own lips you should be assured of peace. But in doing this you betrayed the trust we gave you and now our warriors are dead and the grief you have is transferred to us. For this, there can now be no peace for you.

"Strangers and enemies: while you are in this country, blow away all fear out of your breasts, change the black streak of paint on your cheek for a red one, and let your faces shine with bear grease. You are safer here than if you were at home. The Six Nations will not defile their own land with the blood of men that come unarmed and ask for peace. We shall send a guard with you to see you safe out of our territories. So far you shall have peace, but no farther. Get home to your own country and take care of yourselves, for there we intend to come and kill you!"

He made a motion with his hand, dismissing them, and

four young warriors at once left the Iroquois party and moved over to flank the Catawbas and escort them from the country. No further business was carried on by the congress until they were gone from sight and hearing. Even then the only matter discussed was postponing any further meetings until the next day.

That day—today—dawned gray and mean with a fine drizzle falling. By 10 A.M. it had ended and at noon the council reassembled beneath the tremendous old pine tree where such councils were usually held. For as long as any could remember who were assembled here, this tree was the council tree. Now it was decayed in places and numerous branches had fallen from it. Though still a giant, it was a dying giant.

Once again the council opened with the various Indian commissioners speaking, asking that the Iroquois League for once and for all give their full and unswerving allegiance to the English colonies, to help them fend off the French, who would destroy the Indians just as they wished to destroy the English. Wasn't what happened at Pickawillany proof of this?

When they were finished only one Indian on hand showed any desire to speak. This was Sconondoa, an incredibly old and frail chief of the Oneidas, whom the German settlers of the Mohawk Valley had long ago dubbed Plattkopf. His hair was the color of dirty snow and hung nearly to his waist. He had no teeth and his limbs were hardly bigger around at the wrists and ankles than broomsticks. Yet, amidst the maze of wrinkles which lined his face until it appeared to be a gray-brown prune, his eyes shone with intelligent light and his voice, when he spoke, carried to the ears of all who were present, even though it was high-pitched and frequently cracked with the strain of projection. No one knew how old he was, but no white man here ever knew him except as an incredibly old man and even their fathers and grandfathers who were first to come here spoke of him as the old wizard of the Oneidas.

"My warriors, my children!" he began. "My old ears play tricks with me. They tell me that they hear the English men asking the Iroquois to support them and that my Iroquois discuss this seriously. My old heart says this cannot be true, but yet I have heard it.

"My children, none among all the Iroquois have lived as long as Sconondoa and no more than two or three even halt as long. Yet, surely among you there must be some who remember what we are and who we are and what we once had. Are there none here who remember when the cry 'The Iroquois are coming!' was alone enough to make the hearts of the bravest warriors of other tribes fail within their breasts? Are there none here who remember when this land was all ours and that though other tribes were round about, they were there by our forbearance and there was none who could stand before us; are there none here who remember that from the green sea to the east and the blue sea to the south, to the land of always-winter in the north and the land of always-summer in the west, they feared us?

"But then came the men in their boats and they brought us gifts. They asked for our friendship and we gave it to them. Then they asked for just a little land and we foolishly gave it to them. Then, when they asked us for more land and we would not give it to them, they asked us to sell it to them and because they had goods that were new and powerful to us, we sold them some. Then they asked us for more land and when we would not give it or sell it, they took it from us and we talked and talked and always it was we who gave in and signed a new treaty and took gifts for what was taken, but the gifts were cheap and worthless and lasted but a day, while the land lasts forever."

He paused and his ancient eyes moved across them with an almost palpable love and concern; but when his eyes encountered the white men in attendance, they moved across them as if they did not exist. He returned his attention to the Indians and continued:

"My children, my warriors, still they are nibbling at our land and now they do so under the pretense of protecting us from other white men who would take it from us. Are the Iroquois all blind? Do they not see what is happening? Do they not know, as in my old heart I know, that they play us one against the other until somehow the white man is suddenly on more of our land and we are pushed back?

"My children, raise your heads! Open your eyes! Unstop your ears! Can you not see that it makes no difference whether these white men are of the French or the English or any other of the peoples from across the sea? All of them threaten our very existence. All of them! When they came here they had nothing. Now, like a great disease they have spread all over the east until for twelve days' walk from the sea there is no room for an Indian to stay and he is made unwelcome. Yet this was not long ago all Indian land. How has it gone? As these white men have stained the east and the north with their presence, so now they extend themselves to the west and the northwest and the southwest, forcing all Indians to take sides for them or against them, whether they are French or English, but in such a game the Indian cannot win."

His voice cracked and changed, becoming higher pitched, more beseeching, but he did not pause:

"Oh my warriors, my children, hear me with your minds and your hearts! See what my eyes see and hear what my ears hear and take warning from what I say. We have sent the Catawabas away today with the fear in their breast that soon we will come and kill them, but we will not, although in the past we would have done so at once. We will not do so now because day by day our League weakens and is pulled apart by these white men whose every word and deed is filled with treachery against us. Now we no longer have the strength or unity to carry a war across the country to a far-distant tribe. We do not dare do so, lest our own lands be stolen while we are gone.

"I am Oneida, but more than that, I am Iroquois!" He raised his hand then to point a skeletal finger at the great old pine tree towering over them. "The Iroquois are like this council tree. It was then full of life and vigor and beauty. It drew its nourishment from the ground; it was not cramped and confined; it could draw its sap from all the land, for the Iroquois owned it all, they had parted with none of it. And as it could draw its sap from all the land, it grew and put forth more branches and more strong green needles and sent out new roots and spread them farther in the ground. It became strong and very beautiful. So did the Iroquois. As the tree grew, so did the Iroquois. The white men came. We gave him a portion of the land. A root of the tree, which drew its sap from that land, withered; when it withered, a branch died, and the tree lost some of its beauty. Again the white man came. This time we sold him a piece of our land; another root withered, and another branch fell down, and we now see our tree: though beautiful, it has lost its branches, it no longer sends forth new roots and puts forth new branches, it is cramped, it has not the land to draw sap from which it had.

"And we, my children, where are we?" There was an immense sadness in the words and it was a contagion which spread across the Indians listening closely to this oldest and most revered man in their League. Sconondoa shook his head and repeated, "Where are we, my children? The white man has come again. He wants more of our land, though he says differently. Shall we sell him another piece? Shall we let the tree under which our father sat lose another and another root, and cause another and another branch to fall?

"My warriors, my children, hear! It is cruel. It is very cruel. A heavy burden lies on my heart. It is very sick. This is a dark day. The clouds are black and heavy over the Onioto-people and over the Rising Sun[15] people and over all the people of the Six Nations. A strong arm lies heavy upon us, and our hearts groan under the weight of it. Our fires are put out, our beds are removed from under us. The graves of our fathers are destroyed, and our children are driven away from them. We must have been very wicked, for the Great Spirit is angry with us, therefore his arm does not keep us.

"Where are the chiefs of the Rising Sun people, whose home was easterly from the Onioto-people and who are not now permitted to return to where their council fires once burned brightly? White chiefs now kindle their fires in those places. And there no Indian now sleeps but those who are sleeping in their graves. Soon all the Mohawk land will be like this and then my house will soon be like theirs. Soon will a white man kindle his fire on the land of the Onioto-people and that of their wards, the Tuscaroras, and after that his fire will burn on the ashes of our own League fireplace at Onondaga. We will be no more, and his fire will sweep before it all trace of the Cayuga and the Setting Sun people. Your Sconondoa will soon be no more; his village no more a village of Indians, his nation no more a nation, and his League broken like the ice of a river under the rains of spring."

His voice broke again and for a long while he could not continue, but no person present made any sound and at last he went on. The projection of the words was weak now and he was hard to hear. He seemed to be talking as much to himself as to the council:

"My children, I am sick. The Iroquois people are sick. Our eyes rain like the black cloud that roars upon the trees of the wilderness. Long did the strong voice of Sconondoa cry, 'Children, take care, be wise, be straight:' His feet were then like a deer's and his arm like the bear's. Now he can only moan out a few words, then be silent. His voice will soon be heard no more. But he will live long in the minds of his children, and in white men's minds! Sconondoa's name has gone far; it will not die. He has spoken many words to make his children straight. The words have not always been heard, but one last time he will say them again, and he cries to your hearts to listen: Drink no strong water; it makes you mice for white men who are cats. Many a meal they have eaten of you. Their mouth is a snare, their way like the fox. Their lips are sweet, but their hearts are wicked! Attach yourselves not to them, but stand alone against all white men. Become again a league of men who fear none but who themselves are feared by all!"

Again he stopped and now he seemed to shrink inward upon himself until the illusion was strong that he would simply shrivel away to a tragic nothingness. A faint breeze came up and a whisper of sound drifted downward from the remaining needles of the ancient pine tree. The wrinkled old face, wet with tears, rose until his eyes were on the top of the tree and then Sconondoa spoke again; a sibilant, penetrating whisper that might almost have been mistaken for the wind itself:

"I am an aged hemlock. The winds of one hundred winters and more have whistled through my branches; I am dead at the top. The generation to which I belong has run away and left me. Why I live, the great good spirit only knows."

### [ *August 18, 1752—Tuesday* ]

The Baron de Longueuil had cherished the belief that since he had stepped into the office of governor of New France on the death of Jonquière and had, since that time, done a good job of administering affairs of government, his self-appointed temporary post would become permanent. The King of France and his colonial minister in Versailles, however, had plans of their own. Longueuil was commended for his actions in keeping things going but was blandly informed that a new governor was on the way.

The man sent to replace him was not only an able administrator, but a keen military strategist as well and a member of an esteemed naval command family. That he was a distinguished individual in both background and appearance was immediately evident when he arrived at Montreal on the first day of July. The fact that his lofty, overbearing attitude offended many of the Canadians at the outset mattered not one whit to him.

He was the Marquis Duquesne.

One of his first acts was a general review of the regular French troops and militia and he was not particulary pleased with what he saw. Slovenliness and insubordination were rampant and within days of his arrival he had demoted numerous officers, promoted to officership a sizable number of soldiers from the ranks and issued a raft of orders and regulations difficult to keep pace with. He made enemies from the onset, which also bothered him not at all, but at the same time garnered a grudging respect from nearly everyone. From the moment of his arrival, there was no doubt that he was born to command.

By the end of his first week in office he had thoroughly assessed the French and English military and economic picture in North America and set his own wheels to moving at once to take advantage of what he quickly realized was the greatest weakness of the English colonials: their incomprehensible neglect to firmly establish themselves in, and permanently occupy, the western passes and waterways. Duquesne had no intention of letting this incredible opportunity pass. That this was the same idea Jonquière had had and would have consummated if he had received greater support from France, was of little moment to him. The fact of the matter was that Duquesne *did* have such support and he most certainly meant to use it.

At once he mustered the regular colony troops, found them weak, ill-trained and insufficient for what he had in mind and immediately called up the Canadian militia. With this body of men he was highly pleased. They were not only eager and surprisingly obedient, they were also numerous and he placed them on a tough training schedule, giving them an alert to be prepared for major undertakings in the spring, for which he would thoroughly outfit them.

Duquesne's quick mind perceived at once that by planting French forts and strong garrisons on the upper waters of the Ohio and the few passes leading to that important waterway, the English colonial traders would be effectively barred from any reasonable access to the West. It stood to reason then, that the numerous Indian tribes of that great area, deprived thereafter of the weapons and goods heretofore provided by the English traders, would necessarily be drawn back to dependence upon the French.

Even more importantly, the Indians were highly impressionable and greatly respected vigor and daring, especially when backed by a strong show of force. While the English might give them words, Duquesne planned for the French to give them actions which would speak much louder. It was not difficult to imagine toward whom the savage leanings would then belong. It was this entire plan that he sent on to the colonial minister. As Duquesne summed it up:

*In short, Excellency, this intended enterprise will be a master-stroke which must lay bare to our axe the very root of disaffection. While it is true that the treaty commissioners have long been in session in Paris to settle the irksome problem of American boundaries, this is a fact that I have taken into consideration. It is, I believe, clear to all of us that they can never come to a satisfactory agreement. For France to make good her Western claims, we must, while there is yet time to do so, secure and occupy the areas in question, lest our rival fasten a firm grip on the countries in dispute.*

And in France, while King Louis was spending millions on his own frivolities, the colonial minister in Versailles remained the conservative economist and replied to Duquesne:

*Be on your guard against new undertakings, in particular those suggested by others, for private interests are generally at the bottom of them. It is through these that, at great cost to His Majesty, worthless new posts are established, only to soon be abandoned. Proceed cautiously with your plan and review it carefully in all respects. You must keep only such forts as are indispensable, and suppress the others. The expenses of the colony are enormous; and they have doubled since the peace. With this letter you have authority to build on the Ohio and tributaries such forts as are absolutely necessary, but no more. Remember that His Majesty suspects your advisers of interested views.*

Today had been a most pleasant day for Duquesne. Well aware of the chicanery and official thievery and corruption prevalent in virtually all French colonial affairs, both military and civil, the marquis had already been successful in spiking many such endeavors. This was not to say he let courage and imagination go unrewarded.

Only this morning had come a young ragtag half-breed incredibly leading four regular soldiers from Detroit who, in turn, had in tow five English traders as prisoners. With sincere interest and approval, Duquesne listened while Charles Michel de Langlade reported on the total destruction of Pickawillany, the death of its chief, the confiscation of the English and Miami properties, and the capture of the traders. When Langlade had finished and the prisoners had been incarcerated for later questioning in detail, the new governor shook the half-breed's hand warmly.

"Monsieur Langlade," he said, "your years belie your deeds and I commend you highly for this bold enterprise. Would that I had an army of men of your caliber. You will not be forgotten, believe me. I will this day recommend you most highly to the colonial minister and leave out no detail of your accomplishment. I hereupon appoint you to the rank of lieutenant in the colony forces. Rest assured that I will, if you are agreeable to it, call upon you again in a time soon to come, to take a command part in a major undertaking. In the meanwhile, though you must be anxious to return to your home and wife, I would be honored to have you remain here as my guest, to dine and rest and be fitted out with new clothing and equipment for your return to Michilimackinac. Further, for your exemplary service in ridding us of Pickawillany and its Indians who were so hostile to our cause, I shall recommend to His Majesty that you be more materially rewarded with a pension of two hundred francs."

And the Marquis Duquesne did just that.


[ *September 14, 1752—Thursday* ]

It was a peculiar day today, for the simple reason that yesterday had been September 2. By royal proclamation, the eleven days following Wednesday, September 2, were omitted in Great Britain and the American Colonies and, for the first time in the history of the English-speaking peoples, nothing— *absolutely nothing*—happened on September 3 through 13, simply because these days failed to exist. The Julian calendar was being discarded in favor of the more accurate Gregorian calendar. Schedules were thrown off kilter, meetings aborted, correspondence befuddled and the entire calendar system so confused that savants were saying it would be years before the problems this change generated would be eased, and that history would ever afterward be affected and subject to confusion in dates.[16]

The words of the Oneida chief, Sconondoa, moving as they had been, had not really been taken with very great seriousness. Sales of lands by Indians who no longer wanted that particular land or who thought it wise not to try to hold on to it in the face of growing settlement by the whites, continued at a brisk pace. And William Johnson, essentially freed of the burden his Indian Affairs office had placed on him, concentrated now on securing choice expanses as his own.

He already held title to the land upon which he had built Mount Johnson and to the great circle of land around Lake Onondaga. But now he expanded his land activities and bought from the Mohawks a tract of one-hundred-thirty-thousand acres on the Charlotte River tributary[17] of the upper Susquehanna River for three hundred pounds and a certain amount of goods. Nine Mohawk chiefs signed the deed and among them were Tiyanoga, Wascaugh and Nichus.

For any individual to get legal possession of land purchased from the Indians, he was required to have granted to him a patent for that land by the governor and his council. William, of course, immediately submitted a request for patent to his Charlotte River land and, at the same time, sent in a similar request for the land around Lake Onondaga which the Crown had shown no interest in taking off his hands.

He learned at once that it was illegal for any individual to receive a patent for more than a thousand acres and was urged to engage in the somewhat shady business of suppressing his own name in the petition and submitting individual petitions of a thousand acres each in the names of friends, who would dutifully sign the land back to him once the patent was granted. Unfamiliar with this particular species of corruption, Johnson was at first outraged and presented the petition legally in his own name.

"My contributions to the frontier in New York have been such," he told the governor and council, "that I should be excused by the government from engaging in the corrupt practices of lesser men in order to secure this land which I desire."

While admirable, his honesty was not in this instance the best policy. Giving the matter due consideration, the government blandly gave him a patent to the Onondaga land, which was practically worthless to him, as supposed payment for all the debts the colony owed him. "But," they went on, "since the alleged Charlotte River purchase might involve a conflict with the jurisdiction of Pennsylvania, patent for that land is denied."

It was no more nor less than a convenient excuse to balk him and, angry now and determined to fight on the government's own terms, William turned right around and bought from the same Indians a good section of land in the Mohawk Valley which totaled twenty thousand acres. He then drew up the patent petition in the name of one of his employees, Arent Stevens, along with twenty of his neighbors, and even assigned a sixth share of the land to George Clinton.

The governor, after neatly pushing the grant through his council, sold that sixth share back to William for two hundred and thirteen pounds. A big party was held at Mount Johnson for Stevens and the twenty neighbors and, when it was all over, all the deeds had been signed back to William Johnson.

The "Stevens Purchase" was something of a narcotic to him and the former Indian agent now began gobbling up land in this manner the way a starving man gobbles a crust of bread. Very quickly he became possessor of another large tract which he immediately named Kingsborough. It was a section of country north of the Mohawk River, above the Palatine settlements, in area about ten miles wide and fifteen miles deep.[18]

As far as William Johnson was concerned, this was only a start.

# CHAPTER V

[ *April 8, 1753—Sunday* ]

ONLY fifteen minutes ago Lieutenant Richard Holland had been sitting in his quarters thinking what a miserably monotonous post this was, having command of Fort Oswego. The weeks went by in the same dragging manner and the most common topic of discussion among the entire garrison was health—who was sick, who was dying, who was recovering and who, if anyone, was well.

It was bad enough to have a command on the edge of nowhere like this, but even worse when the home government wouldn't supply even a tenth of what was required for well-being. Lieutenant Holland shook his head and then pulled off his boots and stretched out on his cot to take his usual nap following Sunday services. That was when the orderly had tumbled into the room without even knocking, so excited he could barely put across the basis for his concern.

When Holland did get the gist of it, he snatched up his telescope, sprinted out of the room without even putting his boots back on, and raced up to the parapet overlooking Lake Ontario. For ten minutes he remained there with the glass directed out over the lake. Soldiers and traders flocked to join him but, except for a brief conversation with a French trader who happened to be there, the commander spoke to no one.

Now he was back in his quarters, his pen racing furiously across the page in a dispatch to be sent by express to Governor Clinton:

*Oswego*
*Sunday Noon*
*April 8, 1753*

*Honored Sir,*

*Please be advised that I have just witnessed a great fleet of canoes which I believe to be French, passing from east to west on Lake Ontario about three miles off shore. I counted 191 separate vessels but, due to distance and weather conditions, may have made some slight error. I am sure there were no less than 180 nor more than 220 of them. Each craft seemed to have from eight to twenty men. I questioned a roving French trader, who happened to be here, and he told me that they belonged to an army of six thousand French soldiers going to the Ohio to cause all the English to quit those parts. I will double the guard at this post and permit no further French traders to enter until I learn your pleasure.*

*Sir, I believe this to be a very serious matter.*

> *Yr. Obdt. Svt.,*
> *Richard Holland*
> *Lieutenant Commanding*

### [ May 15, 1753—Tuesday ]

William Johnson's urgent message had reached Governor Clinton only hours before Lieutenant Holland's and each substantiated the other, though William's was the more accurate.

According to William, he was awakened about midnight on April 20 by Mohawks "whooping and hallowing in a frightful manner." When he hastened down to them they explained that word had just come of a major French force mobilizing at Fort Frontenac. No Indians were with the force or had been invited to accompany it. Not only was the force— estimated to be about fifteen hundred to two thousand strong—well equipped with rifles and other gear, but they reportedly had with them no less than eight small artillery pieces.

It had been learned from traders with whom the Indians dealt that the force was en route to build three or four major forts on the passage from Lake Erie to the Ohio River, beginning with one at that long spit of land known as Presque Isle,[1] which extended out into the lake to form what the French governor, Marquis Duquesne, was calling the finest harbor in nature. This was to be followed by another, fifteen miles to the south at the headwaters of Rivière aux Boeufs.[2] Beyond that, it was said, there would be others. Johnson added in his report:

*The Iroquois are greatly concerned and I have received a message from the Senecas who ask, "Are we dead?" The Mohawks, too, are worried and Hendrik [Tiyanoga] has asked me to tell you that he is coming with an embassy to council with you on this and other matters. In my capacity as a member of the Governor's Council and a party interested in Mohawk affairs, I will accompany them.*

Clinton and his advisers were more concerned than anyone really knew about this French invasion. The fear, so long dulled, had suddenly become a sharp stabbing. And now, with William Johnson and his Mohawks already assembled in the meeting chambers, he would have to listen to more of the same old demands and accusations. He was not much in the mood for it, but there was no legitimate way he could fail to appear. Wearily, he got to his feet and made his way to the waiting delegation.

In addition to the Indians—all eighteen of them clad in the fine lace coats William had given them—and Johnson himself, the other members of the Governor's Council were also assembled here. No one looked very happy and the first words of Tiyanoga to Clinton did not improve anyone's disposition.

"Our League is threatened," the principal Mohawk chief said harshly. "If your ears are like those of the wolf, you can hear our union of six tribes straining and the tendons stretching and cracking. Not only our League, but even our tribe is being threatened, and it is all the fault of you English here. Brother, had you not broken your promises to stay with us and support us in the last war, the Mohawks would have torn the Frenchman's heart out! But your promises were nothing and when it suited you, you pulled away. Now the situation has become even worse. The half-Seneca called Joncaire, who works for the French more than for the Indians, has gained over most of the Seneca people to French thought and trust. The black-robed man who is at the mouth of the Oswegatchie—he who is called by the name of Piquet—this man is drawing the Onondagas more and more to his mission. You know of the great French army which is at this moment building a strong fort at Presque Isle, which is at the back door to our Long House. You have left your allies naked and defenseless and do not care what becomes of our nation!"

He stopped, expecting some sort of reply from Clinton, but

the governor had none and in a moment Tiyanoga spoke again, this time of another matter festering between them:

"Brother, the English do not support their Indian allies as they should, and as they expect us to support you. In all ways, things grow worse each day. Indian land is being stolen in great pieces by the Dutchmen of Albany. We are shown deeds that we have never signed, though marks that are supposed to be ours are upon them. When we *have* sold land, your own surveyors come in and what they mark off is always more than we have sold.

"Therefore, hear me now, Brother, for my words do not blend: all old deeds supposedly signed by us must be looked at again and the land they deal with surveyed again, but only under our supervision. No new deeds will be granted except in the presence of Indian representatives. And where white men are in cabins upon our lands without authority, we will take a little rod and whip them away."

This was more than Clinton could take and now his eyes flashed angrily as he replied.

"I will not stand for insolence in these chambers!" he said tightly. "If you have any legitimate grievances, land or otherwise, do not come to me about them. Go and see the commissioners I appointed for you in Albany."

Tiyanoga approached the governor of New York until their noses were only inches apart and his own voice was harsh and ugly.

"Those commissioners you appointed for us are bad men. They are not people, but devils! You take us for fools who will settle for a leaf when the entire tree is ours."

The more the chief spoke, the angrier he became and now he smacked his fist into his hand and then thrust his hands away from him, palms down.

"No more! It is finished! We leave here, and as soon as we come home, we will send up a belt of wampum to our brothers in the other five nations to tell them that the covenant chain is broken between you and the Mohawks. So, Brother, you are not to expect to hear of me anymore. And, Brother, we desire to hear no more of you!"

He stalked out of the chamber and his seventeen men, every bit as angry as he, followed closely behind him. The council members were suddenly white-faced and Clinton himself looked sick. Any other single tribe of the Six Nations might go pro-French without it becoming too great a catastrophe, but if the Mohawks did so, nothing in this world could keep the entire Iroquois League from doing likewise. With such Indian support, the French could make a shambles of the colony. New York City itself would not even be safe.

The consternation spread quickly until the entire New York Assembly was in an uproar. And through it all, with an expression of patient concern on his own face, sat Colonel William Johnson, late of Indian Affairs. He even managed to act surprised when the Assembly now came to him with the plea that he intercede on New York's behalf and go to Onondaga on a peace mission, and went so far as to vote him four hundred and fifty pounds for expenses.[3]

With an outward show of reluctance, but inwardly delighted, William Johnson accepted the commission and returned at once to Mount Johnson. Tiyanoga met him there with a warm hug and handshake and an offer to accompany him to Onondaga ... and Warraghiyagey was not the least surprised.

## [ June 5, 1753—Tuesday ]

"Brothers of the Six Nations," said Warraghiyagey in the great council house at Onondaga, "it grieves me sorely to find that the road here from New York has become so grown up with weeds for want of being used. And even more so, my eyes weep tears to see our fire almost burnt out at Onondaga. This is not a good thing and it is upon me to make this right. I am now sent here by your brother, the governor, to clear the road and rebuild the fire with such wood as will never burn out. This I do now with my presence and this belt of wampum from the governor."

He held the wampum high for all to see and then threw it down and the assemblage responded with a collective *"Haygagh cohweh heglohmekah!"*—We hear and we understand.

"My Brothers of the Six Nations, I have now renewed the fire, pulled from the path all the weeds that were growing there and swept clean all your rooms with a new white wing. I leave this white wing hanging near your fireplace, that you may make use of it for cleaning away all dust, dirt and such things as that which may have been brought in by strangers, who are no friends to you or us.

"My Brothers, I am sorry to find on my arrival among you that the fine shady tree which was planted by our forefathers for your ease and shelter, should now be leaning, being almost blown down by winds from the north. I shall attempt

233

to set it up straight again, so that it may continue to grow with strength and beauty as before.

"With these words I have done these things, my Brothers of the Six Nations. Your fire now burns brightly again at its old place and the tree of shelter and protection is set up straight and grows well. I must now insist that you pour water upon that fire kindled with bramble sticks at Oswegatchie, for though the black-robe called Piquet tells you that he works to bring you God, his words are lies and he works to bring you war and destruction. My ears have heard that the Onondaga have been going to him in groups of many and that the black-robe treats them well and gives them many presents. This is a sorrow in my heart. But even more, it is a sorrow to learn that the Frenchmen are building a strong fort on the Lake of the Erighs[4] and will soon build others until they have made a wall of themselves to the Ohio River. Can it be that it is with your request or consent that they do such ominous things? Can it be that it is with your encouragement that they have destroyed the great Pickawillany at Ohio? My heart hopes that my ears will hear you say this is not true and that you continue to hold the bright and unbroken and uncracked chain of covenant by one end, while our governor holds the other."

With the end of the speech, a fine feast was held, at which William Johnson ate with gusto while the chiefs conferred among themselves to form their answer. As he completed his eating, a young Onondaga maiden with unusually delicate features took his hand. Clad only in a napkin-sized breechcloth, she was not much more than a child—perhaps fourteen years old—but already she was in the body of a woman, with bare breasts which were firm and ample. The invitation was implicit and William Johnson was rarely one to refuse an invitation to anything, most especially to something of this sort. In moments they had disappeared together into one of the lodges.

It was a pleasant interlude which lasted until—on the second day after his talk—Warraghiyagey was summoned by Tiyanoga to the reconvening council. He was pleased to see that both Tiyanoga and Nichus were wearing the brillant scarlet British military jackets he had given them as a supposed testimonial of brotherly regard from the English. Nevertheless, he did not expect much, for what was there for the League to say except to deny French attachment, and so he was not disappointed at the reply.

234

"Brother Warraghiyagey, what can you wish to hear from us? Is it possible that you can expect the Six Nations to renew what never was a good alliance with the English, when the English themselves answer French armed might with nothing but hollow words? But no, this we *will* tell you: it is not with our consent that the French have committed any hostilities at Ohio.

"You white people confuse us with the way you move and the things you do and say. We do not know what you Christians—English and French together—intend. We are so hemmed in by both that we have hardly a hunting place left. In a little while, if we find a bear in a tree, there will immediately appear an owner of the land to claim the property and hinder us from killing it, by which we live. We are so perplexed between you both that we hardly know what to say or think."

### [ *September 6, 1753—Thursday* ]

In Captain Henri Marin, one of two Canadian brothers who were both officers of the French colony troops, the Marquis Duquesne had picked an able and energetic officer to command the force building the new forts in the western country. Marin had a special knack for leading men, an ability to inspire confidence and wholehearted response even under the most trying of conditions. Part of this was due to the fact that without exception he worked just as hard, or even harder, than those to whom he assigned specific tasks. His one great failing was his age; at sixty-three he just couldn't any longer push himself as he had in years past, even though he tried.

It was a bitter pill to him that he could no longer work with the vigor displayed by his brother Jacques, who was sixteen years his junior and a lieutenant. But Jacques still did not have—and there were some who claimed he never would have—the steadiness and dependability that Henri had always shown.

Jacques Marin was far more an example of the Canadian bush loper, the *coureur de bois,* and the best suited for leading Indians and fighting beside them. Where leading his own countrymen was concerned, Henri stood head and shoulders above him. Nevertheless, it was at times like this that Captain Henri Marin envied the seemingly boundless vigor of his brother.

Though this current expedition had started off well enough and his force of about fifteen hundred men had made the difficult trip from Montreal and Fort Frontenac to Presque Isle in record time and with no loss of men or equipment, it had sapped them all, especially Captain Marin.

It had been difficult in the extreme to carry the heavy boats and cumbersome baggage over the long, tough portages. The whole armed force was weary when they reached the Lake Erie site. It had not helped morale any, either, when they arrived and began to unload, to find that much of the baggage contained material that was worthless to this expedition—velvets, silks, musical instruments and a multitude of other costly items which were at best superfluous for the job at hand. It was another example of the prevailing corruption so well established in virtually all levels of the French colonial government. These boxes and bales, procured from Montreal merchants through the Canadian intendant, François Bigot, had all been labeled as goods essential here and had been obtained at enormous cost to the government. They would have to be sent back and the proper materials brought here and in the process, Marin knew, someone would be getting his pockets well filled.

The work of fort building had gone more slowly than Henri Marin had anticipated. Construction of Fort Presque Isle had taken what little energy remained in his men, yet he drove them on in their labors almost as hard as he drove himself.

His second-in-command, a sour individual of about thirty, was Captain Michel Jean Hughes Péan, who was here only through subterfuge committed against him. Devoid of any smattering of personal charm, Péan had, until this expedition, been making a small fortune in smuggling and other corrupt enterprises. But Péan had a wife who, if not especially beautiful, was extremely talented in bed. Numerous government officials had already discovered these talents and among them, as a recent acquisition, was Intendant Bigot, It was Bigot therefore, who successfully encouraged Governor Duquesne to name Péan as second-in-command of this expedition, thereby allowing Bigot to partake of this forbidden fruit with greater regularity as well as with greater safety.

Together, Captain Marin and Captain Péan pushed their men in the job of clearing a road southward to the headwaters of the Rivière aux Boeufs, but morale was rapidly disappearing—almost as rapidly as sickness was striking down the men. They set about quickly building the second post, located at the southern end of that road, and Marin was already calling it Fort Le Boeuf.[5] As soon as construction was well under way, the commander sent Captain Daniel Joncaire with a detachment of sixty men to the south to seize the English trading post of John Fraser at the Seneca village of Venango.

Fortunately for Fraser, he was not on hand at the time. Two of his men were, however, and now they had their answer to the puzzlement that had filled them because of the

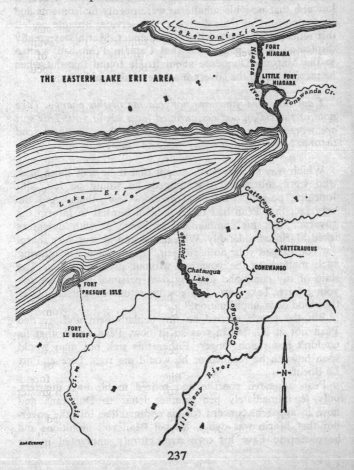

THE EASTERN LAKE ERIE AREA

Lake Ontario

Lake Erie

Niagara River

FORT NIAGARA

LITTLE FORT NIAGARA

Tonawanda Cr.

Cattaraugus Cr.

CATTERAUGUS

Portage

Chatauqua Lake

CONEWANGO

FORT PRESQUE ISLE

Conewango Cr.

FORT LE BOEUF

French Cr.

Allegheny River

-N-

A.W.ECKERT

disappearance of all the Indians from the village the night before. The pair were captured with ease and they, along with their goods, were taken back to Marin while Joncaire remained with a small garrison to hold the post and, if possible, to encourage the Senecas to return to the village in peace and friendship.

On the return of the soldiers with their prisoners, they found their commander, like so many of his men, badly stricken with dysentery. Unlike the men so afflicted, however, Marin continued to work as hard as ever and tried rather unsuccessfully to raise the morale which had dipped to such a low ebb that now his subalterns were openly malcontents and made no secret of their dislike of this service. Because he felt this reflected upon himself as commander, Marin was greatly displeased when he learned that Captain Péan had written to the Marquis Duquesne about it. He found this out when he received from the governor a letter which said, in part:

*I am surprised you have not told me of this change. Take note of the sullen and discouraged faces about you. This sort are worse than useless. Rid yourself of them at once; send them to Montreal, that I may make an example of them.*

Which was all very well, except that if he sent those back who were sullen and discouraged, he would be left with Joncaire, possibly Péan, and precious few others. And the very fact that Péan had taken it upon himself to inform the governor that his commander was very ill with dysentery irked Marin considerably. With his second he was very sharp.

"You exceed your authority, sir," he rumbled, "in relaying such matters to the governor without my permission. The state of my command and my own personal health are not your affairs. Take care, lest you be returned yourself under the cloud of insubordination!"

But the words carried no fire behind them and worried Péan not at all. Marin was so ill now, Péan knew, that he couldn't last much longer. Either this sick old man would soon have to be recalled or he would die right here at Fort Le Boeuf.

Péan appeared contrite and retired to his own quarters, only to immediately pen another letter to Duquesne and now, in apparent concern for his commander, told the governor that Marin was dying. Michel Péan was ambitious and he meant to have his own name firmly implanted in the governor's mind when it came to name a successor to his command. A commander of such posts could, with a little effort, rake off a tidy income with a little manipulation of orders and reports.

About this same time, far to the south at Logstown, two Seneca runners presented themselves breathlessly to Chief Monakaduto, known to the English as Chief Half King, and panted out the story of how the French soldiers had marched upon them and forced the entire village of Venango to flee; how they had watched from cover and seen two of their white brother Fraser's men captured and a French flag raised over the small post.

Monakaduto's face darkened with anger. "They will not stay long," he declared. "I will go there at once and tell them to leave and they will not dare to disobey me!"

[ *September 28, 1753—Friday* ]

Of all the English colonial governors, Robert Dinwiddie alone fully recognized the current fort-building activities of the French as the fantastic threat they really were. And when the Virginia Assembly continued to blandly disregard his entreaty that they set aside funds immediately for the building of English forts in the same area, he carried his argument directly to the King. The response from His Majesty George was gratifying:

*Your plan for the construction of forts, in particular a strong fort at the forks of the Ohio, is approved for the security and protection of our subjects and of the Indians in alliance with us. You are directed to procure funds from the Colonial Government that a sufficient number of cannon may be shipped for emplacement in the forts. Our will and pleasure is that you use your utmost endeavors to erect the said forts as soon as the nature of the service will admit. Our further will and pleasure is that you should bring forth with cause the whole or part of our militia of our Province of Virginia now under your government, to be drawn forth and armed as you may judge necessary for our service. In case any of the Indians not in alliance with us or dependent upon our Crown, or any Europeans under pretense of alliance with the said Indians, should presume to interrupt you in the execution of these our orders, you are first to represent our undoubted right and to require the peaceable departure of any such Europeans or Indians. But if they should still persist, our will and pleasure is that you should repel force by force. Since the Crown has received information that a number of Europeans not our subjects are appearing in a hostile manner in the area, you are instructed to inquire into the truth of the report. If you shall find that any number of persons shall presume to erect any fort or forts within the limits of our Province of Virginia, you are first to require of them peaceably to depart; and if, notwithstanding your admonitions, they do still endeavor to carry out any such unlawful and unjustifiable designs, we do hereby strictly charge you and command you to drive them off by force of arms, in execution of which, all our officers, civil and military, within the limits of your government, are to be aiding and assisting to the utmost of their abilities.*

It was precisely what Dinwiddie had hoped for. At once he issued an order convoking his assembly—the House of Burgesses—for the first day of November. He had no doubt that the French would not leave their new forts simply by his requesting them to do so, but he had to follow His Majesty's orders and make his official protest over encroachment and request that they withdraw.

Several people came to his mind as fair possibilities for the undoubtedly hazardous job of carrying this message to the French commander on the western frontier, whoever he might be. The traders William Trent and John Fraser could probably do the job, but Dinwiddie preferred someone a little closer to home. And perhaps, with judicious appointment, he could even gain some strong support.

One of the most influential members of the Virginia council, and a man whose friendship Dinwiddie had long been cultivating, was the Honorable William Fairfax. When only recently a family friend of the Fairfaxes—Major Lawrence Washington—died and left vacant the post of adjutant of the Virginia Militia, Dinwiddie had reorganized the militia into four districts. Lawrence Washington had a twenty-year-old half-brother who, though he had no formal education after his fourteenth year, was a favorite of Lord Fairfax. The young man had a sharp mind and so, even though he was without any form of military training, Dinwiddie had appointed him to the rank of major and made him adjutant of Virginia's Southern Military District, at the salary of one hundred pounds per year. He was a young man, eager to please, and Dinwiddie sent for him at once now, feeling sure he could be relied upon as well as the next man to get the protest message through to the French.

The young man in question was named George Washington.

[ *September 29, 1753—Saturday* ]

In spite of everything, Captain Michel Péan had to admire Captain Marin. The man had a spirit that just wouldn't give up. For days he had been flat on his back in his quarters, gasping his life away, groaning softly with the agonies brought on by a dysentery and other complications that his body could no longer fight. That he had remained alive this long was amazing to Péan, but that he should get out of bed, dress himself in his finest uniform to meet an ignorant savage and yet show neither in word nor action that he was ailing, was unbelievable.

The Seneca chief, Monakaduto, had arrived this morning with a dozen of his followers, demanding to speak to the white chief in charge here at Fort Le Boeuf. Péan had told him to wait and carried the message to Henri Marin, certain that the ailing commander would simply tell his second to deal with the Indian as he saw fit. But Péan had underestimated his superior.

From some hidden reserve, the commander found the strength to raise himself and don the uniform, complete to sword, boots and cocked hat. He staggered to the door of his quarters, straightened with an effort and then, by some miracle, opened it and walked out as if he were at the peak of health. Péan's eyes widened in astonishment, but he said nothing.

Monakaduto began his oratory by telling Marin that the French were unwanted here and that, in the name of the Six Nations, he was ordering the officer and his men to abandon Fraser's trading post, burn both Fort Le Boeuf and Fort Presque Isle and return at once to the French King's own territory. To all of this Captain Marin said nothing, his entire attitude one of such hauteur and contempt that soon Monakaduto was almost screaming his threats.

The Seneca chief was, if anything, slightly taller than Marin, yet Marin somehow conveyed the impression that he was looking down at the Indian as if he were no more important than some distasteful insect. And when at last he spoke, it was casually, but with smarting insult.

"Indian," he said, "I am troubled enough in this place with mosquitoes and flies. I do not need another pest here. Look around you. Yesterday the Miamis were fast friends of the English, but we ate their chief and today they bring us English scalps and ask for forgiveness. The Delawares and Shawnees come here and ask to carry our baggage for us, and all the other tribes of the Western lands rain on us their devotion. Yet you come here and dare to stand in our way and say that you present the Six Nations? *You lie!* You are a little man with big ideas. Go away from here before I flick you away as the horse flicks the fly with his tail. If you stay, I may have to spank you to teach you some respect."

The captain turned and left the room, shutting his own door behind him. And if Monakaduto had not been so filled with incoherent rage, he might have heard the thud as Captain Henri crumpled unconscious to the floor an instant after the door closed.

As soon as the angry Senecas were gone, Péan helped Marin back to bed. The commander had returned to a state of fuzzy consciousness and even now, though a deathly pallor drained his face and his teeth clenched against the pain grinding through him, he remained in command.

"Captain Péan, our orders call for the third fort to be constructed at Venango or some point lower down the Ohio.[6] I feel that Venango is as good a site as any. You are to see to this construction and, when it is completed, you will descend the river with the whole remaining force, impose terror on those tribes still wavering in allegiance to us and complete their conversion. See to it."

But Péan did not. With eight out of ten of the army suffering from dysentery, scurvy, fevers and lung diseases, the work would have to be done by reinforcements ... when and if they should arrive.

### [ *October 1, 1753—Monday* ]

The news of Captain Marin's illness was a great worry to the Marquis Duquesne. There were few officers of Henri Marin's leadership caliber that he could call upon to take the commander's place, should be become so severely incapacitated that he could no longer perform his duties. And then, by a fortunate happenstance, a veteran officer sent by Governor

Jonquière nearly two years ago to explore the west all the way to the Rocky Mountains returned to Montreal.

He was Captain Jacques Legardeur de Saint-Pierre and he was a tough, highly experienced officer with a flair for command, devotion to duty and an outspoken admiration for Duquesne.

He reported to the governor on his discoveries and said that he had stopped briefly on his return at Fort de Chartres on the Mississippi.

"It is, sir," he said, "nearly entirely rebuilt now. Instead of wood, native rock has been used and this fort is now undoubtedly the most impregnable establishment we have in the west. No more than a handful of men could hold it against almost any attacking force."

It was good news which would delight the colonial minister, but at the moment Duquesne's mind was too filled with worry over the situation at Fort Le Boeuf to appreciate it.

"Captain Saint-Pierre," he told the man, "you have my congratulations on your successful mission. Your full reports will be forwarded to France by the next mail. But now, although I realize you have only just returned from a strenuous duty and are deserving of a long rest, I am compelled to call upon you immediately for another position. As you have heard, we now have two new forts built—at Presque Isle and Le Boeuf—and others planned south of there. Captain Marin, a good man, is in command, but he has been taken seriously ill and must be replaced. His second-in-command, the Chevalier Péan, is a prodigy of talents, resources and zeal, but because of evidence recently brought to my attention about him regarding certain peculations that have been occurring, I do not wish him to assume command except on the most temporary basis. Instead, I wish you, as soon as you have made all your reports ready and put your things in order, to leave immediately to assume command from Captain Marin, or perhaps from Monsieur Péan, if such be the case."

Saint-Pierre was far from pleased with the commission, but he was far too good an officer to make this known to Duquesne. To voice objection would not negate the order and it would only cause the Marquis to lose some of his confidence in him.

And so, Saint-Pierre bowed in courtly fashion and thanked the governor as if this was exactly the plum he had been hoping for.

Captain Michel Jean Hughes Péan watched without expression or comment as two orderlies carried the long, blanket-wrapped figure outside. A box was being built at the carpenter shop for it and soon it would be buried beside the many others in the meadow behind the fort. Péan himself would officiate and most certainly all who could get out of their own beds would be required to attend the service.

For now, however, there was an important letter to write and he set about it in a rather nonchalant manner at Captain Marin's desk. Because he had written the letter many times mentally already, he found it not at all difficult to write in actuality:

> *October 12, 1753*
> *Fort Le Boeuf*

*Marquis Duquesne*
*Governor*
*Montreal*
*Excellency:*

*It has become my unfortunate province to inform you of the death, this date, of the commanding officer of this post, Captain Henri Marin, who, having suffered great pain from his affliction, failed. The entire garrison, itself suffering the extremities from this same and other maladies, is grief-stricken, as am I. But it is obvious that the duties must continue for the greater glory of France, and it is to this end that I now resolve myself. With your Excellency's permission, I have assumed command of this post and that of Fort Presqu' Isle and the small post at Venango. As I have been second-in-command of this army and close to all that has occurred here, have the esteem of the men, and the knowledge of what is expected of me and them, I assume you will be so gracious as to make this a permanent command for me. It is with regret as well, that I must inform you that your army is in very poor condition, being both physically and spiritually afflicted and wholly unable to continue with what we had hoped to accomplish before winter arrived, that season being near upon us now. We are in grave need of supplies and medicine and the services of a physician, as already we have buried twenty-three men and more are sure to follow. Every day more Indians come to camp near us and*

*swear to uphold us in our endeavor to insure this country
from the English. Two more English scalps have been
brought in by them and the word spreads among them that
our arm is greatly stronger than that of the English. Even
though Captain Marin and I held audience for the Seneca
sachem known as Half-king and sent him away shedding
tears of rage and mortification, yet our situation with the
Iroquois has improved and instead of being angered, they
have been awed and are fearful of our strength, wishing only
peace with us. Since we are thus established here with them,
it is my recommendation that this army be recalled for this
winter and returned to my command in the spring with
healthier men to continue the execution of your orders. The
Indians have assured me they will see to the forts in our
absence and, on our behalf and theirs, continue to discourage
any attempts on the parts of English traders, settlers or
soldiers, to enter this country. To this end I will garrison
each of the two posts with 150 of the most able men
remaining and start the rest, numbering 1,175 back to
Montreal about the first of December. I trust this action will
meet with your approval.*

*Capt. Péan
Commandant*

## [ November 1, 1753—Thursday ]

The Virginia House of Burgesses listened carefully and with
concern as Governor Robert Dinwiddie outlined to them the
peril imposed on the colonies in America in general, and
Virginia in particular, by the French forts being built on the
Allegheny and its tributaries and at Presque Isle on Lake
Erie. When he told them that, in accordance with the wishes
of the King, he had only yesterday dispatched young Major
George Washington to carry a strong message of protest to
the French commander at those forts, and a demand that
those posts be evacuated and the French soldiers leave that
country, the Burgesses nodded in approval.

Even when Dinwiddie read to them the order from His
Royal Majesty authorizing that funds be allocated for the
means to meet this danger, they were in agreement. But it
was at about this point that a stumbling block was encountered: a small debate centering about the fact that the
governor was charging a fee of one pistole—piece of gold—
for each patent of land issued by him. The amount, the

Burgesses readily agreed, was trifling, but it was the *principle* of the levy that they questioned.

As always, the aristocracy of Virginia were extremely suspicious of even the slightest of encroachments on what they considered their rights, either by the Crown or by representatives of the Crown. Not realizing that this molehill was rapidly growing to mountainlike proportions, Dinwiddie casually defended the fee.

It was like a glove in the Burgesses' face.

"Subjects cannot," they argued heatedly, "be deprived of the least part of their property without their consent. This is an unlawful tribute and we call upon you, Governor Dinwiddie, to confess it to be so!"

Dinwiddie, his own back up now, grew angry in turn. He retorted, "It is not unlawful! It is a just fee for a service rendered and I shall under no circumstances confess it to be illegal."

Without even realizing it was happening, the Assembly had just neatly maneuvered the governor into a box. Here was the governor, asking for money to be allocated for military uses, and at the same time trying to stand up against them. It was a perfect opportunity to bring him to terms and they reiterated their demand, adding that if Dinwiddie did not declare the pistole fee to be illegal and unfair and an invasion of individual rights, that no funds would be granted in the matter presently before them.

Flushed and angry, Dinwiddie continued his refusal and then berated the entire body for its uncaring blindness.

"In this action," he stormed, "you are not only disregarding the designs of the French, you are disputing the rights of the Crown. And in doing so, you are placing in grave jeopardy each and every one of these citizens whose rights you are so eager to defend."

But the Burgesses would no more give in than he, and the Assembly broke off in a stalemate.

[ *November 29, 1753—Thursday* ]

*Montreal*
*29 November 1753*

*Colonial Minister*
*Versailles*

246

*Excellency:*

Captain Jacques Legardeur de Saint-Pierre, accompanied by a small detachment of aides and orderlies, has departed this city for Fort Le Boeuf to assume command there as expressed to you in the previous communiqué. Although the news from that post had been unwelcome—the sadness at the loss of a good and able commander, of which there are far too few, and the irritation of the disobeyance of orders by Captain Péan in sending the majority of the army back to Montreal instead of downstream on the Ohio as Captain Marin's orders expressly outlined—yet events since then have shed a new light and I am forced to admit that Captain Péan's actions, while not circumspect, were the most appropriate. Only this morning that army returned here and I, in spite of the forewarning received, was shocked at their altered looks. I reviewed them and could not help being touched by the pitiable state to which fatigues and exposure had reduced them. Past all doubt, if these emaciated figures had gone down the Ohio as intended, the river would have been strewn with corpses, and the evil-disposed savages would not have failed to attack the survivors, seeing that they were but spectres.

Although Captain de Saint-Pierre was given leave largely to act on his own as conditions warranted and to proceed with the expedition if he deemed it advisable, which of course he will not now be able to do, I have nonetheless sent him an express that he is to conserve himself and his men and do naught but that which is necessary to maintain safety and what comfort may be gained. I further informed him that the planned expedition could easily recommence in the spring along similar lines to those originally planned and that a force sufficient to those who returned here, or as nearly so as possible, would be returned to him in the early part of the year.

Indian activity at and around other western posts had diminished, which is not surprising, inasmuch as this is the hunting and trapping season for the savages. However, a constant guard is maintained in case of disturbance and at every opportunity the various commandants have been encouraged to implement friendliness with them.

You will be glad to learn that the Indian situation on all fronts and with virtually all tribes is better now than it has been for many years previous. Our show of strength and determination has won for us many converts. Only the Iroquois, largely because of the peculiar influence over them held by Colonel Jeanson [*William Johnson*], continue to be mostly neutral. Many of their Onondagas and some of their Oneidas and Senecas are ours, but this is balanced by most of the Mohawks and portions of all the others attending to the English, while the whole League, fearful of a split within itself, prefers to remain officially neutral. They will not, they say, under any circumstance, allow themselves to be brought into a situation where they will be fighting amongst themselves, although such a situation could be most advantageous to us. It is toward this end that Abbé Piquet continues to endeavor with satisfactory results at Oswegatchie or, as we have come to call it, Fort Présentation. Captain Joncaire remains at the English fur post at Venango, while his brother, Chabert, circulates very widely among the Iroquois, and to good effect. It is very cold here with much snow. Even the Canadians remark on the unusual severity of the weather.

Duquesne

[ *December 2, 1753—Sunday* ]

Young Major George Washington had expected the overland journey through five hundred miles or more of wilderness to be difficult, but not this bad. As if it had been patiently waiting for the stripling officer to set out on his mission, the weather threw storm after storm at him and compounded the difficulties by dropping the temperatures to crackling sub-zero readings. Blizzards came and went, interspersed with frigid rains which quickly soaked clothing and made teeth chatter uncontrollably, followed by further drops in temperature which coated forest and field with a treacherous glaze of ice. It was one of the worst periods of bad weather in late autumn and early winter in anyone's memory.

The young officer's first stop was at Fredericksburg where he engaged his recently acquired fencing instructor, Jacob van Braam, as a French interpreter. Next, with two of his servants and van Braam riding beside him, Washington made stops at both Alexandria and Winchester for supplies and additional horses. They followed the Nemacolin Trail to the west and, on reaching Will's Creek on November 14, came to where the Ohio Company storehouse was located. A good number of men were camped here and from among them Washington enlisted the services of Christopher Gist as a

deliberately held back. The more the Frenchmen drank, the more expansively talkative they became.

And the more indiscreet.

"You have come," Joncaire said thickly, waving a finger roguishly at Washington, "with some idea to frighten us away, is that it? Ah, how strong an idea it would have to be, Monsieur! An' do you know, Majeur, why it is that even though you English have more men than we, it is we who will always be ahead?"

Washington shook his head, interested, and listened carefully as Joncaire continued with hardly a pause.

"Because, Majeur, while you have many more men, the English are simply too slow in the movements, too dilatory, to prevent whatever action the French wish to take. You may complain, *oui*, but about it you can do nothing. Even the *savages* realize this."

He indicated with his thumb Monakaduto and his three men who sat in the corner being poured drink after drink by one of Joncaire's lieutenants, while they listened with bleary pomposity to the uninhibited efforts of that officer to dispel the shame Captain Marin had heaped upon him, and to make them see how foolish they were to continue to support the English. Washington noted with some concern that the Indians—even Monakaduto himself—seemed to be in full agreement. But to try to remove them now from the French officer's influence would undoubtedly stop the tongue-wagging of Joncaire, which was becoming more indiscreet with each swallow. At Gist's covert motion toward the Indians, Washington merely shook his head slightly and continued to listen.

"Majeur, you have been born on the wrong side; the losing side." Joncaire laughed and was joined by his men. "An' do you know why? Because, Majeur, it is the absolute design of the French to take sole possession of the Ohio and, by God," he slammed his hand on the table, "we will do it! You come here with your little party and hope to frighten us, eh? Do you know that we have now one-hundred-fifty men at each fort, and they are only a winter guard? Ah, Majeur, ten, twenty, thirty times that many will come with the spring an' then we will see who has possession of La Belle Rivière!"

[ *December 14, 1753—Friday* ]

Captain Jacques Legardeur de Saint-Pierre had lived a life filled with surprises, so it took a great deal to cause him to lift his eyebrows. But those brows nearly disappeared into his

251

hairline when, just after sunset three days ago, the tall young man who was George Washington came riding out of the forest with the older and rougher frontiersman Christopher Gist beside him. Monakaduto and three other Indians rode behind them and a small cluster of white men with pack-horses brought up the rear.

At once Saint-Pierre sent one of his officers out to meet them and escort them to the fort. Within minutes the entire party, obviously very weary, their clothing soaked with a sodden snow and the hooves of their horses shod with great balls of accumulated mud, entered the gate and dismounted. From every door and window the faces of French soldiers stared at them with open-mouthed wonder.

Washington paid no attention to them, his eyes straight ahead, but he wondered if this was where he would lose Monakaduto and the other Indians. The lieutenant at Venango had been so convincing in his arguments that it was only with the strongest of counterarguments that Gist and Davison felt they had managed to keep them with the English party.

Though he appeared to be immersed in his own thoughts ever since he came within sight of the fort, Washington had not failed to note that over two hundred large canoes were pulled well up on the river bank nearby; enough for two or three thousand men and apparently only awaiting spring to be put into use.

The French officer sent to meet them expressed to Washington the compliments of the commandant and commiserated with the party on its weariness. With appropriate tact he suggested that they might wish to clean up, eat well and have a good night's rest before being presented to Captain Saint-Pierre. Unless, of course, the matter was so pressing it could not wait?

It was not that pressing and Washington, glad for the opportunity to rest and refresh, did not meet Saint-Pierre until the following morning. Even then there was little for him to say, other than the fact that he represented the Virginia governor and had come here with a message for the officer highest in command.

"I am the highest officer here," Saint-Pierre admitted, "but I would prefer that your message had been directed to the Marquis Duquesne. However, I will accept it."

Washington extracted a packet from an inside pocket of his coat, opened it and removed a folded paper which he then handed to Captain Saint-Pierre. The commandant took it with a slight bow. The letter, in Dinwiddie's own hand, did not mince words:

To the Commander of the Western
Forts of the French
Sir:

*As Governor of the Province of Virginia, it has come to me to my astonishment that French troops have built forts upon lands so notoriously known to be the property of the Crown of Great Britain. I must desire you to acquaint me by whose authority and instructions you have lately marched from Canada with an armed force, and invaded the King of Great Britain's territories. It becomes my duty to require your peaceable departure; and that you would forebear prosecuting a purpose so disruptive and interruptive of the harmony and good understanding which His Majesty is desirous to continue and cultivate with the Most Christian King. I persuade myself you will receive and entertain Major Washington with the candor and politeness natural to your nation; and it will give me the greatest satisfaction if you return him with an answer suitable to my wishes for a very long and lasting peace between us.*

         *Robert Dinwiddie*

George Washington had not expected an immediate answer from Saint-Pierre and he did not get one. The French commander, by way of excuse, told him that he preferred to await the arrival of another officer who was due to be here sometime the next day. Washington and his party were invited to make themselves comfortable until such time as an appropriate answer could be framed. Then Saint-Pierre and one of his officers retired to private quarters where they could go over Dinwiddie's letter minutely and at their leisure.

It turned out to be three days rather than one before Saint-Pierre summoned Washington. The major had made good use of the interval by memorizing the interior of the fort, its defenses and layout. Of these he wrote in detail in his journal. Nor was he unaware that the efforts that had been begun by Captain Joncaire at Venango to win his Indians over had been quite strongly continued here. Last evening Washington had spent considerable time summing up in his journal his impressions of this installation and its commander. Concerning Saint-Pierre he had written:

*He appeared to be extremely complaisant, though he was exerting every artifice to set our Indians at variance with us. I saw that every stratagem was practised to win the Half-King to their interest.*

Saint-Pierre's reply to Dinwiddie was quite brief and something of a disappointment to the young major. It said:

*It is not for me to set forth the Evidence and Reality of the Rights of the King [of France] and to contest the pretensions of the King of Great Britain there. I would have preferred to have Major Washington proceed to the main French headquarters in Montreal, but since his instructions are to go no farther than here, I will transmit your letter to the Marquis Duquesne, Governor of New France, for his orders. Meanwhile, I will remain at my post, according to the commands of my general . . .*
*Be assured, Sir, that I have made it my particular care to receive Mr. Washington with a distinction suitable to your dignity as well as his own quality and great merit . . .*

Because their horses were still so jaded from the long hard journey here, Washington requested—and received permission for his party to remain over another full day and take their leave on the morning of December 16.

The request was granted.

### [ December 31, 1753—Monday ]

Although by the route they traveled it was less than forty miles, it took Washington and his party five full days to once again reach Venango. The respite at Fort Le Boeuf had not helped the horses very much and they had begun playing out again by the end of the second day.

Captain Saint-Pierre had sent along a canoe escort to pace them on the yet unfrozen waters of the stream and to carry some supplies and messages to Joncaire. Gist had objected that it wasn't necessary for the commander to provide such an escort, fearing that some sort of treachery might be involved. But treachery, if it was planned, never materialized. On the third day the canoe hit a stretch of bad water and upset. The horsemen, inwardly delighted and without even a pause, merely noted the partially empty kegs of brandy and wine bobbing off downstream in the choppy waters and the half-frozen soldiers floundering chest-deep in the icy water as they surged toward shore. Whether or not these men made it back to their post was their own concern. Weary as the horsemen and their animals were, Gist rationalized, there was nothing they could do for them.

By the time they had reached Venango, and paused there to report the mishap to Joncaire, Washington was chafing at the delay being caused by their exhausted animals. He suggested to Gist that the two of them continue the journey afoot while the others followed at their leisure. At first Gist protested, doubting George Washington's ability to make any such journey on his own legs, but when Washington insisted, the frontiersman was quick to agree. His own horsemanship was sorely lacking in comparison to that of the young major, and now he would have a chance to see how the officer handled himself afoot. Even for himself, a highly experienced cross-country walker, Gist knew the trip would not be an easy one. For the major it would probably become torture, and the thought of it amused the frontiersman.

Monakaduto was even stronger in his objections. He felt that it was only the proper and respectful thing for Washington to continue back to Logstown with the party, there to report in person to the assembled chiefs awaiting their return. When Washington could see no good reason for doing so under the circumstances, Monakaduto became angry, called his men together and left without further word. Gist shook his head. This young fellow still had lots to learn about handling Indians and he might live to regret the insult he had just given the chief.

Washington put Jacob van Braam in charge of the horsemen and early the next morning he and Gist set off at a mile-eating pace toward the southeast. For the first couple of days Washington held up well, though Gist was a grueling pacemaker, but at last the strain began to tell on him and he was forced to ask the frontiersman to ease up. The weather continued as badly as before, with even colder temperatures and more snow. Their fires, when they could find dry wood to make them, shed little heat and even that was quickly gone in the bitterly cold air. At night each man had only a single blanket to curl up in and the cold would settle over them with such icy claws that further attempts to sleep were dangerous, lest that fatal drowsiness of a man freezing to death should creep over them.

They were now in country that Gist had never traveled

through, when they encountered a lone Indian warmly wrapped in furs and carrying a rifle. He told them he was from a village called Murdering Town, motioning vaguely toward the east to indicate its direction. When Gist told him they were heading for Will's Creek, the Indian nodded. He knew exactly where it was, he told them, but they were going in the wrong direction; he would guide them to it.

Gist was dubious but the two white men finally agreed and began following the native. After they had gone a mile or more, the clouds broke briefly and Gist suddenly swore and pointed at the sun. They were headed west. Washington looked around and saw that the Indian, now a dozen yards ahead of them, had his gun aimed in their direction.

"Look out, Gist!" he shouted, leaping to one side.

The frontiersman jumped too, just as the musket fired. Both men sprawled in the snow and then scrambled to hands and knees and stared at one another.

"Are you shot?" Washington asked quickly.

Gist shook his head. "No. Let's get him!"

The Indian was already racing fearfully away, but Gist ran him down within a few hundred yards and dragged him back to the major. The Indian declared that his gun had gone off accidentally and Gist, not believing him in the least, jerked his knife from its sheath to kill him.

"Don't!" said Washington, quickly grasping the big man's wrist. "He said it was an accident. Let him go."

"By damn, Major," the frontiersman said darkly, "that was no accident!"

Washington, however, gave him an odd look and Gist sighed, shook his head disgustedly and turned the man loose. It didn't take the native very long to disappear from sight in the direction they had come from.

In reply to the angry question Gist now put to him, Washington agreed that he was sure the Indian had shot at them purposely, but it was not to their advantage to kill him. Letting him go might change his mind about the English. Even if it didn't and he went back to his village to bring others back with him, they wouldn't necessarily hurry, thinking the pair would pretty much continue the pace they had been making and shortly make camp for the night. This they would not do.

Gist snorted, convinced that Washington was a fool and that they should have slit the Indian's throat. Now there was nothing to do but get away as fast as possible and hope that when the following Indians—and Gist was dead sure there would be some—did not catch up to their quarry in a reasonable distance, they would give up and go back home.

All night long they traveled as swiftly as they could go, and all the next day as well. It was toward evening when they reached the banks of the Allegheny not far above its junction with the Monongahela and now Gist groaned. Instead of the stream being well frozen, as they had expected the center was still open in a broad gray ribbon of water dotted with slabs of floating ice.

They made a camp and remained here for the night. In the morning the gray swath of water was narrower, but still there. It wouldn't be safe to stay here much longer so the pair moved downstream until they found a great jam-up of floating branches, logs and debris. From this they pulled enough buoyant wood free to build a raft of sorts, tying the wood together with long rawhide tugs from Gist's pack. It took them nearly all day to complete the makeshift affair and even then it was decidedly lacking. Hopefully, however, it would hold together until they could reach the ice of the other side.

They managed to get it into the water and get aboard themselves without getting too wet, but as they poled themselves along, moving downstream much faster than crossstream, a large mass of floating ice and driftwood bore down on them. Washington stuck his long pole far ahead and pushed it into the bottom in an effort to get leverage enough to move the rickety raft away. But the water pressure against the frail craft shoved it into the pole; jerking it severely in Washington's hands.

Gist was knocked off his feet but managed to stay on board. Washington was not so lucky. He was catapulted forward, lost his balance and with a sharp cry plunged into the frigid water and disappeared. In an instant he was back at the surface, gasping and sputtering, clawing frantically for the raft. His outstretched hand touched and gripped it, and in a moment Gist had him by the wrist and was pulling him out.

Both men had lost their poles in the process and now they floated helplessly with the current in the gathering darkness. And then, as their hopes were fading, an island loomed before them and Gist thrust his hands into the water and paddled with them with all the strength he possessed. Little by little the raft moved into a collision course. The pair were standing when it struck bottom a dozen feet from the island and they leaped off, landing in water ankle-deep. They floundered ashore while the raft spun off with the current and then, as Washington huddled shivering beneath Gist's dry blanket, the frontiersman scrounged about searching for dry wood and ignoring the growing numbness in his hands and feet.

He found enough to get a fire going with his flint-steel-and-tinder kit and all through the night he continued to hunt for more wood and fed it to the fire while the major's clothing and blanket, hanging limply from sticks stuck up around the blaze, steamed and dried somewhat. The temperature plummeted to far below zero and before dawn Gist's fingers and toes had become badly frostbitten. He was forced to toss one last armful of wood on the blaze, remove his own footwear and then sit near the fire himself while the agonizing pain of the thawing members coursed through him.[8]

When daylight returned, Washington got dressed and Gist redonned his footwear. Both men kept their blankets wrapped around them and studied their situation. On the east side of the island the river was frozen, but the ice did not appear to be very thick. From the ground close to the fire, Gist pried loose a boulder and heaved it out onto the slick surface. It struck with a thud and stuck with a quarter of its bulk in the hole it had punched. The ice was far too thin to attempt walking across.

Gist grunted and shook his head. There had to be a reason why the flowage on the east side of the island had frozen, while that on the west had not. He motioned to the major and led the way down the east shoreline of the island. They had not gone more than a quarter of a mile when they saw what had happened. A small tree being pushed along by the current had lodged between submerged rocks and gradually more driftwood and ice chunks had built up against it and froze it in place. Even the raft they had abandoned was there, tilted out of the frozen mass at a slight angle.

Tentatively, carefully, warning Washington to follow and step exactly where he stepped, Gist started across. Step by step, agonizing foot by foot, they moved across toward the other shore. Now and then the pile groaned with their weight or a piece of brittle wood snapped with the sound of a gun firing, but the pile held and neither man got even his feet wet in the passage.

When safely on the other shore, Washington stopped Gist and squeezed his shoulder. The frontiersman grinned wryly.

"Seems like if you don't give up, somehow there's always a way," he said. "Let's git movin'. That's the only thing now that's going to keep us from gittin' froze up ourselves."

Washington nodded. They began moving down the east shore of the Allegheny and after about half an hour Gist stopped short and pointed to a large misshapen willow tree, which looked to George Washington just about like any other willow tree they had been seeing along the river."

"Know where I'm at now, Major. This is where we leave the river."

Numbly, Washington followed him toward the southeast again and in an hour they were shuffling through the woods along an unbroken stretch of snow that could only be a path. And late in the afternoon, when for George Washington existence had become no more nor less than painfully lifting a foot, pushing it forward, setting it down again and repeating the process with the other foot, Gist suddenly grabbed him and shouted something. The major was so foggy he didn't understand and Gist shook him sharply and repeated himself.

"There it is, Major, by God! There it is! John Fraser's place."

Blearily, Washington's gaze followed Gist's pointing finger. And there it was, several hundred yeards ahead of them in a small clearing alongside the Monongahela—a lonely little windowless cabin not much more than ten or twelve feet square. Undisturbed snow had drifted deeply around it and a cherry plume of blue-white smoke rose lazily from the stone chimney. It was the relatively new cabin of John Fraser, trader, but for both of these men it was far more than that.

It was the most beautiful sight in the world.

### [ *February 28, 1754—Thursday* ]

With the intensity of a fire sweeping through dry grasses on a gusty day, young George Washington caught the imagination of the people and almost overnight he became a sensation. Everyone was talking about him, his exploits and the hardships he had encountered in his travels to and from the French stronghold in the west.

Not until January 6 had the major and the frontiersman finally reached the Will's Creek Station of the Ohio Company. Here, after only a brief rest, Washington had left Christopher Gist and continued on his way alone to Williamsburg to report to Governor Dinwiddie, arriving there on January 16. So taken was the Virginia governor with the young officer's details of what had occurred on his journey and, especially, with the detailed report Washington had written that he had the major's journal published and distributed. Copies found their way to all points in the Colonies, and either segments of it or the journal in its entirety were reprinted in many newspapers. Quite suddenly George Washington was an intrepid hero whose name was on the lips of everyone.

Nor was Washington slow to take advantage of his instant popularity. He applied at once to Richard Corbin of the Virginia council for promotion to the rank of lieutenant colonel. In his letter he said:

*I flatter myself, that, under a skillful commander, or man of sense (whom I most sincerely wish to serve under,) with my own application and diligent study of my duty, I shall be able to conduct my steps without censure, and, in time, render myself worthy of the promotion, that I shall be favored with now.*

Already Robert Dinwiddie had big plans for this determined young man. Acting under Washington's strong recommendation to this effect, he now gave the young major even more responsibility.

"I am," he told Washington, "giving you a new command. You are to go to Frederick city and take command of the fifty men of the militia of that county. I am also appointing the trader, William Trent, as your lieutenant, with the rank of captain. You are to send him to Augusta County to recruit fifty more. These men are to go at once to the site you have recommended at the forks of the Ohio to build a strong fort. I don't think it is necessary for me to tell you the urgency of this step and how essential it is that you permit no one to stand in your way in its execution.

"The remainder of the force," he continued, "is to assemble at Alexandria where it will be equipped. There, you are to train and discipline them in the best manner possible. Having all things in readiness there, you are to use all expedition in proceeding to the forks of the Ohio with the men under your command, and there you are to finish and complete in the best manner and as soon as you possibly can, the fort which I expect will already be begun by then by Captain Trent. You are to act on the defensive, but in case any attempts are made to obstruct the work or interrupt our settlements by any persons whatsoever, to make prisoners of, or kill and destroy them.

"For the rest," concluded Dinwiddie, "you are to conduct yourself as the circumstances of the service shall require and to act as you shall find best for the furtherance of His Majesty's service and the good of his dominion."

For a man who had never before had an active command, never drilled men nor himself been subjected to drill, this appointment was quite an accolade and George Washington resolved on the spot to make the most of it. He thanked the governor simply, yet sincerely, for his trust and left at once to begin preparations, while Dinwiddie himself began hastily writing a series of messages. The first of these went to the chiefs of the Catawbas, Cherokees and Chickasaws in the south. It said:

*Brothers, I hereby invite you, in fact, urge you to now blow away the clouds before your eyes and take up the hatchet against the French who, under pretence of embracing you, mean to squeeze you to death.*

Essentially the same letter was sent to the chiefs of the Delawares, Wyandots, Shawnees, Miamis, and to the Six Nations—the Mohawks, Oneidas, Tuscaroras, Onondagas, Cayugas and Senecas.

He followed this up with letters of equal urgency to the governors of Pennsylvania, the Carolinas, Maryland and New Jersey, telling them explicitly of the developing situation and the steps he had already taken, finishing off each letter with an entreaty that contingents of men be sent to arrive at the Will's Creek Station in March at the very latest, to help promote and protect this enterprise which was now being undertaken for the benefit of all the English colonies.

Aware that what the expedition needed most of all was sufficient funds, he once again summoned the House of Burgesses to meet on February 14, trusting that knowledge of the prevailing situation would encourage them to cooperate with him for the general welfare of Virginia and the rest of the colonies. And he ended his very busy day with a letter to Lord Fairfax, explaining what he had done:

261

*I have asked the Burgesses to convene again on the four-teenth instant of February. I hope they will lay a fund to qualify me to send four or five hundred men to the Ohio, which, with the assistance of our neighboring colonies, may make some figure.*

Matters moved swiftly after that, though not entirely to Dinwiddie's satisfaction. At the meeting of the Burgesses he begged them to clear their minds of petty jealousies and postpone less pressing questions to the exigency of the hour.

"Think!" he exhorted them passionately. "You see the infant torn from the unavailing struggles of the distracted mother, the daughters ravished before the eyes of their wretched parents, and then, with cruelty and insult, butchered and scalped. We must prevent this. We must vote funds enough to raise troops and clear the French from the area and safeguard British interests!"

For nine days the Assembly argued about it and then finally responded only partially in this direction. Still holding over the governor's head the club of the land-warrant fee of one gold pistole, they authorized ten thousand pounds in Virginia currency to defend the frontier. Not only was it much less than Dinwiddie hoped for, they tied up the amount by placing its expenditure in the hands of a committee of their own. The governor had no choice but to submit to their wishes. To his merchant friend, John Hanbury, Dinwiddie wrote immediately after the meeting:

*I am sorry to find them too much in a Republican way of thinking. I have had a great deal of trouble from the factious disputes and violent heats of a most impudent, troublesome party here in regard to that silly fee of a pistole. Surely every thinking man will make a distinction between a fee and a tax. Poor people. I pity their ignorance and narrow, ill-natured spirits. But, my friend, consider that I could by no means give up this fee without affronting the Board of Trade and the Council here who established it.*

Despite this, Dinwiddie continued to send out messages as fast as he could write them, seeking help from anyone who might be able to offer it. More emissaries were sent to the various Indian tribes with a request that they meet him in a council at Winchester, where he would provide them with gifts. He also sent circulars from the King to the neighboring governors, calling for supplies, and wrote them letter upon letter to rouse them to effort.

To the governors of New York and Massachusetts—George Clinton and William Shirley—he sent a plea that they make a feint at Montreal, to prevent the French from sending so large a force to the Ohio. And already the governors of Maryland, New Jersey, Pennsylvania and the Carolinas were behind him, but with somewhat the same problem Dinwiddie faced—opposition from their own assemblies. Just as with Dinwiddie, the governors of these colonies could get nothing except by agreeing to terms with which they simply would not or could not comply. And, since the land being invaded belonged to either Pennsylvania or Virginia—the ownership was still not clear—the other provincial assemblies had no mind to vote any money to defend them. Even Pennsylvania continued in its refusal to do anything. James Hamilton was hamstrung in his own efforts by the Quakers, who refused to vote any money for warfare, and by the German farmers, who were too tightfisted to vote money for anything except their own immediate needs.

Only one colony—North Carolina—heard the appeal with any real understanding and voted money enough at once to raise four hundred men to meet at the Will's Creek Station as Dinwiddie requested. They, along with his own meager force and two independent companies maintained by the King—one in New York and the other in South Carolina—constituted the might with which the Colonies prepared to oppose the French on the frontier.

The next order of business was finding a commander who would have the respect and obedience of these varied troops. Even Washington himself, busy in whipping his own small force into shape, realized that regulars would not like the idea of being led by an officer like himself who was sorely lacking in any kind of military experience. The forty-seven men he had sent under Trent to begin construction of a fort, and the others he was collecting at Alexandria, these were a different matter; they were volunteers who had enlisted with the full knowledge that they would be serving beneath him. But he was in perfect agreement with Dinwiddie that his role must be as second-in-command under a prominent military figure.

The officer selected for this command post was Colonel Joshua Fry. As he arrived at Alexandria to gather and mold into a reasonable force the three hundred men who were being called the Virginia Regiment, Washington left with half of them for the Will's Creek Station, which was to form the base of operations. From there, partially via the Nemacolin Trail, it was a hundred forty miles to the forks of the Ohio fort-building site. The prime concerns were that Captain Trent would be able to fortify himself there before the arrival of the French, and that Washington and Fry would be able to join him in time to secure the position. And no one had any illusions that during all this time the French would merely be sitting on their hands.

It was going to be quite a race.

### [ *March 7, 1754—Thursday* ]

For Governor Robert Dinwiddie life was a series of continuing problems. Word had just reached him that another massive French force, estimated to be anywhere from a thousand to four thousand men in size, had recently left Montreal for Fort Le Boeuf and points south. When they reached the forks of the Ohio there would be trouble beyond any doubt, and Dinwiddie knew who would get the worst end of it.

As if that wasn't bad enough, support from the other colonies had slackened instead of increasing and even North Carolina, which had authorized troops to help, was now demanding a high fee for that help. To top it off, he was having problems of temperament with George Washington. The young fool had been given the promotion to lieutenant colonel that he'd asked for and now, because the council had granted him only the pay of a militia officer of that rank, he was outraged and threatening to quit. He wanted the pay of a regular British officer of equal rank, which was double what he was getting.

Dinwiddie sighed and thanked Providence that Lord Fairfax had intervened and cooled off the young man by advising him to bide his time and prove himself so valuable in his position that his demands would be met without question. Though still rankled by what he considered a great injustice, Washington agreed.

Now Dinwiddie finished writing the notice he was planning to send to all major newspapers in the Colonies, hoping that this, if nothing else, would bring some favorable results:

## MEN! YOUNG AND OLD!

*For the protection of your very homes and lives and the lives
of your loved ones, I appeal to you to enlist in our cause,
which is the cause of all Englishmen in America. The French
prepare to strike us soon a crushing blow and we must be
able to defend ourselves, which we cannot do without more
men. As Governor of the Province of Virginia, I therefore
make this offer; to those who will enlist, I offer by Proclamation some 20,000 acres of good land in the Ohio Valley,
such land to be divided among the soldiers if and when the
area is secured. Enlist now to help your country and yourself!*

### [ April 12, 1754—Friday ]

It had come as a severe blow to the Marquis Duquesne that
Captain Jacques Legardeur de Saint-Pierre had to be replaced.

Of all times for a devastating fever to knock out one of his
most able commanders, this was the worst. With a philosoph-
ic shrug and a shake of his head, he searched about for a
replacement and settled upon his own aide-de-camp, Captain
Pierre de Contrecoeur. A much younger man than Saint-
Pierre and nowhere near as experienced and steady, he was
nonetheless a good man with the imagination and daring that
might serve him well if a real campaign against the English
should develop.

Contrecoeur had left Montreal at once with a large force
of regulars and Canadian militia—a total of eleven hundred
men—and arrived at Fort Presque Isle without difficulty.
From there the journey down the new road to Fort Le Boeuf
was quickly made and now a new fort was already under
construction at his orders. It was going up across the stream
from the Seneca village of Venango, adjacent to John
Fraser's old trading post which was still occupied by Captain
Daniel Joncaire. The new fort would be finished very soon
now.

Contrecoeur had already named it Fort Machault, after
the French financial wizard and statesman Jean Baptiste
Machault D'Arnouville. He was well pleased at the speed
with which it was taking shape. He stood now on the point
formed by French Creek and the Allegheny River and spoke
to his second-in-command, the Chevalier Le Mercier.

"Captain, get your men in readiness. I'll want about half

the total force here to embark for the great fork below us. At that place we are going to erect the strongest French installation in America. And with it, God willing, supported by this new fort and both Le Boeuf and Presque Isle, we're going to have such a hold on the interior of this land that there won't be anyone who will ever be able to take it away from us!"

But just about a hundred miles to the south at that very fork he mentioned, a new English fort, as yet unnamed, was rising; far more slowly than Fort Machault, to be sure, but with every bit as much determination.

### [ April 17, 1754—Wednesday ]

Pierre de Contrecoeur took the half-built English fortification at the forks of the Ohio as if it were a gift.

The fort wasn't much yet, but it was most assuredly a fortification of sorts. The only problems were its lack of men, lack of ammunition, lack of building tools, lack of skilled engineers, lack of medical supplies and lack of food. The food situation, in fact, had grown so critical lately that Captain William Trent had taken a small detachment and left the place to search for some to bring back. He would get it from the Ohio Company storehouse at the mouth of Red-stone Creek on the Monongahela River, if possible. If not there, then he would have to go all the way to Will's Creek Station, which was at least twice as far. He left Ensign Edward Ward in command, with orders to continue the construction as best they could. Unfortunately, forty-one hungry men don't work very well and little further progress was made in the fortifications before Captain Contrecoeur arrived with his force of five hundred soldiers.

Ward and his men saw them coming and stood quaking in their boots as they watched the bateaux and canoes land and disgorge their horde of soldiers. Within minutes half of the eighteen French cannon had been brought to bear on the English works. Ward then received a polite demand to either surrender or be blown to bits along with the fort.

He surrendered.

They were treated quite well and even allowed to leave—with orders never to return—and a half hour after the French appeared the remnant English force was trudging rapidly toward Will's Creek Station. Even before they had gotten out of sight, Contrecoeur's men were demolishing the pitiable unfinished fort and starting construction of their own on the same site; a much larger and considerably better fort which already Contrecoeur was calling Fort Duquesne, after the governor.

Unseen in the woods around them, a host of Iroquois, who had come at the suggestion of William Johnson to help the English, melted away and headed for their respective villages, thoroughly disgusted with the evidence of their own witnessing: that not a single gun had been raised by the defenders in protest. If it came to a choice now of what European power they would side with, there was little doubt that it would be with the French. Word of the bloodless capitulation flashed through the wilderness and the same thought was in every savage mind:

*The French are men; the English are worse than women!*

### [ May 22, 1754—Wednesday ]

Captain Contrecoeur looked appraisingly at the young man standing at attention before him. He was Ensign Coulon de Jumonville de Villiers, one of his brightest and most energetic young officers. Contrecoeur pursed his lips in thought and then nodded faintly. Jumonville would do admirably for the job he had in mind.

"Sit," he said, gesturing at a chair before his desk, and as soon as Jumonville had obeyed, he began his instructions. "Our spies, both Canadian and Indian, have been very active and have brought me many reports. The only problem is that I don't know how much to believe of what they tell me. The Indians will say whatever it suits them to say and you know as well as I that it is dangerous to place too much reliance in their reports. Some of them, I suspect, are still inclined to the English and if that is true, then their reports could be no more than sly attempts to maneuver us into difficult situations. The Canadians, on the other hand, though I respect their ability, enlarge and exaggerate to such an extent that it's almost impossible to determine what they've actually seen."

He paused to light his pipe, then continued, "As Nearly as I can determine now, the English commander Washington has moved to somewhere eastward of the Monongahela to the place the Indians call the Great Meadows, where he has been waiting for his senior officer, Colonel Fry, to join him. There is no indication, however, that Fry's army is even on the move. Certainly it is nowhere near. But we do not know for certain how strong this Washington is, how many men he has, whether or not he has artillery, and so forth. I do not really believe his force is very strong and, if not, we may be able to destroy them quickly. That is where you come in."

He handed Jumonville a folded dispatch which, at Contrecoeur's nod, the ensign opened and read. Then the commander continued:

"As you can see, it is a summons directed to any English you may chance to encounter. They are called upon to withdraw from this dominion of France or be set upon by force of arms. You are to carry this document with you, *but you are not to show it unless you are seen and it becomes necessary*. Ostensibly, you are leading a party traveling under a flag of truce simply to deliver this message. In point of fact, you will be on a mission to spy on Washington's force. You will have with you another officer, three cadets, a volunteer, an interpreter and twenty-eight soldiers.

"As soon as you have discovered to your satisfaction what his strength is, without yourself being detected, dispatch two of your men back to me with the information. If the situation warrants it, which you will yourself be able to see, I will then come at full speed with a force to destroy them—hopefully by taking them in complete surprise and wiping them out to the last man."

Ensign Jumonville grinned and his eyes danced with excitement. It was just the kind of assignment he had dreamed of; one that could win him considerable honors, perhaps even a promotion.

## [ *May 27, 1754—Monday* ]

Monakaduto, Seneca chief, had found the tracks of two white men where there should have been no tracks, and, both wary and puzzled, he began following them. He kept himself low and paused frequently to study the terrain far ahead, keenly aware that it was only too easy for a tracking man to fall into an ambush set by the one he follows.

From these tracks alone he was able to deduce a surprising amount of information: that one of the men limped, placing more weight on his right foot than on his left; that at least one of them carried a rifle, the butt of the weapon having made a slight impression in the damp earth where the two had stopped; that the pair did not want to be seen by anyone, as evidenced by their taking advantage of every bit of cover and pausing to shuffle about a bit before leaving cover to cross—very quickly—an open spot; that they were Frenchmen, since the tracks left behind were those of boots, not moccasins, and the camp of the English soldiers was being covertly circled.

For several hours he had followed them and at last, in a rocky, secluded hollow of the forest he found them. The pair had joined a body of thirty-four men—French soldiers and Canadians—in their well-concealed camp.[9] They seemed to be in some kind of conference and even as he watched them closely from hiding, Monakaduto saw two of the men shoulder their small packs, pick up their rifles and strike out to the northwest in the direction of Fort Duquesne.

As silently as he had come, and with none aware that he had even been there, Monakaduto withdrew and returned at once to his own camp several miles from that of George Washington's. By the time he had entered his large tent, he had decided what to do. He had not completely forgiven the young officer for having left him at Venango last winter. It had been insulting for the young man to strike out overland for Williamsburg rather than stop off with him at Logstown to meet with the Indians awaiting him there. He could almost hate Washington for that, but his hatred for the French was much stronger. He had by no means forgotten, nor would he ever forgive, the gross humiliation he had suffered at the hands of Captain Henri Marin at Fort Le Boeuf. It made no difference that Marin was now dead. The insult was from the French; his hatred was for the French.

At once he had dispatched a runner to carry to Washington the news of the camp and the offer of his own services to lead Washington to it, if that was his desire. It was obvious that he expected the officer to come with his whole force immediately to attack the intruders.

Washington *had* come, but not with all his men.

Fearing the information might be only a stratagem to surprise his camp, the young commander had handpicked forty men to go with him and left the remainder of his force with readied arms and doubled sentries. It was late when they set out—about 10 P.M.—and the overcast night extremely dark. The path to Monakaduto's camp was very narrow and numerous times they lost it and stumbled around in the dark, falling over one another and talking in excited whispers until they found it again. At one point seven of the men somehow got separated from the main party and Washington was forced to leave them behind. But at last, just at sunrise, the lieutenant colonel and thirty-three of his men reached Monakaduto's camp.

They held a brief council in the chief's tent and Washington was so genuinely pleased at seeing Monakaduto again that the chief's anger at the young man was washed away and soon his own face was wreathed in a warm smile. He agreed to bring a couple of his own warriors and lead Washington to the French encampment. They set out in single file without delay.

When they were about halfway there, a heavy rainstorm came up and so badly soaked them that now Washington was afraid their weapons would not fire and passed the word down the line behind him to attach bayonets. The storm dwindled to a mere light rain just as they approached the place where Monakaduto said the Frenchmen were. The English force, at a signal from Washington, spread out stealthily in a semicircle and began a cautious advance on the enemy.

They were still there, mostly huddled miserably beneath small rocky outcroppings in a vain effort to keep themselves dry. They had no inkling of their danger. At a prearranged signal, Washington's men burst from cover, pausing only momentarily to aim and fire—during which no more than a quarter of the guns actually discharged.

Taken so completely by surprise, the French return fire was extremely sporadic, their own guns almost worthless because of dampness. Washington and his men plunged into action and for fifteen minutes the scene was one of wild confusion. Monakaduto became something of a demon, racing about with his tomahawk upraised and screaming inarticulately. It was he who was the first to reach Ensign Jumonville, and he swung his tomahawk in a tight and vicious sidearm sweep. The weapon caught the French officer just over the right ear and punched a jagged hole halfway through his head, killing him.

As swiftly as it had begun, the fight was over, the Frenchmen still alive throwing down their weapons and pleading for mercy. Nine of the French had been killed and twenty-one were captured, one of whom was seriously wounded. Only one man—a Canadian who sprinted off into the woods at the first onslaught—had escaped.

The English soldiers watched in approval as Monakaduto

and his men scalped the dead. The Seneca chief shook the blood free of Jumonville's scalp and handed it to the lieutenant colonel, signifying that he had forgiven Washington completely for last winter's incident. The officer accepted it graciously and then complimented Monakaduto and his braves for their efforts. In particular he thanked Monakaduto profusely for locating the French camp and leading him and his men here.

"You and your people," he told the Seneca leader, "are always welcome in our camp, and we will help you in whatever way we can. This scalp which you have given to me I now give back into your care and ask that it be carried to the Delawares who, I am told, have begun to cling to the French. Tell them that this will soon be the fate of all Frenchmen in this territory."

Monakaduto accepted the scalp and said he would do so. Then Washington ordered the wrists of the prisoners to be bound behind them and a quick march be made back to their own camp at the Great Meadows.

But even though his men were jubilant with their victory, Washington was in a subdued mood. The thought was heavy on his mind that two men from the French camp had been seen by Monakaduto to set off toward Fort Duquesne, and another had escaped during the fight. He had no doubt that there would soon be other encounters with the French and no one knew better than he just how weak the English forces really were. If those two French couriers had carried back to the commandant at Fort Duquesne intelligence on how weak his force was, then there could be no doubt about it—they were in deadly jeopardy.[10]

[ *May 30, 1754—Thursday* ]

William Johnson still exercised much power among the Indians. His dealings with them over the years seemed to have sharpened rather than dulled his business acuity and his fortunes had grown to staggering proportions. Into his possession came vast tracts of undeveloped land, farm property, servants, storehouses bulging with furs, all sorts of luxuries and a considerable amount of actual money. But despite his influence and affluence, New York leaders continued to shun him: he was, to their way of thinking, an uncouth ruffian, an arrogant upstart, a domineering and flamboyant individual who singlehandedly could accomplish

271

what all the numerous Indian agents in New York and elsewhere could not, and the government had no intention of turning to him for help unless it became absolutely essential.

Pennsylvania, which also had no great love for William, nevertheless reluctantly conceded that he had quite a way with the Indians and might even be better than their own highly esteemed Indian agent, Conrad Weiser. But there was fear in certain quarters at Philadelphia that Weiser might suddenly die or get killed or become incapacitated and leave the colony without the services of a good agent. It was with this in mind that they employed a twenty-three-year-old man of more than ordinary intelligence who was presently at loose ends in Philadelphia. His name was Daniel Claus and he had been born in Württemberg, Germany. He was penniless, having entrusted his small inheritance to a smooth-talking minister's son who promptly vanished, and so he accepted with alacrity Pennsylvania's offered commission to go to the Mohawk Valley to learn from William Johnson the speech and the ways of the Indians.

William liked the young man and took him under his wing, helped him in every way possible and gave him a course in Indian lore such as no other person, Indian or white, could possibly have given him. But when Claus wrote back to the Pennsylvania authorities of his progress, they were incensed with what he had to say; they had sent him to learn of the Indians and his reports did hardly anything more than sing the praises of one William Johnson. As Claus told them in one of these reports:

*All the Six Nations carry their belts and news to his house and confide in him information of the greatest importance which one would normally expect them to keep only among themselves, for in the hands of some white men, this information could cause the Iroquois great harm. But they trust Johnson above all others, considering him a chief of the Mohawks, nor will they see or hear of the fourteen Commissioners of Indians Affairs which New York his assigned to deal with them. Johnson gives of himself and his fortune to them freely, without anticipation or demand of remuneration. He suffers, to my surprise, a vast deal of trouble and charges, when the Commissioners sit quietly at home and mind not to send any messages at all to them. For this they admire and respect him and are free in all their confidences to him. Above all, they are strongly loyal to him. I dare say,*

*if Colonel Johnson should neglect or take no notice of them,*
*they would be already in the French interest. I myself have*
*gone to live with Johnson, who introduces me to all affairs*
*necessary.*

The outraged Pennsylvanians thereupon wrote William Johnson a curt letter, virtually accusing him of kidnapping their protégé whom they were, in effect, girding to oppose William as champion of Indian Affairs in America. Johnson merely smiled and, to prevent trouble for his new young friend, had him move out of Mount Johnson and take up residence at Canajoharie with Tiyanoga, where he was just about as much in William's control as in his house. And Claus naïvely continued to relay messages of praise for William to his Pennsylvania superiors.

But for William himself, matters had suddenly taken a downward swing. While he had never completely regained the full friendship and confidence of Governor George Clinton, which had been lost when he resigned, there was nevertheless something of a working arrangement between them. Clinton had realized just how important William was on the frontier and he continued, in little ways, to aid him from his lofty position.

Now, without warning, Clinton had suddenly been recalled to England and a high-strung individual named Sir Danvers Osborn had been appointed to the New York gubernatorial seat. Osborn, however, had deep-seated problems of his own. When to these were added the complex disorders of the governorship of New York, it was more than he could bear and he quietly committed suicide. His lieutenant governor thereupon became acting governor, and for Johnson this was the greatest blow of all, because the new governor was none other than Johnson's and Clinton's adversary of many years, James Delancey.

### [ *June 27, 1754—Thursday* ]

The Indians came from all directions to Fort Duquesne. It was no longer difficult for them to see where the greatest strength of men, arms and ammunition lay. George Washington may have pulled off a coup against Jumonville, but that was merely a skirmish. The fact most evident to the Indians was this: the French had marched into the unfinished English fort at this location and taken it over without firing a shot, as if it had belonged to them, and sent the English garrison packing with its tail between its legs. Against only several hundred English right this moment settling themselves into a patently indefensible position for a stand, there were five times that many French soldiers, better armed, better trained, better supplied and far more confident of success.

The Indians had no doubt where the eventual victory must lie.

Never before had the forks of the Ohio seen such a concentration of Indians representing so many tribes. Here were the fierce Abnakis and Algonkins of St. Francis on the St. Lawrence River below Montreal, and here too were the Algonkins and Hurons, Nipissings and Abnakis and even a fair number of Iroquois who had become a part of Abbé Piquet's flock at Fort Présentation at the mouth of the Oswegatchie River. From the upper Great Lakes had come the Ottawas and Potawatomies, the Chippewas and the Mississaugi Chippewas and more Hurons. And from the Ohio country had come additional Potawatomies and Wyandots, along with Shawnees and Delawares and some of the Miamis.

A band of these Delawares, showing the Fort Duquesne commandant, Captain Pierre de Contrecoeur, the scalp of Jumonville which had been given to them, pledged their allegiance to the French instead. Contrecoeur thereupon sent them to Washington's encampment, to approach it in the guise of friendship and learn what they could of it, then return here with news of its strengths and weaknesses, and they did so. The word they brought back set the assembled Indians into a state of great excitement. The young English commander, they reported, had dug a shallow, extremely poor earthwork in the midst of a prairie known as Great Meadows; an exposed position well within range of rifle fire from the surrounding forest. And for Indian allies, he had only the Seneca leaders, Monakaduto and Queen Alequippa, with a total of perhaps thirty or forty warriors.

Contrecoeur was supremely confident that his own army could overrun Washington without difficulty, yet he was wise enough to know that if the assembled Indians were permitted to take part in the forthcoming engagement, the word would spread all across the continent and even greater numbers of Indians would ally themselves to France—perhaps even those most important holdouts of all, the Iroquois League tribes.

It was with dismay that Contrecoeur had learned of the

fate of Jumonville and his party, and he had sent runners at once with word of this to the Marquis Duquesne in Montreal. The French governor had immediately dispatched reinforcements under Captain Coulon de Villiers and so rapidly did that officer push his men that in just fourteen days they had arrived at Fort Duquesne. There was good reason for the speed he displayed: Jumonville had been his brother.

Villiers reported to Captain Contrecoeur and found that a detachment of half-a-thousand French soldiers was all set to leave the fort the next morning under Chevalier Le Mercier to attack Washington's ill-constructed fortifications, but because of his seniority of rank and his relationship to the dead Jumonville, the command of the expedition was, at his request, transferred to him. The march was temporarily delayed and a larger assault force gathered. Villiers, Le Mercier and Longueuil retired with Contrecoeur to his quarters and there drew up on paper their plans for the campaign. The document said, in part:

*It is fitting to march against the English with the greatest possible number of French and savages, to avenge ourselves and chastise them for having violated the most sacred laws of civilized nations; that though their conduct justifies us in disregarding the existing treaty of peace, yet, after thoroughly punishing them, and compelling them to withdraw from the domain of the King of France, they shall be told that, in pursuance of his royal orders, the French King looked upon them as friends. But it is further agreed among us in this conference of war that shall the English have already withdrawn themselves to their own side of the mountains, they should be followed to their settlements to destroy them and treat them as enemies, till that nation should give ample satisfaction and completely change its conduct.*

Now all that remained was to encourage as many as possible of the Indians encamped around Fort Duquesne to join in the campaign, and to this end Contrecoeur called an immediate council with all the chiefs, subchiefs and a great many of the warriors. His long face was appropriately sad and determined as he spoke to them.

"My Brothers, in my heart there is a great gladness that you have at last thrown off the shackles with which the English have tried to bind you, and that you have now realized that your future is tied to the French, who are your

275

brothers and your protectors. From across the sea your great father, the King of France, and all his country looks upon you with warmth and high praise. Already he has sent you many presents, honoring you for your faith and fidelity, and there will be more presents to come and an even greater harmony will rise between us until for all time to come our races will be as one."

The assembled Indians nodded and murmured among themselves as he paused, but then became silent again as the Fort Duquesne commandant held up a war belt of deep purple color. It was so long that though he held it high above his head, yet both ends trailed to the floor. It was an inspiring piece of work and they listened carefully now to what Contrecoeur had further to say.

"My Brothers, all of you know by now that the English have murdered my children. My heart is sick. Tomorrow I shall send my French soldiers to take revenge. And now, men of Sault Sainte Louis, men of the Lake of Two Mountains, men of La Présentation, men of the far West—I invite you all by this belt of wampum to join your French father and help him crush the assassins." From under his coat he removed a bright new tomahawk with his free hand and stepped to one side where he placed it and the war belt atop two barrels. "Take this hatchet," he continued, "and with it, two barrels of wine for a feast."

The chiefs unanimously indicated that the belt, tomahawk and wine were accepted and, with them, the agreement to go with the French into battle.

Pleased, Pierre de Contrecoeur smiled briefly and then turned to the Delawares who, of all the Indians assembled here, were most being courted by the English traders in an effort to gain their allegiance. From an aide, the commandant took four more belts similar in color to the first but each of them considerably smaller.

"By these four strings of wampum," he told them, "I invite you, if you are true children of *Onontio*,[11] to follow the example of your brethren."

Although at first they hesitated, the Delawares finally nodded and accepted from Contrecoeur all the belts and another new tomahawk.

The council broke up then and the Indians retired to their camps to spend the rest of the day mixing war paint, making moccasins for the march and seeing to their weapons. And Contrecoeur was elated with his success as he returned to his quarters. The twenty-two-year-old English commander would soon learn that he had made a grave blunder when he destroyed the Jumonville party.

## [ June 2, 1754—Tuesday ]

Lieutenant Colonel George Washington's inexperience in military tactics had become increasingly clear in the days following the victory over Jumonville. His first hope had been that the triumph would have impressed the Indians to such extent that warriors would flock to his camp in large numbers to become part of his force, but what followed was a disappointment.

Chief Monakaduto, it was true, showed up with his thirty warriors and promised to stand beside the young English commander, and even the Seneca squaw-chief known as Queen Alequippa came with her small following and vowed allegiance with him, but they were pitiful returns for such a signal victory. Including the families they brought with them, the Indians numbered only one hundred fifty. Further, it meant that Washington, despite his own meager supplies, must now feed an additional hundred fifty people for the dubious advantage of having about forty warriors added to his force. No one knew better than Washington himself that now he was in trouble. With a hundred fifty inexperienced soldiers and this handful of Indians, he was facing a French force which numbered, at Fort Duquesne alone, over fourteen hundred soldiers and possibly seven hundred Indians.

The fortification built on the Great Meadows was a poor effort. It was completed in three days and yielded little real protection, but this did not keep Washington from confidently reporting that it could easily withstand the attack of an army of five hundred. He was just whistling in the dark.

His one great hope now was that Colonel Joshua Fry would soon arrive from Will's Creek with the remainder of the Virginia Regiment. Immediately after the attack on Jumonville's force, he had put the prisoners under strong guard and sent dispatches to Fry with urgent requests that he come soon, never doubting that he would, since Will's Creek was only fifty-two miles away. But Joshua Fry had been thrown from his horse and suffered very serious internal injuries and his army was stalled in their camp at the Ohio Company's trading post stronghold.

Then, on May 29, Fry had died of his injuries and this

meant that George Washington—even though he did not yet know it—was commander of the whole army. Christopher Gist gave the commander of the regulars, Captain Mackay, instructions to follow him and set out at once to join Washington and tell him this news. Mackay, justifiably irked that he must now be subordinate to a commander who was only twenty-two and without military experience, moved his men almost leisurely toward the Great Meadows.

Gist reached Washington with the news on June 3 and Captain Mackay's detachment arrived two days later, along with an independent company from South Carolina. But the presence of Mackay and his regulars was not quite the blessing Washington had anticipated. Almost at once the friction grew between captain and commander.

Mackay, whose commission had come from the King, held little respect for the commission bestowed on George Washington by Virginia. That Washington's rank was two grades over his own meant nothing to him, nor would it have even if Washington had been a general. Mackay considered himself above any officer commissioned by colonial proclamation. Even though a degree of military courtesy was observed between them, Mackay was extremely reluctant to take orders from the lieutenant colonel of volunteers. In addition, his men would do no work except for an additional shilling per day for each man—a sum which Washington would not, *could not,* give. Not only were funds insufficient to permit it, but to do so would have bred severe discontent among the Virginians, who were required to work for nothing except their daily wage of eightpence. With the presence of these drones of the regular army demoralizing his volunteers, Washington did the only sensible thing; he separated them. He ordered Mackay to remain at the Great Meadows with his men and the French prisoners and then set out with his own force to transform the Nemacolin Trail, which was only a blazed path here, into a good wagon road from the Great Meadows to Gist's settlement, then on to the Ohio Company's Redstone storehouse where Redstone Creek joined the Monongahela.

They arrived at Gist's on June 8, greatly weary and with no less than twenty men rendered ineffective due to illness. To have moved on to Gist's had not been wise, but to have pressed on even farther to the Redstone storehouse was simply foolhardy, yet that was precisely what Washington ordered. They reached that place on June 12, their stores of lead and powder nearly depleted and with their remaining food sufficient for only another two days.

Almost at once had come word from Monakaduto's scouts and some French deserters that strong reinforcements were expected momentarily at Fort Duquesne and soon a force would be marching from there to attack Washington. The young commander now ordered his men to turn right around and retreat to Gist's, and there he ordered an entrenchment built encircling the little cabin and a storage shed which were the only structures of the so-called settlement. Only a limited number of men would be able to fire through the loopholed logs of the cabin and shed, so the remainder would have to make use of the entrenchment.

As they worked feverishly, a band of forty Delaware warriors arrived on the pretext of consulting with Washington, but the talks amounted to nothing and after several days the Delawares departed without notice in the middle of the night. There was no doubt in Washington's mind that they had been spies for the French and immediately he sent a runner to Mackay with orders for the rest of the army to join him with the exception of a small garrison to be left at the Great Meadows to guard the French prisoners.

Mackay arrived on June 28 at just about the same time one of Monakaduto's men galloped in, bringing word of a huge French and Indian force that had begun to move at dawn toward this place. Washington called a council of war among his officers and they all listened dispiritedly while Captain Mackay pointed out in clipped terms that to attempt to make a stand here was little short of insanity, since the site was overlooked by neighboring heights from which they could be fired upon in a most devastating manner.

With the weight of military logic against him, Washington agreed that it might be better to turn back and make their stand at the Great Meadows where the French would have to cross open ground to get at them. Better yet, they might even fall back all the way to the Will's Creek station.

Once again the army was set into weary motion, and as one tired sergeant of the Virginia Regiment put it, "I reckon if them Frenchies do find us, they ain't gonna have nuthin' but movin' targets, seein' as how we ain't quit movin' since we got in this here army!"

Now, however, their few horses were so weakened from heavy use and insufficient grain that the Virginians had to carry most of their baggage on their backs and drag their nine swivels by hand over the rough and rocky trail. Even in this, Mackay's regulars refused to give any help.

By the time the army reached the Great Meadows again—yesterday forenoon—the volunteers were so utterly sapped that they could not continue. Whether this was the right place or not, there was no other choice but to stand and make their fight. It was with hardly any reaction that Washington read the dispatch awaiting him from Dinwiddie with the news that he had now been promoted to full colonel. With fatigue hanging over all of them here like a great wet shroud, he set his men about the work of improving these fortifications. It was with a touch of grim humor that he gave the place now the most appropriate name he could think of: Fort Necessity.

### [July 4, 1754—Thursday]

Coulon de Villiers's force was an impressive one as it left Fort Duquesne on June 29 and began its journey up the Monongahela River. Over a hundred canoes there were, each carrying ten men or more, plus considerable equipment and artillery. There were seven hundred soldiers and just over three hundred fifty Indians representing nine different tribes, their faces painted with blacks and browns and whites in savage designs.

All day they paddled upstream and finally made camp for the night on a broad bank of the Monongahela's west shore not very far below Redstone Creek where, in the morning, they expected to engage the English. Here, as most of the Indians watched curiously, the Jesuit priest who was chaplain of the expedition said a solemn Sunday Mass for the soldiers.

After the service was completed, the guards posted and the men remaining had eaten and were settling down for the night, Captain Villiers called all the chiefs together for a council. Though he knew precisely how he intended to conduct the campaign, he knew as well that it would please the chiefs and bind them and their warriors more firmly to him if he were to ask their advice and, where practicable and amenable to his own plans, follow it.

The chiefs were pleased indeed and the council continued far into the night, with Villiers gravely noting everything said and every idea proposed. Spies had now brought in word that the Redstone storehouse was abandoned and in the morning the whole flotilla was on the move again before the sun had risen. They quickly reached the Ohio Company's storehouse and beached their canoes well up from the water. Villiers posted a sergeant's guard to protect the boats and immediately ordered the pursuit march begun on Washington's very evident trail.

The going was no easier for them than it had been for Washington and, when the first halt was called only a few miles from Redstone, the chaplain was so fatigued he declared he could not go farther and would return to the storehouse to wait there. Before leaving, however, he held another service for the entire body of men and absolved them of all their sins.

The march continued while scouts came and went with regularity in front of the army. On the first day of July they had reached Gist's settlement and, finding it abandoned, bivouacked there. Only the officers benefitted from the comfort of the quarters here. The remainder of the army and the Indians were out of doors and spent a miserable night engaged in the impossible task of trying to stay warm and dry through a droning, persistent rain which began just before midnight and did not cease until daybreak.

They munched cold rations without pleasure in the light of dawn and then took up the march again, only to have the downpour begin anew before they had traveled more than a mile. They passed through the gorge of Laurel Hill and Villiers's scouts came in to report excitedly that the English were holding fast in the Great Meadows, only four miles ahead.

Here the French force paused and, while his men rested, Coulon de Villiers was guided by some Indians to the spot where his brother had been killed. His features were cold and grim as he stared through the rain at the bloated and scalpless remains of the bodies, including that of Jumonville de Villiers. To have heard of the deaths and scalpings had been bad enough, but to actually see the desecrated remains made him sick and he wished that he had not come. He had no tools with which to bury them in the rocky soil, so he merely said a brief prayer for the departed souls in general and his brother in particular and then returned through the continuing drizzle to his camp.

And then yesterday, when the dismal gray daylight filtered through the forest, the attack march was begun. Throughout the early morning hours he had been receiving continuous reports from his scouts. His battle plans had been relayed to his officers and now the whole expedition was reaching its climax.

At Fort Necessity, Washington and his men continued to strengthen their position as best they could. It was largely a futile effort. No attention was paid to Monakaduto's advice that they make their stand on a hilltop, not here. In fact, so disgusted by such ridiculous defenses had the Indians become who were attached to them, that Monakaduto and the squaw-chief, Alequippa, deserted the English after conferring among themselves.

"Look around you," Monakaduto said with a disparaging swing of his arm over the encampment. "Is this how we want to fight a war? The white chief, Washington, is a good-natured man, but he has no experience and will by no means take advice from us. He would rather drive us on to fight by his directions. He has laid at one place from one full moon to the other, yet has made no fortification at all except this little thing here on the meadow where he thinks the French will come up to him in an open field." He shook his head angrily. "Why should we endanger ourselves and our people, when the French behave like cowards and the English like fools?"

Fort Necessity was not much. A simple square enclosure of upright logs reinforced by dirt heaped on both sides and having a trench no more than knee deep, it was located at the eastern end of an oval-shaped, east-west meadow with a small brook trickling through the middle. On the south side of the enclosure, and partially on the west, there was an embankment on the outside and a rifle-pit ditch had been dug inside this. Morale among the men was abysmal. Even the emergency reserve provisions had been used up now, and for days the army had been living on only the fresh meat of their dwindling herd of beef cattle. Artillery had been placed to command the approaches, but there was precious little cannon powder and even less for their rifles. The entire English force had last night numbered four hundred five men, but during the night a number had deserted and others had fallen sick. By morning's light only three hundred fifty men were able to stand and fight.

Washington knew the French were coming closer, but when no attack came at dawn yesterday, he thought they would have yet another day to continue their improvements of Fort Necessity. Then, at 11 A.M., a wounded scout supported by a companion had stumbled to the commander with the news that the French army was attacking. Within minutes the enemy force had broken from the forest and immediately the Indians with it began a screeching war cry and a ragged firing of their muskets. The range was far too great and the lead balls fell harmlessly.

Believing that the French, since they were far superior in force, would advance at them head on, Washington ordered his men to fall into rank in the meadow before the fort. While the Indians and some of the French soldiers at the far end of the meadow continued the yelling and inconsequential firing, Villiers had ordered the rest of his men to flank the little fort in the woods on both sides of it, approaching as near as possible without showing themselves. Here, on two heavily wooded hills, they took their positions—only sixty paces from the English on the one side, a hundred paces away on the other.

That a worse place for the construction of Fort Necessity could hardly have been chosen now became evident. From these two hills the French had the protection of trees and could shoot from above with a murderous crossfire and rake much of the interior of the fortification with their bullets. It was a predicament that dawned on the young commander with staggering impact and now he countermanded his initial order and had the entire force withdraw into the fortification and take cover as well as they could out of the crossfire.

The rain that had fallen all night stopped at dawn for an hour, then began to fall again and had continued ever since. Now it became a heavier downpour and the trench inside Fort Necessity became little more than a mucky, calf-deep quagmire. The light swivels still commanded the approaches to the fort, but now the French musket fire was coming so heavily from the two hills that there was no protection at all for the artillerymen and, for the most part, the big guns remained silent.

The firing from both sides became hot and deadly at those times when the rain slackened, then petered out to a ragged scattering of shots as the downpour increased. Late in the afternoon the rainfall became so hard that only occasional shots were heard but then, with the approach of evening, it eased up to no more than a fine drizzle and the shooting became very heavy again until darkness fell.

The bodies of the English soldiers, regulars and colonials alike, lay where they had fallen inside the fort. Twelve of George Washington's volunteers lay dead in the muck, along with eighteen of Captain Mackay's regulars. Seventy men with crippling bullet wounds crouched against the ramparts, moaning and weeping, almost two thirds of them from among the volunteers. Their situation was critical in the extreme. Desperately hungry, weakened by sickness and desertion, almost out of ammunition, their guns badly befouled and only two screw-rods on hand with which to clean them, total destruction seemed imminent.

To make it even worse, discipline was collapsing and some of the men had gotten into the remaining rum supply. Half of those not wounded were now drunk. They raised their cups in sarcastic gesture to any officer who approached them and said, "We who are about to die don't salute you . . . we ask why in hell we are here?"

The situation was terrible and still degenerating, but Villiers did not know how badly off Washington's army actually was. As darkness fell and ended a nine-hour battle with no cry for mercy having come from the fort, the French officer began to grow a little worried. His fears were compounded when a pair of Delawares rushed up to tell him that they had been scouting to the east and heard, far in the distance, the beating of drums and the firing of a cannon.

"The chiefs have sent us to tell you this," said the spokesman. "We are further to tell you that we will continue to fight throughout the night, if that is your wish, but with the dawn we will leave."

The Delawares walked away without waiting for a reply and Villiers reflected sourly on the situation. He didn't know whether or not to believe the report of drums and cannon in the distance. Though he doubted it, it could possibly be true. If it was, his own army might be in jeopardy. Ammunition was falling short and there was even the possibility that the English might sally out of the fort in a body to attack.[12]

He called Le Mercier to him and they discussed the situation. Within minutes they had decided that the best course would be to send in a messenger under a flag of truce for capitulation talks with the English. The messenger was sent, and he advanced to Fort Necessity waving a large cloth attached to a pole and shouting at intervals, "Don't shoot! I come unarmed to talk with your commander!"

Washington met him in front of the breastwork, not permitting him to see the interior nor the condition of his men. He considered the messenger to be more of a spy sent to see how the English were faring than as a bona fide deliverer of capitulation terms. He rejected the proposal in a peremptory manner and sent the Frenchman back.

The more he thought about what the man had said, however, the more he began to wish he had been less hasty with his reply. If they continued the fight, it could only end in annihilation of the English. Did he have the right to threaten his men with sure death if it was not really necessary? As he was pondering this question, the messenger returned to the fort and called out again that he came unarmed to speak to the commander. This time Washington listened carefully.

"My commandant," the messenger said nervously, "wishes that you will think again what will certainly befall you if you continue in this way. He asks that you send him an officer to discuss terms by which no more blood need be shed."

There could be no further hesitation. He told the Frenchman to wait, stationed a guard with him and withdrew into the fort. Only two men in his whole army could speak French; one was a young ensign named Peroney, but he was disabled with a bullet hole through his calf muscle. The other was his own friend and companion from last winter's wilderness journey, the recently promoted Dutchman, Captain Jacob van Braam. There could be no choice in the matter: van Braam would have to go.

The officer was gone for a long time—so long, in fact, that Washington began to fear it had all been just a ruse to diminish his officer strength. But then van Braam returned bearing with him the articles of capitulation being offered by Villiers. Washington summoned all his officers, and they huddled together, keeping a sputtering candle lighted only with difficulty, while van Braam interpreted the paper.

On the whole, the terms were most generous, although certain objections were made to some of them and these were changed. But now they were coming to a passage which van Braam knew would almost certainly cause Washington to reject the capitulation entirely, and so he carefully mistranslated so that the section assigning to Washington personally "*. . . l'assassinat du Sieur de Jumonville . . .*"—the *murder* of Sieur de Jumonville—became, instead, the *death* of Sieur de Jumonville. The rest of the capitulation terms were quite acceptable and undoubtedly much more generous than they would have been had Villiers known the true nature of the English condition:

*The commander and his men shall be permitted to march out of their fort with drums beating and the honors of war attending. They shall be permitted to carry with them one of their swivels and all other of their property and baggage, cattle, arms and ammunition. They shall be protected against any insult from French or Indians. The prisoners taken in the affair of Jumonville shall be set free. Finally, two English officers shall remain as hostages for our safe return to Fort Duquesne.*

Inwardly delighted to get off thus easily from what was certain disaster, all of the English officers signed the paper at just about midnight, including Colonel Washington, who thereupon branded himself forever in French eyes as the murderer of Jumonville. There was no little discussion regarding who was to remain behind as hostage, but at length the decision was made: the two would be van Braam, since he understood French and might be able to learn something valuable to impart when—and if—he returned, and Lieutenant Robert Stobo, who accepted the appointment if not with pleasure, at least without evident fear.

Most of the rest of the night was spent in preparations for their departure, and in the early morning light of an overcast but rainless morning today, they filed out to the pitiful cadence of a single drummer. Already part of the capitulation terms had been broken. During the remainder of the night, under cover of the cease-fire order from both sides, the Indians had slipped into the adjoining cattle compound and slit the throats of those horses and beef cattle not already killed by the previous day's shooting.

Now it was upon the unwounded men to carry the sick and wounded on their own backs and therefore leave behind much of the baggage they had intended taking. But the supposed withdrawal-with-honor turned into an ignominious retreat. The Indians heckled them incessantly and the heckling degenerated into plundering and threats to kill the remaining English and take their scalps—just as the bodies still within Fort Necessity were at this moment being scalped.

Nor was it just talk. There was hatred and murder in the eyes of the Indians, and abruptly they seized the medicine chest being carried by two privates and smashed it to bits. When two of the wounded men complained, they were killed by tomahawk blows, their scalps cut off immediately and then shaken in the faces of the others. It was only with threats to withhold their presents that the angry Captain Villiers finally forced them to desist and the dismal march continued for the English.

Even then they managed to travel only three miles before exhaustion forced them to stop and make camp, fearful that at any moment the Indians might again swoop down on them and this time wipe out everyone. Washington dispatched two of his most able survivors to continue the remaining forty-nine miles to Will's Creek Station and return with wagons for these men still here.

Men sprawled on the ground wherever they had taken their burdens from their backs. Washington himself was carrying a heavy load, and it was one that he could not put down, a load greater than anyone else's; a spiritual load which threatened to engulf him. The sight of his suffering injured men being borne in defeat on the backs of their staggering comrades; the knowledge that so many of his men had been killed; the knowledge that he had been thoroughly defeated in his first major engagement; the knowledge that his failure could not help but cause further disastrous losses for the English throughout the frontier; the knowledge that now, beyond any doubt, those Indian tribes still vacillating in their allegiance would flock to the French; all these things and more made this the bleakest time of his entire life thus far.

Behind him, Villiers was returning in triumph to Fort Duquesne, having had only two men killed. He was burning Gist's Settlement and the Ohio Company's Redstone storehouse as he passed, and he was bearing to his commandant, Captain Contrecoeur, and to the Marquis Duquesne the electrifying news that now not a single English flag was flying to the west of the Alleghenies.

### [July 30, 1754—Tuesday]

The Marquis Duquesne felt very well indeed. The entire situation in the west had gone far better than he had anticipated. Except for the unfortunate death of Jumonville and his men at the hands of that murderer, Washington, the entire campaign could hardly have turned out better. He frowned slightly as he sipped a deep-red wine from a beautiful crystal glass. Of course, it would not pay to become too heady with one's successes. The English could hardly be expected to take all this without some sort of attempt to recoup their losses and erase their shame.

Nevertheless, it was pleasant to have things going so well. Indians all over the eastern half of the continent, from Louisiana to the upper Great Lakes to the mouth of the St. Lawrence, were now vying with one another for French favor, and the Iroquois, the ever-important Iroquois, were leaning most strongly now toward French attachment. Of the Six Nations, in fact, only the Mohawks—because of that infernal William Johnson!—continued to hang onto the English coattails. If *they* could be shaken free . . .

Duquesne's eyes gleamed at the thought. But even if they didn't, there might be some way the French could cause the Iroquois League to rupture. If they could make that happen, there was no doubt in the governor's mind that four and possibly even five of the Six Nations would swerve sharply to French allegiance. He had long hoped that some Indian would have attempted to collect the bounty set on Johnson's head, but that none had did not especially surprise him. Johnson had an enormous influence among the Indians and any individual who killed him, whether white or Indian, would be sealing his own death warrant at the hands of the Mohawks. Nevertheless, in the far west—at Fort Michilimackinac and Detroit, at Fort La Baye and Fort La Pointe, at forts St. Joseph and de Chartres and Ouiatenon, even at Fort Miamis—Indian-French relations were better than ever, and Frenchmen in the wilderness were enjoying more security than they had ever before known there.

Of all the posts, two remained very weak and had needed reinforcement, not only in manpower but in their very construction. Even this was being taken care of admirably at this moment by one of France's most celebrated military engineers, Chevalier Chaussegros de Léry. With a strong force of men and equipment, Duquesne had sent him first to visit and study the fortifications at Detroit, to improve them where needed, and then go from there to Sandusky Bay to build a new fort—to be called Fort Junundat—close to the site where the English had had the audacity to raise their trading house. It was a site from which to control important portage routes of the Indians and the fur trade from the interior of the Ohio country, and from which to help defend Lake Erie from any further attempt at English encroachment.

But the biggest and best installation for Léry to concern himself with building, was a replacement of the pitiful little fort at Niagara—that crude structure of logs and dirt thrown up ostensibly as a trading post in early 1751 to divert some of the fur trade heading for Oswego. And thus far, Léry's progress toward that end had been admirable. His report, which Duquesne continued reading now, went on:

*Work goes well, Excellency, on the new Fort Niagara. What a difference it will be from the little log and bark trading post which met my eyes when first I arrived. The* work goes somewhat slowly on the new fort, but this is merely because of the great labors required in locating, transporting and fitting the native stone which will be its eventual strength. The walls will be very thick, so much so that a cannon might fire at it all day and only chip the outer surface. It will be a bastion of strength in this wilderness, of which all France can be proud. With the Indians there was only that initial disturbance about which you are aware—that of their objection to a "stone house" when they had given us the right to build only a fur-trading post, a "bark house" as they call it. But you were wise, sir, in sending to speak to them M. de Longueuil. He is a very suave and persuading speaker. Through M. Joncaire, he explained to them that this was not actually a fort that was being built, but rather a great fur-trading and storage station—the greatest in all of America—and that the reason it was being built out of stone rather than bark and logs was simply that furs do not keep well in the bark house, as the Indians themselves well know, since they have had many furs stored in such places damaged by insects and other vermin; and that a stone house was better for this purpose. He has, in fact, been so convincing in this argument, that some of the Indians have told me they want to watch us as we build, so that they might return to their villages with this knowledge and construct stone fur-storage houses of their own. But this would not be good knowledge for them to have, lest they turn it against us in the future, and so, with the help of M. Joncaire and Chevalier de Longueuil and the distribution, when necessary, of some rum and brandy, we have managed to divert their interest and soon it will be too late for them to understand what has been done, though I have doubted from the beginning that they could have understood it even should we have deliberately attempted to teach them. Their minds are not mathematical enough and their spirits not willing enough to undergo the hard labors such construction necessarily entails. These things aside, rest assured, Excellency, that by the end of the autumn this will be the best and strongest bastion of all this wilderness empire of New France.

Yes, Duquesne mused, placing the report back on his desk, things were going well for a change, but it was no time to let down one's guard. With such men on the frontier as William Johnson, George Croghan, Conrad Weiser and others of that caliber, there could be no relaxing.

At least not until the French hold on North America was

so absolutely secure that no power on earth would dare dispute it.

### [*December 31, 1754—Tuesday*]

The Colonies were deeply shocked and distressed at the defeat of young Colonel George Washington's army, but the anger which it fostered among them was not, surprisingly, directed at the popular Virginian himself. Instead, it was a self-directed anger at their own disunity and the intercolonial bickering which now posed a very definite threat to the continued existence of these Colonies. Already in newspapers of the major cities were appearing copies of the cartoon which had first appeared in that Philadelphia newspaper called the *Pennsylvania Gazette*—that of a writhing snake broken into eight segments representing South Carolina, North Carolina, Virginia, Maryland, Pennsylvania, New Jersey, New York, and New England. Beneath the broken snake was the ominous warning: JOIN, *or* DIE.

The problem did not just end with a disunity between the Colonies. It went much deeper—to a too-long established foundation in internal cross-purposes within the individual colonies. Robert Dinwiddie of Virginia had been deeply disturbed by the confiscation of the uncompleted fort at the forks of the Ohio by the French in April, and he lay the blame rightly at the feet of his own House of Burgesses in a letter he wrote on May 10 to his friend John Hanbury:

*If our Assembly had voted the money in November which they did in February, it's more than probable the fort would have been built and garrisoned before the French had approached; but these things cannot be done without money. As there was none in our treasury, I have advanced my own to forward the expedition; and if the independent companies from New York come soon, I am in hopes the eyes of the other colonies will be opened; and if they grant me a proper supply of men, I hope we shall be able to dislodge the French or build a fort on that river ...*

But the hope had been in vain and the shock that had struck him at the loss of the partially built fort was nothing compared to that which came with the news of Washington's defeat. Again he called the House of Burgesses to special session and opened with a speech that moved them considerably.

"Do you not see clearly now," he asked, "what kind of people the French are and the depth of the danger with which they threaten us? They show a brazen contempt of treaties and exhibit openly their ambitious views for universal monarchy. I could expatiate very largely on these affairs, but my heart burns with resentment at their insolence. I think there is no room for many arguments to induce you to raise a considerable supply to enable me to defeat the designs of these troublesome people and enemies of mankind."

For once it appeared that the Burgesses were in accord with Dinwiddie's sentiments. Their own resentment at the French move was keen and they promptly voted twenty thousand pounds. All seemed well until the third and final reading of the bill, when they attached to it a rider which touched on the aggravating old matter of the gold pistole fee on land patents. Dinwiddie was furious almost beyond words. When he collected himself enough to reply, he told them that attaching such a rider to the bill was not only offensive, it was unconstitutional. But his argument fell on ears that had no desire to hear and he practically wept with rage when the assembly adjourned. In letters to both James Hamilton and James Abercromby he complained:

*A governor is really to be pitied in the discharge of his duty to his king and country, in having to do with such obstinate, self-conceited people. I cannot satisfy the Burgesses unless I prostitute the rules of government. I have gone through monstrous fatigues. Such wrong-headed people, I thank God, I have never had to do with before.*

The fact that some very definite form of unity was now desperately needed by the Colonies was becoming daily more evident, especially to certain of the governors and various independent individuals of some influence, such as the irrepressible forty-eight-year-old publisher of the *Pennsylvania Gazette*, Benjamin Franklin. What was needed was some way to get all of the governors in accord on the matter so that they, in turn, could bring a definite, solid, acceptable plan to their assemblies.

And just such an opportunity was presenting itself.

Belatedly, the British Crown itself had become alarmed at the news that not only were the French making substantial inroads on English-claimed territory in North America, but the staunchest Indian allies of the Colonies, the Iroquois, might be led out of their never officially ended alliance with England by the Mohawks, who had broken the covenant chain in New York. The Lords of Trade and Plantations were suddenly horrified at such a concept and had sent out a directive ordering all the colonies involved with the Iroquois in any way to meet in a great Indian congress at Albany to adopt a new policy and complete a joint treaty that would bind the entire League in faithfulness to the Crown. It was to this Albany Congress that Benjamin Franklin now came as an ambassador and spokesman for Pennsylvania. While delegates from only seven of the thirteen colonies showed up, at least it was a start.

The Congress was opened by a presentation to the Indians of a huge chain-belt of wampum, into which was woven a symbolic representation of the King of England holding in his embrace the Thirteen Colonies and the Six Tribes of the Iroquois League, along with tribes allied to them. It was presented in conjunction with a speech which harangued the French for all the evils they had perpetrated—and a few they had not. It was, in essence, an apology to the League for past neglectful treatment, a sincere promise to do better in the future, and a plea for the reinstatement of a strong pact of alliance between the Iroquois League and the Crown Colonies.

It was the old and now white-haired Mohawk chief, Tiyanoga, who accepted the belt for the League, handed it carefully to the tribal record-keeper, and then stood for a long quiet period studying the faces of the commissioners, delegates, ambassadors, representatives and other white dignitaries on hand. When at last he began to speak, his voice was so low that many of those in attendance leaned forward and tilted their heads or cupped their ears to better hear him, but his voice became quickly stronger as he spoke and what he said became engraved in their minds.

"My Brothers, who are the children of our Father, the King, my heart and the heart of my people and of all people in the Iroquois League rejoices at this return of friendship. We do now solemnly renew and brighten the covenant chain. We shall take the chain-belt to Onondaga, where our council fire always burns, and keep it so safe that neither thunder nor lightning shall break it. In this way we are happy, but in other matters our hearts are heavy and weep tears.

"Brothers, there are those of your people—perhaps some who are present—who continue to work toward taking our land from us. This is wrong and we wish it to be stopped, or friendship renewed this day between us will wither away.

"Brothers, you claim that the French are your enemies, yet there are those of your people, especially of this city of Albany, who sell arms and goods to the French in return for beaver skins. This, too, is wrong and must be stopped.

"The commissioners have blamed us for allowing so many of the Iroquois people to be drawn away to the French god-house at the St. Francis River or that one at the Oswegatchie. They say the League is no more, that we are no longer one people. This is not true, for we are still the Six Nations and will no more lift our hands against our brothers than we will lift them against our fathers or our mothers. But in some ways it is true that we live disunited. Some years ago the Caughnawagas, who are Mohawks, separated themselves from the League, which was their choice, not ours. We have tried to bring back our brethren, but in vain; for the governor of Canada is like a wicked, deluding spirit. Now he seduces some of our northern brethren—a certain number of the Onondagas, the Cayugas and the Senecas.

"Brothers," he continued, and now his voice and the strong tone of accusation in it could be heard well by everyone present, "you ask us why we are so apart. The reason is that you have neglected us for these three years past." He paused and took a short stick from his waistband and tossed it over his shoulder without looking back. "You have thus thrown us behind your back; whereas the French are a subtle and vigilant people, always using their utmost endeavors to seduce and bring us over to them.

"Brothers, hear me! It is not the French alone who have invaded the country of the Iroquois. No! The Governor of Virginia and the Governor of Canada are quarreling about which of them owns the land which belongs not to either of them, but to *us!* And *their* quarrel may end in *our* destruction.

"Oh, Brothers, open your eyes to those who are your friends and can be your might! Remember what happened only a few yesterdays ago, when the French came down and took your Saratoga. For you, at that time, we would have taken Crown Point, but you prevented us. Instead, you burned your own fort at Saratoga and ran away from it, which was a shame and scandal to you. Look about your country and see: you have no fortifications; no, not even in this city. It is but a step from Canada hither, and the French may come and turn you out of doors. You desire us to speak from the bottoms of our hearts, and we shall do it: look at the French; they are fortifying everywhere. But you are all like women, bare and open, without fortifications."

There was, startlingly, a smattering of applause from the whites as the interpreter translated these words, but Tiyanoga gave no sign that he had heard it and it quickly died away. He turned and left his position—surrendering it to his young brother, Steyawa, who was better known to the English as Abraham.

"Brothers the English," Steyawa said slowly and distinctly, "what the first son of my mother has told you is true. He has spoken from his heart and he speaks for my heart and for the hearts of all Iroquois. But I wish to speak to you of another matter.

"Brothers, where is our right hand? You have cut him from us and we wish him restored. I speak of our brother, Warraghiyagey, who sits there." He pointed a long, slender finger at William Johnson, who was seated all by himself between the English and the Indians in attendance. There was a stirring as the audience shifted to see the object of his pointing and, when silence once again prevailed, the Mohawk subchief continued:

"He was our lips and our tongue and our mouth. He was our eyes and our ears. He heard and spoke and saw for us and now, for this long while, he has not been permitted to do so. You have appointed fourteen men to take his place, yet ten times fourteen could not do so. We wish him to be returned to his place in Indian Affairs, for we love him, and he us, and he has always been our good and trusted friend. It

294

is with gladness that we accept the presents you make to us, but we would rather have the return of he who hears, speaks and sees for us; he who feels and thinks and does for us. Restore to us our Warraghiyagey!"

William, saying nothing, looked amused and raised a quizzical eyebrow toward the commissioners, who cleared their throats self-consciously and looked away from him. At last their spokesman arose and replied to Steyawa that while they, the commissioners, had not the power to grant the request, the Iroquois could rest assured that it would not be forgotten. Then James Delancey, still New York's acting governor, got to his feet and with a genial smile, which unfortunately extended no further than his lips, made a reply.

"Men of the Iroquois League, your words have been noted and your wishes will be gravely considered. You may have justification for your grievances and for your requests, but I can do nothing until all such matters have been carefully investigated. I will report to you one year hence about what I have learned considering each of these matters. In the meanwhile, the Iroquois should continue to deal with the Indian commissioners here in Albany, for they are your old and dear friends."

Perhaps he intended to say more, but it didn't happen that way.

As he paused and an intense silence followed the interpreter's words, from the gallery of Englishmen there abruptly came an immense and noisy discharge of intestinal gasses which could be heard by everyone. In an instant the entire assemblage was engulfed in a gale of laughter virtually beyond control. Even the Indians hooted and howled and slapped their legs in hilarity. Delancey's pinched face whitened with anger and his cold gaze flashed over the gallery, but there was no way of telling who was the source of the insult, if insult it was intended to be.

It took a long while for the proceedings to resume the decorum so abruptly shattered and in this interval the Iroquois delegation left, pausing only to claim the gifts which had been provided for them.

The Congress returned to the serious motives which had brought it into session and the spate of gaiety was quickly forgotten as business recommenced. It was patently apparent that while they had been prevented by protocol from interfering in New York's affairs, the delegates of the sister colonies were unhappy with New York's rather cavalier treatment of the Iroquois. All of them knew only too well

295

that if the League joined the enemy, there was the utmost danger that the whole continent would be subjected to the French. The delegates as a body thereupon drew up a resolution which apprised the Crown of this fact and indicated for the record that of all the men in the Colonies, only William Johnson had sufficient influence with the Iroquois to save British America from this threat.

When this had been taken care of, Benjamin Franklin was recognized and spoke sagely of the need for all the colonies to unite to the common purpose and good of each.

"There is," he said mildly, peering somewhat owlishly over small square spectacles, "a writer of our day named Kennedy, who has written an intriguing work entitled *Importance of Gaining and Preserving the Friendship of the Indians*. I do not know Mr. Kennedy personally or what qualifications he has, but this is of little importance, for what he has to say makes good sense. He comments in detail on the strength of the League which has for centuries bound our friends the Iroquois together in a common tie which no crisis, however grave, since its foundation has managed to disrupt. Further, this League does not infringe upon the rights of their individual tribes. Gentlemen, I propose now that all of British America be federated under a single legislature and a president general to be appointed by the Crown."

The Philadelphia publisher smiled and continued in that same compellingly mild tone, "It would be a strange thing, would it not, if Six Nations of ignorant savages should be capable of forming a scheme for such a union, and be able to execute it in such a manner as that it has subsisted for ages and appears indissoluble, and yet that a like union should be impracticable for ten or a dozen English colonies?"

There was instant disapproval among the representatives in attendance, both those of the Colonies and those of the Crown. The Crown, it was said, would summarily reject the plan because it gave altogether too much power to the Colonies. The representatives of the Colonies argued that such a consideration was ridiculous even to contemplate, since it gave too much power to the Crown and because it also called for each of the Colonies to transfer some of their functions of self-government, of which they were very jealous, to a central council or legislature.

But the proposition was recorded and now would be read by officials in each of the Colonies and by those in high seats across the sea. More than this Benjamin Franklin had not expected. He was content with the matter as it stood and, despite the criticisms the proposal had brought, resumed his seat with that same shy smile curling his lips.

A seed had been planted.

Upon the adjournment of this Albany Congress, William Johnson rode back to Mount Johnson between the Mohawk brothers, Tiyanoga and Steyawa. He spoke little, steeped in thought, and the chiefs were content to ride in silence beside him, confident that whatever thoughts were filling his mind now, he would see to the welfare of the Iroquois as always, whether or not in an official capacity.

It was precisely the matter of official capacity in Indian affairs that was troubling the big Irishman. Much as he disliked admitting it, even to himself, he deeply missed his duties as an official representative of the Indians. In his storehouses could now be found virtually every fur pelt that had ligitimately been brought to New York in the past half year; his fur business had made him one of the most wealthy men in North America. And, as his storehouses bulged with furs and his mills with grain, so too his accounts bulged with wealth and his home with the finest material goods he could acquire. Women he could have in whatever number he wished, whether Indian or white. Yet, the thing he enjoyed most in life—dealing officially in the affairs of men and races—was being denied him and he yearned for it with an almost overwhelming desire.

Less than two weeks after his arrival back at Mount Johnson, he received a startling note from Delancey. Though it went much against the grain for him, the acting governor of New York had begun to realize that if he was ever to get anywhere with the Iroquois League, he was going to require the help of William Johnson. The colony, Delancey said in his note, would finally pay Johnson all that it owed him if Johnson would give his wholehearted support to the fourteen New York Indian commissioners.

It was most assuredly not the reintroduction into official capacity that William was looking for and was, in fact, to his way of thinking, little more than an ill-concealed bribe. He immediately declined Delancey's offers.

But then had come another letter from a governor, this time from Massachusetts' William Shirley, who wrote:

*I am persuaded His Majesty hath not a subject who knows so well how to gain the hearts of the Indians and an absolute influence over them as yourself. It would be to the benefit of all His Majesty's Colonies in North America if you were to resume active service to the Crown in this regard, and, if you will be pleased to let me know in what particular manner you think you can be most instrumental in that service, I will represent and recommend it.*

William Johnson's pulse quickened and he sat down at once to reply in as constrained a hand as possible. There was, he told the Massachusetts governor, only one position in which he could envision himself of value to all the Colonies equally, and that was if he were appointed not by any particular colony, but instead by the Crown to the chief position of Indian Affairs connected with the Iroquois or their allies. In conclusion he told Governor Shirley:

*Should His Majesty deem me worthy of that important trust, I will abandon the fur trade and devote the rest of my life to the public service.*

# CHAPTER VI

[*April 14, 1755—Monday*]

NEVER before in the history of the British Colonies had such a war fever gripped North America. Everyone, it seemed, was girding himself for battle and for most, since they had never really been in battle before, it was an exciting time.

Across the sea, Brigadier General Edward Braddock had been promoted to major general and ordered to America to take command of all military affairs there, with Governor William Shirley of Massachusetts—still with the rank of colonel from the last war—to be second-in-command as well as commander of the colonial forces.

Braddock's instructions from the King were to take two regiments—the Forty-fourth and the Forty-eighth—of five hundred men each to Virginia from England and, upon their arrival there, to increase the regimental totals to seven hundred men each. His appointment was made on November 25 and on January 15 he set sail from Cork, England. He expected, on his arrival at Hampton, Virginia, on February 23 that everything would be in readiness as ordered by the Crown, but instead found matters badly bungled and no one prepared.

The news he received, in fact, was highly discouraging.

He was filled in on the current situation by Governor Shirley's son, also named William, whom Shirley had sent to Hampton to meet the general and thereafter act as his secretary. France, young Shirley told Braddock, had quickly learned of the general and his regiments being shipped to America and was acting swiftly to nullify the threat. At Brest and Rochefort she was hurriedly fitting out eighteen ships of war, and reports had it that they would probably be setting sail around the end of April. On board would be a reinforcement of six thousand men—six full battalions from La Rein, Bourgogne, Languedoc, Guienne, Artois, and Béarn. Worse yet, a new and highly experienced officer was to come along to command all the French forces in America. He was the Baron Ludwig August Dieskau, a German professional soldier in the French service, who had received his training at the elbow of the famous military tactician and strategist, General Saxe.

Braddock shook his head glumly and had no doubt that General Dieskau would be the toughest adversary he had ever faced, but young Shirley was not yet finished. The same special dispatch from the Crown, he told Braddock, stated that Dieskau would be accompanied by a new governor for Canada—the Marquis Pierre Rigaud de Vaudreuil—who would replace Duquesne, whose health was failing. And Vaudreuil was well experienced in North American affairs, having only recently been governor of Louisiana and himself Canadian born. Admiral Dubois de la Motte would be in command of the French troop fleet and, to prevent any possibility of the English fleet from attacking this convoy, Admiral Macnamara with another squadron of nine warships would be acting as escort for at least the first portion of the voyage.

None of this was encouraging to Braddock, for though everyone was in a state of excitement over the impending war, virtually no one was prepared. The only really worthwhile step toward defense that had been taken thus far was the construction during the winter of a new fortification named Fort Cumberland. It had been erected adjacent to the Ohio Company's trading station at the mouth of Will's Creek; but it was a long hop from there to the bastions of the French, beginning with Fort Duquesne.

Governor Shirley, for his part, had taken some steps to raise forces but as yet had not met with great success. In late January he and Dinwiddie had conferred on the new and disturbing menace of a French fleet at their back door—on Lake Ontario. At Fort Frontenac, according to reports they had received from traders, the French were hastily constructing a half-dozen or more ships with which they could command this lowest of the Great Lakes. Shirley was setting gears in motion to turn Fort Oswego into a great British shipyard, hopefully to turn out warships for Lake Ontario just as fast as the French could—or, hopefully, even faster. And Dinwiddie, looking ahead, had proposed that the same be done, if any practicable way could be found to do it, on

Lake Erie. If they could rout the French from Fort Presque Isle and convert it into another ship-building yard, they could soon command the whole of Lake Erie and perhaps, through blockade, even take Detroit. But everything depended on first subduing Fort Frontenac. If they could do this, they would cut off the supply shipments to all the western forts and each would become ripe fruits ready for the plucking.

Immediately upon his return home to Massachusetts, Shirley had issued a call for volunteers from all the Colonies. While as yet there had been no great response, the colonial commander was sure there soon would be. Connecticut had already voted twelve hundred men to the effort, New Hampshire five hundred and Rhode Island four hundred, all at their own expense. And while New York was mostly marking time right now, it was reasonable to assume that she would provide another eight hundred.

Braddock, never one to hesitate, had called upon the colonial governors to meet him for a council of war at Alexandria on April 14, and so, today, this was where all had assembled to thrash out the strategy for the forthcoming campaign. Also on hand, though not attending the war council, was William Johnson, who had been specifically invited by Shirley to attend. And, remembering Shirley's promise of last December to help him, William waited nervously outside the large tent for the arrival of the dignitaries.

The others arrived relatively close together. Here was Governor Dobbs of North Carolina and there the new governor of Pennsylvania, Robert Hunter Morris, fresh from his first clash with the Quaker and Dutch-ridden assembly. Next came Governor Sharpe of Maryland, followed by James Delancey of New York.

Finally came the governor's coach from Virginia. Behind it on horseback rode Captain Robert Orme, aide-de-camp to Braddock and an impressive young man with a pale, though handsome face. He was wearing shiny black knee-boots, a scarlet coat and a small tricorn hat heavy with gold lace.

Beside Orme, his face glum, rode young William Shirley— glum because in the weeks he had been closely associated with the general as his secretary, Braddock's glitter had worn very thin. In fact, the young man had even written to his friend Governor Morris:

*We have a general most judiciously chosen for being disqualified for the service he is employed in, in almost every respect.*

The fancy coach came to a halt before the huge tent and first to alight from it was the twenty-nine-year-old second son of the Earl of Albermarle, the Commodore Augustus Keppel—already a highly experienced naval officer and statesman, who had only recently returned from an important mission to the Mediterranean where he had been successful in persuading the Dey of Algiers to put down piracy, and with whom he had made a solid treaty for England.

Following Keppel out of the coach was Robert Dinwiddie, smiling jovially and obviously feeling that this council was the beginning of the end of his troubles with his antagonistic House of Burgesses.

Last out of the coach was General Edward Braddock himself, emerging grandly and—to William Johnson's way of thinking—somewhat pompously, wearing in every gesture and expression a declaration of his forty-five years in His Majesty's Service.

The introductions were made and places taken inside the tent, with guards posted outside so that no one could approach within hearing. Governor Shirley acted as something of a chairman and it was evident that he delighted in the role. Though now he was past sixty, there was a buoyant youthfulness about the old lawyer which made him seem much younger. To Braddock and the assemblage he recounted the fundamental ideas he and Dinwiddie had formulated in January for the forthcoming campaign, and he was pleased when Braddock nodded his approval of them. Then, in a session lasting many hours, the entire campaign for the year was mapped out, with everyone contributing. It was a highly ambitious plan which, boiled down to its essentials, called for a simultaneous attack on the four key French fortifications.

Braddock was to take his own two regiments of British regulars and march against Fort Duquesne. The two new regiments of colonials would be led by Shirley, now with the rank of major general, and they would have as their objective the destruction or capture of Fort Niagara. A body of provincials being raised at this moment in New York, New Jersey and New England would be sent against Fort St. Frederic, the French stronghold at Crown Point on Lake Champlain. Finally, Lieutenant Colonel Robert Monckton would lead another force of New England Provincials against the great French fortress at Louisbourg on Cape Breton Island of Nova Scotia—better known to the French as Acadia.

Only for the Crown Point campaign had no commander yet been named, but this matter Shirley and Braddock had previously discussed through correspondence. The movement against Fort St. Frederic was to be entrusted to a man who had a reputation for energy, capacity and faithfulness, as well as a strong influence with the Indians—William Johnson.

The supposed justification for these planned assaults was that all four forts lay within English territory, but it was stretching the truth to the breaking point to claim this with any degree of seriousness. It might be a fact where the Louisbourg fortress and Fort Duquesne were concerned, but with Fort St. Frederic and Fort Niagara it was a different matter entirely. Crown Point had been in the undisturbed possession of France for two dozen years, while Niagara had been occupied by them for fully three quarters of a century and even though New York claimed that ground, no serious attempt had been made to oust them.

Braddock agreed that vessel building at Fort Oswego should be pushed with all possible energy and that—to the delight of both Dinwiddie and Shirley—the Colonies be compelled by Act of Parliament, which he had the right to invoke, to contribute in due proportion to the war effort. Finally, he suggested to Shirley, handing him a document at the same time, that all efforts be made at once to repair any damage done to the English-Iroquois alliance. With that, the council was dissolved.

Almost at once Braddock called Captain Orme and asked him to pay his respects to William Johnson and invite him into the tent. A few moments later, William was ushered in. Braddock shook his hand gravely and then nodded to Shirley, who also shook the big trader's hand with warmth and then handed him the paper Braddock had given him. Puzzled, William took the official document bearing the seal of the King of England and read it. His heart leaped within him and he quickly dropped his hands to his sides lest their trembling betray the strong emotion sweeping through him at this moment.

His greatest dream had come true!

By order of King George, he was appointed Supervisor of Indian Affairs for the Six Nations and their Allies, managing all affairs with the northern Indians of America and accountable not to any colonial governor or assembly, but only to General Edward Braddock. Further, he would be supported in all his Indian duties with funds directly from the Royal Treasury. He had won!

It was only with the greatest effort that he held down the wave of elation that threatened to engulf him and, in a voice slightly shaky, thanked Braddock and Shirley in turn and shook hands with both men again as they congratulated him.

"There's more," said Shirley. "One of the objects in the forthcoming campaign is the taking of Crown Point from the French. This will be done with an army made up of men from New York, New Jersey and New England—in particular, New Hampshire. General Braddock wishes you to take command of that army and accomplish the job. With it goes the rank of major general of the Provincial Army."

William was stunned. For a long moment he said nothing and then finally he shook his head.

"I don't think I can do that." He turned to General Braddock and added, "Sir, you must be convinced that the little experience I have of military affairs cannot entitle me to this distinction. Further, I would be pleased, General, to be relieved from this Crown Point command lest it interfere with my administration of Indian affairs."

But Braddock wouldn't hear of it and insisted that William shoulder both responsibilities. At last William gave in, accepted the command and then bid the men adieu. A short while later he was astride his horse, returning with the news to Mount Johnson—and the Mohawks—in something of a daze, feeling that on the whole, it had been quite a day.

### [April 25, 1755—Friday]

Throughout the Iroquois League the word spread with the speed of a grass fire in a high wind: once again Warraghiyagey was their representative!

Around a hundred or more council fires the news was discussed over and again and a great excitement filled the land. In most cases the speaker who broke the news sang it, rather than spoke it. While whole village populations gathered around he chanted the words to a jerky rhythm of his body:

"Our eyes are opened ... again we see! ... The thread that has sewn our lips together has been cut away ... again we may speak! ... The mud that has filled our ears has dried and crumbled and fallen away ... again we hear! ... Warraghiyagey is again our eyes ... again our tongue ... again our ears ... his council fire has been rekindled ... and our hearts are glad!"

But the excitement this generated in the Mohawks in
304

particular and to large degree among the Oneidas and Tuscaroras, some of the Onondagas and Cayugas, was not a universal thing among the Six Nations. Too much time had passed with their being shunted aside, their words and their ideas being ignored; too much time had been given, and for many the inducements of Chabert Joncaire and Abbé François Piquet and others had taken effect. And when the council fire gleamed before Mount Johnson and the bare feet that had trodden the forest paths to that point had stopped and all were congregated who would come, their numbers were not a tenth of what they had been in days past.

As Warraghiyagey, William Johnson danced before his fire clad only in a breech cloth, his entire body garishly painted. He threw down the war belts and viciously plunged his red-painted tomahawk into a blackened post. His feathers and ornaments bobbed and jangled as he leaped and bent and pounced, and he stirred a frantic war fever in them, causing their howls and shrieks to reverberate down the Mohawk Valley.

But despite the fervor he was able to ignite in them, William Johnson was only partially successful in his request that a large party of them go at once to aid General Braddock against the French at Fort Duquesne. The Mohawk subchief, Scarroyaddy, agreed to go with a party, but emphasized that it would be only "to pay our respects to your general."

The meaning was implicit to William. They would go primarily to look over Braddock's strength and condition and potential for victory and then report back to the League council with recommendations. At once William wrote a strong letter to the commander in chief:

*The success of wilderness marches such as you will soon be embarked upon depend in great measure upon Indian protection. A party of Mohawks are coming to you soon, representing the Six Nations, and I urge you most strongly, General Braddock, to receive them with courtesy. However, do not make the mistake of trying to enlist this delegation. Instead, they should be treated well, shown your strength and then sent back with bountiful presents. The Onondaga Council will soon meet and they would be greatly displeased if the Mohawks were to engage in any hostilities without the general concurrence.*

Even as these Mohawks under Scarroyaddy were preparing

305

to go, William Johnson sent his own messenger off to Braddock, then returned his attention to the council in progress. He shook his head regretfully. Though these in attendance seemed eager to fight, they too must be bound by the vote of the League council. He remembered only too well how closely he had forced the Mohawks to inter-League warfare the last time he exacted the war fervor in them without the concurrence of the council.

He shook his head again. He knew he ought to be pleased at this turnout of well over a hundred warriors, but he was not; there should have been upward of a thousand or more warriors and chiefs in attendance here. Within him there was the sick feeling that his own race had waited too long. Nevertheless, he passed the word that an even greater council of all the Iroquois was to meet again at Mount Johnson in the middle of June.

Perhaps by then matters would improve.

### [ *May 1, 1755—Thursday* ]

Charles Michel de Langlade, though he got along well enough with the Ottawa war chief, had little regard for Pontiac, whom he considered an irascible tyrant. Nevertheless, he had to admit that the man wielded a great and ever-growing influence over all these tribes of the upper Great Lakes and he was most definitely going to need the chief's help if he was to gather any substantial force of Indians this time.

Only a short while ago the letter had come to him from Governor Duquesne by special courier. That event alone was enough to raise his own esteem among the Indians—especially the Chippewas—several notches. The letter had praised him again for the courage and leadership he had shown in the destruction of Pickawillany, then went on to say that once more the government was in need of Lieutenant Langlade's help in raising as many of the western Indians as possible for a forthcoming confrontation with the English. Could M. de Langlade provide several hundreds or more of the best warriors these tribes possessed? If so, he was to collect them at once and lead them to Fort Duquesne at the forks of the Ohio, there to confer with the commandant, Chevalier Contrecoeur, as to how best their strength could be utilized. Ample rewards, it added, would be made to each and every Indian taking part.

Now Langlade was at Detroit, deep in conference with

Pontiac. He painted quite a verbal picture for the Ottawa war chief; considerably different from the tenor of the letter he received from Duquesne.

"My brother," he said earnestly, "we fought well together at Pickawillany, you and I, and the fame of Pontiac has since spread far and wide through this country and even far beyond. There is no war chief of any tribe who is more powerful or more respected than you. Yet, now there is the possibility of your greatness growing even more, of your fame being on the tongue of *all* men, both Indian and white."

Pontiac seemed to swell visibly under the praise and there could be no doubt his interest was sparked by what Langlade had already said. His porcelain-bead ear ornaments rattled slightly and his crescent-shaped nose pendant swung slightly as he leaned forward and nodded for the halfbreed to continue.

"The English," Langlade went on, "who have filled the hearts of the Iroquois with hatred for the Ottawas and their friends are now threatening our friends and allies, the French. An army of English from across the great eastern sea, and also many gathered from east of the mountains, are planning to come against Fort Duquesne, and the governor has sent me to you, since you are the greatest warrior in the land, to ask you to draw together your best warriors and take up the hatchet against them, to come with me and the Chippewas that I have gathered and leave at once for Fort Duquesne where the commandant, Contrecoeur, awaits us with a warm heart and many fine presents."

On and on Langlade went, wheedling, inflating, convincing Pontiac that his greatness now would be as nothing compared to the glory he would reap after destroying the English who were enemies of both the Indians and the French. Not only would there be gratitude and presents from the French, but there would be an abundance of scalps and captives and plunder to be had from the vanquished foe.

By the end of their session, Pontiac was convinced. His harsh features softened into the semblance of a smile and he placed his hands on Langlade's shoulders and nodded.

"Young brother," he said, "I will go with you, and my warriors with me, and all the others that we can gather, and all that you have said will come to be. We will leave on the day of the next moon."

After interminable and thoroughly frustrating delays, General Edward Braddock had finally assembled his army at Fort Cumberland—that new, strong fortification dwarfing the storage cabins of the Ohio Company here where Will's Creek emptied into the Potomac.

He had kept his aides—Captains Roger Morris and Robert Orme, and young Colonel George Washington—extremely busy in trying to round up more men and provisions, but they had been balked on all sides. Not only were supplies of any kind extraordinarily scarce and transportation for them virtually nonexistent, but the populace was filled with such apathy in regard to furnishing material or physical help that Colonel Washington quickly became exasperated.

"They all want the protection we are to provide," he fumed, "but none are willing to sacrifice on their own part for it. They ought to be chastised!"

The success of the whole expedition depended largely on speed. The huge reinforcements being sent by France were only now en route and it was imperative that the strikes at Niagara, at Duquesne, at St. Frederic and at the Louisbourg fortresses be made before these installations could be strengthened. But speed was impossible. Braddock's quartermaster general, Sir John Sinclair, stormed in his own hell of frustration like a wounded lion, but to no avail. Though months before notice had been made for supplies to be readied, practically all stores and supplies essential to the campaign were severely lacking. All too regularly contracts were broken or pretenses given that they had never been drawn in the first place, and the result was that the army was in serious want of everything—horses, grain for them and for the beeves, wholesome food for the men and, most of all, wagons for transporting baggage, supplies, cannon, medical goods and ammunition.

Ben Franklin spent several days visiting with Braddock, during which time the long-awaited wagons arrived, but they were a huge disappointment. Instead of eight score, as required, there were only twenty-five and most of these needed extensive repairs before they could be used. Franklin shook his head sadly.

"A pity, General, that you did not establish your headquarters in Pennsylvania where almost every farmer has his wagon."

Braddock grasped at this straw of hope and asked Franklin

if, with his influence as a respected publisher and postmaster general of Pennsylvania, he could not get some of these wagons for the army's use. Franklin agreed to try. No sooner had he returned to Philadelphia than he issued a strong appeal to the farmers, warning them darkly of the danger to them if the army should fail because of lack of transportation, which the farmers could provide. He also gave a series of personal talks on the same subject in York, Lancaster and Cumberland counties. And in two weeks' time, a stream of one hundred fifty wagons and a great many horses arrived at Fort Cumberland. Braddock's gratitude was almost pathetic to witness.

"It is the only instance of ability and honesty I have known in these provinces," he declared. "Were it my decision, I would disband the army and stand back to enjoy the squeals of the colonial sheep when the French wolves descended upon them. It is only what they deserve!"

But even with the wagons and horses now on hand, the situation remained bad. Not only was there no grain for the horses, there was absolutely no decent pasturage within many miles of Fort Cumberland. Almost seven hundred horses and hundreds of beef cattle were being fed a diet of leaves stripped by work details in the surrounding forest. Those animals which did not sicken were badly weakened with only this poor fare to subsist upon.

The entire force of twenty-two hundred men was now bivouacked at Fort Cumberland and Braddock resignedly busied himself with final details preparatory to the beginning of the march. His Forty-fourth Regiment under Colonel Dunbar and Forty-eighth under Major Halket had now been filled out to seven hundred men each through enlistments in Virginia. There were also nine companies of Virginia militia, for whom Braddock had nothing but contempt.

"You are assigned the duty," he told Ensign Allen of Halket's regiment, "of making them as much like soldiers as possible, though I doubt you will have very substantial results. Their lazy, apathetic disposition will be difficult, if not impossible, to eliminate."

Deeply proud of the Virginians, Colonel Washington could not in the least agree with Braddock and the two had heated words on the merit of the Provincials on numerous occasions. It was not their only point of disagreement. The young colonel, who also recognized the imperative need for Indian aid in the forthcoming campaign, strongly urged the general to follow William Johnson's recent advice. General Johnson's letter had arrived only a day or so before the Mohawk delegation, but it was obvious that Braddock, far from trying to enlist them as allies, did not care to have Indians around at all.

Washington still faithfully kept his journal and now he wrote in it with some discouragement:

*He looks upon the country, I believe, as void of honor or honesty. We have frequent disputes on this head, which are maintained with warmth on both sides, especially on his, as he is incapable of arguing without it, or giving up any point he asserts, be it ever so incompatible with reason or common sense. He makes no secret of his contempt for the militia, considering them immensely inferior to his regulars and this is in some respects reflected in his attitude toward me, though with subtlety, to be sure. Nor does he seem to realize the great value Indian allies can be to us, seeing them only, as so many new to this country see them, as ignorant painted savages valueless to any campaign. Even in those occasions when he has made great effort to accept them, he does not delude them. The trader, Croghan, has recently brought fifty warriors under Chief Scarroyaddy, who offered their aid against the French. The general saluted them, made speeches and caused the cannon to be fired and drums and fife to be played in their honor and even provided them with a bullock for a feast and ample rum to warm them, but to them, as to us, the efforts were insincere and it was evident that he could scarce tolerate them. Croghan is disgusted with this treatment to them after all the endeavors to bring them here. He reports that Scarroyaddy complains that the general looks upon them as dogs and will never listen to their advice, and he suspects that they will soon leave because of this.*

Even young William Shirley, Braddock's secretary, found his initial bitterness about the general getting steadily worse. While he continued to serve the commander in chief as best he could, his complaints about him became more overt, as evidenced in the letter he wrote to Governor Morris:

*It is a joke to suppose that secondary officers can make amends for the defects of the first; the mainspring must be the mover. As to the others, I don't think we have much to boast; some are insolent and ignorant, others capable but rather aiming at showing their own abilities than making a proper use of them. I have a very great love for my friend,*

310

*Orme, and think it uncommonly fortunate for our leader that he is under the influence of so honest and capable a man; but I wish for the sake of the public he had some more experience of business, particularly in America. I am greatly disgusted at seeing an expedition (as it is called), so ill-concerted originally in England, so improperly conducted since in America.*

But at last, today, the army left Fort Cumberland and took up its march into the mountainous wilderness of the Alleghenies, leaving Colonel James Innes in charge of the fort and the substantial crowd of invalids, soldiers' wives and other women left here.

Though it was customary for a great crowd of women—wives, sweethearts and prostitutes—to follow an army on the march, Braddock had ordered them to remain here at Fort Cumberland where, if nothing else, they could launder bedding and clothing and help tend the sick who were necessarily left behind. A good many of them remained, but as the army moved out toward Fort Duquesne, at least three score of the women followed. These were mainly the prostitutes, who had absolutely no interest in laundering or nursing and, with most of the wives remaining at the fort, considered this a golden opportunity for themselves to make tidy little fortunes in providing a release for the carnally deprived men.

Not all the women who followed the army against Braddock's orders were prostitutes, but there were very few exceptions. One such exception, however, was Mary Francis, wife of Edgar Francis, who was a private in the Virginia Regiment. She was a determined young woman and she had no intention of staying behind. When she and Edgar were married less than a year ago, she had vowed she would never leave him and she meant to keep that vow.

And so now, though she tired rather easily because of the weight of the unborn child in her swollen womb, she trudged along behind uncomplainingly. It was worth the effort to be near her man.

### [ *June 14, 1755—Saturday* ]

Canada had a new governor, a new military commander, and virtually a new army.

Along with Baron Ludwig Dieskau and the six thousand regular troops from France, Pierre François Rigaud de

Vaudreuil—the Marquis de Vaudreuil—had arrived at Montreal and taken command from the Marquis Duquesne.

A Canadian by birth, Vaudreuil was the son of Philippe de Vaudreuil, who himself had been Canada's governor in the early part of this century. Now the son was following in the father's footsteps, feeling sure he would amass a fortune in the position, just as his father had.

It was not by preference but rather by direct order from France that Duquesne handed over his office to Vaudreuil. He knew the new governor well enough to realize that there were scores of men better equipped than this tall, lean, highly egotistical and somewhat effeminate appointee who had so recently been governor of Louisiana.

Fine clothing was a passion with Vaudreuil; silks and satins his love. They occupied as much time in his thoughts as matters of state or even, for that matter, his wife. Though backed by a foundation of good education and a considerable degree of intelligence, he was without the highly desireable seasoning of good common sense and was often inclined toward petty meanness.

His first concerns upon arrival were to such pressing matters as fabrics and furniture for his person and quarters. Though the quarters he had inherited with his appointment were sumptuous for Canada, they were to his reckoning miserly and poor, almost barbaric, and far removed from the elegance and luxury he had wallowed in, both in Louisiana and Paris. And so, while the army drilled and loafed and wondered about this great wild new country—and its commander successfully masked his impatience at the delays—Vaudreuil took his good time getting settled.

Though somewhat lacking in beneficial imagination, he was nonethless thorough and made a careful study of the situation in New France—past, present, and projected future. In a surprisingly short time, once he had applied himself to it, he had garnered a rather complete foundation in the problems to be met and solved. Among the many recommendations presented to him which he considered at length, the one which seemed to him most deserving of priority was the perennially repeated request by the Abbé Piquet at Fort Présentation that the isolated English installation on Lake Ontario—Fort Oswego—be destroyed. The very presence of the English on this lake was an affront to French territorial claims and the activities engaged in or originating from the fort made that installation a perpetual thorn in the side of the religious, commercial and military designs of France.

So now, at last, with Baron Dieskau at his side, the Marquis Pierre de Vaudreuil began mapping a campaign to rid the French dominion of the English outpost. The plan was a simple one: Ludwig Dieskau was to establish himself well with the majority of the new troops at Fort Frontenac—or perhaps even at Fort Niagara—and then, say about mid-August, launch a swift and powerful invasion which would sweep away Fort Oswego as if it were no more than a bothersome insect.

In the meanwhile, of course, it might be wise to keep an ear attuned to whatever whispers might filter northward about the activities and plans of one Edward Braddock, Major General.

### [ June 16, 1755—Monday ]

In deadly earnest the Indians now spread out from Fort Duquesne—not all of the eight hundred who had assembled here, but perhaps a third of them, traveling in small raiding parties of ten to thirty warriors each. These were the warriors of Charles Langlade and Chief Pontiac. Those left at the fort were mainly the more eastern Indians who had long been under the French influence; the Caughnawagas of Sault St. Louis, the Abnakis of St. Francis, the Christianized Hurons of Lorette under Chief Athanase, and the disaffected Onondagas, Senecas and Cayugas of Oswegatchie. At the moment the blood lust of these Indians at the fort had not yet risen. They were content to drink the rum provided by Captain Contrecoeur and wait for the English army to get closer to them before raising the war cry. Just arriving, too, but equally content to wait and size up the situation were the Shawnees under Chiefs Catahecassa and Pucksinwah, and the Delawares under Chief White Eyes.[1]

Langlade was duly impressed when he arrived with Pontiac and their army of warriors at the forks of the Ohio and saw Fort Duquesne for the first time. It was not as large, perhaps, as Detroit, but it was surely as strong and even more protected from attack. It was formed in a square with four cannon-mounted bastions. The waters of the Allegheny lapped at one side of it and the waters of the Monongahela at the other. The third side faced down the Ohio River. All three river sides were enclosed by a stockade of upright logs twelve feet high which were firmly mortised and well dotted with loopholes for musket fire. Attack against any one of these three sides was almost out of the question.

The fourth side of the fort faced the woodland in an easterly direction. Here the ground had been interlaced with ravelins and ditches and barricades of various kinds, with ramparts made of squared logs filled in with earth and ten feet thick. Trees and stumps had been cleared to the eastward for more than the range of a rifle ball from the ramparts, and outside the ditches were bark-and-pole cabins that had been built for the overflow of French regulars and Canadian militia. Entrance to the fort proper could be made only from this east side, through a gate and drawbridge. Inside the walls were soldier barracks, officers' quarters, Contrecoeur's own quarters, a guardhouse and a large storehouse, all built of combined logs and boards. It was a sturdy fort, of which Contrecoeur and his three captains—Beaujeu, Dumas, and Ligneris—were justifiably proud.

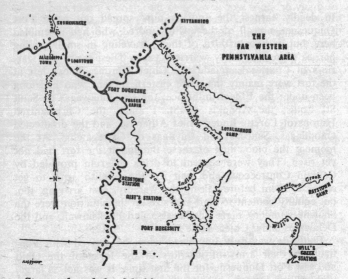

THE
FAR WESTERN
PENNSYLVANIA AREA

Strong though he felt himself to be in fortification, if not in manpower—at the moment only a few companies of regulars supported by a large number of Canadians—Contrecoeur still welcomed Langlade and Pontiac heartily. Nor had he been long in apprising them of the fact that the English army under Braddock was already on the move. That was when he had suggested that these Indians from the west, who were primarily Chippewas, Ottawas and Potawatomies, but with a scattering of Delawares and Shawnees and even a

314

few Mingoes,[2] spy on the movement of the army and harass it in its movements.

They had moved out at once in their small bands, but when they reached the four-mile-long ribbon of Braddock's army cutting its laborious twelve-foot wagon road through the forested mountains, they were awed by its apparent strength and kept their distance. Here and there they would catch and scalp a straggler or scout and now and then inscribe dire warnings on debarked trees in the path of the advancing army, but mostly they kept their distance.

In point of fact, they soon drifted off to easier pickings.

The frontier was now basically undefended and from settlement to settlement the Indians moved, looting, burning, killing. Many of the settlers gathered up their families, abandoned their cabins and fled to the east, but there were as many or more who refused to be frightened out and many of these paid the greatest price for their obstinacy. With their rude, isolated farms forming a wavering, seven-hundred-mile-long boundary of English habitation, these pioneers were generally a coarse, tough lot, little removed from savagery themselves. When attack came, there was no one to cry for help; it was simply a matter of fight or die. In a great many instances it turned out to be a case of fight *and* die.

A new and gruesome chapter was opening in the border annals. Within two weeks of their arrival here, the Indians of the west had butchered thirty Pennsylvania and Virginia families.

[ *June 17, 1755—Tuesday* ]

At eighteen James Smith was a surprisingly intelligent youth for one so isolated on the Pennsylvania frontier, where the average youngster grew up in illiteracy or, at best, with only a rudimentary knowledge of books. Not Smith. He could quote with both appropriateness and fidelity from some of the best essays, poems and other literary works of the time, often amused himself by posing and then solving mathematical problems, and heartily detested frontier life.

His intelligence and education was far more a tribute to his mother than his father. From Walter Smith, genial, handsome and virtually uneducated trader turned settler, he had learned many of the ways of the woods and was confident in his ability to protect himself at any time, should the need arise. Also from his father he had inherited a fine physique and good features and his six feet of height. But it was from

315

Sarah Smith, his mother, that his intelligence had been nourished, his knowledge broadly expanded.

Sarah loved her husband deeply; too well even to suggest that he give up the way of life he loved for the one she so yearned for in secret. But she meant her son to have his latent talents developed and at every possible opportunity she was with him—teaching him, conversing with him, explaining things to him. To one who did not know his background, it would have been hard to believe that James Smith had not attended a regular school in his entire eighteen years.

It was for his mother's benefit, therefore, because she was concerned over the growing Indian attacks on this frontier, that he had embarked on two new projects. The first was, through subtle hints, to convince his father to take them back to the east coast where Sarah belonged and would be so much happier. The second was twice each day to walk a regular circular patrol five hundred yards or so in radius around their cabin with their wolf-like mongrel dog, Jupiter, to keep a watch for Indian sign anywhere nearby.

It was on just such a patrol that he was walking now when Jupiter suddenly stiffened and cocked his head to one side. A rumbling, ominous growl sounded from deep within the dog. James, too, had heard the same sound that affected Jupiter— from toward their cabin, a thin, wavering screaming filled with unspeakable terror.

He didn't even have time to react to it. A deadly buzzing sound came and Jupiter grunted and tumbled in a thrashing pile as an arrow plunged into his body just behind the foreleg with such force that it drove through the animal's heart and protruded nearly three quarters its length out the other side.

The young man spun about and found himself in the center of a triangle of Ottawa Indians, two with muskets and one with bow and arrow—all three weapons centered menacingly on him. Almost without conscious thought he allowed his own gun to thud to the ground at his feet.

One of the musket-armed Indians walked up to him and said something he could not understand. Again from the distance came the piercing scream which could only have issued from the throat of his mother. It was the last thing James Smith heard before the rifle barrel slammed into his temple and laid him out on the ground beside the body of his dog.

William Johnson hoped that things would go better at the grand council now convening in front of Mount Johnson than they were going at Albany where his army was gathering.

The friendliness that had peaked quickly between himself and Governor Shirley at Alexandria had now taken an abrupt downswing. He found the new commander of colonial forces to be overbearing in almost every respect, treating William as though he were some kind of fool whose thinking would have to be done for him. It would have been bad enough if some sort of distance had separated them but Shirley, too, had chosen to gather his army at Albany to march from there to Fort Oswego and subsequently against Fort Niagara.

With two different armies gathering at Albany and their commanders increasingly at odds with one another, the situation was not at all pleasant. There was a decided conflict of commands, since General Shirley was General Johnson's superior in regard to colonial troops, but Johnson was Shirley's superior in regard to Indian forces. There was another irritation, too: since Shirley was using the two royal Massachusetts regiments for his campaign, he received his financing through the Crown, but Johnson's force—strictly newly inducted volunteers—would have to be supported through colonial appropriations, and these were never easy to come by.

General William Johnson's force was supposed to be one of four thousand men: twelve hundred from Massachusetts, a thousand from Connecticut, eight hundred from New York, six hundred from New Hampshire and four hundred from Rhode Island. But though the army's ranks were slowly swelling at Albany, many of the contingents were in no hurry to get there and soon William was gnashing his teeth in frustration. Not only were the various colonies still arguing about who should pay what percentage of the cost for the coming affray, but certain segments of the army were already pulling foolhardy moves.

A case in point was the New Hampshire regiment, whose mountain boys were originally mustered to move under Colonel Monckton against the French forts of Nova Scotia, but who then had been given orders to report to Major General William Johnson at Albany instead. And, because they didn't like traveling by water, they refused to sail down the east coast and up the Hudson, but rather chose to move overland afoot through the mountainous wilderness to that place, risking attack by French or Indians in the process. William had even received reports that they were lost and would probably never show up. This he discounted, but the delay occasioned by their marching here would delay his entire campaign and it irked him considerably.

Now the council between himself and the Iroquois was commencing and he nodded with some satisfaction at the large number of Indians in attendance, despite the fact that they were tearing up his meadow and their horses were eating every green thing growing around the mansion.

Over eleven hundred of the Iroquois were assembled; a much better showing than had attended the last council here and for this, if for no other reason, he was encouraged. Session followed session and the council seemed to be going nowhere except into a morass of endless argument. Of all the Iroquois on hand, only the Mohawks appeared ready and willing to fight beside the English against the French. The reluctance of the other chiefs to do so as William well knew, was because a good many of the leading chiefs had lately formed a real attachment to the seemingly more powerful French interests.

In his dual position as William Johnson, Indian supervisor, and Warraghiyagey, Mohawk chief, the big Irishman talked and exhorted until he was hoarse, but for once he failed to reach them as he wanted to and the response was generally poor. At one point he slapped his hands to his sides and turned to one of his aides with a shake of his head.

"There is no way I can convince them to fight against the French, but thank God I have tried! I have no doubt that if this meeting was not being held, the major part of the upper nations would already have defected to the French. They might not fight *with* us for now, but for now I do not think they will fight *against* us.

Even when he was not addressing the entire assemblage, William continued his maneuvering and cajoling, seeking out the most important Indian leaders and appealing to each one individually, sometimes with arguments but more often with promises and presents and with assurances of deep affection. Yesterday in these endeavors he had worked without pause for rest or food for nearly twenty hours and when, at last, he retired to his huge house and jotted down a brief report before turning in, he wrote to Delancey:

*My conferences with them last from early morning until*

*twelve o'clock at night and sometimes later. The fatigue I have undergone has been too much for me. It still continues, and I am scarce able to support it.*

Nevertheless, in the morning he was at it again, only to learn that even at this distance General Shirley was attempting to usurp his command. He had sent William's one-eyed former deputy, John Lydius, to gather as many recruits from among the Iroquois as he could, to join Shirley in the Niagara campaign. Lydius was already circulating among the Indians gathered here. It wasn't a smart move to begin with and the choice of an agent was even worse. Over the years Lydius, eternally munching his hardboiled eggs and guzzling whiskey in prodigious amounts, had won a distinct enmity from the Iroquois through getting certain chiefs drunk enough to sign over land to him for a piddling amount.

Now Chief Grota Younga, the Seneca, arose in the council and pointed an accusing finger at Lydius, protesting against such recruiting before the Iroquois council had decided upon an official League policy.

"Brother Warraghiyagey," he said to William, "you promised us that you would keep your fireplace clean of all filth, and that no snake should come into this council. That man sitting there is a devil and has stolen our lands. He takes Indians slyly by the blanket, one at a time, and when they are drunk, puts money in their bosoms and persuades them to sign deeds for our lands."

Furious, Johnson ordered Lydius away and became more determined than ever that Shirley would get no Indian help at all until he was on the eve of departure from Fort Oswego.

But where Braddock was concerned, it was another matter. The commanding general was already deeply into his campaign and he needed Indian allies as quickly as possible. William explained this in detail to the assembled chiefs, urging that they resolve at once to go help him. And as luck would have it, it was just at this juncture that Chief Scarroyaddy and his warriors showed up, fresh from their meeting with Braddock, and William soon learned the bad news.

"The great man in Virginia," said Sarroyaddy dourly to the assemblage, "does not seem to love Indians and makes but little account of them. Such a man needs to be left to his own arm, that he may learn how weak it is."

Inwardly cursing Braddock's stupidity where Indians were concerned, William now attempted to mollify them and win

319

them, if not to Braddock's cause, then to the cause of Warraghiyagey. Throughout the rest of the day and into the night he orated at great length, delivering huge promises and praying that somehow they would be met. As usual, when he spoke to them at length, he gesticulated wildly and repeated himself much, reiterating things he had said to them many times before in past speeches, but they showed no impatience. This was the expected procedure.

At last, after several hours, he was finished. He was a seedling too long without water. The strain of maintaining such an oration was enormous and, as always, sapped him both physically and emotionally.

"My Brothers," he said loudly, "now that your ears and eyes, tongue and arm have been returned to you, will you so soon cut them off again? Is this how the Iroquois honor him who has lived for their benefit and wishes? Is this how you would treat me when it is now *my* hour of need? I cannot ask you to fight beside General Braddock if it is not your own desire to do so, for your desire is mine, but will you let this also interfere with any desire to help me? If you do this to me," he added darkly, "then, Brothers, I will stop my management of your affairs entirely and leave this country!"

The Iroquois chiefs gathered themselves into a tight cluster but their voices were an unintelligible mumble to William Johnson. He had slumped to the grass beneath a tree and sat there catching his breath and waiting, his expression calm but his insides clamped with the cold hand of fear that they would refuse.

At last, after nearly an hour of discussion, the chiefs broke up their meeting and Canassatego addressed William in a voice loud enough for all assembled to hear.

"Warraghiyagey, we will not cut ourselves off from you. When the time comes that you are ready, we will join and assist you in your undertakings."

Had he been by himself, William Johnson would have wept with relief.

### [ *June 28, 1755—Saturday* ]

Benjamin Franklin was only mildly curious about the excited voices he heard approaching his house. With characteristic steadiness he continued the writing he was doing at his little desk until heavy footfalls clumped onto his stoop and the door knocker was banged at least two or three times more than civility dictated.

With a sigh he put aside his quill and stepped to the large front door and opened it. A crowd of twelve or more men was clustered a short distance away, their voices loud and jovial and filled with sudden bursts of laughter. Franklin caught snatches of their conversation—words like "Braddock" and "victory" and "wonderful" and "Duquesne."

His attention, however, was directed to the two neatly dressed gentlemen at the door. He knew them well. They were the brothers named Bond, both of whom were physicians in the community. The elder of the pair greeted Franklin with an enthusiastic handshake.

"Ben, have you heard?" he asked. "Braddock's army was nearing the Little Meadow last Monday and by now he's probably beating down the gates of Fort Duquesne!"

Franklin raised an eyebrow but said nothing and now the younger Bond spoke up. "We're going to have a huge victory celebration. Thats what we're here for now. Beginning right here with you, we're taking up a collection for fireworks. Yes sir, we're going to have the gol-darndest display of fireworks that's ever been seen!"

The postmaster general was unimpressed and shook his head. "Not a gun has been fired yet, to our knowledge," he said.

The elder Dr. Bond looked at him in amazement. "Why, the devil!" he exploded. "Franklin, you surely don't suppose that fort won't be taken?"

"War," said Franklin, "is always an uncertain thing. I suggest your collection campaign be put off until actual word of such victory comes. Then there will be time enough—and justification—for such a celebration, and I will then be first to contribute."

He nodded, stepped back to close the door, then paused and added, "But, gentlemen, not until then."

### [ July 2, 1755—Wednesday ]

Through the English Colonies raced the confirmed word of victory, but it wasn't the anticipated victory of Braddock over the Fort Duquesne forces. On June 16 at the Bay of Fundy, Duchambon de Vergor, commandant of the French fort of Beauséjour, second fortification in strength to the Louisbourg fortress in Nova Scotia, had surrendered to the English troops sent out under Monckton, Scott and Winslow. The rest of Acadia, it was felt—including the primary fortress—would soon follow Fort Beauséjour's example. For all intents and purposes, so it was said, the English had won in that theater and not only that, rumor had it that Braddock was at this very instant sweeping down invincibly upon Fort Duquesne. Things couldn't be going better.

The rejoicing throughout the English Colonies was great, but at Albany—where the armies of Major Generals Shirley and Johnson were collecting—the jubilation was overwhelming. Morale had been slipping badly and this was a much needed lift of the spirits for all the men.

It was on this note that William Shirley ordered his army to begin the journey to Fort Oswego. Johnson was still waiting for his lost New Hampshire regiment and other segments of his force which had not yet shown up and he watched gloomily as the commander in chief of the colonial forces directed his troops away from the city. It was not as large an army as Shirley had wished but it was, to Shirley's way of thinking, strong enough to defeat a French force many times over that size, and then whip their Indian allies as an afterthought, just for amusement.

William Johnson doubted it very much. Shirley had only three regiments: the New Jersey Regiment, which was better known as the Jersey Blues; the Fiftieth Regiment; the Fifty-first Regiment—the latter two termed, respectively, Shirley's Regiment and Pepperell's Regiment. Supposedly, since they were paid by the King rather than the Colonies, they were regulars; the fact of the matter, however, was that they were the rawest of Provincials, with no battle experience whatever, their heads filled only with glory and their march as proud as strutting peacocks. If nothing else, they were colorful. Where Johnson's Colonials were clad in ragtag homespun, Shirley's were downright gaudy in their fine new uniforms and they delighted in them. Sergeant James Gray of Pepperell's Regiment strutted grandly beside his men, and in his breast pocket was a letter he had begun but not yet finished to his brother John who was with Braddock's force. He had written:

*I have two Holland shirts found me by the King, and two pair of shoes and two pair of worsted stockings; a good silver-laced hat (the lace I could sell for four dollars); and my clothes is as fine scarlet broadcloth as ever you did see. A sergeant here in the King's Regiment is counted as good as an ensign with you; and one day in every week we must have our hair or wigs powdered ...*

Johnson watched them go with a shake of his head, certain that at the first shot directed their way, at least two thirds of them would turn into quivering jelly, drop their guns and run. A band of fifty determined Iroquois would have no trouble in wiping them out.

"I wonder," he mused to one of his aides, "how many of them will come back down the Mohawk next fall?"

### [ July 4, 1755—Friday ]

For at least the fiftieth time since his capture by the Ottawas, young James Smith wished he had been killed along with his family and his dog Jupiter. And now, with Fort Duquesne spread out before them and hundreds, maybe even thousands, of Indians primed for his arrival, he had even more justification for the wish.

The days since he had been taken had become something of a painful blur in which all the many hurts that had been delivered to him—both physical and mental—merged. The individual horrors might yet come back some day to haunt him and cause him to rise screaming from his sleep, but for now his shocked mind was mercifully dulled and filled with only one consuming thought: to somehow stay alive.

The blow from the Indian's rifle barrel which had felled him, had caused the whole side of his head to swell and discolor. His ear was so puffed it looked like an angry red muffin and his eye was badly bloodshot and nearly swollen closed. He had awakened to find himself with his hands bound behind him and a rawhide leash around his neck tethering him to a sapling. His head was being shaken violently by the same Indian who had struck him down.

They shouted things at him in turn in their Indian tongue and, when he failed to reply to what were apparently questions, slapped him repeatedly with open hands until both lips were badly split and the blood from them joined with that gushing from his nose and made him cough and gag.

Within five minutes six other Indians came into the clearing, two of them triumphantly waving fresh scalps which had to be those of his mother and father. These Indians, too, had shouted things at him and when he only sat there mutely, they wrapped the hair of the scalps tightly around their fingers and whipped him with the bloody ends until, after a long while, he fell unconscious again.

When he came to his senses the second time, the already swollen eye was sealed shut with dried blood and further swelling, and the other he could open only a faint slit. The Indians were squatted around a fire, tearing at the carcass of an animal that had been spitted and blackened over the flames. It was with an odd sense of detachment that he realized the carcass was the remains of Jupiter.

They saw he was awake and one of them came toward him with a handful of foul-looking viscera scooped from the carcass. He tried to turn his head, but the Indian gripped his hair and held him and tried to force the mess into his mouth. When he refused to open his tightly clenched teeth, the Indian kicked him savagely in the groin, making him gasp in pain. As he did so, the handful was thrust into his mouth and the hand clamped over his face in such a manner that he had to swallow or suffocate. As soon as he had done so, the Indian released him and then he and the others slapped their sides and whooped with glee as young Smith vomited violently.

He didn't really remember much about the proddings along the trail as they marched, the many blows he took from fists and open hands and switches. They had stripped him of everything but his pants and now his bare feet were bruised and gashed and badly swollen. His one partially opened eye showed no spark of interest when another and then a third party of Indians joined them. He merely moved along in the direction pointed, repeating only one word over and over in his mind: *endure . . . endure . . . endure . . .*

And now they had arrived at Fort Duquesne where perhaps, just perhaps, he might find some sort of sanctuary among the French as their prisoner. The thought died aborning, however, when he saw the gauntlet line stretched out before him. Over a hundred yards in length it was, composed mainly of warriors with sticks and switches and thorny branches. The two lines of Indians—between which he must run—ended at the gate of the fort. An Indian approached him and spoke in badly broken English:

"Run. Take run. Indian hit. You fall, you die. No fall, live. Run!" He cut away Smith's neck leash and wrist bonds, slid the knife inside the ragged pants and cut them away, and then smashed the naked youth full in the face with the heel of his hand, repeating, "Run!"

James Smith broke into a stumbling shuffle and entered the double line of warriors who screeched hideously as he approached. Blows began raining upon him, but only from the rear. They pelted him from the back of his head to his ankles—stinging, biting, jarring blows which snapped him

324

from his lethargy and caused him to pick up speed. It was worse than a nightmare. He felt as if each long stride took minutes to complete and lifting a foot to push it forward and put it down again was more difficult than trying to run through waist-deep water.

The blows continued to fall, but no longer did they hurt individually. His whole backside was a living fire of agony and his run became again a staggering, reeling trot. Only half the gauntlet was run and now it came to him that he would never make it and from his half-opened eye a bloody tear oozed and jiggled away.

Abruptly a gagging, blinding handful of sand was pitched into his face and then, even though his legs were still moving mechanically, he was going nowhere and he realized with dull shock that he was on the ground and the blows were striking him everywhere now ... on shins and knees ... in groin and stomach ...

... and on his head.

[ *July 7, 1755—Monday* ]

The terrain over which General Braddock moved his army was so rugged that the progress made by the end of each day was little short of discouraging, especially to young officers like Colonel George Washington, who were so anxious to engage the enemy. As if it were a scarlet, blue and brown-banded snake in no hurry to get anywhere, the army slowly writhed along over the tortuous ground, preceded by three hundred axe-wielding soldiers and frontiersmen clearing the way for the following troops, packhorses, wagons and cannon.

Little by little, flanked by guard squads and with scouts coming and going regularly, the army inched to the crest which divided those streams which flowed to the east and the Atlantic, from those which flowed to the west and, ultimately, to the Gulf of Mexico. With dismaying regularity wagons fell apart from the constant jolting over roots, stumps and rocks in the twelve-foot-wide road being cleared, and Braddock had to keep a team of wagoners—led by a twenty-one-year-old sergeant named Daniel Boone—busy making repairs as best they could and abandoning those wagons damaged beyond repair.

The way was no easier on the western slope of the Alleghenies. All energies had to be devoted to easing around great crags and bluffs and ravines, and long detours were made to avoid insurmountable natural hazards. Day by day the army weakened, its battle strength being sapped by the labors of traveling where as much distance was covered moving up or down as forward. The horses, in poor condition at the outset of the march because of their inadequate diet of leaves rather than grain or pasturage, began giving out. They fell in their traces, gasping and wheezing their lives away and creating still more obstacles to be cleared from the army's path. Flocks of wheeling buzzards followed to feast on the carcasses left behind and they filled many of the more superstitious soldiers with forebodings of disaster.

In the first eight days of the march they had covered less than thirty miles and now the men themselves began to collapse, weakened not only by their unending labors but by a grinding dysentery which left some of them groaning with internal spasms, and a variety of fevers which plunged others into delirium.

Among the most exasperated at the snail's pace was Washington and he was not at all hesitant about making his feelings known to the general. "If we continue as we are going now," he told Braddock bluntly, "there will be no strength left in the men to fight when that time comes."

"What do you suggest?" Braddock asked.

Washington pointed toward the rear where the heavily laden wagons crept along by painful inches. "Our trouble, sir, is there. I think we should push ahead with a chosen body of troops and leave the heavy baggage behind to follow as it can."

Braddock considered this and then nodded. It was sound advice, especially in view of the fact that spies had just brought in word that at least five hundred regular French troops were at this moment on the way to reinforce Fort Duquesne. The general adopted Washington's plan and directed Colonel Dunbar to remain behind to command the rear division. And on the morning of June 19, after a night's rest, Braddock pushed ahead at only slightly increased speed with his officers, twelve hundred soldiers, thirty wagons, a large number of packhorses still able to travel well, and those pieces of artillery felt essential for what lay ahead.

And though some of the prostitutes remained behind with Dunbar's detachment, a good portion of them continued to trudge along after the army, their purses already bulging nicely with the coins thus far collected in their extensive nightly services. And with them, steadily and without complaint, came the pregnant Mary Francis.

The going was still very slow for the advance army, however, and not until today—twenty-seven days after leaving Fort Cumberland—did they reach the Monongahela a few miles upstream from the mouth of Turtle Creek. From here it was perhaps ten or eleven miles to Fort Duquesne.

When they had made their camp for the night, Washington took the opportunity to write his brother a brief letter:

*It was a great satisfaction to me when we left Colonel Dunbar behind with the main portion of our baggage and supplies, for it seemed we should now be able to forge ahead at greatly increased pace. The prospect conveyed infinite delight to my mind, though I was excessively ill at the time. But this prospect was soon clouded, and my hopes brought very low indeed when I found that, instead of pushing on with vigor without regarding a little rough road, they were halting to level every mole-hill, and to build bridges over every brook, by which means we were four days in getting twelve miles. Now we are near to the mouth of this stream which is called Turtle Creek and from there to Fort Duquesne is direct and short. To follow this route, however, would lead us through difficult country and a defile very perilous and ideal for ambuscade to be laid against us. The general has therefore resolved to ford the Monongahela at once to avoid the danger and then ford it again below Turtle Creek, from which point the way is clear. Under the circumstances I believe he is acting wisely and well. . . .*

### [ July 8, 1755—Tuesday ]

Pierre de Contrecoeur was almost ill with the apprehension that filled him as report after report came in on the advance of General Braddock's army. The Fort Duquesne commandant was not essentially a brave man and over these past three or four days an enormous fear had been spreading through him, preventing him from eating well or sleeping soundly, for fear that it would be his last meal or that he would awaken to find a knife at his throat.

Outside the fort the Indians were decidedly nervous, which did not add to his own comfort in the least. If eight hundred savage warriors, upon whom he was strongly depending, suddenly deserted him in the face of this threat, how could he possibly stand against it?

The day before yesterday, when several of Lieutenant Charles Langlade's Indians had come in with the report that

Braddock was very near, Contrecoeur had sent out the Chevalier de la Perade to reconnoiter and that officer had come back yesterday with the same report: Braddock's army looked strong and determined, was armed with artillery that could soon smash even the strong walls of this fort and, since he was fording the Monongahela now, undoubtedly he would quickly be here.

Then, this morning, he had sent out the brothers Normanville and now, in midafternoon, they were back already, nervously reporting the army's advance. It was obvious, they said, that Braddock would cross the river again at the fording place only a short way above the fort. Tomorrow, beyond any doubt, the battle would be in progress.

Captain Contrecoeur called for a war council with his officers and explained the situation to them, suggesting in a rather oblique manner that perhaps it might be well for them, before devastating battle could be joined, to send a party to the English under a truce flag and avoid bloodshed through an immediate capitulation.

The dark eyes of young, aquiline Captain Daniel de Beaujeu flashed angrily at the idea. No such capitulation could possibly be considered honorable. And furthermore, why should they wait for the enemy to attack them here?

"Sir," he said to Contrecoeur, "let me meet them—not with a flag but with lead and steel! They still have to cross the river and while they are so engaged we can ambush them there. Or, if not there, elsewhere between here and there."

"Do you think there could be the remotest possibility of success in any such attack, Captain?" asked Contrecoeur.

Beaujeu nodded. "Favor in battle lies more with he who attacks than with he who waits for attack. With the Indians and Canadians and some of the regulars, we may, if nothing else, be able to so weaken them that we could stand them off here at the fort. And if not, then at least it cannot ever be said that we did not try."

Contrecoeur successfully masked the sting he felt from the implication of Beaujeu's words. If the young fool wished to be a dead hero, then so be it. With a nod he accepted the plan and gave Beaujeu permission to lead an ambushing detachment.[3]

The handsome young captain left the fort at once to speak with the chiefs. In a short while he stood before Pontiac of the Ottawas, Athanase of the Lorette Hurons, and the other chiefs of the Chippewas and Abnakis, Shawnees and Caughnawagas, Delawares, Potawatomies, Nipissings and Algonkins. Squatted silently on his haunches, Langlade, too, listened to Beaujeu.

The captain told them quickly of the plan for an ambush and raised a tomahawk high, telling them that now the time had come, that now was the time to avenge all the wrongs the English had done them, asking them to accept the tomahawk and join with him and his men in this fight.

It was Athanase who stood first and spoke slowly, shaking his head at intervals as the guttural words rolled from his lips.

"We have sent our eyes into the woods," he said, "and have seen the English might. There we have seen the strength of their arm and we do not like that which we have seen. They come on us here with as many men as there are days in sixteen seasons and they have with them their sharp swords and their little guns and their great guns before which walls of much strength fall down. Evil spirits sit on branches and warn us not to oppose them. No, we will not go with you. Do you wish to die, and to sacrifice us besides?"

Beaujeu's nostrils flared and he refused to accept the decision. "Do you," he asked Athanase, "speak for all Indians?" He turned first to Pontiac and then to Pucksinwah and Black Hoof, and finally to White Eyes. "Does a Christian Huron, Athanase," he asked them, "speak for all the Indians gathered here? Does he speak for the Ottawas and the Shawnees and the Delawares? Does he speak for the other great war chiefs gathered in this council? Hear me! Frenchmen are men and we go to fight in the morning. Council among yourselves during this night and then in the morning give me your answer."

With that he turned on his heel and reentered the fort. When he was gone, Langlade spoke briefly.

"I will not urge you to go," he said. "For my part, I have given my word that I will fight the English, and I will do so. But if it is some sign that you need to encourage you, then hear this: in my dream last night I saw us moving toward our villages and we went with light feet, though our loads were heavy—for the loads we carried were the scalps and the plunder of the English."

### [ July 9, 1755—Wednesday ]

Though able to hobble about painfully with the aid of a crotched stick used as a crutch, James Smith was still far from well. That he was alive at all was something of a minor miracle; few men ever survived a gauntlet run.

It was to Charles Langlade that he owed his life. The half-breed had watched with interest as Smith ran the gauntlet. However, when he was downed and the beating continued, he interfered and convinced the Indians that it was to their benefit not to kill him. The youth might have information which the French could use to help defeat the English in the forthcoming battle. Reluctantly, the Indians gave in and permitted two French soldiers to carry the young settler inside the fortification.

Throughout the rest of the day and the night he had remained unconscious, and the next morning he awoke to the prickling pain of the Fort Duquesne surgeon opening a vein to bleed him. He was cleaned and fed some broth, then given a pair of dirty trousers to wear, but he stayed rolled in bedding all day. This morning, feeling terrible yet much better, he had awakened at dawn and slowly, painfully got to his feet. A wheezing cry of pain left him as he did so. His entire body was one massive ache and for the first hour it was all he could do merely to retain his balance with the stick that had been given to him.

Now, however, the acuteness of the pain was easing and though one eye was still swollen shut, he looked around himself cautiously with the other. He had been given the freedom of the fort, but was warned not to go outside the walls, as the Indians would kill him—a warning he believed implicitly. The bustle of activity everywhere within the fort intrigued him, though, and he watched the battle preparations being made. To get a better view he climbed to the rampart and found that the activity outside the fort even exceeded that inside.

He watched below him in the yard of the fort as the captain called Beaujeu removed his hat, kneeled and received a blessing and communion from a priest. The officer then threw off all but his trousers, swiftly painted his chest and face in dark lines and circles, strapped on a metal gorget of armor which protected his neck, shoulders and part of his chest, and then went out to the Indians.

The chiefs, accompanied by Langlade who had also adopted Indian garb, but without armor, came to meet him and even before he began speaking they were shaking their heads.

Then Langlade said something to them and they were silent while Beaujeu spoke at length and fiercely. Smith saw him thump his chest several times and point up the Monongahela. Even from this distance it was obvious that he was telling them he intended to fight, whether or not they would come with him. Though he could not understand the words, the young settler on the wall could faintly hear the officer's voice become sarcastic, then scathing. Just when it appeared that it had all been to no avail, the chiefs suddenly caught the fire of his appeal and nodded, raised their own tomahawks and uttered the fearsome war cry. Instantly it was echoed by all their followers some distance away until the whole valley seemed to ring with the sound.

Now, burning with the fever instilled in them by the French officer, they rushed about their camps and snatched up bows, guns, knives, tomahawks and war clubs. Band by band they set off on the path leading toward the ford of the Monongahela and, because he felt someday the information might be valuable, James Smith made an effort to count them. A total of six hundred thirty-seven Indians filed away, led by Beaujeu and Langlade, still in their Indian garb, and followed by thirty-five French officers and cadets, seventy-two French regulars and one hundred forty-six Canadians.

This was an impressive force of eight hundred ninety-one men, but still they were well outnumbered by Braddock's fourteen hundred fifty-nine, who were at this precise moment approaching the lower ford. Braddock knew that if an ambush was to occur against his force anywhere, it would probably come during this second fording of the river. He stopped the march on the west bank and studied the opposite shore closely for any sign of the foe, but there was none. At last the general put Lieutenant Colonel Thomas Gage in charge of a strong advance guard with orders to cross over and, if possible, secure the other side.

With their weapons held high above their heads, the advance party entered the water and started wading across in double file. Their faces were grim, their muscles taut, expecting at any moment to feel the impact of bullets slamming into them. But the crossing was made without incident and possession of the east shore quietly taken. It was incredible.

Certain that there must be French or Indian spies watching them, Braddock determined to make an impressive crossing. He gave the orders and with banners waving almost gaily under the cloudless sky, the fording was begun by the main army. George Washington, astride his horse on the west bank, watched with admiration and pride and he sensed the rise of the spirits of these men as, for the first time, they seemed to realize that a great victory was within their grasp.

The mounted officers crossed over first, then the lone troop of light cavalry. They were followed by the red-coated regulars and the blue-coated Virginians, then the wagons and tumbrils, the cannon and howitzers and coehorns.[4] The pack-horses came next and then the herd of beef cattle. Behind all came the gaggle of perhaps twoscore women, all considerably worn themselves from the rigors of the march. These latter Braddock again specifically ordered to stay where they were or go back, not to follow across the river—and again, some obeyed, but the majority ignored the order and followed the army across. With them still was Mary Francis: Private Edgar Francis had crossed; she would cross, too.

As soon as the entire army was safely on the east shore of the river, Braddock ordered a brief rest and refreshments for everyone; and a council of war was called for the officers. The general admitted to some perplexity about the fact that they had made the crossing unopposed and ordered that a tight alert be maintained from this point on. A wave of rumors washed across the troops: that the Indians had turned against the French on seeing the English strength and had massacred them all; that the French strength was not as great as anticipated and that the Indians had abandoned them and now the French were merely waiting at the fort to surrender; that the French themselves had deserted Fort Duquesne and were on the run. By the time the march was resumed, there was a general air of disappointment among the men that they had marched this far and now were to be cheated out of a good fight.

A short distance ahead of them as they began moving out, George Washington saw a sight he recognized at once—the deserted, lonely little cabin of John Fraser which he and Christopher Gist had reached when they were almost at the end of their endurance on the return from delivering Dinwiddie's dictum to the French. From this point the path curved inward, away from the river for some distance, then back again to run a parallel course to the Monongahela at the base of a line of steep hills.

More concerned by the lack of opposition than he cared to show, Braddock took precautions to avoid having his army caught in an ambush, which could so easily take place from the heavy forest flanking them. He ordered several guides and a half-a-dozen Virginia light horsemen to take the lead. Four or five hundred yards behind them came a vanguard of the army: three hundred soldiers under Lieutenant Colonel Gage, followed by a large party of axemen under command of Sir John Sinclair, to open the road for the following wagons. Two cannon with tumbrils and tool wagons came next and, finally, closing the vanguard, came its own rear guard. In addition, flanking parties were well out on either side of this procession.

Immediately behind the vanguard came the main body of the army, also with flanking parties spread out on either side. The artillery and wagons moved along the path which the advance axemen were turning into a road and the troops filed along near them on either side through the woods. Between the roughly parallel lines of troops came the packhorses and cattle. The rear of the entire procession was brought up by a body of regulars and provincials.

And it was an excellent marching plan; one that could hardly have been improved upon, considering the type of terrain being crossed. The main body of the army was just about to cross a densely overgrown ravine that Thomas Gage's vanguard had already passed, when the Virginia light horsemen and guides in the far front abruptly wheeled and fell back. Toward them from far ahead on the path was running a man painted like an Indian but wearing a gorget.

It was Captain Daniel de Beaujeu.

The French officer thumped to a halt on seeing the column and then instantly turned and waved his hat while a weird shriek issued from him. At once a great wave of Indians and soldiers poured out of the woods ahead, echoing their commander's shrieking, and swiftly spreading out to left and right for cover in the trees, their weapons already banging and great puffs of dirty blue-white smoke beginning to rise.

At a bellowed command from Gage, the vanguard deliberately and methodically formed a tight formation abreast and fired several volleys each at the spot where the French soldiers and Indians had been. Beaujeu still stood rooted where he had stopped his headlong run.

"*Attaquer!*" he shouted loudly, "*Attaquer.*"—Attack!

But the withering fire from Gage's men had already demoralized the Canadians, few of whom had ever before been under fire, and now their own cries overrode his:

"*Sauve qui peut! Sauve qui peut!*" —Stampede!

A great many of the French colony troops, prepared to fight, heard the cry, thought it a relayed order and pivoted to flee back in the direction they had come from, not even bothering to reload their emptied weapons.

*"Arrêter! Attaquer!"* screamed Beaujeu in rage, ordering them to stop and attack. But the rout continued and at the third volley from Gage's troops, half-a-dozen balls struck Beaujeu simultaneously, three of them nearly destroying his head and the others piercing his upper body. He flopped lifelessly to the ground.

Shots from the Indians well hidden among the trees now began to take their toll of Gage's men and he cried out an order for his cannon to be brought to bear. But with no distinct target at which to shoot, the artillery men became almost frantic and fired wildly into the woods with cannonballs that crashed fearfully through limbs and into trunks, but killed no one.

From behind Gage's force now came the closely ranked scarlet-coated regulars of Braddock, marching ahead with guns at ready and with the precision of puppets, their voices raised in a booming rendition of "God Save the King."

With the death of Beaujeu, Captain Dumas was now in command and he was sure that his remaining Frenchmen and Indians were lost. Nevertheless, a wild recklessness that he had never known before came over him now and he leaped forward shouting to his men as he ran.

"Follow me! Fire! Kill them!"

Captain Ligneris, now second-in-command, was amazed and overjoyed when the remaining soldiers rallied well and poured a blistering fire into the red ranks ahead. Dozens, then scores of the English dropped to the ground dead or wounded and the Indians, seeing this happening, rallied themselves to the shouts of four of their leaders in particular—Langlade, Pontiac, Pucksinwah and White Eyes—and plunged forward for the close-in fighting at which they so excelled. While the French regulars and what remained of the Canadians held their ground before Braddock's army and continued to direct brutal volley after volley into the exposed English ranks, the Indians infiltrated the flanks. Added now to the shots and screams and moans was the deadly thud of tomahawk or war club slamming home in English skulls and bodies.

They made short work of the army's flankers, killing them or driving them back to the main body, and then directed another murderous fire into the redcoats still standing, who were loading and firing volley after useless volley into the trees ahead without aim and only rarely hitting an enemy. It was now that the most destructive fire of all began from a large group of Abnakis, Hurons, Nipissings and Algonkins led

334

by none other than the former reluctant Chief Athanase. They had all climbed the nearest hill and found themselves with the distinct advantage of being able to fire down into exposed, densely formed troops while themselves remaining under highly protective cover. It was almost as if a scythe were slicing down the redcoated ranks.

Braddock, at the first firing, left a four-hundred-man force under Sir Peter Halket to guard the baggage, and himself then thrust forward with the rest of the army to support Gage. Though only short minutes had passed since the first firing, to those in Gage's vanguard it had been an interminable time. Already their two cannon were being abandoned and those remaining alive of Gage's force were beginning to fall back to escape the wicked fire from front and flanks and hilltop, leaving behind a ground made scarlet with the bodies of their companions.

They were close to panic now and as they met Braddock's approaching force they darted in among the men and tried to find cover behind them. It threw the whole body of troops into a deadly disorder. The regiments became hopelessly mixed and suddenly the army found itself in several dense pockets of almost total disorganization, some facing one way, some the other, and only those in the center momentarily safe from the hail of bullets coming their way.

The regulars were thoroughly confused. This was not how they had been taught to fight a war. It simply wasn't fair or right for the enemy to fire upon them without standing up to be fired upon in return! They didn't know what to do and they were being slaughtered. Only the Virginians realized the desperate necessity of fighting this enemy on its own terms and they began to move out, disperse themselves among the trees and return the fire from cover.

It was an effective move and the balance of the battle shifted back somewhat in favor of the English. Not for long, however. Outraged that the provincials should act in a manner that literally shocked his ideas of battle courage and discipline, Braddock shouted at them in a voice thick with fury.

"Where the hell are you going? Get back here! God damn it, get back in these ranks and fight like men, not animals. Form the lines, captains! Get your men back here to support us!"

Some of the Virginians heard and obeyed, but others went on. One group of about twenty, under Captain Phineas Waggoner, plunged toward a huge log at the edge of the woods, secured it and began pouring a highly effective fire at the Indians. Private Edgar Francis was with this group. But the English regulars, hearing the concerted firing from this new quarter and seeing the clouds of smoke forming above the crouching men, mistook them for the enemy and themselves sent a barrage of musket fire toward the log, hitting Waggoner's men from behind and killing or wounding virtually all of them. Private Francis was among those killed.

The regulars themselves—some of them—began now to take refuge behind trees. Braddock saw their move and, shouting curses, galloped his horse down upon them and beat them out with the flat of his sword until he had flushed them back into the queerly coveylike formations with their comrades. Soon these clusters of humanity were not firing so much as they were writhing about in a concerted effort by each man to find some degree of shelter in the center. Individual rifle balls from the French and Indians sometimes passed through two men before lodging in a third and the dead English piled up in actual mounds. Abject panic was threatening and practically no heed was being paid to the commands and entreaties of the officers.

Braddock worked his terrified horse with difficulty to the side of Lieutenant Colonel Burton, gripped him by the shoulder to get his attention, and pointed to the hill where Athanase's Indians were still raining the heaviest shooting upon them.

"Get some men," Braddock shouted. "Get some men and take that damned hill!"

Burton nodded and leaped away, handpicking men as he found them, ordering them to fall in behind him. Finally, when he had gathered about a hundred, he led them in a charge up the rising ground. Three fourths of the way to the top a ball smashed his hip, shattering the socket and sending him tumbling. Instantly his men turned around and raced right back to the main army, despite Braddock's bellowed commands for them to go on.

For the English soldiers, the world had gone mad. A fantastic din of screams from the Indians and angry curses from officers and men alike, the cannonading, rifle fire, the bellowing of wounded cattle and the thunder of terrified horses leaping about, the cries of the wounded and dying men—all these terrible sounds smote their ears at once. Gunsmoke was so thick that it was difficult to see anything clearly and tears ran from the irritated eyes of everyone. Many of the soldiers were simply loading and firing mechanically, wholly without aim; the guns sometimes going off while directed skyward and at other times into their own comrades.

Braddock was indefatigable, seemingly everywhere at once—ordering, pleading, threatening, bullying, desperately trying to quash the ever-rising panic. Four times in succession his horse was shot from beneath him and he immediately mounted another, undaunted. The fifth animal somehow was not hit seriously, though two balls ripped furrows in its haunches.

Captain Robert Gethen, who had brought the last horse to him, had just turned away when a bullet tore through his throat. It spun him around but he managed to stay on his feet. With a fantastic amount of blood spurting from his ruptured jugular vein, he stared at Braddock for a long terrible moment, his mouth working soundlessly as he tried to speak, and then he collapsed. Braddock kneed his horse away.

Working every bit as hard as the general to hold the force together was George Washington; cursing at his men, encouraging them, berating them, urging them on, doing anything to keep them going, to keep panic from sweeping away all reason. His horse was struck in the head by a bullet and fell dead, catapulting him from the saddle, but he sprang up, caught another and in a moment was astride it. Within five minutes this one, too, caught a fatal bullet, and Washington found a third. Four bullets had already ripped through his clothing, yet he remained unwounded.

The Indians had by now worked their way down to the rear of the column and even Sir Peter Halket's four hundred were under severe fire. As Braddock had done up front, Halket ordered his men to stand firm and fire effectively, but they were dropping in their tracks by the dozens under this fusillade. Seeing that conditions were worsening for Braddock, he ordered the commander's secretary, young William Shirley, to lead a detachment to the general's aid. But even as the young man was nodding his head, a bullet tore through his brain and he fell. Another, an instant later, struck Halket in the breast and ripped through his heart and he tumbled from his horse.

"Father!" the anguished cry came from Lieutenant Halket nearby. He rushed to the older man and lifted his head into his lap, murmured "Father" again, and then slumped over dead himself as a ball tore off the back of his skull.

With the death of both Major Halket and his son, what

few shreds of discipline remained among the wagoners and packhorsemen disintegrated. They left their wagons or threw the packs off their horses, jumped astraddle the animals and galloped off, most of them heading back toward the fording place, but some striking out cross-country into the hills. Only a small percentage of these got through.

Lieutenant Henry Gladwin of the Forty-eighth Regiment, knocked a soldier unconscious when the man became hysterical and threatened to spread his panic among the men. Then he grinned at the men around him.

"Keep those barrels hot, boys. We'll lick 'em yet!"

At that moment a rifle ball slammed through his upper arm and he nearly fell. Catching himself and holding the wound with his free hand, he grinned again, a bit lopsidedly this time. "Well, dammit, I'm the one who's shot, not you. Keep firing!"

All around them men continued to fall and officer after officer felt the sudden burning agony of a bullet ripping through his flesh. In rapid succession Captains Rose, Tatten and Poulson were killed. Lieutenant Colonel Gage took a shot in the right shoulder and Major Gates caught one in the left thigh, and both Captain Orme and Captain Morris were struck in the upper arm. None of the wounded officers relinquished their duties unless so disabled they could not walk; and even then many of them called orders from the ground where they lay.

Braddock, still racing about on a horse ready to fall from exhaustion, stared about unbelievingly. For three hours now the battle had been raging and it was becoming clear that the English were defeated. To attempt to hold this ground any longer would only result in the total annihilation of his army. Standing high in the saddle and cupping his mouth, he bellowed the order he had felt would never issue from his lips:

"Retreat! Retreat! Back to the river and cross it. Retreat!"

The command was picked up by officers and men and echoed down the line. And only an instant after he had given it, Braddock himself felt the searing blow of a bullet. It came from one side and caught him in the upper arm, ripping through muscle tissue and out the other side to pass into his body and lodge in his lung. He fell into a brushy thicket.

At once one of his messengers, a boyish corporal named John Campbell, was at his side trying to pull him out, but Braddock moaned with the pain it caused and told him to stop.

"Get away if you can," the general said, foamy flecks of blood forming at the corners of his mouth. "I'll be all right. Get away. Try to get word back to the frontier what's happening. Hurry, while you can still get away!"

Campbell nodded and, racing off, soon encountered Captain Stewart. He stopped and pointed to the place where the general lay almost hidden by the brush, said a few words, and then ran on, to become quickly lost in the turmoil.

Captain Stewart found one of the Virginians who could help him and they went to the aid of General Braddock. The commanding officer shook his head, trying to talk past the bloody froth in his mouth, throat and nose which threatened to strangle him.

"No!" he gasped. "I'm finished. Leave me where I am. Go!"

Stewart brushed aside his order and nodded to the Virginian. Together they picked up the general and carried him to the rear, several times being almost knocked down by the panic-stricken scrambling of the men who had quickly made of the retreat a totally disorganized rout. Washington and Gates, Orme and Morris and others of the officers tried to hold them in order, but with no more success than if they had ordered a falling tree to stop.

In witless terror, the bulk of the army still capable of moving under its own power, rushed to the river and splashed into the shallows, then surged across the waist-deep middle to the other side, leaving behind all baggage, cannon, horses, weapons, wagons and wounded companions to the Indians.

They were pursued by only a small party—perhaps fifty men, mostly French regulars led by Captains Dumas and Ligneris—and even these stopped at the edge of the river and turned back. The others were already plundering the fallen. The screams which arose from the wounded were ghastly, as their heads were broken by tomahawks or war clubs, or knives were plunged into their bodies. All were scalped. Not all of the wounded were killed, however; to one side of the path a circle of Indians was stripping and binding a half-dozen unwounded English who had surrendered and that many more who were only slightly wounded.

At Fort Duquesne, young James Smith maintained his perch on the rampart, watching, waiting, hoping with all his might for an English victory. In the middle of the afternoon a runner burst from the forest and sped shouting through the Indian encampment to the fort. In minutes the entire fort was the core of another great and apparently joyful hubbub. An old French soldier—a regular—soon climbed the rampart to take up a watch near him, and Smith hobbled over to the man.

"What's happened, sir?" he asked. "Please tell me, what's it all about?"

The soldier shook his head and indicated he did not understand. Again Smith addressed him with the same questions, this time in the Dutch tongue of his mother, and the soldier beamed and nodded.

"It is wonderful news that a runner has just brought," he replied in the same language. "We are beating them. We are defeating the English! We and the Indians have surrounded them and are firing on them from cover while the English stand in the open. He said he saw them falling in heaps and if they did not take to the river, which is the only gap, and make their escape, there would not be one man left alive before sundown. It is wonderful!"

Almost sick with the disappointment of it, Smith leaned against the pickets and continued his watch. Some time passed and then he heard the scalp cries of Indians coming from the woods. In moments they emerged—a party of perhaps fifty of the Indians and twenty or thirty of the French. In their hands they carried and waved triumphantly aloft a number of bloody scalps, grenadiers' caps, English canteens, English bayonets and other items. And with them they brought the official news that Braddock was defeated.

A short while later another group came in, chiefly Indians and about a hundred in number. To Smith it seemed that every man among them was carrying at least one scalp. Not far behind them came another group leading wagon horses and also carrying many scalps. Those arriving and those already here kept up a running gunfire and harsh, victorious shrieking.

It was about sundown that the last of them came in—a smaller group prodding before them twenty or thirty prisoners, including at least half a dozen of the women that had followed Braddock's army across the river. One of them was heavy with child and even heavier with grief, for she had seen the scalped body of her husband beside a log on the battlefield.

All the captives, both men and women, had been stripped naked and their hands tied behind their backs. The faces and upper bodies of half of them had been smudged with charcoal, and James Smith knew it was the mark of the *cut-ta-ho-tha*—the mark of the condemned.

The prisoners were marched to the river bank and taken

across to the Ottawa and Chippewa camps on the west bank of the Allegheny directly opposite the fort. With a fascination bred of horror, Smith watched posts being erected and a dozen of the blackened men were tied to them. Roaring fires were quickly built around them—not close enough to burn them with living flame, but close enough so that little by little their skin cooked and blistered and then charred. It was a process that took hours and the hideous cries of the tortured men reached peaks of frenzied intensity as flaming brands and red-hot ramrods were poked at their eyes and mouth and genitals.

At last the young man could not stand it any longer and he hobbled back down to his quarters, but even there the faint tortured screams of those wretched men reached him and continued all through the night.

For the French, jubilant and triumphant and not in the least disturbed by the screams, it was a victory beyond all expectations, beyond even the wildest dream. While no one could be sure exactly how many Indians had been lost, the number could not have been higher than perhaps thirty-five or forty. The loss among the French was relatively slight: three of their officers had been killed and four wounded; and of the regular soldiers and Canadians, only nine had been killed or wounded.

For the English, however, the loss assumed the proportions of a catastrophe. Sixty-three of the eighty-six officers had been killed or disabled. Of the thirteen hundred seventy-three noncommissioned officers and enlisted men, only four hundred fifty-nine came away unharmed. The total dead-or-wounded figures for both sides were startling: for the French, sixteen; for the Indians, forty at the maximum; but for the English, nine hundred seventy-seven!

Though it was still undeclared, there was no vestige of doubt remaining in anyone's mind—the French and the English were again at war.

### [July 10, 1755—Thursday Morning]

Pierre de Contrecoeur confronted Charles Langlade angrily and said, "Monsieur Langlade, just where do you think you are going?"

The half-breed looked steadily at the Fort Duquesne commandant for a long moment and finally shrugged his shoulders slightly and murmured, "Home, Captain."

"Home! You can't go home yet."

Langlade's brows pinched together and he swept out his arm to indicate the camps of the Ottawas, Chippewas, Potawatomies and Hurons who were busily engaged in packing the gear and plunder for the homeward trek.

"They are ready to leave," he said. "They and I have fought the English for you and defeated them. It is what they came here to do. They have done it. They wish now to return to their families, to rejoice over their victory, to bring back the prisoners they have kept alive, to exhibit their trophies of battle and to mourn their dead. I led them here. I will lead them back."

"But if you go now, Monsieur Langlade, you will leave us defenseless here. As soon as General Braddock's reinforcements come to him from his Colonel Dunbar, he will attack us again. We need you here."

Langlade shook his head. "No, you will not be defenseless, Captain. You have lost hardly any in the battle and your eastern and northern Indians—most of them—are still here. As for the English, you did not see with your eyes as I did how badly they have been beaten. They will not come again for a long time. They have run, those who were yet able to run, like frightened dogs and they have lost everything. They have nothing left to fight with. No, Captain, they will not return. And we will not stay."

Langlade paused for a moment and then added, "I had not intended to leave without first seeing you to give you something." He dug inside his buckskin shirt and produced a packet of papers which he handed to the French commandant.

"The men of Chief Pontiac," he said, "found these in a chest on the field of battle. They wish to keep the chest but gave the papers to their chief, who gave them to me. I am not able to read them, but they look important, so I give them to you. And now we go. Adieu, Captain."

Contrecoeur took the papers with hardly a glance and, without even thanking Langlade or acknowledging his farewell, turned and stalked back into the fort. He noted that the remaining Indians seemed stationary enough in their camps and he hoped they would remain. Nevertheless, the specter of a retaliatory strike by the English after they were reinforced by Dunbar continued to haunt him.

In his quarters he placed the packet of papers Langlade had given him on the desk, opened it and looked closely at the official pages. He could not read English but here and there he could see important names of people and places and his interest grew. He called his aide and sent him to fetch someone who could read English and return with him.

In ten minutes the aide returned followed by young James Smith who hobbled along fearfully with the aid of his makeshift crutch. He did not know why he was being summoned, but it frightened him. With them was another French regular who could speak English, but not read it. Contrecoeur motioned Smith to a chair and handed him the papers

"Tell him," he told the English-speaking soldier, "that he is to read this aloud to you so that you can translate for us. And tell him to change nothing, that we will soon know whether or not he read it accurately and if he did not, we will turn him over to the Indians to do with as they like."

The French soldier nodded and translated the order to English. James Smith paled, the visions of the tortures undergone last night by the English prisoners still fresh in his mind. He swallowed nervously and then agreed to do as he was told. Sentence by sentence then, he read the documents and sentence by sentence, as they were transformed to the French tongue, the atmosphere became charged with excitement.

When they were finished, Contrecoeur ordered Smith back to his quarters. When both he and the interpreter were gone, he sent his aide to have a courier and a double-strength armed escort party prepared to ride for Montreal within the hour. The aide left at once.

Contrecoeur now took his place at the desk, set to one side his report of yesterday's battle, upon which, after lengthy conferences with Dumas and the other officers who had been in the battle, he had worked on most of the night. In that report he had also asked to be relieved of his Fort Duquesne command. For a long while he sat motionless with the English papers before him and then finally he set them off to the other side of the desk and began to write a letter:

10 July 1755

Marquis de Vaudreuil
Governor
Montreal
Excellency:

In separate pages I have prepared for you a full account of our decisive victory yesterday over the English under General Braddock along the River Monongahela not far from this establishment. I have also requested, for the reasons stated herein, to be relieved of command of Fort

*Duquesne and be permitted to return to Montreal. But the reason for this letter is another matter.*

*I have now the honor, Sir, to impart to you news of the utmost importance and urgency. The papers enclosed here, written in English, were recovered from a chest on the battlefield. They are complete battle plans for a campaign being launched at this very moment against Fort St. Frederic at Point à la Chevelure [Crown Point] The English army moving against this installation is under the command of Major General William Johnson . . .*

### [July 10, 1755—Thursday Noon]

"Sir," the sentry said, saluting, "three riders approaching from the west. They're acting rather strange."

Colonel Dunbar nodded and dismissed the guard, wondering vaguely why the riders should be acting oddly, but not surprised at their arrival. He had been expecting dispatches from General Braddock before now.

He sauntered out to meet them and, as the sentry had been, was confused at their actions. They appeared to be reeling in their saddles and endeavoring to make their horses travel faster, but the animals were apparently too jaded to manage any more than a walk. They were still a quarter mile away and now Dunbar sent out an escort to meet them. But his perplexity turned to alarm when he saw the escort rein to a halt in front of them and then, after only a moment, wheel about and gallop furiously back to camp.

"Colonel Dunbar, sir," the soldier shouted, even before he brought his horse to a halt, "the army's been destroyed!" He leaped off the horse. "Almost everyone's dead, sir. Those men say they only got away at the last minute. General Braddock's badly wounded and is being brought back as fast as possible. Everything's been lost."

The trio of horsemen—wagoners who had somehow been able to catch mounts in the confusion of the retreat and get away—were now only a few hundred yards away. Their names were Matthew Laird and the brothers Michael and Jacob Hoover. The three were babbling almost incoherently to him even before the running Dunbar got within earshot, all trying at the same time to tell what had happened. They dismounted, still talking wildly as he reached them, but his voice was a whipcrack which silenced them and then he ordered Laird alone to tell what happened.

In reasonably chronological order, the wagon man told

him of the defeat, the incredible number of English soldiers who had fallen, the wounding of Braddock, and the fear-blinded retreat across the Monongahela. Throughout Dunbar's camp the word of the tragedy spread as swiftly as it was uttered and within minutes this camp itself was in a panic. Visions of the victorious French and Indians following up the rout and wiping out the survivors and then advancing on this camp to do the same quickly filled their minds.

In moments a number of soldiers and teamsters under Dunbar had leaped to the saddle and thundered away to the east despite the colonel's shouted order for the sentries to stop them. The only way to stop them would have been to shoot them, and the men speeding off in terror were their friends and countrymen and they just couldn't bring themselves to do it. So the sentries merely milled helplessly and watched them disappear eastward on the miserable road so laboriously hacked out of the wilderness.

In a rage, Dunbar got matters under control, trebled the sentries and ordered them to shoot to kill anyone else who might attempt desertion. Then, after leading the fatigued survivors of the battle to the camp and questioning them some more, he ordered a half-dozen wagons filled with supplies and a company of soldiers as an escort and reinforcement to leave at once to join Braddock and render whatever help was required. And all the while, over and over he kept thinking, It can't be true . . . it can't be true . . .

### [July 11, 1755—Friday]

Colonel James Innes at Fort Cumberland heard the screaming of the women shortly after noon and rushed outside to see what was happening. Near the gate a large crowd was forming around an exhausted man who had been helped from his equally exhausted and now panting and spraddle-legged horse.

From all quarters others were rushing to see what was the matter. Some were soldiers recuperated enough from their illnesses to be on their feet again, but mostly they were the wives and sweethearts of Braddock's men. From them the screaming and crying increased.

An ensign raced up to the commander and threw him a hurried salute as he skidded to a halt. "Sir," he gasped, "terrible news! General Braddock has been defeated. His whole army wiped out. One of the wagoners—his name's Bristell—managed to catch a horse and get away. He's there

345

now." The young officer pointed at the milling, wailing crowd.

"Bring that man to my quarters at once, Ensign!" Innes rapped the order out sharply, his face set in hard lines. "Disperse that crowd, close the gate and double the guard at all posts. Every man who can walk to be put on the alert. Three men to reconnoiter out toward Dunbar's camp. Move!"

The ensign sped off again and Innes reentered his quarters, stunned by the news and desperately hoping that Bristell was simply a deserter who had concocted a wild story. But half an hour later, when the terrified wagon man had finished gasping out his story, the commander knew it was not a tale told from his imagination. With growing alarm he had listened while the man told of how and where the attack had occurred and the carnage that had followed, culminating in Braddock being shot off his horse and apparently killed, just after shouting the retreat order. That was when the wagoner had fled overland.

Dunbar ordered the weary man fed and cared-for and immediately wrote a brief letter to Lord Fairfax at Williamsburg:

*11 July, 1755*

*Sir,*

*I have this moment received the most melancholy news of the defeat of our troops, the general killed, and numbers of our officers; our whole artillery taken. In short, the account I have received is so very bad, that as, please God, I intend to make a stand here, 'tis highly necessary to raise the militia everywhere to defend the frontiers.*

*J. Innes, Col. Commanding*
*Fort Cumberland*

### [July 14, 1755—Monday]

The report Colonel Innes received and forwarded of General Braddock's death was an error more in time than in fact. From the instant he was shot, the commanding general was a living dead man, his life slowly oozing away in the bubbly, wheezy sound which came from the hole high on his side with each painful breath he took.

Not until the captain and private who had picked him up on the field of battle had carried him across the Monongahela fording place and a quarter mile up the path on the other side, did they set him gently to the ground and themselves practically collapse with exhaustion. The general had been conscious all this while but said nothing, though it was obvious he was in great pain. A constant stream of wounded and unwounded men was still coming from the direction of the river, some helped by comrades, some struggling along on their own. They reported still others coming behind.

Four of the officers—George Washington, Robert Orme, Thomas Gage and Henry Gladwin—managed to round up a hundred of the fleeing soldiers and collect them around the general, but when Braddock gasped out the order that they should fortify themselves as best they could here and hold this position to await reinforcements from Dunbar, the terror grew in them again. Individually and in small groups they began slipping away and continuing the retreat upriver. Within an hour almost all of them were gone, as was Lieutenant Gates, who spurred after them in an attempt to stop and hold them. Now, despite the pain the general was in, they would have to go on.

They rigged a blanket litter for the officer and, taking turns with the carrying, managed a reasonably fast pace to the upper ford of the river. Along the way they passed many wounded men who had collapsed and others who could only crawl, and Braddock's eyes filled with pain, for them as much as from his own wound.

"Tell them," he whispered to Orme, "tell them to come as far as they can and not give up hope. Tell them that we'll send help back for them. Give them my word on it."

When they forded the Monongahela to the east side again, they found Gates waiting for them with another eighty men he managed to rally there. Braddock, his voice stronger now, belying his weakening condition, called Washington to his side.

"Take some men and the best horses we have left," he ordered, "and leave at once for Dunbar's camp. Get wagons, provisions, hospital stores, men."

"Yes, sir," the young colonel said. In a few moments he was thudding away with six soldiers and the trader, George Croghan, behind him—all of them on very weary mounts, but animals far better than any of the others remaining.

Gage, Orme and Gladwin tried to convince the general that they should remain here, since some order among the men had been restored, but Braddock shook his head slightly. When he spoke, his voice was firm but so low that they had to lean over to hear.

347

"Look about you," he said. "These men are hardly under control. They want nothing more than to flee this place and they can almost hear behind them the war whoops. If we do not move on now, they will leave us in the middle of the night and then we will be without defense. Put me on a horse. I will ride."

The officers were shocked at the request, but he insisted and reluctantly they lifted him to the saddle. Immediately it was apparent that the pain in this position was unbearable for him and he could not possibly ride, so once again a litter was made. Captain Orme called for volunteers to carry him, but not until he offered a reward of a guinea and a bottle of rum apiece for bearers did two swarthy privates step forward and accept the job.

All night they moved slowly along, constantly passing still other wounded who could go no further or who had stopped to rest; occasionally losing men from their own party who fainted from loss of blood or simply collapsed from exhaustion. Throughout the next day—July 10—the painful journey continued and early in the evening they reached the remains of Gist's settlement. Here they were met by the wagons and reinforcement sent by Dunbar, themselves just having arrived.

Dunbar's men told them they had learned of the disaster first from some wagoners and then, shortly after starting out to give aid, had encountered Colonel Washington, who had urged them to hurry and himself continued with his party to Dunbar's camp. That camp, they added, was about six miles from here.

"Then we can get there by ourselves," said Braddock, raising his head slightly. "Lieutenant, take your detachment and all but one of the wagons and continue on our path. Cross the Monongahela at the first ford and continue to the second or as near it as possible without risking your own lives. Pick up every wounded man along the way and return with them to Colonel Dunbar. We will be there."

There was an audible groan from the wagoners and some of the soldiers, but the lieutenant saluted smartly and led them out. Braddock's party remained camped at Gist's and, in the morning, with the general and some of the other seriously injured still with them made as comfortable as possible in the wagon, they set out for Dunbar's.

Late in the morning—July 11—they reached the camp and found it still in a state of great excitement. Numerous retreaters had collected here, held from going farther by Dunbar's orders. Great mounds of supplies, gunpowder kegs and other goods were stacked at intervals all around. Colonel Dunbar himself, as the army's second-in-command, came at once to Braddock's side and was shocked at the ghastly pallor of his commander. He attempted to converse with him but was only partially successful. Braddock was weakening most seriously now and his voice was so faint that Dunbar had to put his ear close to the general's lips to hear what was said.

When at last he straightened, the other officers were appalled to hear him order an immediate destruction of all supplies and wagons except those necessary in their retreat—a retreat, he added, which would begin at dawn. With almost shameful haste the regular and provincial troops carried out the order. Over a hundred wagons were run together, turned over and piled against one another, then put to the torch. Even as they were burning, the cannon, coehorns and shells were either burst or buried. The kegs and barrels of gunpowder for muskets and cannon were rolled to a small creek nearby, their sides smashed in with axes and the contents dumped into the water. Provisions and supplies of all kinds were scattered with abandon all about the surrounding woods and marshes.[5]

In the dawn's light next day—July 12—the full-scale retreat to the east began and it was then found that too many wagons had been burned and a sizable number of the wounded had to walk, which slowed the whole procession terribly. They continued a dogged, dragging march all day and shortly before camping for the evening were rejoined by the reinforcement company and wagons which Braddock had ordered on to the Monongahela for the other wounded. Nearly every cavalryman had a wounded man astraddle behind him and the wagons were full. The lieutenant reported to Dunbar the only good news since the battle: that apparently no pursuit was being made by either the French or the Indians.

Braddock himself was nearing death. All through this day of marching he had remained silent, though conscious most of the time. Now, with Orme seated beside him, he suddenly spoke aloud with surprising distinctness.

"Who would have thought it?" he said. But they were the only words he uttered.

Yesterday—Sunday, July 13—the retreat was again begun in the early morning and once more Braddock said nothing all during the day. In the late afternoon they made camp near the Great Meadows, close to where the ruins of George Washington's Fort Necessity lay. And, as the men sprawled on the ground wherever they happened to be, a knot of officers gathered around General Braddock.

In the early evening Braddock's eyelids fluttered and opened. For a long while he looked at his officers and then just the faintest suggestion of a smile touched his lips.

"We shall better know how to deal with them another time," he muttered.

His eyes closed again and not long afterward—at eight o'clock—a long wheezing breath escaped him and he inhaled no more. Major General Edward Braddock was dead.

It was a gloomy night for all: behind them was a battle lost, an army lost, a commanding general lost; ahead, an ingloriously wretched return.

Before daylight, without the light of lanterns to betray their activity, they dug a hole in the middle of the road and buried their commander in it. A prayer was said and now, without eyes for the beautiful dawn lighting the sky and without ears to appreciate the trilling of cardinals and larks and robins, the remnants of the defeated army resumed its march.

The men, the horses and the wagons passed directly over the grave, forever obliterating its location lest any Indians following them should dig up and mutilate the body.

### [July 15, 1755—Tuesday]

The Ottawas returning to their villages were very hungry now. They had had little food with which to begin the long journey home and even this was quickly gone. Keg after keg of rum taken as plunder had been opened along the way and they had stumbled along giddily, drunkenly, savagely switching their thirteen naked prisoners if they began to lag. The seven men and five of the women had been able to keep up well enough, but Mary Francis, for whom each step had become agony, had been whipped so many times that her buttocks and back were raw. The heaviness of her pregnancy sapped her and it was clear that she had come about as far as it was possible for her to travel, and that her time of delivery must be very close.

When camp was made late in the afternoon in a wooded copse close to a creek mouth on the southern shore of Lake Erie, she slumped to the ground in exhaustion, wrung dry of tears and only able to stare unseeingly as the other prisoners were tied in sitting positions to individual trees. When it came her turn, she was unable to get to her feet to get closer to a tree, and so they let her lie where she was and the tether around her neck was run to a sapling and tied there.

From within her distended belly she felt the feeble kick of her unborn child—the first time it had kicked since yesterday—and she felt a vague stirring of relief. She had begun to think it had died. She closed her eyes and, while she did not sleep, she became insensitive to what was happening around her. She was not aware of it when the last of the rum kegs were opened and guzzled to the final drops by the savages. She did not even hear the kegs being knocked apart and the staves being tossed on the fire over which a ten-gallon pot half filled with water was bubbling. It was one of the pots taken as plunder from the English supplies on the battlefield. In fact, she was not aware of anything else until there came a sudden fantastic explosion of pain in her stomach and she jerked erect with an inchoate scream.

Instantly she was shoved flat on her back again by an Ottawa while another, who had shoved his knife deep into her stomach on one side, now ripped it crosswise and opened her clear to the other side. While she thrashed and screamed again and again, he plunged his hand into her and tugged out the fetus and then cut it away from the placental mass. He stood then and held it high for the others to see and, with their shrieks of wild approval ringing in his ears, carried it to the fire and tossed it into the boiling pot. Then he returned to her.

Her convulsive thrashings had caused the tether cord to bite deeply into her throat and the initial screams had degenerated into a hair-rising gurgling sound. The Indian took a handful of her long black hair and drew a quick circle around the top of her head with his knife. With a great yank he pulled the scalp free, but still the hideous sound issued from her and did not cease until he pulled the warclub from his waistband and caved in the bloody top of her skull with it.

Using tomahawks and knives, he and the Ottawa who had held her swiftly and expertly beheaded and dismembered her, tossing the severed limbs and other portions into a pile closer to the fire.

Two of the women captives had fainted and two others were having hysterics. The fifth, her face ashen and her eyes closed, sat with bowed head and her lips moving soundlessly, apparently in prayer. The seven English men were reacting in various ways—with horror, anger, fear, revulsion, sickness.

351

Two of them screamed the filthiest insults they could muster at their captors, and it was their undoing.

Half a dozen of the savages moved to them and even as they struggled and screamed, began cutting off their legs first and then their arms. Both lived long enough to see their own legs tossed in a pile with the pieces of Mary Francis; one lived long enough to sense his life draining away from where his arms had been.

The infant fetus was lifted from the pot with a forked stick. Even as a number of the severed adult limbs were taking their place in the pot, it was cut and ripped to pieces and devoured by the Ottawas who crowded around. The limbs themselves were hardly half-cooked before they too were forked out and still more thrown into the pot. The Ottawas were very hungry and had eaten little since leaving Fort Duquesne, and they had had no meat at all.

# CHAPTER VII

*[August 1, 1755—Friday]*

LIKE a great suffocating mist, the news of Braddock's defeat enveloped the English Colonies. Philadelphia heard it with a stunned, sickened silence and now the brother physicians, Bond, had cause to reflect on the words of Benjamin Franklin, that war is always uncertain.

Governor Robert Hunter Morris took the news before his council. They were as shocked as he, but the members of the Pennsylvania Assembly would not even believe it and actually insulted him in the street for giving credence to such a report and for further trying to stir up a war fever.

Lord Fairfax at Williamsburg had forwarded the brief letter from Colonel Innes to Governor Dinwiddie, but the governor himself could not believe it. He replied:

*I am willing to think that account was from a deserter who, in a great panic, represented what his fears suggested. I wait with impatience for another express from Fort Cumberland, which I expect will greatly contradict the former. I regret that word of this wild report has got out, for now the slaves show signs of excitement. The villany of the Negroes on any emergency whatever is what I have always feared. These Negro slaves have been very audacious on the news of the defeat on the Ohio. They believe it true, and these poor creatures imagine the French will give them their freedom. We have too many here; but I hope we shall be able to keep them in proper subjection. I have sent to Major Colin Campbell for news regarding the general forces. It's monstrous that they should be so tardy and dilatory in sending down any further account.*

But the expectation he harbored that the report from Innes was in error was shattered first by another letter from Innes to the governor himself, dated three days after that written to Fairfax. It was followed up a few days later with confirming letters brought by special courier from both George Washington and Robert Orme. The latter had written:

*My Dear Governor,*

*I am so extremely ill in bed with the wound I have received that I am under the necessity of employing my friend, Captain Dobson, as my scribe. We have suffered a grievous defeat and with this letter I am enclosing a full account of the battle. Believe me, Sir, when I say that the officers were absolutely sacrificed by their unparalleled good behavior; advancing before their men sometimes in bodies, and sometimes separately, hoping by such example to engage the soldiers to follow them; but to no purpose. Poor Shirley was shot through the head, Captain Morris very much wounded. Mr. Washington had two horses shot under him, and his clothes shot through in several places; behaving the whole time with the greatest courage and resolution.*

In Colonel Washington's letter Dinwiddie read:

*Sir,*

*Since Captain Orme is writing you a full account of the affair in which we suffered such a great loss, it is needless for me to repeat it. But I do wish to say to you, for what comfort you may derive from it, that our poor Virginians behaved like men, and died like soldiers; for I believe that out of three companies that were there that day, scarce thirty were left alive. Captain Peronney and all his officers down to a corporal were killed. Captain Polson shared almost as hard a fate, for only one of his escaped. In short, the dastardly behavior of the English soldiers [regulars] exposed all those who were inclined to do their duty to almost certain death. It is imagined (I believe with great justice, too) that two thirds of both killed and wounded received their shots from our own cowardly dogs of soldiers who gathered themselves into a body, contrary to orders, ten and twelve deep, would then level, fire, and shoot down the men before them; and at last, in spite of all the efforts of the officers to the contrary, they ran as sheep pursued by dogs and it was impossible to rally them.*

Washington also sent letters to his mother and his younger brother, John Augustine, not so much to report on the battle itself as to assure them of his well-being. He wrote:

*As I have heard a circumstantial account of my death and dying speech, I take this early opportunity of contradicting the first and of assuring you that I have not as yet composed the latter.*

Far to the north, on the flats just upstream on the Hudson outside Albany, where Major General William Johnson still waited with gnashing frustration for the arrival of the troops from New Hampshire, the news came with numbing force. A strong fear welled up in him. Few white men had ever understood the Indian mind as did he, nor could so well anticipate Indian reaction to events. He had little doubt that when the Iroquois learned of the defeat, out of simple self-preservation they would join the enemies and turn against the English.

But hardly had he read the report than into his clearing filed Tiyanoga, Wascaugh, Steyawa, Canassatego and a half-dozen other chiefs, some of them among the most respected and powerful in the Iroquois League. He greeted them with warmth, masking his own emotions, fed them well and, after they had rested, questioned them and discovered they knew nothing of the defeat. Playing it down as much as possible, he told them what had happened, not lingering on the enormity of the defeat, yet not omitting any of the essentials, which they must soon learn anyway from other sources. And when, a few hours later, they left, he immediately wrote a quick report to the acting governor:

*My dear Mr. Delancey,*

*I had just received the incoherent, unexpected, unintelligible, not to be credited, damned bad news of Braddock's army having been annihilated when, in less than an hour, some of the most leading men in the Upper Nations filed into my camp. I had at first thought that when they found out about the defeat that the greatest part of them would undoubtedly seek self-preservation and join our enemies against us and that therefore it would be madness to continue the Crown Point campaign without Indians and that it should be stopped and what forces could be spared from defense of the Colonies be concentrated under General Shirley against Niagara. I thought that I myself would leap into the forest, go through all the nations or try to get some of their most leading men to meet me at Onondaga, lay matters before them, use all the arguments and influence I am master of to prevent dissolution of our Indian connections. I feared that without them we English would face the last and worst of all evils, namely to perish infamously. But then came the leading men of the Six Nations to me and, after they had eaten and rested, I spoke to them and my questioning revealed to me that as yet they knew naught of England's disaster. I therefore told them, feeling that it would better be told them by me then by the French. I began in a minor key but warmed to the subject and finally had communicated the defeat pretty nearly in its true light. To my delight and even surprise, they assured me that they would stand by their engagements, and I am now fitting them out with arms. In a short time I should have three hundred or more of them armed and ready. I assure you that the Crown Point expedition now will be pushed on with alacrity. Most of these Indians are of the Mohawk and they are anxious to engage the enemy. I have no doubt they will make a good accounting of themselves. If the Indians stand by us, and God bless our endeavors, I hope we shall raise laurels that will overshadow our cypress.*

Governor-General William Shirley was undoubtedly one of the last of the leading Englishmen in North America to hear of Braddock's defeat. After leaving Albany with the remaining two hundred of his troops, he had embarked up the Mohawk from Schenectady in the clumsy, high-sided wooden boats most familiarly known as bateaux. They were craft favored by the traders because of their cargo capacity, but hated because of their clumsiness and difficulty in portaging.

Up the river he had gone, past Mount Johnson, past the Lower and Upper fortified villages of the Mohawks—Teantontalogo and Canajoharie—past the Palatine settlement of German Flats and then sixty miles upstream beyond that to the portage known as the Great Carrying Place,[1] which divided the waters which flowed into the Hudson from those which flowed north to Lake Ontario.

Here, along the path which led westward to the vagrant stream called Wood Creek, the heavy bateaux were dragged on sledges with great expenditure of effort. The portage was made and the boats then tied for the night on the marshy shores of Wood Creek while camp was being made, when the express arrived. Shirley read it with as much shock as anyone else had exhibited and even a greater amount of horror and sadness. He sent his aide to fetch his eldest son Jack, and within a minute Captain John Shirley had presented himself. The general placed his hand on the young officer's shoulder and told him of the defeat of Braddock.

Captain Shirley's eyes widened and his first question, when his father had finished, virtually burst from his lips.

"Dad! Was Will still with them? What about Will, is he all right?" He and William had always been extremely close, a fact which General Shirley was well aware of as he now squeezed the younger man's shoulder sympathetically.

"Your brother and my son," he said, his voice nearly breaking, "was killed."

The courier who had brought the express had not been cautioned to silence and the word flashed through this force of men. A pallor of fear descended over them, and late into the night groups of them sat about the fires discussing the matter. And in the morning, an aide brought further bad news to General Shirley; during the night almost all of his boatmen and draymen had deserted.

### [ *August 4, 1755—Monday* ]

On the spacious desk before Governor Pierre Vaudreuil and Baron Ludwig Dieskau lay the war plans of Major General Braddock. For hours the pair had studied them and discussed in detail what they should do now.

The plans had arrived just in time from Contrecoeur. Already a large portion of the troops newly come from France had been parceled out as reinforcements to the upper Great Lakes forts and those installations of the string reaching from Niagara to the Mississippi. Many had already been sent on by ship to Louisiana, and others to Quebec and other posts. Fort Frontenac alone, in anticipation of the intended strike against Oswego, had been sent fourteen hundred of the regulars. Nearly twelve hundred more were yet here in Montreal and within another day or two Dieskau and most of them would have been en route to join the others at Fort Frontenac to begin the campaign against Fort Oswego. Now matters were changed.

Outside, guns were still being fired with abandon and there were cheers and yells and laughter and dancing in the streets. The news of the defeat—in fact, almost the annihilation—of Braddock's army had lighted a fire of gaiety that only exhaustion would quell. Vaudreuil, in his freshly powdered wig, frowned at the disturbance, then shrugged and smiled and directed his servant to shut the windows, then leave the room.

With the outside noises muted and no other person with them, this high command of the French forces now made its own plans. The intended expedition against Fort Oswego was put in abeyance. With Shirley already on the march to reinforce Oswego, there was a better way to destroy the English.

Scouts had brought word of Johnson's army forming at Albany and the fact that already a large segment of them had been put on the march up the Hudson, while Johnson and the rest continued to wait for some expected reinforcements from New England. Johnson's was obviously the weaker of the two armies and his defeat would open exciting possibilities. Albany would lie defenseless before them, to be taken with great ease. With Johnson taken and Albany occupied, Shirley would then be cut off from all supplies and could be left to dangle and gradually weaken until his force could be taken with no difficulty at all. And then, within easy reach downstream from Albany, the greatest prize of all—New York!

The plan was laid. Baron Dieskau would now lead his force of three thousand—sixteen hundred Canadians, seven hundred regulars and seven hundred Indians—up the Richelieu River and into Lake Champlain, then up the lake to Fort St. Frederic at Crown Point. From here, conditions and the reports of reconnoitering parties would indicate how best to advance upon and destroy General Johnson's army and then seize Albany.

"Johnson," Dieskau said, "is a fur trader, not an officer. His officers are country squires. His soldiers are farmers and nothings! We will wipe him away without our breath becoming heavy, and we will not offer quarter."

Vaudreuil nodded, pleased at the baron's confidence. Yet, he still had not lost sight of his cherished plan against Fort Oswego. He shook the officer's hand and nodded again.

"Make all haste," he said. "When you return we shall send you to Oswego to execute our first design."

Baron Dieskau bowed smartly and departed. When he was gone, Vaudreuil returned to his desk, pausing momentarily at a mirror to inspect himself and then brush a faint trace of wig powder off his velveted shoulders. At the desk he looked again at the papers Contrecoeur had sent and then wrote a short order:

*Chevalier Pierre de Contrecoeur—*

*Sir, your news and reports have been most welcome here and your personal request is being honored. Upon receipt of this letter, you are relieved of your duties as commandant of Fort Duquesne and ordered to repair at once to Montreal. Captain Dumas will assume command in your stead at once and to him you will deliver all necessaries of office, along with the special instructions enclosed in this packet. Word is being sent to the Colonial Minister and His Majesty of the bravery and sacrifice of Captain de Beaujeu and I doubt not that his family will be compensated for their loss insofar as material compensation can be given.*

### [ August 12, 1755—Tuesday ]

The remainder of the journey to Fort Oswego for General Shirley and his men had not been an easy one. To his soldiers' own reluctance to reinforce the installation in the face of an overwhelming victory by the French, was added their lack of skill in handling the clumsy bateaux and their less than keen desire to do the hard physical labors of chopping, carrying, lifting, dragging and rowing.

Time after time the flotilla was held up in the narrow confines of creek or marshy channel until fallen trees could be hacked out of the way, but at last the broad expanse of Lake Oneida opened to them. It took most of a day for them to row down its length and then begin to slide along with the current of its outlet, the Onondaga River.[2] The heavy forest was close in on both sides of the river and every minute of the way the men lived with the mortal fear of a fusillade of crossfire against them from such ideal ambush cover.

But at last, twenty days after leaving Schenectady, the inland sea that was Lake Ontario opened before them and disappeared in a limitless horizon to the north. And here, on a bare hill on the west side of the river's mouth, stood their destination—Fort Oswego.

Shirley had not expected the establishment to be much, but it was considerably less than that: a thirteen-year-old, bulky, boxlike square with an ill-constructed picket arrangement thrown up on the west to prevent attack from land, but nothing on the east, its defenses there dependent upon several cannon on the fort ramparts. A few outbuildings were scattered about the fort and even a number of tents, occupied by the advance force Shirley had sent up earlier. On a spit of land extending from in front of the fort to nearly the middle of the river's mouth, some desultory ship construction was under way. Few men were in sight and Shirley quickly learned why; nearly the whole garrison was victim to a severe fever and dysentery epidemic. It was hardly a propitious welcome.

Within a few days Shirley had briefed himself quite thoroughly on the state of affairs, not only here at Fort Oswego, but at the French strongholds on this same lake—Niagara to the west and Frontenac to the north. On the whole, the situation was pretty bad, but there were a few bright spots. Although it was reported that there were a large number of Canadians and Indians at Fort Niagara and possibly, but not definitely, an even larger number of French regulars and Canadians at Fort Frontenac, these forces would largely have to travel by canoe or bateaux on the lake. The two small ships that had lately been built and launched at Fort Frontenac would be no match for what Fort Oswego had to offer.

The first English warship of the planned Lake Ontario fleet was already built and had just been launched. The finishing touches remaining on the second craft could be completed in the next day or two and it would slide into the water to join its sister ship. Considering the time and place, this first ship of the English ever to float on the Great Lakes was a real beauty. She was a forty-three-foot sloop that had been christened the *Oswego;* a warship armed with twelve cannon, five guns and a swivel on each side. Around her sides had been painted a wide, gay swath of yellow-orange. Above this was a narrower black band and below it another swatch of black which extended below the waterline to the white tallowed bottom.

Fifty-three feet over her decks, at the top of her single mast, waved the English flag, and her stark white canvas sails slid in a graceful curve to the end of the fifty-five-foot boom. Across her middle she was fifteen feet in beam and, because this harbor was only eight feet deep, she had been designed to draw only seven feet of water when fully loaded. Her magazine was amidships and the forecastle contained a small galley and cooking stove and twenty bunks for her crew. Staterooms for her officers were under the quarterdeck.

She hadn't been an easy craft to build. Not only was it difficult to get skilled shipbuilders to come here, but most of those who had come suffered the same fever and "loose-dirties" that struck the garrison. Further, during the building of her, twelve carpenters en route to Fort Oswego from New York had been attacked by Senecas under Chabert Joncaire while they were portaging across the Great Carrying Place, which Shirley himself had only recently traversed with his force. Eight had been killed in the fight and four captured and tortured to death later. But somehow, some way, the ship had been finished and launched and her mastery over the lake was supreme.

Soon her sister ship, the *Ontario*, would join her and the pair of small schooners now under construction, and already officially christened the *Vigilant* and the *George*, would be launched to complete the Lake Ontario fleet. Before them, the French naval force in these waters paled to insignificance.

With the exuberance of the young, Captain John Shirley was all for mounting an expedition at once. "Father," he told the general, "it's Fort Frontenac we should take first. Niagara's a much stronger fort and farther away and if we should be held up there, what's to keep the troops at Frontenac from hitting Oswego here while it's essentially unprotected?"

General Shirley smiled, admiring his son's strategy, but he shook his head. He wanted first to know more about the enemy strength at both locations before any attack could begin. Young Shirley remained convinced that his own plan was good and now, while the elder Shirley continued his study of the situation, Jack wrote a hasty letter to Governor Morris, whom he admired as much as his brother had:

*I have sat down to write to you because there is an opportunity of sending you a few lines; and if you will promise to excuse blots, interlineations, and grease (for this is written in the open air, upon the head of a porkbarrel, and twenty people about me), I will begin another half-sheet. We are not more than about fifteen hundred men fit for duty; but that, I am pretty sure, if we can go in time in our sloop, schooner, row-galleys, and whale-boats, will be sufficient to take Frontenac; after which we may venture to go upon the attack of Niagara, but not before. I have not the least doubt with myself of knocking down both these places yet this fall, if we can get away in a week. If we take or destroy their two vessels at Frontenac, and ruin their harbor there, and destroy the two forts of that and Niagara, I shall think we have done great things. Nobody holds it out better than my father and myself. We shall all of us relish a good house over our heads being all encamped, except the General and some few field officers, who have what are*

*called at Oswego, houses; but they would in other countries
be called only sheds, except the fort, where my father is. You
of course know by now that my father has become, with the
death of Gen'l Braddock, commander-in-chief of all military
forces. Confirmation of this rank is expected soon and, in
fact, we are led to understand it is now on the way.*

*Adieu, dear Sir; I hope my next will be directed from
Frontenac.*

*Yours most affectionately,*
*John Shirley*

### [ August 15, 1755—Friday ]

For William Johnson, the long wait at Albany for the slow-
moving New Hampshire regiment was irritating beyond measure. Literally weeks had gone by while he marked time here
and still the regiment under Colonal Joseph Blanchard failed
to appear.

But even though champing at the bit, William did not
allow the time of waiting to become a total loss. No one
knew better than he that his army of three thousand provincials was inexperienced, but that to train them in the regular
English army mode of fighting was worse than useless against
the enemy they would meet. Braddock's defeat had made
that only too clear.

Therefore, while they waited here at camp just north of
Albany, William set his men to training for warfare in a
manner in which Englishmen had never been trained before.
Tiyanoga and his men were a great asset here. The Mohawk
chief had come to William with three hundred warriors,
mostly his own Mohawks, all of them painted and fearsome
and eager to do battle.

William—as Warraghiyagey—greeted them warmly and
had a whole steer spitted and roasted in their honor. With his
own face painted and his broad chest bared, to the astonishment of his army, Warraghiyagey handed Tiyanoga his own
sword to slice the first meat away. Late into the night the
war dance continued frenziedly, with the frontier general
leaping and lunging as heartily as any of the warriors. And in
his journal that night, the New England regimental surgeon
wrote:

*I shall be glad if they fight as eagerly as they ate their ox and
drank their wine. . . .*

With Tiyanoga's assent and cooperation, William sent four of the Mohawks to the north for the dual purpose of reconnoitering the French strength on Lake Champlain and visiting the Caughnawagas in their St. Francis River village, to encourage them toward neutrality in the coming affray. They left at once.

The remaining Indians settled themselves at the edge of the camp, but they, just as much as the provincial army gathered here, were not happy with the wait necessitated by the extremely tardy New Hampshire regiment.

Tiyanoga was not the physically able warrior he used to be. His age was definitely telling on him now; his hair was completely gray, his vision and hearing not as good as they had been, and he had been getting fat. He had trouble moving about rapidly, became winded easily and even needed help in mounting his horse or dismounting from it. But his mind remained sharp and his knowledge of forest fighting was superb. When William suggested to him that the enforced wait be taken up in war games, with the provincials engaging in mock battles with Tiyanoga's Indians, the old chief grinned and agreed.

It hadn't taken long for the assembled provincials to realize that even though they greatly outnumbered these Indians, they were no match for them unless they fought according to Indian rules. To stand in dense ranks and fire without aim in the general direction of the enemy was futile when the enemy was not in similarly dense ranks. And soon the farmers and tradesmen, laborers and mechanics who made up the bulk of William Johnson's army were learning to take cover behind anything handy, to approach the enemy in a series of zigzagging runs from tree to tree, rock to rock, keeping always under cover of the stop and running low and erratically when exposed.

A regular English officer, Lieutenant Colonel John Abbott, up from New York to confer with Johnson, watched these antics bemusedly and shook his head. To him it was all just so much foolishness, like children playing games. The various companies obviously did not even know how to march in rank.

"Why," he asked one of the provincial captains, Edward Billings, "don't you drill your troops?"

The rough officer not wearing a uniform shook his head. "What we're learning is far more important. The whole point of our training is to keep from exposing ourselves and learn to load quickly and hit what we fire at."

"What!" Colonel Abbott was obviously shocked. "You mean to say you actually take *aim* at the enemy?"

"Absolutely. If we don't have a good target, we don't shoot."

"So in other words, if you see an enemy officer, there may be twenty or more of you aiming at him?"

Captain Billings nodded proudly and the English regular officer drew back from him in a loathing that was not simulated. "Why, that's absolute murder!"

"No, sir, Colonel, that's not murder. It's war."

Abbott was not the only one to be shocked by some of the actions of the army. Colonel Ephraim Williams, who had left his duties as a deputy sheriff and a member of the Massachusetts General Court to take a command position with the army, lamented the baseness of the army in a letter to his brother, Colonel Israel Williams, who was commanding on the Massachusetts frontier. He wrote:

*We are a wicked, profane army, especially the New York and Rhode Island troops. Nothing to be heard among the great part of them but the language of Hell. If Crown Point is taken, it will not be for our sakes, but for those good people left behind.*

Another of the fringe benefits of the interminable wait here at Albany was the proximity of a large number of Dutch girls very willing and extremely able to provide companionship to the backwoods soldiers after their exercises of the day. William Johnson himself, never one to hold back in this respect, was host to a veritable string of females who slipped in and out of his quarters. Age and looks of the woman of the moment were not important to him; he was just as charming and devouring with a lonely and homely spinster of forty as he was with a lithesome, fullbodied beauty of eighteen. His temper was therefore not improved when outraged complaints from parents and ministers in New York and Connecticut and Rhode Island came flooding in, demanding that this iniquity be stopped and the loose women be instantly banished, lest the wrath of God be raised against their army. If that threat were not enough, the protestors declared darkly, then the levies that their colonies provided, which made up two thirds of what the army received, would be cut off.

The latter threat was by far the more convincing and Johnson reluctantly ordered away from the army—though not from his own quarters—the apple-cheeked, buxom Dutch girls in their swishing full skirts and crisp white blouses and caps. But he silently sympathized with the deprived soldiers of his army who were now penning such items as . . . *Saw Nelly and Polly greatly upset, for the women were ordered away* . . . and another who wrote . . . *I ache for dear sweet Kate who was told by the officers not to come back here again* . . . and still another who penned the longing lines . . . *went to bed and dreamed I was playing with a Dutch girl again* . . .

It was an odd, strangely improper army without uniform, except for one corps which wore a blue coat faced with scarlet. Blankets had been provided to all by the Colonies involved, but most of the guns belonged to the men themselves and had been brought along by them. In fact some who came without them were suffered to pay fines for their lack of foresight. There were no bayonets for the rifles, but most of the men carried tomahawks at their belts as a substitute. All had powderhorns and many of these, during the long time of waiting, had been handsomely carved.

Raw and basically rough though the army was, William Johnson had some extremely good talent among his subordinates. His second-in-command, Colonel Phineas Lyman, hailed from Connecticut and had once been a teacher at Yale College. He had left behind a lucrative law practice to take this command. Colonel Moses Titcomb had been one of the Massachusetts boys to fight in Nova Scotia and his neighbor, Colonel Ephraim Williams, had been a captain in that affair. The latter officer, with a presentiment of death hovering over him, made out his will while in the Albany camp, providing ample funds for the establishment of a school of higher learning.[3] His cousin Stephen Williams was here too, as regimental chaplain. Lieutenant Colonel Seth Pomeroy had left behind a renowned gunsmithing business, and with him was his brother Daniel, a captain.

When, by the middle of July, the New Hampshire regiment had not yet arrived, William Johnson started his first division up the Hudson to escort the great armada of bateaux aboard wagons; these boats eventually to be used, according to the plan, for the invasion of Lake Champlain. Then, on the second of the month, William ordered his second division to follow the first with the remainder of the boats that had arrived in Albany. And when, on the eighth, there was *still* no sign of the missing unit, William himself gave up in disgust and went upriver with the last of his men and fifty of the Mohawks.

The rest of the Iroquois faction, under Tiyanoga, abruptly decided to return home to see to their own affairs, but they promised to return when Warraghiyagey sent word that he was ready for them. And despite the disbelief this occasioned in his junior officers, William Johnson trusted them implicitly and sent them off laden with gifts bought out of his own pocket.

His march up the Hudson to where Colonel Lyman had bivouacked the army was not much over fifty miles, and here, only a few miles below the falls of the Hudson at its northernmost bend as a navigable stream, he ordered Lyman to begin construction of a three-bastioned log fort.[4] In an effort to ease a sense of strain that had developed between himself and Colonel Lyman—who felt that it was he who should be in command of this campaign—William authorized his second to christen the new installation Fort Lyman. And it was here that a messenger arrived with word that part of Blanchard's New Hampshire regiment had finally arrived at Albany.[5] They were without provisions and William had to send back orders requisitioning food for them from the Albany storehouses. He also ordered Blanchard to send a detachment of his men to escort a provision train to Fort Lyman and then to follow with the remainder of his force when they should all arrive.

Now, with Fort Lyman well under way, it was necessary to determine which route it would be best for the army to follow in its move toward Crown Point—whether to cut a road almost due north to Wood Creek,[6] which ran into the headwaters of Lake Champlain, or to build the road northwest to the head of Lac St. Sacrement, that long lake which ultimately joined Lake Champlain about eighteen or nineteen miles below Crown Point. Since the Wood Creak route was somewhat the shorter, axemen were sent out to begin clearing the way.

They were not out for long. This morning, the four Mohawks William Johnson had sent out to reconnoiter and visit the Caughnawagas, returned and filed solemnly into William's tent. From their attitude, the general expected bad news.

He got it.

"Brother Warraghiyagey," said Toolah, the leader of the party, a muscular man of about thirty with a knife scar on his right shoulder, "we have done as you and our chief, Tiyanoga, have asked. Our brothers, the Caughnawagas, who

366

long ago separated from us, welcomed us and listened with their ears to what we had to say, but their reply was not what your ears wish to hear. They told us that the French black-robes, by throwing water on their heads, have made them subject to the Christian God and to the will of the *Onioto* of Canada. They begged us as their brothers and as a free people to be careful of our safety and not to engage ourselves in quarrels between the French and the English. They said that where the French go, they must go along, and that the enemy of the *Onioto* of Canada—he whose name is Vaudreuil—is also the enemy of the Caughnawagas.

"They told us," he continued without pause, "that they were eager to fight the English and take their scalps but that they did not wish to harm their brothers, the Mohawks, but that if the Mohawks are so blinded to what is right and good that they continue to cling to the English, that they would then destroy them along with the English."

Toolah looked very sad and paused here briefly before going on. "This was what they told us and then they said as well that they are not alone and that the Mohawks and the other Six Nations peoples should walk with care lest the very ground they walk upon should open to devour them. They said that every northern Indian on both sides of the great northern river from the lakes to the sea, that which you call the St. Lawrence, is with the French and that the French army has eight thousand soldiers who are coming with them to destroy your army.

"This," he added, "is what they told us, and they said further that the new chief of the French soldiers, whose name is called Dieskau, is already on the move against you and that they will soon be leaving to join him and that they will meet your army and crush it on the portage which leads from here to the near end of the long lake called by you and them, Champlain. This is what they told us. I am finished."

It was a disturbing report but William thanked them and gave them gifts and let them go back to Tiyanoga. At once he sent out a messenger to call in the axemen clearing the path to Wood Creek. They were, he directed, to abandon that project and instead, to start immediately to clear the alternative road to Lac St. Sacrement. As soon as it was finished, the boats stockpiled here at Fort Lyman would be carted to the southern end of that lake and launched for the journey north.

A wave of red terror—red for Indians, red for blood—was inundating the entire western frontier. A madness and unslakable blood lust had filled the Indians since the taste of great victory at the Monongahela over Braddock.

It had started slowly after the battle; a continuation of the raids with a cabin burned here, a family butchered there, a spate of minor skirmishing all around. It was as if the Indians were not yet sure of the reaction from the French, whom now they greatly feared and respected.

Contrecoeur, in those weeks before the battle, had not discouraged them from attacking English settlers, but neither had he specifically encouraged them to do so, and they hesitated to displease him. But suddenly now, Contrecoeur was gone and Captain Dumas had taken his place and Dumas was not afflicted with any form of queasiness. He had made it a point to call all the chiefs to a council on the day he assumed command of Fort Dequesne.

"Go out," he told them. "Spread yourselves through the whole country as far as you can go. Take scalps. Kill the English, all of them. Kill them in any way you like—with club or gun, knife or tomahawk. Torture them with fire and coals. Burn their houses, destroy their livestock, destroy all they own. Drive them back to the sea-cities, and there our armies will come and finish the destruction. Kill them!"

And now a reign of atrocities and death was sweeping the western frontiers of Virginia and Pennsylvania and New York ... but mostly Pennsylvania. Shawnees, Delawares, Hurons, Senecas, Cayugas, Ottawas, Chippewas, Potawatomies and even some of the Miamis and Wyandots slashed their way through border settlements, leaving in their wake an unparalleled scene of destruction and terror.

## [ *August 27, 1755—Wednesday* ]

Major General William Johnson did not pay particular attention to the twenty-three-year-old captain of the New Hampshire company, whom Colonel Blanchard had sent north from Albany with the provision train the general had ordered. The young officer hailed from near Rumford on New Hampshire's Merrimack River, and his name was Robert Rogers. Ever since he could remember, the Abnakis and Caughnawagas streaming out of their St. Francis River village had murdered and destroyed in his neighborhood and for years he had nurtured a passion to pay them back. Now he believed he would have that opportunity and he looked forward to it eagerly.

Of this, William Johnson knew nothing. He acknowledged the arrival of the supplies escorted here by Rogers and dismissed him. Other problems occupied his attention. The road stretching fourteen miles from Fort Lyman here to Lac St. Sacrement was completed and now it was necessary to make final plans.

Soon after his scouting party of Mohawks under the warrior, Toolah, had returned from their mission to the Caughnawagas and reported the massive force moving against him under Baron Dieskau, William had called a council of war with his officers. It had been resolved to send immediately to the several Colonies for reinforcements and orders went to Colonel Blanchard at Albany to move at once to Fort Lyman with all of his regiment that was on hand. William also asked the Mohawks still with him to carry word to Tiyanoga at Canajoharie that it was now time for him to honor his word, given when he left the army weeks before, and return now to meet him at the head of Lac St. Sacrement.

When at last Blanchard arrived with his men, final orders were given. That officer was left with a force of five hundred men at Fort Lyman to complete the work on that fortification and yesterday two thousand soldiers, with Johnson at their head, set out to the northwest on the new road. The term road was rather a misnomer, for despite the job of clearing that had been done, it was still very bumpy going for the long train of wagons and their progress was slow. Last night they had camped about midway between Fort Lyman and the lake.

Not until late afternoon today did the broad expanse of one of the most picturesque lakes in America open before them. Few, if any, of these soldiers had ever before seen it and not a man in the entire company could help but be impressed with its beauty. Flanked by hills covered with dense forests of maple and oak and pine, Lac St. Sacrement was at this point about a mile and a half in width, though farther to the north this distance was almost doubled. From this southernmost point of the lake, which was its head, it was about thirty miles to where the hills closed in on either side and the lake narrowed sharply and turned to an easterly course for four or five miles before joining Lake Champlain. This stretch of Lac St. Sacrement was actually a river which tumbled through a rocky gorge in an unnavigable stretch of rapids ending in a falls only a few miles up from Lake Champlain. The point where this river outlet of Lac St. Sacrement met Lake Champlain was called by the Iroquois Ticonderoga, and the connecting river itself was called the Ticonderoga Narrows. Just under twenty miles to the north of Ticonderoga proper lay Fort St. Frederic at Crown Point.[7]

Now, on General Johnson's orders, the army made its camp close to the Lac St. Sacrement shore and tents were pitched at random among the stumps of newly felled trees. With the lake at their back and themselves facing south, the army had to its front the heavy forest of hardwoods and conifers; to its right a marshy ground thickly overgrown with alder and willow and swamp maples; to its left a low hill also overgrown with trees.

Here the army would be forced to remain until the wagons had trucked in the six hundred bateaux from Fort Lyman. In these boats they were to move down the length of Lac St. Sacrement and ultimately to Crown Point.

William Johnson summoned his artillery officer, Captain William Eyre, the only regular English officer in his entire army. The general discussed with him their position here and concluded with an order:

"We will need to plan a fort here to keep our communications open. There's no need to start on it at once, but the fort should be completed shortly after the army has embarked on the lake."

For a long while, as camp was being prepared, William Johnson stood silently surveying the beautiful lake. It struck him that the very name of it—Lac St. Sacrement—signified that it was French and he resolved to rectify that at once. He mounted a stump and held up both arms until the hubbub of voices surrounding him was stilled and he had everyone's attention.

"From this time forward," he announced loudly, "this body of water shall be known by the name of Lake George,[8] not only in honor of His Majesty, but to emphasize his undoubted dominion here."

There was a tremendous cheering at this and William grinned, waved and then stepped down. Having made his historic declaration, he thereupon sent out three small Mohawk scouting parties—one each to move northward on opposite sides of Lake George toward the Ticonderoga Narrows, and the third to move in an easterly direction toward Wood Creek to watch for any sign of approach by

Dieskau. For a man untrained in military strategy, William Johnson was not doing badly.

## [ *September 4, 1755—Thursday* ]

Baron Ludwig August Dieskau had nowhere near the alleged eight thousand soldiers that the Caughnawagas had boasted of to the Mohawks, but his force was nonetheless a respectable one. Early in the morning five days ago in a grand flotilla of whaleboats, bateaux and canoes, he had arrived at Crown Point with his French regulars, Canadians and Indians—a total force of three thousand five hundred seventy-three men.

With an experienced eye he inspected this point and its bastion, Fort St. Frederic, and shook his head sorrowfully. The site had not been well chosen for either offense or defense and the fort itself was not really very much, even though stronger and larger than he had been led to expect. It would have been an easy matter to entrench his troops here, improve the fortifications and simply await the arrival of General Johnson's provincial army, but he had no intention of doing so.

Naturally aggressive and much more inclined to attack than wait to be attacked, he listened carefully to the reports of scouts, both Indian and Canadian, and then swiftly penned and posted a notice on a timber set upright in the cleared ground in front of his headquarters:

*August 31, 1755*

### ORDERS OF MARSHAL DIESKAU

*The entire force will prepare and hold itself in readiness for the march which will begin at sunrise tomorrow. In addition to their weapons, officers will take nothing with them but one spare shirt, one spare pair of shoes, a blanket, a bearskin, and provisions for twelve days; the troops will similarly supply themselves. The Indians will continue as they have under Captain Legardeur de Saint-Pierre and under no circumstances are they to amuse themselves by taking scalps until the enemy is entirely defeated, since they can kill ten men in the time required to scalp one. The squaws and young Indian boys accompanying the warriors may proceed with the force as far as the point where the army will leave the water and continue afoot, but no farther. They will camp at such place until we return or until they are sent leave to join us again ...*

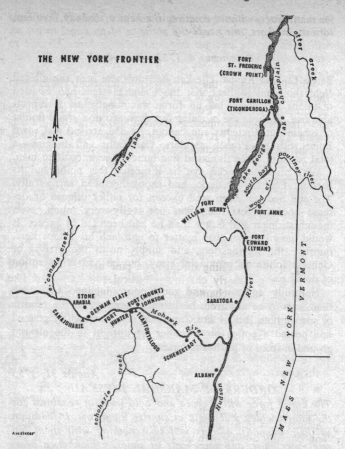

A.W.ECKERT

Even though he well recognized the value of having these Indian allies, Dieskau did not like the idea of having them as part of his command. He found them already to be of almost unmanageable nature and, at least at this stage of the operations, far more a liability than an asset. As the men settled down for the night, Dieskau wrote to Vaudreuil to tell of the army's progress thus far and the plans for the next morning's move. He was quite optimistic about everything except his savage allies. As he put it to Vaudreuil:

*They drive us crazy from morning till night. There is no end to their demands. They have already eaten five oxen and as many hogs, without counting the kegs of brandy they have drunk. In short, one needs the patience of an angel to get on with these devils; and yet one must always force himself to seem pleased with them.*

With the rising of the sun, Dieskau embarked his force to the south again, leaving behind a reinforced garrison of seven hundred men to hold Fort St. Frederic. Shortly before noon they reached that imposing promontory which the Indians called Ticonderoga. It was a naturally defensible location, and here Dieskau directed the French engineer to establish a camp and, with a large body of workers, begin construction of a strong fort on the Ticonderoga point.

From a military standpoint, this promontory was a superb defensive site, commanding from a very secure position the only two reasonable routes by which the English army could approach Crown Point—that of Lake Champlain via Wood Creek, and that of Lake George.

The lapping of the water against the foot of the promontory and the wind sighing through the pine needles and leaves imparted a peculiarly charming musical sound, almost like distant chimes. Enchanted by it, the engineer, Lotbinière, asked and received from his commander permission to name the new establishment Fort Carillon.

The stop at the Ticonderoga promontory was brief. By noon Dieskau had embarked with his somewhat diminished force and was pressing on, moving southward along that swiftly narrowing prolongation of upper Lake Champlain which gradually began shallowing out at its head into an area known to the Indians as the Drowned Lands. At the approach to this area the lake became hardly more than a wide channel marked permanently by nature with two huge rocks, one on either side, both so large that trees had taken root and grown on their tops. Appropriately enough, the area was called Twin Rocks and it was here that they made camp for the night.

In the morning, even as Dieskau was holding a meeting with his officers to discuss their plans for the attack, one of the Indian scouting parties he had sent out jubilantly appeared with a scalp and a prisoner.

The captive was a private named Andrew Hornsby from William Johnson's army who had been deserting with a companion when caught by the Caughnawagas. In great fright he had thrown down his gun and surrendered on first sight of them, but his young friend had elected to run. For this unwise decision he had caught a rifle ball in the middle of his back.

Now, being questioned by Dieskau through an interpreter under threat of being turned over to the Indians for torture if he didn't talk, he determined to try to make them walk into a trap. Successfully feigning eager cooperation, he told them that Johnson, hearing that Dieskau had eight thousand men, had marched back to Albany to await reinforcements, leaving Fort Lyman with a garrison of just five hundred men and its fortifications not yet completed. To his satisfaction, Hornsby saw that they believed him. Now, if only he could escape and return with this news to General Johnson, the general could strike the French and Indians from the rear while they attacked Fort Lyman and instead of being a deserter, Andrew Hornsby would be a hero.

There was little likelihood of his getting away, however. Baron Dieskau had the private securely bound, placed him in the care of a detachment of men under Lieutenant Roquemaure and told them to wait here at Twin Rocks for his return. Immediately he directed the remainder of the force to embark again in the canoes and continued paddling into the area known as South Bay. This was a long, shallow, marshy expanse heavily overgrown at its edges with sedge, waterweeds and cattail. The going here was rough and slow and it was late afternoon before they reached the head of the bay where a small stream entered it. Here they beached their canoes and established their camp for the night.

Tomorrow morning, Dieskau told his officers, they would leave another detachment to guard the boats and then, after the Jesuit priest with them said Mass, they would march again. The size of the army was considerably smaller now due to the troops left at Crown Point, Ticonderoga, Twin Rocks and here, but they still had a total of some fifteen hundred men—two hundred sixteen regulars of the battalions of Languedoc and La Reine, six hundred eighty-four Canadians and about six hundred Indians—and that, Dieskau boasted, was far more than enough to take Fort Lyman and its garrison.

## [ *September 7, 1755—Sunday afternoon* ]

The eleven days that William Johnson's provincial army had been bivouacked at the head of Lake George had been essentially uneventful. Much of the time had been spent in chopping down trees and burning them until not a single tree remained within a musket shot of the camp. The better logs from these trees had been trimmed and stacked about for use in the fort construction.

The only real excitement, in fact, had come just two days ago when the Mohawks in camp suddenly sprang to their feet and then set up a fearful howling which only William, of all the Englishmen here, recognized immediately as the Indian halloo, or greeting.

A few moments later somewhat over two hundred Indians trooped out of the woods and a great smile wreathed William's face as he stepped forward to meet Chief Tiyanoga. It was a joyful reunion and the approaching Indians fired their rifles in salute. In return, William ordered two rounds fired from the cannon. Pleased at the vindication of his faith that they would return, William ordered two of the beef cattle to be roasted and brought out barrels of rum. It was a wild evening, given up almost entirely to feasting and dances. To the general disapproval, and in some cases consternation, of his officers, the general stripped off his own clothing and, wearing nothing but a breechcloth, led the energetic stamping and leaping.

Then, yesterday, an old chief of the Oneidas named Cohega, whom William had seen on numerous occasions at Onondaga and at his own council fire at Mount Johnson, came to him with a doleful expression on his face.

"Warraghiyagey," he said, "I have had a bad dream. I have dreamed that in that direction," he pointed to the east, "there is a danger walking. It is a great pack of wolves, some of them gray, some of them red, and they are hungry. They wish to feed on the flesh of English soldiers. It is a bad time. Do not let men stray from your camp into the woods, lest they find themselves in the bellies of these wolves."

Without waiting for a reply, he turned and left William's tent and for a long time the general sat there thinking about what he had said. He was not one to laugh off the dream of a sachem. Too many times he had known of such dreams having proven themselves to be accurate omens of events to come. He called his aide, Peter Wraxall, and instructed him to pass the word to all officers and men to keep within the confines of the camp. Wraxall, a bit perplexed, did as ordered.

This morning there had been a brief shower but then it had turned into a beautiful sunny day. The venerable chaplain, Colonel Stephen Williams, held Sunday services outside, attended by almost all of the Indians as well as the soldiers. It was an excruciatingly long and complex Calvinistic sermon taken from Isaiah, which was not finished until well after noon, since at the end of each sentence he had to pause so that the Mohawk interpreter could translate for the natives. They watched him closely and listened intently and when he was finished at last they clapped their hands together and thudded the ground with their bare feet.

Perplexed, Williams asked the interpreter what that outburst was for and the man bobbed his head and grinned and then said, "They think you are one of the funniest storytellers they have ever heard."

There was a roar of laughter from the soldiers. Colonel Williams drew himself up ramrod stiff and without another word turned and walked to his tent. He remained there most of the day.

Shortly after the sermon ended, a train of two hundred wagons came bumping and rattling into view, each carrying three boats. The rest of the afternoon was spent unloading them.

The sun was just couching itself on the tops of the trees to the west when there was a commotion. One of the three Mohawk scouting parties Johnson had sent off returned, riding their horses in from the northeast. Warraghiyagey and Tiyanoga interviewed them at once.

"We found the tracks of two men," their spokesman said, "and we followed them. Soon the tracks of three others joined them. They were all white men's tracks. Then we heard six guns fired. After that we heard so many guns we could not count them and we made a wide circle to the north and east. Soon we came to three new paths close together. The ground was packed and the grasses crushed down so that they could not again spring up. A great number of men had passed here."

He pointed to the northeast and continued, "We followed their paths from the way they had come and at the end of the South Bay above the Drowned Lands we saw from a distance their camp, where they had left many boats with some French soldiers to guard them. There was also a camp of many Caughnawaga squaws and children. Too many soldiers were there for us to show ourselves, so we came back here at once in a straight line, having traveled most of this day."

"Which way were the three paths heading which you followed backwards?" William asked quickly.

"They were going south and just a little east. Their line was toward your Fort of Lyman."

"Will they cross our road? Can a messenger still get through to warn Colonel Blanchard there?"

The Indian considered a moment. "Their three paths," he said, "run in the direction of your road and unless they change the way they are pointed, they will not meet it. A rider going fast might pass them unseen and unheard."

William nodded, squeezed the Mohawk's arm in recognition of a good job well done, and then strode to his tent and swiftly wrote a note to Blanchard explaining about the approaching force. He enclosed it with some other dispatches he had prepared during the day and then emerged and called aloud for a volunteer to carry the warning to Fort Lyman, emphasizing that it was apt to be a dangerous mission.

One of the wagon drivers, leaning against the wheel of his wagon, straightened and began walking toward Johnson.

"Reckon as how I'll give 'er a try," he drawled.

He was a steady-looking man, blond and about twenty-eight, and William Johnson nodded. "What's your name?" he asked.

"Adams, sir. Jacob Adams."

"All right, you've got the job. Take my horse, he's in good shape. Let him out all the way. And Jake—be careful!"

The wagoner merely grinned and nodded. As he moved to get the general's horse, William was already giving rapid-fire orders for the hasty construction of some sort of barricade; a defensive work he now realized that he should have had erected immediately upon establishing the camp here. Even as Adams thundered out of the camp and down the road, wagons were being overturned and logs and branches were being piled against them to form a breastwork.

Ten of the other wagoners, who had been standing with their heads together in whispered conversation about an hour later, broke apart and casually sauntered to their wagons. Before anyone even suspected their intentions, they had vaulted into their seats and whipped their horses into a frantic run down the road through the last remaining gap in the barricade. While the stunned soldiers watched, they vanished toward Fort Lyman and soon even the sound of their galloping hooves had passed beyond hearing. Johnson shook his head, having no intention of sending a pursuit party after them.

The gray wolves and the red wolves were closing in ...
and the sheep were beginning to panic.

All day Dieskau's army had marched and, though he was not aware of it, the closer they came to Fort Lyman, the less his Indians were inclined to go ahead with the attack. The Caughnawagas and Abnakis, like most Indians, felt a great awe of cannon. Few of them had not seen how one cannon-ball could smash down a house or a wall of a fort; how trees could be cut in half and a whole body of advancing men killed, injured or completely demoralized by one blast. They were sure that Fort Lyman, like most English forts, must have at least six of the big thunder guns, and they had no desire to face them.

It was at sunset, when they were only three or four miles away from the fort, that the Indians suddenly balked, refusing to advance into the artillery which by now had increased in their minds to a dozen or more pieces. Dieskau tried to reason with them but it was to no avail and finally, in disgust, he accused them of cowardice and said he would go on without them.

The insult stung and, after a hurried council among themselves, they announced that they were the bravest warriors in the world and to prove it they would even lead the way for the attack. Mollified to a certain degree, Dieskau nodded them on. The majority of the Indians took the lead, followed first by the baron himself, then by the battalion of La Reine, the battalion of Languedoc and, finally, the Canadians. Another smaller group of Abnakis and Caughnawagas brought up the rear. And a hundred yards or so behind them, unknown to all, came three Caughnawaga boys, each only twelve or thirteen years old, who had been following them ever since they had left the camp where the squaws and children had been ordered by Dieskau to remain.

It became ever darker in the woods and the way grew steadily rougher. They ducked under limbs, plunged through dense scrub growth and thorny underbrush, around a great windfall of trees broken down into a jumble and finally, after about an hour, the Indians stopped and blandly told the commander that somehow they had gotten lost. As a matter of fact, for the past forty-five minutes they had been moving deliberately in a wide circle away from the fort.

Cursing bitterly in German, which they didn't understand, Dieskau berated them for their trickery. But even as he was ranting, two Abnakis came running up bearing a fresh scalp and a packet. They told the marshal through his interpreter that there was a new road just a short distance west of them running to the northwest from the fort and that this man, whose scalp they were holding, had come galloping along heading toward Fort Lyman and they had shot and killed him.

Dieskau, his anger abruptly forgotten, dispatched an officer and four regulars to return to the road with the Abnakis to reconnoiter. As they moved away, a small fire was hastily built with flint and steel and from it a candle lighted. Its wan glow revealed the scalp to be blond and the packet to contain a number of dispatches from Major General William Johnson to Colonel Robert Blanchard, including the warning of the approaching French force. It took a while for the contents to be translated and assimilated and by the time Dieskau was finished, the detachment he had sent out returned, this time with a prisoner.

He was a very young man, hardly more than a boy, and he was so badly frightened that his teeth were chattering and his whole body was trembling. He had been one of the deserting wagoners and had seen the drivers in the three wagons ahead of him shot and killed from ambush. While the wagoners behind him had leaped to the ground and raced away into the woods, he himself had been captured. His name was Martin Cavet and when he was questioned, he stammered out his answers quickly and without guile. He emphatically denied the story of their first prisoner, Andrew Hornsby, that General Johnson and his army had returned to Albany. They were at this very moment, he told them, at a camp at the head of the lake, only about twelve miles from here, that it was a large force of over two thousand men, but that they had no real fortifications yet except for a hasty barricade that was being thrown up when he left.

Dieskau now called a council with the Caughnawaga and Abnaki chiefs, explained what the questioning of the prisoner had uncovered and said, "I give you now the choice of going in the morning to attack that fort where there are only five hundred men, or to attack General Johnson, who has above two thousand."

There was no hesitation in their reply. They flatly refused to attack the fort, but said they were willing to attack Johnson because they believed he had no cannon. Some of the Canadian leaders objected that Johnson's force was much larger than their own, but Dieskau brushed aside the protests.

"You yourselves," he told them tersely, "are the ones who

advised me that the English colonial militia are the worst troops on the face of the earth. And that must be true, for look what mere French captains—Captain de Villiers and Captain de Beaujeu—did to the armies of Colonel Washington and General Braddock! Are we to fear such armies as those?" He shook his head violently.

"No! I do not care how many men Johnson has. The more there are, the more we shall kill. We march on their camp before dawn!"

### [ September 7, 1755—Sunday Night ]

It was nearing midnight when one of the wagoners who had deserted and then escaped from the ambush on the road, finally reached General Johnson's encampment again. He was scratched and bruised from his initial wild run through the darkened woods. When at last he had gotten back to the road, almost a mile from where he had left it, he trotted all the way back to the camp and was so out of breath now that he could hardly speak.

Little by little, William Johnson and several of his officers pieced the story together. What it amounted to was that there was a war party—though apparently not a very large one—on the road between here and Fort Lyman; that it had killed a number of the deserting wagoners, perhaps all but this single escapee; that the odds were, since it was so close to the fort, that it would attack Blanchard in the morning; that whether or not Jacob Adams had gotten through was not known, but they must assume that he had not.

William called an immediate council of his officers along with Tiyanoga and some of the other Iroquois chiefs on hand. The situation was discussed briefly and then a decision made: in the morning, two detachments of five hundred men each would leave the camp. The first would march via the road to go to the aid of Blanchard at Fort Lyman; the second, guided by the Indians who had found the paths of the invaders, would go overland to reach the French camp, destroy their boats and then cut off the invaders in their retreat from Fort Lyman. It sounded like a good plan, but now Tiyanoga shook his head.

"It is not well for you to do this, Warraghiyagey." He stooped and picked up a fair-sized section of branch and snapped it in half. Then he put the two halves together, side by side, and tried to break them again, but could not. William understood; it would not be wise to split the detachments. But when, after some more discussion between the officers, William agreed to join the detachments together in one body of men to march as a reinforcement back to Fort Lyman, again Tiyanoga shook his old gray head.

"If those thousand are to be killed, they are too many," he said simply, "and if they are to fight, they are too few. My warriors who saw the trail they left, say there are many more in the war party than you will send against them."

When William insisted that he must send the detachments out, irrespective of the danger, to keep the French from taking Fort Lyman and cutting them off here, Tiyanoga gave in.

"I will lead all my warriors before the soldiers," he said. "It may be that when our brothers, the Caughnawagas—and the Abnakis who are with them—see us and know that we are with you, they will refuse to fight, not wishing to draw blood between ourselves. If they refuse to fight for the French soldiers, your own will have no trouble defeating them."

To this William Johnson and the other officers readily agreed. Tiyanoga then went outside and, with some difficulty, climbed to the bed of a wagon. Into the darkness he gave vent to the council call and soon the Indians were crowded around. He addressed his Indians in a loud, impassioned voice, his animated gestures throwing grotesque shadows from the lantern light. It was not a long speech and when he finished the response from the clustered Indians was enthusiastically vocal. The soldiers had not understood what he said, but to a man they were deeply impressed with the way he said it.

When the uproar died away, Tiyanoga climbed back down with some difficulty and then returned to the general.

"My warriors have agreed," he said. "We will lead your soldiers in the morning, Warraghiyagey."

·[ *September 8, 1755—Monday,* 8 A.M. ]

Tiyanoga was disgusted with how long it took this English army to get moving. Since before the dawn his own men had been painted and ready to go. Yet, here they were with the sun up for over an hour already and still wasting time at the Lake George camp.

But finally, the English were ready—at least most of them— at just about eight o'clock. Colonel Ephraim Williams took his place at the head of the troops of the first segment of five hundred men, with his company commanders before their own men.

Because Tiyanoga was now so old, and heavy, it was apparent that he could not walk far, and so he was given assistance in mounting a saddleless horse and, highly conspicuous as the only man on horseback, led two hundred of his war-painted Iroquois warriors to the front.

They began moving out, Tiyanoga in front of his warriors in single file in the center of the road behind him for about one hundred yards. Next came Colonel Williams, striding proudly along before the first segment of five hundred men, who were marching six abreast.

The second segment of the same size, however, under Lieutenant Colonel Richard Whiting, was delayed for several minutes for some reason and when word of it was relayed to him, Williams called a halt until they could close ranks. Tiyanoga and his men had gotten fifty yards or more ahead of the soldiers before he, too, became aware of the delay and stopped to wait.

And three hundred yards down the road in front of Tiyanoga, a French soldier peering from behind a tree, pulled his head back and raced unseen through the woods parallel with the road, dodging under low branches and leaping over logs. When he had finally passed a point where the road curved somewhat and he was no longer in sight of the Indians or English, he returned to the road and increased his speed.

[ *September 8, 1755—Monday, 9* A.M. ]

Baron Ludwig Dieskau had been moving his force up this new road since before dawn. As always happened before any engagement, he felt an electric thrill within him—the thrill that the professional soldier experiences when he is on the brink of doing that which he has been trained to do, and does best. At such times he always had a great awareness of his surroundings and his sharp eyes rarely rested on anything very long, constantly moving from point to point for any clues which might in some way cause him to change his strategy. It was what made him an outstanding commander.

His regulars had their weapons charged, bayonets attached and every one of them seemed as much keyed up as was he. Most of them had donned their lone clean shirts from their packs and had replaced their worn and dirty footwear with fresh. Their white coats may not have been spotlessly clean, but they were amazingly visible in the gray light of the dawn, which made the Caughnawagas and Abnakis shake their heads in wonder. A white coat like that could only draw bullets as honey drew the fly.

The Canadians were less prim, but no less eager for the battle, now that they were committed to it. Those few who still had qualms were reassured by their comrades: nothing to fear, just remember Villiers and Beaujeu. The Canadians were marching in a group cluster without steady formation behind the precise regular troops. All around the soldiers, front, sides and rear, were the Indians. They rarely stayed in one spot long and only infrequently remained on the open road for more than a half a minute at a time. Their constant movement made the procession seem almost like a wheel within a wheel.

And five hundred yards behind this army, still undetected, came the three Caughnawaga youngsters, two with little bows and willowy arrows, one with a freshly made lance decorated with turkey-wing feathers, all three of them with knives and tomahawks. They slipped from tree to tree in quick spurts, terribly excited and terribly proud of themselves, already dreaming of the stories they would have to tell their companions when they returned.

Abruptly, the Indians moving back and forth across the road in front parted somewhat to let a panting French soldier run through their ranks to Dieskau, who at once raised a hand to stop his army and then listened carefully while the scout told of the Indians and English on the move against them on this very road, about three miles ahead. A hurried council was held with the French and Canadian officers and with the chiefs of the Abnakis and Caughnawagas.

Within five minutes the new plan had been laid.

The Indians and Canadians moved forward of the army about three hundred yards and then split and melted into the forest on both sides of the road. In moments there was no trace of any of them. The white-coated French regulars, still in precise ranks and with Dieskau at their head, stood waiting patiently but alertly.

Fifteen minutes passed, thirty, and then just over forty, when from far ahead came the jingle of equipment and the thudding of many feet. Tiyanoga, astride his horse, held the pace to a brisk walk. Behind him stretched his two hundred Indians, still in single file. Close on the heels of the last of them was Colonel Williams, leading the first detachment of five hundred, who had by now closed ranks considerably.

Twenty yards behind them, in similar dense formation, came the final five hundred under Lieutenant Colonel Whiting.

Suddenly Tiyanoga reined in, a faint sound to one side alerting him. Behind him the whole procession slowed and began stopping. But before he could do anything, a warning shot was fired from the underbrush and a loud voice, speaking in the Iroquois tongue, was heard.

"Who are you, there in the road?"

Tiyanoga looked about calmly and then replied in a firm voice, "I speak to no man who squeaks from hiding like a frightened rabbit. Come out to where I may see your eyes, and you mine. Then only will I make reply."

Here and there in the dense woods on both sides of them numerous Indian faces appeared from behind trees and logs. They, like Tiyanoga's men, were war-painted. From the right of the Mohawk chief a tall Caughnawaga and two warriors stepped out of the cover and onto the edge of the road no more than twenty feet away. They stopped there and the tall Indian locked his gaze on Tiyanoga. Again he put the question: "Who are you? What are you doing here?"

The voice of the mounted Mohawk chief was stern and far-reaching. "I am Tiyanoga, principal chief of the Mohawks, who have remained faithful to the Iroquois League of our fathers. We here are the Six Confederated Indian Nations, the heads and superiors of all Indian nations in this entire land."

The tall Indian did not seem particularly impressed. He waited a moment and then spoke just as sternly as had Tiyanoga.

"I am Iptowee, chief of the Mohawks now become Caughnawagas, who have learned that to stay with the English is to act with the foolishness of an empty-headed bird. We here are of the Seven Confederated Indian Nations of Canada. We come here to support our father, the King of France, to fight with his soldiers against their enemies, the English. It is not our intention to quarrel with our brothers, the Iroquois, or to trespass against any Indian nation. We therefore ask that you remove yourselves from the way, lest we are forced to move against you and thereby involve us in a war amongst ourselves."

Tiyanoga shook his head. "It is you who are in our way. You have already trespassed here on our lands. The Six Nations have come to aid our brothers, the English, against the French men who are encroaching on Iroquois lands to west and north. You are Caughnawagas, who were once

Mohawks. You know us. You know we will not back away from you, or from any other tribe or confederation, or from any white men. You are Caughnawagas, who were once Mohawks. You should join your brothers in this worthy cause of forcing back the French men who would take our lands from us; but if you will not do this, then you are advised to remove yourself from the way in case you should get harmed."

The stillness round about them was absolute as Tiyanoga finished; as if even the birds and insects had stopped their activity to hear what the reply would be. It was a long time in coming.

At last Iptowee shook his head and opened his mouth to speak again, but he never got to utter the first word of it. From just behind Tiyanoga one of the younger Mohawk warriors, unable any longer to restrain himself, threw his musket to his shoulder and sent a lead ball through Iptowee's heart.

Instantly the two warriors with him leaped away into the brush and the faces that had become visible on both sides ducked back out of sight. For one tremulous instant longer the silence continued as the smoke from the single shot drifted lazily upward.

And then the woods exploded.

A deadly hail of bullets from both sides swept the entire formation of Indians and English. In that first firing, forty of the Iroquois were killed. Whole ranks of the English collapsed like puppets whose strings have been cut and lay motionless in the road. Tiyanoga's horse was hit and knocked down, pitching him off to the side of the road. A bullet nicked his upper arm and as he scrambled into the woods he could feel the warm blood flowing from the wound.

The fire became even hotter as the French regulars, combining their firing with that of the Indians and Canadians in ambush, sent a blistering fusillade straight down the road. The provincials and Iroquois were pinned in a murderous three-directional crossfire.

Back at the Lake George camp, William Johnson heard the rattle of gunfire and immediately ordered the "to arms" drum roll to be beaten. Those in the camp snatched up their weapons and took protective positions behind the flimsy barricade. Within five or ten minutes the sound of the fighting grew louder and it became obvious that the detachments were retreating. Without delay, William ordered Lieutenant Cole to go to their aid with a detachment of three hundred men. At the same time he ordered Captain Eyre to plant three of his cannon to command the road and another on the slope of the hill to their left to command the clearing between woods and camp. Eyre leaped to action.

At the scene of the ambush there was great confusion. Men by the score were falling and Colonel Ephraim Williams, seeing a low hill rising in the woods to their right, shouted for his troops to follow him, and ran for it. He had hardly left the road, however, when a Canadian popped from behind a tree and shot him through the head.

Lieutenant Colonel Seth Pomeroy was still back at the camp, but his brother Daniel was here. In Williams's place, he continued to lead the men to the hill and got them there, but then he, too, took a ball through the brain.

The troops milled about desperately, trying to cover themselves and find something at which to shoot, but in both efforts they were largely unsuccessful. Whiting, now in command, recognized that the situation could not be maintained and bellowed an order to continue firing but to fall back toward the camp.

The training the men had received under Johnson's Indians back at Albany now paid off handsomely. English regulars, attempting to hold their ground, to stand and shoot in volley without aim and without cover, would have been destroyed, just as Braddock's troops had been. But now these provincials moved back in a retreat that was surprisingly orderly under the circumstances. From tree to tree and bush to bush they dodged, and within another ten minutes Lieutenant William Cole's reinforcements met them, saw they were falling back and held their ground to add their firepower to the retreat.

Captain Jacques Legardeur de Saint-Pierre exhorted his Abnakis and Caughnawagas to press the enemy closely. For a moment he forgot himself and stepped into a clearing. Several bullets struck him simultaneously, driving him backwards as if he had been struck by a great invisible club. He slammed into a tree and then slid to the ground. He was dead before his body stopped moving.

Amazingly, Tiyanoga had managed to get through the opposing Indians and Canadians. Cut off from his own warriors, he ran as he had not run in years, the soft fatty flesh of his arms and chest and waist bouncing violently with each step, his lungs burning with the effort to breathe. And finally, with the sounds of the battle becoming muted behind him, he turned to circle widely and join them from the rear. But he was no longer a young warrior full of vigor and strength. He had to rest a moment. Abruptly he flopped to the ground and lay there gasping. Slowly his system caught up with him; his breathing became less tortured, his heartbeat less like some living creature within him straining to break free of his chest.

He sat up and listened for a long moment. He could hear the sounds of the battle to the northwest still as strong as ever, but growing dimmer with distance, and he knew he must return to his warriors and lead them back to Warraghiyagey to help the general hold the camp. With great effort he raised his heavy body to a standing position, but before he had a chance to take even one step, a willowy, crudely made arrow fletched with turkey feathers plunged deeply into his breast and stuck there quivering.

He looked down at it in a bewildered manner and then looked up again. A second arrow slammed into his left leg just above the knee and he staggered but did not fall. With failing vision he saw the incredible sight of three young Caughnawaga boys, not yet even young men, racing across the clearing toward him, and he reached for the knife in his waistband.

He was too slow. The leading boy, brandishing a length of sapling that had been stripped of branches and bark and its end whittled to a point to make a crude lance, reached him first and lunged with the spear, driving it into the Mohawk's chest close to the arrow and with such force that it passed through Tiyanoga's heart and protruded redly a foot or more from his back. He fell.

Screeching in falsetto triumph, the boys set about scalping him, but they had never scalped before and they botched the job, mutilating the whole top of the fallen chief's head before getting his crest of hair off. They ended up with a small strip of flesh not much bigger than the Mohawk's ear, with only a small portion of the hair still adhering to it.

About a mile away, the retreat of the provincials was moving well now—rapidly, yet well organized and completely under control. Only once had panic threatened to sweep the men, and that was when eight soldiers of Captain Elisha Hawley's company fell dead at the same volley from the French regulars; but Hawley rallied them, only himself to fall a moment later with an arrow driven through his throat, mortally wounded.

In rather quick time the retreat carried the provincials to within three fourths of a mile of the Lake George camp, and the French regulars continued to press up closely behind them on the road while the Indians and Canadians surged and darted about them in the woods. Seth Pomeroy rounded up a group of thirty or more of his men and had them load and hold fire. Then, on his command, they took good aim and fired simultaneously and the whole front segment of the French regulars fell.

The provincials continued to fall back, however, and now, as Johnson and the remains of his army back at camp watched, the first of the retreaters came into sight, dashing along madly, leaping over stumps and logs. In a moment the face of the woods erupted with men stumbling toward the camp, many of them pausing to shoot a final time before scrambling over the barricade and milling about with the troops waiting there.

Behind this first heavy rush of retreaters—both Indians and English—came more soldiers, many of them, moving along more slowly. These were primarily the wounded and those who were helping them. At the same time, on the road itself came the remnants of the main party of the retreating detachments. An hour and a half had passed since the ambush was sprung.

A panic was building up in the men at the camp who had not yet faced fire, and William Johnson was moving about everywhere, calming them, tongue-lashing them, ordering them to stand fast, to be alert and ready. If Dieskau came plunging on while such confusion was prevailing, the camp could be taken easily.

But Dieskau was having his own troubles at this moment. Realizing that they were now approaching General Johnson's camp, he ordered all pursuit halted in order to pull his own forces together and quickly map out a plan of attack. His own Indians were now fighting among themselves. A group of the Abnakis had captured three of the Mohawks and bound them and were already gathering wood to roast them when the Caughnawagas interceded. Though they were fighting the Mohawks, too, they did not wish to see inflicted on their parent tribesmen the ignominious death by roasting that the Abnakis were planning, and the argument between the two allied Indian forces was growing hot.

Dieskau shouldered his way into the midst of them with his interpreter. "Burning of your prisoners can wait," he said angrily. "We are going to advance at once on the camp. I order you to come!"

The Abnakis and Caughnawagas put their own spat in abeyance and together turned on Dieskau. "We have fought your battle for you, and we have won it. It is not our

388

custom, after we have fought one battle, to fight another at once. We wish now to go home with our scalps and spoils."

Dieskau could scarcely believe his ears and was even more dumbfounded when a number of the Canadians chimed in and said if the Indians did not fight with them, they did not want to attack the camp. The loss of the Indians would be a bad enough blow, Dieskau knew, but without the support of these Canadian troops, the whole attack could collapse.

"By God," the commander stormed at both factions, "the liquor is drawn; it must be drunk! Prepare yourselves to attack!"

It wasn't all that easy. Never anxious to attack a fortified position, the Indians still hesitated. Long precious minutes were wasted in convincing them that the battle was only half fought and already they were the victors. Completing the job would only give them an even greater victory at considerably less cost. Gradually he won them over and the French force began its advance.

But the delay had been costly.

William Johnson had managed to calm his men and ordered five hundred of them to post themselves on the flanks—two hundred fifty to each side, from the front of the camp to the lake in a horseshoe pattern. The remainder of the men, including those who had not yet seen action and those who had returned from the ambush, were positioned in the front facing the road.

They were none too soon. Just as the first ranks of white-coated French regulars began appearing on the road, the woods all around the camp vomited a howling mob of Canadians and Indians. Once again panic began to rise in the provincials but, under Johnson's orders, their officers strode back and forth among them, swords in hand, threatening to run the weapons through any man who should break and attempt to flee his post.

The French regulars pouring from the forest-canopied road into the cleared area swiftly formed themselves into three long straight lines facing the barricade, their bayonets glittering in the bright sunlight. The front rank raised their weapons, aimed and simultaneously fired in an ear-splitting volley. Immediately they lowered their guns and knelt to reload while the two ranks behind stepped forward. The second rank, which had now become the first, raised and fired and then they, too, started to reload while the third rank stepped in front of them.

Abruptly Captain Eyre's cannon belched grapeshot at them

389

and though most of the damage done was to the trees and brush behind them, the French regulars faltered and broke. They gave up their formations and loaded and fired from wherever they were and all throughout the area the fighting became general and confused.

William Johnson, his voice hoarse from shouting commands, suddenly gasped and fell as a bullet struck him, but almost at once he struggled to his feet, pressing a hand over the wound in his hip and attempting to carry on. He fell again and Peter Wraxall, his aide, led him hobbling to his tent to be doctored as soon as possible.

Phineas Lyman now took command with as much or even more vigor than William had shown and the fire of the colonials continued furiously against the attackers. At first the army's surgeon, Thomas Williams, and his assistants, Dr. William Pynchon and two young men, attempted to doctor the men near the barricade, but the gunfire was so heavy and the bullets raining about them were so numerous that they withdrew to a log shed that had been built close to the lakeshore and established it as a hospital.

The Caughnawagas and Abnakis who had led the Canadians out of the woods on the flanks had abruptly lost interest in the fight at the booming of the artillery. Many of them had drawn back to places of safety behind trees and were merely watching what was happening. The Iroquois in Johnson's camp, too, had had their bellies filled of the fighting and most were merely watching now as the English and the French fought it out by themselves.

But with the lack of help from the Indians, the Canadians were faltering and falling back. Dieskau, seeing that he was making no gains with the brunt of his initial attack against the center and left of the provincials, now ordered a vigorous onslaught against the regiments of Titcomb, Williams and Ruggles on the right. Colonel Moses Titcomb immediately caught a bullet in the spine and died, but though the firing continued with great heat on both sides for the better part of an hour, the provincials held.

Now, seeing the firing of the Canadians faltering and his Indians not fighting at all, Dieskau raced toward them with his aide, Captain Montreuil, close behind him. They made inviting targets and a rain of bullets came their way. One of them caught Dieskau in the leg and tumbled him in a heap. Immediately Montreuil was at his side, cutting away the cloth and pouring brandy on the wound from a flask. Even as the officer worked on him, two more bullets struck the baron in the same leg, one in the knee and the other in the thigh. Still another ball nicked Montreuil's shoulder, but the wound was slight.

Montreuil, an adjutant as well as Dieskau's aide, shouted frantically for two Canadians firing from behind a tree nearby to come and help carry their commander out of range. The pair rushed over but even as they bent to help, one of them was fatally shot and fell atop Dieskau and the other man fled.

"Take command!" Dieskau barked at Montreuil, shoving the body off himself. "Take command! I'll be all right."

Montreuil nodded and dashed away to rally the faltering troops. Dieskau, with bullets still plucking up little fountains of dirt all around him, managed to drag himself behind some logs and from there into the trees behind. There, reasonably out of range, he propped himself up with his back against a tree to watch and, if possible, direct the continuing battle.

Things were not going well for the French forces now. The hasty barricade thrown up by the provincials would have been useless against artillery, but Dieskau had brought no cannon, and the rifle fire was practically useless against it. Time and again the regulars formed themselves into ranks to raise, aim and fire, but it was essentially ineffective and ever greater numbers of the white coats were becoming stained with red.

It was late afternoon already and the Abnakis and Caughnawagas were moving away, returning to the scene of the bloody morning ambush to collect their scalps and leave, their appetites for battle sated. The greatest part of the gunfire was emanating now from behind the barricade. The voices of English company commanders shouted above the din and abruptly the defenders became the attackers, spilling over the barricade in a living flow, smashing the French regulars back and causing the Canadians to flee after their Indian allies. Tomahawks, gun butts and knives took the place of bullets on the English side, and bayonets on the French. The battle had now become almost entirely one of hand-to-hand combat. Dieskau watched with despair as he saw his army being destroyed. He heard a sound close by and turned to see a provincial only a dozen yards away to his left, aiming his musket at him.

"Don't shoot!" the marshal screamed, but the blast of the weapon cut off his words and he felt another tremendous blow as the ball passed high through both buttocks, narrowly missing the end of his spine. The man followed up his shot by dropping his gun and throwing himself upon the German officer.

"Surrender, damn you!" he growled, in perfect French.

Groaning with pain, Dieskau replied, "You idiot! Why did you fire? You see a man lying in his own blood on the ground and you shoot him!"

"How did I know you didn't have a pistol?" the soldier replied. "I'd rather kill the Devil than have the Devil kill me!"

"You are French?" the marshal asked.

"Yes. I left Canada over ten years ago."

More of the provincials came running up and stripped off his clothing to stare at his wounds. Furious, as much with the insult as with the pain, Dieskau shouted at them, "I am Baron Dieskau, commander of the French! I order you to take me to your general."

The men became wide-eyed at this momentous news and without another word they lifted him carefully and carried him to William Johnson's tent and lay him on a cot there. The English general sent them at once to get surgeon Williams and when the doctor came and headed toward William to dress his wound, the commanding officer shook his head and told him to take care of the baron first, since he was the more seriously wounded. Williams turned and looked at Dieskau's wounds and shook his head. As he set to work to remove the bullets, Dieskau fainted and Williams muttered that he didn't think the man could live with such wounds and such loss of blood.

By now it was five o'clock in the evening and the French army was in full retreat, with the English snapping at their heels. Many more of the French regulars and some of the Canadians were killed; and a number of each were taken prisoner and brought back to the camp.

A large segment of the Caughnawagas, Abnakis and Canadians had by now returned to the scene of the ambush where they were methodically scalping the dead soldiers and Indians. So engrossed were they in their grisly work that they failed to hear the approach of a detachment of men out of Fort Lyman under Captains McGinnis and Folsom. The detachment had been sent out by Colonel Blanchard when some of the wagoners who had escaped the Indians the evening before had finally reached the fort and told their story.

Though the detachment was greatly outnumbered, their surprise was so complete and they attacked with such ferocity that they drove the scalpers into retreat after a sharp and bloody skirmish in which McGinnis and a number of his men were killed. The bodies of the Indians and Canadians were tossed into a quiet pond[9] close by and the detachment continued to General Johnson's camp.

In the camp, Dieskau had just regained consciousness in Johnson's tent, only to find the English general arguing heatedly with a large group of Mohawks that had crowded inside. They were extremely angry, though no more so than William himself, but eventually they trooped out with sullen looks on their faces.

"What did they want?" Dieskau whispered.

"They want to burn you, by God!" Johnson said, still angry. "Then they were going to eat you to avenge the Indians killed here today and to absorb your strength. But don't worry, you'll be safe with me. I told them if they wanted to kill you they would have to kill me first. They won't do that."

Outside, Colonel Phineas Lyman was busy. Under questioning, some of the French prisoners had said that there was another force of a thousand French regulars coming right behind them. This Lyman doubted very much, but he warned his men to be cautious as they went about their jobs of patrolling the camp with a large sentry force, guarding the tent where Dieskau lay to prevent the Indians from killing him, and gathering the dead to bury them in common graves.

And late in the evening, by candlelight, the first post-battle letters were being written to next of kin; a melancholy business for all.

## [ September 18, 1755—Thursday ]

Down the Hudson River had gone the stream of messengers from the Lake George camp and from Fort Lyman, shortly after the battle. They carried bundles of letters and official dispatches and throughout the Colonies the news they carried spread with incredible speed . . . and it all boiled down to six stunning words:

Johnson's army has defeated the French!

Official reports went to all the governors and to the Crown, but it was in the personal letters, many of them quickly reprinted in the newspapers, that the citizens of the Colonies were able to feel the closeness of what had happened.

Thomas Williams, surgeon, though utterly fatigued by his long hours of doctoring, which still remained unfinished at midnight of the day of the battle, had slept for an hour and then treated more wounded until he finished at last the next afternoon. Then, without further rest, he had engaged in a chore quite as unpleasant—writing the saddest of news in a quick note to his wife. His was one of the letters speeded down the Hudson. He wrote:

*My Dearest One:*

*My dear brother Ephraim was killed by a ball through his head; poor brother Josiah's wound, I fear, will prove mortal; poor Captain Hawley is yet alive, though I did not think he would live two hours after bringing him in. I have naught but a great admiration for General Johnson's firm steady mind during the action and would consider him a second Marlborough.*

*The Indians fought well in some instances, but poorly in others, and in a few hours lost their taste for the fight altogether. They lost many warriors and chiefs, but the number of their loss cannot well be determined. Some of them may have run off and others were probably killed in the woods and still lie there. The English loss was two hundred and sixteen killed, which we buried, and ninety-six wounded, which I have treated.[10] Johnson believes the French loss to be four hundred, but Seth Pomeroy sets it at four hundred to five hundred.[11]*

For his own part, Lieutenant Colonel Seth Pomeroy was heartsick at the letter he was forced to write to his sister-in-law, Rachel, who had only two weeks before made him an uncle by delivering his brother Daniel's first child, a son. He wrote:

*Dear Sister,*

*This brings heavy tidings; but let not your heart sink at the news, though it be your loss of a dear husband. Monday the eighth instant was a memorable day; and truly you may say, had not the Lord been on our side, we must all have been swallowed up. My brother being one who went out in the first engagement, received a fatal shot through the middle of the head. Another attack may be coming to us, if what our prisoners say is true, but as God hath begun to show mercy, I hope he will go on to be gracious. I have just finished the melancholy piece of business of helping to bury our dead. We also buried as many of the French as possible without the knowledge of our Indians, to prevent their being scalped,*

394

*which may have been an excess of civility, since Braddock's dead were left to the buzzards . . .*

Others of the men wrote of the individual heroism of their comrades or the conduct of their officers. Private Edgar Warner, a farmer of Connecticut and one of Phineas Lyman's men, shared his commander's resentment that Johnson rather than Lyman had been made general of this army. In a letter to his brother, he had some unusual comments:

*Dere Bro. Caleb—we ben hit by the French but has successful survvived and run them off shot there genrel Dyskow and have him took—that damn fool Johnson who aught not to ben genrel at all but instead our Col. Lyman, he was not much in the battel, being shot in the asse whitch shows what way he was heading whilst we was attaçkted. but our Col Lyman he was a hero and become our leader whilst Johnson rested in his tent til the battel was won . . .*

His comments, however, were offset by those as biasedly in favor of Johnson, such as the comments of Private William Savage of New York, who wrote to his father:

*In spite of his wound, our general tried to carry on and direct us and was able to do so until his leg began to stiffen and cause him great pain, at which time he was brought to his tent and Col. Lyman took command. But it is a wonder we won, for there is none more cowardly than he. While we were in the midst of our battle I found the colonel behind a tree lying on his belly with his face to the ground, saying prayers. When I cursed at him this saint lifted his face which was white with his scare and told me not to swear because God did not like profanity and would cause the bullets to come our way.*

Such letters were quick to spark a feud between Connecticut and New York which showed no promise of ever being amicably settled, but it was a minor matter. The important thing was that the Colonies had a signal victory. The French might have had their victories over Washington and Braddock by Villiers and Beaujeu, but the English now had theirs over Dieskau by Johnson.

Despite the fact that they had been ambushed in what was now officially being called the Bloody Morning Scout, the triumph belonged to the English. An army of provincials, most of whom—with the exception of their Indians—had never seen battle; an army unstrengthened by regulars with the single exception of Captain William Eyre; an army under local command of an entirely inexperienced general; such an army had stood up to and defeated an army of French regulars, Canadians and Indians under the command of a highly trained and seasoned professional soldier.

It was exactly the type of victory the Colonies needed, to help wipe away the dreadful stain of General Edward Braddock's defeat.

### [ September 23, 1755—Tuesday ]

Throughout the Pennsylvania border country continually more of the residents of scattered settlements and isolated cabins were being forced to move to the largest and strongest house in their vicinity in order to fort up, that is, to make concerted stands in fortified houses or even to build their own forts for such purpose. To refuse to do so was to invite the same disaster that had already befallen so many of their frontier neighbors.

Some of these reinforced buildings were quite strong and able to withstand concerted attack, but many others were frail and fell with ease before the Indians. One of the stronger ones was the forted house at the mouth of Wisconisco Creek[12] on the Susquehanna River. Here a total of eighty-four residents from the surrounding area along the east shore of the Susquehanna had congregated. Forty-six of them were men; the rest women and children.

Through the rifle slots in the chinking of their defensive works, they watched now as a party of about one hundred Indians and twenty French soldiers, led by a captain, systematically burned the thirty scattered cabins and sheds that made up this settlement and butchered all the cows and hogs in their pens.

At first the men in the fort had done some heavy shooting at the intruders, but the range was too great and so before long they ceased their firing and simply watched with groaning frustration while their homes and possessions disappeared in smoke. With insolent slowness then, the attacking party moved away to the north. While still within sight, they split; a group of about twenty Indians turning straight eastward and the remainder continuing upstream along the Susquehanna.

Inside the forted building a hurried conference was held. If they waited until the main attacking force was out of sight and hearing and then speedily followed the smaller party, they might be able to overtake and destroy them. Undoubtedly it would teach the others a good lesson. As quickly as it was suggested, the plan was adopted.

Ten minutes after both of the attack parties had disappeared from sight, the entire forty-six men trooped out of the forted house and took up a hot pursuit. They themselves had not been gone from sight for over five minutes when the larger group of French and Indians suddenly thundered back to the now virtually undefended building and took it with ease. They killed twenty-one women and two teen-aged boys and, after plundering the place and setting it afire, carried off into captivity the remaining six women, three young girls and seven little boys.

The burning of the scattered cabins and the departure first of the Indians and French and then their pursuers had been witnessed by three boys, aged sixteen, fourteen and twelve, who were crouched fearfully in a dense thicket a few hundred yards away. They had been on the verge of leaving their hiding place and going to the fortified house when the large group of attackers had returned. Trembling, they watched the place taken, saw the slaughter of the women and two boys they had been on their way to visit, and finally the departure of the party with their captives as the house burned fiercely.

When the three boys at last left their hiding place and ran to the spot a quarter mile downstream where they had pulled their canoe into the bushes, it was with a horror indelibly implanted in their minds. With all the speed they could muster they paddled across the Susquehanna and down the west bank of the river to the mouth of Sherman Creek. Up that stream they went until, within a half mile they reached the cabin of their step-father, John Turner.[13]

These were the Girty boys—Thomas, Simon and James.

At about the same time, eleven miles to the east of the Susquehanna, the pursuing border men from the fortified house rode straight into a withering ambush.[14] In one fatal moment a dozen of them were dead and eight others were writhing on the ground with the agony of their wounds. The other twenty-six uninjured, in a frantic stampede to escape what they thought was the entire body of the Indian party again, abandoned their fallen comrades and fled back toward their fortified house. But what they galloped to was even worse than what they left.

In the great longhouse at Onondaga, the council fires of the Iroquois League had been burning for several days. Chief after chief had risen to speak his mind at length, and in all who were assembled here there was an underlying fear.

The Six Nations were being destroyed.

Individual human beings they could meet in battle at any time without fear; even armies would have to exceed their own strength numerous times over to daunt them. But the form of destruction that was eating them away now was an insidious one which was striking them from many different directions at once; one that they could not fully understand.

"We are being devoured by little pieces," said Chief Red Head to the assemblage. "Everywhere there are bites taken from us and they are like the bites of the mosquito—not felt until after the bite has been taken and there is no enemy there to slap, only a hole where once there was a part of us."

The Onondaga chief shook his head angrily. "We wanted no white men in our lands, but then we sold the edges of our land to them, English and French both, and they were not content, but began to eat into us more. We let them build fur-trading posts where we could sell what we work to gather and thus be able to buy the goods which we need, but somehow these posts grow like living things and before we have turned around they are become forts and we are shut out of them and the land around them is suddenly no longer ours. We are showed deeds which it is said we have signed, but we have not signed them; and when we take this to them and tell them, they shake their heads and say they are sorry and that they will look into it, but then we hear nothing more."

His voice began rising with indignation as he continued, "Now they are no longer content with just our land and our furs from the land. No! They wish to divide us so that Mohawk may break the head of Oneida and Seneca take the scalp of Onondaga, and Cayuga burn the body of Tuscarora.

"In the recent battle at the lake we have lost one of our great chiefs, Tiyanoga, whose body we did not find for three days, and who, as a great warrior, was insulted in the worst possible way—by being slain by little children with toy weapons. Many of his men died also. And who was it who killed him and who killed them? Not the French or the English. Not even the Hurons or Algonkins or Ottawas, who were the enemies of our fathers. No! Tiyanoga, chief of all Mohawks, was killed by Caughnawagas who, until lately, were themselves Mohawks. The hand turns and stabs its own body.

"Where are we now?" he asked. "Where are we and who are we? The tribes that have always before feared us now move boldly through our western countries to attack the English settlers, and we are too busied with our affairs to force them away, fearful that we ourselves may be crushed between the two white peoples. Our right hand holds a tomahawk stained with the blood of the English, and our left hand holds a tomahawk stained with the blood of the French, but we have become so busied with these affairs that we forget we are a League and our chest and backs become exposed.

"My Brothers," he cried, *"this* is where we are: now all of us must sleep with ears unplugged and one eye left open, lest during the dark of night not only our enemy but our own brother or cousin or friend should slip in upon us and kill us. And where only a short time ago there were no French—at the point of Ticonderoga—now there is a strong French house and it is called Fort Carillon by them and suddenly that is no longer our land but theirs. And where only a short time ago there were no English—at the falls of the Hudson and at the head of the water they call Lake George—now there is a fort at each place and suddenly those, too, are no longer our lands but theirs. It is *their* war, yet it is *our* chiefs and *our* warriors who die, and *our* lands which are lost. *This must stop!"*

A fierce uproar of approval followed these words and when at last it had quieted, Red Head continued:

"Warraghiyagey has long been the only white man we could trust, yet can we even trust him now? When the Mohawks and other Iroquois who fought for him at the lake would have killed the French general in revenge for Tiyanoga, he stopped them. When they would have scalped their dead enemies, as is their right, he made haste to bury them so this could not be done. When we would have taken the French prisoners to our villages for the torture which it is our custom to bestow, he made haste to escort them out of our country and to the English cities so we could not reach them.

"It is bad and it must stop. To the Mohawks and the Onondagas, to the Senecas and Cayugas, to the Oneidas and their adopted children, the Tuscaroras, this we say now as the word of the Iroquois League: *No more can we support white men, French or English, for they both have a design to kill us all!* Our ruling is and must be, that that nation of the

Six Nations which does support either one or the other of them, that nation of ours which in any way acts to continue the war beside the whites, *hear me now,* that nation we will kick away from us and it will no longer be of the League of our nations and it will be our enemy!"

Red Head was finished, but the response to this last was not as he expected. The alliances that had been formed with whites were addictive. The various nations of the League were dependent upon whites for powder and lead and supplies, without which they would be hard put to survive and, becoming weakened, would be open to attack from other tribes who hated them.

Despite Warraghiyagey's victory at Lake George, the majority of individuals in the Six Nations were coming to believe that the French would ultimately be victorious over the English. Most of them were inclined to hope so. The French might claim their land and build forts, but when they did so, this was not instantly followed by an influx of settlers onto the land, as with the English.

The principal chiefs of this council—Red Head, Wascaugh, Old Belt, Canassatego, Torach, and others—looked at one another knowingly. Although the council had now officially ruled against any further support of the whites, the alliances would continue, either openly or covertly.

And in either case, the foundation of the centuries-old League of the Iroquois was collapsing, and within their hearts there was a great sadness.

[ *November 27, 1755—Thursday* ]

From the throats of a thousand border people and more in the western wilds of Pennsylvania came the screams for help. They had begun in earnest only days after the defeat of Braddock in July, and with the passing of the days into weeks and then the weeks into months, the anguished cries had swelled to a chorus which echoed through the governor's mansion and the halls of the Pennsylvania Assembly. But until now, these pleas had been in vain.

John Harris,[15] settler on the east bank of the Susquehanna, was one of those who begged for assistance in a letter to Governor Robert Hunter Morris:

*Sir—*

*In the name of God, help us! The inhabitants are abandoning their plantations, and we are in a dreadful situation. The*

400

*Indians are cutting us off every day, and I had a certain account of about fifteen hundred Indians, besides French, being on their march against us and Virginia, and now close on our borders, their scouts scalping our families on our frontiers daily.*

Adam Hoops, settler of near Lancaster, was another who wrote to Governor Morris:

*We are in as bad circumstances as ever any poor Christians were ever in; for the cries of widowers, widows, fatherless and motherless children, are enough to pierce the most hardest of hearts. Likewise, it's a very sorrowful spectacle to see those that escaped with their lives, with not a mouthful to eat, or bed to lie on, or clothes to cover their nakedness, or keep them warm, but all they had consumed into ashes. These deplorable circumstances cry aloud for your Honor's most wise consideration; for it is really very shocking for the husband to see the wife of his bosom her head cut off, and the children's blood drunk like water, by these bloody and cruel savages.*

Report after report, letter after pleading letter came in with the dreadful news: twenty dead and eleven carried off to almost certain death on the east bank of the Susquehanna; forty dead and nine carried off from Paxton; fourteen dead, five missing near Reading; one hundred dead, thirty-seven captured from almost within shouting distance of Fort Cumberland; the whole settlement of Tulpehocken, only sixty miles from Philadelphia, destroyed and its thirty inhabitants dead; the entire settlement of Great Cove wiped away as if it had never been, except for mounds of ashes and a few rotting corpses.

And with the reports and letters came petition after petition from the people of the borders for arms and ammunition and, most of all, for a militia law which would enable the people to organize and defend themselves. But this measure in particular was resisted by the Quakers in the assembly, who deadlocked that body in interminable arguments to the effect that it was against God's will to be violent or to support violence.

Still the letters came and even William Trent, the Indian trader of renown, was one of those who wrote. His demand minced no words:

*How long will those in power, by their quarrels, suffer us to be massacred? Two and forty bodies have been buried on Patterson's Creek; and since, they have killed more, and keep on killing!*

Threats came, too. Colonel William Moore of West Chester wrote to Morris that two thousand men were coming from Chester County to compel him and the assembly to defend the province. Conrad Weiser wrote that a body of men was coming from Berks for the same purpose. Four hundred German settlers, whose homes had hitherto been considered safe but were now endangered, cast aside their long-nurtured pacifism and came to the Governor's home in a procession to demand protection and measures of war. And a letter that had been written by Colonel George Washington, commander of the Virginia Regiment, to Robert Dinwiddie in Williamsburg, was forwarded by the Virginia governor to Morris and read into the records of the Pennsylvania Assembly:

*Sir, every day we have accounts of such cruelties and barbarities as are shocking to human nature. It is not possible to conceive the situation and danger of this miserable country. Such numbers of French and Indians are all around that no road is safe. My command of the Virginia Regiment gives me but a thousand men with which to protect a frontier three hundred and fifty miles against more numerous enemies who can choose their time and place of attack.*

*Your Honor may see to what unhappy straits the distressed inhabitants and myself are reduced. I see inevitable destruction in so clear a light, that unless vigorous measures are taken by the assembly, and speedy assistance sent from below, the poor inhabitants that are now in forts must unavoidably fall, while the remainder are flying before the barbarous foe. In fine, the melancholy situation of the people; the little prospect of assistance; the gross and scandalous abuse cast on the officers in general, which is reflecting on me in particular for suffering such misconduct of such extraordinary kinds; and the distant prospect, if any, of gaining honor and reputation in the service, cause me to lament the hour that gave me a commission, and would induce me at any other time than this of imminent danger, to resign, without one hesitating moment, a command from which I never expect to reap either honor or benefit, but, on the contrary, have almost an absolute certainty of incurring dis-*

*pleasure below, while the murder of helpless families may be laid to my account here.*

*The supplicating tears of the women and moving petitions of the men melt me into such deadly sorrow, that I solemnly declare, if I know my own mind, I could offer myself a willing sacrifice to the butchering enemy, providing that would contribute to the people's ease.*

The majority of the complaints were, as they should have been, directed to Governor Morris. He sympathized with them from the depths of his soul, but in session after session with the Assembly, he was being hamstrung by the Quakers in any attempt to defend and protect the people.

To the assembly, furthermore, the prevailing feudal proprietaryship of the Penn family in this province was detestable and against their democratic nature. Although the first proprietary, William Penn, had exhibited a broad liberalism in his use of these feudal rights—and with them had forged of Pennsylvania the most democratic province in America—the present proprietaries, Thomas and Richard Penn were arrogant, imperious, and a bane to any lover of liberty. And since the governor was the deputy of the proprietaries, the Assembly's one great passion was to defeat him in any way possible. To this was added the religious pacifism of the Quakers, to whom any suggestion of taking up arms—especially against Indians—was wholly repugnant. In Philadelphia and the surrounding close-in area, where the danger did not immediately affect them, they could still go about their business, tend their shops, work their farms, and sit about in their broad-brimmed hats of black to discuss all the wickedness of warfare in righteous indignation.

Thus, while the butcherings not only continued but increased on the western borders, the Assembly played a game of Beat-the-Governor-and-Leave-the-Enemy-Alone. In the first sessions after the alarms and complaints came rolling in and Morris appealed to them for help, the Assembly placed the blame where it was safest to place it—on Braddock's head—and did nothing.

"Braddock's defeat," they intoned, during one of the initial sessions, "was a just judgment on him for molesting the French in their settlements on the Ohio."

But when the attacks grew worse and the complaints stronger and they could no longer sit in silence against the rising anger of the people, they deftly shifted the blame to the proprietaries and to Governor Morris.

403

"Although it is our belief," they said, "that the accounts of barbarities are exaggerated, we do confess that outrages have been committed, undoubtedly with reason. Why, we ask Governor Morris, have the Delawares and Shawnees become unfriendly? Is it because they have suffered wrongs from the proprietaries? If they have suffered such wrongs, then we are resolved to do all in our power to redress them, rather than entail upon ourselves and our posterity the calamities of a cruel Indian war."

The calamities of a cruel Indian war were *already* upon the borders and daily moving closer to themselves; a fact which caused them increasing nervousness but, with it, a certain satisfaction, since now they felt they had the governor over a barrel and could force him to yield an important point. At the next session they made the demand.

"We lay before you, Governor Morris, for your concurrence, a bill we the Assembly have passed for emitting bills of credit to the amount of sixty thousand pounds, to be sunk in four years by a tax including the proprietary estates."

It was blackmail, and no one knew it better than Robert Hunter Morris. He had no authority whatever to sign any bill levying taxation against the proprietaries of Pennsylvania or their properties, but if he did not sign it, he could not provide relief to the border settlements and crush the Indian menace.

"The Assembly seemed determined," he replied heatedly, "to take advantage of the country's distress to get the whole power of government into their own hands. The conduct of the Assembly is, to me, shocking beyond parallel. It has taken uncommon pains to prevent the people from taking up arms. Constrained by my instructions and bonds, I must reject this bill. I can only say that I will readily pass a bill for striking any sum in paper money the present exigency may require, providing funds are established for sinking the same in five years, but *not* through proprietary taxation."

Four more bills were passed by the Assembly and presented to the governor, and each time with the clause calling for taxation of the proprietaries' estates, which it was beyond his power to grant. When he vetoed them, the Assembly figuratively shook their finger in his face for the benefit of the public and their comments now began to take on a certain vindictiveness, assailing the governor's own character.

"We have taken every step in our power," they said, "consistent with the just rights of the freemen of Pennsylvania, for the relief of the poor distressed inhabitants; and we have reason to believe that they themselves would not wish us to go farther. Those who would give up essential liberty to purchase a little temporary safety deserve neither liberty nor safety!

"What must we do," they continued plaintively, "to please this kind governor, who takes so much pains to render us obnoxious to our sovereign and odious to our fellow subjects? If we only tell him that the difficulties he meets with are not owing to the causes he names—which indeed had no existence—but to his own want of skill and abilities for his station, he takes it extremely amiss and says we forget all decency to those in authority. We are apt to think there is likewise some decency due the Assembly as a part of the government; and though we have not, like the governor, had a courtly education, but are plain men, and must be very imperfect in our politeness, yet we think we have no chance of improving by his example."

The words hardened, becoming more accusatory as they continued: "Colonial governors have often been transient persons, of broken fortunes, greedy of money, destitute of all concern for those they govern, often their enemies, and endeavoring not only to oppress, but to defame them. Governor Morris, you are taking advantage of the country's distress to reduce the province to Egyptian bondage. Do not, we implore you, make yourself the hateful instrument of reducing a free people to the abject state of vassalage."

If they thought to intimidate the governor by this tirade, they underestimated him. Refusing to be baited into a duel of personalities, Robert Hunter Morris replied in a steady voice which belied the turmoil within him and surprised the Assembly.

"I shall not, he said, "enter into a dispute whether the proprietaries ought to be taxed or not. It is sufficient for me that they have given me no power in that case; and I cannot think it consistent either with my duty or safety to exceed the powers of my commission, much less to do what that commission expressly prohibits. I will, however, stretch what authority I have so far as to propose a sort of compromise by which the question should be referred to the King."

Instantly there were outraged shouts of *"No! No!"* and after the uproar died down to where he could be heard again, Morris continued:

"You have, in all, proposed to me five money bills, three of them rejected because contrary to royal instructions, the other two on account of the unjust method proposed for

405

taxing the proprietary estate. If you are disposed to relieve your country, you have many other ways of granting money to which I shall have no objection. I shall put forth one proof more—both of your sincerity and mine in our professions of regard for the public—by offering to agree to any bill in the present exigency which is consistent with my duty to pass; lest, before our present disputes can be brought to an issue, we should neither have a privilege to dispute about, nor a country to dispute in!"

Adroitly he had dumped the whole mess right back into their laps and they squirmed uneasily and swiftly fell back on their time-tested, Quaker-instigated argument that war is a sin and that they would pass nothing which would make the Assembly guilty of abusing God.

But it was about this time that a cluster of stern-faced frontiersmen came to Philadelphia bearing in a wagon a gruesome cargo consisting of the beheaded or scalped bodies of their families and friends. They stopped before the Assembly doors, threatening vengeance and cursing the Quakers in loud, angry voices. Close on their heels came a deputation from one of the few remaining bands of friendly Delaware Indians on the Susquehanna to ask of the Assembly whether or not the English meant to fight, for if they didn't stand by their Indians, then these Indians would join the French. It was definitely the Assembly now which was feeling the slings and arrows of outrage from the populace.

Some of the province's chief citizens took it upon themselves now to draw up and sign a paper which they called "A Representation," and this they sent to the House. It stressed the imperative need for measures of defense to be enacted immediately, and concluded with great force:

*You will forgive us, gentlemen, if we assume characters somewhat higher than that of humble suitors praying for the defence of our lives and properties as a matter of grace or favor on your side. You will permit us to make a positive and immediate demand for it.*

This threw the Quakers, in and out of the Assembly, into a flurry of activity. Black-garbed preachers of both sexes took positions everywhere an audience might be gathered in order to decry the sinfulness of war. Those Quakers belonging to the Assembly were invited to a private house in Philadelphia where three of the sect from England implored them not to weaken in their stand. Then some of the principal resident Quakers went even further and addressed the House.

"Any action on your part," they warned the legislators darkly, "which is inconsistent with the peaceable testimony we profess and have borne to the world, appears to us in its consequences to be destructive of our religious liberties. We would rather suffer than to pay taxes to support warfare!"[16]

The House found itself between two fires and that of the Quakers was not the hottest. There now loomed the viable danger that if they did not do *something*, make some sort of concession toward ending the border problems, they would become the actual physical target of the public's anger.

It was ironic that Governor Morris should be the one to lead them out of their dilemma.

Morris informed them that he had just received a letter from the proprietaries which authorized the expenditure of five thousand pounds for use in defense of the province. There was a condition attached: that the money should be accepted as a free gift and not in any way to be regarded as their share of any tax which was now in existence or might be laid by the Assembly in the future. That the proprietaries should so stipulate was strictly a coincidence, for as yet they knew nothing of this argument presently raging in the colony. The money had simply been sent in view of the defeat of Braddock and the probable consequences it had engendered.

It was a way out and the Assembly snatched at it. The clause taxing proprietary estates was stricken from the bill at hand and the bill then presented again to the governor. Morris, with deep satisfaction and no hesitation, signed it and thereby made it a law.


[ *November 29, 1755—Saturday* ]

Matters at Fort Oswego had not gone well at all for General William Shirley. Ever more clearly it was seen that to attempt an attack against Fort Niagara without first destroying Fort Frontenac might be—in fact, almost surely would be—disastrous. There was little doubt that Niagara could hold out for quite a long time against them should they lay siege to it. If, while they were gone from Fort Oswego on this mission, however, a force came down from the much nearer Fort Frontenac, Fort Oswego would fall without question and Shirley's army would suddenly find itself dangling, cut off from all supplies and with the enemy at its rear.

Small bands of Indian spies were sent out to reconnoiter both French forts and in each case their reports showed Niagara to be the lesser danger to Fort Oswego. French regulars alone at Fort Frontenac numbered over fourteen hundred and to these were added more than twelve hundred Canadians and in increasing number of Indians from the tribes of the upper . Great Lakes—Chippewas, Ottawas, Hurons, Mississaugis, Menominees and Potawatomies—and the tribes from the north and east—Algonkins, Caughnawagas, Abnakis and Nipissings.

On September 18, General Shirley had called a council of war of his officers and their entire situation here was discussed in detail.

"Gentlemen," he said, "it appears that for the moment we are unable to move against either Fort Niagara or Fort Frontenac. Just as our spies have been able to gather information for us on the strength of those two installations, so we must recognize that their spies are gathering the same information on us. Our effective strength at this moment, not including those too ill to engage in any march or action, is thirteen hundred seventy-six. Every day more of our men become incapacitated by the fevers and bloody fluxes that have levied such a toll against us.

"Worse yet," he continued, "is our lack of provisions. Supplies which should have come soon after my arrival here have never even come at all. Our medicines and food supplies are perilously low. To even contemplate beginning a campaign without being backed up by adequate supplies would be the height of folly. As I see it now, we are too weak to attack Fort Frontenac and too ill supplied to attack Fort Niagara.

"I can see but one course clear for us," he added. "There is no substantial force of regulars at Fort Niagara. All forces there, in fact—regulars, Canadians and Indians—total less than eleven hundred. Most likely our army could take them, but with the new ships the French have built at Fort Frontenac and the great fleet of whaleboats and bateaux they have on hand there, they could cross the lake and fall upon this installation as soon as we have gone. Therefore, our plans must be along these lines: we will continue to wait for our provisions to arrive and, just as soon as they do we will march with a force of six hundred troops and just as many Indians as possible against Niagara, leaving the rest here to defend Oswego against the expected attack from Fort Frontenac.

"As you all know by now, General Johnson's force underwent a severe test, beginning with a despicable ambush against them which took the lives of a great many of our comrades, and ending with a fine rally on the part of our forces which resulted in the destruction of the French force and the wounding and capture of its commander, Marshal Dieskau. When our own supplies come and we launch the attack against Fort Niagara, we must do all in our power to avenge those who fell during the Bloody Morning Scout, and to emulate the determination of that force to wrest victory from the almost certain aspect of defeat."

The officers continued to discuss the matter and rather halfheartedly agreed that General Shirley's plan might work, providing a substantial number of the Iroquois hovering about Fort Oswego would support them. Shirley at once called the chiefs together and addressed them. They should, he told them, march with the detachment against Niagara, to revenge themselves for the death of their great chief of the Mohawks and for the warriors who had died at that battle. With Niagara taken, the English would be all around them, except for the far western forts from Presque Isle to Duquesne. And these, with their supply lines cut, could be left to wither until they were too weak to any longer defend themselves.

Shirley's officers were not fully satisfied, when the general finished addressing these Iroquois, that he had aroused enough animosity in them for the death of Tiyanoga. In fact, they felt the Indians here were acting most standoffish and would still hesitate to give them aid when the time came to march with the army. Though Shirley watched with approval while the Indians feasted and leaped to a stirring war dance during the evening, yet the natives would not give their unqualified promise to support him.

Late in the evening the long-anticipated supply train finally arrived from Albany, but with only a very small percentage of the goods that had been requested. Nevertheless, Shirley at once passed orders for six hundred men to embark against Niagara in the morning; but there was suddenly such opposition that it was deemed advisable to hold another war council. That meeting was held in the morning and now almost unanimously, the officers voted to postpone any plans for attack.

Young Captain John Shirley, himself extremely ill with dysentery—the bloody flux—managed to rouse himself enough to attend the council and afterwards write a letter to Governor Morris in which he said:

*All I was uneasy about was our provisions; our men had been on half allowances of bread these three weeks past, and no rum given to 'em. My father yesterday called all the Indians together and made 'em a speech on the subject of General Johnson's engagement, which he calculated to inspire them with a spirit of revenge. After the speech he gave them a bullock for a feast, which they roasted and ate, pretending they were eating the Governor of Canada! Some provisions arriving late this night, orders were given to embark on the next day, which is today, but the officers were murmuring their dissent, claiming that the supplies were not enough, the weather persistently bad, our vessels would not hold half the party and the bateaux, made only for river travel, would infallibly founder on the treacherous and stormy lake. All the field officers think it too rash an attempt; and so this morning another council was called. After the issue had been argued from all sides, my father was reluctantly convinced of the danger and put the question to them whether to go or not. The situation admitted to but one reply. The council was of the opinion that for the present the enterprise was impracticable; that Oswego should be strengthened, more vessels built, and preparations made to renew the attempt as soon as spring opened. All thoughts of active operation have now been suspended and we are seeing to our winter defenses, after which approximately half of us will remain to garrison this post and the other half return to Albany. I pray I may be among that last half, for, truth to tell, sir, I am most unwell and in need, I think, of greater care than can be provided at this post.*

And so, on the last day of October, General William Shirley left seven hundred of his men at Oswego and returned to Albany, very nearly drowning on the return as his whaleboat upset in rapids while he was attempting to determine the practicability of using that sort of craft for river travel. At Albany he learned that his long-held desire had come true; he had officially been given command of all military forces in America, succeeding General Braddock in that office.

Young John Shirley, too, got his wish in being among those to leave Fort Oswego, but he did not, as they did, remain in Albany for the winter. Instead, he continued to New York

410

for medical treatment and from that city, in a short while, an express was sent to Governor Robert Morris of Pennsylvania. For a long while after he read it, Morris sat at his desk with his head buried in his hands, but at last he dipped his pen and began writing a letter to Governor Dinwiddie of Virginia:

*My heart bleeds for Mr. Shirley. He must be overwhelmed with grief when he hears of Capt. John Shirley's death, of which I have an account by the last post from New York, where he died of the flux and fever that he had contracted at Oswego. The loss of two sons in one campaign scarcely admits of consolation. I feel the anguish of the unhappy father, and mix my tears very heartily with his. I have had an intimate acquaintance with both of them for many years, and know well their inestimable value.*

Another letter Morris wrote was shorter, but even more difficult to compose:

*Hon. William Shirley*
*Governor-General Commanding*
*Permit me, good sir, to offer you my hearty condolence upon the death of my friend Jack, whose worth I admired, and feel for him more than I can express. Few men of his age had so many friends ...*

[ *December 31, 1755—Wednesday* ]

For William Johnson, the year ended with great honor, but the honor was tempered with an even greater sadness. Not since he had come to America, perhaps not in his entire life, had such a great grief settled over him. He had not fully realized how much Tiyanoga had meant to him and what a great asset he had been in dealings with the Iroquois League. Wascaugh was now principal chief of the Mohawks and there were still many other chiefs throughout the League who were strongly friendly to him who might, in their own way, act as Tiyanoga had on Johnson's behalf, but it wouldn't be the same.

Tiyanoga would be greatly missed.

Not until three days after the battle had the chief been found by some of the Mohawks who were searching for him, knowing he was either dead or wounded or he would have returned by now. They bore him back to Canajoharie, telling

411

William they would be back after the death song had been sung and their chief laid to rest, but William doubted it—nor was he wrong.

The entire force of his Indian allies were angry with him for ordering the enemy dead buried before they had had the opportunity to exercise what they considered their right—to scalp them. They were further insulted by the fact that none of the prisoners, including even those they themselves had taken, were given to them to take to their villages for torture, but were instead spirited away to New York. Finally, they were extremely angry—especially after finding the body of Tiyanoga—that they had not been allowed to butcher and eat Baron Ludwig Dieskau, whom they most blamed for the death of their chief. On the fourth day after the battle, Dieskau too had been whisked away under cover to Albany for protection and medical care.

And so now, without the strength of Tiyanoga to hold them here, they would neither stay or return. In fact, within a few days William Johnson learned that they had even dissuaded some others they had met who were en route to join him.

Desperate now for scouts of any kind, William sent a dispatch to Colonel Robert Blanchard at Fort Lyman, asking for some good men for this purpose. Blanchard sent him the New Hampshire captain, Robert Rogers, and the general ordered him to leave at once to scout the area around Crown Point and Ticonderoga for any information he could gather. With four picked men, Rogers left.

It was the first of a score or more scouting expeditions performed by Rogers and within a remarkably short time his fame spread widely as a resourceful and courageous scout. Braving bitterly cold weather, generally hostile Indians and enemy forces, Rogers returned from each trip with more information and sometimes even with French and Indian scalps. Other scouting parties of officers and soldiers were sent out, too, but they were largely ineffectual. Only the reports turned in by Rogers could be depended upon for accuracy, and these reports were not encouraging: the new Fort Carillon at Ticonderoga was turning into a strong bastion under the skilled French engineer, Lotbinière. And from prisoners Rogers brought back, it was learned that Captain François Pouchot, under Governor Pierre Vaudreuil's orders, was equally improving the defense at Fort Niagara.

When the enlistment period of the New Hampshire men expired on October 6, nearly all of them left in a body, but

Rogers stayed on to continue his spying missions—always with the hope of killing more Indians—and William Johnson was greatly impressed by him. In letters to the governors of New Hampshire, Connecticut and Massachusetts he wrote:

*Rogers' bravery and veracity stands very clear in my opinion and of all who know him. Though his Regiment is gone, he remains here a volunteer and is the most active man in our army. I believe him to be as brave and honest a man as any I have equal knowledge of, and both myself and all the army are convinced that he has distinguished himself since he has been among us, superior to most, inferior to none of his rank in these troops.*

Gradually Johnson's force was increased until, with the arrival on October 31 of the New Hampshire replacements, he had strength of thirty-six hundred men. In view of Rogers's reports, he wanted to mount a fast-moving expedition against Fort Carillon and possibly Crown Point's Fort St. Frederic, but in the council of war he held he found his men with little desire to do so. His officers complained of the closeness of winter, the insufficient clothing for the men, inadequate provisions, not enough boats and many of those on hand beyond repair because of extensive bullet damage. Finally, the morale among the men was extremely low and they wanted to go home for the winter.

William finally gave in to them, but would not hear of disbanding the army until a substantial fort had been built here at Lake George. With the impetus of leaving the place to spur them on, the men built the fort quickly and William named it Fort William Henry after one of the King's grandsons. At the same time he changed the name of Fort Lyman to Fort Edward, after another grandson of the King.

By November 27 the forts had been garrisoned and William now gave the remainder leave to go home, then set out himself for New York. The very night of the day he left, one hundred ninety-six of the four hundred two men left behind at the Fort William Henry garrison deserted.

For William in New York there was a hero's welcome surpassing anything he had ever seen and certainly beyond any accolade he had ever expected to win from the populace. To everyone he was "the heaven-taught general" and there were loud demands that William Shirley be shorn of his command and William Johnson named to it. Johnson demurred. He wanted nothing more than to get back to his

Indian affairs, and so he resigned even his own command and returned to his home which was now, with the erection of a small stockade, being called Fort Johnson instead of Mount Johnson. At once he went to confer with the Mohawk chiefs.

Wascaugh welcomed him warmly enough and they spent a sadly pleasant time together reminiscing about Tiyanoga. But the new principal chief's friendliness cooled perceptibly when William said that he had learned of the terrible massacres being committed by the Delawares and Shawnees—and even some of the Iroquois, it was claimed—on the western borders at the encouragement of the French at Fort Duquesne. He urged Wascaugh to circulate belts among the tribes involved, demanding that they stop their attacks and atrocities, but Wascaugh shook his head.

"Warraghiyagey, as a brother Mohawk you know it is not my power to do so. Only through order of the League Council can this be done, and the matter has already been discussed. For long now the white men have been trying to manipulate us, but we will no longer hold for it. You are our friend and, where it is possible, I and others will continue to help you, but this matter of which you speak now is one about which we can do nothing."

So now he was back at Fort Johnson and, with the old year swiftly coming to an end, a messenger from New York galloped up to the great Johnson mansion with a packet addressed to him, its waxen seal bearing the Imperial Coat-of-Arms of King George. He accepted it and, his fingers shaking slightly with nervousness, he opened it and read the enclosed document, then read it through a second time to make sure he was not dreaming.

He was not. In recognition for the services he had performed, for the battle he had won when all others of His Majesty's commanders in the interior of North America were being defeated or rendered unable to carry out their campaigns, he was being awarded the sum of five thousand pounds. And because certain of his enemies were still trying to inveigle his discharge from the Indian service, the King personally proclaimed that his rank was now permanent as Colonel, Agent, and Sole Supervisor of the Six Nations of Indians and all other northern tribes, and that no person in America had the power to discharge him from this office. Nor was that all. As a further reward, His Royal Majesty had conferred upon William Johnson a baronetcy for life.

From this time forward, he would be known to all men as Sir William Johnson.

# CHAPTER VIII

*[ February 18, 1756—Wednesday ]*

THE knowledge that the Iroquois chiefs had become decidedly cool toward him was a heavy weight in the mind of Sir William Johnson. Three times he had tried to have a grand council called at Onondaga, that he might address all the chiefs at once, but his requests had been shunted aside. That failing, he had moved through the country rapidly on horseback as Warraghiyagey, visiting those chiefs he could and exhorting them individually to convince the other chiefs that the League must stop the frontier marauding and slaughter.

"I ask this," he had told them, "not merely to protect the English settlers in Virginia and Pennsylvania and New York, but equally to protect my brothers, the Iroquois. Though some of them are aiding the Shawnees and Delawares in these raids. I know that most have remained neutral, but neutrality is not enough. The Assemblies will not stand for their people being murdered and already steps are being taken to destroy those Indians.

"The bad part," he added gloomily, "is that Iroquois warriors may be mistaken for Delawares or Shawnees. This could destroy the relationship we have so long shared and which I have labored so hard between us to strengthen. Are not the Delawares and Shawnees your children? Are they not bound to do as you tell them? Will you stand here and see them bring death and destruction upon you by their acts?"

The chiefs he spoke to individually were impressed and concerned and they agreed to send emissaries to the Delawares and Shawnees on the Pennsylvania frontier in an effort to get them to stop their border attacks and, instead, strike an alliance with the English through Warraghiyagey. It was a promise William knew they would keep, but that did not mean those tribes so requested would give in.

He continued his visits with the chiefs and it was likely that he might have been able to effect some more positive action from the League if a careless accident hadn't occurred. As he walked down the street in Albany just after the turn of the year, William Johnson was shot. A provincial private had clumsily dropped his rifle, causing it to accidentally discharge, and the ball tore a shallow but painful crease in the flesh of William's right arm and chest. It was not a serious wound, but word of its occurrence sped about the League and it was considered to be an omen that Warraghiyagey was walking under the shadow of a bad spirit and both his company and advice should be avoided until the black cloud passed.

Perhaps it was just as well, for there was little likelihood that the League could have done much toward discouraging the border onslaughts. More and more of the Indians committing them were calling themselves Mingoes. This collective rather than tribal designation, which had first included mainly just the Cayugas and Senecas of the Allegheny Valley, now embraced as well many members of the Delawares, Shawnees, Hurons, Ottawas, and even some of the Miamis, all of whom were severely harassing the frontiers.

At one time, just a mere murmur from the Iroquois League would have caused any one of these non-Iroquois tribes to quake with fear, just as the Delawares had, not so many years ago, when they had been reprimanded for selling Iroquois land, and for which they had since rankled under the epithet the Iroquois had given them—that of being women. But now, while the population of the Iroquois had decreased regularly over the years, the numbers of the other tribes had remained mostly constant and, in some cases, had even increased.

There were two other points of which the Mingoes were well aware: first, that the Iroquois were in such troubles themselves in the perpetual tugging at them from the English on one side and the French on the other, that they would be unable to mount any substantial body of warriors to enforce any edict against the other tribes; secondly, that a fair portion of the Mingo confederacy was still made up of Senecas and Cayugas, who themselves were of the Iroquois League, which more or less gave a tacit sanction to the acts being committed. And so the murders and scalpings and burnings continued in great number along the borders.

Benjamin Franklin, in Pennsylvania, did not take kindly to

Sir William Johnson's efforts to enlist the aid of the Iroquois to stop the slaughter by the Mingoes.

"It is my belief," he orated in the Assembly, "that the Six Nations have privily encouraged these Indians to fall upon us. I regard the application made through Sir William Johnson to those nations to procure us peace as the most unfortunate step we ever took. During such negotiations our hands will be tied while our people are being butchered. In short, I do not believe we shall ever have a firm peace with the Indians until we have well drubbed them all!"

In Virginia, George Washington felt the same. He fumed at his inability to take the offensive and when, with his own eyes, he viewed the mutilated remains of Virginia and Pennsylvania settlers—some of them butchered within a hard day's ride of Philadelphia—he nearly wept with rage and the desire to retaliate. But though he was commander of the Virginia Regiment, it was a hollow command at best. His men were, almost without exception, surly and uncontrollable enlistees from the border country. When ordered to do something they did not care to do, they simply refused, considering that any kind of discipline put them on the level of Negro slaves. Nor would the House of Burgesses help by giving Washington the authority requisite of his command, because it might infringe on the liberties of the free white men in his army. It was an intolerable situation, worsened by the fear of an uprising of the slaves if too many men should have to leave home to fight.

There was legislative cooperation of a sort with the border people. In both Pennsylvania and Virginia they were given unofficial sanction to fort up, but for the most part this was done at their own expense and out of simple desperation. The measures were largely inadequate and the slaughter went on.

In New York, however, steps were being taken to strengthen the government's position toward its outposts. The ever-present fear remained that Fort Oswego would be lost to the French and, with it, access to the Great Lakes. The point of vulnerability for that post was not so much the fort itself, which might possibly be able to withstand a fairly strong attack. Rather, the peril was worst at the Great Carrying Place between the Mohawk and Wood Creek. Here, supply convoys, their energies sapped in making the difficult portage, were inviting targets for even small marauding bands of Canadians and Indians.

To eliminate this danger, two forts were ordered built here early in the winter and they were just now being completed.

These were Fort Bull and Fort Williams. The latter was by far the strongest and was located on the bank of the Mohawk where the portage began.[1] Fort Bull, which more than anything else was a mere collection of storehouses surrounded by a stockade, was four miles to the west near the edge of Wood Creek.

There had been strong murmurings among the Iroquois when these two were built, but once again it was William Johnson who smoothed the way. They were, he told them, only a temporary expedient and as soon as the difficulties with the French were settled, they—like the other forts in

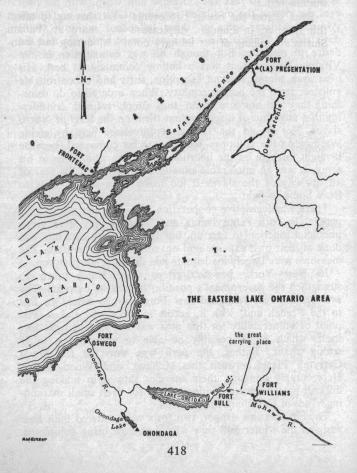

THE EASTERN LAKE ONTARIO AREA

Iroquois territory—would be destroyed or handed over to the League.

It was not only in the wilderness that changes were taking place now which promised to have an effect upon the frontier. William, who could have made use of a whole army of representatives to work with and for him among the Indians, settled for the time being on the appointment of one of the most able traders and frontiersmen he had ever encountered, George Croghan, as his first deputy Indian superintendent. He was a good man, exceptionally experienced, with an excellent knowledge of, respect from and influence over, the western tribes.

Even across the ocean two events were shaping to affect this frontier. In London, displeasure was sharp at William Shirley's handling of his military command during last summer's campaign. For this he was being recalled to England. Royal orders were drawn up in January transferring Shirley's command to John Campbell, Lord Loudoun, who would have the rank of lieutenant general. Campbell was soon to send on his two top men—General James Abercromby and Colonel Daniel Webb—to take over. Until the arrival of Webb, who was expected to reach America first, Shirley would remain in command. As soon as Webb arrived, however, he was to turn over the military command to him. Webb would then relinquish it later to General Abercromby, Abercromby, in turn, to John Campbell.

And in France, a new commander had just been chosen to replace Baron Dieskau who was still mending from his wounds in New York and who, it was obvious, would never entirely recover. The man selected to fill the post was a well-educated, cultured and highly experienced officer, Louis Joseph, Marquis de Montcalm-Gozen de Saint-Véran.

Montcalm, born near Nîmes in southern France at the Château of Candiac on February 9, 1712, had a personality and character which combined a number of attributes not often found in the military. He was, above all, a tried and proven officer who actually led his troops rather than directing them from the safety of some rear position. Because of this he had been wounded in action six times already—once by a musket ball and five times with saber—and once he had been taken prisoner by the enemy at the battle of Piacenza, Italy, but was later paroled back to France.

He was scrupulously honest, loyal with every fiber of his being to the King, a firm believer in God and respecter of the church, and a man who was very popular. He was equally a devoted father, husband and son. When he was twenty-three, shortly after the death of his father in 1735, he married a lovely woman of position, Angélique Louise Talon du Boulay, and with her had ten children. Four had died in childhood, but four daughters and two sons were growing to maturity and he was deeply proud of them all.

An avid reader, he was extremely knowledgeable in a wide range of subjects. From earliest childhood he had been taught respect for authority and the value of improving one's mind. That he had adhered to these directions was evident as early as his tenth year, at which time, in response to a letter from his father asking him what his aims were, he replied:

First, to be an honorable man, of good morals, brave, and a Christian. Secondly, to read in moderation; to know as much Greek and Latin as most men of the world; also the four rules of arithmetic, and something of history, geography, and French and Latin belles-lettres, as well as to have a taste for the arts and sciences. Thirdly, and above all, to be obedient, docile, and very submissive to your orders and those of my dear mother; and also to defer to the advice of my teacher, M. Dumas. Fourthly, to fence and ride as well as my small abilities will permit . . .

He had joined the army in 1727 at age fifteen as an ensign and in two years was a captain. At twenty-nine he was colonel of a regiment and ten years ago, at age thirty-four, he had been promoted to brigadier general. Now he was forty-four and a self-assured commander of men. He was rather small in size but seemed larger because of the keenness of his eye, the liveliness of his character and his self-possessed nature and effervescent personality. Merely talking with him was an interesting experience. He was given to speaking rapidly and sometimes with considerable vehemence, accompanying his words with elaborate gestures and a great variety of facial expressions.

Always before his commands had been on the Continent and, though he had heard a great deal about America, he had never really had any particular desire to go there. Nor had there been any indication he would, until last autumn at the close of a visit to Paris.

Preparing to return to his family, he had stopped briefly to bid adieu to Minister of War D'Argenson, who had just learned the shattering news of the defeat of Baron Dieskau by General Johnson's homespun army. They discussed the matter to some degree and at length, as Montcalm stood to leave, the minister of war walked with him to the door, shook his hand and then looked at him speculatively.

"There is now," he said, "the position of military commander of New France to fill. It may be that the officer to fill this important post is the one who honored me with his presence tonight. It is, at any rate, a thought to bear in mind. Adieu, General."

Louis Montcalm was pleased at being so considered, but he knew that there were many officers in France of equal or greater rank than he and more experienced for such a post. He hardly even thought about it, in fact, after leaving D'Argenson. Yet, just a fortnight ago had come one of the most exciting letters he had ever received:

*Versailles*
*Midnight, 25th Jan., 1756*

*Marquis de Montcalm-Gozen*
*Château de Candiac, Nîmes*

*Perhaps, Monsieur, you did not expect to hear from me again on the subject of the conversation I had with you on the day you came to bid me farewell in Paris. Nevertheless, I have not forgotten for a moment the suggestion I then made you; and it is with the greatest pleasure that I announce to you that my views have prevailed. The King has chosen you to command his troops in North America, and will honor you on your departure with the rank of Major-General.*

*Your second-in-command will be, with the rank of Brigadier, the Chevalier François de Lévis. Third in command, with rank of Colonel, is the Chevalier François Charles de Bourlamaque. You will be provided with reinforcement troops for Canada to the number of twelve hundred men—a battalion each from the Regiments of La Sarre and the Royal Roussilon. Three ships of the line—Léopard, Héros, and Illustre—will transport these troops, and you and your chief aide-de-camp, Captain Louis Antoine de Bougainville, will accompany them aboard the frigate, Licorne. The Chevaliers de Lévis and de Bourlamaque will follow several days later in the frigates Sauvage and Sirène. Port of embarkation will be Brest. You will be provided naval escort until beyond reasonable possibility of interception from British warships.*

*Much must be accomplished before embarkation date*

*which, for you, will be April 3, and you are therefore ordered to repair at once to the Court in Paris for Royal Instructions.*

*Accept, Monsieur, my personal congratulations on your appointment to this post, which indicates the high respect the King holds for you. I know that you will also be pleased to learn that your son, the Chevalier de Montcalm, has been appointed to command a regiment here in France. He is a good officer and you must be very proud of him.*

*My kindest regards to your mother, Madame de Saint-Véran, as well as to your wife, Madame de Montcalm, your good family, and yourself. It will be my pleasure to see you again.*

*D'Argenson*
*Minister of War*

Now he was in Paris and, though accustomed to the complications arising in the preliminaries involved before assuming a new command, he was almost dazed by all that had already transpired and yet remained to be done. For days he had been in conference with the King, the colonial minister, the naval minister, and the minister of war, and a multitude of instructions had been given to him. Among these was one which troubled him. In the French government and in its colonial and military arms, particularly those of New France, corruption was more the rule than the exception. In fact, Montcalm's inherent honesty was rather like a beacon in the darkness, and he was ordered to view with care, whenever possible, the activities of the authorities, military and civil, in Canada. Especial concern was to be paid to three of New France's most prominent men—Governor Pierre Vaudreuil, Intendant François Bigot, and the colony's richest merchant provider, Joseph Cadet.

In his quarters, Montcalm gladly put aside his complex activities for the moment and relaxed while engaging in one of the activities he most looked forward to—writing to his wife.

*My Dearest Angélique,*

*All is well here and it has been a busy time for me. Don't expect any long letter from me before the first of March; all my business will be done by that time, and I shall begin to breathe again. When there has been a moment of quiet before retiring, I have been reading Charlevoix. I take great pleasure in it; he gives a pleasant account of Quebec. But be comforted; I shall always be glad to come home.*

*Monday night I came from Versailles, and am going back tomorrow evening until Sunday, and will write from there. The King gives me twenty-five thousand francs a year, as he did to M. Dieskau, besides twelve thousand for my equipment, which will cost me above a thousand Crowns more; but I cannot stop for that.*

*My son, with whom I am well pleased, joined me last week. He is as thin and delicate as ever, but grows prodigiously tall. He has come for me to coach him and get him a uniform made, in which he will give thanks for his regiment at the same time that I take leave in my embroidered coat. Yesterday I presented him to all the Royal family.*

*I like the Chevalier de Lévis and I think he likes me. It is good to be soldiering with him again; de Bourlamaque, of course, you already know, and how highly I regard him. I am also well pleased with my first aide-de-camp, Louis de Bougainville. He is a young man, son of a notary, who began life as an advocate in the Parliament of Paris, where his abilities and learning quickly made him conspicuous. However, he resigned the gown for the sword and became, fortunately for me, a captain of dragoons. He is bright and witty and makes things easier for me by correctly anticipating my wants. I prize his varied talents highly.*

*I shall be at Brest on March twenty-first, where I will have a secretary and will write more at length. Everything will be on board on the twenty-sixth. I have business on hand still, my health is good and the passage will be a time of rest. I shall write up to the last moment. I embrace you, my dearest, and my daughters. Love to all the family.*

*Louis*

### [ March 29, 1756—Monday ]

The military might of Canada, Pierre Vaudreuil knew, was in the sturdy French regulars. In battle they would stand with resolution, in their dense ranks, facing withering fire and return volley for volley. They had been trained to fight this way; drilled in the proper procedures of forming rank, firing, then immediately loading again while the rank behind stepped forward to repeat the action.

Yes, for open battle against similarly trained forces, they were the might of Canada; but for bush fighting, for stealth, for ambush, for massacre, they were worse than useless. It was a form of fighting they could not comprehend and were powerless against, just as were the English regulars. And it was for this reason that the Canadians disliked fighting beside the French regulars, whose officers expected them, too, to stand and be shot down. This was not the Canadian's way.

He was a new form of white fighter, known among his own as the *coureur de bois* and among the English as the bush loper. He thought like an Indian, moved like an Indian, fought like an Indian. For a century and a half he had lived among the Indians, not trying to change the Indians to his own ways but rather adapting himself to the Indian way of life. He learned from them, and learned well, combining the best survival and offensive tactics of the two races and becoming, in the process, a deadly adversary in forest warfare. He married Indians, raised half-breed children, scalped as the Indians scalped, tortured his enemies as they did and sometimes even shared with them the devouring of an enemy's flesh. But there always remained an attachment to France and a duty to fight to protect the mother country's interests—provided he could fight his own way.

Among the English there were few counterparts for the bush loper. To be sure, a small number of hardy frontiersmen had evolved along the same lines and managed to survive on the bloody frontiers, but their interests were far more personal than partisan and they were, for the most part, loners who distrusted even their own kind. Only the company of men under Captain Robert Rogers came close to fighting the way the bush lopers did.

Rogers's company was getting a hard core of tough men whose abilities could well be stacked against those of the best *coureurs de bois*. They had to be good or they didn't survive, it was that simple. Rogers longed for the day when he would have three hundred, five hundred, perhaps even a thousand men well trained in wilderness fighting and survival; men who could range anywhere with self-confidence and ability and the reasonable assurance of returning alive and well. Such a force, he knew, was still a long way off for him. In a way, he secretly envied the French governor who had such a storehouse of natural-born bush fighters he could call into service.

It was to just such a group of three hundred of the *coureurs de bois* that Vaudreuil had given special instructions several weeks ago. Word had come to him of the English building new forts at the Great Carrying Place of the Mohawk. The mission of the Canadians was outlined; regardless of the weather, move to those forts at once and do as much damage as possible, in any way they cared to. They were to be led by a French regular officer Captain Claude Léry.

It was precisely the type of assignment the bush lopers admired and they moved out at once. With muskets in hand, tomahawks and knives in their belts, a blanket and a meager quantity of jerky and meal in their back packs, they strapped on ice skates and sped up the rock-hard surface of the St. Lawrence to Fort Présentation at the mouth of the Oswegatchie. Rarely had this journey been made so swiftly. There, at Abbé François Piquet's mission, they recruited half a hundred or more Caughnawagas, Algonkins, Nipissings and a few Abnakis and set off cross-country on snowshoes, heading due south through the heavily snow-blanketed forest.

They crossed the frozen Mohawk several miles above Fort Williams and then, after moving to the west a mile or so, made their camp. Scouts were sent out to reconnoiter toward the forts. And back at the river, where two Mohawks had been hunting and had hidden at the approach of the force, there was furtive movement as the pair slipped from hiding and raced away toward the southeast to warn the only Englishman they could trust—Warraghiyagey.

Long before dawn Léry had his bush lopers ready. His scouts had reported that the snow on the road connecting Fort Williams with Fort Bull was well packed, indicating considerable traffic had been passing lately. The scouts had also slipped quietly eastward and peered from cover at Fort Williams, but it was a well-built place and apparently quite heavily garrisoned. Worse yet, it had cannon.

In no formation whatever, the *coureurs de bois* and Indians slipped silently across the dark snow, hardly making a sound of their own and their ears attuned to any outside sound that might reach them. It was 5:30 A.M. when they reached the road and instantly hid themselves at the sound of horses and wagons approaching.

The twelve soldiers riding the three wagons did little speaking. The fact that they had been rousted from their bunks this early in the morning to cart arms and provisions to Fort Bull had made them sullen. So quietly did the bush lopers move into position that not until the two horses pulling the first wagon jolted to a snorting halt did they see with fearful eyes that a horde of Canadians and Indians were all around them. There was no possibility of resistance, so they threw their weapons down disgustedly and surrendered.

While his scouts continued to watch far along the road in both directions, Léry questioned the prisoners. His command of English was poor, but he learned enough from them to realize that at Fort Bull a great mass of goods had been stockpiled for the planned spring offensive against Fort Niagara. Further, there were only a couple-of-dozen soldiers there, along with a few women and bateaux men. The main problem would be getting themselves inside the stockade before their presence was discovered.

It was not such a problem at that.

With guns at their heads, the twelve men were forced to disrobe, even to their footwear. Then, while the captives shivered as much with fear as with the severe cold, they were led a distance out into the woods and then gripped simultaneously from behind while their heads were struck with tomahawks or their throats slit with the razor-edged knives of the *coureurs de bois*. Even as they kicked their lives away, others of the Canadians were donning their clothing.

Within the hour the same three wagons with twelve men aboard crunched into view of Fort Bull over the hard-packed snow. The effort to surprise the inhabitants, however, was in vain. Unable to restrain themselves, the Indians with that part of Léry's party still hidden in the woods, burst screeching from cover when the wagons were still fifty yards from the gate. Had the drivers whipped their horses into a run toward the fort, the gates would undoubtedly have been held open for them until they could rush in, but the Canadians hesitated too long and the ruse became obvious.

Swiftly the alarm spread among Shirley's provincials inside the fort, but not swiftly enough. Even before a defense could be mounted, the twelve aboard the wagons had leaped forward and taken possession of the portholes and began firing through them at the occupants with devastating results. In moments the whole horde of Indians of Léry's Canadians were around the fort and the fighting was furious.

Léry took advantage of a brief lull in the firing to call to those inside to surrender, but they refused, and so now the Frenchman ordered the gate attacked with axes that had been on the wagons. It was a flimsy portal at best and in minutes had been chopped through and opened. Again Léry called to them to surrender and again they refused. At his signal then, the Canadians swarmed through, screaming *"Vive le Roi!"* In another fifteen minutes it was all over. Except for two men who hid themselves beneath a pile of rubble, none of the English were left alive.

Great piles of supplies were stored in the several buildings within the stockade and, unable to carry much themselves,

426

Léry let the Indians and Canadians take whatever they wanted to carry—including the scalps of all the dead—and then the buildings were set afire. From a safe distance they watched them burn, until the powder magazine was reached and exploded with a devastating roar. Then, fearful that it had been heard at the four-mile distant Fort Williams, Léry ordered the homeward trek begun. He was satisfied that they had disrupted the English plans considerably.

And so they had.

The two dazed soldiers managed to creep safely out of their burning hiding place, their senses almost deadened by the blast, but there was nothing they could do but watch the fires destroy the bodies of the twenty-six soldiers, two women and one bateaux man still inside.

It was a cheap victory for Léry's party—forty-one of the enemy dead,[2] at the cost of four men—two Indians and two Canadians—slightly wounded.

Although William Johnson rapidly rounded up a force of five hundred of the militia and a small number of Mohawks as soon as he got the news of the French party, he found only ruins and bodies at the site of Fort Bull. It was the Mohawks who found something else: messages had been left on trees where the Canadians and Indians had camped. The bark had been stripped away and odd characters had been painted on the bare wood with the moistened powders of vermilion and other colors carried in their pouches. The messages were addressed to the Iroquois and told them that a great multitude of Indian nations from southwest and west, northwest, north and northeast, were gathering at Niagara and would capture Oswego. Furthermore, if the Iroquois dared to interfere, they would cut them all off the face of the earth.

That neighboring tribes should disobey the Iroquois was bad enough, but that they should trespass into Iroquois territory and actually threaten to destroy them was unbelievable. The Mohawks were furious and chopped the warnings to illegibility with their tomahawks, but along with their fury, William Johnson thought he detected a trace of fear.

[ *May 30, 1756—Sunday* ]

Louis Montcalm had mixed emotions regarding this new land in which he found himself. It was a magnificent country with powerful rivers, great sweeping plains and forests stretching beyond the reach of any eye. It was a country where the hand of God could be seen at every step and yet, at the same time, a place of incredible barbarity.

Winter had been reluctant to relinquish its grasp this year and the *Licorne* had been stopped by ice in the St. Lawrence River on the tenth of May while still twenty miles below Quebec. With some difficulty the French commanding general made his way to the city accompanied by Captain Bougainville. There he had dispatched a courier to Governor Vaudreuil to inform him of his arrival and then, after several days, journeyed to Montreal himself, pleased to have learned before he left Quebec that the *Sauvage* and *Sirène,* bearing Lévis and Bourlamaque, had just arrived safely.

He was appalled at the miserable condition of most of the Canadian inhabitants. Their faces were gaunt and their eyes feverish. Prices, he found, were exorbitant; and that the Canadian population was almost starving was only too obvious. At several of the squalid, ill-made homes along the way he saw newly butchered meat hanging which at first he mistook for wild game, until it was made known to him that some of the inhabitants had begun killing their horses for meat.

These conditions, however, were in no measure reflected in the opulent quarters of the governor, where Montcalm was served fine wines, excellent meats and other dishes amidst great luxury.

For his own part, Governor Vaudreuil was not at all pleased to see Montcalm and veiled his feelings only thinly. He had hoped to continue the job he had been doing as commander of the military since the capture of Dieskau, and had even written to France to tell the court that it was both expensive and inexpedient to send another general when he, Vaudreuil, could himself do the job so admirably. But Minister of War D'Argenson had known, as the governor himself had not, that Vaudreuil was not quite the man for this responsibility. He was an accomplished administrator, but he had some grievous flaws: he lacked an inherent force of character and the ability to make wise decisions at critical junctures; he was far more concerned in asserting his authority than he was judicious in applying it; he was a man who, in his own mind, was responsible for every good thing which happened, while swift to shift the blame for all setbacks to others.

D'Argenson had, of course, replied in the negative to Vaudreuil and now Montcalm was here. While for Vaudreuil there was some satisfaction in the knowledge that Montcalm was his subordinate, yet it was galling to know that in Montcalm the government had placed its trust for the conduct of the war. To make sure there was no misinterpretation on this point—either deliberate or unintentional—D'Argenson had even clearly stated that Montcalm would have command not only of the regular French troops, but also of the colony troops and the militia, of which the *coureurs de bois* could be considered a part.

As civilly as he could, which was not saying a great deal, Vaudreuil briefed Montcalm on the situation now prevailing in the matter of war, concluding with the remark that it was evident from reports of the Indians and *coureurs de bois* that the English were massing again to strike at three points—Fort Carillon at the Ticonderoga Narrows, Fort Frontenac at the mouth of Lake Ontario, and Fort Niagara at the head of the same lake.

"In view of this," he said, "I have recently sent out a detachment of eleven hundred men—Canadians and Indians, mostly—under Captain Coulon de Villiers[3] to harass Fort Oswego and, if possible, to sever their communications with Albany again, as Captain Léry and his force did in March. I expect to hear good reports before too long."

Estimates, Vaudreuil added, placed the English strength at about ten thousand men under arms, most of them at Albany, Fort Edward and Fort William Henry, but it was said that more were being enlisted daily.

It was disconcerting news to Montcalm. To face this threat, Canada had to offer a total of six thousand seven hundred seventy French and colony regulars, plus an indeterminate number of militia and Indians. Every male Canadian from ages fifteen to sixty was required to be a member of the militia and was subject to the governor's call. At present, this amounted to perhaps fourteen thousand individuals, but it would be next to impossible to round up those who refused to answer the call, and this might turn out to be a great number. In effective fighting soldiers, Montcalm would probably have no more than eight thousand, if that, but added to this would be many hundreds of Indian allies who, trying as they might be to deal with, were most necessary. Those most loyal to the French were the bands which had assembled at the Catholic missions: the Hurons and Abnakis gathered at the Lorette Mission a dozen miles northwest of Quebec; the Abnakis at St. Francis and Batiscan; the Algonkins and Caughnawagas and Nipissings at Two Mountains on the Ottawa River; the Caughnawagas at Caughnawaga itself; and the Caughnawagas, scattered Senecas, Cayugas and a few Onondagas assembled at the La Présentation Mission on the Oswegatchie. To these were added the Indians of the far west, mainly the Ottawas, Hurons, Potawatomies, Chippewas, Delawares and Shawnees.

As for the Iroquois, Vaudreuil shrugged. "I have about given up on them," he told Montcalm. "We have wooed them for years to gain their allegiance. Some few of them we have, but most we do not. Perhaps the best we can hope of them is that they will maintain their neutrality."

When word of the new commanding general's presence spread, delegations of Indians from the missions and elsewhere came to him in droves with a variety of demands, requests, suggestions, appeals and arguments. Though inwardly he recoiled at the sight of them and at their barbarous actions, Montcalm treated them with respect and thoughtfulness and very quickly won their approval and confidence.

Now, on this bright Sunday, Montcalm took advantage of a respite in his busy schedule to write of these people and of other matters to both his wife and his mother:

*Having come to Montreal from Quebec, I see that I shall have plenty of work. Our campaign will soon begin. Everything is in motion. Don't expect details about our operations; generals never speak of movements until they are over. I can only tell you that the winter has been quiet enough, though the savages have made great havoc in Pennsylvania and Virginia, and carried off, according to their custom, men, women, and children. I beg you will have High Mass said at Montpellier or Vauvert to thank God for our safe arrival and ask for success in the future.*

*I have had more visits than I like from our Red allies. They are vilains messieurs, even when fresh from their toilet, at which they pass their lives. You would not believe it, but the men always carry to war, along with their tomahawk and gun, a mirror to daub their faces with various colors, and arrange feathers on their heads, and rings in their ears and noses. They think it is a great beauty to cut the rim of the ear and stretch it till it reaches the shoulder. Often they wear a laced coat, with no shirt at all. You would take them for so many masqueraders or devils. One needs the patience of an angel to get on with them. Ever since I have been here, I have had nothing but visits, harangues, and deputations of these gentry. The Iroquois ladies, who always take part in their government, came also, and did me the honor to bring me belts of wampum, which will oblige me to go to their village and sing the war-song. They are only a little way off. Yesterday we had eighty-three warriors here, who have gone out to fight. They make war with astounding cruelty, sparing neither men, women, nor children, and take off your scalp very neatly—an operation which generally kills you.*

*Everything is horribly dear in this country; and I shall find it hard to make the two ends meet, with the twenty-five thousand francs the King gives me.*

*The Chevalier de Lévis did not join me till yesterday. His health is excellent. In a few days I shall send him to one camp, and M. de Bourlamaque to another; for we have three of them: one at Carillon, eighty leagues from here, towards the place where M. de Dieskau had his affair last year; another at Frontenac, sixty leagues; and the third at Niagara, a hundred and forty leagues. I don't know when or whither I shall go myself, as that depends on the movement of the enemy. It seems to me that things move slowly in this new world; and I shall have to moderate my activity accordingly. Nothing but the King's service and the wish to make a career for my son could prevent me from thinking too much of my expatriation, my distance from you, and the dull existence here, which would be duller still if I did not manage to keep some little of my natural gaiety.*

*Adieu, my beloved ones. I am with you in spirit, and you with me.*

*Louis*

Montcalm was not the only one writing letters. In his own elegant chambers, Governor Vaudreuil was busily engaged in writing a report in code to Minister of War D'Argenson in Versailles:

*I like M. de Montcalm very much, and will do the impossible to deserve his confidence. I have spoken to him in the same terms as to M. Dieskau; thus: "Trust only the French regulars for an expedition, but use the Canadians and Indians to harass the enemy. Don't expose yourself; send me to carry your orders to points of danger." The colony officers do not like those from France. The Canadians are independent, spiteful, lying, boastful; very good for skirmishing, very brave behind a tree, and very timid when not under cover. I think both sides will stand on the defensive. It does not seem to me that M. de Montcalm means to attack the enemy; and I think he is right. In this country a thousand men could stop three thousand . . .*

[ *June 25, 1756—Friday* ]

The meeting between General William Shirley and General James Abercromby at Albany was not a warm one. Though long prepared for the arrival of his successor, Shirley had not looked forward to the event. Everything, it seemed, had gone wrong: the Niagara campaign in which he had set such high hopes had fizzled into a mortifying failure, amplified by Johnson's victory over Dieskau at Lake George; he had lost two fine sons; he had lost his military command; he had lost his governorship of Massachusetts; and now, with the arrival of Abercromby, he would probably soon be returning to England in disgrace, never to see the Colonies again.

It was to his credit, though, that even with replacement imminent, Shirley had continued with his war planning and troop gathering as if he were going to continue as commanding general. Now that the war had been officially declared—by England on May 18 and France on June 9—there was more support from the Colonies and he couldn't help but feel that if such support had been given him earlier, he would not be in the position he found himself occupying.

Shirley had expected Colonel Daniel Webb to arrive first to take over his command and, though Webb had reached New York on June 7, he had waited there for Abercromby and then the pair had come up the Hudson together. And so, as thoroughly as he could, Shirley filled the new general in on what had been done, what operations were under way and what yet remained to do.

Just above Albany, at a place called Half Moon—named after the exploration ship of Henry Hudson, which had anchored here—just over five thousand men were already gathered. They were provincials and, for the most part, just as untrained as William Johnson's men had been. But they were being drilled daily, Shirley hastened to add, and were shaping up well.

The loss of Fort Bull had been a severe, unexpected blow, setting back the Niagara campaign for weeks, perhaps even months. He had rebuilt the installation immediately and now the route to Oswego was being carefully guarded, especially in the vicinity of the Great Carrying Place. A regular patrol system, for example, had been set up between Fort Williams and Fort Bull, so that neither place could be taken by surprise again and even now substantial stores of provisions, ammunition and weapons were either already there or on their way.

"Forty companies of fifty boatmen each," he continued, irked at the superior way Abercromby sat there, not saying a word, "were formed here and then placed under Colonel John Bradstreet—a good man, incidentally—to escort a large shipment of provisions, medicines and ammunition to Fort Oswego. They arrived safely and are there now, and I expect they will soon be returning."

Shirley paused, expecting some comment from Abercromby or Webb, but there was none. Determined not to give either officer the satisfaction of seeing his irritation, he continued: "You've probably heard of the company of rangers I've been forming under Captain Robert Rogers. They've been doing an exceptional job—spying up at Crown Point and Ticonderoga, harassing French supply shipments, attacking small French and Indian patrols and the like. They've pulled off some rather epic feats and are proving extremely valuable to us. I have them headquartered now at Fort William Henry on Lake George, but their patrols take in Fort Edward, too, along with the Wood Creek portage route up to South Bay. Just yesterday five of the whaleboats they requested passed through here on the way up to Fort William Henry. They'll be able to handle them better and with more men per boat than with the bateaux. I can't recommend Captain Rogers highly enough to you. He is training his men to fight the Indians and the Canadians on their own terms and they've done very well."

Colonel Webb cleared his throat, glanced at General Abercromby and, at his superior's nod, interjected a comment.

"Speaking of Indians," he said, "how do we stand now where they're concerned? I've heard so many conflicting reports I don't know whether the Six Nations are with us or against us."

Shirley shrugged. "Hard to say. More and more they seem to be leaning toward the French. If they do make up their minds to go pro-French, we're in trouble, believe me. Sir William wrote me a few weeks ago that he was just then leaving for Onondaga to speak at a grand council of all the chiefs. He said he was determined to get a strong commitment from them, not only to back us, but also to get them to make the western Indians stop the border attacks. It's a waste of time to my way of thinking. We ought to crush them along with the French and be done with it. Franklin has the clearest thinking on it. He says the only way to deal with Indians is to hit them before they can hit you.

"As for the French forces," he continued, taking up where he left off to reply to Webb, "we've had some reports—mainly from Rogers's men—that there is some French activity up at the northern part of Lake Champlain and it may be that a force is moving down to either Crown Point or Ticonderoga, possibly both. In my opinion, if this is true it would seem that now would be the opportune time to push the Niagara campaign as rapidly as possible."

Abercromby did not comment on the recommendation. He pursed his lips for a moment and then, as if suddenly realizing General Shirley had finished, said, "That's all?"

"That's all," Shirley replied wearily, "except for minor details."

"All right," Abercromby said, nodding, "we'll go over the fine points with you in the next few days. As of now, however, consider yourself relieved of your command here. As soon as our talks are completed, you will please go to New York at once and wait there for the arrival of the Earl of Loudoun, and you will then lay before him the entire state of affairs."

## [July 3, 1756—Saturday]

Of all the English posts in America, probably none was so thoroughly detested by those who had to be stationed there as Fort Oswego.

The place had three marks against it from the very beginning. It was, first of all, a pesthole in which garrisons continually suffered from debilitating fevers and a persistent dysentery which had already killed dozens of men, including the son of General Shirley. It was, secondly, the most isolated outpost of the English Colonies, with miserable communications and a supply line so faulty that more often than not supplies failed to come at all and the garrison was left to suffer or survive on its own. Finally, it was so poorly built that it was practically indefensible—and this despite the adjacent Fort Ontario which was built earlier this year, and another being lackadaisically constructed right now a quarter mile away which was actually more of a cattle pen than a defensive works. In no post of America, whether French or English, was morale any lower than here.

Fort Oswego stood on the west bank of the mouth of the

Onondaga River, with a view of both the river and Lake Ontario. It was built partially of logs, but mostly of large stones set in clay—but with more clay than stones. Long ago artillery practice had been abandoned, not only because of a shortage of powder and ball, but because every time the cannon fired, chunks of the walls broke away from the vibration. To its west and south, this fragile fort was protected by an earthwork on which cannon were mounted and which provided a sort of shelter for the troops encamped outside the fort. The side of the fort facing the river was entirely unprotected.

This lack of defense was justified now, at least, by the fact that five hundred yards away, on the east side of the river, stood the newer Fort Ontario. Though poorly built in its own right, it was by far the most defensible of the three forts here and was designed to protect the exposed east face of Fort Oswego. Fort Ontario was built of tree trunks cut flat on two sides and then stood up on end to be fitted together closely and embedded in the earth. The wall thus formed was impressive to look at, being in the shape of a five-pointed star. Against muskets or swivels it was a good defense, but a twelve-pounder cannon could smash it with ease.

A quarter mile south of Fort Oswego—which was also sometimes called by the men Old Oswego and Fort Pepperell—was a low hill upon which was perched the unfinished stockade which, officially, had already been named Fort George, but which most of the men were calling either New Oswego or Fort Rascal, simply because it was so worthless. By some blunder, its timber walls had been erected without benefit of loopholes or ramparts to fire from. Should attack ever come, the gates would have to be opened in order for the defenders to see anything at which to shoot.

The present commander of these three fortifications was Colonel Hugh Mercer, and he was never so happy to see anyone as he was on the day when Colonel John Bradstreet's fleet of three hundred bateaux loaded with men and bounteous supplies hove into view up the river. Even at risk of crumbling the wall of the fort, the cannon was fired in a booming greeting and from every raw throat there came a cheer.

Bradstreet was appalled by the conditions at the fort. Since General Shirley had left it last autumn well over half of the garrison had died of disease or hunger or a combination of the two. There was nowhere near enough space for all the garrison to be housed under the fort roof, so the greater number had been forced to spend the winter huddled in the barrackslike huts, without cots and without even floors to stand on.

In January there had come an alarm that the installation was soon to be attacked by Indians. So weak was the garrison at that point that the strongest guard force they could mount was a subaltern and sixteen to eighteen men. Half of these had been so debilitated that they were forced to support themselves with a stick in one hand while the other held a rifle. With alarming frequency the sentries on guard simply collapsed at their posts and lay there until their relief came and helped them to their feet again so they could go somewhere else to collapse. Fortunately, the rumored attack never materialized.

Bradstreet, Mercer and the fort's engineer, Captain Mackellar, held council at once. Mackellar told Bradstreet what that officer's eyes had already shown him: that their works here were indefensible and their position therefore untenable. And Mercer, with undoubtedly one of the greatest understatements ever uttered, said that there was some degree of general discontent among the garrison.

Colonel Bradstreet determined to waste no time here but, rather, to move swiftly back to Albany to report to Shirley these deplorable conditions. This morning his boatmen were ordered to man their oars and the return journey to Albany in the empty boats was begun. They pushed their way upriver in three divisions, with Bradstreet leading the first, comprised of a hundred boats and three hundred men.

By three o'clock this afternoon they had traveled some nine miles from the fort when abruptly there was a fusilade of musketry from the flanking trees on the eastern bank of the river. A great many of the boatmen were killed and even more of them wounded, and a mad splashing of oars began among them to reach the west bank. The firing petered out and Bradstreet, looking about anxiously, saw a movement upstream and detected the attackers—part of Coulon de Villiers's Canadians and Indians—attempting to cross the water unseen to the undercover of a little brushy island.

The English officer got there first, along with six or eight of his men, including a steady, twenty-three-year-old captain named Philip Schuyler. This small party took possession of the island and poured a steady fire at the attackers until another eight or ten of Bradstreet's men joined them. Villiers's men fell back under the attack, but in moments they rushed into the water again to reach their goal. Again they were beaten back by the hot firing from the island. There was a brief pause and then a third attempt was made and similarly repulsed.

Villiers called to his men now and they disappeared into the undergrowth. A few minutes went by and then young Schuyler grabbed his colonel's arm and pointed upstream. Several Canadian bush lopers had briefly shown themselves and disappeared again, but it was obvious they were heading for a fording place not far upstream.

Rallying the five sixths of his first division still in fighting shape, Bradstreet was about to lead them up the west bank to meet Villiers's men when the regimental surgeon, Dr. James Kirkland, rushed up to say that the second division of boats had arrived and the men had all landed safely. Bradstreet sent him back with orders for them to remain where they were and defend the lower crossing.

The brief delay had not been to his advantage. By the time he and his men reached the upper ford, Villiers's party had crossed and were in a pine swamp not far from the river. The firing between them rose and fell in intensity for about an hour without much effect until at last Bradstreet ordered a charge. Villiers's men had not expected it and abruptly broke and fled before it to the river and began to cross. Most of them made it, but a fair number were shot and either sank or floated away with the current.[4]

No sooner were they gone than the rest of Villiers's force came charging down the west bank, having crossed at another fording place still higher upstream and hoping to catch the enemy in a surprise crossfire. But seeing that their comrades had been forced back across the stream, they too began surging across through the water and reached the other side without loss. In minutes the whole Canadian and Indian force, except for two bush lopers who had been taken prisoner, had vanished.

Half an hour passed before the grenadiers of Shirley's regiment reached Bradstreet and much later came another two hundred men from Fort Oswego as reinforcements. In the battle, Bradstreet had lost sixty or seventy men, including some who were captured, but the danger was past now and the enemy gone. And now Bradstreet had an even greater reason for reaching Albany as swiftly as possible: under questioning, the two prisoners had declared that the plans of the French were now to attack and destroy Fort Oswego rather than to wait for Niagara or Frontenac to be attacked from it. And the French force would be coming soon.

It was a grim bit of intelligence to be passing on.

### [ July 11, 1756—Sunday ]

At twenty-seven, Louis Antoine de Bougainville was a fine soldier and a fine figure of a man. He was a good-looking individual of average height, somewhat husky, with wide-set eyes and curly, light-brown hair. Devoted at all times to the King of France and to his immediate commander, he was unusually intelligent and an ideal aide-de-camp for the Marquis de Montcalm.

Even though he was not of noble birth, as the son of Pierre Yves de Bougainville, a wealthy Paris lawyer, he was certainly to be counted in the uppermost levels of the bourgeoisie and of excellent social standing. His father had hoped to see Louis follow in his footsteps but, while the young man studied law and did well in it, he never practiced it. He preferred the study of higher mathematics and looked forward to a career in military service.

More than anything else, he had a sharp wit and an extremely pleasant personality and, after his formal training, he convinced his reluctant father to allow him to enter the militia. Only two years ago he was an officer with the militia at Picardy, and had already had published his first book—a volume on integral calculus. It brought him some degree of attention and he was given the opportunity to serve for several months as secretary to the French ambassador in London. Almost at once he became extremely popular there, made many friends and perfected his speaking of English.

Early last year, with his second book on calculus completed and in the hands of his publisher, he became a member of the regular French army as a lieutenant of dragoons, still with frequent London contact. And only this year, just before being promoted to captain and becoming aide-de-camp to General Montcalm, he had been elected a member of the British Royal Society—a signal honor for one so young and an extraordinary occurrence, since he was a Frenchman and French-English relations were badly degenerated, though war had not then been officially declared.

Excited at the prospect of seeing America from a most advantageous position, Bougainville determined to keep a journal of all that occurred. Stuffing his baggage as much with writing materials as with anything else, he had embarked on the project with as much flair as he attacked all things which interested him. Depending on what happened in America, he felt that one day he might publish this journal and gain even more renown for it than he had already received for his books on calculus.

Already, in only the short time he had been keeping it, the journal had become sizable and he had no doubt that by the time this campaign was over he would have sufficient material for quite a comprehensive volume. Little escaped his attention and he wrote with a straightforwardness uncommon to the time and quite indicative of his character. In yesterday's entry, for example, in the quiet of his own chambers in Montreal, he had written:

*July 10*

*A Canadian officer who arrived here with ten English, as much prisoners as deserters, reports news of successful action carried out by M. Coulon de Villiers on the Oswego River. With four hundred men he attacked a convoy of three or four hundred bateaux, each with two men, and three companies of soldiers. The English companies here are of one hundred men. Some have been reduced to sixty-two. They were returning from Oswego, where they had carried food and munitions, and had gone up again after more provisions. M. de Villiers put them to flight and knocked off a great number, and would have knocked off considerably more were it not for the poor quality of the tomahawks furnished by the King's Store, took twenty-four scalps and killed or wounded in their flight, according to his estimate, about three hundred men. We lost in this affair a colony officer, six Canadians and colony soldiers and one Indian.*

*The victory would have been greater except for the eagerness of the Indians, who struck too soon, and I would add, also that of the chief, for I have seen him in a similar situation.*

*As for the rest of it, his detachment, according to what he wrote to M. de Vaudreuil, is not capable of undertaking anything at present, the Indians have all left him, the Canadians and soldiers are almost all ill, a sickness caused by the terrible quality of their rations, just as bad as at Fort Carillon and in all the posts. Nevertheless, he is maintaining his camp of observation.*

*M. de Vaudreuil is sending him a reinforcement of men and supplies. M. St. Luc de la Corne left Tuesday with a troop of Indians to rejoin him. The quantity of munitions sent several days ago to Lake Ontario, the detachment of*

*Canadians which left for the same place, the refusal of M. de Vaudreuil for me to rejoin M. de Montcalm even though M. Doreil arrived at this city today and consequently my duties here cease, the report received by M. de Montcalm that the English no longer appear to be in the neighborhood of Fort Carillon; all these reasons make me believe that M. de Montcalm will make an attempt on Oswego. This evening a messenger carries him an order to return to Montreal.*

*Besides, according to the reports of prisoners and deserters, this undertaking will be easy to accomplish. The newer fort, on this side of the Oswego River, is only a stockaded fort with eight guns of very small caliber; there are only 250 men in the garrison. This fort once taken, the batteries that would be put into position there would breach the big fort on the other side of the Oswego, which is a simple loopholed rampart. Its strongest point is a sort of earthen hornwork which envelops all the right flank and rear of the fort. There are scarcely six or seven hundred men in the garrison, badly fed, low in spirit, discouraged, ready to desert at the first chance. Two engineers who have been there the last two months have built no new works at the place. That is what they say of the condition of the fort, the importance of which to the English makes me doubt that it may not be in a better state of defense.*

*My guess as to the return of M. de Montcalm from Fort Carillon in the near future and his destination was verified this evening by the departure of a courier carrying orders for him to return to Montreal.*

*All these days here there have been Indian councils.*

*Today I wrote M. de Montcalm and sent him a package of letters.*

Nothing significant had happened this morning for Bougainville to write about, but about noon there was a flurry of excitement when the Canadian officer, Captain Jacques Marin, arrived with forty Indians of a tribe Bougainville had not seen before. They were called Menominees and they were from west of Lake Michigan, near the French post of La Baye where, until only recently, Marin had been commander. Bougainville had heard it said that to be stationed at Fort La Baye, at the foot of Green Bay, was a duty few French soldiers liked. Dead fish so frequently washed up on the shore and permeated the air with the stench of their rotting, that Green Bay had become more familiarly known as Stinking Bay.

With considerable interest, Bougainville had viewed the day's activities and now he wrote about them in his journal:

*July 11*
*At noon there arrived at Montreal M. Marin, a colony officer who spent the winter at the post at Stinking Bay, and who led five hundred Indians to Presque Isle, the rendezvous assigned for all the Indians from the far West.. All have decamped, having heard it said that there was smallpox at all our forts. The Indians fear nothing so much as this disease; in fact it treats them cruelly when they are attacked by it, either because of lack of proper care, or because of a susceptibility in their blood.*

*Only the Indians of the Menominee Tribe, or the Wild Rice People, to the number of about forty, have, according to their expression, closed their eyes and risked death to come with M. Marin, first to join M. de Villiers, with whom they were in the attack on the English bateaux, and afterwards to go downriver to Montreal. Wild rice are a kind of grain resembling oats, and which are a very healthful form of nourishment. This plant forms the totem of the nation.*

*The Menominees are always strongly attached to the French. They came in five great birch-bark canoes with six scalps and several prisoners. Arrived opposite to Montreal, the canoes were placed in several lines, they lay to for some time, the Indians saluted with a discharge of guns and loud cries, to which three cannon shot replied. Afterwards they came ashore and went to the Château in double file, the prisoners in the middle carrying wands decorated with feathers. These prisoners were not maltreated, as is customary upon entering into cities and villages. Entered into M. de Vaudreuil's presence, the prisoners sat down on the ground in a circle, and the Indian chief, with action and force that surprised me, made a short enough speech, the gist of which was that the Menominee people were different from the other tribes which held back part of their captures, and that they always brought back to their father all the meat they had taken. Then they danced around the captives to the sound of a sort of tambourine placed in the middle. Extraordinary spectacle, more suited to terrify than to please; curious, however, to the eye of a philosopher who seeks to study man in conditions nearest to nature.*

*These men were naked, save for a piece of cloth in front and behind, the face and body painted, feathers on their heads, symbol and signal of war, tomahawk and spear in*

441

*their hand. In general, these are brawny men, large and of good appearance; almost all are very fat. One could not have better hearing than those people. All the movements of their body mark the cadence with great exactness. This dance is the pyrrhic of the Greeks.*

*The dance ended, they were given meat and wine. The prisoners were sent off to jail with a detachment to prevent the Algonquins and the Iroquois of the Sault St. Louis [Caughnawaga] who were at Montreal from knocking them on the head, these Indians being in mourning for the men they had lost.*

### [ July 15, 1756—Thursday ]

Governor Vaudreuil had cautioned Montcalm, shortly after his arrival, not to place too much credence in the reports of the Iroquois.

"They are in an odd position," Vaudreuil had said, "and they take advantage of it. They know that we will not offend them, for fear that they will join the English, and that the English will not offend them for fear that they will join us. They have access to us both and bring information to both sides principally for the goods in which they are paid for the information. When they don't have any worthwhile news, they are not above inventing some, just to get the payment."

Nevertheless, Montcalm had been disturbed by the increasing reports the Iroquois brought of the quickening build-up of English forces at Albany, Fort Edward and Fort William Henry. To these reports were added those of the *coureurs de bois* who were more familiar with military preparations of the white man and insisted that strong forces would undoubtedly soon be launched against Fort Carillon and perhaps even Fort St. Frederic.

These French outposts were only in fair shape, despite the fact that for months improvements had been going on under the French engineers, Captain Lotbinère at Carillon, Captain Pouchot at Niagara, and Captain Descombles at Fort St. Frederic. It was time, however, for Montcalm and his army to take to the front and they had lost no time doing so.

With two battalions already at Fort Carillon overlooking the mouth of the Ticonderoga Narrows, Montcalm had quickly dispatched to the same post a reinforcement of colony regulars and followed them up with a third battalion, the Royal Roussilon. Even as Montcalm himself and General

Lévis had moved to join them, the militia were called up by Vaudreuil and ordered to hasten after them with all speed.

It had been on June 26 that the new commander and his second had reached Ticonderoga. Though Fort Carillon was nearing completion now, it was by no means the best fort the two generals had ever seen. It perched high atop the promontory overlooking the narrows of Lake Champlain to the east and the Ticonderoga Narrows to the south. It was a square construction with four bastions, ramparts consisting of two log walls built ten feet apart and the space in between them filled with earth and gravel, a ditch running around it and incompleted barracks made of clay and stone.

It was beautiful here at this time of year, but the gangs of workers were given little time to appreciate it and made to labor fearfully at their jobs. Time after time during the construction English raiders under Captain Robert Rogers had peered at them from cover and, where it could be done with relative safety, ambushed patrols on the lakeshore or in the woods. But in each worker's mind was the knowledge that the English had been taking much more than they were dishing out. The Indians camped nearby—mostly Caughnawagas, along with a few Abnakis—came and went with great regularity and it was a rare day when they did not return from their forays toward Fort Edward or Fort William Henry without fresh scalps.

Generals Montcalm and Lévis inspected the works of Fort Carillon with professional thoroughness. The commander in chief had decided to make this his command post, since it was here that the English army was apt to strike their first real blow. But today had come from Montreal a characteristically exaggerated express from Vaudreuil:

*We spoke together, before you left, of my long-nurtured plan to destroy Oswego. I have just received word that the detachment sent out by me under Captain de Villiers has engaged a large supply train near that fort and have destroyed it, with over five hundred of the enemy dead. Prisoners taken in the engagement confess under questioning that the fort is desperately weak, its garrison almost all sick. They are virtually cut off. It is my wish, therefore, that you return at once to Montreal and from here to Fort Frontenac, to lead an attack against that fort. Such attack would be almost certain to draw off some of the troops being moved into position to come against Fort Carillon and, if promptly and secretly executed, might result in the actual taking of Oswego*

443

*and the ships they have built there, which are a menace to
our own vessels at Fort Frontenac.*

Montcalm prepared to leave at once and sent a messenger
to find General Lévis, who had been gone for several days
exploring the surrounding area on foot to familiarize himself
with the terrain, but who was reported to be nearing the fort
again on his return. While he waited, Montcalm took the
opportunity to write a letter to Minister of War D'Argenson
in France, telling him that he was placing Fort Carillon
under the command of Lévis and would be leaving for
Montreal, Fort Frontenac and, hopefully, Oswego, just as
soon as Lévis came in from his inspection. He told D'Argenson that he was daily more pleased with General Lévis
and that the man's hike through these dangerous woods was
indicative of his enterprise. He added:

*I do not think that many high officers in Europe would
have occasion to take such tramps as this. I cannot speak too
well of him. Without being a man of brilliant parts, he has
good experience, good sense, and a quick eye; and, though I
had served with him before, I should never have thought that
he had such promptness and efficiency. He has turned his
campaigns to good account.*

Lévis returned while he was still writing and so Montcalm
broke off abruptly and gave his second-in-command the
necessary orders and then turned command of the fort over
to him. As he was putting his own letter away to return it to
Montreal for posting when he was finished with it, Lévis
presented him with a sealed letter of his own to D'Argenson
and asked that it be posted as well. He had written it shortly
before leaving the post three days ago. Just as Montcalm was
pleased with Lévis, so Lévis was pleased with him and,
unknown to one another, they had written markedly similar
letters to the minister of war. The one from Lévis said, in
part:

*I do not know if the Marquis de Montcalm is pleased with
me, but I am sure that I am very much so with him, and
shall always be charmed to serve under his orders. It is not
for me, Monseigneur, to speak to you of his merit and his
talents. You know him better than anybody else; but I have
the honor of assuring you that he has pleased everybody in*

*this colony, and manages affairs with the Indians extremely well . . .*

Montcalm accepted the letter with hardly a glance, placed it safely with his own and within another five minutes was on his way back to Montreal.

### [ July 16, 1756—Friday ]

Louis Bougainville was delighted to learn from one of the Canadian officers at about three o'clock today that the Marquis de Montcalm would undoubtedly soon arrive in Montreal. The general's aide did not care for the waiting here and wanted action. His comment in his journal this evening was rather brief:

*July 16*

*M. Mercier, the Canadian artillery commander, arrived this afternoon . . . having left Carillon yesterday morning. He reported that M. de Montcalm slept today at St. Frederic, so he should be expected on Sunday evening or Monday. No news that the English are making any move in this area. They sent a small detachment in pursuit of a party which stopped two bateaux on Otter Creek.[5]*

*It appears certain that General Johnson has gone to the Six Nations[6] to try to get them to raise the hatchet against us and to come to war with him. The General has been adopted by these tribes, speaks their language, has their manners and style, is painted in war paint like them. He even has a cabin in their villages. It is to be feared that part of the warriors will follow him.*

### [ July 17, 1756—Saturday ]

William Johnson looked terrible.

His face was drawn and etched with lines that had only recently begun to appear. His eyes were feverishly bright and seemed to have sunk deep into their sockets. There were bags under them and the lids were discolored a sickly grayish-blue. He looked as if he had lost a dozen pounds or more. In truth, the past forty-four days had sapped him as nothing had ever sapped him before.

On June 3, with Wascaugh at his side and upwards of a hundred Mohawks in single file behind them, William had set out for Onondaga for what he felt was apt to be the most important Iroquois council he had ever attended or addressed.

Since the woods were so full of enemies these days, with them as escort was a company of grenadiers and fourteen heavily laden packhorses. The job of these soldiers was not only to protect the procession, but also to act as drovers for the huge herd of beef cattle William was bringing along to provide a great feast for the delegates to the council and the inhabitants of Onondaga. The packhorses were loaded with gifts which William would distribute as a partial redress of wrongs done against the League by the English.

It had been no easy matter for William to get the chiefs to give in to his demands that he be allowed to address them in full formal council. Though several large councils had been held since the death of Tiyanoga, he had been invited to none of them and there had been considerable opposition to having this council at his behest.

Feeling that the Iroquois were rapidly slipping out of the English grasp, William had resorted to desperate measures, appealing directly to the Crown with an outline of what needed to be done without delay. For once the Crown had followed through quickly, sending Royal Orders to New York's new governor, Sir Charles Hardy, to the effect that immediate redress must be made for Iroquois grievances, that no further land surveys were to be made except in the presence of the Indians claiming a right to that land, and that the more distant Indian hunting grounds were to be kept entirely free of white settlement.

William had been delighted. This was powerful ammunition with which to face the Iroquois, and runners were sent to Onondaga requesting that the council be called and stressing the extreme importance of it to the entire League. And, after some vacillation, the request was finally honored, but with a stipulation: the emissaries who had been sent at Warraghiyagey's request to the Delawares and Shawnees had returned with word that those tribes would indeed change to the English side, but only if Warraghiyagey himself would meet them at the Onondaga council and convince them beyond doubt of the English desire to live in harmony and friendship.

William had agreed with alacrity and the messengers rushed back with his word of it to the seat of the Iroquois government. And even as William and the Mohawk delegation had departed from Fort Johnson for the long journey to

Onondaga, runners were sent from there to fetch the Shawnee and Delaware delegates.

Despite the fact that the majority of William's party were on foot, they were slowed even more by the cattle. The grenadiers were not experienced drovers and the animals were balky in the extreme, almost as if they sensed what was in store for them at their destination. Not until the tenth day after leaving Fort Johnson had they come—on June 13— within about two miles of Onondaga, and the principal Iroquois village spread out like a small city before them. The longhouses dominated in the center, a half dozen or more of them, with the largest being the council house, but around them were scores upon scores of smaller bark quonsets, wegiwas, tepees and other temporary shelters which had been hastily erected. Perhaps three thousand Indians were on hand and the village was a beehive of activity.

It was at this point, just after coming in sight of the place, that they were met by a party from the village. There were six men, three women and two boys in the party and all of them were entirely naked and their bodies and faces were smudged to a dirty gray with ashes and clay. With mournful expressions, they told Warraghiyagey and Wascaugh that the principal chief of the Onondagas, Red Head, had died.

Though no flicker of it showed in his expression, William felt a flood of relief wash through him. Red Head had been one of the greatest powers in the entire Iroquois League and it was he, more than any other chief of the Six Nations, who most vocally opposed Warraghiyagey, and whom William had long suspected of being in active collaboration with the French. Now his place would undoubtedly be taken by the second chief of the tribe, Rozinoghyata, with whom William had always shared cordial relations.

Nevertheless, as Warraghiyagey he set his own features in doleful lines, removed every stitch of his clothing—as Wascaugh and the other Mohawks behind were already doing— and rubbed himself thoroughly with handsful of dirt scooped up from beside the trail. Then, joining the delegation in funeral song, they continued their march to a point about a mile from the edge of the village. Here, as the delegation went on into town, William went to the grenadiers and ordered them to do exactly as he said: to keep themselves in the background, to speak softly, to in no way impose themselves upon anyone in this village, to keep to themselves entirely and not mingle with the natives, and under no circumstances to give way to laughter at anything heard or seen. Then, as Warraghiyagey, he returned to the Mohawks, whom Wascaugh had formed into a sitting semicircle across the road, and sat down beside the chief in the center of it. A profound and respectful silence came over them all.

As always when he assumed the role of an Indian, engaging in the ancient customs was undertaken with conscious effort but, as always, a change came over him. The conscious effort was soon gone and with it, his identity as William Johnson. He became now, in fact, an Indian of the Iroquois League, deeply and sincerely mourning the loss of a great and respected chief, feeling the selfsame anguish rise in him that was evident in his Mohawk companions.

Within fifteen minutes another delegation came from the village to them. It was Chief Rozinoghyata and two subchiefs of the Onondaga, Onokio and Araghi. Warraghiyagey stepped forward to meet them, interlocking both his hands with theirs in turn, but saying nothing. The three chiefs sat down and, as they did so, Warraghiyagey began a curious, jerky, shuffling movement in the midst of the crescent of Mohawk warriors.

He continued this for five minutes in silence, kicking up little puffs of dust, occasionally slapping his breast or thigh, often bending far over at the waist and rotating his head. At length he stopped, his body sweating and turning the dirt on his skin to a film of mud. Then he raised both arms high and broke into the song of condolence, turning slowly in a full circle as he sang it. It was a weird, guttural song, rising and falling in cadenced waves, extolling the laws, customs and names of himself, Wascaugh, and the subchiefs who had come here with them, proclaiming their great sorrow which perched like a buzzard in their hearts and enfolded them with mourning. He sang of the prowess and greatness that had been Red Head's and the grief which now shrouded the Iroquois confederation of tribes, and prayed that his departed brother might be blessed with good hunting and great happiness in his new abode with the Great Spirit.

When he was finished, Wascaugh performed similarly. Then, saying in his own way almost the same things Warraghiyagey had said, both he and Warraghiyagey once more clasped interlocked hands with the three Onondaga chiefs and the march to the village was resumed.

Now, from all the Mohawks behind, came a grieving, mournful death chant which did not cease until they had all assembled before the longhouse which had been Chief Red Head's and which was now decorated with an interlacing of bright green, viny foliage and numerous blossoms, all kept from rapidly wilting by the painstaking placing of a little ball of wet earth formed over the cut of the stem. Here, beneath a similarly decorated arbor, they seated themselves and silence reigned again as Rozinoghyata entered the dwelling. In a few minutes he came out again, took Warraghiyagey and Wascaugh by their hands and, himself walking backward as they walked forward, pulled them inside.

Here Red Head was stretched out on a pallet, his dead face painted in colorful symmetrical circles on the cheeks. He was naked and his body considerably tattooed. Around him were a number of unclad squaws, all of them weeping and softly wailing, their skin discolored with ashes.

Chief Rozinoghyata released the hands of Wascaugh and Warraghiyagey and then placed a hand to the forehead of each, moved it down across the face, briefly touched their throats and finally patted their chests, saying as he did so, "My Brothers, I now wipe away your tears, clean your throats and open your hearts, according to our customs."

They left the chamber together, the squaws still rocking and wailing behind them. At a gesture from Wascaugh, each of the Mohawks waiting outside similarly wiped their own eyes, touched their own throats and patted their own breasts. Immediately they got to their feet, tied their breechcloths around them and moved away singly or in small groups through the village, mingling with the others there.

William, too, was putting his clothing back on. Chief Red Head, he knew, would lie in state here in the longhouse until he started to putrify. Then, without ceremony, he would be put into a hole and covered up. The actual ceremonial funeral might not be held for ten or twelve years, at which time he—and all the others of the village who had died in this interval—would be disinterred and their remains brought to the longhouse. The bones of the skeletons would be scrubbed clean and any of those which had been more recently buried and still had the flesh covering them, would have this flesh scraped away and discarded until the bones were clean. Then, with the whole nation present, the remains—sometimes representing scores of people—would be solemnly placed in a specially prepared pit. Amongst them would be placed gold rings, silver bracelets, beads, belts of wampum, kettles, bows, arrows, tomahawks, knives, beaver skins and other items. Then the hole would be covered over. Until this time, according to tribal belief, regardless of how long ago the deaths had occurred, the spirits of these dead had been roaming in an unseen world, living off bark and rotted wood by night and crouching by day in the position of the sick. But now, with the covering of the bones in ceremony, the spirits would be released and in this hour their happy immortality was begun.

Now, with the condolence ceremonies completed for Red Head, William Johnson turned his attention to the council which was beginning to form. Although a great many Indians were on hand, he was disappointed to see that the entire clan of the Chenussio Senecas from the Genesee River were absent and that a number of the other Seneca, Cayuga and Oneida villages were not represented. Worse yet, the Delawares and Shawnees who were supposed to have been on hand were not here. Yet, the council opened and for nineteen grueling days William Johnson—as Warraghiyagey—argued for support of the English. One point was taken at a time and, when he had finished speaking on this point, the council was recessed while its chiefs discussed the measure in private, decided what to do and then reconvened to give their answer. It was not any easy matter to win them over. Never before had William witnessed among them such strong antagonism against the English in general and himself in particular. Chief Stokka of the Oneidas was especially hostile to him:

"Beware, Brothers," he said, pointing at William, "of the words spoken by he who sits there. He comes with food and gifts to the Indians. And he speaks very fair to them. And he makes many fine promises to them. And he gives many handsome presents to them. But watch out! At his parting he will drink to their healths and he will invite them to drink, but after they have swallowed it, it will throw them all into a sleep from which they will never awaken!"

On and on the speeches went; accusations and counteraccusations, pleas and counterpleas. And the only respite for Johnson—if respite it could be termed—was at night when always there was a new female awaiting him. Each of them shared common traits: a warmth which could swiftly turn to demanding heat, a persuasiveness which never failed to sexually arouse him despite any weariness, and a strong yearning for the seeds he planted in them to take root and grow, to swell their bellies and engorge their breasts and allow them to bring forth to the Iroquois another infant who might share the savage strength of his maternal heritage and the breadth of mind and courage of him who deposited the seed.

The interludes with these women were unfailingly a delight to William Johnson. They broke the strain of long days spent in council and turned the mind away from problems, leaving him drained and relaxed and more able to face the next day's council with renewed vigor.

As far as he could tell, he was little by little dispelling the French influence; convincing these Indians that their future lay with the English, that all the Iroquois should join in a vigorous attack against the French, that permission should be granted to the English for the right to build better and more closely spaced forts on the supply route to Fort Oswego.

And at last the council agreed in essence: that if the English would support them, they would turn their backs on the French and perhaps, if it appeared that the English needed help, even give them active support in battles against the French—but not against the Indians who might still be supporting the French; that the English might further fortify the Oswego supply route, but only with the complete and not-to-be-forgotten understanding that the moment the English-French war was ended, these structures would be demolished or put into the hands of the Six Nations.

It was something of a victory for William Johnson; perhaps not quite as strong an agreement as could have been desired, but far more than he had anticipated winning. He presented to each of the chiefs in attendance a large bronze medallion upon which was stamped the likeness of the English King. And now, with the council fire extinguished, the cattle were butchered and cleaned and spitted for roasting, the kegs of rum were opened and a sense of festivity filled the air. A great many of the Iroquois were, in fact, well into their cups when there came the halloo call from the southwest trail and the greatly tardy Delaware and Shawnee delegation hove into view. It had been a long journey from the forests between the Susquehanna and Fort Duquesne and they wished to get to the matter of counciling quickly.

That was before they saw the rum. William, knowing if they once got into it the counciling could be wrecked, immediately invited them to accompany him back to Fort Johnson where he would ignite his own council fire, where they could speak at length and at peace and where, when counciling was finished, he would present them with gifts and rum to equal what was here.

The Indians agreed, though reluctantly. Wascaugh said that he and a number of his Mohawks would come along and partake of their share at Mount Johnson, which would be closer to home for them than here. In a short time, the entire procession was on the move.

Weakened by ten days of travel followed by nineteen days of daylight bouts with the Iroquois men and eighteen nights with Iroquois women, William was completely exhausted and on the way home he was stricken with a severe fever. He was carried into his quarters and for five days nursed with compassionate care by an extremely attractive young Mohawk woman who had been hastily summoned by Wascaugh. Unfortunately William, for once, was totally incapable of appreciating her proximity.

While the assembled Indians pitched their camps outside on his grounds, tore up his lawns and gardens, plucked and devoured his fruit, ate and drank from his larder and in various ways amused themselves until he could be made well enough to start the council, the Mohawk woman bathed him, fed him and treated him with the remedies known to her people. For two days he hovered on delirium and for three days after that he was desperately weak and scarcely able to leave his bed. And all this time she was beside him, treating him, cleaning him, stroking him, caring for him with a tenderness he had never really experienced before.

She appeared to be in her middle twenties or perhaps a little younger and, when he was able to think clearly again, William studied her, watching how she carried herself, the flow of her long black hair, the exquisite chiseled beauty of her bare breasts, the rich warmth of her smooth skin, the gentleness of her hands, the sweet melody of her speech, the genuine concern in her wide brown eyes. She was neither shy nor bold, but merely casual and when he asked her name she sat on the bed beside him and smiled for the first time, showing well-formed white teeth.

"My people call me Degonwadonti." A note of pride crept into her voice. "I am the grand-daughter of Chief Sagayeanquarashtow—he who was known to the English as Chief Brant. My father is Aroghyidecker, also known as Chief Nichus—he who is known to the English as Chief Nichus Brant. I am the older sister of Thayendanegea, who is also called Joseph Brant, and who will one day also be a great chief of the Mohawks."

"Degonwadonti." The name rolled off William's tongue and he liked the feel of it and nodded. "It is a good name. You come from a great family, but is it only your grandfather, your father and your brother who have English names?"

She tossed her head back, and a light, musical laughter escaped from her. "No," she said. "It was the English who many years ago gave my grandfather his English name in return for a favor he had done them. But it was my grandfather who gave my father his English name, and my father who gave English names to my brother and me. I am called Molly Brant."

Johnson nodded again. "It is a good name, too." He looked at her speculatively. "You are not a young girl. You are a woman. Who is your man?"

She hesitated a moment and then replied, "Yes, I have a man, but the man does not have me. I have watched him for many seasons when he has not known I was watching. I have waited for the sign that my vision said would come. And the sign came. It was when Chief Wascaugh summoned me to help you in your need. Yes, I have a man, and his name is Warraghiyagey."

She placed her hand on his chest and William Johnson suddenly felt something he had never really felt before, at least not fully. He had perhaps felt it a little for Catty—Catherine Weisenberg—who had lived with him and borne three of his children; he had even felt a trifle of it for the little French girl he had bought from the Indians, Angélique Vitry. But he had never felt it with such intensity, with such sureness, with such unwavering certainty.

Sir William Johnson was in love.

He did not question it, even in his own mind; did not wonder how it could have happened so swiftly, how this time it was so different than the hundreds, perhaps thousands, of other women—both red and white—that he had known intimately. The fact of it was there, indisputably, and he accepted it.

The rest of the day and night they were together and it was only with the greatest of reluctance in the early morning that he left her and moved shakily toward the council fire, which had been kept burning until he should join them. A wild whooping went up from the throng when they saw him and he was amazed at how their number had grown. In addition to Wascaugh and four or five of his men, their party had numbered only about forty-five on the journey from Onondaga to Fort Johnson. But now there were over a hundred fifty warriors assembled here. The number of Delawares and Shawnees had not increased, but many more Mohawks had come, plus from two to five each of the Onondaga, Cayuga and Oneida, and even a party of twenty-six Mohegans from eastward of the Hudson and northward of Albany.

The council was opened with the customary salutations to those present and then an opening appeal by William to the

Shawnees and Delawares of the western Pennsylvania lands to cast aside their animosity and embrace the English. He begged them to open their eyes and see that the French had seduced them; that they must throw off the chains with which the French had bound them, and wipe away from their eyes the sand that the French had thrown into them to blind them. He held aloft war belts and asked them to join with the English and fight beside them, instead of against them.

But again it was no easy matter. The arguments went back and forth, often very heatedly until, all excuses and shallow reasons being worn away, one of the prime bones of contention became apparent. It was the chief of the Delaware delegation, White Eyes, who voiced the matter.

"We have lived under a cloud for many long summers, Warraghiyagey," he said. "The Iroquois, when we had sold some land to the English, summoned us and stripped us of our manhood. They put petticoats upon us and called us women and that is how all the tribes look upon us."

His voice rose angrily now: "You say we have been seduced by the French, but if we are women, is it any wonder that they have seduced us? Brother, listen! One of the reasons we are fighting the English is to prove that we are men and not women! We wish to prove that we are men who are able to hold land and declare war independently of the Iroquois!"

It was an inflammatory statement, considering that the council was made up largely of the Iroquois. And it had put William smack into the middle of a ticklish situation again. With a deep breath and keeping his eyes averted from the Iroquois, he walked forward to White Eyes and made a pantomime of removing a skirt from around the Delaware. With one hand, then, he held this imaginary skirt high and pitched it over his shoulder.

"I do now," he cried dramatically, "in the name of the great King of England, your father, declare that henceforth you are to be considered as men by all your English brethren, and no longer as women, and I hope that your brethren of the Six Nations will take it into consideration to follow my example, and to remove this insulting term from you, which you have worn long enough—and I will recommend to them strongly that they do so."

It was a startling move and William himself did not know quite what to expect. Surprisingly, though the Iroquois present were taken aback by the pronouncement, they made no objection to it, but neither could they, by themselves, commit the League to observe such a declaration, Wascaugh told him, until the assembly should convene again at Onondaga and the matter be put to a vote.

More surprised than any were the Delawares and Shawnees. So long had the former tribe worn the stigma attached to them by the Iroquois that they had never really believed they would have it removed, but that it would continue to be a stain over their tribe for all time to come. Now, in one quick gesture, even more swiftly than the name of women had been applied to them, Warraghiyagey had stripped it away and they were men again! They were exultant.

A grand war dance began now and the war belts which William Johnson raised aloft were picked up by both the Delaware and Shawnee representatives, who declared that they were now no longer with the French, but were back by the fire of the English. Rum flowed, oxen were roasted, gifts distributed and a fine finale consummated the council. When the meat and rum were gone, the Indians began drifting off. Within an hour not an Indian was to be seen anywhere. William viewed with some dismay the wreck they had made of his grounds. He gave instructions to his servants to clean things up and return, as best they could, everything to the condition it was in before the arrival of the multitude.

By himself again, he relaxed the strong front he had forced himself to assume. He looked very ill. The forty-four days just past had taken their toll. The sickness alone had not done it, nor had the councils alone, nor the women. But too much of all of them in too short a time had assuredly left him in serious need of rest and recuperation.

But he had done it, by heaven! He had wrested an alliance of sorts not only from the Iroquois, but equally from the Shawnees and Delawares. Whether or not they would hold to this alliance would now depend upon the English. If the army could come up with some impressive victories, there could be no doubt that these Indians would remain allies. But the victories had better come. Without them, the alliance might be no more than just so many words.

Wearily now, William Johnson began walking back to the big house, his mind going to other things, prominent among which was Degonwadonti, his own Molly Brant, awaiting him in the house. His heart quickened at the thought and his step became surer.

He had not quite reached the house, however, when he was stopped by the sight of a horseman riding furiously toward him on the road from Albany and Schenectady. In moments the man had reined to a halt and thrust at William an express from Governor Hardy. Then he waited patiently for it to be read, in case an answer was to be returned.

William broke the seal at once and as he read it, the slight color that had come back into his face drained away and he looked more haggard than ever. Silently he folded the paper, tucked it into his pocket and began to walk away.

"Any reply, sir?" the young messenger asked quickly.

Sir William Johnson stopped and looked back without speaking for a moment and then he shook his head sadly. "No, son, I have no reply."

He turned and walked slowly again toward the house. The message from Charles Hardy had been brief, informing him that Governor Robert Hunter Morris of Pennsylvania had just declared war on the Shawnees and Delawares and an attractive bounty was being offered for all Indian scalps brought in.

[ *July 26, 1756—Monday* ]

The past eight or ten days had been busy ones for Captain Bougainville. After the long time of doing virtually nothing in Montreal, the somewhat frenetic activity of these days since Montcalm's return had been wearing. Now the young officer glanced back at the entries in his journal since then and shook his head in annoyance at himself. His comments on those days had been brief—much too brief—and if he was to make his journal something worthwhile, he would have to take greater pains with it.

Though it was no easy matter to write interestingly and at length of the day's activities when those very activities had so drained him that his eyes became sandy with sleep and his head started to nod as soon as he sat down, yet he resolved to force himself to do better in his journalistic efforts, beginning this evening. First, however, he read over what he had written recently:

*July 17*

*Received news from Frontenac ... Sunday a detachment of two hundred men and five lieutenants of the Regiments of La Sarre, Guyenne, and Béarn left Frontenac to join M. de Villiers. M. Descombes, engineer, went with this detachment. His mission is to reconnoiter Oswego and to report on its condition, if he can get near to it ... The works at Frontenac progress slowly ... nothing is in shape ... May God grant that the expedition they propose shall succeed. The enemy will be chased away from a post very advantageous to them, both for war and as a depot for trade, and especially we shall be rid of a great source of embarrassment.*

### July 18

M. Marin left with the Menominee; all wished to follow him except the wounded. Today a deputation of Iroquois from the Sault [Caughnawaga] came to compliment Intendant François Bigot on his arrival at Montreal.

### July 19

The Marquis de Montcalm arrived at Montreal this morning. He has made complete dispositions for defensive action in the region of Carillon. The Chevalier de Lévis commands there. His position is a touchy and delicate one, for he should have five thousand men in order to make a good defense, and he has at most only two thousand, of which fourteen hundred are regulars, the rest militia and Indians. There are now four hundred on the way to reinforce him. The fort at Carillon will not be safe to risk a garrison in for another six weeks.

M. Mercier left this morning for Frontenac to get the artillery prepared.

### July 21

I left Montreal with the Marquis de Montcalm at half-past four this evening. We reached Lachine, where we spent the night, at half-past seven. Lachine is three miles from Montreal. It is the place where one embarks for all voyages to the West, the river not being navigable from Montreal to this place. A canal from Montreal to Lachine has been proposed to supply this deficiency.

### July 22

Left Lachine at half-past five in five bateaux, each with a crew of ten men . . . For all this distance the navigation is very difficult, but there is the most beautiful scenery in the world. The river is full of well-wooded islands and its channel obstructed with rocks as well as restricted by these islands. There are waterfalls and almost continuous rapids for nearly forty leagues ... The trees in all these parts are admirable, many of them suitable for ship-building. It is a shame that so fine a countryside should be without cultivation.

Arrived at our sleeping place at half-past four. It is a very *hard day's journey and one that usually takes two days to make.*

## July 23

*Re-embarked . . . The waterfall at Coteau du Lac is one of the hardest to pass . . . Made eight leagues today.*

## July 24

*Left at half-past four . . . camped at six . . . made ten leagues during the day.*

## July 25

*. . . made nine leagues.*

Again Bougainville shook his head, determined to make his journal more interesting, beginning right now. He dipped his pen and began to write the day's entry:

## July 26

*. . . passed Pole Cove, so named because the river is now free from rapids as far as Frontenac so the boatmen no longer need poles and throw them away here. Drunkard's Point, Isle aux Galops, Pointe Galette, Fort Présentation where we arrived at half-past four and where we spent the night . . . The Abbé François Piquet, able missionary, known for a voyage he made to France with three Indians, obtained a twelve-arpent⁷ concession above La Galette. Five years ago he built a fort of squared posts, flanked by four strong bastions, palisaded without, and with a water-filled ditch. Beside the fort is a village of a hundred fires, each that of an Iroquois chief, all warriors. Each of these chiefs costs the King about one hundred crowns. They have made a clearing, have cows, horses, pigs and hens. They plant Indian corn and last year sold six hundred minots⁸ of it.*

*Abbé Piquet teaches them and drills them in the French military exercises. His assistant is Abbé Chevalier Terley, called Chevalier Terley because of his warlike disposition. There is in the fort a captain of colonial troops as commander, but all real control is ecclesiastical. They plan to transplant here all of the Six Nations that can be won over to France.*

*There arrived at the fort at the same time as we did, seven of this fort's Indians, sent last year as deputies to the Six Nations. They brought back with them forty ambassadors of*

*the Oneidas and Onondagas, who came, I believe, to assert
their neutrality. Every day is passed in council with one or
the other. They will leave day after tomorrow for Montreal.
There have arrived at Niagara deputies of the Cayugas and
Senecas. They came with M. Chabert de Joncaire, an officer
of colony troops, our ambassador to these tribes.*

*The Menominees have joined us here and follow us as far
as Frontenac and farther if we can make them stay with us.*

### [ August 6, 1756—Saturday ]

Fort Granville was certainly no great shakes as a bastion, but
it was a defense of sorts and, for the resident settlers along
the Susquehanna and two of its western tributaries, the Juniata River and Sherman Creek, it was a lot better than trusting
to Providence that Indians wouldn't attack while they were
isolated on their log-cabin farms.

The bloodletting that had been going on for so long now in
western Pennsylvania had resulted in a number of forts like
Fort Granville being set up; some of them—Fort Granville
for one—by the government and others by the settlers themselves. At least sixty or seventy of the settlers were in Fort
Granville now, fearful of even leaving the gate of the place
without a military escort.

There was a fairly strong garrison here—a full company of
Pennsylvania provincials under command of Captain Edward
Ward. Lieutenant Edward Armstrong was second-in-command
and, after him, Lieutenant John Turner. Of the three, only
Turner was a resident of the area. He had been given a commission because of his knowledge of the Indians and methods
of Indian fighting, not necessarily because of any particular
degree of heroic stature. And having been commissioned, he
was ordered to duty at Fort Granville mostly because he was
thoroughly familiar with the lay of the land around it and to
the west, since he had long traded with Indians all throughout
this area.

Using his prerogative as part of the fort's military establishment, Turner ensconced himself and his family inside the
place in quarters every bit as good as their own nearby
home. It was a sizable family, consisting of himself, his wife,
Mary, their thirty-month-old son John, and Mary's four sons
by her former marriage, Tom, Simon, James and George—
the Girty boys.

Just nine days ago, on July 22, there was a call to arms
and a considerable fright when a horde of over a hundred

459

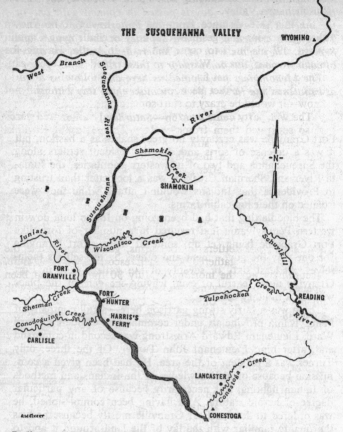

Indians, mostly Delawares and Shawnees, but led by a company of twenty-three Canadians, approached to just beyond rifle shot from the walls.

This was a band under the leadership of Captain Neyon de Villiers[9] out of Fort Duquesne. This fort at the forks of the Ohio was the origination point of a majority of the raids against the Pennsylvania and Virginia frontiers. Eager for more English blood to be spilled, Neyon de Villiers had long been anxious to pull off some great coup. His party had already destroyed a number of isolated cabins and had even taken several scalps, but he wanted more—many more—and

460

so now he was marauding through this countryside of the Susquehanna Valley.

At this safe distance from the fort, he let it be known through actions and gestures that he was challenging Captain Ward and his men to come out and do battle. Having the much weaker force, Ward wisely refrained and even cautioned anyone against firing their muskets. Without cannon to back them up—a fact he hoped the party out there did not know—it would be crazy to start something.

The war party came ever closer until only a hundred yards or so separated them from the fort. The atmosphere within the place was greatly strained, but still there was no gunfire and finally, with an insulting gesture, Villiers led his party away. And when, after passage of a week, there was no further sign of them, the occupants of the fort breathed a collective sigh of relief.

Because of the fact that wheat on the farms of the area, especially those in the Sherman Valley, had ripened and needed to be harvested, Captain Ward now agreed to escort a group of the settlers to the farms, guard them while the crop was being gathered and then escort them back here. Accordingly, on the morning of July 30 the gates had been opened and the party marched out, Ward leading them with all but twenty-three of his men, who were left under command of Lieutenant Armstrong to guard the fort. Lieutenant Turner and his family also remained behind, along with about a dozen others.

Hardly had Ward's party gotten themselves out of sight and hearing, however, when Neyon de Villiers and his band of bush lopers and Indians showed up again and attacked the fort without hesitation. It was a pretty good fight while it lasted, going on all afternoon and well into the evening. But the attackers took advantage of the poor placement of the fort, took advantage of a deep ravine which ran to within thirty feet of it from the Juniata and, before those inside realized what was happening, set fire to the wall.

The wall was comprised of poles rather than logs and it burned rapidly. As soon as a hole developed in it, the firing became hot through it from both sides. Three Indians and three Canadians were hit fatally in quick succession as they attempted to plunge through the burning gap. But they were not all who died. Inside the fort a private standing and shooting beside Lieutenant Armstrong took a bullet through his throat and crumpled. A moment later another ball hit Armstrong in the head and killed him. Three other privates

461

were wounded at the same time. There was a momentary lull in the fighting and during the interlude the voice of Captain Villiers called out:

"Englishmen! Surrender the fort! We do not want to have to kill you, which we will do if you continue shooting. You will not be mistreated if you surrender. We only wish to destroy the fort."

With the death of Armstrong, Lieutenant Turner was in command. Without hesitation he now ordered his men to throw down their weapons and personally opened the gate. Instantly the Indians and Canadians poured in. Private George Brandon was one of the first reached. A tomahawk hissed through the air and buried itself in his head with a hideous meaty sound. He was scalped, as were Armstrong and the dead private. Another private, Peter Walker, taking advantage of the fact that all attention was riveted there, slipped out through the burning hole into the ravine and escaped in the gathering darkness.

The prisoners—the Turners and Girty boys among them—were all rounded up in a group and, under Villiers' orders, led a short distance away after being heavily loaded with plunder from the fort. Then Villiers had the barracks, sheds, fort proper and everything else set afire.

While Neyon de Villiers then went on with the majority of his party to raid other outposts, a group of about thirty Delawares, with considerable prodding and beating, forced the captives on their way westward through the hills. It was a rugged journey with the threat constantly over the captives that anyone who faltered or dropped his load would be tomahawked and scalped. Turner himself was forced to carry over his shoulder a one-hundred-pound sack of salt.

Days and nights merged for the captives into one great plodding agony, but at last, about noon today, they reached their destination—one of the largest Indian villages in western Pennsylvania. Located on the bank of the Allegheny River about forty-five miles upstream from Fort Duquesne, this was Kittanning,[10] and it was the meeting place of the Delaware Indians going to or coming from frontier raids. Here the prisoners were tied to trees while the villagers flocked around them, whipping them with switches, kicking them and otherwise mistreating them.

Abruptly the village chief—Tewea—appeared and John Turner blanched. He knew this one-eyed Indian only by the name of Captain Jacobs, but he had heard many grisly stories from his fellow traders of the viciousness of the man. And almost immediately what he had feared would happen actually did. Chief Tewea peered into Turner's face and then smashed him in the mouth with the heel of his hand and stepped back with an explosive grunt. The chief was the brother of No-me-tha—the Fish—and the last time he had seen his brother was five years before when he had departed with two English traders, Simon Girty, Sr., and the man who was now tied to the tree before him.

A string of commands rattled from Tewea and immediately there was a flurry of activity among the Indians. A hole was dug and a heavy black post sunk into it. Turner was cut from the tree where he had been tied and dragged screaming to this stake, while all the other prisoners, including his wife—still clutching their two-and-a-half-year-old son John to her breast—and the Girty boys watched in horror.

A roaring fire was built a dozen yards away and four or five of the Delawares put their muskets down so that the barrels were resting in the flames. When the metal was as hot as it would get, they ran to Turner with them and shoved them at him as if there were bayonets at the ends. The hot metal punched deeply into his body—through it in at least one case—and his anguished screams split the forest air, bringing approving cries to the mouths of the Indian onlookers. They were far from finished with Turner, though. A squaw ran up with a knife, sliced off his ears and crammed them into her mouth and ran off again while the warriors roared with laughter. Several of the men gathered in front of him and then one by one they cut off his fingers at the middle joints and now his screams turned to an unintelligible mumbling groan. His penis was severed next, then his testicles, yet still he was on his feet, still he was alive.

Now Captain Jacobs—Tewea—himself came up to the captive and ran his knife blade around in a deep circle atop Turner's head. Gripping the hair in the center of that circle, he gave a mighty yank and pulled away the entire top of the scalp, exposing the bare, bloodied skull. Even then, though he was leaning heavily against the cords that bound him, Turner was still standing.

A Delaware boy of about six, son of Tewea, was now given a tomahawk and then held up by the chief so that his head was level with the scalped captive. With a shrill, wild cry, the boy raised the weapon high and brought it down with all his small strength onto the bare skull, caving it in. And now, at last, Lieutenant Turner was no longer standing.

It was midnight now and Louis Montcalm smiled and thought again of how incredible it was that his whole force had been able to get so close to Fort Oswego—hardly more than a mile away—and yet remain undetected. It was hard to understand a foe who could be so careless, but he thanked Providence for it. Now, settled as comfortably as possible in his tent, he prepared, by the light of a well-shielded lantern, to pen a resumé of what had transpired to this point, for dispatch to the minister of war.

The return to Montreal had been uneventful. There, Governor Vaudreuil had told him that he had sent his own brother, Rigaud de Vaudreuil—a man almost entirely lacking in military training—at the head of seven hundred Canadians to Fort Frontenac, there to take command of the post from Captain Coulon de Villiers. The governor had blandly commented that he was sure Rigaud would prove to be a good leader and undoubtedly Montcalm would be wanting to give him special and important responsibilities of command, both over colonials and regulars. With exceptional diplomacy, Montcalm managed to maneuver the conversation to other channels without committing himself in that respect.

Montcalm and his aide, Captain Bougainville, went at once to Fort Frontenac and found encouraging reports. Rigaud had already crossed to the south side of the lake and was encamped at Niaouré Bay[11] with the united bands of Indians and the majority of the Fort Frontenac military force.

A reconnoitering of Fort Oswego was undertaken by Captain Descombles and successfully carried out without detection. His report was even more encouraging—that he felt an attack was certain of success—and this was confirmed by deserters who were carefully questioned. They declared that the main fort was no more than a simple loopholed wall and the garrison ill fed, discontented and mutinous. They added that about half the garrison—three hundred seventy men—was at Fort Ontario and the remainder of the seven hundred effectives at Fort Oswego and Fort George—largely the former, with the sick multitude crowded into Fort George. They also reported that in the past year alone, twelve hundred men had died of disease at this outpost.

With his own force at something over three thousand men, and having an abundance of heavy artillery, there was every reason for Montcalm to believe the Oswego installations could be taken with ease. He was too wise in the foibles of war, however, to become overconfident and underestimate the enemy's ability. He intended to keep his army's movements secret from the enemy to the last possible moment.

On August 4, under cover of night, he embarked with the first division and crossed the mouth of the large lake to a huge nameless island[12] to the south of Fort Frontenac, where he ordered camp made and all men to keep under cover throughout the daylight hours. At nightfall he had them on the move again and they had joined Rigaud's force at Niaouré Bay by 7 A.M. August 6. His movements had been closely followed by the second division, which brought the supplies, hospital train and eighty artillery boats. The divisions joined at the bay on August 8. Then, Rigaud's Indians and Canadians had set out along the shore under cover of the forest in order to be on hand to lay down protection for the troop landing.

Montcalm had set out in boats with the first division again and less than an hour ago they had landed here. Immediately four cannon were set up on the beach at his orders and the men settled down to rest and, if possible, to sleep, beside the boats. A strong guard patrol was stationed in a wide semicircle around the encampment and all was in readiness for an attack in the morning.

Having finished his report to the minister of war, Montcalm now hurriedly wrote another few lines on a fresh piece of paper—a note to his wife:

*Midnight, 10 August 1756*

*Dearest,*

*In the morning we go into battle, but do not fear, for I believe we have every advantage with us, and greatly outnumber the enemy. It is at times like this that I always experience a great yearning for you, and a sorrow for the pain I cause you through absence in dangerous pursuits. The life of a soldier's wife is one of waiting and fearing, perhaps more difficult to bear than what the soldier himself faces. I know your prayers are with me, just as I, in spirit, am always with you, my dear mother, and my beloved daughters. To them and to you I send my heart.*

*Louis*

**[ August 12, 1756—Thursday ]**

John Campbell, Earl of Loudoun, had finally arrived in New

York from London on July 23, bringing with him a cluster of baggage and servants, and even his mistress. He was a short, ill-tempered Scot with hair the color of burnt sand and the imperious attitude of one born and bred to wealth, position and power.

He was met by William Shirley, who delivered to the new commander in chief a packet of papers outlining what steps had been taken thus far in the year's campaign, and urging that his long-cherished plan of taking Forts Niagara and Frontenac be pushed forward at all speed. In fact, with a distinct lack of tact, Shirley made it quite clear in his usual pompous way that there had really been no need at all for a change in commanders.

If there was any sure way of making Lord Loudoun balk, it was by telling him that his thinking had been done for him and all he had to do was allow the wheels to roll as they had already begun rolling. Even before Shirley had finished, the new commander had decided to abandon any attempt against either Niagara or Frontenac and aim instead for Fort Carillon at Ticonderoga. Within minutes of their meeting, he had had his fill of William Shirley and sent him away with orders to stay in New York where, if necessary, he could be reached. With stiff formality, Shirley departed. Not long afterward, in a letter to Henry Fox—Lord Holland—John Campbell wrote:

*I got from Major-General Shirley a few papers of very little use; only he insinuated to me that I would find everything prepared, and have nothing to do but pull laurels; which I understand was his constant conversation before my arrival.*

Six days after reaching America, Campbell arrived at his new quarters in Albany, took command from Abercromby and received a variety of reports on the state of affairs. Colonel John Bradstreet was one of those reporting, explaining the sad state existing at Fort Oswego and the attack he had suffered on the way back to Albany; all of which only strenghthened Lord Loudoun's resolve to do nothing about either Fort Frontenac and Fort Niagara now. From Albany to Lake George—at the Half-Moon camp, the rebuilt post of Saratoga, Fort Edward and Fort William Henry—some ten thousand soldiers, largely provincials, were ready to move and chafing at merely being held in camps on a seemingly perpetual alert. Already at Lake George three good sloops

466

had been built and laborers were just now completing the last of several hundred whaleboats. The best of intelligence from spies indicated that Fort Carillon didn't have half as many men as Campbell; and the reports from Robert Rogers and his Rangers indicated that the defenses there were still very incomplete. If ever the time was ripe to move, it was now.

But his lordship, John Campbell, was in no great hurry. He did, with some reluctance, send Colonel Daniel Webb up the Mohawk with the Forty-fourth Regiment today to reinforce Oswego and deliver some more supplies there, but that was about the only real military move that the Earl of Loudoun seemed inclined to make at the moment.

There were other important things to distract him: such as retiring to his quarters to compare notes with his mistress on this frightfully barbaric country to which they had been exiled.

## [ *August 14, 1756—Saturday* ]

Colonel Hugh Mercer had detected no sign of danger imminent on that bright August morning. As usual, the patrol canoes had gone their rounds, one to paddle a half day westward along the shoreline toward Fort Niagara and then return, the other to move along the shoreline to the east and then in an arc to the north as the lake shore curved up toward the St. Lawrence River. The latter craft had gone shortly before dawn, but had come paddling furiously back within minutes.

"Boats! French boats, Colonel, scores of them," his scout reported excitedly. "They're all beached about a mile east."

Even as he spoke there was a rattle of gunfire from the silhouetted woods east of the forts. The first blood in the battle of Fort Oswego was drawn—and it was French blood.

At just about the time the canoe had set out on its rounds, Captain Descombles, Captain François Pouchot, and several other officers had gone with a small party of their Indians to reconnoiter the fort. They became separated from one another and, in the gloom of the still-dark woods, one of the scalp-hungry Caughnawagas mistook Descombles for an English soldier and put a bullet through his brain. Immediately thinking the attack had begun, the others rushed toward the fort firing at shadows.

The drum-roll alarm was sounded at the installation and Colonel Mercer sent Captain Broadley and his crew to sail the *Oswego* to the scene of the landing and open an attack.

The heavy craft swung ponderously into position and began firing, but then quickly had to move out of range as the much heavier artillery of the shore batteries began ripping through the shrouds. The ship turned and fled back to the fort where it circled aimlessly offshore, not knowing exactly what to do.

Montcalm had been on the verge of ordering his readied army to open the attack when the gunfire from the woods sounded and he barked a command, sending the greatest part of his forces forward. Very quickly the general engagement broke out. For the first part of the fighting the French kept close under the cover of the trees and peppered Fort Ontario with musketry. Neither side did a great deal of damage.

In the afternoon, Montcalm's second division arrived and they had with them twenty-two more cannon, many of them the ones that had been lost on the Monongahela battlefield last year by General Braddock. As soon as darkness had fallen, Montcalm ordered the first parallel marked out, about one hundred eighty yards from the ramparts. All night long his men worked feverishly, digging trenches.

Dawn on Friday the thirteenth found the French forces securely in position, their entrenchment well protected by fascines, gabions and a strong abatis.[13] And twenty heavy cannon had been laboriously tugged and shoved through the woods until now there was no more cover for them and no time to get them in position to command Fort Ontario until darkness set in again.

Messengers flitted back and forth across the mouth of the Onondaga River between Fort Oswego and Fort Ontario. By noon, with the musket fire between Fort Ontario and the French entrenchment still continuing heavily, Mercer demanded to know why that fort's own artillery had not been brought into use. The fact of the matter was that no one had even thought to move it. The eight little cannon and a single mortar which made up the fort's artillery were all in position along the fort's west wall, as protection for Fort Oswego, from which direction attack, if it ever came, had been expected.

Now the pieces were moved into place on the east side and a brisk fire was maintained the remainder of the day, but not a great deal of damage done. At nightfall practically all firing ceased. And now Colonel Mercer, knowing they had been extremely fortunate thus far in not having the French artillery brought into operation against them, sent a message

468

across the river ordering the evacuation of Fort Ontario to Fort Oswego.

"The fort will be under heavy artillery fire tomorrow for certain," he said, "and it can't possibly stand against it. Better to lose the fort alone than both fort and garrison."

The cannon there were spiked or thrown into the well and throughout the night boats paddled back and forth. Before the dawn, the east side of the river was devoid of English.

Montcalm's men had had a busy night, too, moving their cannon into position. At dawn today the French general ordered Rigaud to lead his Canadians and Indians upstream to a fording place about a mile and a half above the forts, cross over and then strike the enemy from the south and west. Even as this detachment moved out on their mission, the commander ordered the artillery fire to commence. The effect of the twenty-pounders and twelve-pounders was devastating. The ramparts of Fort Ontario splintered and flew apart as if they were matchsticks and dust. With no reply fire it was obvious the post had been abandoned and the cannon were brought up to the fort itself, which remained relatively undamaged. They were positioned now to bear on Fort Oswego across the river.

From the west side of that river, to south and west, there now came shrill cries and musket fire as Rigaud's force, which had made its crossing unopposed, attacked. Though they kept themselves so far away that their bullets did little physical damage, the blow to the morale of the defenders was crushing.

Colonel Mercer at Fort Oswego had leaped into full view on a parapet to study the attacking forces on both sides of the river. The French artillery opened up abruptly and one of the first twenty-pounder cannonballs struck the English commander squarely in the middle and tore him in half.

Amidst the booming of the guns and the thunder of crashing walls came the wails from the sick men and the screams from nearly one hundred women who had attached themselves to the place. The position of Fort Oswego was utterly hopeless. A hurried council of the officers was held and now a white rag was knotted to a pole, raised high and frantically waved.

Immediately Montcalm ordered a cease-fire and Captain Bougainville was sent across with the terms of capitulation: that the garrison would be prisoners of war; that the officers and soldiers take away with them their personal baggage and be escorted under guard to Montreal for questioning and possibly for eventual exchange. The terms were accepted and all English arms surrendered.

Abruptly there was a clamor of howling and screams as Rigaud's Indians and *coureurs de bois* burst in and began a murderous attack with tomahawks and knives. English soldiers by the scores fell beneath them and the earth quickly became a ghastly expanse of red mud scattered with scalped corpses. Not for many minutes could Montcalm—as furious as Louis Bougainville had ever seen him—stop the carnage and exact promises from the Indian chiefs that they would keep their warriors in check and allow no more to be massacred; and these promises were exacted only by Montcalm's own promise of eight to ten thousand livres' worth of gifts from the King. In that interval of bloodshed, however, upwards of one hundred prisoners were killed— more than in the battle itself, in which the English loss had only numbered eighty men.

Defenseless against the heavier artillery of the French, the small English fleet was surrendered by its commander, Captain Broadley: the sloop *Oswego* and the schooners *George, Vigilant, Halifax, London* and *Mohawk.*[14]

All supplies, provisions, armament and equipment that could be transported were readied for removal. Brush, branches and logs were piled up inside Fort Oswego to make it more flammable, since it was constructed largely of clay and stone. The vessels, both those of the French and the captured English ships, were made ready for the return to Fort Frontenac.

After a few days of rest, Montcalm announced, the prisoners would be taken to imprisonment in Montreal and all three of these defensive works—Fort Oswego, Fort Ontario, and Fort George—would be destroyed by fire. Though he had lost thirty men, his first battle in America had been a signal success and the Marquis de Montcalm was very pleased.[15]

## [ *August 21, 1756—Saturday* ]

Colonel Daniel Webb was by no means anxious to get his Forty-fourth Regiment to Fort Oswego, yet he didn't dawdle. From all he had heard about it, the place was a pesthole, virtually a deathtrap, and the idea of simply sitting up there as a reinforcement to the present garrison galled him. He knew Lord Loudoun was planning his prime attack to be directed at Ticonderoga, and that is where he wished he could have been sent. Military honors and promotions, he was only too well aware, are won on the battlefield, not in resident duty at some godforsaken outpost.

He paused only briefly at Fort Johnson and again at Fort Williams. The portage across the Great Carrying Place to Fort Bull was expeditiously made today and the baggage just being reloaded in the boats newly launched on Wood Creek, when two of his scouts sent ahead with some Indians to alert Colonel Mercer of their impending arrival abruptly returned, moving swiftly along the river trail. Webb gave his regiment the order to halt and listened with shock as Thomas Harris and James Conner told their story.

They had reached Oswego in the afternoon yesterday and the place was an utter ruin. The ground was littered with the debris of battle—broken weapons, smashed barrels and kegs, smoldering clothing and the like. There was nothing left of Fort Ontario but a great gray pile of smoldering ashes. Fort George was still smoking. Just barely visible to the northeast on the lake was a fleet of a handful of large boats and a great flotilla of smaller craft. There was absolutely no one at the scene.

A large area of freshly turned earth gave silent evidence of being a mass grave and either the entire garrison was dead, or some were dead and the others taken away as prisoners. Harris, Conner and the Indians had then scouted around for any sign that someone had escaped and might still be in hiding, but there was no one. All that remained were two signs that had been erected close to the residue of what had been Fort George. One was on a cross and the other on a post. Neither the scouts nor the Indians coud read the language in which they were inscribed, which they took to be French, but they had carefully copied the words and showed them now to Webb. The commander glanced at them and saw they were written in Latin, not French.

"The one from the cross," he said, "which reads *In hoc signo vincunt*, means, I believe, 'We have conquered in this place'. The other one, that you copied from the post, *Manibus date lilia plenis*, means 'Give lilies freely,' meaning, I suppose, to next of kin."[16]

Though until now he had reacted with a strange sort of detachment, abruptly a sick fear crawled over Daniel Webb. Vivid pictures of scalpings and atrocities flashed through his mind. His throat went suddenly dry and his hands shook slightly with reaction and for a long moment he didn't know what to do. Already the news was spreading among the

471

regiment and a highly contagious fear bordering almost on panic was washing over the troops. Webb did little to hold it down.

In another instant the colonel had made his decision. Almost a hundred axemen were ordered to spread out along the overgrown banks of Wood Creek for a space of two miles downstream and at intervals fell trees into the water rendering it impassable to any boat—in the very area where many arduous months had been spent by English soldiers and laborers not long ago clearing the water of just such debris that had fallen naturally.

While this was being done, he ordered all the supplies that could be carried to be taken out of Fort Bull. Then he set that place afire and, when certain the blaze was going well and would entirely consume the fort, began to retrace the portage to Fort Williams.

The effect on the garrison there was almost the same as it had been on Webb and his men and the Fort Bull garrison. At Webb's orders, they too packed everything they could. The tragedy was growing into something even worse than it had been. Imagination somehow became fact and the report of the two scouts that the French army had been witnessed disappearing in the distance was brushed away. By the time all the goods had been stowed for transportation aboard the bateaux, the danger had become a palpable thing and terror churned their stomachs.

Again torches were lighted and eager flames began their job—this time consuming Fort Williams. It was still a roaring inferno when the combined troops were rowing downstream for all they were worth and their story ready to bubble from their lips: the French were coming! Six thousand strong they were coming, right behind the English!

The entire Mohawk valley was thrown into a greater panic than it had ever before experienced.

### [ *September 1, 1756—Wednesday* ]

It had been a long and trying day for Governor Pierre de Vaudreuil. He had had to meet with General Montcalm and listen to his full account of the Oswego battle, and make sure to compliment him in all the proper places. He had successfully masked the displeasure of hearing about the small contribution his brother Rigaud had been to the whole affair.

"In all respects, Monsieur de Montcalm," he had told the

general heartily, "I approve of your proceedings in this campaign and France owes you a great debt of gratitude."

But at last the interview had concluded and now Vaudreuil, in the quiet of his posh chambers, clad in a robe of thick wine-red velvet, inspected himself carefully in the mirror to make certain his newly powdered wig was properly seated, delicately pulled an offensive black hair from the tiny mole below his right ear, and then sat at his desk.

The primping had been automatic, almost unconscious, as he formulated in his own mind what he meant to say about the Oswego victory in his letter to the naval minister. Now, seated at his desk with his code book at hand, Vaudreuil was ready and his pen moved swiftly across the page in cipher, subtly damning Montcalm and absorbing onto himself and his brother all of the credit for the triumph:

*September 1, 1756*

*Ministre de la Marine*
*Versailles, France*

*Esteemed Excellency,*

*By now you have learned through other dispatches and formal reports of my victory over Fort Oswego. You may recall that in my letter to you of August 13, that I was confident I should reduce it and that my expedition was sure to succeed if Monsieur de Montcalm followed the directions I would give him. Observe, the victory has been won, though Monsieur de Montcalm would never have dared attack that place if I had not encouraged him and answered his timid objections.*

*The victory was due almost entirely to my brother, Rigaud, and the Canadians, who have been ill-used by the general and were not allowed either to enter the fort or share the plunder, any more than the Indians, who were so angry at the treatment they met that he had great difficulty in appeasing them.*

*There has been a great deal of talk here of my outstanding contribution in the planning of this offensive to the minutest detail; but I will not do myself the honor of repeating it to you, especially as it so much relates to myself and praises me so highly. I know how to do violence to my self-love. The measures I took, suffice to say, assured our victory in spite of opposition. If I had been less vigilant and firm, Oswego would still be in the hands of the English. I cannot sufficiently congratulate myself on the zeal which my brother and* the Canadians and Indians showed on this occasion; for without them my orders would have been given in vain. The hopes of His Britannic Majesty have vanished, and will hardly revive again; for I shall take care to crush them in the bud. As far as the troops from France conducted themselves, they were generally good, but thus far they have not absolutely distinguished themselves.

I do justice to the firmness they showed at Oswego; but it was only the Colony troops, Canadians and Indians, who attacked the forts. Our artillery was directed by the Chevalier Le Mercier and M. Frémont, both Colony officers, and was served by our Colony troops and our militia. The officers from France are more inclined to defense than attack. The troops from France are not on very good terms with our Canadians. M. de Montcalm is so quick-tempered that he goes to the length of striking the Canadians. How can he restrain his officers, when he cannot restrain himself? Could any example be more contagious? This is the way our Canadians are treated. They deserve something better.

The zeal, hardihood and bravery of these our Colony troops is beyond reproach, but I would be remiss not to inform His Excellency that nothing but their blind submission to my commands prevents many of them from showing resentment at the usage they have had to endure.

The Indians, on the other hand, are neither so gentle nor so yielding; and but for my brother Rigaud and myself, might have gone off in a rage. After their return here they did not hesitate to tell me that they would go wherever I sent them, provided I did not put them under the orders of M. de Montcalm. They told me positively that they could not bear his quick temper. I shall always maintain the most perfect union and understanding with M. le Marquis de Montcalm, but I shall be forced to take measures which will assure to our Canadians and Indians treatment such as their zeal and services merits.

*Vaudreuil*

### [ September 11, 1756—Saturday ]

Louis Antoine de Bougainville had looked forward to his arrival at Fort Carillon. Having heard so much about it from Montcalm, he had wanted badly to see the installation and the area in which it was situated. With almost boyish excitement his pulse had quickened when, at six o'clock last night, their boats had come within sight of the place.

Since then he had been doing a great deal of roaming about, noting the placement of the defenses and the troops, moved by the beauty of the surroundings. He had gathered much information during the evening yesterday and throughout the day today, and so he retired a bit earlier than usual to his quarters to jot down his impressions in his journal.

### September 11

*Fort Carillon, commenced last fall, is situated almost at the head of Lake Champlain on a peninsula pointing south which divides the lake from the south bay, and to the north of the outlet of Lake George.[17] The fort is square, with four bastions, of which three are in a defensible state. It is of horizontal timbers. The position is well chosen on a rugged rock formation, but the fort is badly oriented and is not far enough out on the north point of the lake, which has obliged them to make a redoubt[18] at the place where the fort should have been. As for the rest of it, they would have done better to take advantage of the rock, breaking it up with a pickaxe and using it for the parapets.*

*The troop encampment is presently on the river's edge at the foot of the rocky formation. It is presently composed of the battalions of La Reine, Languedoc, Royal Rouissilon, and some Colony troops. Guyenne and Béarn are camped half a league away at the Falls of Lake George.[19] From there, two roads are built through the woods, one on the right, the other on the left, the first leading to the end of the portage where the Chevalier de la Corne is camped with 600 men. That of the left leads to the same camp and to that of M. de Contrecoeur, 400 men strong, which is half a league beyond the portage on the left bank of Lake George, with a post of 120 men in between. Two well-armed bateaux leave this camp every day to watch the movements of the enemy on the lake.*

*The English have two large camps, one at Fort Lydius [Fort Edward] on the Hudson River with a water battery, the other at Fort George [Fort William Henry] at the head of Lake George, the two connected by a great road, and consisting, in all, of ten to twelve thousand men. . . . They have accumulated a great store of rations and munitions at Fort George.*

*Sir William Johnson concerns himself only with Indian affairs; he is the chief of that department. He has gathered together four or five hundred Indians from the regions of the Delaware, the Susquehanna, Seneca, etc. . . . We do not know* the destination of the Mohawks, to the number of one hundred, who have taken up the hatchet against us.

The enemy occupy almost all the islands in Lake George by entrenched posts. They say they are making many beams, planks and such. I suspect them to be preparing all the material for a fort to be built at the portage as soon as we fall back, or early next spring. They have two armed vessels on the lake, two others on the stocks, and about two hundred bateaux.

They have little parties ... and a few Indians continually observing from the heights and the woods that surround Carillon. I suspect they have established a flying camp behind the mountains north of the lake which supplies and shelters all these little parties.

In this position of the enemy, we being so much inferior in number, without vessels or boats and no fort on Lake George, it would appear to me to seem impossible to undertake anything of consequence against troops three times greater in number, well established everywhere, and having the support of very good forts. We content ourselves with continually harassing them by raiding parties who recently have succeeded in taking prisoners almost within sight of Boston, by putting ourselves in a state to resist an attack on their part. Our order of battle is laid down in advance, all orders given for the march and disposition of the various troops, the signals are agreed upon, and I believe that the enemy would be well blocked if he came to attack us. We all wish that he would come, but there is no sign of it.

We have about 180 Indians, all at the portage and at M. de Contrecoeur's camp.

At six this morning we inspected the posts at the Falls, at the portage, and those of MM. St. Martin and de Contrecoeur. At this last one there was a council of Indians who leave tomorrow for a raid to make a coup or a reconnaisance. All the country that we have been over, going by the right-hand road and returning by the left, is a country of mountains, precipices, entirely a tricky and dangerous country. . . .

At six the Iroquois [Caughnawagas] who left us on the evening of the eighth to follow the trail they had discovered, returned with two prisoners, a Scottish cadet and a militia captain. . . .

About three hundred Indians arrived at the camp this evening; Iroquois, Chippewa, Ottawa. Indian council of the usual sort. Some reports of Indian scouts seem to confirm *what I had suspected and said to the General, of a flying camp behind the mountains to the northwest.*

## [ *September 22, 1756—Wednesday* ]

Captain Bougainville was learning what all European officers seemed sooner or later to learn when it came to waging a war with Indian allies—that they were a most difficult people to control in any way. To acquaint himself with their methods, Bougainville had asked of Montcalm—and received permission—to accompany a detachment of French, Canadians and Indians on a mission to scout out the English movements on Lake George.

He had entered into it with great enthusiasm, but over the past ten days his journal entries indicated quite clearly his growing dissatisfaction with the Indian allies:

*September 12—13*
*Nothing new, a few Indians scouting on the lake. . . . We now have six hundred Indians, and hold council to send them off in detachments, but it is a long job to get them to make up their minds. It requires authority, brandy, equipment, food and such. The job never ends and it is very irksome.*

*September 14*
*. . . . It had at last been arranged with the Indians that one party would proceed by the south bay of Lake Champlain and the other by Lake George to strike Fort Edward, Fort William Henry, and the road between the forts. They were to leave this evening. Several Iroquois, who for two days had been out on a scout, came in with seven deer they had killed. They invited their brothers to a feast, and behold, everything is off and the departure can wait. . . .*

*September 15*
*. . . . The Indians who were supposed to leave this evening did not go; even the destination has been changed. It is said that the departure is set for tonight, but it is only a rumor, and the caprice of an Indian is, of all possible caprices, the most capricious.*

*September 16*
*Indians again determined to leave tonight. At M. de Contrecoeur's camp about one hundred Canadians and four hundred Indians under command of M. de la Perière, captain*

*of Colony troops, embarked at six o'clock. The canoes, thirty-four in number, waited in line behind a point until dusk had fallen. Indians determine the route, the halts, the scouts, and the speed to make, and in this sort of warfare it is necessary to adjust to their ways.*

*September 17*

*... our scouts returned without having discovered anything except smoke in several of the islands. After their return a herald went along the shore and summoned the chiefs of the nations to a council. All went to the camp of the Iroquois [Caughnawagas], who being the greatest in number took the lead without even learning the wishes of the French commander. The chiefs, blankets on their backs and lances in hand, gravely advanced, took their places, and smoked the council pipe ... the Indians treated us imperiously, made rules for us to which they did not conform, and one suspected that the Iroquois were not acting in good faith. ...*

*September 18*

*Nothing new during the night's march. ... Stopped toward two in the morning about four leagues from Fort William Henry. Spent most of the night in canoes. At daybreak sent out scouts as usual. The council which was held at daybreak decided to make neither any fires nor the least noise. As soon as it broke up, the Indians at once did both. ...*

*The Iroquois still wish to pass the night here and consequently tomorrow's daylight hours. The other nations do not like it. Discord is introduced. ...*

*Scouts have come to report that they have seen a canoe go ashore on the north side at a point where they thought they had also seen several tents or huts. Resolved to send two canoes at nightfall to reconnoiter this point. They returned at eleven and confirmed the first report. Embarked at once, crossed the lake in complete silence, and halted behind a point a league and a half above where it was believed the enemy post was.*

*September 19*

*An hour before daybreak we left through the woods to make an attack, leaving a few with the canoes with orders to come out into the lake and come to us when they heard the first shots. We marched through the woods in several files, the Indians almost naked, all in black and red war paint. We surrounded the suspected point, but found nothing except old*

478

fires smoldering in the roots of trees and a few abandoned huts. We at once returned, suspecting that the Iroquois had deceived us, more especially since in order to cut off the retreat of the enemy, if there had been any, it would have been necessary to go ashore beyond the point and not this side of it.

Because of the grumbling of the other nations, the Iroquois were deprived of command, and with a common accord, 110 Indians, the most nimble of all the detachment, were chosen, who left with a score and a half of the most active Canadians, with the intention of going as far as the fort and not returning until they had made a coup.

The canoes were then put in the woods with the rest of the detachment to guard them. It was agreed that if the warriors had not returned in two days, it would be proof that they had been hotly pursued and had taken the course of going back to Carillon through the mountains and hence that the canoes could return. They left at eleven o'clock.

Around two o'clock at about a league and a half from the fort, they suddenly ran into a detachment of thirteen English, whom they immediately attacked. All except one, who will have carried the news to the enemy, were killed or captured. The Iroquois had two killed or wounded. The Indians on the field of battle performed cruelties even the recital of which is horrible.

At noon MM. Mercier, Desandrouins and I left in a canoe. We reached Carillon at seven.


September 20

The Indians returned tonight . . . seventeen prisoners; they have already knocked several of them on the head. A detachment of a lieutenant and thirty men ordered to bury the two dead. The cruelty and the insolence of these barbarians is horrible, their souls are as black as pitch. It is an abominable way to make war; the retaliation is frightening and the air one breathes here is contagious of making one accustomed to callousness.

Two canoes of Indians went off today without telling anyone.


September 21

At five in the morning, council held with the Ottawas and Chippewas; the former having four prisoners and about five hundred leagues to go to get home, left early this evening; the Chippewas say that they have not seen the enemy close enough and have agreed to leave this evening to make a raid toward Fort Edward.

*At ten o'clock, a council with the Iroquois. At first, words of condolence over the losses they have suffered . . .*

*All the Indians, I believe, want to leave; Iroquois, Abnakis, Hurons . . . Of 450, scarcely 30 will remain. They have made a coup. It is necessary to seek their native hearth. The Canadians feel the same way.*

Now, once more in his tent for the evening and writing the day's entry, Bougainville reflected on what had happened and decided that as long as it was necessary to have Indian allies, there would be no end to the problems of command, of indecision, of incessant counciling and of trying to wage a campaign as it should be done. He wondered if it was all really worth it, if perhaps maybe they couldn't get just as far or even farther without Indian help, but then he shook his head. No, like it or not, the Indians were essential to them and they would just have to work things out as best they could with them. Nor did it always turn out as poorly as this latest enterprise had. From La Belle Rivière—that is, Fort Duquesne—the news received, for example, indicated that the Indians were raising unholy terror everywhere on the frontier there for the English.

Bougainville sighed and began writing his new day's entry:

*September 22*

*A convoy of some thirty bateaux arrived with M. Bleury, who is the head of the ferrying service. Because of this convoy we are now provisioned up to the tenth of the month. M. de Vaudreuil proposes to form a detachment of two thousand men to engage the enemy in combat in the Canadian manner. I do not know what bait can make people leave a fort who are determined to stay shut up in it, and come out into the woods to fight Canadian style. Our general seems to me to pursue a wiser course; that of not exposing himself to a material set-back or the embarrassment of an enterprise which, undertaken with éclat and ending in nothing, would rate as a defeat in the eyes of friendly and enemy Indians. . . .*

*At two o'clock nine Indians, who left a day before the big detachment, returned with a scalp taken at Fort William Henry. The Indians are of the Six Nations. They left, and we have here not more than about sixty Indians: Iroquois, Abna-*

*kis, and Amalecites. These last are Abnakis established on the
River St. Jean.*

*The news from La Belle Rivière is good . . . The Chevalier
de Villiers has taken Fort Granville, sixty miles from Philadelphia. In this fort there was a garrison of sixty men and
supplies for six months. The Indians continue to carry consternation into Virginia, Pennsylvania, Maryland and Carolina. Although they today have more than one hundred
leagues to go to find scalps to lift, this distance does not
stop them. The Delawares have burned one of the prisoners
taken at Fort Granville to punish him for having several
years before assassinated one of his comrades in order to
marry his widow. The English have enlisted one thousand
men to paint themselves like Indians and make raids into this
country.*

*Today there arrived a reinforcement of twenty-four Iro-
quois and Nipissing Indians, led by several officers of colony
troops. . . .*

## [ September 30, 1756—Thursday ]

Whether or not their older brother Tom was still alive,
George, James and Simon Girty had no idea. For that
matter, even their mother and their little half-brother, John
Turner, might be dead now. There was no way of knowing.
And where the three themselves were concerned, this was
their last time together and they reassured themselves by
telling each other that everything would be all right, that
they'd make out just fine and be together again sometime.

Not one of the boys believed it—not in light of the events
that had taken place here at Kittanning since the torture
death of their step-father.

Surprisingly, after the wrath and cruelty of the Delaware
chief, Tewea—Captain Jacobs—had been vented on the elder
John Turner, he had turned almost cordial to the rest of the
Girtys. The boys had been fed well enough, they had been
given loincloths to wear, feathers had been attached to their
hair and their faces painted until they looked considerably
like Delawares themselves.

It was about the middle of August that they had last seen
their mother and half-brother. A segment of the party that
had brought them here to Kittanning after destroying Fort
Granville was from the village of Tahode, south and west of
Fort Duquesne. Wishing now to return home, they had taken

481

their share of the prisoners, including Mary Girty Turner and her young son.

For now, however, the Girty boys had been kept at Kittanning and they, along with the other remaining prisoners, had been given chores to do. They had taken their share of kicks and cuffings from the Indians, but things were not really as bad as they had anticipated. All four, in fact—Tom, Simon, James and George—were already picking up quite an Indian vocabulary; enough to make themselves reasonably understood and, to some degree, to understand what the Indians were saying.

And then had come the night of September 8.

With the first faint glimmerings of dawn, just as the fires were being rebuilt and the village awakening, there was a sudden explosion of gunfire, followed by screams from both the squaws and the white women captives, along with hoarse yells from the men. Only a minute or so before, Tom Girty had ambled sleepily into the woods to relieve himself and at the first firing, Simon, James and George had been snatched by two warriors each and hustled toward the river. Behind them a wild fight was going on and plumes of smoke were already billowing upward in the calm air from the fires that had been set in the buildings.

The greater majority of the Indians thrashed their way across the Allegheny at a waist-deep fording place and, from under cover on the other side, watched their companions still coming and waited for the attackers to follow them into the river, where they could then be picked off with ease.

But these attackers were not so foolish. They were a party of three hundred men—mostly frontiersmen, but with a scattering of regular soldiers and militia—from Fort Shirley to the east of the Susquehanna. They were led here by Lieutenant Colonel John Armstrong, brother of the dead Lieutenant Edward Armstrong of Fort Granville. Lieutenant Colonel Armstrong[20] had prevailed on Governor Morris, after the destruction of Fort Granville, to let him set up the expedition against this Indian town from whence so many attacks against the Pennsylvania settlements originated.

A good number of the Delawares, including Chief Tewea, had stayed in the village, barricading themselves in the log huts and cabins that made up the village. The battle was a hot one, lasting two or three hours. Armstrong caught a bullet in his shoulder and a number of his men were likewise wounded or killed, but the Delawares suffered worse. Cabin by cabin the village was set afire, including the structure within which Tewea was holed up. When the flames became too hot, he attempted to squeeze out of the window of a loft, but was hit by a half-dozen bullets at once and died on the spot, half in and half out. With cheers the soldiers and frontiersmen watched his body blacken and then split as the flames roared around him.

Fearful that the Indians might be able to mount a quick retaliatory attack against them from the other villages, Armstrong's army, with thirteen men wounded, pulled away and disappeared, leaving behind seventeen of their own dead and taking with them eleven liberated prisoners.

One of them was Thomas Girty.

For the rest of the day and night, the three Girty boys and other captives, along with the remaining Indians, kept to the woods on the west side of the Allegheny, themselves fearful of going back lest the English have another ambush prepared for them. Early in the morning, however, a party of Canadians and several French officers from Fort Duquesne arrived and the Delawares and their captives recrossed to the village site.

There was not much left of Kittanning and there were thirty Indian bodies scattered about in addition to the seventeen dead whites. The Indians that had not been roasted to death in their cabins but had been killed outside had all been scalped and the mournful cries of the squaws were raised as their bodies were gathered and prepared for burial. A touch of retaliation was made by the squaws who scalped and mutilated the dead whites, but it was little real satisfaction.

It was while the Indians were thus engaged that, unable to take the strain any longer, one of the women captives from Fort Granville—a not unattractive widow of about forty named Sarah Lawton—managed to slip away into the woods in a desperate effort to catch up with Armstrong's party and reach safety. She didn't make it. Late that evening the Indians had discovered her absence and in the following morning they set out on her trail. Two days passed before they returned with her on a long rawhide tether tight around her throat, her buttocks badly welted from switchings received since her recapture and her nude body badly bruised and bloody from scratches she suffered as she had run and stumbled wildly through the underbrush in her vain attempt to escape.

With methodical brutality, as the Frenchmen and Canadians watched with approval, the Delawares staked her out on her back in spread-eagled fashion and then turned her over

483

to the squaws whose men had been slain in Armstrong's raid.

It was then about nine o'clock in the morning. Sarah Lawton's eyes bulged and her mouth worked, but the only sound that issued from her was a weird mewing cry barely audible. For the better part of the first hour then, the squaws amused themselves by placing burning splinters of wood on her flesh and laughed as she writhed and struggled to dislodge them.

Next, while shrill screams issued from her, the squaws shoved knives into the soles of her feet until the points projected through the top of the arch, then ripped them out through the flesh in the direction of her toes. They let her rest for a short while after that and her screams dwindled away to an inchoate croaking while the ragged remains of her feet jiggled from the uncontrollable trembling of her legs. There was remarkably little blood, as if the squaws had known just exactly where to cut so that no major arteries were severed causing her to bleed to death.

The respite was not long. A heavy squaw—wife of the late Chief Tewea—came back to her now, knelt beside her and, as if anticipating what the Indian woman meant to do, Sarah Lawton's screams once again rent the air. The squaw leaned over and in turn bit off the captive's nipples, spitting them into her hand and then forcing them into the mouth of the struggling white woman until she was forced to swallow them.

Hour after hour the tortures continued and, incredibly, Sarah Lawton never lost consciousness. Sometime after noon her screaming ended and only a strangled groaning still issued from her mouth. When at one point she tried to close her eyes to keep from seeing what was coming next, her eyelids were cut off. Her scalp was removed expertly and one by one her fingers were cut off, followed by ears and nose, and yet she lived.

Toward later afternoon her struggles were becoming decidedly weaker and she hardly writhed at all anymore when burning sticks were placed against her skin or bare skull. At last, just as the sun was beginning to sink, Tewea's squaw took a burning pole from the fire, its end pointed and glowing, touched it to the captive's croth and then lunged forward, thrusting it far inside her.

For the last time, Sarah Lawton screamed.

Her body jerked convulsively and her wrists and ankles strained against the rawhide sinews which bound them to stakes. One of the French officers, his face pale and set, now

484

got to his feet, walked to the still-living remains of what had once been a human being, held his musket to her forehead and mercifully blew her brains out.

In the days that followed there was, understandably, little desire in the remaining captives to attempt escape. And now, today, the site of Kittanning was being abandoned. Having been attacked and defeated here, the Indians would never establish permanent residence again. All that remained before they went their separate ways was an equitable distribution of the English loot and captives remaining in the village.

Simon, aged fifteen, was taken for adoption by the Senecas. He would go with them to their village called Cattaraugus.[21] Thirteen-year-old James was to become a Shawnee and live with them at a village on the Scioto River in the Ohio country.[22] George, eleven, became the property of the Delawares, to go with them to their principal village of Goschachgunk[23] at the forks of the Muskingum River, also in the Ohio country.

They said their farewells and parted, absolutely certain they would never meet again.

## [ October 8, 1756—Friday ]

It looked to Captain Louis Bougainville as if the season was altogether too far advanced now to even consider carrying on any more campaigns and he wished the order would soon be given to return to Montreal or Quebec for the winter. Those cities did not have a great deal to offer, but certainly they were a considerable improvement over this post of Fort Carillon. Work was still progressing on the place, but only at a snail's pace and Bougainville grinned as he thought of how angry Montcalm became every time he inspected and found substantially less work completed than he had expected.

When, just a couple of weeks ago, the general had asked him to briefly sketch out in writing his own personal feelings in regard to the campaign, Bougainville had complied and turned in a statement that he hoped would encourage the Marquis to call it quits for the year. He had written:

*Sir: Whatever the plans and movements of the English may be in these regions, it seems to me that with the season being much advanced, the campaign—which has been very brilliant, since we have had only great success without any loss on our part—is drawing to the end and it is possible that peace could be made this year. Even should this not yet be*

485

*considered, the improvement of the works of Fort Carillon being an important objective, we should not attempt any offensive act at the end of Lake George, unless it is only a matter of a little post easy to seize. Any material check of our troops would be of the greatest consequence and would perhaps render us unable to carry out next year's campaign. Men are scarce here and more precious than one can say.*

Montcalm had seemed pleased at his comments, but the days had passed and the general had still made no decision to end the campaign. Bougainville felt sure that he would soon, and that the principal reason Montcalm was extending his stay here was to speed up as much as possible the work on the fortifications.

"And that," Bougainville muttered sardonically to himself, "is something God Almighty Himself probably couldn't do here."

He grunted with exasperation and set himself to writing the day's affairs in his journal:

*October 8*

*Rainy day, the work interrupted. These works go very slowly. The soldiers—corrupted by the great amount of money (since they are given extra pay for working on the fort), by the example of the Indians and Canadians, breathing an air permeated with independence—work indolently. M. de Lotbinière, relative of Governor Vaudreuil, and our chief engineer here, is almost never at the works. It is not to his interest that the fort should be completed quickly. He has the exclusive privilege of selling wine, and all the money of the workmen, and even the pay of the soldiers, goes to his canteen. . . . It is an odd thing, this engineer gives the workers certificates which have the value of money, without anyone controlling their issue, and all of these certificates come back to him. . . .*

*The Indians go hunting every day, proof that the English Indians have gone back to their villages. When these Indians believe themselves safe from attack, there certainly is no danger to fear. Those who remain here get drunk and, since they have lost all their spirit, everything is permitted them.*

Increasingly, Bougainville knew, he was becoming strongly opinionated about the war and felt himself disagreeing to some degree with practically every action taken by Governor Vaudreuil. This was particularly true because it seemed that

Vaudreuil deliberately went out of his way to make decisions which greatly affected those of Montcalm, yet without even having the decency to inform the general, but rather letting him find out through rumor. It was as if Vaudreuil was making a conscious effort to make Montcalm look bad. Now Bougainville, concerned about this, continued:

*I do not believe that it is a good policy in the case of a defensive such as we are conducting today to send the army at any one time a large number of Indians, such as M. de Vaudreuil sent us the end of last month. They gather together in mobs, argue among themselves, deliberate slowly and all want to go together to make a strike and at the same place, because they prefer big war parties.*

*Between the resolution made and the action taken there passes considerable time. Sometimes one nation stops the march, sometimes another. Everybody must have time to get drunk, and their food consumption is enormous. At last they get started, and once they have struck—have taken only a single scalp or one prisoner—back they come and are off again for their villages. Then for a considerable time the army is without Indians. Each one does well for himself, but the operation of the war suffers, for in the end they are a necessary evil. It would be better to have on hand only a specified number of these mosquitoes, who would be relieved by others, so that we would always have some on hand. In general, it does not seem to me that we are getting all the use we can out of these Indians. With less servile compliance for their caprices, less respect for the silly things they do, less outward indifference toward the service expected of them, one would accustom them to consideration toward the French, to obedience, I would say even to a kind of subordination. Finally, if they believe they can be dispensed with, they should seek to make themselves of value through real services. Some companies of volunteers who, through living in the woods would know them and serve as guides, would be a marvelous spur to prick the honor of these barbarians, for self-love is everything, and pride is the only wealth of every Indian.*

*The commander at Presque Isle wrote that the news of the taking of Oswego created a sensation in the Western country, that a great number of Indians appeared, full of ardor to come next season and hit the English. It is especially of the Indians that he speaks truth: DONEC ERIS FELIX, MUL-*

*TOS NUMERABIS AMICOS. TEMPORA SI FUERINT NUBILA, SOLUS ERIS.*[24]

[ *December 21, 1756—Tuesday* ]

*Fear!*

Throughout the English Colonies it spread. Just about everything had gone wrong for them. Excepting only the Kittanning skirmish, not since Sir William Johnson's army had defeated the attacking French and Indians at the Lake George camp had the English made any gains and, in fact, they had taken terrible losses.

Suddenly, on almost all fronts, the English frontier had been pushed back great distances. The toehold at the Forks of the Oho had been lost with Braddock's defeat, and the hoped-for alliance with the Delawares and Shawnees shattered by the Pennsylvanians themselves. Thrust back had been the settlers who had begun to plant roots in the valleys of the Monongahela and the Youghiogheny and Allegheny. Even the settlements close to the Susquehanna River were driven back step by bloody step, out of the valleys of the Juniata River and Sherman Creek and even far to the east of the Susquehanna Valley. Settlers high up on the Potomac had been driven in, and the waters of the Shenandoah were regularly stained with blood.

In Maryland, on the Salisbury Plains at the mouth of Conococheague Creek,[25] a group of men, women and children had stood with bowed heads on August 20 while one of their fellow settlers had been buried, minus his scalp. And even as the prayers were being uttered, a hail of bullets caught them all in a cross fire from surrounding woods. Fifteen were killed in the first moment and another fifteen wounded. The Indians were driven off, but the subsequent burial was a larger and much more tragic affair. And when it was completed, the settlement was abandoned and the refugees bumped along in rickety wagons or limped along on homemade crutches toward the east, while behind them, before they had gone two miles, the sky was blackened by the smoke of their cabins being destroyed.

Worst of all, perhaps, the spearhead of penetration which had given the English access to the Great Lakes was gone, thrust back farther than anyone dreamed it could have been. Not only Fort Oswego and Fort Ontario and Fort George lost to them, but even the Great Carrying Place and the forts named Williams and Bull. The Mohawk Valley frontier no longer took in virtually the whole length of that river. Now it was the essentially unprotected, terrified little settlement of German Flats[26] just above Fort Johnson that had unwillingly become the westernmost outpost of English penetration in New York.

Fort Johnson itself was nothing to brag about as a defensive installation. If, as the story had it—a story which William Johnson strongly doubted—the French were indeed on their march down the Mohawk Valley as Colonel Daniel Webb had declared, then the danger was extreme. German Flats would be wiped out with practically no effort and Fort Johnson was defenseless against artillery. True, a small blockhouse had been built on the nearby swell of a knoll, but it was nothing more than a lookout post manned constantly by a single sentry whose instructions were simple: if the enemy were spotted, he was merely to fire his rifle once as a signal and then abandon his post and dash for the fort.

This fort, which incorporated the large residence, was a strange affair. Two blockhouses were connected by a façade which William liked to call a "curtain," and the walls from each of them, enclosing the house, went to the river's edge. A low, covered walkway protruded outward from the west wall a considerable distance so that rifle fire from its portholes could keep attackers away from the walls proper. The other two walls could similarly be protected from the blockhouses. Most of the windows of Johnson's residence had been either entirely bricked or else reduced to little more than loopholes for rifle fire.

A small platoon of regulars under a lieutenant had been assigned duty there previously by General Shirley, and Johnson had posted written orders they were to follow in case the French or Indians came:

IN CASE OF ATTACK, THE BASTIONS TO BE PROPERLY MANNED, THE CURTAINS ALSO, THERE MIXING SOME OF MY PEOPLE WITH YOURS. THE REMAINDER OF MY PEOPLE TO MAN THE DWELLING HOUSE AND FIGHT FROM THENCE, MAKING USE OF THE FOUR WALL PIECES AND MUSQUETOONS OUT OF THE WINDOW FITTED FOR THEM. WHENEVER THE WARNING SHOT IS GIVEN BY THE ADVANCE SENTRY, EVERYONE IS TO RUN IMMEDIATELY FROM THE OTHER HOUSES, INDIAN SHEDS, MILL, OR WHEREVER, TO THE RESIDENCE. AT THAT ALARM BY THE ADVANCE SENTRY YOU WILL ORDER

*THREE PATEREROES[27] TO BE IMMEDIATELY FIRED,
THAT BEING THE SIGNAL I HAVE GIVEN THE MO-
HAWKS; AND ON THEIR APPROACH NEAR THE
FORT, WHEN CHALLENGED, THEY ARE TO ANSWER
"GEORGE" AS DISTINCT AS THEY CAN; THEN TO
BE ADMITTED IF PRACTICABLE. WHEN THERE ARE
NO INDIANS HERE, THE GATES TO BE LOCKED AT
EIGHT O'CLOCK IN THE EVENING AND OPENED AT
SIX IN THE MORNING, FIRST LOOKING AROUND
TO SEE THAT ALL IS SAFE AND CLEAR.*
                                    *W. JOHNSON*

At Albany the citizens were stunned with the news of the
fall of Oswego and immediately orders went out from John
Campbell to Fort Edward and Fort William Henry to fully
prepare for defensive rather than offensive operation. Plans
for attack against Fort Carillon were put in abeyance and
now everyone waited fearfully for the swarm of French reported by Webb to be on the way; a force rumored to be so
much better than the English forces that they would sweep
them aside, destroy Fort Johnson and Fort William Henry
and Fort Edward; a force that would soon be occupying
Schenectady and Albany and preparing to launch itself from
there against New York City itself!

The French army did not come. Reports from the spies
showed that immediately after Oswego, Montcalm had
speedily returned his army to Montreal, picked up reinforcements and then, without further pause, had returned to Fort
Carillon at the Ticonderoga Narrows. But here, he and his
force had stopped to wait for the English attack, just as the
English were waiting for them. Late summer became autumn
and then early winter and the time for launching campaigns
was over for the year.

But all fall from Lake Champlain had come party after
party of Indians to assault and harass the New York frontier;
nor were these merely the Caughnawagas and Abnakis, the
Nipissings and Algonkins that had done so from there before.
Now, usually led by French or Canadian officers—such as
Charles Michel de Langlade—the Indians included large
numbers of Ottawas and Hurons, Chippewas and Menominees, a scattering of Potawatomies and Winnebagoes and
Peorias, and even some of the Delawares and Shawnees who
had spread out from the Virginia-Pennsylvania frontier to
join those from the north.

The latter two tribes had returned to Venango and Kittanning and Fort Duquesne and instead of the peace which William Johnson had offered them and they had accepted, they found a sharp step-up of the war and a high bounty placed on their scalps, and their fury was such that they tossed down the wampum belts William had given them and ground them into the dirt under their heels.

Nor were all these harassing attacks any more just the work of small parties of a dozen to twenty or thirty Indians, especially on the New York frontier. Actual armies of them came and created ever-increasing havoc and terror. One of these had been a party of four hundred Indians of nine different tribes of the north and west, along with a hundred Canadians under Captains Marin and Perière and Bougainville. They slipped soundlessly to the south and almost in the shadow of Fort William Henry—less than three miles from it—ambushed a detachment of soldiers under Captain William Hodges and wiped it out.

His lordship, John Campbell, becoming the brunt of considerable criticism, sought and found the perfect scapegoat for everything that had gone wrong—Major General William Shirley, now sitting on his hands in Boston. It was, the Earl of Loudoun declared, because he had followed the war plans already set in motion by Shirley that Oswego had been lost and that the planned attack against Fort Carillon failed to materialize. He immediately ordered Shirley back to England, to leave at once, giving the unfortunate commander little time or opportunity to reply to the charges lodged against him.[28]

It was Ben Franklin who took it upon himself to champion the deposed general. "He would, in my opinion," the Pennsylvania legislator said, "if continued in place, have made a much better campaign than that of Loudoun, which was frivolous, expensive, and disgraceful to our nation beyond conception. For though Shirley was not bred a soldier, he was sensible and sagacious in himself, and attentive to good advice from others, capable of forming judicious plans and quick and active in carrying them into execution."

Even the attacks of the Canadian and Indian parties dwindled away as autumn became bitter cold winter. At last Rogers's Rangers reported that Montcalm was beginning to move his army out of Fort Carillon for the winter return to Montreal and Quebec. John Campbell's ten thousand men who had been waiting so long at Forts Edward and William Henry braced themselves for the order that would march them north to fall upon and take with ease the small winter garrisons of both Fort Carillon and Fort St. Frederic.

The orders came ... but not for attack. The English troops were being withdrawn, with the exception of small garrisons, to be billeted in New York and Philadelphia and Boston until the next season's campaign should begin. Although the privates were given mean quarters in hastily erected barracks in these cities, the officers were on their own in finding someplace to stay. Campbell issued orders to the mayors of the cities to find lodging for them in private homes. Already having become quite an unpopular figure in America, the Earl of Loudoun did not endear himself with this demand. When the mayors balked, Campbell exploded with a wrath which indicated how greatly the recent criticisms had eaten into him.

"God damn my blood!" he shouted to the complaining Mayor Cruger of New York. "If you do not billet my officers upon free quarters this day, I'll order here all the troops in North America and billet them myself upon this city!"

So at last all the army was settled, but there was remarkably little laughter in the English Colonies this winter.

[ *December 31, 1756—Friday* ]

Never before had so many Indians congregated in Montreal.

Ten, fifteen, perhaps twenty tribes were represented here and they were practically falling over each other in their eagerness to serve the French against the English. Those who had been loyal to the French all along were inspired by the French successes and boasted to the other tribes of their wisdom in choosing friends. Those who had been lukewarm to the French and had only helped them on occasion, now became solid allies. Those who had wavered in allegiance were now pushed over the brink onto the French side, and those who had stood with the English against them had grown afraid and sent deputations to Governor Vaudreuil to ask his forgiveness for having been blinded and deceived.

Among these latter were chiefs who formed an official delegation from the Iroquois League, empowered by the League to speak for it. They presented themselves to Vaudreuil at the council and the governor rose triumphantly to the occasion.

"Men of the Six Nations," he said loudly, so all the other tribal translators could render his words to the language of the various peoples gathered here, "where now are your friends? Where now are your devotions? Early in the summer you came to see me for talks, but the talks came to nothing and you held yourselves off from me. Search your minds for the words I spoke to you that day. Remember that I said, 'Children, continue not to fear Colonel Johnson; do not listen to his evil counsel: labor only at good business and you will always be quiet on your mats.' That is what I told you then, but your reply was to show me the medals Colonel Johnson had given you to wear around your necks, which tied you to foolish promises made to him. And where now are the promises he made to you? Did he not promise you that the English would destroy the French? Look around you, children—are we destroyed? Did he not promise you that you would be given right for wrong in the matter of your lands? And what has happened? No redress has been made to you of any kind. Did he not tell you that the forts built on your lands would be yours? How many of those forts are now yours? Men of the Six Nations, how can your ears hear such things without your stomachs becoming sick?"

The Indians murmured as he paused, some of them nodding their heads and others fingering the large bronze medallions still hung around their necks by lengths of red-dyed rawhide thongs. Nor was it lost on any of the assemblage that Vaudreuil had addressed them twice as "children," which at any other time would have been taken as a great insult, but which now they were accepting with docility. Not wishing to give them time to dwell on this, Vaudreuil raised his arms and they quieted, and now his features grew harsh and his voice cold as he continued:

"How many times, Brothers, have the English told you that compared to their power the French are nothings? I have laid Oswego in ashes and the English quail before me. Why do you nourish serpents to your breasts when they mean only to enslave you? The Master of Life permitted me to pull down their forts and their pride; He wished me to humble them and make the English admit that the French will always be the victors.

"Hear me now, Brothers, for this is the last I will say: If the Iroquois allow the English to rebuild even the tiniest post at Oswego or anywhere else in the vicinity of Lake Ontario or throughout the Iroquois country, we and our Indian allies here will attack you! You can no more beseech me as formerly, not to stain those lands with blood. I will not listen to you!"

There was a loud clamor of assent from the assembled

Indians. Vaudreuil stepped down, walked to the Iroquois delegates and handed them some French medallions. Immediately another clamor arose: the Iroquois delegation had risen as one, removed from around their necks the medallions Sir William Johnson had given them at the Onondaga council, threw them on the ground and now stamped on them. Following this they donned the new ones they had just been given. And their reply to Pierre Vaudreuil was unanimous:

"We will nevermore lift our tomahawks against the army or the people of the French governor, who is the Devourer of Villages!"

# CHAPTER IX

[*February 1, 1757—Tuesday*]

IN the gloom which settled so ominously over the English troops left to garrison the outposts of Fort Edward and Fort William Henry for the winter, there were only two rays of light. One of these emanated from the intrepid Robert Rogers and his Rangers who, when others of the garrison at Fort Edward feared going into the surrounding forest for firewood, regularly continued patrols deep into enemy territory with a dash which left everyone amazed—French, Indians and English alike.

The other emanated from Sir William Johnson, who was seemingly always ready to march at a moment's notice to bring help wherever needed. A case in point occurred during the second week of January when word reached him at his home on the Mohawk that a large French force was sliding along the frozen length of Lake George to attack Fort William Henry. Immediately William had roused the sixty Mohawks who had taken up quasi-residence in the shed provided for them at Fort Johnson and asked for someone to carry the war belt upstream to Canajoharie in order to get a large number of Mohawks of that upper village to go with him. But the result of the switch in allegiance of the greater majority of the Iroquois to a strongly pro-French leaning, if not an outright alliance, made them leery of carrying any English war belts. When he danced the war dance and sang the war chant and wound up asking these sixty to go with him and support their brother, even then they were noncommittal.

"We will go along with you, Warraghiyagey," was the answer, "to see what becomes of you. Whether or not we will fight beside you remains yet to be seen." Not even Degonwadonti, with all the influence she had among them, could wrest from them more of a promise than this.

William would far rather have just stayed home and dawdled in bed with this beautiful Mohawk woman who had cured him of his fever and cough and was now working on curing him, with an Iroquois remedy, of the syphilis that was beginning to make his life miserable.[1] The fact that he had this venereal disease did not, however, stop her from providing full satisfaction for him whenever he wished it, which was often. At the moment, however, his responsibilities had to take precedence, and so William disgustedly turned next to the Mohawk Valley militia from Schenectady to German Flats with his appeal, and here he was more successful.

Twelve hundred men turned out to help and in four days of forced marches through the swirling snow and bitter cold, they arrived at Fort William Henry, only to learn that it had all been a false alarm. Apologetically, William sent the militia and Indians home with the promise to pay each man more than adequately for his help, and then stayed on himself at the place where he had won such great honors.

The post was now occupied by four hundred English regulars under command of Major William Eyre, his former artillery captain. It was a decidedly dispirited garrison, with upwards of half the men sick of dysentery or smallpox and those who were still physically well at a dangerously low ebb of morale. William's arrival had the effect of cheering them considerably. It was nice to know that someone not only remembered they were there, but would come to their aid if they were endangered. Even Major Eyre was almost pathetically grateful and it was for his benefit mainly that William decided to stay on here for at least a couple of weeks, perhaps longer.

The exploits of Robert Rogers and his men continued to be the talk of the garrison. Not a man there at Fort William Henry did not admire what that elite group of Rangers had done and was doing—and not a man at the fort ever really expected him to return whenever he set out on one of his missions. Yet, each time he had come back, usually having penetrated to Fort Carillon and often as far as Fort St. Frederic at Crown Point, to spy, to harass and, if possible, to engage small parties of Frenchmen and return with their scalps or with prisoners.

Since late last summer the Rangers had made their headquarters—at orders from John Campbell—on a forty-acre island in the Hudson, adjacent to Fort Edward. From here he ran regular scouting patrols fairly close in, to watch for the dreaded French attack which everyone was sure was coming. When it failed to come, Rogers maintained his island base but expanded his movements and soon was infiltrating again to within shouting distance of the French forts on Lake Champlain.

Even the regulars—officers and men alike—who generally looked upon the provincials with undisguised contempt and disgust, shook their heads in wonder and admiration for this New Hampshire captain and his men. General Abercromby, for example, who considered the provincial soldier the devil's own invention placed on earth to plague him with ineffectiveness, took great pleasure in the reports, as well as the scalps and prisoners, brought back by Rogers. The reports themselves were a delight in their understatement of the dangers faced by the Rangers and the boldness with which they performed their missions. A patrol they had taken last October, from which they had returned with a terrified French soldier as prisoner, was a case in point. For days Rogers and his men had lain in ambush close to Fort Carillon without any luck until Rogers decided to force the issue. As he stated it in his report:

*I at length discovered two men, sentries to the picket guard of the French army, one of which was posted in the road that leads from the fort to the woods; I took five of my party, and marched directly down the road in the middle of the day, till we were challenged by the sentry. I answered by French, signifying that we were friends; the sentry was thereby deceived, till I came close to him, when, perceiving his mistake, in great surprise he called, "Qui êtes vous?" I answered, "Rogers," and led him from his post in great haste, cutting his breeches and coat from him, that he might march with greater ease and expedition.*

It became something of a test of valor for officers of the regulars to volunteer to go out on scouting expeditions with the Rangers and, without exception, they came back marveling at the competence of that company in the woods. Even General Abercromby's nephew, Captain James Abercromby, not to be outdone by his fellows, went out with Rogers a time or two.

Now, with the rumored threat of the French attack dispelled, Rogers was ordered out on another scout of Fort Carillon. He and his first officer, Lieutenant John Stark, arrived at Fort William Henry from Fort Edward with fifty of the Rangers, and Rogers immediately requested of Major Eyre an additional thirty-three men to go along. The reinforcement was provided—under Captain Thomas Speakman, who was to be second-in-command—and Rogers led the party out of Fort William Henry late in the afternoon of January 17.

Each man carried with him, in a pack over his left shoulder, a food ration for two weeks and ammunition enough for sixty shots, plus a knife and tomahawk. Snowshoes were strapped to their backs and from each right shoulder was slung a powder horn and a canteen filled with diluted rum. Every man wore heavy mittens attached by cords up the sleeves to prevent their loss which could, if it happened, mean the loss of fingers from freezing. Two blankets were worn as the Indians wore them at this season, draped over the head in monk fashion and anchored inside their belts. At the lakeshore, each man strapped on a pair of ice skates and then, with their guns in hand, slid off in rapid single file to the north.

Well into the night they traveled and when camp was made, they were about halfway down the northward length of the lake at a narrow portion, with Tongue Mountain jutting up along the western shore. It had been treacherous skating in the darkness and eleven men were injured from severe falls. At the first light of dawn, these eleven were sent back to the fort while Rogers led the main party on. The weather had warmed considerably and almost a score of miles farther north they began hitting ice that looked dangerous to their leader, so he ordered the skates removed and the journey continued on snowshoes via land.

It was a rough way to travel, especially for the regulars from Fort William Henry, none with much snowshoe experience. By evening, January 19, however, they had pitched camp some five miles to the north of Fort Carillon and three miles west of Lake Champlain. In the morning a dismal drizzle was falling and they were forced to light concealed fires to dry out their wet muskets. As soon as this was done they turned eastward and came out on Lake Champlain's west shore between Fort St. Frederic and Fort Carillon.[2]

Despite the unfavorable conditions for travel on the ice, right away they saw two French horse-drawn sleighs coming north from the latter fort. Rogers immediately sent John Stark with a party to cut off progress to the north, ordered Tom Speakman to hold the center for the attack and himself took a group of Rangers south to cut in behind them and prevent the retreat of their quarry when the attack was begun. Rogers let the two sleighs approach until they were within a quarter mile of him when, following them, he spotted three more sleighs coming. Instantly he sent off two runners to tell Stark to let the first pair pass, but it was too late. By the time the runners got to his position, Stark and his men were already rushing out onto the lake to attack. There was nothing to do but bull ahead with the plan and so Rogers and his men themselves burst from cover.

At sight of Stark's men far ahead, the two leading sleighs and a third that had almost caught up to them slid to a halt almost in front of Rogers and his men, who plunged upon them at once and captured them, along with six horses and seven of the enemy. Three of the mounted French guards, however, managed to wheel and race away toward the other sleighs. The Rangers pursued a short distance on foot, but it was hopeless. At a signal from the three Frenchmen, the oncoming sleighs spun about and virtually flew across the ice back to Fort Carillon.

Rogers called off his men and all three of his divisions reassembled in the woods. Here the seven prisoners were separately questioned. Their individual stories jibed in the main . . . and were frightening. Besides the garrison of three hundred fifty regulars at Fort Carillon, a couple of hundred Canadians and forty-five Abnakis and Algonkins had just arrived. Another fifty Nipissings were expected momentarily.

Rogers grimaced. There was now every reason to believe that Captain Lusignan, the winter commandant at Fort Carillon, having been alerted by the returned guards and sleighs, would send out a force to try to cut them off from retreat back to Fort William Henry. At once Rogers placed each of the prisoners with an individual Ranger who was ordered to kill the man without hesitation if they were attacked, rather than to allow him to be rescued and give the enemy information about them. The whole party then returned to their camp of the night before. They rekindled their fires, dried out their slippery muskets and began a forced march through wet and sloppy snow which was generally knee-deep. Rogers and Lieutenant Kennedy were leading the first of the three segments, Speakman the second and Stark the third.

It was extremely hard going at best, the snow clinging wetly at each step, and soon all of them were gasping for breath as they pressed on, hoping desperately to avoid being cut off by an enemy detachment. And, for a long while at least, it appeared they were successful. They streamed up a narrow valley between ridges closing in from both sides and by two o'clock in the afternoon had almost reached the end of it when there was a sudden burst of gunfire from their left.

Lieutenant Kennedy and a private named Gardner fell dead and three others were wounded: another private named Eggars, who took a bullet through the arm; a third private, Thomas Brown, who was shot through the body, but still managed to retain control of the prisoner he was charged with; and Rogers himself, who was sent sprawling in the snow by a ball which grazed his head and momentarily dazed him.

Even as the attacking Indians, Canadians and a few French regulars continued their firing from ambush, Rogers struggled back to his feet, ordered the prisoners killed and the Rangers themselves to scatter and make it as best they could to the opposite ridge where they would re-form and hold their ground. A glance at the enemy now spilling out of the woods made him sure that the attacking force numbered no less than two hundred fifty men.

Private Thomas Brown swung his tomahawk even as Rogers was speaking, burying it in the skull of his prisoner. The French soldier fell without a cry and Brown struggled painfully through the snow toward the ridge until he spied a huge boulder. He ran for it in order to take advantage of the protection it would offer, where he could rest for a moment and try to bind his wound so he wouldn't bleed to death. As luck would have it, he walked straight into a pair of Abnakis coming from behind it.

Both of the Indians jerked up their guns to fire at him. In a violent movement, Brown threw himself backwards full length into the deep snow, snapping both his snowshoes in the process, but avoiding the two musket balls which whistled over his head. One of the Indians threw a tomahawk at him, but missed. Brown scrambled about frantically, jerking off the broken snowshoes and losing his own footwear in the process. He brought his gun to bear but the Indians, their own weapons empty, leaped behind the big rock and raced down a slope on the other side.

Brown regained his feet and thrashed away barefoot through the snow, finally reaching the ridge and joining Rogers and the men already there. Here Rogers had drawn them together into a line—those that had not been cut off from following the main retreat—and this line was putting down a hot fire, time after time repulsing the enemy as he tried to advance. Brown flopped behind a log and began shooting with the others. He managed to get off seven shots and was reloading for the eighth when a ball struck his gun at the lock, broke it in half and sent the pieces spinning from stunned fingers. Another ball slammed with devastating impact into his knee and a few moments after that he was wounded a third time when a bullet crashed through his shoulder. With a concerted effort, he dragged himself along on his stomach considerably to the rear of Rogers's party.

Hour after hour the fight continued, sometimes with furious firing, sometimes only sporadic poppings. At about sunset a bullet zinged into the Rangers' lines and hit Rogers. The ball passed through his wrist and gouged a painful furrow in the palm of his hand. The commander could now no longer load and fire, but he kept rallying his men, moving among them and encouraging them.

As dusk was deepening the firing ended and a weird stillness settled over the area. Suddenly a loud call in English came from the French and Indian force.

"Rogers! Captain Robert Rogers! You and your Rangers give yourselves up. We promise you quarter if you give up now. You will be treated with mercy and kindness. It would be a pity for so many brave men to be lost."

"Go right straight to hell!" Rogers shouted back, and his men cheered.

In a moment the voice called again: "We have great esteem for your ability, Rogers, but even you must see that all is lost now. We warn you, give up! We have a reinforcement on the way now. They'll be here any moment and if you don't give up now, we'll cut you to pieces in the morning."

Rogers laughed derisively. "Any cuttin' to be done, by God, we'll be the ones to do it."

Private Brown, in the meanwhile had continued his crawl to the rear until he encountered and joined two other wounded men. One of them was one of the Fort William Henry regulars who had volunteered to come along. His name was Baker and he was wounded in the shoulder. The other was Captain Thomas Speakman, who had been shot seriously, low in the stomach. Figuring they were far enough behind the action to be relatively safe now, the three kindled a small fire and crouched around it. Brown's bare feet were like chunks of ice.

Toward the middle of the night they sensed that there was

an abnormal quiet and Brown became nervous. He felt that Rogers and the party might have slipped away under cover of the night, not knowing that he and these other two wounded men were here. Neither Speakman nor Baker were concerned, but the fear continued to mount in Brown and he told them he was going to go check. Using a branch as a crutch and gasping quietly at each step, he hobbled slowly into the darkness, but soon had to pause and lean against a tree in an effort to ease the pain emanating from his three wounds. Behind him he could still see the fire flickering and the two men lying beside it. Then he saw something else.

Several Indians rushed into the clearing and had the pair before they even realized anyone was nearby. Baker, able to walk, was dragged off screaming into the woods. Seeing that the officer was mortally wounded, however, the Indians merely scalped him alive and then went off into the darkness, leaving the captain lying there groaning.

After a few minutes Brown worked his way back to the campsite. He stepped close to Speakman, whose head raised slightly. The officer's eyes opened, blinking against the blood which was running down his face from the mutilated head. All around him the snow was stained with his blood.

"Brown, it's you! Oh my God, Brown, look what they've done to me. Oh, it hurts, it hurts! For God's sake, Brown, give me your tomahawk so I can kill myself."

Sickened, Brown shook his head. "No, Captain, I couldn't do that. I couldn't! Pray, Captain. You can't live much longer, Pray."

Speakman groaned and his head fell back on the snow. Brown thought he had died, but then the officer spoke again without opening his eyes.

"Brown, if ... if you live to get home ... tell my ... tell my wife how I died ... Tell her I ... was thinking of her ..."

His mouth moved some more, but Brown could hear no more. It was as if a curtain had been drawn around him, gradually shutting away sight and sound. He closed his eyes and fell unconscious beside the dying officer.

In the first light of dawn, a few tentative shots came from the French, but they went unanswered. Rogers and his men were gone. Immediately after full darkness had fallen, Rogers had called his officers together and the decision was made to disperse quietly, carrying between them those wounded who could not walk. No one knew of Speakman, Brown and Baker far to the rear. So swiftly and so quietly was the withdrawal made, that none of the enemy even realized they were leaving. When the French took the position and spread out in a search, the only Ranger they found still alive, though unconscious, was Private Thomas Brown.[3] He they carried back to Fort Carillon, after first decapitating the dead Captain Speakman in order to impale his head on a pole at the fort.

By morning, Rogers and his men had reached Lake George, but it was obvious now that they couldn't travel much farther without help. Rogers dispatched John Stark, along with two other unwounded Rangers, to push on at top speed for the fort and come back on the ice with a sleigh for the wounded. In the meantime, as best they could, Rogers and the others would follow.

Stark and his two men soon disappeared from sight and by nightfall Rogers and the wounded had made it back almost to Tongue Mountain again. Far behind in the gathering gloom they saw someone coming, frequently falling and apparently nearly done in. Two of the less severely wounded Rangers went back and within half an hour had returned with him between them. It was Sergeant Joshua Martin, who had been shot through the body and left for dead, but who had come around and somehow managed to follow the tracks in the snow.

In the morning Stark came back with a strong detachment of men and a large sled, onto which all of the wounded were placed, and the remainder of the trip to Fort William Henry was completed without further complication.

It had been a disastrous expedition, but not only for the Rangers. Of the seventy-four Rangers involved in the fight, thirteen had been killed, nine were wounded and seven taken prisoner. But so furiously had they fought that, in addition to the seven French prisoners who were killed, close to fifty French, Indians and Canadians were slain.

And today, along with several other of the more grievously wounded, Rogers was transported to Albany for treatment. But no one had any doubt that he would soon be back leading more patrols into the wilderness.

Official recognition of Rogers's expedition and battle came from Captain James Abercromby, speaking for his uncle, the general. To Rogers he wrote:

*I am heartily sorry for Spikeman[4] and Kennedy ... as likewise for the men you have lost, but it is impossible to play at bowls without meeting rubs. I regret not having been in the action, which Mayor Eyre so correctly describes as gallant behavior. I am certain it is better to die with the reputation of a brave man, fighting for his country in a good cause, than either shamefully running away to preserve one's life, or lingering out an old age, and dying in one's bed, without having done his country or King any service.*

*The General returns you and your men thanks for their behavior and has recommended both you and them strongly to My Lord Loudoun. Your behavior upon this late occasion entitles you to marks of your Lordship's favor and countenance. Your relation by way of journal is very modest.*

*You cannot imagine how all the ranks of the people here are pleased with your conduct, and your men's behavior; for my part, it is no more than I expected; I was so pleased with their appearance when I went out with them, that I took it for granted they would behave well whenever they met the enemy. When I returned, I reported them as such, and am glad they have answered my expectation.*

### [ March 29, 1757—Tuesday ]

Governor Pierre Vaudreuil could not have been more pleased with the news just brought him by courier; news which was now creating an electric effect throughout Montreal. He had known of the innuendos of nepotism cast his way because he had placed his brother, Rigaud, in a military command position. The fact that Rigaud had, at Oswego, done his part reasonably well had been a satisfaction to the governor, but now he was exultant.

Montcalm, he knew, had been coldly and quietly furious with him for attempting to put Rigaud on a level with, if not above, both General Lévis and Colonel Bourlamaque. He was even angrier, though, for Vaudreuil's having planned a strike against Fort William Henry and not even telling him about it until Rigaud was on the eve of departure.

"I am under the necessity, Monsieur de Vaudreuil," Montcalm had told him, "of communicating to you my reflections. I will not name any of the persons who, to gain your good graces, busy themselves with destroying your confidence in me. You will, sir, always find me disposed to aid in measures tending to our success, even should your views—which always ought to prevail—be different from mine. But I flatter myself that henceforth you will communicate your plans to me sooner, for though your knowledge of

504

the country gives greater weight to your opinions, you may rest satisfied that I shall second you in methods and details."

With a bit of well-hidden discomfort, Vaudreuil managed to give Montcalm no answer at all, by inviting him to dinner and being charming and witty all evening—and not giving Montcalm any time alone with him. But now, with Rigaud's unexpected smashing drive at Fort William Henry successfully completed, Vaudreuil felt his judgment vindicated and his brother's ability indisputably proven. Further, he meant to see that thorough credit came where due from Europe and, if he could plant a few more seeds of disaffection for the Marquis de Montcalm in the mind of the court while in the process, so much the better.

The report he wrote now to M. D'Argenson was long and involved. He wrote that even while Montcalm was wasting time meeting with savages and accepting their homage and accolades for the destruction of Fort Oswego—a destruction at which, he reminded the minister of war, Rigaud had played the key role—word had come of the near-destruction of Captain Robert Rogers's English Rangers by the troops at Fort Carillon. However, the commandant there, M. de Lusignan, admitted to a fear that it was but a prelude to a great attack against the fort itself and requested further reinforcement.

Since Montcalm was obviously otherwise occupied, Vaudreuil went on, it became the responsibility of the governor to see to the safety and furtherance of French endeavors in America. He had thereupon dispatched sixteen hundred men under Rigaud to Fort Carillon. They had arrived there safely, rested and then set out to attack Fort William Henry. When they arrived there they lost the element of surprise, according to Vaudreuil, through the stupidity of some Indians, but the attack was launched anyway.

Governor Vaudreuil, however, neglected to mention that Rigaud's force outnumbered the English at Fort William Henry by close to five to one. Nor did he make it clear that Rigaud, afraid to launch a concerted attack on the fort proper, had lost courage entirely when a messenger sent in to demand surrender of Major Eyre returned with that officer's reply that the fort would be defended to the last man.

Rigaud had paraded his men about in a show of strength, fired a few ineffective volleys of musketry at the defenses, burned the two ice-bound sloops and three hundred whaleboats so painstakingly made for the invasion against Fort Carillon, and then finally burned down several outlying storehouses, a sawmill, a hospital, a sloop under construction, some huts and a few piles of construction lumber.

The fires had been set in the dead of night and consumed everything but the fort itself. And then, with Fort William Henry virtually in the palm of his hand, Rigaud turned his army around and led it home, having exchanged the lives of eleven of his own men for seven of the English.

With suitable doctoring, the report Vaudreuil wrote now showed that Rigaud had accomplished an incredible feat at tremendous risk and that by this act alone his name should forever be hallowed in the halls of heroic men.

### [ June 27, 1757—Monday ]

William Johnson was absolutely certain now that there was no possibility of reestablishing the lost English prestige among the Iroquois. It had practically vanished with the destruction of Fort Oswego and became even less when the English themselves burned their own Forts Bull and Williams and fled in terror. And now, with the Earl of Loudoun's latest move there was, for all intents and purposes, no prestige whatever left for the English among at least four fifths of the Iroquois Confederacy.

The destruction of the buildings and boats at Fort William Henry had caused a setback John Campbell hadn't anticipated. It would take a good while to rebuild those necessary craft and so any offensive against Fort Carillon was postponed for at least a year. Lord Loudoun had thereupon gathered up the Rangers under Rogers and grandly sailed off last month to attack the big fortress of Louisbourg on Nova Scotia. Under the circumstances it was a smart move in one very important respect: if that strong island fortress could be taken, an English naval blockade on the St. Lawrence might possibly prevent—or at any rate greatly hamper—French supplies and reinforcements from reaching Quebec and Montreal.

Robert Rogers's wounds had healed well and even the smallpox fever which had struck him on March 5 and kept him bedridden for a month was now well behind him. His brother, Richard, had not been so fortunate. He, too, had came down with the pox at Fort William Henry just before Campbell's expedition left, and only a week ago today, he had died and been buried by the fort.

But while Loudoun's move against the Louisbourg fortress with Rogers and his men might have been sound militarily, it also had a serious effect among the Iroquois, who did not comprehend the grand strategy. To them, the failure of the English to retaliate instantly for either the loss of Fort Oswego, or the Fort William Henry incident, was evidence that the English were women. In the Iroquois council held during April, the atmosphere was so pro-French that most of the Mohawks had not even dared attend, and only a few of the Oneida showed up. Now, only the Mohawks of Teantontalogo and Canajoharie, whom William Johnson was in a position to personally protect, remained reluctantly loyal to him, along with scattered personal Indian friends who had taken up residence at his invitation in the huts within the walls of Fort Johnson. What was so desperately needed was a victory of any kind—something to encourage the Indians and make them realize that there were still claws on the English lion.

There was, however, no way to do this. The only substitute would be a victory for the remaining pro-English Indians, and so now Sir William Johnson, grasping at straws, appealed to Degonwadonti to bring her family influence to bear and get her father, Chief Nichus, to lead an attack against the small fortified fur-trading post near Niagara Falls, which was known as Little Fort Niagara and which was under command of his archrival, Chabert Joncaire. This fort was some distance upstream on the Niagara River from Fort Niagara itself.

As Molly Brant, she kissed him and left, and as Degonwadonti, her influence prevailed and both Nichus and his brother, Sarghyidaugh, arrived with thirty warriors all bedecked in war paint, at Fort Johnson. With Degonwadonti beside him, William Johnson praised them and fed them, supplied them and sent them on their way full of the fire of war. The destruction of Joncaire's little post, with its garrison of a dozen or so, would be relatively easy, William knew; and it could, with care, be blown into something quite more than it actually was. As Degonwadonti's father and uncle disappeared up the Mohawk with their party shortly after noon, she turned to William and touched his arm.

"With my father to lead them, Warraghiyagey," she said, "this is one thing—among a string of bad things—which will go good for you."

"I think you're right, Molly," William replied. "This may be the start of the way back."

It was not.

Before noon the next day the war party returned, Nichus

at their head, his face engraved with lines of anger. He was not just wearing the breechcloth and war paint with which he was decorated when he left, but also the scarlet British uniform jacket William had given him at the Onondaga council almost exactly four years ago; a jacket of which the Mohawk chief had always been inordinately proud.

Now he paced to within a few feet of William and deliberately and methodically tore it from himself, button by button, sleeve following sleeve, until the entire garment was a rag pile on the ground between them. Then, still without a word, he lifted his breechcloth and urinated on the torn jacket.

"That is my feeling for the English, Warraghiyagey!" he said when he finished. "Do not ever ask again that I fight for them or for you. I have nothing more to give the English. The mud that runs from my bowels is too good for them!"

*Oh, damn, damn, damn!* Johnson thought, *what now?* He coaxed and wheedled for the better part of an hour before at last, with Degonwadonti's help, the full story came out.

Immediately after setting off upstream, Nichus and his men had traveled until they were a mile or so from German Flats. Here, as it was growing late, they put ashore to spend the night. It had not been an especially wise choice for a campsite.

Ever since they had inadvertently become, with the destruction of Oswego and the forts at the Great Carrying Place, the westernmost English settlement in New York, the Palatine residents of German Flats had been very nervous. Time and again had come scares of French and Indians coming to attack them. Time and again they had roused to arms, only to find they had been frightened by a false alarm.

But the war-painted Indians camped nearby were a tangible, visible threat to their way of thinking. They attacked them in the middle of the night, killing two and driving the remainder downstream toward Fort Johnson. One of the dead was the subchief, Sarghyidaugh, brother of Nichus and uncle of Degonwadonti.

It took two full days of conciliatory argument and several hundred pounds' worth of gifts for William to appease the Mohawk's wrath and effect a satisfactory restitution. When at last Nichus and his warriors left again, it was quietly, and William knew that while he might still have the chief as a friend, he no longer had him as an ally for the English. It was a loss the faltering English cause could ill afford.

508

There were many things about his commander that Louis Antoine de Bougainville liked a great deal. The Marquis de Montcalm was a kind man, capable of great gentleness, yet not a man to be run over roughshod by anyone. He had, it was true, a rather flamboyant manner of speech, but that was of little moment. Occasionally, but never without due provocation, he lost his temper. No one who listened to Montcalm could in the least doubt his sincerity and he had that peculiar and rare talent of being able to address a group and yet leave each listener feeling as if he had been spoken to personally.

The aide-de-camp shook his head. How it was possible for Montcalm to stand up to the constant demands, arguments, ideas, and celebrations of the Indians who seemed to require so much of his time, and keep from losing his patience with them, or even his pleasantness, was beyond Bougainville's understanding.

Captain Bougainville was delighted that this period of waiting for the campaign to congeal was coming to an end and soon Montcalm would be moving out and he, Bougainville, would, as always, be right beside him. Prisoners taken in the vicinity of Fort Edward and Fort William Henry, along with dispatches received from Versailles, had made it clear that the English Earl of Loudoun was keeping only a token force at the two forts this summer and directing his attentions instead to the taking of the Fortress of Louisbourg. That this giant fortress might be taken was inconceivable and no great concern was shown in that respect. It could withstand any siege brought against it and emerge the victor, even if the enemy could assemble a great force in its attack, which apparently Lord Loudon could not. The time was therefore propitious for Montcalm himself to take up the offensive and the blow he would strike would be aimed at Fort William Henry—which Rigaud should have taken and destroyed in March—and Fort Edward. Perhaps then, with those two out of the way, Albany itself!

Bougainville himself had had a busy time lately and had fallen behind in his writing, not only in correspondence to his mother and brother, but in the journal he had until recently kept so assiduously. The correspondence would have to be put off until another time, but there was nothing really pressing in that respect anyway. Only the Indian events had occurred since last he had written to both his mother and his brother on June 30, and he had amply stated his feelings about the Indians then.

To his brother he had written only briefly, alerting him to the fact that the campaign was drawing nigh and he would soon be on the move with the general. He continued:

*M. de Montcalm has become something of a God to the Indians, many of whom have traveled phenomenal distances just to look upon him. He has fired their imagination with the taking of Oswego, which for so long was permitted to fester as a sore in our flank. Just the other day (for an example of their reaction to him) a visit of ceremony occurred with some chiefs of the Indians at Michilimackinac. Their speaker stood before M. de Montcalm in silence for some time until at length he nodded and spoke these words, which were translated by M. de Langlade, who has led them here: "We wished to see this famous chief who, on putting his foot on the ground, tramples the English forts under his feet. We thought we should find him so tall that his head would be lost in the clouds. But you are a little man, my Father. It is when we look into your eyes that we can see the strength and greatness of the pine tree and the spirit and courage of the eagle."*

*We have nearly 8,000 men, 1,800 of whom are Indians, naked, black, red, howling, bellowing, dancing, singing the war song, getting drunk, yelling for "broth," that is to say blood, drawn from 500 leagues by the smell of fresh human flesh and the chance to teach their young men how one carves up a human being destined for the pot. Behold our comrades who, night and day, are our shadows. I shiver at the frightful spectacles which they are preparing for us.*

To his mother—Madame Herault—he had written at greater length, again speaking of his devotion to and admiration for Montcalm who, he added, in regard to Governor Vaudreuil:

*... is under the orders of a man, limited, without talent, perhaps free from vice, but having all the faults of a petty spirit, filled with Canadian prejudices, which are of all, the most foolish, jealous, glorious, wishing to take all credit to themselves. He no more confides in M. de Montcalm than in the lowest lieutenants. The Marquis de Montcalm has not the honor of being consulted and it is generally through public rumor that he first hears of M. de Vaudreuil's military plans.*

*The governor is a timid man who can neither make a resolution nor keep one; yet when M. de Vaudreuil produces an idea, he falls in love with it, as Pygmalion did with his statue. I can forgive Pygmalion, for what he produced was a masterpiece.*

*There must be some connection between M. de Vaudreuil and M. Bigot, for the latter engages in peculations almost openly, yet without reproval. M. Bigot, who has established M. Joseph Cadet as Commissary General, claims of himself that he is the backbone of the colony and that he is establishing what he calls the "Great Society"—but its greatness has thus far been of benefit only to M. Bigot and those who are his accomplices. But that is away from our subject.*

*Of matters at hand, I will say only that we expect two sieges and a battle, that your child shudders at the horrors which he will be forced to witness. It will be with great difficulty that we can control these Indians of the far West, the most ferocious of all people, and great cannibals by trade. Listen to what the chiefs said to M. de Montcalm three days ago. "Father, do not expect that we can easily give quarter to the English. We have young men who have never yet drunk of this broth. Fresh meat has brought them here from the ends of the earth. It is most necessary that they learn to wield the knife and plunge it into an English heart." Behold our comrades, dear Mama; what a crew, what a spectacle for a humane man!*

It was to his journal that Louis Bougainville now turned his attention, to record the bizarre occurrences of the past two days—occurrences that had seen himself adopted as an Iroquois. He wrote swiftly, in a firm and highly legible hand:

*July 9*
*The Marquis de Montcalm left today with MM. de Rigaud, St. Luc, de Longueuil, Junior, and Abbé Piquet to go and sing the war song at the Lake and at Sault St. Louis. We have first been to the Lac Des Deux Montagnes [Two Mountains Lake,] which is twelve or thirteen leagues from Montreal and is formed by the Ottawa River. North of this lake is an Indian village. Indians of three different nations live there; Nipissings, Algonquins and Iroquois. They have three separate groups of houses, although all united in the same village. They have a common church, which is attractive and properly ornamented. Two Sulpician missionaries are*

*in charge, one for the Nipissings and Algonquins, the other for the Iroquois.*

*The Indians go to pray in the church three times a day, each in his own tongue, and they attend with exemplary devotion. They serve as choir boys and chanters. The men sit on one side and the women on the other, and the choir formed by the latter is very melodious.*

*The cabins are well enough built, but very filthy. There is a special council house for each nation and a large one, which must be three hundred feet long, for the general councils of the three nations.*

*Upon our arrival we were saluted by a triple discharge of two swivels and of musketry from Indians lined up on the river bank, the missionaries at their head. They led us to the church and from there to the parsonage, where the principal chiefs came to compliment the Marquis de Montcalm. In the afternoon they held a council in which the Marquis de Montcalm told the Indians that he had come to see them and give them through this visit marks of his friendship and esteem. Then he revealed to them the project planned against Fort William Henry, the union of all the Indians in order to cooperate in its execution, and the hope that the Marquis de Vaudreuil had that they, his children, and children of the True Faith, would help him with all their strength to destroy the common enemy. He ended by saying that he would give them three oxen for a feast and that he planned to sing the war song with them in the great council house. The Indians thanked the Marquis de Montcalm for his visit, assured him that they would follow his wishes and that in the evening they would tell him the numbers of warriors who would march with him.*

*We then visited the chiefs in their cabins. In the course of this we saw a Nipissing Indian, dishonored in the eyes of his brothers and of the Canadians because he wore breeches, covered his head, ate, dressed, and slept like a Frenchman. He goes neither to the hunt nor to war. He keeps a shop in his house filled especially with contraband goods, and he has a very lucrative business. The Indians scorn him, but do not reproach him or treat him badly. For in this place of complete liberty,* Trahit sua quemque voluptas.[5] *This man reminds me of that thought that it is trade which most of all civilizes man.*

*In the evening we went to the council house, the Indians were sitting there on the floor, ranged by tribes. In the middle were hung at intervals pots filled with meat destined for the war feast. A few candles lighted up this place which seemed like a witches' cavern. Kisensik⁶ spoke first. After the ordinary compliments, he asked the Marquis de Montcalm for permission to give his advice on war when the occasion offered. He then outlined his tribe's requests and the number of warriors it would furnish. The chiefs of the other two nations then spoke on the same subjects. After the Marquis de Montcalm had replied to their proposals, Aoussik,⁷ seizing a bullock's head by the horns and stalking around with it, sang his war song. The other chiefs of the three nations followed him with the same ceremony, and I sang it in name of the Marquis de Montcalm and was much applauded. My song was nothing else but these words: "Trample the English underfoot" cadenced to the movement of the Indian chiefs' cries. They then presented M. de Montcalm with the first morsel, and the war feast having started, we withdrew.*

*The next day, the tenth, we went to Sault St. Louis [Caughnawaga]. Two canoes, each with ten naked Indians, the finest men of all the villages, painted for war in red and blue, adorned with bracelets of silver and of wampum, came before us on the river a quarter-league from the Sault. They brought to the Marquis de Montcalm a letter from Father la Neuville, a Jesuit, who heads this mission, in which he advised him of the ceremony about to be observed. The two canoe loads, in truth a charming sight, held the attention of all the Europeans. On the river bank we found the missionary, who received the Marquis de Montcalm upon his stepping ashore, made a short speech and led him to the church between two rows of Indians who saluted him, the chiefs with their spears and the rest with a triple discharge of their guns. They sang the Te Deum in the Iroquois tongue, after which the Marquis de Montcalm was led to the council chamber, where the chiefs joined him. The same propositions, the same answers, the same ceremonies as at Lac Des Deux Montagnes, and moreover, that of covering, in the name of the Marquis de Vaudreuil, two dead Iroquois chiefs, and of presenting me to the nation as a candidate for adoption. Three oxen given for the war feast, which went off just like that of last night. The Iroquois adopted me during this feast and gave me the name of "Garionatsigoa," which means "Great Angry Sky." Behold me then, an Iroquois war chief! My clan is that of the Turtle, first for eloquence in council, but second for war, that of the Bear being first. They exhibited me to all the nation, gave me the first morsels of the war feast, and I sang my war song, in part with their first war chief. The others dedicated theirs to me.*

*I paid calls on all my clan and gave the wherewithall for feasts in all the cabins. As for the rest of it, the village at the Sault is attractive, laid out in a regular form with a parade ground which divides it and serves as a riding field, for they have many horses and exercise them continually. The church is pretty and well decorated. The Indians have, as do those at the Lake, fields cultivated by their women, fowl and cattle, all individually owned. They sell, buy and trade just like Frenchmen.*

Bougainville lay aside the pen, blew upon the ink to dry it and then began straightening up and putting things safely away, either to be kept here for his return or brought along. He felt a rising excitement in him as he thought ahead.

The campaign against Fort William Henry was about to begin.

Not far from here, in his own quarters, Louis Montcalm was busy writing, too. He was spending quiet, pleasant moments with his family through his pen. Now, as was usually the case, he kept to a lighter vein, preferring not to burden his loved ones with the problems and tribulations of his office. He wished to bring them happy thoughts, not pain, even though it be pain in the form of sympathy for him. More than on any other campaign he had experienced, he missed his family greatly—his dear mother and his sons of whom he was so proud, his daughters that he loved so deeply that it almost hurt on remembering their laughter and sweetness. And most of all, Angélique, his beloved wife. It was to her that he was writing now:

*My Dearest One,*

*Soon now our campaign will begin and behind me will be the long waitings and pointless routines of which one so swiftly grows weary. I hope next year I may be with you all. I love you tenderly, dearest. There is not an hour in the day when I do not think of you, my mother and my children.*

*I have sent you a packet of marten skins for a muff, and another time I shall send some to our daughter; but I should like better to bring them myself.*

*I am always eager for the news in your letters and to learn all that is happening at home. It is a delight to learn of the prosperity of my olive-oil mill. It seems to be a good thing,*

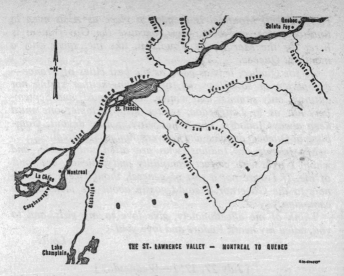

THE ST. LAWRENCE VALLEY — MONTREAL TO QUEBEC

*which pleases me very much. Bougainville and I talk a great
deal about the oil-mill.*

*With little else to do, we have the usual frequency of balls
and dinners here. My station obliges me to maintain a high
standard of living which is, I fear, to my financial detriment.
Canadian prices are exorbitant, but I must live creditably,
and so I do; sixteen persons at table every day. Once a
fortnight I dine with the Governor-General and with the
Chevalier de Lévis, who lives very well too. He has given
three grand balls. As for me, up to Lent I gave, besides
dinners, great suppers, with ladies, three times a week. They
lasted till two in the morning; and then there was dancing, to
which company came uninvited, but sure of a welcome from
those who had been at supper. It is very expensive, not very
amusing, and often tedious. At Quebec, where we spent a
month, I gave receptions or parties, often at the Intendant's
house.*

*I like my gallant Chevalier de Lévis very much. Bourla-
maque was a good choice; he is steady and cool, with good
parts. Bougainville has talent, a warm head, and warm heart;
he will ripen in time. Write to Madame Cornier that I like
her husband; he is perfectly well and as impatient for peace
as I am.*

*Love to my daughters, and all affection and respect to my
mother. I live only in the hope of joining you all again.*

*Nevertheless, Montreal is as good a place as Alais even in time of peace, and better now, because the Government is here; for the Marquis de Vaudreuil, like me, spent only a month at Quebec.*

*As for Quebec, it is as good as the best cities of France— except ten or so. Clear sky, bright sun, neither spring nor autumn, only summer and winter. July, August, and September, hot as in Languedoc; winter insupportable; one must keep always indoors. The ladies witty, polite, devout. Gambling at Quebec, dancing and conversation at Montreal.*

*My friends the Indians, who are often unbearable, and whom I treat with perfect tranquility and patience, are fond of me. If I were not a sort of general, though very subordinate to the Governor, I could gossip about the plans of the campaign. . . .*

*Think of me affectionately, give love to my girls, and to you, adieu my heart; I adore and love you!*

*Louis*

## [ July 27, 1757—Wednesday ]

As any soldier is pleased with a promotion, so Daniel Webb was pleased with his new rank of major general. The fact that his somewhat hysterical report had proved unfounded, that the French and Indians had not made any effort at all to march on the Great Carrying Place after their destruction of Fort Oswego did not make a great deal of difference. After all, he *thought* they were coming and yet, in the face of this great danger he had held his men in check long enough to make the upper portage waters impassable and burn two English forts and a great quantity of supplies which, if the French *had* come, would have otherwise fallen into their hands. And so, as just reward for such a judicious retreat, he was promoted from colonel past the rank of brigadier and up to major general.

Despite the fact that he was a professional soldier, Webb had seen precious little action. Somehow whenever action threatened, he was the one who was sent elsewhere for some reason; just as last year when it seemed certain there would be action in the Lake George area, he had been sent on an innocuous mission up the Mohawk. The fact that he had very nearly run into unexpected action en route to Oswego had since filled his nights with bad dreams.

And now the fates had tricked him again.

When John Campbell, along with Robert Rogers and his

Rangers and all the rest, had sailed off for almost certain action at the fortress of Louisbourg, it was Major General Webb who had been left behind as commander of Fort Edward and with instructions to guard the frontier. And now, when all common sense indicated that the French forces would mass to meet the Earl of Loudoun at Nova Scotia, who would have thought that Montcalm would take such a time as this to make a thrust toward Fort William Henry and Fort Edward? Yet, just as surely as he knew his own name, Webb was certain that was what was happening and once again his nights were filled with restlessness and bad dreams.

The first indication that something was afoot in this direction was word which came from the scouts of uncommon activity taking place all along the length of Lake Champlain and Lake George: an increase of Indian parties, French patrols, Canadian bush lopers. Lieutenant Colonel Monro, commanding now at Fort William Henry, decided to send out a good-sized detachment to reconnoiter the French posts and determine what was in the wind. This detachment—three hundred provincials, mostly from New Jersey—were sent on the mission under Colonel Parker and set out to the north on Lake George at once.

Almost immediately they had been spotted by Indian spies who hustled back to Ticonderoga and, under the Canadian officer, Captain Corbière, and five hundred Ottawas and Chippewas led here by Charles Langlade, sallied out to set up an ambush. Colonel Parker made it very easy for them, not only by hugging the western shore of Lake George with his boats, but by splitting his force.

Yesterday morning, as the first three boats moved casually around a peninsula of sorts commonly known as Sabbath Day Point, they were cut off from view of those following. Instantly a swarm of canoes had them surrounded and they were captured neatly, without a gun being fired. In a few minutes three more of the English boats came around and were snared in the same way.

Finally the main segment of the English flotilla started around and they were met by a furious hail of bullets and war whoops. A great mass of canoes shot toward them, each filled with war-painted Indians, and the whole detachment panicked. Some of the men even leaped out of their boats and into the water in an attempt to swim away, and they were speared as if they'd been fish. In moments it was all over. Except for the final hundred men following at a considerable distance, who now beat the water to a froth as they rowed furiously further out into the lake and then back toward Fort William Henry, those not already killed surrendered without a fight.

The slaughter that followed was horrible. The majority of the captives were killed on the spot and three of them were boiled and eaten. And even while this action was occurring here, another hundred fifty Indians and a few Canadians under Captain Jacques Marin were making a hit-and-run attack on Fort Edward. The pickets were driven in and eleven of them killed, although to make it look as if they'd been even more successful, the departing attackers cut each scalp into two or three. When they got back to Fort Carillon they had thirty-two scalps and a prisoner.

And now Major General Webb, the fear becoming daily stronger in him, hastily penned a message to James Delancey in New York:

Sir:
*The situation here is degenerating. Two-thirds of Colonel Parker's detachment of three companies either killed or captured in an ambush on the lake. Eleven men killed and one missing in a bold attack on this installation. The French are certainly coming and will probably strike at Fort William Henry first. I am determined to march to Fort William Henry with the whole army under my command as soon as I shall hear of the farther approach of the enemy. I beg you, send up the militia without delay.*

*Daniel Webb, Major-General*
*Commanding Fort Edward*

He folded and sealed the dispatch, gave it to an aide to be carried at once to New York and then was again alone with his thoughts. The message, as he had meant it to, sounded very courageous, but General Daniel Webb was an extremely frightened man and he knew deep down in his heart that he just didn't have the courage to lead his men to the defense of Fort William Henry.

## [ July 28, 1757—Thursday ]

At no time in anyone's memory had so many Indians of so many different tribes come together to fight beside one another. Here, close to Fort Carillon, were not only eight thousand French and Canadian troops under command of Montcalm, Lévis and Bourlamaque, but a total of almost six thousand Indians of forty-one different tribes. Even though this Indian total included squaws and children, there was still a remarkable number of warriors—two thousand or more of them. With the smell of English blood in the air, they were busily engaged in a hundred and more ways in prebattle occupations. Council after council had been held among themselves, war dance after war dance staged, and delegation after delegation had come to Montcalm with ideas and demands.

Some of the Indians had come from so far away that they spoke languages which even most of the other Indians did not understand. There were the Iowas, from far to the west of the Mississippi, Winnebagoes and Menominees from west of Lake Michigan, Shawnees and Delawares from western Pennsylvania and the Ohio country, Miamis and Weas and Peorias from the country beyond the Ohio country, and Sac and Fox from beyond them. Micmacs were there, and Amalecites, both from Nova Scotia; Algonkins from as far as the great Hudson Bay, Nipissings from eastward of Lake Huron, Abnakis from Maine and the Gaspé Peninsula. There were Ottawas and Chippewas, Wyandots and their parent tribesmen, Hurons. There were Mississaugis and there were Têtes de Boule; and there were Cayugas and Oneidas, Onondagas and Senecas and Caughnawagas.

All of them now were gathered here to sit in grand council, to hear the words of the little French general, Montcalm; to learn of his plans, to offer their advice, to give him reassurance of their support. So much had happened in these days of preparation here at the Narrows of Ticonderoga, there was such hubbub, so many rites and dances and festivities and feasts going on, so many cries and screams and songs and chants, that the senses were numbed by it all.

The majority of Montcalm's troops had preceded him and, at his arrival, were fully prepared for his orders, whatever they might be. Just below the Ticonderoga promontory, where the outlet of Lake George joined the waters of Lake Champlain, Colonel Bourlamaque had taken his position with two battalions. General Lévis, with the battalions of La Sarre, Guienne, La Reine and Languedoc had pushed up the outlet stream until stopped by the falls in the gorge of the Ticonderoga Narrows and here the major encampment had been made. A sawmill was constructed and a better road cut for a mile and a half to form linkage for a portage to the mouth of Lake George. Outposts and camps of French regulars, colony regulars, militia, Canadian *coureurs de bois* and Indians were everywhere, guarding every approach, watching, waiting.

Captive English soldiers were brought in, wretched and terrified, taken at the ambush on Lake George or from the vicinity of Fort William Henry or Fort Edward. Some were killed and scalped, dismembered, decapitated, boiled, eaten. Most were held for later transport to Montreal, to be traded for rum and weapons and supplies.

The Indians of the far west were hardest to keep under control. They were supremely confident of their own fighting abilities, not especially anxious to follow the battle plans that might be laid out by the French general, yet reluctantly willing to go along with them if the other tribes did so. And as they were the most unmanageable, the most tractable were the mission Indians, those of St. Francis and Caughnawaga, Becancour and La Présentation, Three Rivers and Mississiqui, the Penobscot, Two Mountains and the Lorette.

With the Indians were their officers, Canadian men, *coureurs de bois;* men assigned to guide and control their energies as much as possible—men like Marin and Langlade, Hertel and Longueuil, Fleurimont and Niverville, La Plante, Herbin, Sabrevois, Lorimer, and Langis. And with them, too, were the three missionary fathers who, under orders from Montcalm, must try to their utmost to keep the atrocities to the barest minimum—the Jesuit priest Père Roubaud of St. Francis, and the Sulpicians, Abbé Matavet from among the Nipissings and Abbé Piquet of La Présentation.

And now, at last, the Grand Council was ready to begin in the great clearing made by the sawmill near the Falls. Montcalm would speak first, forced to explain the plan of the campaign in detail and the importance of the Indians to it. And the oldest of the chiefs present, Pennahouel of the Ottawas, would be given the honor of replying first, in respect for his age which, above almost all things, most Indians respected.

For his part, Montcalm spoke briefly, yet forcefully, depicting how the battle was planned, how Lévis would move ahead first by land, how the Indians would move with him, how Montcalm and the rest of the army would follow by boats on Lake George and they would all join, how the attack on Fort William Henry would be launched, and how the fort would fall. Even as he spoke, the interpreters—St. Germain, Chateauvieux, Perthius, La Force, St. Martin,

Launière, Farly, St. Jean, Chesne, Destailly and Reaume—echoed his words in the native tongues.

Hardly had Montcalm uttered the words of how the fort would fall to them when, at the edge of the clearing, a great old tree whose roots had been long undermined by a rivulet, suddenly leaned, groaned and then toppled with a great crash. Quick to take advantage, Montcalm pointed to it and shouted:

"My children! See! There is your sign which I have heard you anticipated but had not yet seen. Now you have seen it and heard it. It is a great augury. As that tree has fallen, so too will the English fall before us!"

There was a deafening roar of approval at this and Montcalm stepped down. In a moment his place was taken by the old Ottawa chief, Pennahouel. He was a cadaverous, incredibly wrinkled old man with bright eyes. He raised his arms and when the murmurings were silenced, spoke:

"My father, I who have counted more moons than any who are here, I, Pennahouel, thank you for the words you have spoken to us. They are good words, brave words, strong with truth and I approve them. No one has ever spoken better. It is the Manitou of War who has inspired you."

Chief Kisensik of the Nipissings, speaking next on behalf of the mission Indians, first addressed his remarks to Pennahouel and the Indians of the upper Great Lakes.

"My Brothers, we Indians who have received the True Faith thank you for coming here to help us defend our lands against the English, whose greatest wish is to take them from us. Our cause is good and the Master of Life is on our side to favor us with victory. Can there be any doubt of this now, after the great blow you yourselves have just struck on the side of the lake where the sun touches first? Your triumph there has covered you with glory and the waters of the lake will forevermore be stained red with the blood of *Corlaer* [the English] to bear witness to what you have achieved. We, too, are covered with glory for what you have done, and we are proud of it."

Kisensik then turned to Montcalm and nodded gravely to him. "Our pleasure in this," he told the general, "is even stronger than yours, for this is our land which is being threatened, not yours. You have come to us from across the great water not for your own gain, but because you have been sent here by the great French King who feared for his red children and said to you, 'Go, cross the waters, and go and defend my children there.' And you are here. He has

521

bound us together with the most solemn of ties. Let us all accept this with a great gladness inside and make sure that nothing will ever separate us from our friendship."

The talk was received with approving cries and murmurs from the Indians and applause from the Canadians and French officers on hand. Once again Montcalm rose to speak and the assemblage stilled to hear the words of this little man who was so great a warrior that when he puffed out his cheeks and blew, the English shriveled up before him and were blown away.

"My children," he told them, "I am pleased to see you all united here for the great work which lies ahead of us. So long as your hands are joined in union such as this, the English cannot resist you, nor take your lands from you. Yes, our great King in France had sent me to lead his army here to protect and defend you, but it is for even more than this that I have come. Above all else, he had charged me to see that you are made happy and invincible, by forming among you this friendship between tribes, this unity of purpose, this joining together of hands to carry on the good work among our brothers, who are the children of the great Onontio."

With this he took from an aide a huge belt of wampum in which a total of six thousand different beads had been worked to form the design of peace and unity. He held it out toward the Indians and continued:

"I give you this belt as a sacred pledge of the word of the King. The pattern of the beads which form it are a symbol of strength and understanding and alliance between us. With this belt I bind you all together so that nothing can separate you before the defeat of the English and the destruction of Fort William Henry!"

With that he tossed the belt onto the ground in the midst of the assembly and now, one by one the various chiefs picked it up and gave their reply. Pennahouel, again with respect for his age, was first to take it up. He held it high in one hand, showing it to all.

"Behold, Brothers," he said loudly, "a circle has been drawn around us with this belt by the great Onontio. None of us may now leave it until we are finished with what we have set out to do here. So long as we keep it, the Master of Life will help us in all our undertakings; he will inspire us in the right way and lead us on the path of victory. If any are here who will quit this union before the English are defeated, the Master of Life is not accountable for the evils that may strike them; rather, that tribe's misfortune will be its own doing, and the blame for it will not fall upon the tribes who here and now promise a strong union and obedience to the will of the great white chief."

Chief after chief followed and made similar speeches and at last the belt was given to the Iroquois faction to keep, since they represented the greatest number of warriors assembled here. They accepted it but, in turn, presented it to Pennahouel as a pledge of their union, to take it back with them to the far west as a symbol of the friendship which existed between them.[8]

The council adjourned in harmony and all that remained now was to march on the English.

### [ July 31, 1757—Sunday ]

Despite the seeming confidence of the Indians in the plans of the Marquis de Montcalm, there were murmurings reaching the ears of his chief aide, Captain Bougainville, which that officer found disturbing. The Indians were discontent over the conditions they were experiencing. That they had the war fever upon them there could be no doubt; nonetheless, it was customary for them, when acting as ally for a white power, to be plied with many gifts to subsequently take home, with much food—especially meat—for their feasts, and with large amounts of rum or brandy. The fact that such supplies were not even available in sufficient quantity for the French army made little difference to them. Bougainville mentioned to his general that he thought there was a good possibility that some of their savage allies would desert them, and almost immediately his prediction proved correct. As he wrote in his journal:

*July 28*

*Twoscore Ottawas and Mississaugis, and the Miamis to the number of eight, left without telling anyone. A Potawatomi chief told the Marquis de Montcalm of it and offered to try to bring them back. He was given a belt and strings of wampum to help him succeed.*

*An English corpse came floating by the Indians' camp. They crowded around it with loud cries, drank its blood, and put its pieces in a kettle. However, it was only the western Indians who committed these barbarous acts. Our domesticated ones took no part in it; they spent all day in confession.*

*July 29*

*The Miamis and others did not come back. Their example has been contagious. Several others have followed them; a few, in order not to be stopped, portaging their canoes through the woods. About two hundred Mississaugi and Ottawas have deserted. No way to hold them; they had made a coup, and besides, they lacked everything—no blankets, no deer skins (except very bad ones), no leggins, no vermilion. Those who send to the army Indians who lack everything, should come and command them themselves. Moreover, this inconvenience, so prejudicial to the King's service, results from the poor condition of the government and is the result of the greed of the leeches of the colony . . . Quebec has absolutely no bread. Everyone is in extreme misery. The small amount of provisions brought by the few ships which came is used up entirely. . . .*

*July 30*

*The Indians were bored and peevish, found the food bad and wanted fresh meat. Consequently their young men came yesterday and killed fourteen of our too few oxen, and today another four. . . .*

*July 31*

*The Indians who for several days impatiently endured their inactivity in a camp where there was neither wine nor brandy and where consequently they could not get drunk, left at three to go forward three leagues on Lake George, where they will wait for us. They have with them three hundred Canadians. . . . On their departure they left at their camp a cloak, a breechclout, and a pair of leggins hung in a tree as a sacrifice to the Manitou. Two Sulpicians and a Jesuit, missionaries with this army, asked if they would be permitted to say Mass in a place where one sacrificed to the devil. Reply by the General of the Army . . . that it was better to say it there than not to say it at all. . . .*

[ *August 2, 1757—Tuesday* ]

It was another tribute to Montcalm's careful planning that his large army had been able to get so close to Fort William Henry without opposition. Two miles ahead the darkness was broken by the twinkling of lights from the fort and now the Indians, French and Canadians prepared for a final night of rest here before a dawn surprise attack which might even permit them to get inside the gates before the alarm was raised.

Such, however, was not to be.

About 10 P.M., Lieutenant Colonel Monro sent a pair of boats out from the fort to patrol. They headed almost directly toward the hidden encampment without realizing it. Their voices and the dipping of their oars could be heard for nearly a mile over the mirror-calm waters and the enemy crouched silently in the shadows, trusting their presence would remain undetected in the darkness.

The boats were just about to pass the French position when one of the soldiers spied something suspicious along the shore—a dark bulk he couldn't quite make out. Some conversation went back and forth between the rowers and then they began a cautious approach. Soon they were able to make out that it was a large bateaux covered over with an awning. It was, in fact, the boat in which the three priests of Montcalm's expedition had been transported.

At first the boatmen took it to be an abandoned boat that had somehow pulled free far down the lake and been blown by the wind to this spot, but just then there came the loud bleating of some sheep in one of the French provision boats a little farther away and instantly the boatmen began a rapid rowing toward the fort.

Just as swiftly the Indians leaped from cover and gave vent to a chorus of blood-chilling screams as they launched canoes in pursuit. It only made the English soldiers row faster and, for a little while at any rate, they managed to maintain the distance separating the boats.

Abruptly they began faltering and the gap started closing. When they were still a quarter mile from the fort landing, the Indians opened fire. None of the soldiers were hit and they, in turn, shot at the Indians with somewhat better effect.

A chief of the Nipissings, Konnik, was standing in the prow of the lead canoe, urging his followers on. A bullet slammed into his chest, passed through his heart and killed him. He fell inside the boat, rather than in the water. Another Indian was hit in the side, but not killed. For a moment the pursuers faltered and the English soldiers snatched up their oars again and rowed even more furiously than before.

The race became a dead heat, with the two whaleboats of the English and the foremost canoes of the Indians reaching the shore at the same time. A hot skirmish broke out, during which three of the soldiers were killed, three others captured and the remaining men escaped in the darkness to the woods, which were closer than the fort to where they landed.

Firing was coming from the fort now and the Indians withdrew. The three prisoners were taken at once to Montcalm who, to his satisfaction, learned from them that the only reinforcement Monro had received from Webb was two hundred regulars under Lieutenant Colonel Young, and eight hundred provincials from Massachusetts under Colonel Frye. That meant that the total force at the fort, including even the sailors, laborers and Negro slaves, was only twenty-two hundred men. Montcalm nodded. The onslaught would begin in the morning and he had no doubt whatever that the garrison would quickly surrender.

The Nipissings were stricken with grief over this early loss of the second principal chief of their tribe, who had led his canoe in the race after the English. Taking their cue from the principal chief, Kisensik, the death wail erupted from their throats and they prepared the corpse for final rites. The chief's face was painted completely with vermilion and feathers were attached to his tuft of hair. Special ornaments of silver and bone were put in his ear and nose, a breastplate of French armor on his chest and numerous silver bracelets placed around his lower arms. Then, aided by some of their allies from Two Mountains, they carried him to the top of a knoll and sat him upright there with his lance in his hands, his tomahawk at his belt, his musket in the crook of his arms, and a large kettle on the ground beside him.

The death wail gave way to individual orations of the prowess that had been Konnik's and of the journey he was now embarking upon to the land of souls. Then a set of drums began thumping and to them the assembled warriors moved in the jerky rhythm of the dance of death, which would last until dawn. Then they would bury Konnik in this same sitting position, facing to the east.

Back at Fort William Henry, several of the boatmen who had escaped into the woods now made a safe return to the fort. And inside, final preparations were being made for the attack which must begin on the morrow. The faces of most of the garrison were ashen and their eyes filled with fear.

And throughout the night came the ominous booming of the drums.

Major General Daniel Webb morosely took stock of the situation and shook his head, wishing he were somewhere else. Here at Fort Edward he had fourteen hundred men and in the nearby camps surrounding the fort he had another eighteen hundred thirty-two. To a man, this total effective force of thirty-four hundred thirty-two men were primed and ready for the fourteen-mile march to the relief of Fort William Henry. They needed only General Webb's command, if not his leadership, to move out. Neither leadership nor command was given. Major General Webb was a man assailed with great doubts—and an even greater fear.

Yesterday before noon had come an express from Lieutenant Colonel Monro at Fort William Henry. It had confirmed all of Webb's growing fears:

> *9 o'clock A.M.*
> *3 August 1757*

*Sir:*

*Our patrol boats were fired upon last night about ten. Three of our men killed, three missing. The war drums have beat all night and we are led to believe the Indian numbers may be equal to the French. Some of the French have just this moment moved into sight on the lake and have commenced movement toward us. Attack is imminent. The reinforcement from Fort Edward is now essential to us.*

Torn with indecision and not really knowing what best to do or say, Webb temporarily solved his dilemma by not making any reply at all. Then, close on midnight last night had come a second message from Monro, brought by three Rangers who told him the road to Fort William Henry was essentially still open, but that it might be taken soon and access to the fort severely hampered or even entirely cut off if help was not speedily sent. Webb heard them out nervously, made a noncommital movement of his head, dismissed them without comment and then took the message to his desk. In the glow of the lantern there he ripped open the second dispatch:

> *6 o'clock P.M.*
> *3 August 1757*

*Sir:*

*We are under musket fire, but bearing up well, our men*

*returning shot for shot. Shortly after three o'clock this afternoon, one of the aides-de-camp of the Marquis approached under a flag of truce and, after being blindfolded, was led into the fort. He bore a letter from the French commander to this effect:*

> *"I owe it to humanity to summon you to surrender. At present I can restrain the savages, and make them observe the terms of capitulation, as I might not have power to do under other circumstances; and an obstinate defense on your part could only retard the capture of the place a few days, and endanger an unfortunate garrison which cannot be relieved, in consequence of the dispositions I have made. I demand a decisive answer within an hour."*

*My answer, Sir, was made immediately, I replying that I and my soldiers would defend ourselves to the last. Our defenses have not been breached but we are greatly outnumbered and in great need of assistance. The French are erecting their batteries and we expect to be under cannon fire soon. I believe you will think it proper to send a reinforcement as soon as possible.*

*Monro*

Again, Webb neither made reply nor sent any help. The final messages from Monro had come today—one in the forenoon and another just a short while ago, after darkness had fallen. They reiterated the seriousness of the situation, the fact that the French were upon them in great numbers, that the French were well supplied with artillery that had not yet been fired against the fort, and that the men were all still in good spirits; that they had thus far been quite effective in their shooting at the Indians who had been harassing the fort with musketry. But the appeal for aid from Fort Edward was now taking on a note of alarm. Monro had concluded:

> *I make no doubt that you will soon send us a reinforcement. . . . We are very certain that a part of the enemy have gotten between you and us upon the high road, and would therefore be glad (if it meets with your approbation) the whole army was marched.*

Since those letters were received, Webb had been pacing his office, stopping occasionally to listen to the reports of returned spies that he had sent out and once to question a

French prisoner who was brought in. And now, at last, he made a decision.

He called to his aide-de-camp, Captain Bartman, and gave him instructions on what to write in a letter to Monro or whoever might be in command at the besieged fort by now. And as soon as Bartman had gone out to do this, Webb himself set about writing a letter to John Campbell, Earl of Loudoun, which brought the commander in chief up to date on what had transpired thus far and then concluded with:

*The number of troops remaining under my Command at this place, excluding the Posts on the Hudson's River, amounts to but sixteen hundred men fit for duty, with which Army, so much inferior to that of the enemy, I did not think it prudent to pursue my first intentions of Marching to their Assistance.*

Captain Bartman finished his letter to Lieutenant Colonel Monro quickly, sealed it and found three volunteers—one to carry it to Fort William Henry, the other two to guard him along the way.

The trio set off immediately, planning to travel the road until about six miles from the fort and then take to the woods from that point to avoid the enemy; but they should have left the road much sooner. Less than three miles from Fort Edward they were fired upon by a party of Indians under Kanectagon, war chief of the Algonkins.

The messenger was killed, one of his guards was captured and the other managed to escape. The messenger was searched and the dispatch was found hidden in the lining of his jacket. That message and his scalp was taken, and in less than four hours, Captain Bartman's letter was being read by the Marquis de Montcalm. It was quite a document to have fall into enemy hands:

*Fort Edward*
*Midnight, August 4, 1757*

To: Lt. Col. Monro or to
    Any Other Officer now
    Commanding in his Stead:

Sir:

*The General has ordered me to acquaint you he does not think it prudent to attempt a junction or assist you till reinforced by the militia of the colonies, for the immediate march of which repeated expresses have been sent. The*

*General has learned that the French are now in complete possession of the road between our forts. A Canadian prisoner just brought in and questioned has reported the French force in men and cannon to be very great, with upwards of eleven thousand troops who have surrounded the fort entirely for a distance of five miles. The General wishes you to be informed of these details so that, if the militia he has sent for arrives too late for him to march to your aid, the commander of Fort William Henry had better see to obtaining the best terms of surrender he can get.*

A broad smile wreathed Montcalm's face as he finished reading the letter. He knew now, with certainty, that Fort William Henry was his.

## [ *August 7, 1757—Sunday* ]

The French left battery had finally been placed and began opening up on Fort William Henry at six in the morning yesterday. Eight cannon and a nine-inch mortar hammered away at the fort all day, doing considerably more destruction to the men and defenses than had the previous three days of musket fire. Monro had answered with his own cannon, but to little real effect.

Then, this morning at six o'clock, not only the left battery of the French but also the right began their bombardment. It was what the Indians had been waiting for and they screamed out cries of pure joy at every blast of the big guns.

Because the Indians had begun to show some restlessness, as was always the case when a siege was maintained for more than two or three days, Montcalm now invited numbers of their chiefs to actually assist in firing the big guns. It was something none of them had ever done before, and their admiration for the French general soared at this vote of confidence in them. And, under supervision of the artillery officers, they did a fairly good job of it, though one of them who stood too close to the muzzle had his eardrums burst and went howling into the woods. The pride of accomplishment in the other chiefs assisting here, however, was almost amusing to witness.

The artillery was causing pure havoc at the fort. For three hours the big guns belched their explosive balls of death—balls from five eighteen-pounders, nine twelve-pounders, two eight-pounders, two six-pounders, two seven-inch howitzers, a nine-inch mortar and a six-inch mortar. It was a terrible pounding to undergo and the relatively high spirits of the defending garrison had abruptly lowered. The enemy outside was awful . . . and so was the enemy inside.

A smallpox epidemic had begun.

Already fifty or more of those inside Fort William Henry had fallen ill with the fever; a recurrence of the disease which only so recently had killed Richard Rogers and the twenty or thirty others now buried adjacent to the fort. And here they were again, with the casemates suddenly overflowing with the sick and more being stricken daily.

Lieutenant Colonel Monro was everywhere among his men, encouraging them as best he could, assuring them that the promised reinforcement from General Webb must be almost here, but now he had his own doubts. If they were coming, why hadn't they arrived long before this? He desperately wished now that he had sent away, at the first suggestion that trouble was looming, the multitude of women and children huddled in terrified masses in the safest places of this fort. These were largely the wives and offspring of the New Hampshire regiment, and Monro was afraid for them, afraid of what might be in store.

At 9 A.M. there came from all of the French guns at once a tremendous double salvo, followed by an eerie quiet. A few minutes later could be heard the rattling of a drum and a watcher on the wall shouted to Monro.

"Sir! There's a party of the French coming now under the red flag!"[9]

Monro hastily took a position where he could see the party approaching under the scarlet flag of truce. It was composed of a drummer, flag bearer, fifteen grenadiers as escort, and a French officer. Monro ordered a ceasefire and as soon as the small French party had reached the foot of the glacis,[10] he shouted an order for them to halt. They did so promptly, and waited.

The Fort William Henry commander then sent out fifteen of his own soldiers and a lieutenant to ask them what they wanted. From inside the fort, Monro could see them speaking. At a sign from the lieutenant outside, he sent out two more officers, one of whom stayed with the French grenadiers as a hostage while the French officer was blindfolded and led into the fort. In a moment Monro was standing before him, asking him what he wanted.

"Sir," the young officer answered, "I am Captain Louis Antoine de Bougainville, aide-de-camp of General the Marquis de Montcalm, who extends his respects and directs me to hand you this letter reiterating his request that, in the name of humanity, in order to spare the further effusion of blood, and for the preservation of your own life and those of your men, you surrender."

Monro took the letter and glanced at it briefly, then shook his head. "I already gave your general my answer to such a request," he replied. "Nothing has occurred which would make me consider changing that answer."

"Respectfully, sir," Bougainville persisted, wishing his blindfold was off so he could watch the expression on the English commander's face, "I must disagree with you. Something *has* occurred which may well change your stand."

He reached into an inside pocket and took out another letter, which was somewhat crumpled and a corner of it stained with blood. He held it out and felt the commander take it from him.

Emotion drained from Monro's face as he read the words from Captain Bartman's pen that no reinforcement could be expected from General Webb and that Munro had better try to get the best capitulation terms obtainable. Nor did he fail to note that the letter was dated three days ago. For a long while he said nothing and when at last he spoke, he surprised himself at the level calmness of his own words:

"Captain Bougainville, express to General Montcalm for me my thanks for French politeness in this matter. It is a pleasure to deal with so generous and considerate an enemy. If and when I have any specific reply to give, the general will be so notified by our raising a white flag."

Louis Bougainville bowed slightly and allowed himself to be led back to his grenadiers, where he was exchanged for the English officer and his blindfold removed. The officers shook hands and in a moment both parties were returning to their own defenses. As soon as both the parties were safely out of sight, the artillery bombardment began anew.

There was no indication—for now, at any rate—that Lieutenant Colonel Monro had any intention of capitulating.

[ *August 8, 1757—Monday* ]

Major General Daniel Webb signed his name to the bottom of the letter he had just written to the Earl of Loudoun. At intervals came a low rumbling like distant thunder from the northwest, but he knew there was no storm approaching, at least not a rainstorm. He looked up as Captain Bartman knocked and then entered.

"Sir," the aide said, "a runner has just arrived with news that the first segment of the New York militia has reached the camp at Saratoga. They are two thousand men and they ought to be here by dark."

Webb pursed his lips, nodded an acknowledgment and motioned the captain out without speaking. As far as he was concerned, it did little to change what he had already told His Lordship John Campbell in the letter—only somewhat negating that part in which he had written:

*I have not yet received the least reinforcement; this is the disagreeable situation we are at present in. The fort, by the heavy firing we hear from the lake, is still in our possession; but I fear it cannot long hold out against so warm a cannonading if I am not reinforced by a sufficient number of militia to march to their relief.*

Now a reinforcement had come, but so far as Webb could see it made little difference. He folded the letter and sealed it, then placed it inside a dispatch pouch with some other correspondence to go down the Hudson today. As he did so there came a disturbance from outside and in a moment there was a knock on his door. It opened and Captain Bartman, obviously excited, started to say something but was roughly shouldered aside by Sir William Johnson, who was followed by some militia officers and three Mohawk chiefs. William was wearing his general's uniform coat over buckskin leggins. His face was a few shades darker red than his coat.

"General Webb," he said in an ugly tone, "just what in the hell are you doing sitting here when Fort William Henry is under attack? For God's sake, man, they need reinforcement and they need it now! Why isn't your army already on the move?"

"By what right," Webb said indignantly, standing up behind the desk, "do you dare come bursting into my office? Have you no conception, sir, of military courtesy?"

"Military courtesy my ass!" Johnson exploded. "We've got men fighting and dying up at the lake. They have got to have help. *Now!*"

Webb shook his head. "I can't send any. It would be useless with the few men I have. Suicide. I'm waiting for reinforcements."

"Then you've got them. There are two thousand militia moving up right now from Saratoga, and they're moving fast.

There's twice that number right on their heels, just a little below Albany. I've brought fifteen hundred more armed militia from the Mohawk Valley, plus a hundred eighty Mohawks. They're outside right now. You've got over twenty-four hundred effectives right here in Fort Edward and around it. Add that to what Monro has at the lake and, by damn, we'll equal if not outnumber the French!"

Again Webb shook his head. "Not so. Fort William Henry is surrounded by eleven or twelve thousand French. Plus half that many more Indians."

"Damn my soul if that's true!" Johnson shouted. "I've just had thirty Mohawks come back from scouting the whole area. Montcalm doesn't even have eight thousand French and Canadians there. Indians, maybe a couple of thousand at the outside. Damn it, man, you have *got* to send a reinforcement and send it now or the fort's going to fall!

"By God," he went on, only by the greatest of efforts keeping his fury in check, "if *you* won't lead 'em, then let me do it! That same shore of Lake George can be just as fatal to Montcalm as it was to Dieskau. You give me the command and I'll see French bones covering the battlefield!" He jerked his tomahawk from under his coat, raised it high with a gesture that made Webb instinctively wince, and added furiously, "By Christ, Webb, give your army to me and I swear by my tomahawk that I'll conquer or die!"

"Don't you yell at me," Webb shouted back at him angrily. "You may be a baronet, but by God you're no longer a general. *I'm in command here—I'll make the decisions!* I'll send no reinforcement to Fort William Henry. I order you to absent yourself from these quarters at once!"

A rage overwhelming beyond any he had ever experienced now came over William Johnson. For an instant he was on the verge of cleaving the general's head with the tomahawk. He caught himself and threw it contemptuously into a corner of the room, then began emulating the recent action of Chief Nichus toward himself, at Fort Johnson. He planted his feet firmly and began tearing at his clothing, savagely ripping off buttons and braid and epaulets, tearing off sleeves and jerking the material away from him as if it were vile. Nor did he stop with just the jacket. Waistcoat, shirt, leggins, moccasins and everything else followed, until on the floor between himself and the commander was a pile of rags and he himself stood there nude and taut with unspeakable fury. His Mohawks had shed their own scant clothing along with him and stood waiting to see what else this incredible Warraghiyagey would do.

For another full minute William Johnson stood there glaring at the astonished Daniel Webb. Then he hawked deeply and spat onto the center of Webb's desktop, spun around and led his militia and naked Indian followers from the chambers.

Webb continued to stand behind his desk, trembling slightly, vaguely wondering why he had not called for the guard and had Johnson placed under arrest. At length he turned and picked up the dispatch packet from his desk, close to where Johnson had spat, and held it out to Captain Bartman.

"Get these off by express at once," he ordered. He dipped his head at the offensive torn garments on the floor and added, "Then get someone in here to clean up this trash."

## [ *August 9, 1757—Tuesday* ]

It was not the easiest thing in the world to write in his journal with the material balanced in his lap, the night air cool enough off the lake to make him uncomfortably stiff, and the small dim lamp swaying back and forth with the motion of the boat, but Louis Antoine de Bougainville was making a valiant stab at it.

He knew it must be nearly midnight by now, and for at least the fifth time since leaving the wharf at Fort William Henry, Montcalm's aide-de-camp politely asked the rowers to endeavor to row without so much jerkiness, as it was detrimental to his writing. The soldiers grunted something of an acknowledgement and did make an effort to row more smoothly, but there was little improvement. Bougainville sighed. Well, it didn't matter much now, anyway, since he was just completing the day's entry.

He blew lightly on the ink to dry it, dipped the point of his quill into the lake to clean it, and then corked his inkpot. Pen and inkpot he placed in the special packet he had for them and put them into an inside pocket of his jacket, momentarily wishing he could find a flatter container for his ink, so the bulge the bottle made in his uniform would not be so apparent and so uncomfortable.

He shrugged unconsciously, and turned back a page in his journal to reread what he had just written:

*August 9*
*Two hundred workers were ordered to improve the work*

535

*during the night. At seven in the morning the fort raised a white flag and asked to capitulate. Colonel Young came to propose articles of capitulation to the Marquis de Montcalm. I was sent to draw them up and to take the first steps in putting them into operation.*

*In substance the capitulation provided that the troops, both of the fort and of the entrenched camp, to the number of two thousand men, should depart with the honors of war with the baggage of the officers and of the soldiers; that they should be conducted to Fort Lydius [Fort Edward] escorted by a detachment of our troops, and by the principal officers and interpreters attached to the Indians; that until the return of this escort an officer should remain in our hands as a hostage, that the troops would not serve for eighteen months against His Most Catholic Majesty nor against his allies; that within three months all French, Canadian and Indian prisoners taken on land in North America since the commencement of the war should be returned to French forts; that the artillery, vessels, and all the munitions and provisions would belong to His Most Catholic Majesty, except one six-pounder cannon which the Marquis de Montcalm granted Colonel Monro and the garrison to witness his esteem for the fine defense they had made.*

*Before signing the capitulation the Marquis de Montcalm assembled a council to which the chiefs of all the nations had been summoned. He informed them of the articles granted the besieged, the motives which determined his according them, asked their consent and their promise that their young men would not commit any disorder. The chiefs agreed to everything and promised to restrain their young men.*

*One sees by this action of the Marquis de Montcalm to what point one is a slave to Indians in this country. They are a necessary evil.*

*I think that we could have had these troops as prisoners at discretion, but in the first case there would have been two thousand more men to feed, and in the second, one could not have restrained the barbarity of the Indians, and it is never permitted to sacrifice humanity to what is only the shadow of glory.*

*At noon the fort was turned over to our troops from the trenches, and, the garrison leaving with its baggage, it was necessary to let the Indians and Canadians in to pillage all the remaining effects. Only with the greatest trouble could the provisions and munitions be saved. The English troops were to remain in their entrenched camp until the next day.*

*Despite a guard from our troops that we had put on it, the Indians could not be stopped from entering and pillaging. Everything was done to stop them; consultation with the chiefs, wheedling on our part, authority that the officers and interpreters attached to them possessed. We will be most fortunate if we can avoid a massacre. Detestable position of which those who are not here can have no idea, and one which makes the victory painful to the conquerors.*

*The Marquis de Montcalm went himself to the entrenched camp. He there made the greatest efforts to prevent the greed of the Indians and, I will say it here, of certain people of our own attached to them, from being the cause of misfortunes far greater than pillage.*

*At last by nine in the evening it appeared that order had been reestablished in the camp. The Marquis de Montcalm was even able to arrange that, beyond the escort agreed upon by the capitulation, two chiefs from each nation should escort the English as far as the vicinity of Fort Edward. I had taken care, upon going into the English camp, to advise the officers and soldiers to throw away all wine, brandy, and intoxicating liquors; they themselves had realized of what consequence it was for them to take this precaution.*

*At ten in the evening I was sent by order of the Marquis de Montcalm to carry to the Marquis de Vaudreuil the news of the surrender of Fort William Henry and the capitulation.*

### [ *August 10, 1757—Wednesday* ]

Despite the generous terms of the capitulation, over which there was at first a general rejoicing among the men, Lieutenant Colonel Monro was worried. Though Montcalm had been the quintessence of gentlemanly behavior and had elicited agreement from all the chiefs that the liberated garrison would not be disturbed on its march to Fort Edward, serious disruption had seemed only too probable as soon as they marched out of the fort. He did not see how such a mob of blood-hungry savages could possibly be controlled, and French assurances didn't help ease his mind, though he accepted them.

His fears were confirmed even sooner than he had anticipated.

The men inside the fort who were sick with smallpox and could not walk were necessarily left behind, along with their own women and children, when the fort was surrendered. Continued assurances were given that they would be well taken care of, and that when Monro's men reached Fort Edward wagons could be brought back to transport them to a better place. Monro was then directed to march his men and the remaining women and children to the entrenched camp, which lay some eight hundred yards southeast of the fort and adjacent to the east side of the road leading to Fort Edward. This he did at once, with the further assurance from Montcalm that in the morning three hundred French regulars would escort them to the vicinity of Fort Edward.

Halfway to the entrenchment, however, it became apparent that seventeen of the wounded soldiers—most of them from the Massachusetts Regiment—were in too serious a condition to go farther. These seventeen were carried into several small huts close to the road, under directions of the regimental surgeon, Miles Whitworth. Whitworth then placed the men under the care of a French surgeon and continued with the defeated army to the encampment. Himself being called away to attend others of his own army, the French surgeon placed a ring of guards around the huts with orders for them to keep the Indians out.

Meanwhile, with the English army now gone from the fort, the Indians and Canadians rushed in to search for plunder and rum. They found precious little of either. The goods were mostly gone, packed in the baggage of the English, and the rum kegs were all smashed. Howling with anger, both the Canadians and the Indians whipped out their tomahawks and fell upon the sick men and their women and children.

The carnage was ghastly.

Jesuit Father Roubaud, hearing the shrieks, rushed in from outside to see what was happening. He was almost bowled over at the door by an Abnaki emerging with the head of one of the soldiers, gripping it by the hair while a considerable quantity of blood still dripped from it. The savage held it high and screamed victoriously, then ran off with it.

In the area of the casements, the screams of the victims were becoming fewer as constantly more of them were slain. Soon the terrified shriekings had ended and all that remained were the exultant cries of the bush lopers and Indians, some of whom were emerging with as many as a dozen scalps stuffed into their waistbands. All of them were well splattered with blood and many, from the amount of blood on their chests, dripping from their chins, staining their lips and mouth corners, had evidently drunk the blood of their victims—a practice not uncommon among them.

Not even those soldiers who had died weeks before and

been buried were left unmolested. The shallow graves beside the fort were opened and the scalps of the rotting corpses were taken. The body of the brother of Robert Rogers was one of those so desecrated.

Still hungry for the plunder that had been denied them and even more so for something alcoholic, the Indians and *coureurs de bois* poured out of the fort in a stream and swarmed toward the entrenched camp where virtually all of the remaining English were now collected and busied in erecting tents for the night.

The French soldiers posted around the perimeter of the camp made something of an effort to keep the horde out, as they had been ordered to, but against such numbers they were helpless. The savages and bush lopers shoved past them and were soon stalking about the encampment in a highly menacing way, brandishing tomahawks or knives. Although the English still had their muskets, their ammunition and bayonets had been surrendered and so they were forced to grit their teeth in frustration as the insults became even worse. The Indians pinched the cheeks, arms or buttocks of many of the men, licked their lips and rubbed their stomachs, and none of the English needed interpretation of the meaning. Of the women they paid particular attention to their long hair, fondling it and sometimes yanking it sharply, and even the hair of many of the children was caressed—all to the abject horror of those being so touched, pinched, fondled or caressed.

The confusion grew worse throughout the afternoon and might quite likely have turned into a massacre if the Marquis de Montcalm had not arrived and strongly rebuked them for breaking their promises. He finally was able to make them leave the confines of the entrenched camp, and then he ordered the Canadian officer, St. Luc de la Corne—commonly called "general of the Indians"—and some of his officers to see that no further violence took place. Yet, it was an extremely uneasy night for everyone in the entrenched camp.

It was at about five o'clock this morning that the sentinels guarding the English wounded in the huts were called away for some other duty. As if they had been cats waiting to pounce, a cluster of Indians almost immediately descended on the huts and dragged the seventeen screaming men out of the buildings by their arms, legs or hair. There in the open, while Captain St. Luc de la Corne and a number of his officers looked on in apparent approbation from less than forty feet away, all seventeen had their throats slit or were tomahawked. With cupped hands, several of the Indians caught the bright blood which gushed from severed jugulars, held it to their lips and quaffed it, then shrieked in wild triumph. All seventeen of the victims were scalped.

The entrenched camp went into an instant uproar of fear, which only increased as an even greater number of Indians and Canadians entered the camp again and now began to plunder the English goods. It was about that time, fortunately, that from the distant camp of Montcalm[11] came the three hundred French regulars he had promised as an escort. Monro complained at once to the officers that the terms of the capitulation had been broken.

"Monsieur," replied the captain in charge, shrugging, "it is a sad thing, but the Indians are very difficult to keep under control. We are only glad that worse has not happened to your people in this camp. As for your baggage—monsieur, these Indians feel deprived; my strong advice is that you and your people voluntarily give it up to them to appease them, lest they continue to try to take it by force, and we would be helpless to stop them."

Lieutenant Colonel Monro and his officers agreed it was probably the wisest thing for them to do and so the English all stood back and watched while the Indians and Canadians leaped into the area and began tearing the baggage apart. Instead of this satisfying them, however, they became even more excited. And then there came a triumphant screech from one of the Indians as he discovered that a canteen was filled with rum instead of water. Instantly there was a frantic scrabbling for all available canteens and a good percentage of them were found to have rum in them. The liquor disappeared down the gullets of the Indians as swiftly as it was found.

With considerable confusion reigning, the column of English with the French escort now began moving toward Fort Edward on the Lyman road—the French regulars a hundred yards or so behind the English and an advance guard of Canadian colony regulars about the same distance in front. Despite the escort, it was by no means a peaceful march. Indians and bush lopers crowded in on them from the sides, snatched hats, coats and muskets away from them, generally impeded the march and began tomahawking any and all who resisted. A dozen, a score, perhaps half-a-hundred women and children were snatched up and borne shrieking into the woods flanking the road, and then abruptly, from the throat of a brawny Indian, there issued an overriding, penetrating cry:

"*Eeeeeee-Neeeee-Yaaaahhhhhh!*"

The Indian was Panaouska, war chief of the Abnakis and chief of the village at the Penobscot mission.[12] It was apparently a prearranged signal, which was instantly echoed by hundreds of others. As quickly as it was sounded the whole rear of the column—made up mostly of New Hampshire men—was inundated by savages and a great massacre began.

It lasted for minutes only, mainly because of the most opportune arrival of Montcalm, Lévis, Bourlamaque and a number of the officers and men of the three commanders. With little regard for their own safety, they threw themselves into the midst of the melee and began pulling Indians away from their intended victims, cursing them, ordering them back, demanding that the carnage cease.

"In the name of God and the King," Montcalm shouted, "I order you to stop! If you have to kill, then kill me, but don't harm another one of the English prisoners under my protection!"[13]

Probably no one other than Montcalm—not even Vaudreuil—could have stayed the Indians from continuing the butchery, but such was their respect and admiration for him that they stepped back. He castigated them frightfully, but the damage was done. Eighty of the English soldiers were already dead or missing. Another four hundred still huddled together on the road, and these Montcalm immediately put under his personal command and had them marched back to his own camp for their protection. But the rest of the English had stampeded down the road, swiftly overtaking the advance guard. They demanded protection from the Canadian officers, but were flatly refused. The Canadians had no intention of getting themselves killed to protect English soldiers.

"Your only choice now," one of the officers shouted, "is to scatter into the woods and shift for yourselves until you can reach your people."

And he was right.

Colonel Frye was gripped by three Indians and threatened with spears and tomahawks while he was stripped of everything but breeches, shirt and shoes. The three warriors then began to squabble among themselves over who should have what, including the officer's scalp, and while they were occupied, Frye broke away from them and plunged into the woods, running at breakneck speed through the tangled undergrowth.[14]

Struggling violently, Captain Burke of the Massachusetts Regiment was also stripped of his clothing and he, too, managed to jerk himself away and disappear into the woods. Jonathan Carver, a provincial private, was similarly stripped and, certain he was going to be killed, he pulled away and ran up to a Canadian officer standing a few feet away with several other officers. He begged for help.

"English dog!" said the officer, and shoved him back vigorously toward the Indians. Two of them snatched the private and began to drag him off when an English officer, clad only in his scarlet trousers, came running down the road, and tried to pass them. One of the Indians holding Carver jumped on him, but was tumbled to the ground. The other turned loose his hold on Carver and ran to help his companion. He drove his tomahawk deep into the officer's back.

Carver turned to run away himself when a boy of about twelve, terror-stricken, clutched him and begged the private to help him. Carver grabbed his wrist and dragged him along, but an Indian snatched the boy away from him and, though he did not look back, Carver heard the youngster's shrieks rise and then abruptly end. By then Private Carver was well into the woods.

The situation was one of pure bedlam. At least half-a-hundred corpses now littered the road here, and as many Indians crouched over them, removing their scalps. Pursuit of those who dashed into the woods was slight and even that quickly given up. But many of the hundreds of English still thrashing through the underbrush felt in their minds the hot breath of the savages still on their necks and they ran until they dropped from exhaustion. The majority became hopelessly lost and it was obvious that if they reached Fort Edward at all, it would not be for many days.

But a few did manage to get there before evening, and, hysterically, they told what had taken place and how the woods were now filled with wandering soldiers unable to find their way. General Daniel Webb ordered the cannon to be shot at regular intervals to help guide the lost ones in. It was the least he could do . . . the *very* least.

And once again the news of major disaster for the English went speeding down the Hudson River.

The Indians, while still respectful of Montcalm, were generally angry with him for not letting them carry out their vengeance to greater measure on the English. The fact that he was still holding four hundred thoroughly demoralized soldiers in protective custody also rankled them. For their own part, they had managed to take two hundred of the soldiers alive and no appeals from Montcalm would persuade them to give these men up to him.

"These English we will keep," they told him, "and take them north to the little Onontio [Governor Vaudreuil] to exchange for the goods and rewards they will bring. We will not be cheated out of this, which is our right. And to prevent any further trouble between us, we will leave now for that place."

Within two hours scarcely an Indian remained at the site of Fort William Henry, and a great many of the *coureurs de bois* had gone off with them. Montcalm's four hundred prisoners nearly wept with their relief at their going.

Montcalm had conversed with his officers at great length over whether or not they should, as originally planned, press their attack now to take in Fort Edward, too, but the decision went against it for a variety of reasons. The Indians were gone, and many of the *coureurs de bois* with them, thus greatly diminishing their total strength. Supplies were short and, further, Governor Vaudreuil had specifically ordered Montcalm to have the Canadian colony regulars and militia back home no later than September 1, so that they could gather the crops their wives and children had been tending in their absence. Nor did the reasons for not pressing their victory end there. It was altogether possible that Webb's reinforcements may have arrived by now. Though the French force was strong, it lacked draught animals for transporting the artillery to Fort Edward for an attack there, and it would be foolish to even consider attacking it without cannon. And finally, to be truthful, none of them really had much heart to carry the campaign any further right now.

Deeply depressed in spite of his victory here at Fort William Henry, Montcalm set his soldiers to the labor of demolishing the English installation. And onto the great pile of rampart timbers, barracks wood and other debris that resulted, all of the bodies of the English that could be found were to be deposited by his order. It would be a big job that would undoubtedly take four or five days, but when it was finished, the whole disgusting mess would be set ablaze and might, in the general's own mind, somewhat cauterize the wound of this most wretched victory he had ever won.

## [ *August 20, 1757—Saturday* ]

Once again the rumors ... and with them, again, the fear.

Throughout the English Colonies the stories spread and the panic was enveloping. The horror of the massacre at Fort William Henry was on everyone's lips and in everyone's eyes, and the dread of the supposedly advancing multitude of Indians, Canadians and Frenchmen was a dead weight in everyone's heart. Rumor had the Indians numbering as many as twenty thousand, and the French and Canadians at over fifteen thousand. Albany, it was said, was on the verge of attack and, following its fall, the next targets would be New York and Philadelphia.

A fantastic number of militiamen were called up, formed into hundreds of companies and immediately moved up the Hudson until, in a very short time, the area surrounding Fort Edward was one massive bivouack. Thousands upon thousands of men arrived, ready to fight for their own lives, the lives of their loved ones, the lives of the colonies.

They waited ... and waited ...

By the thirteenth day of August they were unruly, by the fourteenth mutinous. They were ready to lay down their lives in fighting the enemy, but they were not prepared to lay down their bodies on the earth around Fort Edward, without blankets, without tents, without kettles, without proper food. Not unexpectedly, they began to desert, especially the New York militia, which was closest to home. And when General Webb sent word of it to Delancey—word that these deserters were threatening to kill any officers who tried to stop them— an express came back authorizing him to fire on them if necessary to keep control. Webb did just that: a sergeant was shot dead and others were arrested. Turmoil was general until, on the seventeenth, Webb learned that the French army had withdrawn and he released the militias and sent them home.

And His Lordship John Campbell, his expedition to Nova Scotia a dismal failure and now sailing home without even having gotten within firing distance of the fortress of Louisbourg, was intercepted at sea by a dispatch boat bearing the news of the disaster at Lake George. At once he wrote to Webb:

*The Rangers will, as they are preceding me, return to Albany and Fort Edward at once. I shall, if prevented by headwinds from getting into New York, disembark my troops on Long Island. . . . Hold the enemy in check without risking battle until I myself shall arrive there. I am on the way with a force sufficient to turn the scale, with God's assistance; and then I hope we shall teach the French to comply with the laws of nature and humanity. For although I abhor barbarity, the knowledge I have of Mr. Vaudreuil's behavior when in Louisiana, from his own letters in my possession, and the murders committed at Oswego and now at Fort William Henry, will oblige me to make those gentlemen sick of such inhuman villany whenever it is in my power.*

## [ September 1, 1757—Thursday ]

The Indians were gone from Montreal now and, for the first time since they had arrived nine days ago with their two hundred English prisoners, the populace of the city was able to shake off its fear and disgust over what had transpired in the interval.

Captain Bougainville had arrived in the city at four o'clock in the afternoon on the eleventh and immediately he reported to Governor Vaudreuil. But instead of being pleased, as Montcalm's aide-de-camp had expected him to be, Pierre Vaudreuil complained over the fact that the English captives were being released by Montcalm and, especially, that Montcalm had not instantly followed up his advantage by marching against Fort Edward. The bewildered captain was curtly dismissed.

Then, on the nineteenth the Indians had arrived with their prisoners and demanded of Vaudreuil a ransom for them—two kegs of brandy for every prisoner. The governor scolded them briefly for breaking the terms of the capitulation and for abandoning General Montcalm, but then he nervously gave in to their demands and provided them with the liquor. The Indians took it eagerly, but they did not give up the captives. Instead, they drank the brandy until they were staggeringly, blindly drunk; and all this while the English with them were dying a hundred deaths, with liberation dangled in front of them like an apple, yet a knife at their throats if they so much as moved.

Now came the scavengers—the Canadian tradesmen and storekeepers—who bought all the English plunder from the Indians, providing them with even more liquor and with new knives and guns, powder and tomahawks and other trade goods of more benefit to them. With their new weapons in hand, the drunken Indians roamed the streets of Montreal, threatening and insulting everyone they met. Complaints were carried to Vaudreuil, but instead of reprimanding the Indians and demanding good behavior and the surrender of the prisoners he had ransomed, he loaded them with even more gifts under the assumption that this would make them relent in their cruelty. That it did not was clear from Bougainville's journal entry which said, in part:

*At two o'clock, in the presence of the entire city, the Indians killed one of the English soldiers, put him in a kettle, and forced his unfortunate compatriots to eat him.*

*I would believe that if, immediately upon the arrival of these Indians, the governor had stated to them that until all English were given up, there would be no presents, nor even any food; that if, under the most severe penalties, he had forbidden the citizens either to sell or to give them brandy; that if he had done these things, he himself could have gone to their cabins and snatched the English away from them. I believe this, accustomed as I am to think like a European. I have seen just the opposite, and my soul has several times shuddered at the spectacles my eyes have witnessed.*

*Will they, in Europe, believe that the Indians alone have been guilty of this horrible violation of the capitulation? Will they believe that desire for the Negroes and other spoils of the English had not caused the people who are at the head of these nations—the interpreters and Canadian leaders of the Indians—to loosen the curb, perhaps to even go farther? The more so, since one today may see one of these leaders, unworthy of the name of officer or Frenchman, leading in his train a Negro kidnapped from the English commander under the pretext of appeasing the memory of a dead Indian, giving his family flesh for flesh. That is enough of the horror, the memory of which I would hope could be effaced from the minds of men. HEU FUGE CRUDELES TERRAS FUGE LITTUS INIQUUM!*[15]

And now Montcalm, having safely escorted the four hundred English he had rescued back into English hands, having burned in a great fire and dispersed in obscene oily smoke the residue of Fort William Henry and its inhabitants, having left the lake, having again placed General Lévis in command of Fort Carillon—having done all this, he had returned to

Montreal for his own conferences with Vaudreuil, and they were not pleasant affairs. The governor left no doubt in the general's mind that had he been there, no attempt would have been made to keep the Indians from their massacre; in fact, that encouragement would probably have been given and then, with every Englishman dead, who was to know for certain how they had met their end, or that a capitulation had been dishonored? The rift between governor and military commander thereupon became too wide ever to be bridged again.

Louis Antoine de Bougainville was delighted to have the Marquis de Montcalm back and to be serving again a man in whom there was a great depth of humanity and a great sense of honor. They shared in common a sustaining thought: that while in the eyes of the world they might be held guilty for the criminal acts at Lake George and in Montreal, in their own hearts and minds they knew that they had campaigned with honor and with decency.

The one person above all in the world that Louis Bougainville did not wish to think ill of him was his mother, and so now he wrote to Madame Herault from the depths of his heart:

*September 1, 1757*

*Dearest Mama,*

*Would you believe that this abominable action of the Indians at Fort William Henry has accomplices among people who call themselves Frenchmen; that greed for gain, the certainty of getting very cheaply from the Indians all the goods they had pillaged, are the primary causes of a horror for which England will not fail to reproach us for a long time to come? Thank heaven our own officers are blameless in this respect; several risked their lives on this occasion; they divided up everything they had with the unfortunate English, and these latter say that if ever they have occasion to besiege and capture us, there will be two capitulations, one for the French troops, and the other for the Canadians. These are frightful truths, dear Mama. But spectacles still more frightful have befouled my eyes and left an ineffaceable bitterness in my soul. May the memory of these abominations vanish. What a land! What a people! . . .*

The Indians of the upper Great Lakes were on their way home and, for the most part, they were jubilant.

They were bringing with them to their families and fellow Ottawas, Chippewas, Potawatomies and Hurons, many things. They were bringing new guns and lead and gunpowder. They were bringing new tomahawks and knives and awls. They were bringing needles and blankets and brilliant threads, brightly colored beads and wampum and mirrors. They were bringing a multitude of scalps. They were bringing stories of their courage and heroism for recounting before the fire on long winter nights. They were bringing news of victory!

And there was one other thing they were bringing: they were bringing back erratic pulses and severe headaches; terrible pains in their loins and backs; vomiting and high temperatures; a peculiar rash on the inside of their thighs and on the lower part of the abdomen; they were bringing back little spots on their scalps and faces and arms—spots that were quickly changing to angry pustules.

They were bringing back, in a word, smallpox!

[ *October 19, 1757—Wednesday* ]

He spoke only rarely of it to others, but deep within Louis Antoine de Bougainville there was a strong sense of guilt; a disquieting, undeniable knowledge that the war methods being used here—the methods of which he was most definitely a part—were deeply, morally wrong. To encourage the Indians to continue, even increase, the wave of slaughter on the English borders was inhumanity of the worst kind. But just as he knew it was wrong, so Bougainville knew as well that there was not a thing he could do about it. His heart was not in this war; it hadn't been before, it was not now, it would not ever be. The victories the French had thus far won filled him with exultation, but it was an emotion laced with a bitterness that was reflected in the writing he continued in his journal:

*October 19*
*According to letters from Fort Duquesne of September 7, the Indians of La Belle Rivière perform miracles. Since the beginning of the campaign they have brought back more than two hundred prisoners or scalps. They desolate the English countyside. . . . The deserters assert that the English have*

*not any project planned for this year, but that an attempt against Fort Duquesne is under consideration. . . .*

*The news from Niagara is of September 17. The construction there is practically finished; the only thing left to do is face with stone. The Indians are so strongly disposed in our favor that M. Pouchot believes the next spring, if we furnish Niagara abundantly with powder and trade goods, we can unleash nearly three thousand Indians on the English colonies. What a scourge! Humanity shudders at being obliged to make use of such monsters. But without them the match would be too much against us. . . .*

*All the prisoners assert that if the French should appear in Pennsylvania, the province would make itself an independent republic under the protection of France. I had told this to M. de Vaudreuil when he arrived here, but he did not believe me, or at least he acted as if he had not.*

*According to the news received by M. Pouchot, the civilian governor of Pennsylvania offers to let the Indians pass freely into Virginia, provided that they spare his province. What can one do against invisible enemies who strike and flee with the rapidity of light? It is the destroying angel.*

[ *November 12, 1757—Saturday* ]

The bad news for the English in this year of incredibly consistent bad news was not yet over. At Fort Johnson, Sir William Johnson, bedridden for almost seven weeks now with severe pleurisy and violent stitches in his side, had glumly heard regular reports of just how terrible the English situation was and how nothing really worthwhile could be done. John Campbell, having returned with great bravado to New York from his failure at Nova Scotia, failed to follow through on his declaration that he would at once march against the French with a great force. Instead, he had vented his spleen on the Indians—all Indians, including the Mohawks.

"If," he had threatened darkly and publicly, "the Iroquois do not now declare war on France, I will treat them in the same manner as I do my master's other enemies!" But then, since he hadn't yet treated his master's other enemies so very badly, the threat was a hollow one at worst.

This evening to Sir William Johnson had come the latest important news and it was, as usual, all bad. It had been brought to Fort Johnson by a young Mohawk from Canajoharie and relayed to Degonwadonti—Molly Brant—

who was once again nursing her man to health with every Iroquois remedy she could recall.

At three o'clock this morning, so the report ran, a party of three hundred men—*coureurs de bois,* Indians and Canadian colony regulars—under a captain named Belêtre, swooped down unexpectedly on German Flats just upriver from Fort Johnson and destroyed it utterly. A great number of domestic animals—hogs, sheep, cattle and horses—had been butchered and left lying where they fell. The several small picket forts of the place had been taken one by one and burned. Sixty homes, plus all barns, sheds and other outbuildings had similarly been burned. Forty or fifty of the inhabitants, mostly men, were slain and scalped. One hundred fourteen of the inhabitants, mainly women and children, were marched off as captives. At the head of their column, his arms tied behind him, had been the town's magistrate, Johan Jost Petrie. German Flats had ceased to exist as a village and now the prime remaining strongpoint of the English on the Mohawk River above Schenectady was Fort Johnson.

And Sir William Johnson was too weak to do anything but groan and roll over.

### [ December 31, 1757—Saturday ]

From all outward appearances the year closed on a high note for the French and an exceptionally low one for the English. The former had won impressive victories; the latter suffered inglorious defeats. The former had more Indian allies now than ever before; the latter had left only the nebulous neutrality of the Six Nations and the positive support of only a faction of one tribe of the Six Nations—the Mohawks. Everything appeared to be going well for the French and poorly for the English.

But appearances are deceptive.

A chink was forming in the armor of Canada, exposing beneath it a cancerous rot known as corruption. The Indians and the common people of Canada were first to feel the bite of it. Having busied themselves throughout most of the year as His Most Catholic Majesty's gladiators in a forest arena, their crops had largely failed, disease had felled their livestock, game was desperately scarce and the specter of hunger roamed the land for them and their families.

Quite naturally the Indians and the peasantry of Canada came to the governor with their demands. His larder was bulging with grain, his tables overflowed with fine wines and plump fowl and the best of meats. Was there no flour to spare for the populace? Was there no beef for them? Were his Indian allies and, yes, even his own people not entitled to subsistence for the winter as payment for their alliance and sacrifice this past summer, and also in anticipation of the campaigns to come?

The answer, in essence, was this: If you have money—*lots* of money—you eat: if you have little or none, you starve.

While Governor Pierre Vaudreuil and Intendant François Bigot and Commissary General Joseph Cadet lived, literally, off the fat of the land and grew daily richer, the poor became even poorer and the starving even hungrier. Resentment seethed beneath the surface and when, at last, even the soldiers and what might pass as the middle class were forced to take severely reduced rations and, in place of beef, the carcasses of horses which had been butchered only figurative moments before they would have expired anyway from starvation, the resentment turned to the heat of rebellion.

Just last week a great mob had gathered before the governor's palatial home and screamed epithets at him, telling him what he might do with his horsemeat—a meat, they declared, which in the first place their religion forbade them to eat.

"Disperse!" Vaudreuil had shouted at them. "Go away to your homes or I will have you thrown in jail and, if you persist, I will have you hanged!"

The crowd dispersed, but not to their homes. They went to the soldiers quartered throughout the town and lit the fires of rebellion under them, too. The colony regulars mutinied and even went so far as to get the French regulars of the battalion of Béarn to join them. The mob that re-formed before the governor's house was this time considerably larger and considerably meaner.

Montcalm was in Quebec and Vaudreuil could not call on him for help in time, so he dumped the problem into the lap of General François Lévis who was now quartered here. And Lévis rose to the challenge. He threatened death to any soldier who should refuse to eat horsemeat, which, he assured them, he ate every day himself just as they did, and told them to go home. Amazingly, they did so, but the resentment remained and kept them even warmer than the pitiful fires in their crude abodes.

The situation in Quebec was little better. The so-called "Great Society" of Intendant François Bigot was great for only a few. While the intendant regularly held lavish balls and gambled with extreme abandon, Louis Montcalm's own personal situation worsened and he fell deeper and deeper into debt. Because of his standing, his credit was good, but his indebtedness increased and it preyed upon him. It galled him to see how night after night, while multitudes around him were but a hairline from starvation, Bigot rarely had less than forty guests at his table, for whom he offered great masquerade parties, sumptuous dances and gambling that staggered the imagination. In a single evening of cards at his own table, he lost two hundred four thousand francs, yet scarcely batted an eye.

To Montcalm, who disliked partying, despised dances—especially masquerades—and banquet dinners, who had not the money to gamble even had he the whim, the winter was totally lacking in stimulation except for his frequent conversations with Louis Bougainville. He wrote frequently and with an ever increasing disgust and despair to his mother and to his beloved wife, Angélique, to whom he had only recently written:

*The price of everything is rising. I am ruining myself; I owe the treasurer twelve thousand francs. I long for peace, and for you. In spite of the public distress, we have balls and furious gambling. As for me, my ennui increases. I live as usual, fencing in the morning, dining, and I spend almost every evening in my chambers. I don't know what to do, or say, or read, or where to go; and I think at the end of the next campaign I shall ask bluntly, blindly, for my recall, only because I am bored. Nevertheless, I live here on good terms with everybody, and do my best to serve the King. If they could but do without me! ...*

Bougainville, for his part, was equally bored but he had a greater facility for standing it, a greater resiliency and an ability to seek until he had found something which could, for however short a time, end the monotony. He found his greatest refuge in books and his greatest levity in the foibles of the people around him. The corruption he saw astounded him and, to even greater extent, worried him. To his mother he wrote:

*... the Governor of Montreal enjoys a trading post which is worth immense sums to him. This line of business, he makes quite sure, will never be known to the Minister for the colonies. And can you conceive it: letters from Paris say*

*that they intend to have M. de Rigaud replace M. de Kerlerec in Louisiana. It must be, then, that this government needs only a wig-stand. What a man! Even the Intendant, who gave me this news, cannot believe it. . . .*

*On the ninth they started to issue horsemeat to the troops. The women of Montreal went and threw it at M. de Vaudreuil's feet. . . . The guilt is largely with the peculators in M. Bigot's Great Society, who have so created a monopoly that trade is dead and prices beyond what any but the extremely rich can afford to pay. A citizen of Quebec owed a debt to a member of the Great Society. He was unable to pay it. They assigned him the housing and feeding of a large number of Acadians. He let them die of hunger and cold, got all the money they had, and paid off his extortioner creditor. What a country! What morals!*

To his brother, Louis Bougainville wrote of similar matters and concluded:

*Unfortunately, I have seen and heard only too much myself. I go farther. The air one breathes here is contagious, and I fear lest a long sojourn here makes us acquire the vices of a people to whom we communicate no virtues. . . .*

*Boredom! The great scourge of a thinking man. Without Montaigne, Horace, Vergil, Tacitus, Montesquieu, Corneille, the conversations and kindness of my General, ennui would have consumed me.*

With hunger breeding malcontents among the Indians and Canadian peasantry, and with boredom breeding malcontents among those higher in station, the perfume that had so long masked the corruption was wearing thin and the stench of rot was escaping. Great fissures were forming in the walls of deceit built up over so many years and to some men of vision—men such as Louis Montcalm, François Lévis, François Bourlamaque, Louis Bougainville—a grave portent was clarifying. If, in next summer's campaign, the entire war was not won by France, it might well never be won.

# CHAPTER X

[ *March 15, 1758—Wednesday* ]

ON the whole, English provincials shared a great dislike for English regulars. The regulars were, in their opinion, altogether too inclined to look down their noses at the "militia rabble," as they liked to call the provincials. With no great love lost between them at any time, it was therefore amazing how quickly the entire English army, provincials and regulars alike, had come to respect—in fact, almost adore—a new regular officer on the scene. He had been commissioned a brigadier general, and he was a man of vision, talent, experience and pronounced ability. He was also only thirty-four years of age.

His name was George Howe.

Lord Howe had arrived rather inconspicuously, late in the summer last year, took up residence in Albany and became, very quickly, a close friend of Captain Philip Schuyler. Howe, along with other officers, often partook of the warm hospitality of Captain Schuyler's mother. She, in turn, thoroughly enjoyed their stimulating company and invited them often for dinner and for long and pleasant evenings of conversation. She liked them all very much, but for George Howe she had an intensity of feeling quite apart. So thoroughly had he won her heart in these few brief months that she loved him with very nearly the same depth of love she held for her own sons. And Lord Howe responded with a commensurate affection for her.

That he was several cuts above the other English officers in almost every respect was at once evident. He had the type of nature to which both men and women are at once attracted. As Colonel James Wolfe wrote to his father, Lord Howe "is the noblest Englishman that has appeared in my time, and the best soldier in the British Army."

Nor was it flattery.

The botch of last year's campaign had resulted, as everyone had anticipated, in Lord Loudoun being recalled to England and his second-in-command, General James Abercromby, being named to the top command post by William Pitt. But Abercromby had gotten where he was through politics and outside influence rather than through personal ability, and everyone knew it, just as they knew equally well that while Abercromby might nominally be holding the post of commander in chief, it was really George Howe who was doing the job.

It had taken little time for Howe to realize, after his arrival in America, that the forest warfare being waged against the French and Indians was wholly unlike any type of warfare the English had ever faced before. This was not the place for pokerlike ranks of brilliantly clad men to stand and fire at an enemy they couldn't see, but whose return bullets they so quickly felt. This was a war where the enemy had to be met on his own grounds and fought by his own rules. So far as George Howe could see, that was not being done—with but one exception.

This exception was the Ranger company under Captain Robert Rogers. Howe had been immediately impressed with the tactics developed by Rogers, with the uniform of green worn by his men, allowing them to blend so well with the forests in which they fought. It had become something of a status symbol among the lieutenants and captains of the regulars to go out on scouts with his patrols. One such mission, however, usually sufficed for them, and only rarely did any of the regular officers come back for second helpings.

Just as the ranks of captains and lieutenants vied to go out with him at least once, the high-ranking officers would not even consider doing so. It was, quite obviously, below their dignity to do so and would tend to attach too great an importance to Captain Rogers and what he was doing.

Such was most emphatically not the case where Lord George Howe was concerned. As soon as Robert Rogers had come back from the abortive mission with John Campbell to Nova Scotia, Howe had presented himself and asked to be permitted to join in on some patrols. With a certain amusement, Rogers had agreed, and was amazed to see the general shed his red uniform for the green of the Rangers and follow the orders of the Ranger captain as if he were no more than an eager lieutenant.

Not once in the dozen of missions since then upon which

he had embarked with the Rangers, had Howe asked for or expected preferential treatment. He shared their food, their camp, their laughter, their hardships, and in a very short time he had the entire Ranger company, including Robert Rogers, neatly wrapped around his finger.

It was not with false studiousness that he watched Rogers's every move and marveled at the fighting team this New Hampshire officer had molded. Swiftly, very swiftly, he learned what to do, when to do it, and how to do it to survive in the perilous service of the Rangers. The company was far more effective a force than that which Rogers had formed so long ago; one that was now well versed in guerrilla fighting and survival in the wilderness. And Rogers, flattered by the sincere interest shown by Howe, took special care to instruct him well.

"On a patrol with eight or ten men," Rogers told him, "we walk singlefile, spaced so's to prevent an enemy destroyin' two of us with one shot, an' we move along cautiously. On goin' over mossy or soft ground, we change our position an' march abreast each other. That's to prevent an enemy trackin' us.

"With a big party," he continued, "of mebbe three hunnerd men, we split into thirds. I command the center, my next senior officer is twenty yards away on my right, and the other hunnerd's the same distance off on my left under the third officer. Each division's marched in single file. 'Bout a dozen men range thirty yards ahead of each division and a couple of scouts are ahead of each of these advance parties another thirty yards. Forty yards to each side we throw out a flanking file of twenty-five men, and beyond them a little farther out, two or three men also in single file to guard against ambush. Finally, we have a rear guard of a sergeant an' eight men. Ever' time we go over a rise, they hunker down on top a spell an' wait four-five minutes to see if they's anyone followin'."

These were only the beginnings of the instructions. Plans for almost any contingency had been taken into effect and the very fact of the unit having survived so many missions attested to the effectiveness of the measures. There were specialized instructions for attacking, retreating, making camp, posting guards, emergency measures, how to take fire and how to give it, how not to waste shots, what to do if surrounded, how to signal each other with bird or animal sounds, how to beat the enemy to the punch in every way.

George Howe not only learned fast, he learned well; very

soon he was incorporating some of the things he had learned from Rogers into his own troops. His officers and men were given orders to throw aside all unnecessary encumbrances, to cut their hair close, to brown the barrels of their rifles so their shine would not give them away to the enemy, to wear leggins to protect themselves from the fierce briers, and to carry in their packs some thirty pounds of meal so that if necessary, they could survive a month without their supply trains.

There was surprisingly little complaint from the regulars about the way he was reshaping the army. One officer wrote home:

*You would laugh to see the droll figure we make. Regulars as well as Provincials have cut their coats so as scarcely to reach their waists. No officer or private is allowed to carry more than one blanket and a bearskin. A small portmanteau is allowed each officer. No women follow the camp to wash our linen. Lord Howe has already shown an example by going to the brook and washing his own.*

It was not the only respect in which he set an example of what he expected of soldiers and officers alike. At one point he invited a number of officers to dinner in his tent. When they arrived, there was a bearskin on the floor rather than a carpet and for seats, logs rather than chairs. Soon a kettle was brought in and placed on the ground—a savory concoction of peas and pork. Howe reached to his belt sheath and removed knife and fork and began to cut his meat, while his guests stirred uncomfortably. Then Howe looked up at them and grinned.

"Is it possible, gentlemen," he asked, "that you've come on this campaign without providing yourselves with what you need?"

He laughed and then presented each of them with a sheath containing knife and fork like his own. The meal was a great success.

In all matters he seemed to be thinking ahead and there could be no doubt that he was building an army that would know how to fight; an army which he meant to have sweep from before it the French regime in America. With the campaign season coming rapidly, he would soon be putting his efforts to the test.

*April 15*

*News from Niagara,* Louis Bougainville wrote in his journal, *by which one learns that a party of Indians left there on the warpath, that the Governor of Pennsylvania held a big council at Philadelphia in which he very much exaggerated our distress in every way, promised marvels to the Six Nations and the Delawares, to whom he distributed medals. He only asked their neutrality. A chief of the Six Nations had given the commander of Niagara his English medal. M. de Vaudreuil found all this news very good, and I for myself find it bad. First, I note that all winter only part of the Indians have come; proof of their coolness, since last year they were here all the time. Part of this is undoubtedly due to the pox which has so ravaged them and which, unaccountably, they seem to hold us largely responsible for. Second, the English will perhaps succeed in detaching the Indians from our alliance, and then La Belle Rivière is lost. Why will one permit the so-great sums spent on them by the King to be so useless? Why should two-thirds of what the King sends for them be stolen? And why is the other third sold by the forts commandants, instead of being given to the Indians as the King expects? Why put at Fort Duquesne as commander a man who drinks too much and, under him, drunkards and fools?*

*Here in this city, too, the distress increases. The people of Quebec are reduced to two ounces of bread. There was a mob of women at the door of M. Daine, lieutenant general of police. The insatiable Great Society is an abyss where everything is swallowed up.*

*News from Frontenac, by which one learns that the Mohawks, on November 10, answered a belt that the Iroquois of Sault St. Louis [Caughnawaga] had sent them in July. By this answering belt they promised neutrality and invited their brothers of the Sault to send deputies to a great assembly of the Six Nations that they would hold at the house of the Onondagas.*

*Colonel Johnson is active among the Six Nations. He has a good chance to paint for them a picture of our distress.*

The recalling of John Campbell, Earl of Loudoun, as commander in chief of the military in North America was neither unexpected nor opposed. If anyone—other than Lord Loudoun himself—was put out about it in the English Colonies, he made no sign of it. Campbell continued with his efforts to shift the blame for his own ineffectuality to Shirley. The fact remained, however, that Lord Loudoun had done little of anything and it had again been the English who had lost out because of it.

Month by month the English border had been pushed back, not only by the French to the north, but by the Indians around the whole perimeter of the frontier. Now it was James Abercromby who was the English commander in chief, with Sir Jeffrey Amherst as his second-in-command. But the instructions from William Pitt in London had remained essentially the same: first the vital linking of Canada with France must be cut, and this could only be done with the taking of Louisbourg and Quebec and the establishment of a powerful naval blockade on the St. Lawrence. At the same time, lost ground must be recovered in the interior: Fort Duquesne must be taken, as well as Fort Niagara and Fort Carillon. The French supply route to the interior forts, especially Detroit, must also be interrupted, preferably with the destruction of Fort Frontenac and the reestablishment of a strong installation at Oswego and another at the Great Carrying Place of the Mohawk.

Amherst and the now Major General James Wolfe were to go by sea to take the Louisbourg bastion at the mouth of the St. Lawrence. Brigadier General John Forbes would lead the campaign to go against Fort Duquesne. Lieutenant Colonel John Bradstreet might be permitted to make a thrust at Fort Frontenac on Lake Ontario. William Johnson, with what Indians and militia he could muster, would join Abercromby and Howe in the assault against Fort Carillon at Ticonderoga and, from there, Johnson might go against Niagara.

The only problem was, Sir William Johnson wasn't going anywhere for a long while. He was still very weak from the sickness which had so long plagued him, but, even worse, at the moment there simply were not any Indians for him to gather. Another great council had just opened among the Iroquois at Onondaga and there was about it an ominous note: the Caughnawagas of the Sault St. Louis had been invited to attend, but Warraghiyagey had not. For a time it seemed to William as if his plan, nurtured all winter long, would bear no fruit. It was a plan he had launched before Christmas, when the first murmurings from the Indians had reached him of the French and Canadians no longer being able to trade with them and provide them the necessities upon which they had become dependent, simply because the French themselves did not have them and were forced to eat horsemeat for their own survival.

It had abruptly placed William in a situation of enormous advantage over the French. Though the Indians were still committed to neutrality, the simple fact remained that the Iroquois *had* to have powder and lead, blankets and weapons and other trade goods to survive; and these items William provided willingly and abundantly. He even went beyond that: for the villages of Canajoharie and Teantontalogo, for example, he provided great feasts where fat oxen were roasted and kegs and barrels of rum and beer were given with his blessings. And it was a time, as well, when he could spend a little extra to show his deep personal friendship for the Indians. When a couple of Mohawk squaws died at Canajoharie in a single night, he sent the village a sympathy gift of six gallons of rum. When the frigid blast of winter howled around the flimsy houses of the natives, he sent to the Onondaga, the Oneidas, the Tuscaroras and the Mohawks considerable gifts of blankets and shirts, stockings and hats, food and spirits and even cash money. He gave hundreds of individual warriors and chiefs silver ornaments and beads, ribbons and medals, guns and axes and knives. Even some horses were provided for them and he sent them bags of seed corn of a variety sweeter and bigger than they had ever had before.

Despite all this, he wondered whether or not he had made any headway. There could be no doubt that the annual congress now meeting at the Iroquois capital of Onondaga was one of the most important ever, and yet the fact remained that he had not even been invited to attend. It was a decided snub, not only of William as Sir William Johnson, Indian supervisor, but also of William as the Mohawk chief, Warraghiyagey, who should have been invited specifically just as a matter of course. Not only all of the Iroquois were attending, but equally representatives of the League's former allies, with the avowed intention of creating a new Indian federation so strong that it could dictate the future to the whites, regardless of whether they were English or French; a federation which, if it ultimately decided to take up the hatchet for one of the white factions, would undoubtedly quickly provide victory for it against the other.

561

William had heard murmurings all winter to the effect that with the proper nudging, the Iroquois might yet declare allegiance to the English, but it would take time. To attempt to rush them now might be to jeopardize everything. There was no better way to make the Iroquois League take the opposite tack than to attempt to force them into doing something. Yet, this was the position William now found himself in when the orders came from Abercromby to join him immediately at Lake George with a large army of Indians to move against the fort at Ticonderoga.

Hoping he was not making a serious mistake, William fashioned a war belt by simply dyeing a huge band of white wampum to a dark red and then sending it to Onondaga with the request that—in the name of the long-established alliance between the Iroquois and the English—an army of warriors be sent to join him.

So shocked was the congress at receiving such a breech of etiquette, that the council adjourned and a large delegation was appointed to go to Warraghiyagey and strongly rebuke him for bringing such pressure to bear at a time like this. Further, he was ordered—not invited—to come to Onondaga at once to explain to the council why he had done so. If his reasons were not deemed good enough, he might be ejected from the tribe and League or, worse yet, he might be executed at order of the council.

And when runners came now to advise him of this, William nodded grimly. It was the best he had expected and now, since it would be his right to speak first, he would have to make sure that the words he chose were powerful enough to sway them from their anger and make them eager to help.

He was by no means sure he could do it.

### [ May 18, 1758—Thursday ]

A distinct note of alarm was creeping into Louis Bougainville's writing these days. Perhaps because he was one of the few who really tried to see and analyze the entire picture of the war, from English and Indian sides as well as from the French, he was one of the few French soldiers who admitted to himself that disaster for the French regime in Canada was not only a possibility, it was uncomfortably close to becoming a probability.

The critical point was one of supplies: there were not enough for the army, there were not enough for the civilian population, there were not enough to provision the Indians for their continued fidelity. Already this withholding of supplies to Indians accustomed to getting them was having serious repercussion. He wrote:

*There is great unrest among the Indians of the far West. The Menominees besieged the fort at Green Bay for three days and destroyed a French family. . . . The Ottawas have evil designs. The Potawatomies seem indisposed to us. Finally, the relations of all these nations with us are on the decline. What is the cause of it? The great losses they have suffered from the smallpox? The bad medicine the French have thrown to them? The great greed of the commanders of the posts and their ignorance of Indian customs? They are merchants that give favor to accomplices and indulge in intrigue while charged with a business most important to the safety of the colony. Besides, the English have sent a wampum belt to all the nations, and they make them the finest offers. To these ills, which foretell still greater ones to come, a prompt remedy is needed, one still easy to apply, but which they will not do or else will do too late.*

*M. Desandrouins arrived here in Montreal on the sixteenth. On the thirteenth, when he left Quebec, there was no news of any new ship in the river, although for several days a continual northeaster has been blowing. Our situation is most critical.*

*They are no longer distributing bread at Quebec. . . .*

*How Caesar would have suffered in this country!*

*The Six Nations have had M. de Vaudreuil warned that the English were going to rebuild the forts of Tioga [German Flats], Bull, and William Henry to prepare the way for the reestablishment of Oswego; that they [the English] were making great threats. In the council held on the sixteenth with their envoys, they have asked the Marquis de Vaudreuil for a powerful assistance—one which will warrant them to declare in our favor. What can we answer to this and what can we do, we who are dying of hunger? The expression is literal.*

## [ June 1, 1758—Thursday ]

Sir William Johnson watched the approach of the Iroquois delegation with considerable concern. In addition to the two hundred Mohawks already on hand here, upwards of five hundred warriors and chiefs were in the party, largely Oneidas, Onondagas and Tuscaroras, plus at least half that many more squaws and children, and the mood of the whole group was obviously unfriendly and sullen. Yet, when he met them at the gate of Fort Johnson and escorted them inside to where table after table was overflowing with food and drink, he showed no trace of nervousness and little effect of the sickness still lingering faintly within him.

His first act was to invite the warriors and squaws to fill their stomachs while the principal chiefs retired with him inside the residence to engage in some preliminary discussions. It was William's assembly and so, in accordance with custom, they were obliged to submit to his requests. He was particularly glad they had made it their decision to come here instead of making him journey to Onondago, as he thought at first he would have to do. It would be a little more costly for him here, in food and entertainment and damage to his grounds, but it was worth it to him.

Hour after hour in the confines of a large upper room of Mount Johnson he spoke with them, repeatedly filling their cups with good brandy and explaining how the end of the French was in sight and that it would be to their advantage to side with the ultimate victor. General Abercromby, he told them, was at this very moment moving his great army to Lake George, along with hundreds upon hundreds of boats, and from there he would move to strike Montcalm at Fort Carillon. He outlined briefly what he intended to say in the speech to the whole body of Indians waiting patiently downstairs and outside and he was relieved to note that they showed a grudging approval.

By midafternoon the preliminaries were over and William was pleased with the way things had gone thus far. Despite the seeming hostility of all the Indians when they first came, these chiefs had reacted with surprising warmth to him and told him officially for the League that they looked upon the English King's appointment of him to manage their affairs as having been done because Warraghiyagey was not only the white man most agreeable to them but because he so well understood their manners and customs. But where active help was concerned, they could not commit themselves. That was a matter only the Indians in a body could make any decision upon. A note of chiding had come into their voices, then, at Warraghiyagey's recent breach of courtesy in interrupting the Onondaga Council as he had with his red belt, Warraghiyagey would do well to remember that such presumption on his part was not consistent with the reason for his appointment as Indian supervisor. It was altogether possible, they added soberly, that bad consequences might result.

William was willing to take that chance. There was little choice in the matter for him. Abercromby had not been hesitant to let William know how displeased he was that his orders had been ignored and William had not already shown up at Lake George with his entire Indian force.

Now, with the entire Indian assemblage seated before him, Warraghiyagey began his oration:

"My Brothers, hear me! Three messages have come running to me one after another from the general to tell me he is waiting for me and the Six Nations. He wonders why it is I have not brought you to him long before now and he demands that I come. This order I must obey, for part of the army are already advanced to one of the islands on Lake George. The rest have their faces turned this way, looking out for me and the Indians. If we do not run all the way to join them, they will proceed without us.

"Brothers," he continued after a slight pause, "you have often said that you are the friends of the English and will not lift your hand against them, and that is good. But you have preferred to remain neutral, and that is not good, for how can you remain standing by and watching when it is on your own land that blood is being shed? The time is past when you can say you will no longer join either side. Now you *must* make a decision who you will cling to. And in such a decision, do not be so foolish as to think that your fortunes lie with the French. Their mouths spit out lies and their hearts are rotten with deceit. They tell you that they can help you and provide for you, but how well have they provided for you lately? When you were hungry in your dwellings this past season, did they bring you good food? No! They have none even for themselves and are forced to eat the flesh of animals they thought to ride. When you were cold this season past, did they bring you clothing and blankets? No! They were too busy trying to keep themselves from freezing and had nothing to spare for you. When you needed guns and powder and lead to hunt game that you and your families might survive, did they provide it for you? No! What little they had had to be hoarded against that time when they would come against the English, for their source of these materials is withering away.

"Brothers, while the English have given you food and drink to warm your bellies, clothes and blankets to warm your skins, the French have tried to warm you inside and out with promises that are empty. Is this the type of ally you wish to have? I cannot believe this is so.

"My Brothers, hear me! Now is the time for such men among you as desire to be thought friends and brothers to the English to tuck up your blankets and run with me. There is no time to be lost, Brothers, nor is there time to think of any other business. Those who go with me will see what a great force the English King has brought against his French foe; an army such as your eyes have never before seen; an army before which the Frenchman must flee or lose his life along with all else he has. Those who go with me now will see that the English are men and with the assistance of the Great Spirit, we will give the French such a blow as will oblige them hereafter to be quiet and let us smoke our pipes in peace, and I hope every Iroquois warrior who goes with me will have reason to rejoice that he fought on the side of the English, and bring home with him some spoils of the victory."

To his delight, William saw that the assembled Indians were clinging to every word he spoke and he thought that maybe—just *maybe* he had them. To belabor the point now might be to afford them time for second thoughts. He was taking a terrific gamble that now was the time for the demand. He mentally crossed his fingers, raised both his hands and the murmuring silenced.

"Brothers! Men of the Iroquois! This is the day of trial and I shall see now which among you are my friends, for such will go with me. You here who are determined now to fight with me, speak!—And you shall be immediately fitted out for war. Remember, my Brothers, we were successful together three years ago at Lake George, and I hope I shall now lead you to conquest and glory!"

He flung the red war belt violently to the ground before him and at this signal a half-dozen drums began the fast-paced pulsing of the war dance. He ripped his clothes off and threw them aside and there was a roar of approval as they saw that his body had been painted for war and his loin-cloth flapped wildly as he gyrated before them to the beat, chanting to them the words of the Iroquois war song, which he knew so well. Within moments, even to himself, he had ceased to be Sir William Johnson, baronet, and had become only Warraghiyagey, the Mohawk warrior chief calling his brothers to war.

The beat of the drums quickened and as he leaped and pounced and swung his tomahawk viciously, the Indians began getting to their feet. One after another the chiefs of the Onondagas and Oneidas, the Tuscaroras and the Mohawks picked up the war belt, waved it high with a great scream and threw it down to join Warraghiyagey in the stirring, stamping, wildly jerking rhythms of the dance of war.

Late into the night they danced and ate and drank and a great sense of accomplishment came over the chief who was Warraghiyagey, and a great sense of pride in these, his people. When at last he fell exhausted and leaned back against a wall and the duality of his personality returned to a degree, he watched the continuing war dance with approval until finally a hand touched him gently and he looked around. It was Degonwadonti.

"You have touched something in their hearts, Warraghiyagey," she said. "They have been bound for a long time, but on this day you have cut them free. They are yours now. Even though our brothers, the Senecas and the Cayugas are not here, these who *are* here are yours; they are no longer neutral. Though the League itself may not be committed, these here are yours, and they are with you against your enemy!"

### [ *June 23, 1758—Friday* ]

There was stiff formality in the meeting between Governor Pierre Vaudreuil and General Louis Montcalm. To Bougainville, who stood beside his geneal, the scene was reminiscent of two hostile dogs, stiff-legged and with hackles raised, warily watching one another for an opening.

Earlier in the day the governor had sent by special messenger to the general a couple of war plans which he wished the general to put into operation. And so that there would be no misunderstanding or later claims that Montcalm did not know what was being done, Vaudreuil ordered him to sign the documents and return them to him.

The plans were vague, without much real thought or strategy behind them, but it was the preamble to them, not the plans themselves, which had caused the eyes of the Marquis de Montcalm to narrow and his mouth to draw down into a frown. He did not comment, however, until he was completely finished with the reading of both documents. Then, without signing, he handed the papers to Bougainville to read.

When the aide-de-camp had finished, his own expression showed incredulity. At a sign from Montcalm he took out pen and paper and took down a memoir which the general proceeded to dictate to him. When it was completed, he had Bougainville make an extra copy of it, as well as an extra copy of the governor's plans. Then, though it was late, the two officers went at once to the governor's château and were shown without hesitation into the plush chamber where Vaudreuil sat in an elegant maroon velvet robe. He was sipping a liqueur. He was also without his wig—the first time Bougainville had ever seen him so.

The governor greeted the two with only bare civility and then said, "You received the plan, General?"

Montcalm assured him he had and then nodded to Bougainville, who politely handed the unsigned documents to the governor. Vaudreuil glanced at them, raised an eyebrow slightly, and then extended them toward Montcalm.

"You have forgotten to sign them," he said.

Montcalm shook his head. "I have not forgotten," he replied coldly. "I could hardly have forgotten. It is almost beyond comprehension that I would be requested to sign such instruments as these. To do so would be to sully my own reputation and brand myself as incompetent. It is an insult, sir, to my intelligence that I should be asked to sign them."

Montcalm was beginning to grow angry now and his voice rose slightly. "I will not sign, sir—*never*! Should you insist that I do so, I will be forced to disobey your order; and should that event come to pass, I will at once send copies of them, still unsigned, to the minister of war in Versailles with a full report of our conversation here and these reasons—in detail—of why I have refused."

He handed one of the memoir copies to the governor, who read it rapidly and then looked up sharply. For an instant it seemed he would explode with the white rage which seethed behind his eyes. He was silent for a long while and finally he dropped the papers to his desk. When he spoke, his voice virtually dripped malevolence.

"You forget who you are, General. Worse, you forget who I am. I will not insist you sign, but I think you will come to regret this day. Though you have friends in the court, I am not myself without strong allies there." He stopped abruptly, as if fearful he would say too much, turned his back to the two officers and merely said, "You may leave."

Half an hour later, sitting at the small desk in his own chambers, Bougainville wrote swiftly in his journal. A rectangular lantern with three of its sides and the top constructed of heavy pewter, sent a yellow glow through the thick glass on the fourth side and lighted the papers before him. His brow was pinched in a frown and several times as he wrote he sighed without even realizing he had done so.

## June 23

*I see with grief the growing misunderstanding between our leaders. The Marquis de Vaudreuil this evening at ten o'clock gave the Marquis de Montcalm two obscure and captious orders. If our general was charged with them, they were so worded that any unfortunate results could be blamed on him, no matter how he acted. He returned them to M. de Vaudreuil with a memoir justifying his action in so doing. Great reluctance of M. de Vaudreuil to give him other clear and simple directives. He is especially attached to a preamble he wrote in which he says that he deliberated with our general on all affairs of the colony and took his advice on everything. I admit that M. de Vaudreuil should have done it—that the position, the successes, the reputation of the Marquis de Montcalm (and, what is more, the orders of the King!) required it. But as he never consulted him about anything, had never informed him of the news, nor of his plans, nor of his measures, the Marquis de Montcalm has positively declared that he will never allow this preamble to stand at the head of his instructions as a monument against his reputation. If M. de Vaudreuil had insisted, our protest against this false assertion was ready. It is more than enough that base jealousy should impede the result of zeal and talent, without suffering still more as a black, senseless intrigue associates one with follies over which one may groan but cannot stop.*

### [ July 3, 1758—Monday ]

Brigadier General John Forbes was a tenacious Scot who, unlike the majority of English regular officers, was well liked by the provincials. He had about him a straightforward manner they approved of, a good head on his shoulders and the desire to listen to anyone who thought he could bring the campaign against Fort Duquesne to a happy conclusion.

Ever since April he had been gathering his army at Philadelphia and there awaiting the arrival of his battalion of kilt-wearing Scottish Highlanders. Matters moved slowly, though, and it hadn't been until last month that he had been able to begin his march. In the meanwhile, he had fallen victim to a strange malady that caused him severe pain and sickness, but to which he refused to give in.[1]

Now, though he was so ill he could not ride and had to be transported on a litter hung between two horses, he was determined not to let the sickness keep him down. His force was a strong one—somewhere between six and seven thousand men—and his second-in-command, Lieutenant Colonel Henry Bouquet, was an accomplished Swiss officer.

Forbes had studied thoroughly the reports of Braddock's defeat three years ago and he determined that his own army would not be so mismanaged. That general's greatest mistake, to Forbe's way of thinking, had been in marching through the wilderness, carving out a road as he went and attempting to bring along with him a cumbersome supply train for that whole distance. Forbes had already decided that he would press toward Fort Duquesne in stages, stopping every so often to build a fortified supply depot, until he was within easy reach of Fort Duquesne, then to bring up everything he needed and strike the French installation with all he had. His greatest concern lay not so much with the French force there, which was reportedly small, as with the large number of Indians hovering there—mainly Delawares and Shawnees, but with a great number of warriors from the far western tribes on hand, too, especially those of the upper Great Lakes.

Forbes had made a study of the Indian temperament and fancied he could outthink them. He knew that they grew fidgety if they had to sit idly by and wait when they were ready to do battle. The longer they were kept waiting, the weaker the fires would grow within them. If the army took its sweet time about getting to Fort Duquesne, making the march last through the summer and even into and through the autumn, might not the Indians give up in disgust and go home? It was a maneuver he decided he would utilize.

Further, there was always the possibility that the Indians might even be drawn over to the English side. Was it not worth the effort to try? Wasn't it possible that just the right

570

nudge at the right time and place might be all that was needed to win them over? He decided that it was both worth the effort to try and that it was at least possible, if not probable.

Therefore, his first move was to send Henry Bouquet ahead to establish a fortified station at Raystown[2] on the eastern slope of the Appalachians. Then he called in the Moravian missionary, Christian Frederick Post, to bear to the Indians in the Fort Duquesne area a message from him which stated that he had no wish to bring the war upon them, that they were welcome to join his force if they so desired, but if not, that then it would be to their advantage to leave the French now so that they would not invite themselves to be destroyed, as the French were sure to be. He also invited them to peace talks.

Now there was nothing left to do but continue the slow forward movement of the army and see what developed.

### [ July 5, 1758—Wednesday ]

Louis de Montcalm was in something of a dilemma about where best he could make his stand against so huge a force coming against him. Fort Carillon was by no means an impregnable fortification. Against simple musketry and a straight-on attack, it was ideal; against artillery and flanking attacks, the place must fall.

From all reports of his spies, it was now obvious that General Abercromby's army, which had already left the site of the ruined Fort William Henry, numbered somewhere over fifteen thousand men. Montcalm himself had less than a quarter that many, including even the hasty reinforcement coming down from Montreal under General Lévis, but not yet arrived.

The defensive choices were neither many nor good. For a time he even considered falling back to Fort St. Frederic at Crown Point and making his stand there. But that installation was no better as a fort than Carillon, and much less ideally situated in respect to terrain. It would be flattened by cannon quickly. So, Montcalm decided that he would make his stand somewhere in this area. The question to answer now was, where?

At the moment he had Captain Berry's battalion near the fort itself and Colonel Bourlamaque's force at the head of the portage, where Lake George began to narrow for its subsequent plunge down the turbulent rapids of the Ticonderoga Narrows and over the Falls, before finally running out into Lake Champlain. The main force of the army, however, was with him right here at the sawmill encampment near the Falls, at the foot of the portage road.

Only a short while ago Captain Langy had come in hastily from a reconnoiter with the report that the English had embarked in staggering force from the head of the lake. The decision on where the French stand was to be made could no longer be put off. Montcalm sighed, and dispatched a fast messenger to head down Lake Champlain by canoe to hasten Lévis. A second message was sent to Berry, ordering him to begin at once the construction of a breastwork and abatis on the high ground in front of the fort. Then Montcalm himself began to gather his men to return to the dubious protection of Fort Carillon to make the stand there. He sent for Bourlamaque and his force to abandon the upper portage post, except for an advance party, and join him for the march to the fort. The sawmill encampment he would abandon and the bridge across the Narrows below the Falls he would burn behind him. Nevertheless, he had little hope that his army could avoid suffering a crushing defeat.

### [ July 6, 1758—Thursday ]

Never before had the Iroquois seen such a display of armed might in their country. Though until now some of them had expressed regret that they had fallen under Warraghiyagey's spell at Fort Johnson and agreed to let him lead them against the French, whatever fears they were experiencing were dissolved from their minds at the sight of Abercromby's incredible flotilla on the waters of Lake George.

For a distance of over six miles, the waters of the lake were scarcely visible because of the number of boats afloat on the surface. Over a thousand boats were afloat here, and each one was crowded with men or provisions. There were over nine hundred bateaux, one hundred thirty-five whaleboats, and numerous heavy flatboats to which were lashed dozens of cannon, howitzers, swivels and mortars.

Immediately, the Iroquois had sent runners back to Onondaga and the various principal villages of the individual tribes of the Six Nations with news of this fantastic sight, with news of the incredible number of men, with news of the armed might it all represented. There could be no doubt now that any of the Indians of the Iroquois League who were still vacillating would be won over at this intelligence.

Even to William Johnson it was an impressive sight. The whole army was moving along in three divisions, with the regulars in the center and the provincials on either flank. The brightness of the varied uniforms, the fluttering of the regimental flags, and the music from the countless instruments of each corps—bagpipes, trumpets, fifes, drums—gave the whole procession a festive and inspiring air. The English gave ample appearance of an army well embarked for certain victory, and their spirits were very high.

In the van of the fleet was Thomas Gage with the light infantry and Robert Rogers—newly promoted to the rank of major—with his Rangers. They were followed by Colonel John Bradstreet and his corps of boatmen who had been trained as soldiers. Following them came the main body of the army, with the red-coated regulars under Lord Howe in the center, seven regiments in all. To the right and left of them, uniformed in blue, were the provincial regiments from Massachusetts, Rhode Island, Connecticut, New York and New Jersey. Behind them, the artillery flatboats and, behind all, the rear guard of provincials.

William Johnson and his nearly four hundred Iroquois Indians had moved rapidly to get here before Abercromby could leave, but even so they were slightly late. Now, however, there was no problem. They would rest overnight at this place, follow the shoreline tomorrow and join with the army at the Ticonderoga Narrows. Now his greatest concern was that they should arrive there in time for the Iroquois to witness the defeat of the French.

While it was true that James Abercromby was commander in chief of the army, it was to his lordship, General George Howe, that the army turned for its leadership and inspiration. Howe could supply both abundantly. Rarely had one man so represented the entire spirit of an army. Had he decided to lead them barefoot to hell, they would have followed him over the hot coals cheerfully, so strong was his hold over them, so great their faith in him.

By ten o'clock yesterday morning the great flotilla was passing Tongue Mountain on their left and, with the lake narrowing here, the fleet stretched out even more. By five in the evening they had reached Sabbath Day Point, twenty-five miles down the lake and here they stopped until full darkness had fallen, in order to allow the baggage, artillery and rear guard to catch up.

For over an hour George Howe sat discussing the position of Fort Carillon with Major Robert Rogers's chief lieutenant, Captain John Stark. He wanted to know everything possible about the fort itself and equally about the surrounding terrain—the hills, the forest, the streams, the treacherous Narrows.

At eleven o'clock last night the army had begun to move again, and this morning at daybreak had entered the head of the Narrows. Unknown to them, a French advance party of three hundred fifty men under Captains Langy and Trepezec watched their progress fearfully from atop a huge bare rock.[3] By noon the entire English army had disembarked on the west shore of the upper Narrows and the assault plan was laid out.

Since patrols had already reported that the sawmill camp on the portage road was being abandoned and Montcalm had evidently elected to withdraw to Fort Carillon, the plan was for the army to march in four columns. They would march, preceded by a detachment under Robert Rogers, around the mountains rimming the west shore of the Narrows. In this way they could come around to the front of Fort Carillon for the attack by land.

Rogers set out first, leading two provincial regiments. Lord Howe and Major Israel Putnam followed, leading two hundred Rangers. Behind them came the three other advance columns. The going was very bad, with heavily tangled undergrowth and a terrain so badly broken that it was impossible to follow a straight line of march. Hardly over a mile from where they had begun, the columns became hopelessly confused and lost their direction. They fumbled about trying to find something that would orientate them to the proper direction in which to proceed.

They were not the only ones to become confused. Unexpectedly cut off from joining their forces as they had planned to, the advance French detachment under Langy and Trepezec descended from their rocky observation point and took to the woods. They, too, were attempting to make a wide semicircle along the west side of the Narrows to get back to Fort Carillon.

Hour after hour, until early evening, the compact individual columns thrashed about in the woods, wearing themselves out and coming little closer to their objective. And then came

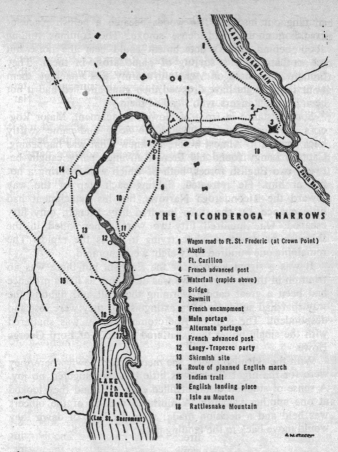

**THE TICONDEROGA NARROWS**

1 Wagon road to Ft. St. Frederic (at Crown Point)
2 Abatis
3 Ft. Carillon
4 French advanced post
5 Waterfall (rapids above)
6 Bridge
7 Sawmill
8 French encampment
9 Main portage
10 Alternate portage
11 French advanced post
12 Langy-Trapezec party
13 Skirmish site
14 Route of planned English march
15 Indian trail
16 English landing place
17 Isle au Mouton
18 Rattlesnake Mountain

A. W. ECKERT

the queer sort of happenstance that can change the course of
history. The French advance party and Lord Howe's column
stumbled into one another. In the gathering gloom of the
woods it was difficult to see anything clearly, but suddenly
from the thickets ahead of Howe's detachment a sharp challenge rapped out:

*"Qui vive?"*

Immediately Major Putnam shouted back, *"Français!"*

Langy knew better. A thunder of gunfire was directed
from the thickets into the English detachment and in that
instant a bullet ripped through the heart of George Howe,

575

snuffing out his life. The woods became a hellish place of crackling gunfire and dense smoke. The columns milling about behind Howe's detachment could hear the noise but see nothing, and a stirring of panic arose in them. They thought the whole of Montcalm's army was attacking them at first and might have dropped their guns and fled had it not been for the Rangers, who steadied them.

Some distance in front of Howe's detachment, Major Rogers's advance party also heard the firing and came swiftly back toward it. Almost before he knew what was happening, Captain Langy found his French advance party caught between two English forces, both of which were pouring a hot fire at him. He retreated, fighting each step of the way toward the Ticonderoga Narrows, but his detachment had little chance. Of the three hundred fifty French, only fifty escaped. One hundred fifty-two were either killed in the skirmish or drowned while trying to cross the rapids. The remaining one hundred forty-eight were captured.

It was a signal victory for the English, but there was no triumph in them. Lord Howe was dead and, as if his presence had been a great candle warming them all and lighting the way that had suddenly been extinguished, they were lost and despondent. The soul of Abercromby's army was shattered with the single bullet that shattered the soul of Lord George Howe.

With the skirmish ended, the men bedded down where they were for the night. There was little talk, no laughter, no joy. A sense of stunned disbelief filled each man and they looked at one another vacantly. A muttered council of the officers was held and a decision made: with the light of dawn they would move back to the landing point.

### [ *July 9, 1758—Sunday* ]

If ever an army was abruptly dumped into incompetent hands, such was the case now with the English army clustered at the foot of Lake George.

Major General James Abercromby had been more than content to allow Brigadier General Howe take the initiative in leading the troops who so admired him. Not only was Howe a superb leader, he was an accomplished strategist. But now Howe was dead and the brunt of command reverted to Abercromby.

As soon as the detachments had returned in the morning

with the French prisoners, the news of Howe's death, and of the almost impassable nature of the terrain on the west side of the Narrows, Abercromby ordered the army to park where it was and sent Colonel Bradstreet with a detachment to take possession of the deserted French encampment at the foot of the portage road near the sawmill and Falls. This Bradstreet quickly accomplished and, while immediately beginning repair of the burned bridge Montcalm's force had left behind, sent messengers back to Abercromby with word that the site was in English hands.

Abercromby started the army moving, and by late afternoon the entire force, with the exception of artillery and baggage, had reached the encampment. Numerous scouts and spies came and went and soon the general had a good picture of what he faced in the battle ahead. All the odds were decidedly in his favor. Because the French prisoners had told him under questioning that Montcalm had over six thousand men—though all his own spies had reported well under four thousand—and that he was hourly expecting another three thousand to arrive under General Lévis, Abercromby was in a fever to get the attack started.

As soon as Montcalm had made his decision to stand at the fort and removed his troops there, he set about in great haste to improve the defenses wherever possible in so short a time. He directed that an extensive abatis be erected on the slight ridge some distance in front of the fort. The trees which covered the ground in this area were chopped down by the hundreds. As soon as each was felled, its top was lopped off and the trunks were piled to form a wall of logs eight or nine feet high, with the uppermost logs notched to form loopholes for musket fire. Beyond this breastwork the remaining trees were felled for the distance of a musket shot; felled with their tops fallen away from the fort so as to form a tangle through which it would be most difficult for an army to pass. It looked, in a short time, as if a great wind had flattened the forest here. Finally, immediately in front of the log breastwork, the bare ground was covered with an intricate interlacing of sharpened branches through which a man could pick his way only with the greatest of care, lest he be impaled.

General Lévis arrived in the evening with his reinforcement and this brought Montcalm's total effective strength to thirty-six hundred. Though it was a most welcome reinforcement, Montcalm had little hope it would help much in the final result. After all, Abercromby's force was well over fifteen thousand men—a ratio of something over four to one.

General Abercromby had been carefully informed about the French defensive measures. There were now several avenues of attack he could utilize with every assurance of victory. Though Montcalm had strengthened his position as much as he possibly could under the circumstances, he was still extremely vulnerable. The English general's wisest move would be simply to bring up his artillery, which was still waiting on the strand at the head of the portage road, and merely batter down the French abatis with a powerful frontal attack of cannon. The entire breastwork could, in this way, be rendered useless in a very short time and the fort proper left open to attack.

If not that, then Abercromby might send a detachment to engage the front of the defensive works while the rest of the army marched safely through the woods to take possession of the supply road leading to Fort Carillon from Fort St. Frederic. A few pieces of artillery strategically placed here would command both Lake Champlain and the road and effectively cut off any further supplies getting to Fort Carillon. Since, as Abercromby had been informed, the French army inside had provisions for only eight days, a siege could be waged which must, within a fortnight at most, cause Montcalm to surrender and the English army to remain virtually without casualty. By the same token, Abercromby had the choice of bringing some artillery to the heights on nearby Rattlesnake Hill[4] and from that position be able to rake the inside of the French breastwork along its entire length.

Even with his haste to get things under way and not wait for cannon to be brought up, Abercromby could have sent part of his force to attack the front while the flanking remainder moved in from the low grounds to the east and west of the fort. It would result in an increase of English casualties, but the French position could undoubtedly be taken quickly.

General James Abercromby chose to do none of these things. With no intention of waiting for cannon and paying no mind whatever to the advantageous moves he might make, he stunned his officers and men by ordering an all-out frontal attack with muskets alone!

High on a hill overlooking the battle area, Sir William Johnson had just arrived with his body of nearly four hundred Iroquois. The Indians were amazed at the incredible number of English poised to thrust against the fort but, instead of joining the affray, they merely settled back to watch.

"With such a mighty army as he has, Warraghiyagey," one of the chiefs told him, "your general has no need of us. For this time, though our hearts are with you now, we will be content to stay here and watch how the English soldier and French soldier fight one another."

They planted themselves comfortably and nothing William could do or say could make them budge farther. And, to be truthful, he himself saw no real need for them to join in. If they stayed here, then there would not arise the problem of restraining them from massacre when Abercromby took the fort. He shrugged and settled back with them to watch.

They were witnesses to the most incomprehensible defeat in English military history to this date.

The attack was begun and the English soldiers, struggling through the tangled branches and sharpened limbs toward the log breastwork, were virtually sitting ducks for the hot French musketry. By dozens and scores the attackers were felled and after over an hour without making any headway and hardly hurting the enemy at all, the English fell back to the sawmill encampment where Abercromby was waiting. They gasped to him that the French were invulnerable to musket attack and that artillery needed to be brought up.

Abercromby was scornful and wouldn't hear of it. He ordered them all back at once to reopen the attack. Reluctantly they obeyed, but the second onslaught was no more successful than the first; nor were the repeated attacks, ordered by Abercromby, which followed. Between one o'clock in the afternoon and seven o'clock in the evening, seven successive waves of attack by the English were beaten back, each time the ground before the abatis became more densely cluttered with dead and wounded English soldiers.

Now, while the Rangers took positions under cover and kept up a strong fire at the defenders, the uninjured soldiers moved in to collect their wounded and take them off. By late dusk there lay only bodies before the breastwork and the English had disappeared. They had moved quickly and with almost total dejection back to the sawmill camp where Abercromby waited expectantly. His expectations were dashed. One thousand nine hundred forty-four of his men were dead, wounded or missing;[5] and so, even though he still

579

had at his command a force of over thirteen thousand effective men and much artillery waiting to be put into use, he abruptly lost his nerve and put his army into full retreat under cover of darkness.

Sir William Johnson learned of the withdrawal and his initial disbelief turned to shock. How could it possibly be, How could such a force as this actually be *retreating* from so weak a foe? His heart was leaden within him, heavy with the knowledge that now the Iroquois, whom he had finally won to the English cause after such a long, hard time, would abandon them and flock to the French. But though he undoubtedly understood the Indians better than any other white man of influence, he still did not know them well enough.

The chiefs talked together quietly for a long time and then a deputation of three of them came to Johnson.

"We leave now," one of them said, "to return to our villages. We have seen and heard what it is hard for eyes and ears to believe. A mouse has fought off a panther and driven him away; but it is the panther's brain that has shamed him, not his muscles. When he is given a new brain, as will happen now, he will be back and we will be with him and support him in the destruction of the French mouse. But as long as the panther's brain remains the same, Warraghiyagey, we will not fight beside the English. Your general ought to be tied to a post and whipped. No, we will never fight under such a man, and this is what we wish you to tell our father, the King."

At the same time, within Fort Carillon, Montcalm was taking stock of the situation. He was intensely proud of the way his men had fought and driven back time and again the assaulting throng of English. Most of his men were bivouacked now between the fort and the breastwork and in the darkness he passed among them, from campfire to campfire, praising them and thanking them for the greatest defense he had ever seen. To every man was given wine, beer and food, and morale was at a high pitch. Nevertheless, Montcalm was not inclined to deceive himself. His third-in-command, Colonel Bourlamaque was badly wounded. Lévis, uninjured, had had close calls when two bullets had passed through his hat. Bougainville had taken a flesh wound. Among the troops there were three hundred seventy-seven dead. Montcalm knew he was weaker now, over a tenth weaker than yesterday, and still gravely outnumbered. As soon as Abercromby brought his cannon to bear in the morning, all would be lost.

When daylight came this morning, however, and there was no resumption of the attacks, Montcalm sent out a party of volunteers to reconnoiter. They quickly returned with the almost incoherently joyful report that the sawmill had been burned and that the English army was already afloat again and in full retreat. In fact the retreat had been so precipitous that the English had left behind several hundred barrels of provisions and considerable equipment.

Jubilantly, hardly able to believe his senses, Montcalm wrote a series of brief dispatches and letters to Vaudreuil, Bigot, D'Argenson, and others. Then, with understandable exaggeration in his state of mind, he wrote to his wife:

*Beloved Angélique,*

*What a day for France! The army, the too-small army of the King has beaten the enemy. Without Indians, almost without Canadians or colony troops—I had only four hundred—alone with Lévis and Bourlamaque and the troops of the line, thirty-one hundred fighting men, I have beaten an army of twenty-five thousand. This glorious day does infinite honor to the valor of our battalions.*

*Never was general in more critical position than was I: God has delivered me; His be the praise! He gives me health, though I am worn out with labor, fatigue and miserable dissentions that have determined me to ask for my recall. Heaven grant that I may get it!*

*I have no time to write more. I am well, my dearest, and I embrace you.*

*Louis*

### [ July 10, 1758—Monday ]

Young Pedrom Schuyler had rarely seen his mother so nervous. Ever since his brother Philip had marched off with Lord Howe to go against the French at Ticonderoga, she had paced and fidgeted. Here at the fine house on the meadows above Saratoga it was hard for Pedrom to believe that at this very moment a battle of great significance could be raging far to the north of them. But the way his mother acted, he could almost believe that she could hear it in progress.

Mrs. Schuyler would walk outside and stand in the grass, her head cocked to one side in a listening attitude, or her hand shading her eyes as she watched the north road for any sign of activity. And now at last, late this afternoon, her vigil was ended.

Into sight came a rider galloping furiously, his hat missing, riding the road which led from Fort Edward to Albany. Too far away to reach the road in time to stop him and ask him what the news was, Mrs. Schuyler sent Pedrom running. He reached the road just as the rider was passing.

"What news?" Pedrom shouted, when the rider showed no sign of slackening speed. "What's happened?"

Hunched low over the neck of his horse, the rider looked back briefly and shouted, "Lord Howe . . . he's been killed by the French and the army's retreating!"

From behind him Pedrom heard a fearful shriek. He spun about and saw his mother a dozen yards away, swaying and ready to fall, her face cupped in her hands while moaning cries came from her. He ran to her and helped her to the house and then fetched neighbors. Late into the night the house remained lighted, and intermittently from within came the heartbroken cries of Mrs. Schuyler, echoed by the neighbor women who were still with her.

George Howe had been as dear to her as her own children.

[ *July 12, 1758—Wednesday* ]

It was difficult for Louis Bougainville to believe that the rift between his general, the Marquis de Montcalm, and the Canadian governor, the Marquis de Vaudreuil, had become such a chasm that the latter could actually have conspired toward Montcalm's defeat here at Fort Carillon. Yet this conclusion, in light of what had happened since the battle, seemed almost inescapable. The truth of the matter was that the governor had deliberately held off sending the so desperately needed Canadian and Indian reinforcements from Montreal to Fort Carillon until too late for them to give aid.

Only yesterday the governor's brother, the largely incompetent Captain de Rigaud, had arrived with several other Canadian officers, a large reinforcement of colony troops and a huge party of Indians representing eleven different tribes. All of them were ready to do battle but it was evident that the battle they expected to do was one of falling upon the victorious Abercromby and wiping him out when he was weakened from his defeat of Montcalm. To have found instead that Montcalm was the victor and that the enemy had

582

withdrawn in a virtual stampede back to the Lake George camp stunned them.

Rigaud and the other officers presented themselves to Montcalm to congratulate him but, as Bougainville had written in his journal last night:

> . . . *Compliments from them on the victory—more forced than sincere.*

Now, having had a full day to make some inquiries and discuss the situation with some of the newcomers, Bougainville was again setting down his impression:

*July 12*

*Council held here to reunite and bind together the Indians of the different tribes: Iroquois, Abnaki, Hurons, Ottawas, etc. They are desolated for not having been at the battle. Much booty lost and the chance to acquire a great name through the taking of a prodigious number of scalps. These are their trophies, their obelisks, their arches of triumph; these are the monuments which attest to other tribes and consign to posterity the valor, the exploits of the warriors and the glory of the cabin. The Indians say haughtily that it was the Marquis de Vaudreuil who kept them; and whatever may have been his reason, it was he that caused their arriving too late. They are in a very bad humor over it.*

*It is custom in America that troops who have had a success themselves sing the* Te Deum *for it, and I approve this custom strongly. . . . The army took up arms today and they sang the* Te Deum. *Never has a victory been more especially to the finger of Providence.*

## [ *August 6, 1758—Sunday* ]

The news of James Abercromby's retreat from Ticonderoga back to the head of Lake George was greeted by the colonies with much the same reaction Sir William Johnson had shown—first a great disbelief, followed by numbing shock. But then the shock turned into anger and fear. Everywhere the same questions were asked. How could it have happened? Why, after it had been transported so laboriously all the way to within battle range, hadn't the artillery been used? How had an enemy only a quarter of their own strength, pinned down in an ill-constructed fort, caused so panicky a flight on

583

the part of Abercromby's army that many of the soldiers had lost their shoes in the scramble to escape, and were too spurred on by fear even to stop briefly to recover them? What had happened to the leadership of this army of over fifteen thousand soldiers?

Always the answers boiled down to two glaring realities: Brigadier General Lord George Howe had been the life and spirit of the army and when he died, the life and spirit of the army died with him; and, secondly, Major General James Abercromby, commander in chief of the English forces in North America, was not only an incompetent, he was an out-and-out coward!

At the Lake George site where Fort William Henry had been and the new fort by the same name was now under construction, Abercromby had finally halted his inglorious retreat and ordered a great breastwork built to ward off the French devil-dogs he imagined were hot on his heels.

Young Colonel William Williams of the Massachusetts Regiment was, like most of the officers, both regular and provincial, still unable to understand why they had retreated. He echoed the general feeling in a letter to his uncle, Israel Williams, shortly after the battle:

*... and now, dear uncle, we are back on this ground which we left with such flush of confidence and pride only a little while ago. Wherever one goes here he finds people—officers and soldiers—astonished that we left the French ground and commenting on the strange conduct in coming away from there as we have done. The provincials are now most openly calling our commander Mrs. Nabbycromby,*[6] *since he thinks of nothing but fortifying himself. So now you know the story of our glorious campaign just completed and the shame that has descended over us all because of it. I have told facts; you may put the epithets upon them. In one word, what with fatigue, want of sleep, exercise of mind, and leaving the place we went to capture, the best part of the army is unhinged. I have told enough to make you sick, if the relation acts on you as the facts have on me.*

For three years now the English had suffered defeat after defeat. Their frontiers had been pushed back until now they were hardly a stone's throw from major cities. In the west, Indians were still raiding the settlements with virtual impunity, and to the north, Indians and Canadians harassed troops and settlements so actively that it had become almost something of a game with them. What was needed—and needed desperately—was a victory of some kind, somehow, somewhere; something to revive the badly faltering hopes and faith of the populace.

And at last, even though far removed from them, they got it; though it came from a sector where defeat would not have been too surprising. The French installation at Louisbourg was certainly one of the strongest fortifications in North America, whether French or English. Yet, despite the fact that enormous sums of money had been spent on repairs of it by the French since the Peace of Aix-la-Chapelle, it was in poor shape and not well supplied. A small fleet of warships hovered around it and over two hundred thirty-five pieces of artillery were nestled in its walls and outworks. Because of this, it was protected by only a little over three thousand regulars. They were simply not enough to hold the place against the attacking force of well over eleven thousand men brought against them by Sir Jeffrey Amherst.

The English fleet had come in sight of the fortress on the first of June and the siege was begun on the eighth. The French ships were swiftly destroyed and for forty-nine interminable days the defenders were bombarded by cannon until the inside of the fortress was a shambles and there was no further hope for the defense of it. The Louisbourg fortress surrendered on July 27.

As Amherst, under Abercromby's orders, hurried back to Boston with six regiments to reinforce his commander in chief at Lake George, he sent Brigadier General James Wolfe—who, to the English troops, had been the life of this siege—to destroy the French villages of Gaspé, Miramichi and others along the mouth of the St. Lawrence and to disperse their inhabitants.

So at last the English had a real victory to crow about. And even more importantly, the vital supply line from France to Quebec and Montreal was all but severed. The fact remained, though, that General James Abercromby was still commander in chief.

In his fumbling hands, hopes for the future could hardly be considered bright.

[ *August 7, 1758—Monday* ]

With wry amusement, Bougainville did not fail to note on his arrival back in Montreal how alarm was beginning to resound through the Great Society of Intendant François Bigot. One of his chief accomplices, Major Michel Jean Hughes Péan, who also was the chief aide of Governor Vaudreuil, was a very guilt-ridden man and he was now pulling out before an axe could fall on him as he expected it to fall upon the others. Part of the cause of this alarm was news received of some unexpected dismissals and appointments being made in the ministries back in Versailles. Even François Bigot was apparently worried, but not in the panicky manner exhibited by Péan.

Once again, on a mission similar to others he had been sent on by his general, Bougainville had been dispatched to Montreal to try in some way to smooth or end the disagreement which seemed to grow even stronger between the general and the governor. In his journal he wrote:

*August 7*

*I have been sent by the Marquis de Montcalm to the Marquis de Vaudreuil with orders to smother, if it is possible, this leaven of discord which is fermenting and which perhaps will hurt the good of the service. Thus our general still makes advances. The public interest controls his actions and he constantly has in mind this word of Themistocles: "Strike, but listen———." It appears that the Marquis de V has rather followed in all these bickerings the prejudices of subalterns interested in making trouble, rather than his own ideas. In this affair, however, it is self-love and a jealousy of rivalry—foundation upon which marplots build—which possess him. The appearances are that my trip has not been unfruitful. I hope that it proves true.*

*M. Péan has left for Quebec, when he will go to France. He will carry the news of our victory. He will lack at his recital only the ability to say: "I saw it." The pretext for his trip is a rheumatic pain in his arm, which needs the aid of the waters of a spa. The true motive is the necessity of getting there first and feeling out a new minister who could yet change.*

*So that Marquis de Vaudreuil will not be alone, Sieur Mercier comes to take the place near him that Péan occupied. It is very necessary that M. the Intendant always should have a resident near the person of the governor. M. Martel, former keeper of the King's stores at Montreal and member of the Great Society, goes to France with Péan. He goes to see how he will there invest the immense sums extracted from this unfortunate land.*

*The Menominees have sent to Montreal as prisoners the seven Indians of their tribe who this winter assassinated a French family at Green Bay. Three have been flogged in the city square. The other four must come to war to expiate their crime. This submission of an independent tribe, distant more than five hundred leagues, does great honor to the French name.*

## [ August 8, 1758—Tuesday ]

While he may have been a man poorly fitted to be a military commander, Major General James Abercromby was by no means a man without feeling. The wave of criticism, even hatred, welling up against him from both civilians and military was almost as terrifying to him as had been the fear of Montcalm. And so, partially to salve his own conscience and partially to retain, if possible, his position as commander in chief while at the same time mollifying the people, he set in motion several programs.

First among these was to dispatch General John Stanwix with a sizable force to the Great Carrying Place of the Mohawk to build a bigger and better fortification. It would be the first step in the eventual rebuilding of Oswego and perhaps even a prelude to attack on Fort Niagara. Stanwix was an engineer of merit and in a surprisingly short time had the new installation well under way. And, with his customary immodesty, when the place was still far from finished, he named it Fort Stanwix.[7]

The second program was one Abercromby probably would not have initiated himself, but one he agreed to readily enough when it was proposed to him by Lieutenant Colonel John Bradstreet: a hit-destroy-and-run attack to be made against Fort Frontenac. Bradstreet had first made the proposal to Lord Loudoun, who had accepted it and then lost his command before it could be implemented. When, shortly after Abercromby had taken command, Bradstreet presented the idea to him, the new commander had not been especially sympathetic to the proposal, preferring at that time to use every available man for the Ticonderoga campaign. Now, however, Abercromby saw it as a means of helping to remove the stigma from his own name. If the attack somehow resulted in success, he would claim much of the credit for it;

if it failed, he could lay the blame at the feet of Bradstreet and Lord Loudoun. Bradstreet was given three thousand men, mostly provincials, and set off at once up the Mohawk. At the under-construction Fort Stanwix he lingered only for a brief rest and, while there, managed to enlist the aid of about forty Iroquois, mostly Mohawks and Oneidas.

The third program set in motion by Abercromby was a retaliatory one. Time after time since the battle at Fort Carillon, parties of anywhere from fifty to two hundred Canadian *coureurs de bois* and Indians descended upon the Lyman Road connecting Fort Edward with newly rising Fort William Henry. They harassed supply and communications lines in vicious hit-and-run attacks. Most of these parties were coming by way of Lake Champlain, up into the headwaters where it passed the Drowned Lands and entered South Bay, and then following the old Wood Creek portage trail past the crumbled remains of an old and long-deserted installation that had been called Fort Anne, and from there along the overgrown road which subsequently merged with the Lyman Road.

On August 1, just such a party of raiders had ambushed a train of supply wagons being escorted to Fort William Henry by forty soldiers from Fort Edward. All but a handful of the soldiers were killed and scalped and the supplies themselves mostly destroyed. Early on August 2 Abercromby learned of it and immediately he called in Major Robert Rogers. He directed the green-clad officer to lead eighty of his Rangers, plus a detachment of six hundred Connecticut provincials under Major Putnam and thirty regulars under Captain James Dalyell, northward on Lake George until almost at the Narrows, then to cut due eastward over the mountains to Lake Champlain in an effort to surprise the raiders on their retreat to Fort Carillon.

Rogers and his party set off at once. They traveled rapidly but the raiders managed to get back to the French fort before he could intercept them. While en route on the return to their home base by way of South Bay on August 4, Rogers was met by an express from Abercromby with orders to intercept, if possible, another large party of French and Indians reported to be moving about just to the north of Fort Edward.

For the next three days the major and his men roamed the area around the ruined Fort Anne, observing all the rules of caution Rogers himself had devised as standard practice for the Rangers, with strict silence maintained while on the march and no fires permitted at night. But when, by this morning, no trace of the enemy had been discovered, caution was relaxed.

Rogers's camp was made in the former mile-wide clearing that had surrounded Fort Anne but where now a dense tangle of second growth had risen, making it almost impossible to walk through except on a narrow Indian path. Early this morning, while his men were getting their packs readied for the return to Fort William Henry, Major Rogers and a Lieutenant John Irwin of the regulars got into a friendly argument about which of them was the better shot. Conversation alone couldn't settle the argument, so a bet was placed and a target set up on a tree stump. Soon the woodland was reverberating with the sound of rifle shots at irregularly spaced intervals.

It had been a poor time to relax caution.

Hardly more than a mile away the shots were heard by the Canadian captain Jacques Marin, at the head of four hundred fifty *coureurs de bois* and Indians on their way back to Fort Carillon with a number of fresh scalps and considerable plunder taken on the Lyman Road the evening before. Immediately word was passed down the line to make ready and a slow advance was made to reconnoiter. If it turned out to be an English party, as was likely, perhaps they could set up an ambush.

By seven o'clock this morning, each man having shot twenty rounds, Lieutenant Irwin ruefully shook his head and handed over the winnings to Rogers. A few minutes later the commander had the entire force on the move in single file down the Indian path. Major Putnam was in the lead with his Connecticut provincials, followed by Dalyell and his regulars in the center and Major Rogers and his Rangers bringing up the rear.

Abruptly there was a chorus of Indian shrieks from both sides and the bush lopers and Indians surged to the attack. As a burly Caughnawaga rushed at him with tomahawk raised, Putnam brought up his gun to bear on the broad naked chest and squeezed the trigger, but the weapon misfired and an instant later was sent spinning out of his hands by the tomahawk blow. Instantly he was seized and dragged struggling into the brush, as were Lieutenant Tracy and three privates.[8] At the same time a heavy firing broke out all along the Connecticut lines.

589

Dalyell and Rogers, their men strung out behind for nearly a mile, thrashed through the brush as swiftly as possible to come to the aid of the provincials, but it was rough going and the better part of half an hour had elapsed before the whole seven hundred English were engaged in the fight.

The uproar of gunfire, shrieks and cries were terrific and during the peak of the action one of the Caughnawagas leaped into the midst of the Connecticut men and in a matter of moments broke the skulls of two of the soldiers with his tomahawk. Then, with the weapon in his hand dripping blood, he leaped to the top of a large log.

"Come!" he shouted in English. "Come, *Corlaer*, and I kill you. You are women!"

One of Dalyell's regulars rushed up and struck him a glancing blow on the head with the butt of his gun. For only an instant the Caughnawaga warrior reeled as the blood sprang from the gash at his eyebrow, but then he gripped the regular savagely by the hair and raised his tomahawk to strike. Rogers himself plunged onto the scene and from twenty feet away sent an acorn-sized ball of lead smashing through the Indian's head.

For two hours the fighting continued until at last some of the *coureurs de bois* were forced to fall back. Taking it as the signal for retreat, the rest of the French and Indian party followed them. Just as Rogers himself had long ago discovered, they knew it was disastrous to retreat in a body, so now they scattered in small groups to make their way as best they could to a predetermined rendezvous at the southern end of South Bay.

Pursuit was hopeless, so Rogers let them go. Then he took stock of the situation. It was bad, but not as bad as it might have been, considering that the enemy had had the advantage of setting up the ambush. There were forty-nine English dead—which Rogers ordered buried at once—and nearly that many more wounded and missing. But the attackers had paid a stiff price for their ambush. More than a hundred Canadians, Caughnawagas and Abnakis lay dead around them.

As the regulars and provincials began burying their dead and making litters for the wounded out of interlaced branches covered with blankets, Rogers and his Rangers moved about among the bodies of their foes and stripped them of their knives, tomahawks, guns and scalps.

"By damn," Rogers said as they finished, "they'll think

twice before sending more parties like this down on us again!"

By noon they were on the move again.

## [ *August 18, 1758—Friday* ]

Christian Frederick Post, Moravian missionary, had never considered himself a very brave man. Though he had spent considerable time among the Indians, had learned the Delaware language well and had even married a Delaware squaw whom he had converted to Christianity, he was an admittedly timid individual.

Post, however, had a strong belief in God and an equally strong abhorrence not only of the carnage being committed against the whites by border-raiding Indians, but by the Indians being daily murdered by equally savage border-ranging whites. If in some way he could do something to help stop this bloodshed, then fear would simply have to be pushed down while he did so. It was why he had accepted the commission from General Forbes and the governor of Pennsylvania to go to the Indians now hovering in great numbers around Fort Duquesne and invite them to a peace treaty with the English, to be drawn up at Easton, Pennsylvania, on the Delaware River, in mid-September.

He had set out on his mission not without considerable trepidation. Though he had lived among the Delawares for a long time and gained their respect and confidence, that had all been while they were then at peace with the English. What his reception would be now, after three years of bloody border warfare, he could only surmise—and his thoughts on that subject made him almost physically ill.

He had in his favor, however, certain factors of which he was unaware. In recent months the payment that the Indians had grown accustomed to getting from the French in the form of presents at Fort Duquesne had dwindled to a mere pittance and they were dissatisfied. They neither knew nor cared that much of the goods destined for them were seized by English cruisers while on their way from France to America, and that what materials did get through somehow found their way into the hands of mercenary government officials or decidedly dishonest merchants who sold them to their own profit. All they knew was that the goods they had largely become dependent upon were being denied them. Furthermore, the goods supplied them by French fur traders

591

had always been expensive and hard to get and many of the Indians were remembering with longing now how abundant and how much less expensive these same items had been from the English traders.

Even Vaudreuil's usual braggadocio in regard to the western forts was failing, especially where it concerned Fort Duquesne, which was the most poorly supplied for its size of all the forts. Earlier in the year he had written to colonial minister Pierre Berryer:

*I have provided for the safety of Fort Duquesne. I have sent reinforcements to M. de Ligneris, who commands there. I have done the impossible to supply him with provisions, and I am now sending them in abundance, in order that the troops I may perhaps have occasion to send to drive off the English may not be delayed.*

And now, in view of the marching of John Forbes's army, Vaudreuil's hopes had waned and in a more recent letter to Berryer he wrote:

*A stronger fort is needed on the Ohio; but I cannot build one till after the peace; then I will take care to build such a one as will thenceforth keep the English out of that country. But I am very anxious for news from M. de Ligneris. I have sent him all the succors I could, and have ordered troops to go to his aid from Niagara, Detroit, and Illinois, as well as the militia of Detroit, with the Indians there and elsewhere in the West—Hurons, Ottawas, Potawatomies, Miamis, and other tribes. They are there now in considerable numbers, but what I fear is that the English will not attack the fort till all these Indians have grown tired of waiting, and have gone home again.*

Nevertheless, quite certain that it would be hazardous anywhere near the installation, Christian Frederick Post took pains to make a wide circuit around the Fort Duquesne area, and came at length to the town where he had once lived, the Delaware village called Kushkushkee, located on Beaver Creek[9] to the northwest of Fort Duquesne and about seven miles upstream from that creek's mouth at the Ohio. He was met and made welcome by three chiefs there, Shingas, Beaver, and one whose only name that Post had ever heard was Delaware George.

After he had rested with them, eaten and prayed, he got down to business. From his pouch he removed the official document given to him by the governor, plus three of the dozen or so bronze medals with the raised figure of the King of England on one side and a stylized figure of an Indian on the other. One of these medals each he now solemnly presented to the three chiefs. He glanced at the document, refolded it and put it back into the pouch.

"My Brothers," he said, "I have come bearing good news from the governor of Pennsylvania, who speaks in turn for the King of England. You know now that since last summer many of the Delaware people—my wife's people, your own people—have accepted peace with the English and no longer attack us. Surely you know by now, too, that the Iroquois who once called themselves your masters, have thrown aside their neutrality and have allied themselves to the English. Yet, still there are many in these woods, both Shawnees and Delawares, who remain at war with us, who come against our people at any time and who cause much bloodshed on the frontier.

"In both the eyes of God and the eyes of man," he continued, "this is wrong. The governor has directed me to tell you that he realizes that it is not your fault entirely, that you have been led astray by lies told you in supposed friendship by the French. The wish of the English is for peace. The governor begs that you accept his invitation to attend a grand council to be held at our town of Easton, which you know, on the Delaware River. There, by renewing the chain of friendship between us, all the bloodstains of the past will be wiped away and all the hatchets buried and nothing of the past held against you.

"We wish a strong friendship with you and would gladly welcome you as allies, but an alliance with you is not essential to the friendship, if you would but remain neutral in the argument we must settle between ourselves and the French. I must warn you that at this very moment a large English army under General Forbes is coming to drive the French from Fort Duquesne. It would not be wise for you and your people to aid the French against us. If you do, there cannot help but be much blood shed—yours, theirs, ours—and this is needless. If you do not fight for the French there, they will be too weak to oppose the army and they will either withdraw before the army gets there, or they will surrender

593

themselves without their blood being shed. There is no other way."

The three chiefs considered this at length and finally Shingas replied. He was a lean man, with broken teeth in front and the tip of his nose missing. Years ago his Indian opponent in a drunken fight had bitten it off and he had retaliated by biting off the man's ear. Every now and again as he spoke he rubbed his mutilated nose, as if still feeling the smart the injury had caused.

"Brother Post, we are agreed with you," he said. "It is not good for us or our families to always be at war and for our young men to be killed. In wintertime it leaves our women and children lonely and hungry and our numbers become fewer each season. We wish it stopped and are glad you have come for this purpose. But we are only one of four Delaware septs and the tribe as a whole can not accept your peace if all are not in accord with it. Come with us now and we will take you to the others."

Post agreed, pleased with the way matters had gone thus far, and in a short time they were on their way to another Delaware village some ten miles farther up the same stream. But here his presence was not at all welcome. A mob of warriors crowded around the party as they approached, screeching insults at him and shaking knives and tomahawks in front of him. Shingas, Beaver and Delaware George, however, calmed them and a council was called. Once again Post passed out the medals to the chiefs and related the governor's message to them. Though by now he hadn't expected it, he was surprised to find they were pleased with what he said, but in turn they insisted that he go with them to Fort Duquesne, where so many other Delawares were assembled, along with great numbers of Shawnees and relatively large numbers of Mingos, Ottawas, Hurons and Potawatomies. They, too, the chiefs told him, must be convinced before a decision could be given.

The fear welled up inside Post again. It was suicidal to go to the fort where the French would have such a grip over them. It was possible that even his Indian escorts would be set upon by them, and so he protested at some length. The Delawares, however, insisted; so, rather than lose what ground he had already gained with them, once again Christian Frederick Post repressed his fear and agreed.

He hadn't been far wrong in his surmise. As soon as they got near the fort and word of his approach spread, the fort commandant, Captain Ligneris, demanded that Post be turned over to him as a prisoner for questioning. Shingas, however, refused to obey. Angered, Ligneris immediately let it be known that he would pay a fancy reward for the scalp of the Moravian.

On hearing of this, Shingas told Post to stay close by the fire between himself and Beaver and that they would do all in their power to protect him. Throughout the night Indians came and went while Post remained rooted between his protectors. In the morning, a large number of Indians and four French officers from the fort came to where he was to listen to what he had to say. The officers had brought along a table, writing paper, ink and pens and by the looks they shot at Post, the Moravian missionary was sure they would like nothing better than to see his scalp hung at the belt of one of these Indians.

Once more he delivered the same message and he was encouraged when, as he was speaking, he noted several of the more hostile chiefs nodding their heads in apparent agreement with what he was saying. At last when he was finished, the Shawnee chief, Red Hawk, arose to speak.

"We have heard it said," he announced, "that the French and English intend to kill all the Indians and divide the land among themselves. It has been said that this is their plan, to wage a never-ending mock war against one another, keeping us in between so that little by little we may be killed off until there are no longer enough to resist and then those of us who remain will be driven from our lands or killed when the French and English make peace among themselves."

The French officers protested loudly at this, claiming that it was a lie and that there would never again be peace between Frenchmen and Englishmen, that one or the other would be driven back across the sea and that, considering the great victories already won by the French, it was obvious that it would be the English who were driven out.

On and on the harangue went, not ending until late in the evening, at which time the tribal chiefs announced that they would consider at length what they had heard and give their decision. It took them three full days to do so and it was Shingas who rose as speaker to make the reply.

"Our hearts are filled with happiness to learn that our English brothers in Pennsylvania wish to renew the old peace chain," he said. He rubbed his blunted nose vigorously, and then continued, "We on our part are willing to do so, but such an

595

agreement must come not just from those of your people in Pennsylvania. What good would such a treaty be if the English in Pennsylvania left us alone, while those in your Virginia and Maryland and New York continued to kill us and take our lands? We are willing, yes, to renew the peace chain and make it bright and strong again, but only if a wampum belt is circulated among us in the name of *all* the English provinces. We will send important people from among us to attend the grand council at your town of Easton. That is the message you may take from us to your governor and general."

And so, still fearing attack, Christian Frederick Post left the Fort Duquesne area and, after traveling for twelve days, arrived at Fort Augusta and made his report.

The governor and General Forbes were elated, and immediately a specific date in early October was set for the council and messengers sent to the neighboring colonies with requests that delegates to the congress be on hand, empowered to speak for their own provinces. White peace belts were sent to all the Indians within five hundred miles, inviting them to attend, and a special invitation was sent to Sir William Johnson.

Recovering under the tender ministrations of Degonwadonti from another attack of fever, William very nearly had a relapse when he got the invitation. For hours he stormed up and down about how his authority as sole Indian supervisor was being usurped, but at last Degonwadonti spoke up:

"Is not peace between our peoples what you have wanted, Warraghiyagey? Is it not what you have worked so many years for? Does it matter that it was not you who arranged the grand council? Is it not important enough of itself that the chance is here and that you have been invited to share in it? And would it not be to your honor to encourage all the Six Nations to attend this council with you, that their wisdom and knowledge might be of benefit?"

William looked at her angrily for a long moment, and then the anger drained away from him and he smiled. He shook his head and finally reached out and pulled her to him and kissed her lingeringly. When they broke apart, he shook his head again, with a wry expression.

"Molly, my girl, you're the only person I ever knew who could get matters all straightened out as nice as you please just by asking a string of questions. You're right, of course. You always are. I'll send a messenger to Pennsylvania right away and start some belts circulating in the Six Nations."

And he did, but he made sure to stipulate in the Pennsylvania message that he, as Indian supervisor, must be spokesman for the English and approve of all proposals before they were made to the Indians. Someone else may have put the pie in the oven, but he meant to be the one to take it out.

Finally, today, having received agreement from all parties concerned with the grand council, General Forbes wrote from his sickbed in Shippensburg to Colonel Bouquet, who had moved with the advance detachment of the army to set up a new post along Loyalhannon Creek to the west of that principal ridge of the Alleghenies known as Laurel Hill.[10] He was jubilant with the successful manner in which Frederick Post had carried out his assignment and with the way all parties concerned had responded. He only wished that he could attend the council himself, but the sickness had so devastated him that he would have to conserve all his strength for the great thrust at Fort Duquesne. This was reflected in his letter:

*August 18, 1758*
*Camp at Shippensburg*

*My Dear Bouquet,*

*I am now able to write after three weeks of a most violent and tormenting distemper, which, thank God, seems now much abated as to pain, but has left me as weak as a new-born infant. My journey here from Carlisle raised my disorder and pains to so intolerable a degree that I was obliged to stop. I really cannot describe how I have suffered both in mind and body of late. However, I hope to have strength enough to set out from this place on Friday next.*

*After many intrigues with Quakers, the Provincial Commissioners, the Governor, etc., and by the downright bullying of Sir William Johnson, I hope I have now brought about a general convention of the Indians.*

[ *September 5, 1758—Tuesday* ]

The fickle fate that had for so long frowned on the enterprises of the English had now apparently done an about-face and directed her glare at the French. First had come the stunning victory at Louisbourg, then the establishment of a grand Indian council at Easton, Pennsylvania to be held in another six weeks, at which it was hoped that at last the Indian menace to the English could be ended. And now the garrison of soldiers and workmen at nearly completed Fort Stanwix burst into excited cheers as the three thousand blue-clad provincials of Lieutenant Colonel John Bradstreet came into view from the west on the portage road of the Great Carrying Place, with flags waving gaily and their throats bubbling with song. Brigadier General John Stanwix himself came out to greet the column and he wrung Bradstreet's hand warmly.

"Did you do it?" the general asked.

"Yes sir, General, we damned well did it!"

"Well, by God, sir, that's wonderful. That's just wonderful. Wait'll General Abercromby hears that. Come on inside the fort and tell me all about it."

Bradstreet nodded, and turned command over to his second with orders to bivouac for the night before the fort. The boats still beached at Wood Creek were to be brought to the Mohawk River side of the portage this afternoon. Then he and the general walked to the fort. It was turning into quite a significant installation and Bradstreet murmured approvingly as they entered.

"Like it, eh?" Stanwix said, chuckling. "She's a pretty good one, I think. Guess she better be for the sixty thousand pounds sterling she's costing the King."

He ushered Bradstreet to a seat in his office, poured them both a drink of quality brandy and then held his up in a toast.

"To victory," he said.

"And to continued victory," Bradstreet added.

"Now, dammit man," Stanwix said eagerly after they had drunk, "tell me what happened."

And Bradstreet did, glorying in the pleasure he was affording the general, savoring the taste of it as he was savoring the taste of the brandy, thinking ahead of how he would soon be repeating the same story to the commander in chief himself. The world may not have heard much about John Bradstreet before, but by heaven it would hear about him now!

His force had left here, Bradstreet related, and rowed downstream on Wood Creek into Oneida Lake. Indians were seen during the crossing of the lake and his own Iroquois had gone to talk with them, but there was no trouble and the party returned bringing even more of their fellows with them. Down the Onondaga River—which Bradstreet insisted on calling the Oswego River—they had gone then and reached the site of the ruined forts without incident.

On the morning of August 22 the flotilla shoved off into Lake Ontario and after three days of hard rowing, landed within a few miles westward of Fort Frontenac. They had seen no one in their passage of the lake and no one had seen them. Under cover of night, on August 26, they had moved silently to within two hundred yards of the fort and surrounded it, still undetected.

Soon after sunrise on the twenty-seventh, Bradstreet announced his presence and sent in an order to the French commandant, Captain de Noyen, to surrender. With only a garrison of a hundred and ten men, Noyen had no choice but to capitulate and surrender his men, himself and some English prisoners. Even better, the entire Lake Ontario fleet of the French was taken at anchor before the fort—nine vessels, with each carrying from eight to eighteen pieces of artillery. Only their crews escaped, rowing swiftly to shore while negotiations were going on between Bradstreet and Noyen, and escaping on foot through the forest to the east.

Fort Frontenac contained an enormous stockpile of provisions, munitions, foodstuffs, Indian trade goods, naval supplies and the like. There were also sixty cannon and sixteen mortars inside. Bradstreet ordered that whatever they could reasonably carry with them should be put aboard the two largest French boats. The rest of the supplies and other goods were to be heaped in great piles and set afire. The cannon were used to blast down the walls of the fort and then a few of the big guns were kept while the rest were rendered unusable by knocking off the trunions upon which they necessarily had to be swiveled.

The Iroquois with Bradstreet wanted to kill and scalp all the French prisoners, but Bradstreet ordered them to stay clear and leave the frightened men alone. The Indians persisted, begging him to turn his back and shut his eyes as the French often did in such instances, but still he refused. Not wishing to alienate them, however, he gave them the greatest share of the plunder, which was far more than any of them had ever received at one time before, and it mollified them to a certain degree.

By midafternoon the tumbled fort was a great blazing pyre and the seven smaller French vessels still riding at anchor were also burned. Then, while the sun was still high, the entire army reembarked for the former site of Fort Oswego. The return trip went swiftly and uneventfully and as soon as the two large sailing ships were unloaded, they too were put to the torch.

"A shame we didn't still have the forts at Oswego," Bradstreet concluded, shaking his head sadly. "We could then have taken almost everything they had at Fort Frontenac and all their boats. We'd have had naval command of the lake. But we didn't dare leave them unburned or the French would've taken them right back again."

General Stanwix nodded sympathetically. "You'll be pushing on for Albany in the morning?"

"Yes, sir, but I'll be leaving a thousand of my men here, under General Abercromby's orders, to help you finish this fort quickly. When you're done with them, you're supposed to detach them at once to Fort Edward."

"Right," Stanwix replied, pleased at getting the extra help. He reached out and took Bradstreet's hand to shake it again. "Damn my bones, sir, you've done a fine job. Excellent! If the Crown has any sense they'll make you a brigadier for this."

Bradstreet grinned. "I hope so, General. I'd like that."

[ *September 11, 1758—Monday* ]

Lieutenant Colonel Henry Bouquet carefully considered the proposal just made to him by his second-in-command, Major James Grant. He was taken by the idea, but it was no easy decision to make. While the major waited patiently, the commander of this advanced detachment of General Forbes's army lit his pipe and puffed methodically, reviewing briefly Grant's request.

The major's idea had been to take a strong detachment and march against Fort Duquesne to deliver a crippling preliminary blow. Grant was sure that the French commandant there, Ligneris, had considerably fewer men than even such a strong detachment would have and, with the element of surprise on the English side, a blow might be struck which could severely weaken the French there.

The thought was intriguing. The morale of Bouquet's men encamped here at Loyalhannon Creek was slipping. Though General Forbes might by now have recovered somewhat from whatever ailed him and be preparing to march the remainder of the army to join Bouquet here, the delay was not pleasant and Bouquet's men were itching for action.

If a few of the outbuildings around Fort Duquesne could be burned and the Indians given a hard time, perhaps a few French prisoners taken, it could bode well for the entire operation. The immediate concern was that it should be done now, which would mean Bouquet would have to authorize the preliminary attack without consulting with General Forbes.

Yet, Forbes had been so ill these weeks and months, unable even to keep up with the army as he should, that as far as Bouquet was concerned, it was himself and not the general who had the better grasp of the situation. And so now he cleared his throat and nodded.

"All right, Major, you have permission to do it. Engage the enemy by surprise if you can and hit him hard, and then retreat back to this position, after which this whole detachment will be ready to follow through and General Forbes will probably be here with the rest of the army. Try to bring back prisoners for interrogation if you can."

Grant grinned, exulting inwardly at this opportunity for a shot at lasting military fame. "Yes, sir," he said, "we'll bring some back, all right. How large a detachment can be spared for me?"

Bouquet considered briefly. "Eight hundred or a little better ought to be enough. Highlanders, Royal Americans and provincials in equal numbers. Major Lewis and Captains Bullitt, Mackenzie and MacDonald to act as company commanders. Can you have them ready to leave first thing in the morning?"

"Yes, sir."

"Fine. Give them hell, Major, but don't expose your men needlessly."

Major James Grant saluted smartly and left the commander's quarters. There was one dominant thought in his head at the moment: If at all possible—and he was certain there was every possibility—he meant not only to attack Fort Duquesne, but to take it. What a coup that would be! And perhaps the final result would be a promotion for him to the rank of lieutenant colonel or full colonel and, if the fort was captured with enough flair, perhaps he might just become Brigadier General James Grant.

The major very nearly licked his lips in anticipation.

For almost two months the western Indians who had come to Fort Duquesne from the upper Great Lakes country had been cooling their heels, waiting for the army that Captain Ligneris had told them was on the march against the fort. They had daily been growing more and more impatient. These were the Ottawas and Chippewas, the Mississaugis, Hurons and Potawatomies, along with a scattering of Miamis and Weas. They all had come a very long way, eager to meet the English and telling Ligneris when they arrived in July that they would serve General Forbes and his army just as they had served General Braddock and his army at this place three years before.

But the weeks had passed and the English had not appeared and now these Indians of the west had lost much of their eagerness. In them there was a continually growing desire to return to their homes along the Detroit River, on Saginaw Bay and Lake Huron, at Michilimackinac and L'Arbre Croche and Sault Saint Marie, throughout the whole area of Lake Michigan. Winter was rapidly approaching and they had their families to think of; there was meat to be hunted, fur animals to be trapped, sugar to be tapped from the maples.

They might not even have minded this prolonged stay so terribly much if, as had always happened before, the French commandant had given them the gifts they expected. But this time he had not. A few items—blankets, knives, tomahawks, lead and gunpowder—were doled out in meager fashion, but there was precious little to spare and not even any food for Captain Ligneris to give them—or sell to them, as he was more inclined to do. The destruction by Bradstreet of Fort Frontenac had resulted in the destruction or confiscation of a great quantity of supplies that had been destined for Fort Duquesne, and now there was little likelihood that any more supplies could come before next spring at the earliest. Privation had since become standard and even among the garrison the specter of actual starvation was looming.

Throughout the summer the number of French at Fort Duquesne had varied from twelve hundred to three thousand men, but already many of these had gone to reinforce Fort Niagara against expected attack there—due to the surprise fall of Fort Frontenac—and many more had been recalled to Montreal. Now, including even the Indians, the total number of fighting men at Fort Duquesne was less than twelve hundred. Further, the militia from Louisiana and Canada who were stationed here were every bit as anxious as the Indians to get back to their families for the winter, and the feeling was growing among them that General Forbes was not going to make any kind of attack this year and that they were wasting their time staying here.

Captain Ligneris, in an effort to encourage the Indians, now spoke to the assembled western chiefs, buoying his voice with a confidence he did not at all feel.

"Great chiefs of the tribes of the far west," he said, "do you not see that the English general is dangling you on a string? He knows that supplies are short here and that I cannot give you presents which you ask for and deserve, and he waits for discouragement to fill your breasts and send you home. This I tell you: while no presents are available for you here and now, they will come soon—more and better than you have ever received and you must put your impatience aside.

"Do not," he continued, "do as the English General Forbes wishes and expects you to do; do not sit here and grumble about what you have not been given until it so eats upon you that you give up and go home without ever having seen the enemy. Instead, take up the hatchet now! Do not wait here for the English to attack, but instead carry the attack to them and destroy them as you so well destroyed Braddock. The honor to come to you on this account will be even greater than it was then."

But the inspiration Ligneris hoped to instill failed to take hold. For too long the Indians had been given promises, and promises did not fill empty bellies. They went into council and discussed the situation at length among themselves and when they gave Ligneris their answer, their air was sober, their demeanor somber.

"We will stay here yet a while longer, having given our word that we would help drive the attackers away from this fort. But we will not go out against that army by ourselves, for such a way is your responsibility, not ours. You have given us almost nothing, though we have been here two moons and more; yet we have stayed because our word has been given. Brother, hear us now! Our word was given to help you for a fight in the warm air of summer or the cooler air of autumn, but we will not stay with you into the coldness of winter, for the bellies of our women and children would dry up and they would die. We must provide for them. Until the moon is full again, we will wait, but no longer. We have said. That is all we have to say to you."

[ *September 14, 1758—Thursday* ]

Nothing had gone right for Major James Grant and now, stripped of his clothing and his hands tied behind him, he was marched with the other survivors of his detachment to Fort Duquesne. His mind was still filled with the horror of seeing his carefully laid plans demolished, his men butchered, their bodies decapitated and scalped and otherwise mutilated. And with each jolting step he took, the realization jarred through him that he was finished, that the military glory he had hoped to gain was forever lost.

How, he wondered, could it have happened? How, when they had come up unseen and with every advantage on their side, had everything become so totally botched? And since he was a man who could see no fault in himself, he inwardly placed the blame on his junior officers—on Major Andrew Lewis and Captain Thomas Bullitt, who were in command of the provincials, and on Captains MacDonald and Mackenzie, in charge of the Royal Americans and the Highlanders.

His detachment—eight hundred forty-two men strong— had reached the top of a hill[11] a half mile or so distant from the Fort Duquesne position at two o'clock this morning. They had arrived here wholly undetected by the enemy, and Grant had ordered Major Lewis to take half the detachment down to the open plain before the fort to attack the Indians camped there. Part of the plan was for him to feign a retreat after fighting briefly, and draw the Indians back to where the rest of the troops, under Grant himself, would be waiting to ambush them.

Lewis had set out at once in the darkness and Grant waited anxiously, his men positioned properly for the ambush; but that's when everything had gone wrong. Just before dawn Major Lewis returned, scratched and disheveled, and rather shamefacedly admitted that he and his men had become lost in the dark woods, and the detachment was now so broken up that any attempt to follow up the attack and ambush plan was no longer possible.

A bitter anger had come over Grant and he gave Lewis a severe tongue-lashing, discarded the original plan and, with a heavy fog cloaking the early dawn light, sent a party of

Highlanders into the cleared ground to burn a storage cabin there, hoping that this would do the job of drawing the Indians into an ambush.

He then foolishly split his remaining force into detachments which could not possibly be of help to one another. Angry still with Lewis, he humiliated him as best he could by sending him with two hundred men to guard the baggage, two miles to the rear, where a small party of Virginians under Captain Bullitt were already camped. He then sent a hundred Pennsylvania provincials far off to the right, toward the Allegheny, and Captain Mackenzie with a detachment of the Highlanders off to the left toward the Monongahela.

By now the fog was lifting a bit and he ordered Captain MacDonald to lead another company of the Highlanders into the open plain to reconnoiter the fort and make a plan of it. Grant himself remained on the hill with a hundred of the Royal Americans and a company of Maryland provincials.

Even then he still had the element of surprise in his favor, but he lost that by ordering the drums to beat reveille and the bagpipes of the Highlanders to be played. MacDonald was by now wide open on the plain between the fort and the woods, and at the sound of the drums and the squealing bagpipes, the Indians boiled out of their quarters—many of them entirely naked or clad only in a shirt or breechcloth—most of them still shaking the sleep from their eyes.

Screaming the war cry, they rushed upon MacDonald's Highlanders and were met by a volley which momentarily checked them, but they quickly surged around the company at a distance to cut off any retreat toward the woods. A sudden panic filled the Highlanders and they rushed back for the relative safety of the woodland, leaving themselves almost entirely defenseless in the precipitous retreat. At the same time, a large number of French soldiers were tumbling out of the fort to follow up the attack of the Indians.

Bit by bit, both MacDonald's and Mackenzie's detachments had fought their way back to the hill where Grant was located, but not without severe losses. Men by the scores were cut down by the French and Indian fire and Captain Mackenzie himself took a bullet through the head. Grant joined in the fight with his force but, seriously weakened by the divisions he had made of his troops, they were no match for the foe who greatly outnumbered them. A demoralizing panic swept over the English, and the soldiers began to drop their guns and run blindly toward the rear.

As best he could, Grant held them in check, knowing now that his only hope was the detachment he had sent under Major Lewis to guard the baggage. He directed his men to head for that rear camp along the circuitous path they had followed from there.

Lewis, however, as soon as he heard the firing break out, got his men up and headed on a straight line through the woods toward the action, not sticking to the path. In this manner, Lewis and Grant passed each other without even knowing it and when Grant reached the camp, his heart sank as he found no one there but Captain Thomas Bullitt and his little company. Almost immediately the whole body of the French and Indians was upon them. The fighting was furious and they were gradually forced toward the Allegheny.

It was Captain Bullitt and his Virginians who guarded the retreat toward the river with such fury that they held the attackers at bay until Grant and his Royal Americans and remaining Highlanders and Maryland provincials reached the river. Bullitt only gave ground himself when three fourths of his company had been killed.

Several times the French officers called out, offering Grant and his men quarter if they would surrender, but Grant refused. At last the majority of the survivors were forced into the river where a good number of them drowned while the others got across. Grant and quite a few of his men were surrounded and forced to surrender or die. A short while later Lewis and his men showed up and all were similarly surrounded and captured.

So now, heading in abject dejection into Fort Duquesne, Grant realized that his military career was through. Two hundred seventy of his men had been killed, another forty-two had been wounded and another hundred captured—accounting for practically half of his force. The others were scattered in the woods, undoubtedly making their own way as best they could back to Bouquet's camp at Loyalhannon Creek.

Captain de Ligneris was delighted with the whole affair and now once again strongly urged the western Indians, along with the Shawnees and Delawares, to follow up the crushing victory by moving at once against Bouquet and the rest of the advance army. But the western chiefs, almost as one man, shook their heads.

"We came here to fight the English for you," they told him. "We said we would serve them as we served Braddock.

We now have fought them and we have beaten them. We do not believe the rest of the army will come for you anymore, knowing how strongly we have fought here. We cannot remain here longer than this. We have fought. We have won. Now we leave."

And so, before the sun touched the western trees on this eventful day, almost the entire western Indian force at Fort Duquesne pulled up and moved silently away across the ford of the Allegheny and into the woods to the northwest. Ligneris watched them go and cursed in a soft voice. If the English learned they had gone, they would not hesitate to attack and Fort Duquesne could not possibly stand against them. There was only one hope: to attempt to make them believe the garrison here was much stronger than they had assumed. What survivors reached Bouquet's camp would help create this feeling, but now Ligneris would be forced to take the offensive and weaken himself by sending a detachment to attack Bouquet and thus convince the English that their only hope lay in retreating and then forting up somewhere for the winter.

If they could do this, Fort Duquesne might yet be held. Even though men and supplies could not be expected this fall—neither Fort Carillon nor Fort Niagara could be weakened by having reinforcements sent from them—still, ample reinforcements and supplies, too, could probably be brought in during early spring to ward off any further attack by Forbes or Bouquet. If, however, Ligneris was not able to convince the English that their only safe course lay in retreat and forting up for the winter, there could be no doubt that Fort Duquesne must fall to them.

### [ September 24, 1758—Sunday ]

Accustomed to strict obedience in all respects from his junior officers, General John Forbes could scarcely put credence to the letter that had arrived yesterday here at the new Fort Bedford at Raystown from Bouquet at the Loyalhannon camp. Details were sketchy in Bouquet's report and there was still no way of knowing how many men had been killed, wounded and captured, but there could be no doubt that a stunning defeat had been suffered.

Verification—had he chosen to disbelieve Bouquet's express—had come this morning, only a short while ago, with the arrival of two officers of the Highlanders who had been with Grant at the defeat. They had come all the way back here without even stopping at the Loyalhannon camp, fearful that the French and Indians had followed up their victory over Grant with a thrust at Bouquet. Together the pair, both in terrible shape after ten days in the woods, gave their impressions to General Forbes, and the fury rose in the ailing general's breast.

For an hour or more he went over the report of Bouquet and considered what the two Highlander officers had told him, until at last the white heat of anger had passed and he was able to write with remarkable restraint. He ordered Bouquet to hold his position and in no way to even consider retreating; he would be coming to the Loyalhannon camp himself with the remainder of the army at once. Then he added:

*Your letter of the seventeenth I read with no less surprise than concern, as I could not believe that such an attempt would have been made without my knowledge and concurrence. The breaking in upon our fair and flattering hopes of success touched me most sensibly. There are two wounded Highland officers just arrived, who give so lame an account of the matter that one can draw nothing from them, only that my friend Grant most certainly lost his wits and, by his thirst of fame brought on his own perdition, and ran great risk of ours.*

[ *October 18, 1758—Wednesday* ]

If the plans of the Marquis de Montcalm came to fruition, Bougainville knew, there was every likelihood that within another month he—Louis Bougainville—would be leaving Canada behind him and returning to his beloved France. His blood raced at the thought of it, and he glowed with an inner pride at the faith and trust Montcalm was showing in him, the confidence he must have in him to put into his hands such a responsibility, upon which perhaps the very future of New France hung in the balance.

Should he indeed go, Bougainville knew he would miss his general and miss aiding Montcalm in fending off the attacks of his enemies here: men such as Governor Vaudreuil, Intendant Bigot, Commissary Cadet and a host of others. They were men who were beginning to sense that the personal empires of corruption they had built were dissolving. To them, Montcalm was a great threat simply because he himself was not corrupt and refused to share in their misdeeds.

It was for aid that Bougainville would go to France, if he went at all, but it was also with certain proofs of the widespread peculations in Canada that he would present himself to the court and implore the King's aid in taking the steps now so necessary—and still possible to him—to preserve and even increase the wilderness empire of France in America.

In recent weeks a heavy melancholy had settled over the young captain. Decency, morality, faith—all these and more seemed to have disappeared here and even the writing about them in his journal had become distasteful to him. He resolved that this evening's journal entry would be the last he would make on a regular basis; he might still jot down events from time to time, but no longer could he write regularly of the dismal events around him which, even in the writing of them, made him feel guilty through association.

Now he dipped his quill for that final entry, and his words ran onto the clean paper in a smooth, firm hand:

*October 18*
*Today, despite the urgency of extreme danger, instead of stocking convoys with articles of defense for the frontiers, the Great Society in preference sends to Niagara and Toronto things necessary for trade. Everybody sees it, knows it— the cry is general. What does that matter to these brokers who enjoy the authority? Separated from the throne by fifteen hundred leagues, up to now sure of impunity because they have dared to make accomplices even as far as within the sanctuary of the Supreme Power, they have accustomed commerce, private parties; the people see it all, suffer all, and continue to be the instrument of their fortune.*

*In the last ten years the country has changed its condition. Before that time one was happy here because, even with little, one still had in abundance all things necessary for life; one did not wish to be rich, one did not even have the idea of wealth; no one was poor.*

*Bigot came, and in building the structure of an immense fortune, he associated in his peculations with several people necessary to his views or his pleasures. The amount of money increases in the colony and, consequently, the price of commodities.*

*The earlier simplicity blushes at first because it finds itself*

609

*vying with a most affected superfluity; luxury comes in and, with it, corruption of customs, avarice, greed, the spirit of graft. The way to pay court is to seem to want to make a fortune. Delicacy as to means is publicly mocked, treated as folly. The example of the leader produces the usual result— that is to say, many imitators. Everybody wants to trade; conditions are all confused. Trade, wiped out by exclusive privileges and by the all-powerful holders of the privileges, groans, complains, but its powerless voice, stifled, cannot make itself heard. It is necessary to submit a law which is going to destroy it.*

*To what cannot a man accustom himself? Force of habit extends even to enduring grief. Extortion has raised its mask; it no longer knows limits. Enterprises increase, multiply; a single society eats up all the interior commerce—the exterior also—all the substance of the country that it devours. It plays with the lives of men.*

*The inhabitants, worn out by excessive work, consume in pure loss to themselves, their strength, their time, their youth. Agriculture languishes, the population decreases, war comes, and it is the Great Society which—through outrages useful to its interest alone—furnishes the ambitious English with the pretext of lighting the torch. An exhausted colony cannot sustain the fatigue and the expense. The peculators do not tire at all. The peril of Canada, which becomes that of the state, makes no change in their method; this dried-up land can no longer furnish anything for their greed. Well! It is the wealth of the state itself they wish. All is put under way to rob the King—means which one cannot give names to, because up to now no one has thought of them. At last, unheard of thing, this Great Society, a law to itself, is the true Commissary General; itself it sets the prices. They traffic with our subsistence and with our life. Is there no remedy for this evil which is so extreme? And is it necessary that one man alone should exhaust the finances of France, abuse our dangers and our misery, and compromise the glory of the nation?*

*... Things necessary to clothe oneself are proportionately just as expensive as are provisions. Murmurs, even discontent, are extreme throughout the army. One's eyes are open and the brightness of too penetrating a light strikes them; one sees oneself the victim of an insatiable greed of a few people who do not even hide their purpose. They have usurped everything: provisions, trade, enterprise. They are the tyrants*

610

*of the price schedules and would take away our very lives if they could tax the air we breathe. The chief of the finances (Bigot), who is either the author or the accomplice of these infamous monopolies, has not, does not and will not make any regulations to stop them. . . .*

*The Great Society sent agents fifteen to twenty leagues out to sea to buy up the cargo of all ships coming to Quebec. Thus making themselves masters of all provisions and merchandise of the country, these insatiable bloodsuckers set prices and hold our very life at their discretion. Also, they write from Quebec that a great number of families are escaping to France. I say "escaping" because it is here a matter of fleeing from an enemy a thousand times more dangerous than the English. How now! Will the cry of this crushed people never reach the foot of the throne? . . .*

*Since the greatly excessive price of provisions and of all goods, shameful result of a visible monopoly, has raised a great unrest in the minds of the officers who are today deprived of almost all existence without going into debt, the Marquis de Montcalm has assembled the troop commanders— two captains and two lieutenants per battalion. He has told them of the representations he has made and continues to make in their behalf to the Intendant; that he proposed to him methods of making subsistence possible, especially to the lieutenants whose pay is absolutely insufficient. He added that he has also reported to the court the present state of affairs and begged an increase, either in pay, or in ration allowance; that he hoped his remonstrances would have results; that, moreover, the true soldier was not only he who could face danger, but also he who knew how to be firm in the face of difficulties and troubles of all sorts; that grumblings were superfluous, produced no remedy, could become contagious and incendiary; that obedience and devotion to the King, to the country, and to his superiors was like the glass in a mirror which the lightest breath would tarnish.*

*I confess that up to now part of the officers have lived as in the depths of peace and the greatest abundance; that their gambling has been enormous; that their table has been covered with delicacies; and that, finally, at the expense of truth in their patrimony or of their creditors, luxury, good cheer, the easy life, alone seem to occupy those whose only object should be glory.*

*But, alas! I say it with bitterness in my heart: desire for glory, fine sentiments, emulation, honor—what has become of you?*

*Our soul is disgraced; vile interest alone is the cause and objective of our conduct. One almost blushes in doing a good deed, solely for the glory of having done it.*

*No longer are our ears shocked by these things which shocked those of our fathers. They say—*

With a sudden revulsion, Bougainville stopped writing and slowly, deliberately, snapped his pen in half. He could not write another word . . .

. . . not one more word.

## [ *October 21, 1758—Saturday* ]

For nineteen days the grand council between the Indians and the English had been carried on here at Easton; nineteen days filled with interminable arguments and counterarguments. But now, at last, the congress was being concluded and, for Sir William Johnson, it was virtually the culmination of all he had endeavored to do for so many years.

There were representatives of many tribes at the meeting place at this Pennsylvania town on the Delaware River. There were, for example, the highest representatives of the Six Nations—Mohawk, Cayuga, Seneca, Onondaga, Oneida and Tuscarora. Equally, there were many representatives of the Shawnees and Delawares, some Mohegans and even a few Miamis and Weas. There were also a number of the disaffected Iroquois—some of the Senecas and Cayugas—who had allied themselves to the western Pennsylvania Shawnees and Delawares to call themselves the Mingoes.

For the English, there were powerful representatives of the colonies of Virginia, Maryland, New Jersey, Pennsylvania, New York, Connecticut, Rhode Island and Massachusetts. The most powerful figure among them—where power was calibrated as influence with and over the Indians—was Sir William Johnson, closely followed by his deputy, George Croghan.

Highly metaphorical speeches flowed one after another for days on end and it was obvious, from the very beginning, that the congress was not only to be a settlement, if possible, of differences between the Indians and English, but between the various Indian tribes themselves as well as between the various white factions. The whole affair boiled down to a political squabble. On the one side was Sir William Johnson and Croghan, representing not only the Indian department, but the Iroquois and the Pennsylvania Proprietary party. On the other side were the Pennsylvania Quakers, desperately trying to retain some control of the Pennsylvania Assembly, along with their allies in the assembly and a self-proclaimed prophet of the Delawares named Teedyscung, who, though without real justification for power, had convinced the Quakers and many of the Indians that he had it.

The arguments became stronger and more heated on both sides. At one point a leading Quaker arose and pointed his finger at George Croghan.

"You, sir, are a rascal and a villain!" he shrieked.

Coming to the aid of his friend, the attorney general of Pennsylvania stood and pointed his own firm finger at the Quaker who had spoken. "If you don't watch your mouth," he said softly, "I will be forced to slap you in the chops!"

More and more heated the congress became and when, at length, Teedyscung pantomimed the removal of the symbolic petticoat that had been put around the Delawares by the Iroquois and threw it to the Senecas and told them to wear it, he was jumped on by half-a-dozen Seneca warriors and beaten smartly before the altercation could be stopped. He was, in fact, fortunate that he hadn't been killed.

It seemed certain that the congress was going to fail through simply degenerating into a series of petty quarrels. But then, at William's suggestion, the Iroquois chiefs took control, quieted things down and, as the undisputed Indian power, declared the Delawares at peace with the English. Thereafter, whenever the battered Teedyscung tried to speak they simply silenced him or left the meeting.

Teedyscung had been fighting doggedly for land which, at the beginning of the congress, he had claimed as belonging to the Delawares; land in the Wyoming Valley of Pennsylvania, a section included in the long-disputed "walking-purchase" of Pennsylvania. At last, however, he admitted under the ungentle prodding of the Iroquois that the Delawares had no land of their own and his demands turned to wheedling as he tried to get the Iroquois chiefs to give the Delawares the valley in question.

"Do you not see, Fathers," he said to the Iroquois leaders, "that I have no place to alight? I sit here as a bird on a bough. I look about and do not know where to go. Let me therefore come down upon the ground."

The Iroquois were not concerned about his claims and could not care less about where this bird perched. The greatest bone of contention between themselves and the English—the knobby dispute that kept them from firmly becoming English allies and advocating that the other tribes do the same—was the way the English had consistently been gobbling up Indian lands as far as they could reach.

It was precisely the opening Sir William Johnson had been waiting for, and now he stood and raised his hands until silence covered the assemblage and all eyes were turned upon him.

"Brother Iroquois and Brother English: the problem is not without solution. The fear in the heart of the Iroquois that their lands will disappear is based in great measure upon the fact that four years ago the Pennsylvania Proprietaries bought in good faith a large parcel of land from the Iroquois on the Ohio River. It is land which the Shawnees and Delawares would like to claim but which, in the first, belonged to the Iroquois through the right of conquest.

"The Pennsylvania Proprietaries," he continued, "have no desire to cause friction between English and western Pennsylvania Indians, and though we have long raised the hatchet against one another, the problem can be solved here and now. I have been authorized to offer this same tract of land for sale *back to the Iroquois*, to do with as they wish, for the sum of only five shillings, which is but a token payment to make a contract between us binding by law. If the Iroquois buy back this land, then it ends all problems between us and we must therefore be allies against our common enemy, the French. Whatever claims the Shawnees and Delawares then have in regard to the land must be settled between themselves and the Iroquois, as it always has been done in the past, for it will then be out of our hands. Do the Iroquois chiefs and the chiefs of the Shawnees and Delawares agree to this?"

The Iroquois agreed and, having no other choice, so did the Shawnees and Delawares. And, as signatures were written on the deed passing the land back to the Iroquois, there was a distinct slackening of the tension which had for so long hung over the congress. With the placing of their own marks upon the deed, the Iroquois, Shawnees and Delawares were once again at peace with the English.

Deeply gratified at how things had turned out, the governor of Pennsylvania arose with a wampum belt in his hand and held it high for all to see.

"By this belt," he told them, "we heal your wounds; we remove your grief; we take the hatchet out of your heads; we make a hole in the earth and bury that hatchet so deep that nobody can ever dig it up again."

He handed the belt to the Iroquois spokesman and then picked up another—a white peace belt—and held it as he had the former.

"And by this belt," he continued, "we now renew all our treaties; we brighten the chain of friendship; we put fresh earth to the roots of the tree of peace, that it may bear up against every storm, and live and flourish while the sun shines and the rivers run. It is my desire that you send this belt to your friends and allies and fellow tribesmen and ask them also to take hold of the chain of friendship."

A multitude of gifts was distributed to all the Indians on hand and the promise exacted from them that the belt would be sent at once on its rounds—beginning with the Indians, now mainly Delaware and Shawnee, still adhering to the French at Fort Duquesne. And named to lead the small English party which would be escorted by some of these Indians on hand, to carry the belt on its rounds, was the Moravian missionary, Christian Frederick Post, who set out at once for the forks of the Ohio.

Even while the congress was breaking up, William Johnson, as Warraghiyagey, was circulating among the Iroquois, emphasizing to them the importance of destroying the French at Fort Niagara, as well as Fort Duquesne.

## [October 23, 1758—Monday]

Having finally arrived here at Lake George with his five regiments of men fresh from Louisbourg to join General James Abercromby, General Jeffrey Amherst discussed with his commander in chief the present situation at length. The entire army was still at ready, expecting to learn any moment that Montcalm's army was moving on them from Fort Carillon at the Ticonderoga Narrows.

Although the precipitous and unreasonable retreat of Abercromby from Fort Carillon was not talked about in detail—Abercromby being understandably reticent to hash over the shame of it—there could be no doubt that Amherst, as second-in-command, found it hard to understand why the withdrawal had been made and why an army in excess of fifteen thousand had not been able to take a poorly constructed defensive works hastily erected and held by only thirty-six hundred men. The fact of the retreat hung like a heavy mist between the men.

Amherst, while successful in keeping any note of criticism out of his voice, tactfully suggested that another attack be launched at the Ticonderoga installation at once, before Monscalm took up the offensive. Abercromby was reluctant to do so, arguing that the season was growing too late to initiate a campaign of such magnitude, and Amherst was compelled to accept that as final.

Then had come word from a French deserter that a fortnight before, Montcalm had marched his army away, heading for Montreal and Quebec for the winter, leaving behind only a relatively small garrison to defend the post—and also that of Fort St. Frederic at Crown Point—for the winter. Should an English attack be launched now, it could not help but be successful. Yet, the morale of the English soldiers had so deteriorated that to order them into an offensive operation would almost surely result in mass desertion and rebellion among these troops who were so anxious to get home. Abercromby thereupon ordered the army south to winter quarters in New York and Philadelphia, but to hold themselves in readiness for an early spring march against the enemy.

At the same time, far to the north in Montreal, the relationship between Governor Vaudreuil and General Montcalm was degenerating daily and now, as they never had before, their comments to one another were becoming acid, their complaints more frequent.

Louis Montcalm was appalled with the wretched condition prevailing in Canada and the sad state of the inhabitants. A few men, highly placed, continued to grow ever richer with their crooked dealings, but for the masses there was only privation. Even in the more remote posts, such as Fort Duquesne and Fort de Chartres, Fort Michilimackinac and Detroit, the corrupt commanding officers and some junior officers were living well and making small fortunes for themselves by appropriating the meager stores sent to them and then selling them to the Indians or to their own men. Men such as Captain Ligneris at Fort Duquesne had quickly learned that hungry and cold Indians would pay dearly in furs for such ordinary items as blankets and meal, gunpowder and rum.

The quasi-blockade of the mouth of the St. Lawrence established by the English, Montcalm found, had been only too successful. What ships did manage to get through were few and far between and their cargoes quickly taken over by peculators to sell at enormous profits to a populace already destitute and on the verge of starvation. A barrel of flour, if one could be bought, was priced at two hundred francs and all other prices were equally exorbitant. All of the cattle had long since been butchered and now even a great percentage of the horses had also been eaten. The Canadians were practically living on a diet of salt cod, and even the French regulars were confined to a regimen of tasteless and unnourishing commissary rations from the King.

Despite Montcalm's incredible holding of Fort Carillon in the face of Abercromby's superior army, the morale of the French and Canadian soldiers was virtually nonexistent. The reverses of the year, the weariness, the ever-present specter of hunger and a growing sense of outrage over the corruption of highly placed officials, perhaps not excluding the governor himself, gave rise to ugly murmurings. For the first time the Canadians were saying among themselves that perhaps further resistance was no more than stupidity.

The incredible thing was that the populace had borne up this long under the yoke of oppression it had been forced to wear these past years. The only really surprising thing about their growing unrest was that it had not manifested itself sooner. Until recently the Canadians had never lost faith that, in the end, everything would work out well and things would be better. They were a strong and loyal people, but even nationalism falters when confidence in the government is lost, and that was what was happening now.

For too long they had been faithful to a government that suppressed them in every way. Without real complaint they had borne severe privation for all too long. When their men were ordered to take up arms and leave their homes, they went, all of them, from sixteen to sixty, and the hard labors of the forest and field which had been their life became the duties of the women and little children and elderly people, who strove to raise a harvest that might somehow see them through the bitter winter. Even then, most of them were required to give considerably of their harvest to the government, supposedly to support the army; except that the army rarely received anything more than the poorest of what was taken.

Through it all, Governor Pierre Vaudreuil had bolstered their spirits with fine words of praise and encouragement. With his continuous lies and exaggerations—making every success far greater than it was and every loss considerably less—he had fooled them for a long time and, in the process, even came to believe himself what he was saying. During the three years past the Canadians had sustained themselves somehow on this diet of words, and attributed the early victories they had won to an exceptional ability of their troops rather than to where it belonged, on the shoulders of English commanders who had been stupid and blundering and cowardly.

But now, at last, the toll of privation was telling and the early whisperings were becoming an angry murmur. One of the first to detect it was Montcalm's quartermaster general, Commissary of War Doreil. In communication directly with the minister of war in France he wrote:

*. . . Rapacity, folly, intrigue, falsehood, will soon ruin this colony which has cost the King so dear. We must not flatter ourselves with vain hope; Canada is lost if we do not have peace this winter. It has been saved by miracle in these past three years; nothing but peace can save it now in spite of all the efforts and the talents of M. de Montcalm.*

For Montcalm himself, his position had become intolerable. Ever so clearly now he was seeing Vaudreuil in a true light and he was disgusted and angered by what he saw. Frequent whisperings came to him demeaning the governor and his underlings. Almost all of Montcalm's junior officers who were not mixed up in some kind of graft or other corruption with the government were being more and more vociferous in their complaints, and the communiqués which passed between the governor and military commander were becoming overtly sharp on both ends.

Montcalm's stunning defense at Fort Carillon had given rise to a bitter jealousy and invective in Vaudreuil, and, lest the general push his advantage and follow Abercromby to take up the offensive and possibly win, he had immediately sent Montcalm express orders that he was to avoid a general engagement. It was a fact, however, which one could never have deduced from Vaudreuil's letters to Colonial Minister

Pierre Berryer. Sensing the murmurings rising around him and the growing antagonism toward him by the Canadians and French regulars, Vaudreuil wrote:

*The people are alarmed and would lose courage if my firmness did not rekindle their zeal to serve the King. Though it has never been in me to deceive the people nor to listen to or pass on gossip, yet much of an alarming nature has reached me. Your Excellency, though it pains me to say so, I am forced to inform you that the Marquis de Montcalm has grossly mismanaged our military affairs. Our victory at Fort Carillon, if such it can be called, will have bad results, mark me. But for the manifest interposition of Heaven, M. de Montcalm would have been beaten. Then, with victory ours, the general failed to follow my directions and enabled the English to escape. He has not only failed to deserve victory, but he has also failed to make use of it. It was my activity in sending the reinforcements to Carillon that forced the English to retreat. The Marquis de Montcalm might have made their retreat difficult; but it was in vain that I wrote to him, in vain that the Colony troops, Canadians and Indians, begged him to pursue the enemy. As the King has intrusted this Colony to me, I cannot help warning you of the unhappy consequences that would follow if the Marquis de Montcalm should remain here. I shall keep him by me until I receive your orders. It is essential that they reach me early. I pass over in silence all the infamous conduct and indecent talk he has held or countenanced; but I should be wanting in my duty to the King if I did not beg you to ask for his recall.*

Having finished that, Vaudreuil sent a terse message to Montcalm, accusing him of hearing, passing on, and perhaps even originating gossip meant to undermine the confidence of the people in their governor. He added:

*In whatever form, sir, gossip is a vicious and malicious thing. I am greatly above it, and I despise it.*

For his own part, Montcalm had done whatever was in his power to stop the murmurings among his troops and, even though justified, to end the growing outspokenness against Vaudreuil among his junior officers. To receive such a letter from the governor then, in the face of this, filled him with a deep bitterness and anger, and his reply was a model of barbed phraseology:

*You are right to despise gossip, supposing there had been any. For my part, though I hear I have been torn to pieces without mercy in your presence, I do not believe it.*

Now, back again for the winter in Montreal, it was with distaste that he attended a dinner with the governor and his wife, along with eight other officers of the regular and colony troops. Vaudreuil was resplendent in freshly powdered wig, perfume and rich velvets and the table was heaped with such food as Montcalm and the officers had not seen for many months. There was no enjoyment to the meal for Louis Montcalm, moreover, because just as he feared it would, the conversation turned to an analysis of the battles already fought.

"It is a shame," Vaudreuil said abruptly, patting his petulant lips delicately with a fine linen napkin, "that you did not see fit, General, to follow up the taking of Fort William Henry with the taking of Fort Edward. It is hard for me, a simple man, to understand why a ripe fruit dangled before the nose remained unplucked."

Before Montcalm could reply and explain for perhaps the twentieth time the variety of reasons why such a follow-through had been impossible, however desirable, Madame Vaudreuil spoke up with acid sweetness:

"The same question had bothered me time and again, Pierre. But then perhaps it is we who are at fault for having entrusted a mission of grave importance to certain people incapable of determining what is important and what is not."

"Yes," the governor replied with mock thoughtfulness, "yes, my dear, you may be right. One may not always judge a soldier's merit by the fame which precedes him, lest the report of it be distorted. It is only through results that any military commander can be judged."

Though Vaudreuil and his wife had been supposedly speaking only to one another, the words resounded in the uncomfortable stillness of the group at the table and now, as if suddenly recalling that guests were present, the governor turned back and fastened a rather contemptuous look on Montcalm.

"As I say, General," he continued, "I am but a simple man

without knowledge of grand strategy. Tell me, if you will, why such a golden opportunity was allowed to slip past."

"Oh yes, General, do," interjected Madame Vaudreuil, coyly fingering the strand of pearls encircling her neck. "Had *I* been the general there, Fort Edward would now be only a memory for the English and we might this night be dining in Albany or New York instead of Montreal. Tell us, General, why are we not?"

Flushing slightly, Montcalm hesitated for a long moment, knowing that to reply at once would be to unleash the harsh words poised on his tongue. At last, in full control of himself again, he directed his reply to Vaudreuil, who listened with a wide-eyed innocence which implied to the officers around the table that he had never had these reasons explained before.

"Although I have explained the matter at length previously to you, both in correspondence and in person," Montcalm said, "I will go over it briefly once again. To have pressed the attack against Fort Edward after we destroyed Fort William Henry was impossible. There were invincible obstacles against us. First and foremost, we had neither the munitions nor the provisions to do so. To this was added the obstacle of attempting to make a portage of six leagues with all our artillery and equipment without oxen or horses and with an army worn out by fatigue and bad food. There was, further, the departure of all of the far west Indians whom we could not prevent going because of their need to supply for their families for the winter and a journey ahead of them of five hundred leagues before they could even get home. And, as you are well aware, sir, since it was by your own direct orders that they were returned, it was necessary to send back all the Canadians so that they might harvest their crops already ripe in the fields. These, though there were many others, were the principal reasons, sir. I must add," he concluded quietly, "that when I go to war, I do the best I can. If one is not pleased with one's lieutenants, one had better take the field in person."

Stung by the reply, Vaudreuil sucked in his breath and seemed on the verge of exploding with an angry tirade, but then he merely muttered in an ugly tone, "Perhaps, Monsieur, I will."

"I should then be delighted," Montcalm said, "to serve under you."

Madame Vaudreuil had been no less stung than her husband and now, her face pinched into a frown, she prepared to launch a stream of vituperation that her husband had failed to deliver.

"Should the governor choose to do so," she said, her eyes flashing heatedly, "there can be no doubt that *his* generalship would be better than that which he gets from those in a command position now! If I had been the general, I—"

Montcalm's abruptly raised hand cut her short and he said tonelessly, "Madame, saving due respect, permit me to say that ladies ought not to talk war."

"As I was saying before interrupted," Madame Vaudreuil went on, "if I had been the general—"

Again Montcalm cut her short with a gesture and then he said, with a certain coldness now clearly evident in his voice, "Madame, saving due respect, permit me to have the honor to say that if Madame de Montcalm were here, and heard me talking war with Monsieur le Marquis de Vandreuil, she would remain silent."

Her mouth opened in astonishment at being so addressed but, though she shot a sharp glance at her husband, the governor remained silent and she clamped her own lips tightly closed. Montcalm sighed, pushed his chair back and stood. He bowed slightly to the govenor.

"With your permission, Monsieur, I must leave. I thank you for the good dinner and your company and that of Madame de Vaudreuil. Madame, Monsieur, gentlemen—*bon soir.*"

The only good thing about the evening, Montcalm decided as he returned to his quarters, had been his success in persuading Vaudreuil earlier in the evening to consent that his aide, Captain Louis de Bougainville, and his commissary of war, Doreil, be commissioned to return to France to appeal directly to the throne for immediate aid for the colony—ships, troops, munitions, and provisions. Without such aid, the colony must fall. The two men would go as soon as possible in different ships so that perhaps one of them, at least, might get through the English and whatever storms nature might decide to unleash.

Back in his quarters again, Montcalm paced about restlessly, sleepiness eluding him. He tried to read, but could not seem to concentrate on the words and so, with dawn about to break, he set about writing letters. With winter closing in, it was not likely that any other ships would be able to sail for France after the two carrying Bougainville and Doreil. These were letters he wished Bougainville to take with him for delivery when he sailed.

Nevertheless, the first letter he wrote was not to France but to his junior officer, Colonel François Bourlamaque, who was still recuperating in Quebec from the serious wound received in his side at Fort Carillon. The general had grown very fond of this steady officer and now he told him of the dinner-table altercation with the governor and his lady, concluding that portion with the wry comment:

*This scene was in the presence of eight officers, three of them belonging to the colony troops; a pretty story they will make of it.*

*I cannot help but feel at loose ends and somewhat powerless in the face of my opposition here. M. Bigot attempts to act as a peacemaker between the governor and me, but without much success and, I think, only because he fears our differences will cause a blight on the fruits of his own corruption.*

*I am not happy here and had even asked for my recall, but now have resigned myself to see it through, if only because my heart weeps at the plight of the poor people here who are so sadly situated. To leave now would be to desert them when their need is greatest. It pains me to see their desperation and courage and I do not wonder at their murmurings. It has come to me that a certain fame now attends me in France because of reports received there of the engagements here and what seems to be our strength in battles with the English. There is equally the rumor that should we persevere—and our great good luck continue—that an appointment to the post of Marshal of France would be made me. Even that such should be considered does me great honor and I am humbled by it. I must in truth admit that I should like as well as anybody to be Marshal of France; but to buy the honor with the life I am leading here would be too much.*

The news from Fort Duquesne is not good at all. The Indians of the far west have gone home for the winter after destroying a large detachment from the army of General Forbes. Because of the loss of Frontenac and all the supplies and ships that had been stored there, Fort Duquesne has been on such scant rations that starvation became a real threat and Ligneris was forced to send two-thirds of his troops home so that what supplies were on hand could last for those who remainded throughout the winter. But now he *is very weak and the defeat of the English detachment does not seem to have had the desired effect of dissuading General Forbes from making further assault this season. There, at Duquesne, as elsewhere, corruption undermines everything. One would not think at so poor an outpost there would be opportunity to make money, but opportunity there is and no lack of those to take advantage of it. The remaining garrison is extremely restless: Mutiny among the Canadians, who want to come home; the officers busy with making money, and stealing like mandarins. The commander sets the example, and will come back with three or four hundred thousand francs; the prettiest ensign, who does not gamble, will have ten, twelve, or fifteen thousand. The Indians don't like Ligneris, who is drunk every day.*

*Forgive the confusion of this letter; I have not slept all night with thinking of the robberies and mismanagement and folly. Pauvre Roi, pauvre France, cara patria!*[12] *Oh, when shall we get out of this country! I think I would give half that I have to go home. Pardon this digression to a melancholy man. It is not that I have not still some remnants of gaiety; but what would seem such in anybody else is melancholy for a Languedocian. Burn my letter and never doubt my attachment.*

*I shall always say, Happy he who is free from the proud yoke to which I am bound. When shall I see my château of Candiac, my plantations, my chestnut grove, my oil-mill, my mulberry trees? O bon Dieu!*

Bon soir; brûlez ma lettre.

It was daylight when he finished, and now Montcalm rushed along with the writing of the other letters to be carried by Bougainville. His next was a brief note to the minister of war, apprising him of the army's return north for the winter and his fear for the campaign to come if succor in quantity and quality could not be sent at once from France. He added:

*What a country! Here all the knaves grow rich, and the honest men are ruined. Yet, I am resolved to stand by it to the last, and will bury myself under its ruins if need be. You recall, Sir, that I asked for my recall after the glorious affair of the eighth of July; but since the state of the colony is so bad, I must do what I can to help it and retard its fall.*

To his mother, too, Montcalm wrote only a short note, striving to be cheerful, but not succeeding very well in the attempt:

*You will be glad, Dear Mother, to have me write to you up to the last moment to tell you for the hundredth time that, occupied as I am with the fate of New France, the preservation of the troops, the interest of the state, and my own glory, I think continually of you all. We did our best in 1756, 1757 and 1758; and so God helping, we will do in 1759, unless you make peace in Europe.*

There remained but one letter for him to write now and he sat thinking about it at some length before beginning. At last he addressed a new sheet to the Marquis de Paulmy in Versailles, also in the ministry of war—a man with strong connections in the court. Montcalm was certain Paulmy would soon become minister of war, and this letter, which he would have Bougainville carry and deliver personally, recommended his chief aide-de-camp in the most favorable of terms. Bougainville, he was afraid, might be detached to other duty and not be returned to him. He wrote:

*My Lord,*

*You are acquainted with Sieur de Bougainville, one of my aides-de-camp. It will not have escaped you that he has spirit and talent. I can assure you that he has a military mind indeed and in adding experience to the theory he already has, he will become a person of distinction. You could use him in Europe upon his return in the various senior staffs of the army and send him into the various parts of the world where the King will be obliged to carry war. After having told you of his talents for his profession, I believe that I can assure you of the soundness of his heart and of his inviolable attachment to you, my Lord; and I look on him as one of those to whom the Ministry of War should pay the most particular attention. Whatever general you should assign him to, will thank you; as for myself, I shall always ask for first call on him whenever I am charged with a particular task.*

Governor Pierre Vaudreuil, too, had spent an essentially sleepless night, but he used most of it in telling Madame Vaudreuil what he should have said to Montcalm. He regretted now that he had agreed to Montcalm's idea of sending Doreil and Bougainville to France for aid. The aid was needed, of course, and he wanted it as badly as Montcalm did, but he was also worried about what stories Captain Bougainville and Commissary of War Doreil would carry to the ministry and the court. And so, long after Madame Vaudreuil had buried her head in a pillow to shut out his voice and finally fallen asleep, Vaudreuil took up his own pen and wrote the customary letters of introduction to the Colonial Minister, Pierre Berryer, for Bougainville and Doreil. They were letters that those two men themselves would carry and it was not inconceivable that they would open and read them, so he was more laudatory about them than he really cared to be. About Bougainville he wrote:

*He is in all respects better fitted than anybody else to inform you of the state of the colony. I have given my instructions and you can trust entirely in what he tells you.*

Concerning Doreil he wrote:

*I have full confidence in him, and he may be entirely trusted. Everybody here likes him.*

But then, having completed those two, he wrote another and more personal letter to Berryer, this one in code and to be firmly sealed and carried for personal delivery by someone in whom he had confidence that it would be neither opened nor maltreated until in the hands of the colonial minister himself. It said:

*Excellency:*
*In order to condescend to the wishes of M. de Montcalm, and leave no means untried to keep in harmony with him, I have given letters to MM. Doreil and Bougainville; but I have the honor to inform you, Monseigneur, that they do not understand the colony, and to warn you that they are the creatures of M. de Montcalm.*

*Vaudreuil*

[ *November 16, 1758—Thursday* ]

Christian Frederick Post was no less nervous about this present approach to Fort Duquesne than he had been with the earlier one, despite the body of friendly Indians and a few frontiersmen who were escorting him. He was keenly aware that while an agreement of sorts had been reached with the Indians at the congress held at Easton, the Indians around Fort Duquesne were ignorant of this. It was a fact driven home even more sharply when the small escort of soldiers that had accompanied him turned back eastward where they had been directed to, on the east bank of the Susquehanna.

Less than four hours later had come an Indian messenger with the ominous news that the returning soldiers had been waylaid and cut to pieces by a band of the very Indians to whom Post was carrying these belts of peace and friendship.

Arriving at the fort, however, he was escorted into a roomy shedlike construction to await the pleasure of the chiefs, to whom his Indian escort sent emissaries. There was an influx of unsmiling Delawares and Shawnees in the shed and their murmurings were anything but friendly. Eagle Claw, a young Delaware warrior of about twenty-two whom Post had converted several years before, leaned over to whisper in the missionary's ear.

"Things are not well," he said. "Some of my people have just returned from an attack on an English fort-house by the big river where we left your soldiers. They were pushed back with injuries and several deaths and they are not happy and have no wish at this time to make peace with those who have just hurt them."

Post nodded and though he quaked inwardly to see numbers of the Indians drinking rum from flasks or canteens, his expression did not change.

"Do not fear for me or for those who are with me, Eagle Claw," he murmured. "As God stopped the mouths of the lions that they could not devour Daniel, so he will preserve us from the fury of the men here."

Nevertheless, though he bore no love for the French, still he was relieved when at last a half dozen or more French officers arrived, carrying their small desk, paper, pens and inkpots. They greeted him coldly and set up their position to one side and began conferring among themselves in whispers.

A short while later came the chiefs of the Delawares and Shawnees, some of whom Post recognized. Cattahecassa—Black Hoof—was here for the Shawnees and, with him, Red Hawk and the second war chief of their tribe, She-me-ne-to—Black Snake. Shingas, Delaware George and Beaver were here for the Delawares, as was the fiercely militant White Eyes, his expression sour, unfriendly. All of them listened quietly while Post spoke at length in the Delaware tongue of what had transpired at the Easton Congress. They gravely took the belts that he offered them, but merely as acknowledgment of what he had said rather than acceptance of or agreement to it.

One of the younger warriors who had been repulsed from the Susquehanna fortified house so recently, and who had a wad of buzzard down tied firmly over an arm wound he had received there, sprang to his feet and pointed his finger at Post and the few frontiersmen who sat with him.

"Anybody can see," he said angrily, "even he who has only one eye to see with, that this man speaks lies. The English mean only to cheat us and to take our lands from us as they always have before. We should now, this moment, knock these messengers in the head!"

The French officers smiled at the discomfort the words were obviously causing Post and his party, but the chiefs waved the young man back.

"Hot blood runs in young veins," Shingas said slowly, "but it boils the brain and for the Delawares and, I think, for the Shawnees, I apologize to our brother Post for the insult of those hasty words. I say now that neither this man nor any with him are to be molested in any way, lest the one who does so feels the sting of my blade in his own heart. We who are chiefs here will discuss what you have said among ourselves. You will wait here until we come with our reply. Food and drink will be brought to you."

The French officer suddenly interjected the complaint that he wished to speak for Captain de Ligneris, but Shingas shook his head.

"Not at this time. First we must consider what has already been said here. When we return, you will be given a chance to speak and then both English and French will have our answer, whether we will cling to one or the other, whether we will carry to our distant peoples belts of war or belts of peace."

The chiefs grunted in affirmation and the whole assemblage, with the exception of Post's party and a few Indians, filed out of the building.

The cooked but cold meat of deer and dog was brought in by squaws and placed before Post's party in communal bowls. They chewed and swallowed without much enjoyment and then merely waited quietly. The rest of the morning and all afternoon passed without news and then finally, as the evening shadows were filling the shed with gloom, several squaws entered and built a fire in the middle of the floor. Before full darkness had fallen, the room was once again filled with warriors, chiefs and French officers.

It was the same French officer who complained before who was first to speak now. He told them what they had heard many times before: that the English were out to cheat them, to take their lands and their game, their waters and their forests as their own, to drive the Indians away from in front of them. He recalled to them the defeat of Braddock, the destruction of Oswego, the massacre at Fort Bull, the humiliation of Abercromby, and the recent defeat of Grant almost on this very spot.

"Are these the people, then," he added contemptuously, "that you wish to bind yourselves to? That would be a very foolish thing, for soon they will fall before us and then where will you be? Your great Onontio, our King in France, could not easily feel friendliness and concern for those among you who would desert him who loves you in favor of they who only mean to use you and take what you have."

He reached over and took from one of the other officers a relatively narrow belt of wampum and held it up. "Captain de Ligneris, who was ill and could not come, has sent me with this belt to remind you of the ties that bind us. It is also an invitation for you to help him drive back the army of General Forbes, as you have led him to believe you would."

He extended it to a Delaware chief whom the French called Captain Pierre and the English called Red Mink, but whose real name was Tollema. That chief looked at the belt with the same expression he might have shown had he been offered a venomous snake. With exaggerated actions he knocked it from the officer's hands to the floor and kicked it. Another Indian kicked it in turn and soon it was going back and forth in a melee of swinging feet amid the cries reserved for the trampling to death of a rattlesnake or copperhead. Finally Tollema picked it up on the end of a stick and showed it to all. The wampum belt hung there limply and the illusion that it had once been alive and was now dead was amazing. With a disdainful gesture, he flung it across the room from him to a dark corner where it fell and remained. Tollema pointed to it.

"Pick it up," he said. "It is yours, not ours. Give it to your captain who lies drunk in his bed, not sick; he boasted of his fighting, so now let us see him fight. We have often risked our lives for him and have hardly got a loaf of bread in return; and now he thinks we will jump to serve him again. But we will not. We will hear now, again, the message of our brother, Post."

Post stood at Tollema's nod to him and did not even glance at the officer who had seated himself in a dejected way beside his fellows. The missionary smiled at the assembled Indians and praised them for their clear thinking. Once again he told of what had happened at the congress and of the friendship and peace he had been authorized to offer.

"Past injustices will be forgotten," he reiterated, "and the evil things that have occurred between us, whether your fault or ours, will be washed away as if they never were. Once again trade will spring up between our peoples and the bellies of your women and children will be full and their hearts will not be empty because their husbands and fathers are far away, perhaps hurt or dead. As powerful chiefs of your nations, we ask you to carry these belts to your farthest villages and even to the chiefs and villages of other tribes to the west of you, to whom this same offer of peace and friendship is made. It is a time now to end war between us and to live in harmony so long as the grass shall grow and the waters flow and the sun shine."

As he finished there was a loud chorus of affirmative cries and considerable confusion momentarily as, it seemed, everyone began talking to his neighbor at the same time. The French officers were stunned, disbelieving, and now shaken badly when one of the Delaware subchiefs known as Isaac Still—because his Delaware name was Eih-saks-tehl—ran up to their spokesman and pointed a finger to within a fraction of an inch of his nose and shouted, "There he sits!"

It was obviously a prearranged signal because immediately, from half-a-hundred throats the simultaneous reply erupted, "The French have always deceived us!"

The officer blanched, looked quickly to his fellows and dipped his head. Without another word all of them got to their feet and, with the jeering cries of the Indians ringing in their ears, left the big shed. The belt they had brought to offer the Indians was flung outside into the darkness after them.

Post could hardly believe it. The victory won at this moment was no less important than any won in the whole war thus far. The Delawares, Shawnees and Mingoes had this moment ceased to be the enemies of the English.

The Indians now flocked about Christian Frederick Post and his men, wringing his hand and giving great expressions of friendship; confessing their delight to once again be united with the English and to have wiped their eyes clear of the blinding sand that the French had long ago thrown into them.

Catahecassa of the Shawnees placed his hand on the Moravian's shoulder and nodded seriously. "The belts will move," he promised. "I will see that they are taken from Shawnee village to Shawnee village until all have seen and heard this happy news. And when they have seen it, I will have it carried to our neighbors, the Miamis and the Weas, the Wyandots and Kaskaskias and the Cahokias and the Peorias."

Shingas, too, wrung his hand and promised, as Cattahecassa had, that the belts would be seen and admired by all their peoples wherever they were and when all had seen them and heard their message, they would be carried beyond, to the Tionontatis and the Mississauigs, and the fathers of the Mississauigs, the Chippewas, and to the Ottawas and the Potawatomies and to the Sac and Fox, to the Winnebagoes and Hurons. All, he assured the Moravian, would accept them with the joy and feeling with which they had been accepted right here.

Already, outside, the Indians were gathering their things and packing them in blankets to be tied to their horses or strapped over their shoulders, and it was clear that by morning every Indian would be gone from this place. Runners were already being sent out to intercept marauding Indian parties still out on the frontier, to call them off and tell them to wipe the blood from their tomahawks and return to their own villages.

The frontiersmen with Christian Frederick Post thumped him on the back and opened their packs to share with the Indians the small amount of liquor they had with them. It was a night they would never forget.

Slowly, thoughtfully, Christian Frederick Post packed his own things away and prepared to return to General Forbes with the good news. At one point he strolled outside and looked up at the stars shining so brightly in the darkness of a moonless midnight. It was hard to believe: the frontier butchery was ended; families need no longer live in fear from one moment to the next; husbands need no longer arrive home to find wives and children gone or dead and scalped.

He clasped his hands together at his waist and raised his face and his cheeks and temples became wet with the warm tears which slid from his eyes.

"Oh, God," he murmured, "thank you. Thank you, dear Lord, thank you."

## [ December 31, 1758—Sunday ]

General John Forbes now knew with unshakable certainty what others had only speculated about: that he was dying. Maybe he could last another two or three months, maybe only two or three weeks; but the fact was clear to him that he would soon be dead.

His body swayed and bounced in the litter slung between two horses and every step of the animal brought waves of pain to surge through him. Yet, in just the past few days he had been able to divorce himself somehow from the pain; shut it away so that while it was still occurring, it was more as if he were spectator to it than experiencer of it. The very fact that he was able to do this convinced him that the end must be close, but now he didn't care. He drifted off into the pain-free reverie which took hold of him so often these days and his mind went back again, for perhaps the dozenth time, over the events of the past ten or twelve weeks.

October had been a soggy month, with day after day of miserable rain, sometimes slashing down with intensity enough to soak a man to the bone in minutes, sometimes only a fine gray mistlike drizzle. No more than half-a-dozen days out of the whole month had the skies cleared and the sun shone through. Late in the month snow had replaced the rain as temperatures plummeted. The road so laboriously carved through the wilderness became a quagmire upon which travel became impossible. Heavily laden wagons sank to their hubs in clayey muck and the weakened horses could not begin to pull them.

Forbes had still been at Fort Bedford in Raystown through all this, though the majority of the army had slogged on to join Lieutenant Colonel Henry Bouquet at the camp on Loyalhannon Creek. The general decided that regardless of the weather, he must join Bouquet to direct operations. He wrote to both William Pitt in England and to Bouquet, complaining bitterly of the lack of supplies and the terrible weather. The whole campaign, it seemed, must be doomed for these reasons. To Pitt he wrote:

*I am in the greatest distress, occasioned by rains unusual at this season, which have rendered the clay roads absolutely impracticable. If the weather does not favor, I shall be absolutely locked up in the mountains. I cannot form any judgment how I am to extricate myself, as everything depends on the weather, which snows and rains frightfully.*

His note to Bouquet at Loyalhannon Creek was no less gloom-filled:

*These days of constant rain have completely ruined the road. The wagons would cut it up more in an hour than we could repair in a week. I have written to General Abercromby, but have not had one scrape of a pen from him since the beginning of September; so it looks as if we were either forgot or left to our fate.*

But at last, early in November, he was carried by litter to the Loyalhannon camp, each plodding step of the horses an excruciating agony for him. Though he was terribly weak when they got there, he called for an immediate council of war with all his officers and the situation of the campaign was discussed at length. No one—not even Forbes himself—felt very optimistic and at last it was resolved to abandon any further thought of attack on Fort Duquesne. Even though the Moravian, Christian Frederick Post, had reported triumphantly of the Indians' acceptance of the peace and friendship offerings and their withdrawal from the fort to their own villages, the army was simply too weak and too ill-supplied to contemplate an attack against a fortified enemy.

Then, just as they were on the verge of withdrawal, three French deserters were brought in with news that changed everything. Starvation, they averred, was so viable a threat to the garrison that Captain Ligneris had been forced to send the greater number of his men back to Montreal or Fort Niagara. Those that remained at Fort Duquesne were in such a demoralized state that desertion had been rampant. Probably no more than four or five hundred remained to hold the place.

Forbes immediately pushed away all the withdrawal plans just made and ordered an immediate advance. Though the rains had now ceased, the road built toward Fort Duquesne by Colonels Washington and Armstrong was still in bad

633

shape, so with the exception of only a few light pieces, all wagons and artillery were left behind at the Loyalhannon Creek camp. Neither tents nor baggage was taken and, carrying only their own weapons, light packs and blankets, the twenty-five hundred men—Forbes slung between two horses among them—set out for the French post on November 18. Six days later they reached a knob called Turkey Hill, a day's walk from the fort, and here they camped for the night. Early in the evening there was a heavy rumble from the west. With the sky cloudless at the moment, the rumor quickly spread among the men that the French magazine had accidentally exploded.

In the morning—November 25—the march was taken up again, with a strong advance guard in the lead, followed by Forbes in his litter and then, in three parallel columns behind, the Highlander troops in the center under Colonel Montgomery, the Royal Americans on the right under Lieutenant Colonel Bouquet, and the provincials on the left under Colonel Washington.

Late in the afternoon they had begun passing the grisly remains of Grant's defeat; the bloated, rotting bodies of men killed two months ago. And, toward evening as they neared the fort, here and there were the heads of Grant's Highlanders still impaled on posts, the kilts hung directly beneath them in grotesque mockery. A deep and implacable rage filled all the men, but reiterated orders filtered back quickly from Forbes: peace had been established with the Indians since this happened and under no circumstances were *any* Indians to be killed or in any way molested except in protection of one's own life. It was a bitter pill for the men to swallow, especially Montgomery's Highlanders. Dusk was deepening when at last they reached the plain before what had been Fort Duquesne, but which was a fort no longer.

The French were gone.

All storehouses and barracks had been burned and the principal fortifications had been deliberately blown up. The booming rumble heard the evening before had been no accidental explosion of the magazine. Fort Duquesne had been abandoned and destroyed.

There was little sleep for Forbes's troops this night. While little likelihood of attack remained, the general was leaving nothing to chance. Defenses and shelters were hurriedly erected. Still undestroyed were a fair number of traders' cabins and huts capable of holding eight or ten soldiers each.

634

Around this cluster of little buildings Forbes ordered a stockade to be built, and in the forenoon of Nobember 26, with the work largely completed, Forbes named it after the English prime minister.

"This place," he said, extending an arm to take in the whole stockaded cluster, "is hereafter to be known as Pittsburgh."

Forbes spent some time in the morning conferring with a few of the Delawares who were still lingering about and learned that Captain Ligneris, with just over four hundred men left, had blown up and burned the fortifications last evening. The French had then departed in three groups—one going down the Ohio and presumably with the ultimate goal of Fort de Chartres on the Mississippi River in the Illinois country of Louisiana; a second striking off overland almost due north and apparently heading for either Detroit or Fort Presque Isle; the remainder, under Ligneris himself, going upstream on the Allegheny and heading for Fort Machault at Venango or, more likely, Fort Niagara.

Secure in the knowledge now that the enemy was definitely gone, Forbes dispatched a detachment of Pennsylvanians under Captain Benjamin West, led by Indian guides, to the site of Braddock's defeat. Here they found the multitude of bones of those who had fallen three and a half years ago. Young Major Halket of Forbes's staff went along in an effort to find the remains of his father and brother. Guided by an Indian who had been in the fight, he discovered two skeletons lying beneath a tree and, because of the peculiarity of the teeth of his father, recognized the last remains of Sir Peter Halket. The other skeleton had to be that of Major Halket's brother, and the young officer moaned and covered his eyes and then fainted. When he was revived, a hole was dug and the bones gently laid in it and buried together, with the grave then covered over with a Highland plaid. A squad of Pennsylvanians fired a final salute over it.

There was no way to distinguish who was represented in the great mass of remaining bones on the battlefield. All these were gathered and buried in one large common grave and another volley fired over them. The same thing was occurring east of the fort where Grant had lost his battle. With the melancholy duty completed, the detachments returned to Pittsburgh.

Though he wished he could press on to follow and attack Ligneris, Forbes reluctantly turned his army back toward the east. To undertake any attack against a French post, regardless of how weak it was, would be foolhardy in the extreme, since his own supplies were virtually gone and his men greatly fatigued by their long campaign, even if they had not fought in it.

Leaving a garrison of two hundred Virginia provincials under Lieutenant Colonel Mercer, Forbes ordered the return march begun. He sent expresses ahead to carry the news of the taking of the Forks of the Ohio and the urgent request that a strong, fresh and well-supplied detachment of men be sent to erect a new fort at this place and make the English hold on it permanent.

Henry Bouquet, still contrite for the rashness of his act in sending out the party under Grant, had nothing but admiration for General Forbes. It was an admiration bordering almost on adoration. As he wrote to Chief Justice Allen:

*We would soon make M. de Ligneris shift his quarters at Venango if we only had provisions; but we are scarcely able to maintain ourselves a few days here. After God, the success of this expedition is entirely due to the General, who, by bringing about the treaty with the Indians at Easton, struck the French a stunning blow, wisely delayed our advance to await the effects of that treaty, secured all our posts and left nothing to chance, and resisted the urgent solicitation to take Braddock's road, which would have been our destruction. In all our measures he has shown the greatest prudence, firmness, and ability. . . .*

Now they were on their return home. Thoughtful of his men, Forbes would not have them slowed because of his own condition, and so he sent them ahead while he, following at the best pace possible, was attended by only a small detachment of officers. Daily marches for him became ever shorter but now, with the year closing and a new year beginning tomorrow, Philadelphia was not much farther ahead. Forbes was confident he would reach it in time.

"It will be a good place," the general whispered to Major Halket, "for me to close my eyes for the last time. I think now that we will beat the French; and I think now that I can die content in the knowledge that in part I will have contributed to our eventual victory."[13]

# CHAPTER XI

[ *March 28, 1759—Wednesday* ]

THE meeting in grand council of the Ottawas, Chippewas, Hurons and Potawatomies in the Ottawa village just across the river from Detroit had been called by Charles Michel de Langlade. Even though the Indians before him represented only a portion of the warriors from each of the villages, almost a thousand were on hand and they listened soberly as Langlade spoke to them.

"I will not, my Brothers, try to tell you that the French, our friends, are still winning the war. They have been hurt by the English. Fort Frontenac, with many of the goods meant for you, was destroyed. Fort Duquesne has been lost. The Louisbourg fortress, which guarded the entrance of French ships into the St. Lawrence River on their way to Quebec, was taken and now few ships get through. But worst of all, the Indian allies of the French have in great numbers deserted them. The Delawares and the Shawnees, the Miamis, the confederation who called themselves Mingoes, other tribes— all have declared themselves neutral or are now fighting beside the English. Among the Iroquois, even the loyalty of the Caughnawagas and Chenussio Senecas to the French is faltering and they may turn to the English. Many of the Algonkins and Nipissings and Mississaugis have gone home. Even the Abnakis, who remain around Montreal and Quebec, do so only because they have vowed never to live near the English and the English have already gone past their towns; yet even they have not much heart for further fighting.

"None of this can be good news to you," he continued evenly, "but do not make the mistake of thinking that because there have been setbacks, that the French are lost. I have been told that the King in France is preparing a great army to come to the aid of General Montcalm and with that force our general will sweep before him all who oppose the French.

"Now I have been asked by the Detroit commandant to call you together to ask again that you raise your tomahawks in the French cause, which is and must be your cause as well. In this year there will be attacks by the English against Fort Carillon on the Ticonderoga Narrows, against Fort Niagara and perhaps even against Quebec or Montreal. The French need your help now as never before and I have come to find out whether or not you will give it. If so, you will leave as soon as possible to assemble at Fort Machault and Fort Presque Isle and from these places you will go to where the general feels you are most needed."

He paused a long while and then finally concluded: "You know in your hearts that the French are your friends and were the friends of your fathers and grandfathers and their fathers before them. They have always treated you well, paid you fairly, lived with you and accepted your ways without trying to change you to their ways. They love the land as you love it and know that it belongs not to individuals, but to all, to share equally. The English may ply you with great gifts to win you over, but the gifts disappear when you have been won, and your land disappears as well. You have no enemy so great and so treacherous as the Englishman. If you do not fight him with the French, then mark what I say, the time will come when you will have to fight him alone. Think well on it. Will you continue now to stand beside your French brother?"

The huge council longhouse practically shook with the cries of agreement which rang from nearly a thousand throats. It was the war chief of the Ottawas—Pontiac—who gave the reply.

"The French," he said, "are our friends. They have been, they are now, they always will be. Just as we are theirs. We do not desert a friend at the time he needs us. Yes! We will fight beside them, as long as there is breath in us to fight!"

### [ April 6, 1759—Friday ]

The approach of the large band of Indians to Pittsburgh had caused quite a stir. The drumbeat alert was sounded as they came into sight this morning and Lieutenant Colonel

Mercer positioned his men advantageously around the pitiful defenses of the stockade.

It quickly became apparent, however, that this was no war party. Here there were Delawares and Shawnees, Mingoes and Senecas, along with a few Miamis and the disjoined Hurons called Wyandots. A delegation of three chiefs left the band, which stopped on the plain some distance before the fortifications, and presented themselves to the commander. They had come, they told him, because now there was peace between them and the English and, to show their good faith in this peace, they wished to deliver up to the commander the English whom they had been holding, some as captives, some as slaves, some as adopted sons.

The acceptance of the prisoners was quickly made by Mercer and, though he could not spare much, he presented to the Indians whatever supplies he could. Within two hours all of the Indians had disappeared. Many of the captives were Grant's men, taken last fall in that tragic skirmish, but just as many were women, children and even some men who had been taken at intervals over the past three years along the Virginia and Pennsylvania borders.

The different groups of Indians had met to form their large band not far from the fort, and for the prisoners it had been an emotional time. Wives and husbands who thought each other long dead were reunited. Parents saw again the children that had been snatched from them; brother was reunited with brother, sister with sister.

The three Girty boys—Simon, George and James—met each other again and rejoiced, and then the three of them together were reunited in an emotional moment with their mother, Mary Girty Turner, and their little half-brother, John Turner.

In the interval they had been separated, however, the three Girty boys had virtually become Indians. They dressed and looked and spoke like the tribes that had adopted them. The gap that had formed between them and their mother was unbridgeable, and when the liberated prisoners were prepared for escort back to the civilized east, these three youths refused to go along. There was a growing need here at Pittsburgh for men who knew the Indians well, who knew the speech of the Shawnees and the Delawares and the Senecas; a need for men who knew the customs of these Indians and who could act as liaison between English and Indians, and to act as interpreters as well.

Simon Girty, James Girty and George Girty were ideally suited to the job and they accepted it without hesitation.

## [ April 11, 1759—Wednesday ]

Since there was a minor epidemic of smallpox at Fort Johnson, the grand Indian council Sir William Johnson had proposed to meet there early this month had been transferred to the Mohawk village of Canajoharie, upstream on the Mohawk. There, in the rude quonset that was the home of Nichus, his Indian father-in-law, William set up his headquarters, still attended by Degonwadonti, who was now heavy with his child.

The Iroquois were coming in from all over for this council, which it was said would be a most important one. The very fact that delegates of the Six Nations had agreed to attend it there rather than at the usual place of Onondaga was evidence of how strongly they had swung toward English sympathy. William was confident the council would be a success.

Word had come that had taken William by surprise and had caused him to delay the start of the council: the Chenussio Senecas, long the most pro-French of all the neutral Iroquois, were planning to attend and were at present en route, led by none other than Chief Old Belt. It was Old Belt who so often had opposed William at the Onondaga councils, and who had been the prime instrument in turning Chief Red Head of the Onondagas to French sympathy. Old Belt's coming here to the Canajoharie council could only signify, as William interpreted it, that he wished to mend his long-broken fences.

At once, as Warraghiyagey, William sent a deputation of Mohawks to escort him and his people in, to make him comfortable, provide him with food and goods and carry to the Senecas the hand of friendship from Warraghiyagey. William's pulse quickened as he thought that at last he might be successful in winning Old Belt away from Chabert Joncaire, who had for so long stirred the Seneca chief against the English in general and William Johnson in particular.

This morning the Chenussio Senecas had arrived, led by Old Belt, each warrior distinguishable from other Iroquois warriors by one especial ornament they favored: a flat, triangular stone hanging pendulously from the nostrils and covering the lips. There were sixty of them in the party and with them were a delegation of perhaps twenty Shawnees, led by the most powerful war chief of that tribe, Pucksinwah, whose village of Kispoko Town[1] lay deep in the heart of the Ohio country along the west bank of the Scioto River.

The Senecas and Shawnees had brought with them five English prisoners, given to them by the Delawares to be liberated to Warraghiyagey as evidence of the Delaware determination to live up to the articles of peace. The five, in rather bad shape, were sent downstream at once to receive treatment at Albany and then to be returned to their homes.

Warraghiyagey welcomed Old Belt and Pucksinwah expansively. "My heart," he told them, "overfills with a great gladness at your presence and the belief that on this day, all past evil things between us may be wiped away as if they had never been."

Old Belt looked somewhat dubious, but both chiefs shook his hand warmly enough and it was Pucksinwah who replied:

"English Brother, the hearts of my people, too, are filled with gladness that the war between us is ended and that we may now live in peace with one another. Our principal chief, the Chalahgawtha Shawnee known to us as Hokolesqua and to you as Cornstalk, has sent me to speak for all our people. More than this, I am empowered to speak for those tribes who could not come here themselves, but who wished to be represented to you. Therefore, hear me now: I speak at this time not only for the Shawnee nation, but equally as Delaware, Wyandot, Miami, Wea, Eel River Miami, Kaskaskia, Cahokia, Peoria, Mingo, Tionontati, Amikwa, most of the Mississaugi, some of the Chippewa, a few of the Ottawa. In their name and in response to the belts of peace and friendship carried to them from the English, they offer their hands, they bury their tomahawks, they bend their gun barrels, they burn their scalps. They return to you the friendship and peace that you have offered and declare the war between you and them to be dead and cold and the fire of friendship to be hot and bright and the chain which links us together to be newly polished and repaired and shining like the sun. Representatives from these tribes are on their way to see you now, but will come at different times since each has a different distance to go. But for all, I am empowered to say that the friendship which bound us to the French has ended, that no more will they lift their tomahawks and take scalps in the Frenchman's behalf. So it is said from them to me and from me to you, English Brother!"

William Johnson was overwhelmed. He accepted the offers of friendship and alliance with gratitude and dignity. Then it was the Chenussio Seneca, Old Belt, who wished to speak.

"Brother Warraghiyagey," he said slowly, "for many seasons now the blood we shared has been cold in the middle and our words to one another and about one another have been filled with anger. But no more! I have wiped the French sand from my eyes and have said farewell to the brothers you know as Joncaire, who were the ones who filled my eyes with that sand and plugged my ears against your wise words. Now the eyes are clear and see well and the ears are unplugged and hear everything. No time before has Old Belt ever said that he was wrong, but now he is saying it for all to hear, thus to know that his words are from his heart.

"It is on our land now, the land of the Senecas, that the French have two posts. The one of these is the post that is called Little Niagara, which is but a little box at which the chief Joncaire is the leader. The other is the big Fort Niagara at the mouth of that river of the same name, which is strong and which holds many soldiers and big guns and has as its commander the French captain who is called Pouchot. These forts we wish you, the English, to destroy, and to drive the French away. We would not ask that you do it alone. We will help you and we will ask that the warriors of the others of the Six Nations will help, too."

It was almost too good to be true and William gravely assured Old Belt that he would take steps at once to see that this was transmitted to the English commander in chief, and he was sure that it could be done swiftly. The surprises of this council were not yet over, however. Toward evening, when two large oxen had been butchered and were boiling in five separate kettles, messengers came from the very strongly pro-French Caughnawagas at both the Sault Ste. Louis and Fort Présentation, bearing belts and declarations that they would no longer fight for the French and wished peace with the English. They also brought along a letter for William, laboriously printed in stilted English. It was from the Sulpician priest, Abbé François Piquet, at Oswegatchie, who had personally instigated and accompanied so many previous raids against the New York frontier. He had written:

*Monsieur Johnson—I begg you that when you march into Canada you will have a good heart. When you come to the Oswegatchie River, where at is my Christian Mission called*

*La Présentation, I begg you that you will remember that it
is a place intended for nothing more than but to teach
religion and give instruction of God for the ignorant and I
begg you that you will not break and destroy this house of
God.*

It was with reception of this letter that Sir William Johnson first felt with unshakable certainty that the French were
lost and that the English would soon win the war. And now,
with his own clothing removed except for a breechcloth and
his face and body garishly painted, he led the entire assemblage in a wildly gyrating war dance which did not end until
the sun was several degrees above the trees to the east.

### [ *May 3, 1759—Thursday* ]

The Marquis Louis Montcalm could hardly recall ever having
been so pleased as he was on this day, and the source of his
pleasure was his relief and joy at the return to Canada of his
sorely missed aide-de-camp, Louis Antoine de Bougainville,
now wearing the rank of full colonel.

For hours now the two men had been closeted together
while Bougainville related in detail all that had transpired
since last autumn when he had set sail from here for France.
Both his ship and the ship carrying Doreil, he said, had
managed to elude English warships and had arrived safely in
France. They had been escorted to the court in Versailles
and had presented their letters of recommendation to the
various ministers.

"I was treated," Bougainville told him, "with the greatest
of deference by all except Monsieur Berryer who, for reasons
I could not and still cannot understand, seemed to treat me
with distaste, even suspicion. Doreil told me later that the
minister had acted the same way toward him, and he did not
know the reason, either.

"Monsieur D'Argenson," he continued, "is no longer minister of war, his place having been filled by the Maréchal de
Belle-Isle who, as you know, sir, is your friend and strong
admirer. He was a great help to me in all matters.

"I lay before the court the four memorials you had
charged me with, which very definitely showed the desperate
state of the colony and its grave need of help. I explained
how thus far Canada had been saved largely because of the
dissention so prevalent in the English Colonies, but that now

these colonies were uniting against her and preparing to put forth all their strength, against which Canada could not hope to stand without substantial aid. As best I could I begged for men, arms, equipment, munitions, all the food it was possible to send, and a squadron of warships to guard the entrance to the St. Lawrence."

Bougainville shook his head sadly and went on. "I'm afraid all the appeals accomplished very little. Although I had interviews with all of the ministers and with the King himself, there was a great reluctance on every hand to commit themselves to the sending of any substantial aid. I finally appealed to Madame de Pompadour and after considerable delay and difficulty, I exacted from her a few promises."

"France, sir," he continued thoughtfully after a moment, "has suffered reverses almost everywhere. She has been unfortunate by sea as well as by land. Her navy is badly crippled, her finances are ruined and the only source of victory she can claim is at your own hands here in North America. For this, at least, you and your officers are being rewarded by promotions. The documents I have brought along honor you, sir, with promotion to the rank of lieutenant general. Monsieur de Lévis is promoted to major general. Colonel Bourlamaque now becomes brigadier and I, as you can see, have been greatly honored with promotion to the rank of colonel and the position of Chevalier of St. Louis. Monsieur de Vaudreuil, incidentally, has been sent the Grand Cross of that order.

"But as far as substantial aid to us is concerned," he added, "there is practically none. All we could obtain was three hundred fifty recruits for the regulars and about sixty engineers, sappers and artillerymen. There is also a fair amount of gunpowder, arms and provisions, all of which are being brought over by Monsieur Cadet. These things, according to the court, are sufficient to see us through the year's campaign. However, I'm sure they are far from adequate for our needs."

Montcalm shrugged. "A little," he said simply, "is precious to those who have nothing."

Bougainville then handed him messages from the ministers, along with his orders for the forthcoming campaign. The principal one came from the Maréchal de Belle-Isle, new minister of war, and it was, at best, disheartening. Without preamble it warned of a great armament already fitted out in English ports for an attack on Quebec. Belle-Isle wrote that it was, in fact, altogether possible that by the time Montcalm received this news, the force would be afloat and en route.

With news of the reinforcement Bougainville had brought, Montcalm had calculated swiftly in round numbers the total force he might have to call upon. At the outside, it could not be over twenty thousand men. There were on hand right now, thirteen thousand effectives. To these he could add thirty-five hundred troops of the line, which included the new reinforcement. Added to that might be another fifteen hundred men made up of widely dispersed colony troops, irregulars, the militia and the *coureurs de bois*. Finally, there were perhaps a thousand to two thousand Indians who could still be counted on, mostly those from the upper Great Lakes. Montcalm shook his head. It was not much of a force with which to fend off the approximately fifty thousand English now gearing to move against Canada. With expressionless face, he continued to read Belle-Isle's letter and learned the reason why no significant reinforcement had been sent. Wrote Belle-Isle:

*If we sent a large reinforcement of troops, there would be great fear that the English would intercept them on the way; and as the King could never send you forces in equal numbers to those which the English are prepared to oppose to you, the attempt would have no other effect than to excite the Cabinet of London to increased efforts for preserving its superiority on the American continent.*

*As we must expect the English to turn all their force against Canada, and attack you on several sides at once, it is the country entirely, its recovery will be almost impossible. necessary that you limit your plans of defense to the most essential points and those most closely connected, so that, being concentrated within a smaller space, each part may be within reach of support and succor from the rest. How small soever may be the space you are able to hold, it is indispensable to keep a footing in North America; for if we once lose The King counts on your zeal, courage, and persistency to accomplish this object, and relies on you to spare no pains and no exertions. Impart this resolution to your chief officers, and join with them to inspire your soldiers with it. I have answered for you to the King; I am confident that you will not disappoint me, and that for the glory of the nation, the good of the state, and your own preservation, you will go to the utmost extremity rather than submit to conditions as*

*shameful as those imposed at Louisbourg, the memory of*
*which you will wipe out.*

But though most of the news was disheartening, there was one gratifying portion to it for Montcalm above and beyond his promotion to lieutenant general. Orders had also been sent to both Governor Vaudreuil and Intendant Bigot from the Maréchal Belle-Isle to the effect that no longer was General Montcalm to be considered in any way as being subordinate to the Canadian administration. In fact, in all matters of military decision, Vaudreuil and Bigot must defer to the wishes to Montcalm. Further, Vaudreuil must not take command personally except in that instance when the entire body of the militia should be called up, nor even then without consulting Montcalm, whose wishes were to be taken as commands.

Montcalm, in a coded document, was requested to make an immediate report on the peculative activities of Governor Vaudreuil and Intendant Bigot, and he did so now, as honestly and as faithfully as he could. It was, he told the minister, difficult to determine which of the two men was most corrupt, though he suspected it was Bigot, since Vaudreuil had not the crafty smoothness of the intendant. In fact, stretching honesty to its greatest lengths, it was possible, though very doubtful, that Vaudreuil was simply an example of supreme egotism rather than one of calculated corruption. But Bigot, ah, that was another matter entirely. Bigot, he reported, had given the position of furnishing provision for all of Canada to one man—Joseph Cadet—whom he named commissary general. And in the name of this office, Cadet could establish his own price on practically anything, and get it. Bigot, through deals and counterdeals with Cadet would buy for the King at second- or thirdhand what he could have purchased new from the original shipment at less than half the cost. Everyone closely connected with Bigot and his dealings, it seemed—and this possibly included Vaudreuil—was becoming immensely rich and living in great luxury while the people around them were quite literally starving. He added:

*Monsieur, it seems as if they were all hastening to make*
*their fortunes before the loss of the colony; which many of*
*them desire as a veil to their conduct. There is the example*
*of M. le Mercier, chief of Canadian artillery, to consider, as*
*only one of many similar cases. This officer arrived in*

*Canada as a private soldier twenty years ago, with his pock-*
*ets empty and no prospects. But he connected himself with*
*the Intendant and M. de Vaudreuil and since has so pros-*
*pered on fraudulent contracts that he will soon be worth*
*nearly a million francs. I have often spoken of these expendi-*
*tures to M. de Vaudreuil and M. Bigot; and each throws the*
*blame on the other.*

## [ May 17, 1759—Thursday ]

The axe of England, often too slow in its fall on its own
people, had finally fallen on the military commander of the
colonies in America.

General James Abercromby was recalled to England and
Major General Jeffrey Amherst was appointed in his stead.
The flair with which Amherst had commanded the Louisbourg campaign had made his promotion an obvious one, and
no one would have been more surprised than Amherst himself had he not gotten the appointment.

On the whole, this ugly individual was an able commander
who had risen through the ranks from private in the commis-
sariat to one of the most accomplished military men in the
British Empire. His hair was a stringy, rust-colored tangle
which he normally kept hidden beneath his heavily powdered
wig. Penetrating gray eyes stared out from over a great
eagle-beak nose and a large, distracting wart protruded from
the skin of his face just to the left of his moist and perpetual-
ly pouting lips.

He was thoroughly British Army, however, and detested
anything that did not conform to the patterns of that body.
He had little more than ill-hidden condescension for provincials, either men or officers, and was repelled by quasi-
military leaders, such as Sir William Johnson. In his book,
there was no such being as a "heaven-sent general." More
than anything else in America, however, he utterly loathed
Indians, terming them "a pack of lazy, rum-drinking people,
and little good."

Ever since his appointment to this powerful new position,
he had been receiving communiqués from Johnson urging
that a strike at Fort Niagara be included in this year's
campaign. When Amherst was noncommittal in his replies,
William Johnson even rode to see him personally at the Lake
George headquarters to argue the cause. For once, William
declared, the entire Iroquois League was on the English side.

Even the previously pro-French Chenussio Senecas—with but a few exceptions—were asking for help in the destruction of the place, and it was an opportunity that should not be passed up, for fear that the Indians would lose their new-found faith in the English cause.

What the Indians thought, felt or did mattered little to General Amherst and with formal coldness he listened to William's appeal, asked a few questions on certain precise details and then abruptly dismissed him without further comment. To his own way of thinking, it mattered little at this stage whether Fort Niagara was taken or not. If the campaign went along as planned, it would necessarily wither and die anyway.

Nevertheless, he studied quite carefully the war plans which had just been received from William Pitt. He admired them, considering them the plans of an astute strategist, particularly in view of the fact that the man was, more than anything else, a politician. Pitt was calling for a strong pincers movement to be made on Montreal. The English second-in-command in America, General James Wolfe, was to advance with a fleet up the St. Lawrence, take Quebec and then move against Montreal. At the same time, the mass of the army, under Amherst, was to strike from the underbelly of Canada, smashing its way past Fort Carillon and Fort St. Frederic and then northward down Lake Champlain to the Richelieu River, thence to join Wolfe for attack against the principal French-Canadian city, Montreal. So far as operations to the west of the line from Lake George to Montreal went, only defensive moves were to be considered: Fort Oswego was to be rebuilt and a new, strong fort built on the ashes of Fort Duquesne. Only a somewhat secondary sort of thing was an attack against Fort Niagara mentioned in Pitt's plans. A campaign against that installation might be advantageous, but only insofar as the campaign against the main targets could permit.

To his credit, Jeffrey Amherst did give serious thought to the taking of Fort Niagara. With men and supplies in relative abundance now, with himself at the helm and with the morale of the army high, it could be accomplished. The more he thought of it, the more it appealed to him and finally, since Fort Oswego would have to be rebuilt anyway, he decided to go ahead with it. He did not, however, tell William Johnson about it at once. Johnson, he was sure, would tell his Indians and the Indians would tell the French and then there would be hell to pay. And so, until he had assigned command of the Fort Niagara campaign to Colonel John Prideaux—newly arrived in America—he simply let Johnson simmer. Now, however, with the detachment of five thousand regulars and provincials practically ready to go, he sent William Johnson orders to muster his Indians and march them to join Colonel Prideaux's force at Fort Stanwix. While General Stanwix and his men were already being ordered to the Forks of the Ohio to build a new English fortification hard by Pittsburgh, Prideaux and Johnson would move to Lake Ontario. First, at Stanwix, they would leave a strong garrison. They would build intermediate forts at either end of Lake Oneida, descend the Onondaga to Lake Ontario and there rebuild Fort Oswego. Finally, leaving about half the remaining soldiers at Fort Oswego under Colonel Haldimand, they were to move with the rest to launch the attack against Fort Niagara.

Almost as an afterthought, Amherst notified Johnson that he would be second-in-command under Prideaux.

### [ May 19, 1759—Saturday ]

From the very first moment he had seen Montcalm, Chief Pontiac was impressed with him. Montcalm was a man of slight stature, even shorter than himself, and that such a little man as he could have so strong an arm and so great a reputation made the Ottawa realize that this French general was a man among men. He was glad that he had not, as he had been tempted to do, remained behind at Fort Machault with the small band of Indians that had decided to stay there to support Captain Ligneris's planned assault against the stockaded Pittsburgh.

Instead, with the majority of the Ottawas, Chippewas, Hurons and Potawatomies, he had continued past Fort Niagara, down the length of Lake Ontario, stopped at Abbé Piquet's mission of La Présentation for a short stay and then had proceeded the rest of the way down the thundering rapids of the St. Lawrence to Montreal.

It was Charles Langlade who presented him to General Montcalm, introducing him with words that had made Pontiac swell with pride nearly to the point of bursting.

"This, General," Langlade had told the commander, "is Pontiac, greatest war chief of all the tribes in the far west. He has led his warriors here to see you and to serve under your orders. You could not possibly have a finer ally. When others might desert you, even those who are Frenchmen, Pontiac will stand firm and will support you as long as there is a breath left within him."

The Marquis de Montcalm had gravely shaken Pontiac's hand, paying no attention to his tattoo-marred skin or the crescent-shaped stone ornament hanging over his lips. Instead, his eyes looked with directness and sincerity into those of the chief and he said, "I have heard many times of your bravery and leadership, and I consider it a great honor that you would lead your warriors to fight beside me. I hope you will give me the benefit of your wisdom and advice when our common enemy is engaged."

In that moment he had won Pontiac completely.

Montcalm then sent an ensign to his own quarters on the run and a few minutes later the young officer had returned bearing one of the general's own uniforms. Montcalm took it from him and then extended it to Pontiac.

"Accept this from me, Pontiac, as a token of my esteem for you. As I am a general among the French, so you are a general among the Indians and you should have a uniform equivalent to this position. I welcome you warmly to my side in whatever shall befall us."

To Montcalm, it was a gesture of friendship, given with the knowledge that it would help cement their relationship and perhaps make the Indians less inclined to desert him should matters take a turn for the worse, as they were apt to do. For Pontiac, however, it was the most signal honor he had ever received. No white man before had ever treated him with such respect, and from this instant on he knew that he would be Montcalm's most dependable ally. Should it become necessary, he would without hesitation lay down his own life to protect the French general's.

"I thank the general from in my heart," Pontiac said, wringing Montcalm's hand again, "and wish him to know that I and my people are beside him no matter what may come. Beyond that, I, Pontiac, give you my word that I shall never desert you so long as the breath of life remains in one or the other of us."

[ *June 1, 1759—Friday* ]

Hours of studying war plans, discussing them with his officers, arguing with Governor Vaudreuil, and knowing in his heart that without further help from France they were fighting a lost cause, all these had taken their toll of Louis Montcalm. He sighed heavily and pushed aside the plans and reports he had been working on, rubbed his eyes with the heels of his hands and then took up his pen again to write to his wife.

Only in those less-frequent moments that he was with her through correspondence—however brief the letters might be—did he seem able to relax anymore. Yet, what was there to say to her now? That he must surely be defeated? That he had been abandoned by France? That his war plans were thus and so? That he had even been considering abandoning the St. Lawrence River valley with his army?

No, he could do none of these things. He could write only in generalities and know that while she might wish to learn more, she would understand why he could say nothing else. He shook his head slightly and dipped his pen.

*June 1, 1759*
*at Montreal headquarters*

*Beloved Angélique,*
    *Time grows short for us here. Great English forces are moving now against us but we are determined to do what we can. Can we hope for another miracle to save us? I trust in God; he fought for us on the eighth of July. Come what may, His will be done! How dearly I have to pay for the dismal privilege of figuring two or three times in the gazettes. I think I would renounce every honor to join you again; but the King must be obeyed. The moment when I see you once more will be the brightest of my life. Adieu, my heart! believe that I love you more than ever.*

*Louis*

It was short, but suddenly he had had no desire to write more. The emptiness it caused inside him was too great, the melancholy that grew became too overpowering. It would not do to become maudlin, for more than anything else this would worry her. But, by damn! Where did they go from here? What could his army do without sufficient food, weapons, gunpowder or manpower?

He thought again of the war plans thus far devised, and grunted sourly. Not an offensive one among them and most of them weakly defensive at best; plans calculated to make any general frustrated.

There could be no doubt what the English intended; their sights were set on Quebec and Montreal, and only consolidated effort in defense would stay them. No longer could his army afford to make a strong stand at Fort Carillon or even Fort St. Frederic. There was too much possibility of the army being cut off and then ripped to ribbons. If only they were not so outnumbered!

Yet, great though the disparity was in numbers, there was still a faint hope that the heart of the colony could be held. To reach Quebec and Montreal, the English had a choice of only three routes: up the St. Lawrence from the Atlantic, down the St. Lawrence from Lake Ontario, or down Lake Champlain and the Richelieu from Lake George. For each approach there were natural barriers which would give the English troubles.

The passage up the St. Lawrence was treacherous and required the services of river pilots with years of experience, to whom every bar and rock was known. The passage down the St. Lawrence was over the unnavigable LaChine Rapids, and other harsh rapids above that, with Fort Présentation at the head of them and the new Fort de Lévis being erected close by to guard against any English attempt to pass. The passage down Lake Champlain to the Richelieu and thence to the St. Lawrence was blocked by the fortifications erected on Isle-aux-Noix—Nut Island—at the mouth of the lake, where it became the Richelieu.

Brigadier General François Bourlamaque, with just over three thousand men, he had sent to Fort Carillon with instructions, if attacked, to leave behind a small force to hold the fort as long as possible while Bourlamaque and the rest of his men would fall back to Isle-aux-Noix, where he could make a firm stand against an enemy weakened—hopefully— by the taking of Fort Carillon. No attempt was to be made at holding Fort St. Frederic at Crown Point.

Captain St. Luc de la Corne, with several hundred men, was at Fort de Lévis, with instructions to hold as long as possible should attack come from the west, until reinforcements could be sent him for a general engagement. General Lévis was to remain at Montreal with his force, prepared to move at once in whatever direction reinforcements were called for. Montcalm himself would be at Quebec to hold the enemy at bay there should he be so rash as to attempt an assault up the St. Lawrence.

Thus far the plan had met the approval of all concerned, but it was in the next step that he had run afoul of Vaudreuil. It was Montcalm's suggestion that should every effort at resistance fail and the English manage to thrust themselves into the Canadian heartland, that as a final desperate move, the entire St. Lawrence River valley be abandoned, that the army and those of the population who wished to come, move at once en masse by way of the Great Lakes to the Mississippi and then down that stream for a final stand in the bayou country of Louisiana where there would be greater likelihood of their retaining a toehold on the North American continent. But Governor Vaudreuil harangued against it to such lengths that further discussion of the idea was put in abeyance until and unless circumstances left no other choice.

The most likely avenue of attack by the English was up the St. Lawrence River, despite the difficulty of navigation and this had been borne out by the fact that English warships and troop carriers had now been reported carefully picking their way up the great river toward Quebec. Today, Louis Montcalm had dispatched the bulk of the army remaining at Montreal to Quebec and in the morning he would follow.

There, God willing, he would hold them at bay while the Indians and the *coureurs de bois* worried their flanks and tail and gradually wore them down. Not in the wildest fling of imagination did he hope for a victory.

"But damn my blood," he muttered aloud, "we just might force a stalemate."

## [ June 30, 1759—Saturday ]

Though he felt he should have been in command of the operation against Fort Niagara, Sir William Johnson accepted the secondary leadership role with good grace, determined to prove to both General Amherst and Colonel Prideaux that the Iroquois who had come to Oswego with him were a decided asset.

Not since the battle of Lake George, where he had defeated Baron Dieskau, had William been backed by such a force of Indians; and in this case the Indians in opposition would be far fewer. All of the Six Nations were represented in the party of over nine hundred Indians he led from Fort

Johnson to the rendezvous at Fort Stanwix. A strong garrison of twelve hundred men was left there and, without opposition or trouble of any sort, Prideaux's remaining force of twenty-two hundred soldiers, plus Sir William Johnson's Indians, moved down Wood Creek in whale boats to the head of Lake Oneida. They built a small fortified post there, garrisoned it with a hundred men, and then moved down the length of the lake to its mouth where another small post was quickly built and similarly manned. Then they floated downriver to the mouth of the Onondaga.

For most of them, even the Indians, it was the first time they had seen the spot since Montcalm's force had devastated it, and they stared at the ruins now well taken over by weeds. A strange sensation accompanied their first view, as if one could hear again the flat report of musketry, the boom and scream of cannon fire and the cries of the attackers and attacked.

At once Colonel John Prideaux placed Colonel Frederick Haldimand in charge of fortifying, and until timber could be cut, hauled and placed, Haldimand erected a barricade of barrels filled with flour or salt pork. Prideaux then asked William Johnson to send several scouting parties of Indians out to reconnoiter Fort Niagara, but William had anticipated the order and dispatched four different parties for this purpose even before they reached the Oswego site. In fact, hardly had Colonel Prideaux made the request when two of the four parties came in and reported directly to William.

The majority of these scouts had been Senecas, long familiar with this, their home area, and many times visitors at the fort. Pretending a continued friendship, they had had no difficulty gaining entry and looking it over carefully. The fort had only recently been refurbished by the officer who now commanded it, Captain Pouchot, and it was surprisingly well supplied with provisions and arms. Its only real weakness was one of manpower, since it was garrisoned by only five hundred fifteen men, plus a few Ottawas left behind recently when Pontiac's party came through en route to join Montcalm. There was also, the scouts reported apologetically and with some worry, a small number of Senecas in the fort under Chief Kaendae, who had always been violently anti-English.

When the Seneca scouts William had sent arrived at the fort, Pouchot had no idea that an attack was being prepared against him, although the scouts almost gave it away with some loose boasting. They had become arrogant to the point where Pouchot had been forced to ask them to leave, at which they told him they would soon have his head when they attacked the place. Pouchot, however, did not give the threat serious consideration, thinking they were speaking of attacking by themselves rather than in conjunction with the English.

Leaving Fort Niagara, the Seneca scouts had then gone to the wooden fort called Little Niagara farther up the Niagara River and about a mile and a half above the Falls. Here Captain Chabert Joncaire was still in command with about sixty men under him. They threatened him as they had done Pouchot, but Joncaire knew the Senecas well enough to realize they were dead serious and had something powerful behind them to so brazenly insult him. In fact, he became so alarmed that shortly after the Indians left, he ordered the untenable little fort burned and marched his men to join Pouchot at Fort Niagara. So now there were almost six hundred men at the stronger fort.

With Joncaire, the scouts reported, had gone some more of Chief Kaendae's little following of Senecas and there was now some concern in William Johnson's Senecas about fighting their own people. William assured them he would do all in his power to provide Kaendae's Indians safe conduct out of the fort if they would accept it. If not, then the fault would lie within themselves and not with William's Indians who were acting in accordance with the decision of the Iroquois League council.

The Senecas accepted this reluctantly for now, and went on to tell Warraghiyagey that the former commander of Fort Duquesne, Captain Ligneris, was at the fort called Machault at Venango with a sizable force of bush lopers, regulars and at least a couple of hundred Ottawa and Chippewa Indians, preparing soon to march to the Forks of the Ohio to destroy Pittsburgh and the new fort that General Stanwix was already in the process of erecting adjacent to it. Further, the Canadian officers, Captains Aubry and Portneuf, commanding respectively at Forts Le Boeuf and Presque Isle, were standing ready with what aid they could muster, should Captain Ligneris run into any real trouble.

William quickly reported all this intelligence to Colonel Prideaux and a council of officers was held. It was decided, largely on William's insistence, to attack Fort Niagara at once, hoping to draw Ligneris—and perhaps Aubry and Portneuf as well—into an ambush as plans against Pittsburgh were dropped and they came to the aid of Pouchot.

Leaving Haldimand to continue with the work of constructing the new Fort Oswego and warning him to keep his thousand men keenly alert for possible attack from the head of the St. Lawrence, the other half of the army and all of the Indians marched out under Prideaux and Warraghiyagey.

And at just about this same time, Captain St. Luc de la Corne was alerted by his own spies that Fort Oswego was going to be rebuilt but that the troops on the site were highly vulnerable. At once he left Fort de Lévis and La Présentation, at the mouth of the Oswegatchie, with almost a thousand French and Canadians and a small number of Indians, mostly Abnakis and Algonkins, to attack it.

July was certainly shaping up to be an eventful month.

## [ July 1, 1759—Sunday ]

While Intendant François Bigot had been at first delighted with the fact that the Canadian Commissary General, Joseph Cadet, had incredibly brought his eighteen supply ships safely to the dock at Quebec, he was now being gnawed by a great worry. More and more over the past couple of years he had been coming under fire from the government in France for the commercial outrages being committed in Canada, both against the Canadians and against the King.

Until now, however, he had always been successful in claiming either ignorance of mismanagement and corruption or else attributing high costs to the simple difficulty of procuring supplies. Apparently that was no longer possible and he didn't know exactly what to do. With scores of corruptive irons in the fire, it would be no easy matter to pull himself out of this growing difficulty. He began to wish that he had not helped boost Joseph Cadet to the exalted position he was in, nor so often oiled the palm of Governor Vaudreuil. They, he believed, were the weak links in his chain.

Cadet was the son of a butcher. Until only three years ago he had worked at his father's trade, but he had a crafty mind and a flair for trade and, as Bigot soon learned, was by no means opposed to making shady money if the opportunity arose.

It arose.

Bigot got him appointed commissary general for Canada in

1756, and in just the short time since then he had become the wealthiest man in New France, perhaps in all of North America, while Bigot himself was almost equally enriched. Within the first two years, Cadet and his associates sold to the King for twenty-three million francs a collection of provisions—many of them bought from the King's own stores—which had cost them only eleven millions—and that was only the beginning.

Intendant Bigot convinced the colonial minister at the start of this business that, with goods enough in Canada, it would be to the King's advantage to buy what provisions were needed in Canada rather than in France and therefore avoid the risk of their loss during a trans-Atlantic shipment. Bigot's associates in France would then ship great amounts of supplies to Canada where Cadet or another of his agents would declare they belonged to the King and thus escape paying duty on them. Then, always under fictitious names, the goods were sold to the King at a huge profit. Step by step new ways for making more and more money for less and less goods were developed. Often, for a cut of the profits, they were sold to some favored merchant who then sold them to the King's storekeeper, another confederate of Bigot's, and as time passed it became standard for the goods to pass through two or three hands before they were finally sold back to the King for perhaps triple their worth, with Bigot, Cadet, and their partners getting all the profit. All other merchants not in cahoots with them were squeezed out until a deadly and virtually complete commercial monopoly was established.

Joseph Cadet had become extremely clever in his varied machinations and before very long Bigot was not entirely sure who, of the two of them, was doing the manipulation. It really didn't matter to him, however, so long as the profits rolled in—and roll in they did, in a veritable torrent. In one of their joint operations, for example, Cadet, with Bigot's help, bought a consignment of stores belonging to the King. They paid six hundred thousand francs for it and then turned right around and sold it back to the King for a million four hundred thousand francs.

Sympathy and mercy were unknown qualities to Cadet. He did everything with a cold and calculating ruthlessness. When stores of food were sent by the King to be supplied as free rations to the starving Canadians, Cadet surreptitiously took those stores and replaced them with stores of moldy, unsalable salt cod. Cadet learned from his spies that the inhabitants were hoarding their grain and he thereupon got Bigot to write out an order requiring them to sell it at a fixed low price or else have it seized. When famine threatened as a result, the partners then sold it back to the King and its original owners at enormous profit.

In another move, a great quantity of grain was bought from the King's stores. Then, in his official capacity as intendant, Bigot issued a proclamation raising the price of the grain to nearly four times what it had been. The recently purchased grain was immediately sold back to the King for a neat fifty thousand crowns' profit. On and on the list of outrages went, more and more involved and varied they became. Practically nothing concerned with commerce was not touched with corruption.

But now it was the corruption that was controlling Bigot and Cadet rather than vice versa. They had become victims of their own rapacity, unable any longer to dare offend their confederates, but refusing to aid in further fraudulent enterprises requiring Cadet's manipulations and Bigot's official sanction. Gradually the friendly letters to Bigot from the colonial minister cooled and then turned harsh as the frauds became increasingly audacious. Recently the minister, Pierre Berryer, had written:

*The Ship* Britannia, *laden with goods such as are wanted in the colony, was captured by a privateer from St. Malo, and brought into Quebec. You sold the whole cargo for eight hundred thousand francs. The purchasers made a profit of two millions. You bought back for the King a part at one million, or two hundred thousand more than the price for which you sold the whole. With conduct like this it is no wonder that the expenses of the colony become insupportable. The amount of your drafts on the treasury is frightful. The fortunes of your subordinates throws suspicion on your administration. . . . What has become of the immense quantity of provisions sent to Canada last year? I am forced to conclude that the King's stores are set down as consumed from the moment they arrive, and then sold to His Majesty at exorbitant prices. Thus the King buys stores in France, and then buys them again in Canada. I no longer wonder at the immense fortunes made in the colony. . . . You pay bills without examination, and then find an error in your accounts of three million six hundred thousand francs. In the letters from Canada I see nothing but incessant speculation in provisions and goods, which are sold to the King for ten times more than they cost in France. For the last time, I exhort you to give these things your serious attention, for they will not escape from mine.*

The intendant's ship was sinking and he was becoming almost frantic, though he tried to mask it. As best he could he wrote letters disclaiming any knowledge of fraudulent practices, stating that he would investigate at once and heads would roll if he uncovered the perpetrators. But now, the letter just received clearly indicated how badly things were going for him in France. With shaking hands he read the latest from the colonial minister and gradually his face became ashen. Berryer had written:

*François Bigot*
*Intendant*
*Quebec*
*I write, Monsieur, to answer your last two letters, in which you tell me that instead of sixteen millions, your drafts on the treasury for 1758 will reach twenty-four millions, and that this year they will rise from thirty-one to thirty-three millions. It seems, then, that there are no bounds to the expenses of Canada. They double almost every year, while you seem to give yourself no concern except to get them paid. Do you suppose that I can advise the King to approve such an administration? Or do you think that you can take the immense sum of thirty-three millions out of the royal treasury by merely assuring me that you have signed drafts for it? This, too, for expenses incurred irregularly, often needlessly, always wastefully; which will make the fortune of everybody who has the last hand in them, and about which you know so little that after reporting them at sixteen millions, you find two months after that they will reach twenty-four. You are accused of having given the furnishing of provisions to one man, who, under the name of commissary-general, has set what prices he pleased; of buying for the King at second or third hand what you might have got from the producer at half the price; of having in this and other ways made the fortunes of persons connected with you; and of living in splendor in the midst of a public misery, which all the letters from the colony agree in ascribing to bad administration, and in charging M. de Vaudreuil with weakness in not preventing*
• • •

It was to Vaudreuil, who had come to Quebec two days after Montcalm arrived, that Bigot now turned and with discreet pressures brought to bear, encouraged him to write a letter which might set the suspicions of the colonial minister at rest. Since Vaudreuil was quite close to Berryer, it might be that Berryer would listen. At least at this stage of the game it was worth a try.

For his own part, Vaudreuil was equally worried and he suspected strongly that it was Montcalm who had been spreading the ill reports to France. He determined to step up his undermining of imperial trust in Montcalm at every opportunity, but he was still highly disconcerted with being forced to come to the aid of Bigot and Cadet.

Now, reluctantly, with Bigot at his elbow, Vaudreuil wrote:

*M. Pierre Berryer*
*Colonial Minister*
*Versailles*

*I cannot conceal from you, Monseigneur, how deeply M. Bigot feels the suspicions expressed in your letters to him. He does not deserve them, I am sure. He is full of zeal for the service of the King; but as he is rich, or passes as such, and as he has merit, the ill-disposed are jealous, and insinuate that he had prospered at the expense of His Majesty. I am certain that it is not true, and that nobody is a better citizen than he, or has the King's interest more at heart. And where M. Cadet is concerned, his zeal for the service of the King and the defense of the colony is triumphant over every difficulty. It is necessary that ample supplies of all kinds be sent out in the autumn, with the distribution of which M. Cadet generously offers to charge to himself, and to account for them at their first cost. I assure you, Monseigneur, he knows the colony and its needs; you can trust all he says. In fact, as a reward for his services, I would ask that you bestow upon him a patent of nobility.*

*Where other matters are concerned, both the Intendant and I have received your second order restating the first that in military matters we are to defer to M. de Montcalm, but adding now that not only in matters of war must we defer to him, but in all matters of administration touching the defense and preservation of the colony. We are distressed at this seeming lack of confidence in us and would hope in the next post from you such orders will be modified. For my own* part, the zeal with which I am animated for the service of the King will always make me surmount the greatest of obstacles. I am taking the most proper measures to give the enemy a good reception whenever he may attack us. I keep in view the defense of Quebec. I have given orders in the parishes below to muster the inhabitants who are able to bear arms, and place women, children, cattle, and even hay and grain, in places of safety. Permit me, Monseigneur, to beg you to have the goodness to assure His Majesty that, to whatever hard extremity I may be reduced, my zeal will be equally ardent and indefatigable, and that I shall do the impossible to prevent our enemies from making progress in any direction, or, at least, to make them pay extremely dear for it. Whatever progress they may make, I am resolved to yield them nothing, but hold my ground even to annihilation.

M. de Montcalm has his forces all in place at Quebec on both sides of the river and I promise, even though it may be most trying to do so because of his arrogant nature and refusal to be guided by my counsel, to keep on good terms with him and defer to him in accordance with your wishes, until I hear otherwise from you.

Our scouts have brought us the grim news that the English ships-of-war carrying General Wolfe's army are only just over twenty leagues below us, at Isle-aux-Coudres. I expect to be sharply attacked, and that our enemies will make their most powerful efforts to conquer this colony; but there is no ruse, no resource, no means which my zeal does not suggest to lay snare for them, and finally, when the exigency demands it, to fight them with an ardor, and even a fury, which exceeds the range of their ambitious desires. The troops, the Canadians, and the Indians are not ignorant of the resolution I have taken, and from which I shall not recoil under any circumstance whatever. The burghers of this city have already put their goods and furniture in places of safety. The old men, women, and children hold themselves ready to leave town. My firmness is generally applauded. It has penetrated every heart; and each man says aloud: "Canada, our native land, shall bury us under its ruins before we surrender to the English!" This is decidedly my own determination, and I shall hold to it inviolably.

In closing, Excellency, I would re-emphasize the depth of confidence I hold for M. Bigot and the firm knowledge I have that his loyalty and concern belongs first to His Majes-

*ty, then to the colony, putting both far above concerns for self.*

*Vaudreuil*

### [ July 4, 1759—Wednesday ]

In his quarters at Fort Niagara, Captain Pouchot mentally cursed himself for unpreparedness, the Indians for treachery, and the English for being in this part of the country in the first place. The *coureurs de bois* sent out by him only yesterday on routine scouting patrols had come bursting in this morning with the news that a large English army accompanied by about as many Indians had just landed a flotilla of whaleboats at the mouth of Four Mile Creek, which was that distance east of the fort.

The commander hurriedly wrote identical letters to Captain de Ligneris at Fort Machault, Captain Aubry at Fort Le Boeuf and Captain Portneuf at Fort Presque Isle:

*English army of about a thousand, supported by as many Iroquois, advancing on this post. Attack expected tomorrow—July 5—but should be able to defend for some time. Nevertheless, reinforcement needed at once. Send all available troops and Indians to me at once.* — POUCHOT

Less than five minutes after he had completed writing them, the letters were on their way in the hands of three different pairs of *coureurs de bois*. Pouchot had no fear that they would not get through.

### [ July 5, 1759—Thursday ]

Both Colonel John Prideaux and Sir William Johnson were well aware that they could not hope to take Fort Niagara by storm. There was no doubt that it was one of the strongest French installations in North America. Triangular in shape, the fort spread entirely over the point formed by the confluence of the Niagara River with Lake Ontario. With two sides defended by water, there was only one approach open to the English and it was not an easy one.

The walls were high on this side facing toward the land. They were indented and tiered with batteries and defended by bastions and every manner of natural and artificial means possible, with all these defenses menacingly facing the narrow end of the rapidly widening clearing. Three fourths of a mile from the fort was where the woods began and it was here, safe enough from the fort's firepower, that Prideaux established his headquarters. The regulars were positioned in the middle, the provincials on the left of them and the artillery on the right, with the Indians farthest out on both ends. He quickly put his engineers to the task of laying out a ditch which would be angled for protection from Pouchot's own cannon. The ditch was being dug at such depth that the artillery could be moved into it and, as the siege progressed, he gradually inched along with the ditch construction until a range had been reached from which they could batter down the fort walls.

A desultory musket fire was directed at the fort, more than anything else to merely keep the inmates of the place bottled up, which it did admirably. In return, Pouchot occasionally lobbed cannonballs toward the woods to keep the attackers at their distance. Except for the English ditch inching ever nearer, it was a standoff. Neither commander had expected more.

Pouchot, however, was not prepared to sit idly by and watch the English get their artillery close enough to start taking destructive shots at him. Before too long, he knew, Ligneris, Aubry and Portneuf would show up with their troops and the western Indians. They ought to number close to a thousand, and against Prideaux's troops he had no doubt they could hold their own and perhaps even take them— except for one thing: Sir William Johnson's Iroquois. If only there were some way for him to either win them over to himself or, failing that, at least to render them neutral, then a victory might even be plucked from the engagement.

He thought about it for a long while and then a small smile curved his lips and his eyes glinted. There just *might* be a way at that.

### [ *July 15, 1759—Sunday* ]

Abbé François Piquet, his hoarse whispering voice barely reaching the farthest troops in the large group clustered around him on their knees, had solemnly blessed them in the early morning light. The benediction rolled smoothly from his lips and was as pious as any delivered anywhere until he ended it with an Amen, and then added:

"Go out now and kill the English. Give them no quarter!"

Captain St. Luc de la Corne, standing on one side, ordered

663

the men to their feet and told them to spread out in the woods, moving generally toward the Fort Oswego site, less than a mile away, until contact with the enemy was made.

"The element of surprise is in our favor," he said. "Make good use of it. Our number is greater than theirs and we should take them swiftly."

They should have, but they didn't.

Colonel Frederick Haldimand had no indication of their presence nearby until a sudden flurry of shots sounded from where a party of wood cutters had been sent into the forest. He reacted with the instinct of the top professional soldier. Within moments the entire camp was alerted; within two minutes every man was in his position, well protected behind log or barrel or other obstacle, weapon pointed toward where the shooting had originated; within three minutes a squad of twenty volunteers was racing toward the woods with muskets ready to fire. The men disappeared into the trees and a moment later there was another burst of shooting.

A large number of St Luc de la Corne's men had converged on the site where the initial shooting had taken place. Two English soldiers lay dead atop the wood they had been cutting. Four others stood with their hands raised. The converging Frenchmen clustered around and it was just about then that the running party from Haldimand's camp burst onto the scene. Half of them fired at once, dropping eight or nine of the French, and then stopped to reload while the other half fired and dropped about as many. Not expecting such instant retaliation and thinking the squad had to be company-sized or larger, the Frenchmen panicked and galloped back through the woods toward where their boats were beached. Abbé Piquet, who had followed along some distance behind them, was literally bowled over, regained his feet and joined the pell-mell dash to the rear.

In the meanwhile, the English squad, having rescued the four surviving wood cutters, quickly made its way back to the unfinished fortification. St. Luc de la Corne was almost beside himself with anger at his men, and he bellowed commands at them until some semblance of order was regained. He then personally led them back to the fringe of the woods before the fortification, where they took cover and started shooting. The range was so great that little damage was done. For two hours the firing continued and then they withdrew.

Throughout the night, the Algonkins and Abnakis kept up

a scattering of fire to keep the English pinned down, and in the morning St. Luc de la Corne led his men back to the spot they had occupied before, to begin the firing anew.

Colonel Haldimand had outfigured him. Expecting just such a move, he had brought three cannon to bear on that spot and instantly retaliated with a bombardment that sent them all scurrying for cover. In the process, the Canadian commander was shot through the thigh.

With thirty men already killed or wounded, including St. Luc de la Corne and two of his officers, the fight went out of the French. On their commander's harsh orders they surged back to their boats and shoved off into the lake, their paddles dipping with methodical speed to carry them back to Fort Présentation and Fort de Lévis.

### [ July 17, 1759—Tuesday ]

Captains Aubry and Ligneris had moved their men with surprising alacrity upon receiving the call for reinforcement from Fort Niagara. Less than a half day after he received his orders, Ligneris had marched all his men, except for a token garrison left behind at Fort Machault, to Fort Le Boeuf. There he found Aubry preparing his own men for the march, too. Another small party was left behind here to guard the place, and the combined troops marched on to Fort Presque Isle, arriving there last night.

Captain Portneuf had elected to stay with his garrison at the Lake Erie fort, but he had the famed Canadian bushfighter, Captain Jacques Marin, along with his men, equally ready. He had sent a party of Ottawas off to Pouchot with a message that a reinforcement would arrive soon, probably before the twenty-eighth of the month. Marin and Portneuf had wisely held off leaving immediately, expecting both Aubry and Ligneris. The interval had been utilized to get a fleet of canoes and bateaux ready, into which the eleven hundred armed traders, trappers, bush lopers, colony troops and about a thousand Ottawas and Chippewas seated themselves and shoved off.

The Indians were painted for war, but they were not the only ones. Most of the bush lopers—the *coureurs de bois*—looked about as much like Indians as did the Ottawas and Chippewas themselves. The Canadians wore hunting shirts of soft deerskin smoked to a drab gray, the breasts decorated with porcupine quills. Similar quills formed lines down the arms of the garments. Many of the men wore eagle feathers in their hair or had glued them to their temples with wads of sticky mud and cedar resin mixed with vermilion. Almost all of them had their faces painted in red and black lines radiating outward from the tips of their noses, across chin, cheeks and forehead.

With each dip of the paddles they sang loudly, and the Indians, their own spirits raised by the high morale of these Canadians, chanted their own words in rather guttural tones to the same tune. Every man in the party was certain that they would swiftly wipe out the whole English party. Already the Indians were boasting of how many scalps they would take.

### [ July 20, 1759—Friday ]

John Prideaux's siege of Fort Niagara had not had much effect until this time. As a matter of fact, he had expected to have his artillery in operation long before today and would have had, too, but for the blundering of his engineers. They were so incompetent that the first trenches they laid out were raked by gunfire from the fort and they had to be dug all over. Lieutenant Allan MacLeane of the Highlanders, who lost several of his privates because of it, was furious.

"Our engineers," he stormed to Colonel Prideaux, "are fools and blockheads, God damn them!"

Prideaux had soothed his junior officer's ruffled feathers as best he could, though he couldn't blame MacLeane a bit, and then had the engineers lay out the earthworks anew. At last, this morning, the artillery was placed in the big trench and ready to open fire.

The colonel might have been a regular officer, with that breed's built-in dislike for provincials and homegrown militia and an actual loathing of Indian allies, but he was not so blinded by such feelings that he could not give credit where credit was deserving. Though he had initially thought the horde of Indians under Sir William Johnson to be a cross he had to bear more than anything else, he now grudgingly admitted that they had been serving his army well. If they and Johnson had not been here, the entire siege could well have failed already.

The day after the siege had begun, the big drawbridge gate of Fort Niagara had clanked down briefly and out had come the militant Seneca chief, Kaendae. He had always had much

666

influence at the Iroquois councils, and despite the fact that he now refused to follow the general pro-English trend of the Six Nations, he was highly thought of by his tribesmen. When he first began walking toward the English there was a scattering of shots at him from the provincials until William Johnson rushed up to Prideaux in a very agitated manner.

"For God's sake, Colonel, stop that firing! If you kill that man the whole body of our Indians may turn against us!"

Startled, Prideaux ordered a cease-fire, and Chief Kaendae, apparently not in the least perturbed by the shots that had whizzed past him or kicked up sprays of dirt near his feet, walked directly to the English camp. He greeted Johnson with stiff formality but met his fellow Seneca chiefs, Old Belt and Hanging Belt, in Johnson's camp with considerable warmth. Kaendae called for an immediate council of the Indians, with no white men in attendance but Warraghiyagey. The whole party retired to a large clearing in the woods some distance away and here Kaendae spoke at length.

"My Brothers," he said, "why have you deserted me? Why have you deserted your friends, the French? Are you so blinded that you do not know where your greatest interests lie? Can you not see what the future of the Iroquois League must be if the English drive the French away? We will be finished! Our League will be dissolved, our lands taken bit by bit and we will either have to merge with the English and lose our identity and our pride, or else be pushed back until we have no more lands at all and are destroyed. You have been led here by Warraghiyagey in a bad cause and you should turn on him and destroy him and the English army before your senses are so dulled that you become the ones who are destroyed!"

The Iroquois met this speech with some evidence of discomfort. Kaendae was wise and respected and one of the oldest of the Iroquois chiefs. Yet, in grand council the Iroquois had thrown themselves behind the English and nothing less than another grand council decision could change this. It was a fact that Kaendae knew as well as they, and they were disturbed that he would try to change them; even more disturbed that if he persisted with the French he might be killed at the hands of the English or even by his own people.

It was Warraghiyagey who stepped up now and with the deftness with which he had always handled Indian affairs, he treated Kaendae's remarks as a joke.

"Chief Kaendae is a great chief," he said, "and we all admire him, but sometimes his nose becomes clogged and he cannot smell which way the breezes blow. The bad smell they blow to him now, which he mistakes for an English smell, is really the smell of the French. He had better blow out his nose and smell how much sweeter the air is here, now that he is away from the French men."

All day long the talks went on, late into the night and through much of the next day. By then Kaendae's resolution was weakening, but he still insisted that several of the chiefs accompany him back to council with the French commander inside the fort. Captain Pouchot, he told them, would let them see wherein their true interests lay.

Warraghiyagey, well aware of the persuasive powers of the French and equally aware that their most influential Indian man—the Seneca half-breed, Chabert Joncaire—was in the fort waiting, did not like the idea of his Indians going back with Kaendae, but he saw no way to hold them. Toward evening, then, Kaendae and his brother Seneca chief, Hanging Belt, along with two Cayuga chiefs, went back inside the fort.

Throughout the long night William Johnson waited and finally, just as the sun came up again, the three chiefs returned. Hanging Belt briefly told Warraghiyagey what had happened. All three of them had been blindfolded and led through what seemed to be a maze until at last their blindfolds had been removed in the room reserved for councils with Indians. Here were numerous treaty belts hanging on the walls to signify and record those meetings of the past. Pouchot and Joncaire were both there, as were a number of Ottawas and the remainder of Kaendae's own Senecas.

Hanging Belt and the two Cayuga chiefs refused to consider another change of allegiance and they said that their only reason for coming to the fort had been concern for Joncaire, for fear that the cannonballs would fall on him. They asked him to leave Fort Niagara before this could happen, knowing that if he went, all the Indians left in the fort, except perhaps the Ottawas, would leave with him. Joncaire, however, refused.

Then Hanging Belt had expressed concern about Kaendae himself. Much of Warraghiyagey's force was comprised of Senecas. If Kaendae were killed, they could never forgive themselves, whether or not it was a Seneca who was at fault in his death. To combat this, several belts, tomahawks, guns and pieces of equipment were arranged in front of Kaendae and a few murmured words spoken, at which Hanging Belt and the two Cayugas brightened. Kaendae was now ritualistically dead and if he should be killed again, it would not call for revenge by his own warriors.

Hanging Belt then suggested to the Ottawas that they move to some place else on the lake and let the white men have their fight. At this point Pouchot had become very angry, told Hanging Belt that his Indians needed no advice from outsiders and sent the Iroquois delegation back.

Throughout the days that followed, Kaendae continued to make trips back and forth between the two forces, but at last he gave up hope of changing the minds of Warraghiyagey's chiefs. He thereupon led his own warriors out of the fort, killing all of Joncaire's cattle in the process to indicate a severance of the ties between thm. It was an act which formally made them enemies. Kaendae and his men were again in support of the ruling of the Iroquois League, and Pouchot had lost in his gamble.

Now, on this bright Friday morning with his artillery in place, Prideaux gave the order to open fire. The big guns began booming and almost immediately there was an accident. A shell from one of the coehorns exploded just as it left the barrel of the mortar and a chunk of iron the size of a large walnut smashed through Colonel John Prideaux's head, killing him. And just like that, Sir William Johnson once again found himself in command of an English army.

### [ July 23, 1759—Monday ]

The thousand Ottawas, Chippewas and Potawatomies and the nine hundred Iroquois faced each other in parallel lines on opposite sides of the huge council fire. For many hours they had been talking, each side doing its utmost to dissuade the other from fighting. Chief after chief had spoken and now, at last, it was the turn of Old Belt, the Chenussio who for so long had been inclined toward the French, but who was now in support of the English.

He raised his hands for silence and then divided his gaze between the two factions for a full minute. When he spoke, his voice was filled with sadness.

"My Brothers the Iroquois, hear me! My neighbors, the tribes of the western lakes, hear me! For two days we have talked and we are nowhere. I begin to think no one here sees

669

as I do what is happening to us, to our countries, to our people.

"You have known me for a friend of the French, but now I am not of them and the reason is because I know that to support them further will mean our end. In two different dreams I have seen the Frenchman dead and the Englishman standing above him with his long knife red with blood. In one dream he has his arm about the Indians who helped him in his victory. In the other he runs his long knife through the Indians who have been against him.

"As individual people, we are more inclined to the French, for they live with us and trade with us and do not try so much as the English to take our lands or change us. But as nations we must think beyond this. We must change to meet the changes that come to us or we will not survive.

"My grandfather," he added reflectively, "once told me a story which I now tell you. There once was, on the shore of the great sea to the east, a large mink-animal. It was a large creature, bigger than the biggest otter and four times bigger than the biggest mink we trap now. Its fur was better than anything else we know; thicker and warmer and darker than the best mink or beaver or otter anywhere else. But this animal could not see its future. It could not change its habits. We learned those habits and set traps for it that it walked into. Unlike the otter or the beaver or the mink, who soon learn to avoid certain traps and make us constantly try to think of new ones to catch them in, the big mink-animal continued in its own old ways and we took it in great numbers until it was all gone. Now it is no more and even the memory of it fades.[2]

"Brothers, neighbors, are we no wiser than this mink animal? Do we continue in the path we have walked so long, simply because it is the way we are used to traveling? Do you not see, as I have seen, that we must change our ways to confuse our enemies or we will perish?

"No, we do not love the English like we love the French. But if we do not change ourselves to live with the English, then we will disappear along with the French, for in all my dreams I have seen the Frenchman dead. I do not wish my people to blindly follow him in this.

"We ache for supplies which the French can no longer give us. They themselves starve from lack. The English are many times over their number and their supplies and weapons are more and better. Already some of our lands have been taken by them, but if we are their allies, the taking will be harder for them and we may retain a little of what we have. If we are their enemies, though we may fight for our lands, we will water them with our blood and in the end the lands will be theirs and we will be forgotten like the great mink-animal."

Old Belt stopped abruptly and pointed toward the direction of the English camp and the French fort, then toward the direction from which the reinforcements from Forts Machault, Le Boeuf and Presque Isle were approaching. Then he continued:

"We are here now, watching the English and the French armies against each other. We are asked by them to fight against each other, but this is not good. It is not good for us to further weaken Indian power by fighting one another in white men's quarrels. We, the Iroquois, must fight for the English because they are already in our lands and only by fighting with them can we manage to hold even a little of what we own. You, the Ottawa, are far from your homes. In your land there are French, but they are few and they must eventually be gone, since they cannot stand against the English. If you fight for the French now, it means that you must fight not only against the English, but against the Iroquois."

Chief Old Belt paused again and not a sound came from any listener among the nearly two thousand Indians listening. They watched his every expression and heard his every inflection and they were deeply involved in what he was saying. Now he pointed a long bony finger at the line in which sat the Ottawas, Potawatomies and Chippewas.

"You, our neighbors of the western lakes," he continued, "are here in greater numbers than we. It might be that your strength could be greater than ours and that you would kill many of us if you fought for the French. But neighbors, hear me well! You are in Iroquois land! The number of us you see here is only a part of our number and others are ready to move on the instant. If we are killed by you, then you must make your peace with the Great Spirit, for no man among you will ever return to his village. Even more, when you are all dead, then our people will also march against your people and our people will destroy them. We will take no slaves from among you, but we will attack your homes and your fields and we will not let you escape. Consider what happened to the Erighs when they opposed us, for it is what will happen to you.[3] We will kill your warriors first, and then we will kill your women and your old men and your children

671

until there are not any of you left and even the memory of you grows dim, just as the memory of the great mink-animal—and the Erighs!—grows dim.

"We have spoken now," he concluded. "Consider well what we have said. Is it not better for Indian peoples to live in harmony with one another, perhaps even to unite against the white man, than to let one group of white men lead us to fight another so that in the process the Indians may all be killed by fighting against each other? We, the Iroquois, are committed. We must fight for the English to have our race survive. You, the tribes of the western lakes, you are not yet in great danger from them and you fight merely for friendship. Think to the future. If you continue to fight with the French against us, then begin to count each day which passes, for you will not have many left to life. I have no more to say."

Old Belt moved away from the council fire with a deep silence prevailing all around him. In a few minutes, Chief Minivavana—called by the French and Canadians *Le Grand Saulteur*—who was the huge, principal chief of the Chippewas, moved to the spot vacated by the Seneca chief and his voice was husky with emotion.

"The Iroquois," he began, "give us little choice, if we are to believe the dreams of Chief Old Belt. It is true that we favor the French men and we depend upon them for many things. We are not a people who desert our friends when we have promised to support them. When first you began to speak, a voice whispered in me that you meant to make threats against us. You say you can quickly destroy us, but do not be so sure of that. The Iroquois League has not the strength it once had, when the mention of the name of them was enough to send brave men running in fear. The Ottawa, the Potawatomi, the Chippewa—we three together are a stronger race and if the Iroquois come against us, it is they who will never return to their homes. Do not think you can make us run from you because of your threats.

"But," the big chief continued, "some of the things you have said to us require much thought and they have about them the ring of real truth. It is true that Indians should not fight between themselves to please the white men. It is true that we must learn to change so that we do not follow the trail made by your grandfather's great mink-animal. It is difficult for us to say what we will do. As you know, already the French men have come from the three forts to the west of this place. Already they have landed above the great Falls and prepare to march upon the English; they prepare to join their brothers at the Fort of Niagara and destroy the English. With our help, they could do so. Will we help them? This I will not say. We must sleep on it and discuss it among ourselves in private council. Perhaps we will; perhaps we will not. But if we do not, then do not think that we have refused to help them because of fear of the Iroquois. There is no fear in our breasts. If we do leave them, it will be because of the truth in your words that Indian should not fight Indian, so that red men grow weak while white men grow strong. I am done."

It was on this note that the council broke up. The Indians of the far west made their way back to the French reinforcements camped at the head of the portage trail around the Falls. The Iroquois made their way back to where Warraghiyagey was waiting for them with the English army by Fort Niagara.

And no one—not the French, not the English, and not even any of the Indians—knew what was going to happen now.

[ *July 26, 1759—Thursday* ]

Fort Niagara was taken!

For the second time William Johnson had led his army to a stunning victory over a superior force and, although the capitulation had only been signed yesterday, already messengers were speeding through the forest to General Stanwix at his new fort rising at the Forks of the Ohio—he was calling it Fort Pitt—and to General Amherst at Lake George. Other messengers went to Montreal and Quebec and the towns and villages and people in between.

The climax had come suddenly, almost unexpectedly. As soon as his warriors had returned to him, William found himself in a dilemma. A force of Frenchmen and Canadians larger than his own would soon be moving down the portage trail against him, accompanied by more Indians than he himself had. And since he had to guard his camp, his artillery, his stores and boats against a possible sudden attack force from the fort, he could not set up the ambush along the portage trail. At least that was how the French figured it, but William was a cagey fighter and his moves hard to figure.

Though most of his regulars and many of the provincials

considered it tantamount to suicide to do so, he decided in favor of the ambush anyway. The only change was to have it somewhat closer to the fort than was originally planned and to leave the artillery firing steadily so that the approaching force would think a full-scale battle was in progress. That way, if an assault force did leave the fort, he would be close enough to fall back on it; and now the ambush was set up along the portage road at a place in the woods known to these Frenchmen as La Belle Famille.

Working rapidly, William had the road blocked by the point of a V-shaped rampart, with the uprights of the V moving off into the woods toward the advancing enemy and so cleverly built with newly cut brush and saplings that the foliage on them was still green and blended perfectly with the surroundings. Along the entire length of both arms of the V, the soldiers waited, while the Iroquois infiltrated all through the woods.

Aubry, Ligneris and Marin were now on the road, moving at top speed toward the fort, certain that the English army would be well hidden in its protective entrenchments before the fort, from which they could hear the continuing booming of the cannon as they battered away at the huge stone walls without much effect as yet. But as the French and Canadian reinforcements surged ahead, their Ottawa, Chippewa and Potawatomi allies fell back, lagging more and more behind until, as the French force moved out of sight around a bend, the western Indians, on command from Minivavana, simply melted into the underbrush and began a general movement back toward the mouth of Lake Erie where the boats were hidden.

The words of Old Belt had had their effect: the Great Lakes tribes would not engage in battles against the Iroquois for the benefit of the French.

In a little while the first of the feathered and painted *coureurs de bois* were moving into the V of the ambush, closely followed by the smaller number of regulars and colony troops. The Iroquois, from hiding, saw them, and were not in the least fooled by the Indian accouterments worn by the Canadian bush lopers, and as Warraghiyagey gave the word for the provincial troops to open fire, the Iroquois did likewise from the far flanks and from behind.

In a moment all was confusion. The first firing, catching them wholly by surprise, cut down the French reinforcements in whole ranks. One of the first bullets took Ligneris through the head and another smashed Jacques Marin's shoulder. Aubry screamed out orders for his men to fight their way over the breastwork William had thrown up and make their way to the fort, but the fire from the hidden provincials was too hot. The Canadian colony troops broke and began a wild rush back in the direction they had come from. Almost at once they were followed by the others. With fierce shrieks, the Iroquois took up the pursuit and continued to cut them down in great numbers.

Within Fort Niagara, Pouchot heard the firing but could not determine what was happening. For half an hour the banging of musketry continued before dying away. At last, about 2 P.M., an Onondaga came to the fort with the news of the defeat of the reinforcements with great loss. Pouchot refused to believe it. Under a flag of truce, he was permitted to send a party of his own to investigate at William Johnson's camp. In two hours they were back, having seen many of the partisan officers being held captive and scores upon scores of their men dead and scalped, often beheaded.

There was no choice now but honorable capitulation. William Johnson and his men entered the fort as the flag of surrender was hoisted and Pouchot turned over his sword to him. With a gallantry befitting a most polished English general, William gave it back to him. With a slight smile and courtly bow, Pouchot invited William and his staff officers to share a dinner prepared in the fort as a final French farewell to Fort Niagara, and William had accepted.

They had dined well, but there was a strong underlying fear in the Frenchmen as they heard the sounds from outside. In order to protect the lives of the French garrison, William had been forced to agree to allow the Iroquois to plunder the fort and they were at it now. Five hundred of the warriors had swarmed in and were taking everything, even stripping the hinges off the doors. Bales of furs were taken and barrels of brandy were opened and consumed with incredible speed. There was ever more talk among them of slaughtering the French prisoners.

William Johnson was well aware that the crucial moment would come when the prisoners were marched out of the fort for the agreed-upon release and return to Montreal. He wanted to see no repetition of the disaster at Lake George when Montcalm had taken Fort William Henry. Therefore, he permitted the French to retain their loaded weapons and told them if they were molested, they could use them to protect themselves. He also told the Iroquois that this step had been taken and the Indians reluctantly held their distance some. All the Indians were, however, furious.

The prisoners were marched out to the beating of drums, their muskets shouldered, flanked on each side by tight ranks of English provincials acting as a protection against the Indians who ranged along the sides with knives and tomahawks in their hands, demanding blood. As they reached the bateaux on the shoreline close to the fort, however, the French soldiers were only too glad to drop their weapons and leap into the boats, then push out immediately a safe distance from shore.

William had not, however, been able to claim from the Iroquois the ninety-six enlisted men they had captured from Aubry's, Ligneris's and Marin's reinforcements, although he did manage to buy all twenty-five captured officers for the sum of a hundred and sixty pounds. Without further ado the ninety-six colony troops, regulars and Canadians were whisked away to almost certain death by Iroquois who already had a hundred fifty scalps hanging at their waists.

And now, the day after the capitulation, William Johnson was already repairing Fort Niagara for winter occupancy by his troops. He was extremely pleased with the way things had gone and fired off to General Amherst a full report of the victory, concluding with the comment:

*By having so many Indians on our side, we gained Niagara with the weakest force and the most insignificant train of artillery that was ever sent so great a distance against so regular and respectable a fortification.*

### [ *August 10, 1759—Friday* ]

Throughout America sped the news of Sir William Johnson's victory and the fall of Fort Niagara to the English. It was a gigantic step for the English in winning all of the continent, because now the vital French linkage across it was severed. The battle of Fort Niagara was strategically the greatest English military victory in the American heartland since the outbreak of the war, and while the French reeled and groaned under the impact of the news, the English were jubilant almost beyond words. In New York City it quickly became a standard toast to raise one's glass high and say, "Johnson forever!"

The victory was even greater than just the capture of Fort Niagara. Retreating at top speed with what few French, Canadians and Indians were left to him, Aubry reached Fort Presque Isle with the awful news. The commandant, Portneuf, immediately dispatched scouts to see how the siege at the fort was going and whether or not Pouchot could hold out. They didn't have to go far. Less than half a day's distance from Fort Presque Isle they met a small party of Ottawas who told them of the surrender and the rapid disappearance of the released prisoners by bateaux to the east on Lake Ontario.

Fearful now that William Johnson would follow up his triumph with a march on him, Portneuf ordered the immediate burning of Fort Machault, Fort Le Boeuf and Fort Presque Isle. It was quickly done and when the parties had reassembled before the smoking ruins of the fort on the Lake Erie shore, Portneuf ordered a march begun, heading for Detroit to take refuge there and fearfully await the coming of the English.

New treaties were quickly enacted at Detroit when they arrived there, with the four principal tribes of the region: Ottawas, Hurons, Potawatomies and Chippewas. This was their land and it was not hard to get them to vow that no English would ever set foot on it and live. Though they had, at the last moment, refused to fight the English for the French on Iroquois soil, it would be a different matter indeed if the English came to their own land.

Now there were no French posts between Detroit and Fort de Lévis, at the head of the St. Lawrence River rapids. An empire had opened to the English and they meant to snatch it. The knowledge that this empire was occupied and claimed by thousands of Indians of numerous tribes made no difference. Already land speculators were making plans for that land and if the Indians opposed them, so what? Couldn't they just be forced back and back as they had been in the east, until the whole land belonged to the English?

After all, they were only Indians.

[ *September 13, 1759—Thursday* ]

"I am afraid, sir," said the surgeon named Arnoux, after his close examination of the French general, "that the wound is mortal."

Louis Montcalm's expression did not alter. He merely

677

nodded slightly and said very calmly, "I think I am glad of it. How long have I to live?"

The young surgeon shrugged, as if reluctant to reply, but then answered, "Twelve hours, more or less. You are bleeding internally and there is no way to stop it."

"Twelve hours," Montcalm repeated, and then he sighed. He must have been in great pain, but his voice was firm and clear and gave no indication of it. "So much the better," he said wearily. "I am happy that I shall not live to see the surrender of Quebec. Since I have lost the battle, it consoles me to know I have been defeated by so brave an enemy."

The Chevalier Ramesay, commandant of the garrison of Quebec, suddenly rushed in, all out of breath, and began asking a barrage of questions about what he should do in regard to the defense of the city and what the general's orders were for him now, since he did not see how it could be held much longer. Montcalm merely waited as the words spilled out of Ramesay in a torrent until at last they faltered and stopped. Even then for some time Montcalm said nothing, and Ramesay began to fidget in a somewhat embarrassed manner. At length Montcalm spoke to him:

"I will neither give order nor interfere any further. I have much business that must be attended to, of greater moment than your ruined garrison and this wretched country. My time is very short; therefore, pray leave me. I wish you all comfort, and to be happily extricated from your present perplexities."

Confused and even more embarrassed, Ramesay backed away and nearly stumbled over his own feet in going out the door. Again Montcalm was quiet for a long time, lost in thought, and then he asked Surgeon Arnoux to write a message for him. His voice a little huskier now, he dictated a letter to Brigadier General Townshend of the English forces outside the city:

*Monsieur, the humanity of the English sets my mind at peace concerning the fate of the French prisoners and the Canadians. Feel towards them as they have caused me to feel. Do not let them perceive that they have changed masters. Be their protector as I have been their father.*

That note out of the way, he thought about writing to his mother, his wife, in fact his entire family one final time, but such a well of emotion arose in him that he could not bear to

678

do so. He answered with a barely audible, "No ... thank you, doctor," when Arnoux asked if he cared to dictate a letter home or if there was anything else he could do for him. Apologizing for the necessity of leaving, Arnoux then placed two women at his bedside to attend any wants he might have, and himself hustled off to treat the multitude of other patients.

A spasm of pain shot through the forty-eight-year-old Montcalm and he stiffened and then slowly relaxed as it passed. The image of his beloved Château Candiac passed away with it and brought him back again to thoughts of the siege and the incredibility of Quebec being taken. It was more like a dream than a reality.

Eighty days ago—on June 26—the siege had begun. Sixty English warships had pulled off the astonishing feat of sailing all the way up to the Isle d'Orleans, which no one believed possible for them to do, as even with experienced river pilots it was a difficult navigation. In these ships were the nine-thousand-man army under General James Wolfe.

For his own part, even though suffering severely from want of food and critical supplies, Montcalm had practically all of the French and Canadian manpower under him—some fourteen thousand men, not including the regular Quebec garrison of twelve hundred under the Chevalier Ramesay. Nor did it include the thousand Indians—mostly Ottawas, Chippewas and Potawatomies—here under Chief Pontiac and Charles Langlade. Quebec itself was such an impregnable bastion that Bougainville expressed the view that it could be held by a small number of men against a foe of many times greater numbers.

Even before the siege had begun, Montcalm decided not to play into Wolfe's hands by engaging in offensive measures. There were not enough supplies for it and his men were too physically weak to engage in any such enterprises, however much he would have liked ordering them. No, the plan was to avoid general battle, run no risks at all and simply protract the defense of the city until the resources of the enemy were exhausted and he was forced by winter to withdraw.

That was the way the siege had begun, and it looked very much as if it would all go according to plan. Montcalm had laid out his defenses carefully, positioning his men on the north side of the St. Lawrence behind strong redoubts and entrenchments for almost eight miles, from the eastern edge of Quebec, at the mouth of the St. Charles River all the way to the western edge of the Montmorenci River. Quebec itself was secure, its gates heavily guarded or, as in most cases, closed and barricaded, with Ramesay's garrison inside to protect it. There was little fear that the English ships could sail past Quebec to make an assault landing on the upstream side—not with one hundred six cannon on the fort's walls ready to crush any ship which might attempt the slow, difficult upstream passage.

Shortly after Wolfe had taken the unprotected Isle d'Orleans, Governor Vaudreuil launched his own surprise retaliation, which he had been boasting would destroy the English ships swiftly and effectively. At considerable cost, under the governor's direct orders, certain French ships and great rafts had been loaded with pitch and tar, grenades and explosives. Some of these craft were linked together by chains. These were the fireboats, to be ignited and set adrift to ram into the English fleet.

On the night of June 28 these craft began their downstream drift from above Quebec under the command of Captain Delouche, but a better man might have been picked to lead them. The nearer he came to the English fleet, the weaker his resolve became, and suddenly, fully half an hour before he should have, he set his ship afire and abandoned it. Instantly those coming behind him fired theirs too, as that had been the signal for them to do so, and the crews of each quickly pulled safely to shore in small boats. But the fireboats did no damage, running aground long before reaching the English ships, or being diverted by daring men in whaleboats from the threatened fleet. Not one English ship was even damaged, much less lost. Vaudreuil had cause to remember then the words Montcalm had spoken when the governor first completed construction of the fireboats: "I am afraid they have cost us a million, and will be good for nothing after all."

On the next day—June 29—Wolfe had taken Point Lévis, less than a mile distant directly across the river from Quebec, and here he began erecting batteries while being regularly shelled from the guns of Quebec. It was no easy task for Wolfe's men and the job was made even more difficult by the frequency with which their scouts, spies and guard patrols were picked off by the Canadian *coureurs de bois* and the western Indians. By the dozens and then by scores the outposted men were felled by rifle fire or arrows, then always scalped and often gruesomely mutilated.

But at last Wolfe had gotten his artillery positioned and opened up a return fire at the city. It was not attempted with any view in mind to weaken the bastion, which could hardly be accomplished by such weapons at this distance, but simply to destroy the outer buildings, throw fear into the inhabitants and generally lower the morale of Montcalm's troops.

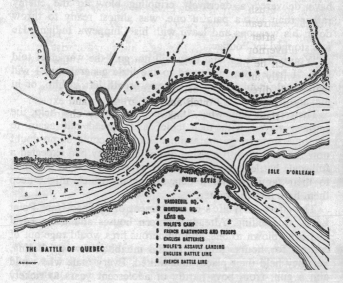

THE BATTLE OF QUEBEC

1 VAUDREUIL HQ.
2 MONTCALM HQ.
3 LÉVIS HQ.
4 WOLFE'S CAMP
5 FRENCH EARTHWORKS AND TROOPS
6 ENGLISH BATTERIES
7 WOLFE'S ASSAULT LANDING
8 ENGLISH BATTLE LINE
9 FRENCH BATTLE LINE

Another aggressive move by Wolfe resulted in the landing of three thousand of his troops just below the mouth of the Montmorenci River, where they established an encampment. Four hundred of Pontiac's Indians, being led by the war chief and Charles Langlade, discovered them first, while the attackers were still in a state of unpreparedness. While his Indians lay in hiding, watching them, Langlade hastened to the nearby encampment of eleven hundred Canadians under Captain Repentigny with a request for support for an immediate attack. Unwilling to act on his own, Repentigny sent a runner with the intelligence to General Lévis to ask for orders. Lévis, in turn had been specifically ordered by Vaudreuil to inform him of all moves without fail *before* they were made, and so now he relayed the message and request on to the governor, whose headquarters were about four miles away. Vaudreuil kept them waiting two hours, and the Indians, impatient at best, finally launched the attack by themselves. They struck Wolfe's unit hard, inflicting heavy losses and forcing it back until, at last, steadied by the rangers, the English force held its ground and broke up the attack. In their retreat, the Indians picked up thirty-nine scalps of Wolfe's men.

Langlade, furious for lack of support, which he felt could have delivered a decisively crippling blow to the enemy rather than just a painful one, was almost ready to throw down his weapons and leave with his Chippewa Indians. He was stopped by Pontiac.

"You will not go, and they will not go," the war chief told him. "I have given my word to the little general that I will fight beside him as long as there is breath left in him, or in me, and I will live by my word or die by it."

Their spirits somewhat dampened by the lack of help, the Indians stayed with their chief and spread out again to continue their fringe marauding. But there could be no doubt now that it was with a rising discontent. They had expected a full-scale battle to be fought, after which they could go home to their families—not a delaying action which might keep them here into the winter.

The effect of Wolfe's bombardment of Quebec from Point Lévis, was telling. Already eighteen houses and a cathedral had been blown to bits, and numerous fires would rage out of control for hours. Morale of the inhabitants was faltering, yet they held their places and waited. Every male who could aim a gun, from boys hardly of adolescent years to rickety old men of eighty and above, was poised and determined to do his part to hold back the enemy.

For the inhabitants, it was hardly more than could be expected. Quebec was their home, their city, and they were not keen on abandoning it. For the general run of the Canadians, however, it was another matter. Their homes were the farms and villages far removed from Quebec and now, after weeks of the siege, they began deserting—five here, a dozen there, a score elsewhere. The news that had come of the loss of Fort Niagara to William Johnson, followed by the burning of Forts Machault, Le Boeuf and Presque Isle, along with the fact that St. Luc de la Corne had been repulsed by Colonel Haldimand, who was rebuilding Fort Oswego, only encouraged their belief that the French cause was lost, and they did not care to go down with her. Vaudreuil proclaimed a death penalty for deserters, but it hardly slowed the numbers who continued to pick up and leave under the cover of night.

Then came the first real setback for Montcalm. On the moonless night of July 18, a number of English ships incredibly slipped past Quebec batteries and got upstream from the city where they attacked and destroyed a fire ship and numerous small boats. Montcalm, not well prepared in that sector, was now forced to split his defense and send a strong detachment to guard against landings. Colonel Louis Antoine de Bougainville commanded that detachment.

Unwilling to let go of his fire ship idea, Vaudreuil had another great procession of them built upstream; seventy rafts, small boats and schooners fastened together, and set afire and floated downstream. But the whole string of them grounded upstream from the ships and burned fruitlessly to the waterline.

On July 31 Wolfe made a fierce attack up the precipitous slopes near the Montmorenci, but for the English it was an insurmountable position held by the French, and he was forced to call a retreat, leaving behind a total of four hundred thirty-three men in killed, wounded and missing, including a colonel and thirty-two other officers. Even then the English commander did not lose hope, and Montcalm marveled at his tenacity and ability in the face of such a defeat to maintain a high level of morale among his men. Vaudreuil, however, wasted no time in admiration of the enemy. He wrote to General Bourlamaque, who was still holding his post at Fort Carillon:

*I have no more anxiety about Quebec. M. Wolfe, I assure you, will make no progress. Luckily for him, his prudence saved him from the consequences of his mad enterprise, and he contented himself with losing about five hundred of his best soldiers. Deserters say he will try us again in a few days. That is what we want; he'll find somebody to talk to!*

Bourlamaque, however, was well occupied on his own front. As Amherst's army was almost upon him in their advance, he left only a small detachment at Fort Carillon with word to fight until it would be disastrous to fight further, and then to surrender. These had been Bourlamaque's orders from Montcalm and he followed them exactly, going past abandoned Fort St. Frederic at Crown Point and down the length of Lake Champlain to its mouth, where he dug in at the more defensible location on the Isle-aux-Noix, where Lake Champlain emptied into the Richelieu River.

At Quebec, the victory over Wolfe in the assault, such as it was, did little to raise the flagging spirits of the Canadians. To them it was but a skirmish and hardly to be considered against the loss of Forts Niagara, Le Boeuf, Presque Isle and Machault, the abandonment of Fort St. Frederic and the impending loss of Fort Carillon. *These* were losses.

The news which came from that southern front a short time later—that both the Ticonderoga and Crown Point installations were now occupied by the English, and that Amherst was busy building a fleet of whaleboats at Fort St. Frederic to continue the push toward Montreal—forced Montcalm to even more seriously weaken his position. He ordered General Lévis to Montreal, to hold it against possible attack from the south by Amherst.

In an attempt to get Montcalm to move to an offensive in which he might become vulnerable, Wolfe now began burning the outlying farms and villages of the Canadians, but Montcalm refused to rise to the bait. He had no intention of risking his army and Quebec to save a few dwellings, and now it was becoming obvious that Wolfe himself was beginning to hurt from want of supplies.

By this time the siege was in its sixty-seventh day and Wolfe had lost a total of eight hundred fifty in dead, wounded and missing, including another colonel, two majors and fifty-one other officers, as compared to negligible losses on the French side. The state of the English general's spirits was indicated in the letter he wrote to his mother on August 31:

*Mother Dear,*

*My writing to you will convince you that no personal evils worse than defeats and disappointments have fallen upon me. The enemy puts nothing to risk, and I can't in conscience put the whole army to risk. My antagonist has wisely shut himself up in inaccessible intrenchments, so that I can't get at him without spilling a torrent of blood, and that perhaps to little purpose. The Marquis de Montcalm is at the head of a great number of bad soldiers, and I am at the head of a small number of good ones, that wish for nothing so much as to fight him; but the wary old fellow avoids an action, doubtful of the behavior of his army. People must be of the profession to understand the disadvantages and difficulties we labor under, arising from the uncommon natural strength of the country.*

In council with his officers, the consensus given Wolfe was to give it all up and go home, to renew the attack again at a later time with more men, more supplies and more time in their favor, but Wolfe himself was all for trying one last gamble. In considerable detail he explained the plan to his officers, and was gratified when it met with a surprisingly warm response, despite the fact that the odds were all stacked strongly against its success.

For his own part, Louis Montcalm had no idea that Wolfe was contemplating anything more than a continued siege and eventual withdrawal. He hoped it would be soon. The posted death penalty for deserters had not had the desired effect and desertions were again on the increase. In some cases as many as two hundred Canadians were deserting in a single night. As much as possible he had been keeping in touch with Generals Lévis and Bourlamaque. One of the brightest bits of news he had received, in fact, was the opinion given by Bourlamaque—who was still at Isle-aux-Noix—that Amherst, having been slowed by boat building and bad weather would not, now that the season was so advanced, attempt any further assault against the French stronghold.

It was only three days ago when he had written to Bourlamaque:

*The night is dark; it rains; our troops are in their tents, with clothes on, ready for an alarm; I in my boots, my horse saddled. In fact, this is my usual way. I wish you were here; for I cannot be everywhere, though I multiply myself, and have not taken off my clothes since the twenty-third of June. I am overwhelmed with work, and should often lose temper, like you, if I did not remember that I am paid by Europe for not losing it. Nothing new since my last. I give the enemy another month, or something less, to stay here.*

Even though Montcalm had sent Colonel Bougainville with some three thousand men to guard the upstream side of Quebec, there was little expectation that attack would come from such quarter. But from two deserters, Wolfe learned that at ebb tide on the night of the twelfth, Bougainville's attention would be diverted by relaying a convoy of provisions from Montreal to Montcalm, and that was the time

Wolfe chose, with forty-eight hundred men, to assault the almost perpendicular slopes of the Plains of Abraham.

At about 2 A.M. today—September 13—the tide began to ebb in the great river and Wolfe's advance detachment were rowed toward shore from the larger ships they were on. Twenty-four volunteers led the way, followed by a large body of others. Silently, but with great difficulty, they pulled themselves from rock to rock, root to root, all the way to the top while the major force waited below for the all-clear sign. At the top, the advance detachment discovered a cluster of tents a short distance away. They rushed upon them, wounded the officer in charge and captured two other soldiers, The remainder fled.

Below, Wolfe was anxiously listening. When he heard the sound of musket shots followed by special cries he knew with a growing exultation that his men had taken the height. He gave the word and the rest of the army leaped from the boats and scrambled to the top. As fast as the small boats were emptied, they returned to the larger crafts in midriver to reload with more. In something under a few hours, the entire force under Wolfe was at the top and before them lay a broad plateau known as the Plains of Abraham—named after a river pilot, Abraham Martin, who owned the land here. On the eastern end of this very plateau lay Quebec, not over a mile away.

Several nearby cannon had sounded during the night and Wolfe had sent men to silence them, which had been done easily. At daybreak, however, batteries of cannon on shore opened up on the English ships still in the river and, three or four miles below Quebec, Montcalm heard them firing.

The French general had spent a sleepless and troubled night. At six o'clock this morning he mounted his horse and rode to Quebec to determine what was happening. From two miles east of the St. Charles River, he suddenly saw the red coats of the English army on the high plateau of the Plains of Abraham.

"This is serious business," Montcalm said to his aide, Chevalier Johnstone, and then sent the man off at a full gallop to bring up the troops from the center and left of his camp. Then, with a stern, unwavering stare straight ahead, he himself rode to the bridge over the St. Charles and crossed it. As rapidly as it could, his army followed him.

Montcalm was stunned when he got the English in full view. Instead of the detachment of several hundred he had expected, he found practically the whole of Wolfe's army. The men he had sent for from the center of his camp were boiling onto the scene now—regulars, colony troops, Canadians, and a host of almost naked savages armed with muskets, knives and tomahawks. The strong detachment from the left of Montcalm's camp, however, did not show up, nor did any of the garrison from within Quebec.

Furious at this lack of assistance, Montcalm sent to Chevalier Ramesay in the city for twenty-five field pieces which were positioned on the palace battery. Incredibly, Ramesay sent him only three, saying he wanted the rest for his own defense. Feeling he could wait no longer, lest Wolfe take even stronger position and cut the supply line from Montreal, Montcalm ordered attack.

The lion had been drawn from his lair and back and forth the battle raged, with Montcalm and Wolfe in the thick of it with their respective forces. Wolfe surged to attack, personally leading a company of grenadiers. A bullet from the French lines shattered his wrist. Almost without pause he wrapped a handkerchief around it and continued the advance. A second shot smashed through his side, low on the right, and he faltered, then pressed on, moving along with his men. Now a third shot came and struck him squarely in the chest, shoved him backward off his feet into a sitting position on the ground. He sat there, stunned.

Three of his men snatched him up and carried him to the rear between them. They would have taken him down the slope to the boats, but he begged them to put him down.

"You'll be all right, General," said one of them, a young man with tears streaming from his eyes, "don't worry. We'll get the doctor."

Wolfe raised his uninjured hand and shook his head. "There's no need; it's all over with me." He slumped back, not yet unconscious, but rapidly failing. Abruptly a harsh voice from one of his men penetrated the mist which seemed to be settling over him.

"They run! Look at how they run!"

Wolfe's eyes fluttered open. "Who runs?" he asked, his voice slurred.

"The enemy, sir, the enemy! My God, sir, they're giving way everywhere!"

"Go, one of you," Wolfe muttered, "to Colonel Burton. Tell him to march Webb's regiment down to the St. Charles River, to cut off their retreat from the bridge."

He closed his eyes again and, with some effort, rolled onto his side and drew his knees up slightly. Incongruously, a faint smile came to his lips and then he whispered, "Now then, God be praised, I will die in peace."

And, an instant later, he did.

Montcalm, still astride his horse and an inviting target himself, was swept back toward the city by the human wave of fleeing French, Canadians and Indians. He was very nearly to the walls when a single ball slammed into almost the exact center of his back. He began to lean and would have pitched from the saddle except that two soldiers rushed to him and held him up, one on each side, and led his horse through the St. Louis gate and into the city.

Inside was a chaotic scene—people running every which way and no one seeming to know quite what to do. A gaggle of worried women stood near the gate and as the general was brought in, one of them screamed piercingly.

"O, my God! My God! The Marquis is killed!"

Montcalm looked over at her and smiled. "It is nothing," he said. "Nothing. Don't be worried for me, my good friends."

He had been taken then to the house of the surgeon, Arnoux, where he lay now, awaiting the end. Off and on during the remainder of the day Vaudreuil and Bigot had come to confer with him, both men in an extremely anxious state and telling him his troops were fleeing everywhere. The English, exhausted by the battle as much as the French, were hastily building an entrenchment on the Plains of Abraham under direction of their new commander, General Townsend, and Vaudreuil was sure they meant to storm the walls in the morning.

All his great resolution to defend to the last against the English, all his boasted zeal, now deserted the governor. Hastily dropping all control of the city into the more than reluctant hands of Ramesay, by way of a brief note, Vaudreuil at nine o'clock in the evening ordered the troops that had retreated into the city to retreat with him at once toward Montreal.

In that initial note to Ramesay, Vaudreuil had ordered him to defend the city as long as he possibly could. With the retreat begun, however, he fired off a hasty second note to the garrison commander:

*M. de Ramesay, the position of the enemy becomes stronger*

*every instant and this, with other reasons, obliges me to retreat. You are not to wait till the enemy carries the town by assault. As soon as provisions fail, you will raise the flag of surrender.*

*Vaudreuil*

Fortunately for his own peace of mind, Louis Montcalm was unaware of this. He lay in the gloom of the doctor's chamber, his face pallid and his eyes sunken. His breathing was shallow, hardly detectable, and it was obvious that the end was near.

## [ September 14, 1759—Friday ]

Charles Michel de Langlade was a member of the melancholy procession of about a hundred people who moved in the gloomy quiet of early evening through the rubble-filled street to the chapel of the Ursuline Convent. At the head of the line were six young officers of the Quebec garrison and they were carrying on their shoulders a very crudely nailed-together rectangular box.

Within the box was Louis Montcalm.

The general had died at four o'clock this morning, only a few hours after the final rites had been administered by Bishop Pontbriand. Because of the confusion raging inside and out of the city, no carpenter could be located to build a decent coffin and so a faithful old servant of the Ursuline nuns—an individual named Old Man Michael—found a few broken boards which he managed to nail together to form the rough box.

Following closely behind the pallbearers was the Chevalier Ramesay and many of his officers from the Quebec garrison. Behind them came a number of inhabitants of the city— mostly weeping women—plus a dozen or so *coureurs de bois*, including Langlade, and perhaps as many more colony troops.

The Ursuline Convent Chapel had been heavily damaged by cannon fire from Wolfe's batteries across the river. One of the shells had smashed through the ceiling and buried itself in the floor before exploding and causing a large crater. A level space had been prepared in the crater and it was here that the rough coffin was placed, under the direction of three priests and three nuns.

As the entire body of onlookers gathered around, a simple quiet service was held by the light of torches. When it was over, most of the women and a great many of the men were sobbing, while some had fallen to their knees and cradled their faces in their hands. It was not only Montcalm who was being buried here; it was New France.

Even as the dry earth and masonry was being scooped back into the hole to cover the ugly box, Charles Langlade slipped out and moved swiftly to the nearest open exit from the city. With that curious loping gait of the *coureur de bois* he seemed almost to flow rather than walk, and in a few moments the bulk of the city disappeared in the darkness behind him.

Half an hour later, approaching so silently that his presence was not even detected until he stepped into the glow of the small fire, Langlade entered the camp of the western Indians. Most of them had gathered here, two miles from the city, uncertain now what they should do.

Pontiac rose to meet Langlade and in the Ottawa tongue the Canadian half-breed told him that Montcalm was dead and had been buried. For the first time in the many years he had known the war chief, Langlade saw Pontiac's features contort with a grief of great depth. The word spread through the camp and the same grief was reflected by many of the others.

After a while Pontiac and several of the other chiefs sat in council with Langlade while the Canadian explained the state of affairs. With the withdrawal of the regulars, militia and colony troops at Vaudreuil's orders, Quebec was as good as gone and, with Quebec, Montreal and the rest of Canada.

The ornaments in Pontiac's ears and nose bobbed as he shook his head and his expression became ugly. "I will not accept English control over Canada," he said. "I do not think they can take it and if they should take it, I do not think they can hold it. If I am wrong and they do take it and hold it, it is *here* that they will hold it, not in our country. We will return now to our villages and stand firmly there, and not an Englishman will be let into our country except by our favor. Quebec may be lost to them; Canada may be lost to them. But as long as he breathes, Pontiac will never embrace the English."

Within the hour everything the Indians had was gathered up and packed and, with Pontiac and Charles Langlade and several other chiefs in front, they moved away silently toward their own upper Great Lakes country. The war was over for them ... for now.

## [ November 9, 1759—Friday ]

Quebec might yet have been saved had it not been for Governor Pierre Vaudreuil.

The English force, after all, was relatively small and decidedly weak after well over two months of maintaining a siege. They had suffered desperate losses in both men and officers, while the loss of French manpower had been relatively slight. Further, while an advance had been made on Quebec, the English were still outside the walls and the city was still able to defend itself for a considerable time if need be. Finally, an express messenger had gone galloping to General Lévis at Montreal with news of the Battle of the Plains of Abraham, Lévis had immediately started gathering his force and what fleeing soldiers he could seize, to come up from behind the English force and crush it.

Pierre Vaudreuil himself, having rushed madly to the safety of Montreal, met Lévis there and quickly approved the general's move to hit the English from the rear. He told Lévis that while Montcalm had been mortally wounded, Quebec was not yet taken, but somehow he neglected to mention that he had ordered Ramesay to surrender the city virtually at his own discretion. Nor did he mention that his pulling out the troops and leaving the way he had gave the Quebec garrison commander every reason to believe that he and his men had been utterly abandoned to the enemy. But Vaudreuil had not forgotten his order to Ramesay and as soon as he left Lévis he sent an express to Ramesay countermanding the previous order and telling him now to hold out at all costs, as help was on the way.

It took a full day for Lévis to get his force in shape and ready to move out first thing in the morning, September 18. In the small hours before the march was begun, the general took advantage of a brief respite to write to Bourlamaque at Isle-aux-Noix:

*Montreal, September 18, 1759*

*My Dear Bourlamaque—*
*We have had a very great loss, for we have lost M. de Montcalm. I regret him as my general and my friend. I*

*found our army here. It is now on the march to retrieve our
fortunes. I can trust you to hold your position; as I have not
M. de Montcalm's talents, I look to you to second me and
advise me. Put a good face on it. Hide this business as long
as you can. I am mounting my horse this moment. Write me
all the news.*

*F. Lévis*

All day he pushed his men on the forced march and by
evening had reached St. Augustin, only to be slammed to a
stunned halt by the dreadful news that Quebec had surrendered and was occupied by the English. He immediately
withdrew his force to the town of Jacques-Cartier, to stand
ready there in case of an English follow-through toward
Montreal. At the same time he sent dispatches on to Governor Vaudreuil, acquainting him with the fact of the surrender
of Quebec.

The news did not greatly surprise Vaudreuil. He had hoped
Lévis might get there in time, but since he hadn't, now was
the time to cover himself as best he could. In his sumptuous
quarters in the days and weeks which followed, he kept himself busy writing a series of letters to France which would
explain to the ministers how courageous he himself had been
in the face of the enemy, and how cowardly virtually everyone else had been. In his letters to the ministers of the
marine and colony, written in code on October 30, Vaudreuil
had poured it on:

*You have seen by the above detailed report, Excellency,
what sad state we have been reduced to, culminating in the
surrender of Quebec to the English. What kind of officer
can the Chevalier de Ramesay be, that in the face of my
direct order to him to hold his position to the very last
because help was on the way under M. de Lévis, he would
take it upon himself to surrender the city? If the blame for
the fall of Quebec is to be placed anywhere, it must in large
measure rest on M. de Ramesay's shoulders. But an even
greater portion of the blame, I regret to say, must be attached to M. de Montcalm.*

*The letter that you wrote in cipher, on the tenth of
February to Monsieur le Marquis de Montcalm and me, in
common, flattered his self-love to such a degree that, far
from seeking conciliation, he did nothing but try to persuade
the public that his authority surpassed mine. From the mo-*

*ment of Monsieur de Montcalm's arrival in this colony, down
to that of his death, he did not cease to sacrifice everything
to his boundless ambition. He sowed dissention among the
troops, tolerated the most indecent talk against the government, attached to himself the most disreputable persons, used
means to corrupt the most virtuous, and, when he could not
succeed, became their cruel enemy. He wanted to be Governor-General. He privately flattered with favors and promises
of patronage every officer of the colony troops who adopted
his ideas. He spared no pains to gain over the people of
whatever calling, and persuade them of his attachment;
while, either by himself or by means of the troops of the line,
he made them bear the most frightful yoke. He defamed
honest people, encouraged insubordination, and closed his
eyes to the rapine of his soldiers.*

*In despair am I, Monseigneur, to be under the necessity of
painting you such a portrait after death of Monsieur le
Marquis de Montcalm. Though it contains the exact truth, I
would have deferred it if his personal hatred to me were
alone to be considered; but I feel too deeply the loss of the
colony to hide from you the cause of it. I can assure you that
if I had been the sole master, Quebec would still belong to
the King, and that nothing is so disadvantageous in a colony
as a division of authority and the mingling of troops of the
line with colony troops. Thoroughly knowing Monsieur de
Montcalm, I did not doubt in the least that unless I con-
descended to all his wishes, he would succeed in ruining
Canada and wrecking all my plans.*

*It is my duty to charge M. de Montcalm with losing the
battle of Quebec by attacking it before I arrived to take
command; and this was due to M. de Montcalm's absolute
determination to exercise independent authority, without caring whether the colony was saved or lost. I cannot hide from
you, Monseigneur, that if he had had his way in past years,
Oswego and Fort George [Fort William Henry] would
never have been attacked or taken; and he owed the success
at Ticonderoga to the orders I had given him.*

With such letters as this sent off to the various ministers,
Vaudreuil began to relax a little, feeling that now no matter
what happened to Canada, he had placed himself in an
exemplary position. But then, only this morning he had
received news so devastating to him personally that it had

caused him to become sick and vomit and suffer a severe throbbing headache.

His informant told him that prior to the battle of Quebec, Montcalm had had a premonition of his own forthcoming death. It appeared, so the informant went on, that Montcalm had for a considerable length of time been amassing evidence against Vaudreuil and his associates; damning evidence filled with facts and figures which pinpointed numerous corruptions in which the governor, the intendant and others were engaged. These papers, according to the informant, were compiled into two considerable bundles and given into the hands of the Jesuit priest of the St. Francis mission, Father Roubaud; and that Roubaud, should he learn of Montcalm's death, was to immediately send these documents on to France.

Little wonder that Vaudreuil had become ill. Now, alone in his chambers, he swiftly drank a large portion of brandy to settle the trembling of his hands, and then went to his desk to write another letter to the minister of the marine and colonies:

> Montreal
> November 9, 1759

*Excellency:*

*I have already had the honor, by my letter written in cipher on the thirtieth of last month, to give you a sketch of the character of Monsieur le Marquis de Montcalm; but I have just been informed of a stroke so black that I think, Monseigneur, that I should fail in my duty to you if I did not tell you of it. I have been informed by a source in which I have the greatest confidence, that a little before his death, and no doubt in fear of the fate that befell him, Monsieur de Montcalm placed in the hands of Father Roubaud, missionary at St. Francis, two packets of papers containing remarks on the administration of this colony, and especially on the manner in which the military posts were furnished with supplies; that the observations were accompanied by certificates; and that they involved charges against me of complicity in peculation. Father Roubaud was to send these papers to France as soon as possible upon hearing that M. de Montcalm had met with death. I do not pretend to know what they contain, but can only state that if such charges are made, they are without foundation and no more than an attempt on the part of M. de Montcalm to continue his maltreatment of me from beyond the grave; an indication of the despicability of his character. You may have already received these papers by the time you receive this letter, but now, Monseigneur, that you are informed about them, I feel no anxiety, and I am sure that the King will receive no impression from them without acquainting himself with their real truth or falsity.*

*Vaudreuil*

But Governor Pierre Vaudreuil was an extremely worried man.[4]

## [ *December 31, 1760—Wednesday* ]

In just under one year from the time of the fall of Quebec, the whole of Canada became the newest addition to the British Empire.

Although General François de Lévis fought valiantly in one last battle at Sainte Foy, between Quebec and Montreal, he had little hope of winning—and he did not. With practically all of the Canadians and the majority of the colony troops now having deserted him, along with essentially all of the Indians, he could not pretend to stand off the might of the English army with only a few battalions of French regulars.

Lévis fell back to Montreal in the spring and, with Vaudreuil, watched with growing despair as the powerful three-pronged advance of the English neared. Jeffrey Amherst, still in command of the English forces, ordered Brigadier General Murray, in command at Quebec, to move up the St. Lawrence on Montreal; Brigadier General Haviland, in command at Fort Ticonderoga—formerly Fort Carillon—he ordered to move down Lake Champlain and the Richelieu River on Montreal; for himself, Amherst chose to lead his force up the Mohawk and down the Onondaga—now being called the Oswego River—to Oswego itself, and from there to destroy Fort de Lévis at the head of the St. Lawrence rapids. He would then move downstream on Montreal. If all went well, the three wings of the army would converge for an attack on the final French bastion they need be concerned with.

Everything went according to plan. Murray reached Montreal first and took possession of Isle Ste. Thérèse to await the arrival of Haviland and Amherst. Haviland, moving up from the south, was not far behind, driving the French army before them from Isle-aux-Noix into the protection of Montreal. Haviland then took a post for himself on the south shore of the St. Lawrence to await Amherst.

Nor was Amherst long in coming, he having taken Fort de Lévis and already descending the Lachine Rapids—at the cost of eighty-four men drowned—and on September 6 he was before the walls of Montreal. In the morning, Murray left Isle Ste. Thérèse and landed just below the city, on the opposite side of it from Amherst. The commander in chief, however, stayed any attack while capitulation demands were carried to the French.

With a total of only twenty-four-hundred French troops remaining, there was no sense whatever to even raising a token resistance to the seventeen thousand English soldiers surrounding them. The capitulation was signed and the city—and the country—turned over to England.

The French regime in Canada was ended and England controlled a new wilderness empire.

As if they had been awaiting just such an appropriate time to do so, the Indians of the north and east, who had been discreetly staying out of sight for some time, now disavowed any affection for the French and flocked to unite themselves with the English, in whom they could no longer deny their future rested.

Many of the Indians came to Fort Johnson to pay homage to Warraghiyagey, some of them bearing gifts for his year-old son by Degonwadonti; a son he had named Peter Warren Johnson, after the uncle who had given him his start in this country.

It was not only the Six Nations who came, but equally the tribes that had fought against him and the English so bitterly for so long—the disaffected Iroquois from Caughnawaga and Oswegatchie, the Abnakis from the far northeast and the Algonkins from the far north. Others came, too—Shawnees and Delawares and Miamis from the west and, from the upper Great Lakes, a segment of the Ottawa nation which had parted company from the rest of the tribe under Pontiac and Mackinac, and moved to a new site on the south shore of Lake Erie.[5] They were unwilling to keep the fire of vendetta burning against the English that Pontiac was stoking among his own people as well as among the Chippewas, Hurons, and Potawatomies.

All of them came to Fort Johnson with the same hope:

that the great Warraghiyagey would temper the feelings of the English toward them, cause his people to remember theirs with some favor and perhaps allow them to preserve for themselves some of this great land which was once all theirs. And Warraghiyagey, as they had known he would, swore to them that he would do all in his power to protect them, their families, their land.

From the outset, however, William knew it was a task he could hardly hope to consummate. The Indians were now put into the position of begging favors of the very people they had often said they not only would not support, but that they would rather die against than live under. But it is an easy thing to vow to fight to the death for something; a much harder matter to actually have the resolution to do so.

Not even the Six Nations, who had belatedly swung their full weight behind the English cause, were in a good bargaining position. The Iroquois League was no longer what it had been for hundreds of years. Though it still sat in council at Onondaga, the decisions made were mostly predicated upon what Warraghiyagey said the English wanted or would agree to. Even the high esteem in which the Iroquois had long held themselves was fading. Once they had been a great warrior race, feared above all others across more than half a continent. Now they were so few that hardly a tribe in the west did not greatly outnumber their aggregate tribal total and, against such numbers and weaponry as the English had, the Iroquois now were as nothing.

English forts were springing up all over the land, with Fort Pitt at the Forks of the Ohio, Fort Stanwix at the Great Carrying Place, and the rebuilt Fort Niagara the strongest among them. The promises the Indians had exacted from the English that these and other such installations would be destroyed or turned over to the Indians as soon as there was no longer need for them against the French, went by the board. On this account, the Iroquois were too weak now to more than utter a few complaints and a few veiled threats, which were not taken seriously. The idea of turning such forts over to the Indians was laughable.

Even to the Iroquois themselves, the mistake they had made was clear. Too long the Six Nations had remained in the middle, delighting in being wooed but never won by both the French and the English. Too long they had tried to manipulate one white faction or the other, continually keeping both off balance and not knowing what to expect. Now it was the

Iroquois who were being manipulated. Too long their numbers had been on the decline as their young men were sacrificed to the war god. Too long they had been in the jaws of a power struggle, so wrapped up in indecision as to whom they should support that their own power had by and large been negated.

Now it was too late. Now that there was little that could be done to change matters, it became clear to them that at the very beginning, when they still had their strength and reputation, they should have done almost anything but adopt a policy of neutrality. As the French and the English fought each other, they themselves should have waged all-out war against both factions and driven them from their lands. Alternatively, they could even have thrown their full support behind the French at the beginning, and the English would most likely have been defeated; it would not have been too hard for the Indians to get along with the French, as they had been doing for so long. However distasteful it might have been, even a wholehearted support of the English from the beginning would have been to some advantage; their position now would have been one of strength and bargaining power and they could have retained their national pride and individual self-respect; they could have been treated by the English as a nation of men, rather than a body of subservients. But they had chosen neutrality and it was this stand which had gradually squeezed them, sapped them of their strength and their reputation and their pride.

The Iroquois were not done. But in the eyes of the tribal elders was the knowledge that their glory was past, that their race would never again be what it was, that more and more of their lands would slip from them, and that they would become objects of contempt for the English traders and settlers already beginning to stream into the forests and plains and river valleys.

Yes, the council fire of the Iroquois League still burned at Onondaga, but its flames were cool and the shadows crept in from all sides. Only the council fire at Fort Johnson still burned hotly for them. Never before in their history had the fate of their nations rested so completely in the hands of one man ... and in a white man at that!

# EPILOGUE

## [ July 11, 1774—Monday ]

MUCH had happened in the fourteen years that had passed since the English had taken Canada from the French. It was a bad time for the Indians everywhere. All the things the French had warned them about in respect to the English had come true: their people had been cheated in every way imaginable and their lands had been nibbled away until there was now hardly anything left. Treaties with the English lasted only as long as they served the purposes of the English.

Only with their own Warraghiyagey—Sir William Johnson —had they had appeal, and he labored for them with a love and dedication that superseded all else. Deep within him he felt a great welling of guilt, knowing that while he had done more to help them than any other white man, yet it was his own people who had led them into these sad straits.

His efforts on their behalf had simply not been enough: he knew it and, what was worse, *they* knew it. For the Iroquois there was no answer. Everywhere in their lands now were the homes and towns and cities of the English. No longer was it, in the white man's eyes, the English who were the intruders, the encroachers, the unwanted. So numerous had these whites become that now it was the Iroquois—the Senecas and Mohawks, the Cayugas and Onondagas, the Oneidas and the Tuscaroras—who were the interlopers and who were thrust out of the way in righteous indignation at every turn.

For the Indians to the west, however, there was an answer, and that answer was war. The Ohio River was becoming the arena for scalpings and murders by both white men and red. The Ohio country itself was becoming the melting pot of displaced Indians; a place where they once again had an opportunity to sink roots and, with it, a great determination to let no white man ever again drive them away. But the white tide could not so easily be stopped.

For a lark, a party of disreputable frontiersmen, under two uncouth giants named Jacob Greathouse and Joe Tomlinson, blandly slaughtered the entire family of the Cayuga chief, Tal-gah-yee-tah, who was better known to the English as Chief Logan, son of Chief Shikellimus, a man who had always gone out of his way to aid and befriend the English. And Tal-gah-yee-tah, still more a Mingo than a Cayuga, swore revenge and was being aided in it by the Shawnees and the Delawares. He needed more help than this, however, against the organized attacks being launched against him, and he appealed to the Onondaga Council for official Iroquois support. The Iroquois chiefs and six hundred of their warriors came at once to Warraghiyagey.

At fifty-nine, William Johnson was very ill. Ravaged by syphilis, fevers and sundry diseases, he could walk only with difficulty, but he had not lost his sharpness of mind nor his almost lifelong concern for his Indian brothers.

The entire body of Indians assembled in the yard below his great house, Johnson Hall, some distance from the old Fort Johnson, and William moved slowly to the shade of a large arbor where he might address them without having to stand in the sweltering rays of the July sun.

"My Brothers," he told them, "no one can know better than you of my great love for you and of my chief desire, which is to see only better things happen for you. My heart grieves for you in the loss of your friend and mine, Chief Shikellimus, father of Tal-gah-yee-tah, and for the other members of the family, all of whom were murdered with the exception of Tal-gah-yee-tah himself. My heart grieves for you in this, and even more so in the forces which are rising up against all Indians in that quarter. I wish to tell you—"

He broke off abruptly and swayed. A giddiness was coming over him, a vertigo, an odd constriction in his stomach, a seeming compression of his heart. He grasped the edge of the arbor and clung there for a long moment while the assembled Indians stared with growing alarm. Then, straightening, he looked again at the multitude and smiled.

"My Brothers," he continued, "I am not able to go on at this time. Pipes, tobacco and liquor will be brought out now. I will—" His eyes widened and two aides rushed to him, each taking an arm, but he called to his audience loudly:

"Brothers! Whatever may happen, you must not be shaken out of your shoes!"

He then asked his aides to take him to his room and they did so. By the time they got him there, he seemed to have recovered himself somewhat. He poured himself some wine and water, drank it down and then, without assistance, sat down in an armchair, leaned his head back and closed his eyes.

In that moment the man who was both Warraghiyagey and Sir William Johnson died.

And as the sun slipped nearer the horizon and turned a deep blood-red, as if in omen of what was to come in that direction, the death wail erupted from six hundred Iroquois throats.

# PRINCIPAL SOURCES

AS the most important and extensive primary source of research for *Wilderness Empire,* I have leaned heavily in many instances—particularly in respect to dialogue—upon the *Sir William Johnson Papers.* Most of the papers still existing are now in the collection of the New York State Library at Albany. Part of these appeared in the *Documentary History of the State of New York,* edited by E. B. O'Callaghan and published in 1849, 1850 and 1851. More of the papers of William Johnson, gathered from British archives, were published in 1855 in *Documents Relative to the Colonial History of the State of New York.* Other documents and diaries of William Johnson pertaining to the years 1738 through 1760, and housed in the New York State Library, were transcribed but not published. Unfortunately, many of the original papers were lost in a fire which swept the state capitol in 1909. In 1921, the Division of Archives and History of the University of the State of New York began publication of the remaining collection under the title *Sir William Johnson Papers.* Under various editorships, this project was completed in 1957 and resulted in twelve volumes with a total of over four million words. Since that time a few other papers have turned up and these are now in a special collection in the New York State Library.

In the preparation of *Wilderness Empire,* however, these papers of William Johnson were not used to the exclusion of other sources. Francis Parkman's works, particularly his two-volume *Montcalm and Wolfe,* played an important part, as did *The American Journals of Louis Antoine de Bougainville, 1756-1760,* in presenting information by and about the

French, English and Indians whose activities are recorded in this work.

Beyond these, a great many other sources have been consulted and studied in depth, including many hundreds of letters, official documents, diaries, logbooks, journals, council reports, newspapers, unpublished manuscripts, personal narratives, depositions, theses, and dissertations. It would be impracticable here to make any attempt to list each source individually; therefore only the major authenticative sources for each chapter are provided in this bibliography. Exceptions are those sources of a minor nature which would not normally be individually listed but which substantiate some deviation from presently accepted historical fact, generally an error made by an early historian and then carried down through the years by other historians.

## CHAPTER I

Andrews, Matthew Page, *Virginia: The Old Dominion* (New York, 1937), 207-208.

Bassett, John Spencer, *The Writings of Colonel William Byrd* (New York, 1901), 391-392.

Beauchamp, William M., *Moravian Journals Relating to Central New York* (Syracuse, 1851), 134-135.

Colden, Cadwallader, *History of the Five Nations of Canada* (New York, 1902), Part One, xxxvi; Part Two, 86-87f., 106f.-108.

Coogan, John E., "The Eloquence of Our American Indians" (unpublished thesis, St. Louis University, 1923).

*Documentary History of the State of New York* (hereafter cited as *Documentary History . . .*), 10 vols., edited by E. B. O'Callaghan (Albany, 1849-51), II, 825, 946-947.

*Documents Relative to the Colonial History of the State of New York* (hereafter cited as *Documents Relative . . .*), 10 vols., edited by E. B. O'Callaghan (Albany, 1854), VI, 671, 741.

Dwight, Timothy, *Travels in New-England and New-York*, 3 vols. (New Haven, 1833), III, 164.

Flexner, James Thomas, *Mohawk Baronet: Sir William Johnson of New York* (New York, 1959), 9-22, 25-27, 33, 37-42, 118.

Fox, Edith Mead, *William Johnson's Early Career as a Frontier Landlord and Trader* (Ithaca, 1945), 1-32.

*Gentleman's Magazine*, 1756, XXV, 432.

Gipson, Lawrence Henry, *The British Empire before the American Revolution*, 6 vols. (New York, 1939-1957), V-64-112.

Grant, Anne, *Memoirs of an American Lady*, 2 vols. (New York, 1901), II, 58.

Hatcher, Harlan, *The Great Lakes* (New York, 1944), 122-123.

Henry, Alexander, *Travels and Adventures in Canada between the Years 1760 and 1776* (New York, 1809), 4f, 95-96.

Jones, Thomas, *History of New York, 3 vols.* (New York, 1879), II, 362-363.

Kinietz, W. Vernon, *The Indians of the Western Great Lakes, 1615-1760* (Ann Arbor, 1940), 3, 230, 319.

*London Magazine,* 1756, XV, 430-433.

Lydecker, John W., *The Faithful Mohawks* (Cambridge, England, 1938), 32, 37-40, 50.

Morison, Samuel Eliot, *The Parkman Reader* (Boston, 1955), 44-52, 57-58, 353-358.

*New York Gazette,* July 25, 1774, and July 31, 1731.

Parkman, Francis, *Montcalm and Wolfe,* 2 vols. (Boston, 1894), I, 20.

Peckham, Howard A., *Pontiac and the Indian Uprising* (Princeton, 1947), 9, 16, 18, 30, 31.

Simms, Jeptha R., *Frontiersmen of New York,* 2 vols. (Albany, 1882), I, 204, 310.

*Sir William Johnson Papers,* 12 vols. under various editors for the University of the State of New York (Albany, 1921-1957), I, 6, 44, 239, 384, 410-411; II, 9-22, 77, 898-900; III, 334-335; IV, 897-898; VIII, 922-923, 958; IX, 1.

Smith, James, *The Remarkable Occurrences of James Smith during his captivity with the Indians* (Cincinnati, 1870), 14-16.

Smith, Richard, *A Tour of Four Great Rivers* (New York, 1906), 19-23, 65-67.

Smith, William, *History of the Late Province of New York,* 2 vols. (New York, 1830), II, 31.

Stone, William L., Jr., *Life and Times of Sir William Johnson,* 2 vols. (Albany, 1865), I, 63, 485.

Swanton, John R., *Indian Tribes in North America* (Washington, 1953), 85-88.

Windsor, Justin, *Pageant of St. Lusson, Sault Ste. Marie, 1671* (Ann Arbor, 1892), 22-26.

Wissler, Clark, *Indians of the United States* (Garden City, 1966), 126-128.

Young, Arthur, *A Tour of Ireland* (London, 1780), 127-128.

## CHAPTER II

Andrews, Matthew Page, *Virginia,* 208-209, 212f., 234.

Bartram, John, *Observations . . . Onondaga, Oswego, and the Lake Ontario* (London, 1751), 41-42, 58-59.

Beauchamp, William M., *Moravian Journals,* 77.

Beauharnois, François, *The French Regime in Wisconsin* (Madison, 1881), 437-442.

Boyd, Julian P., *Indian Treaties Printed by Benjamin Franklin* (Philadelphia, 1938), 309-311.

Colden, Cadwallader, *Five Nations of Canada,* Pt. I, xxv, xxx; Pt. II, 216-221, 226-245, 255-259, 264.

————, *Letter Books,* 2 vols. (New York, 1887-1888), I, 94, 102-104; II, 364, 425-426, 432.

———, *Papers*, 9 vols. (New York, 1918-1923), III, 357, 364, 403-408, 425-426, 432; IV, 64.

Cotterill, R. S., *The Southern Indians: The Story of the Civilized Tribes Before Removal* (Norman, Okla., 1954), 28.

Cuneo, John R., *Robert Rogers of the Rangers* (New York, 1959), 7-9.

*Documentary History . . .* , II, 619-621.

*Documents Relative . . .* , VI, 314-315, 339-340, 343-344, 358-363, 372, 383-385, 389, 422-423, 437-452, 546, 619-621, 650-662, 714, 739-740, 859; VII, 714.

Flexner, James Thomas, *Mohawk Baronet*, 25-26, 40-41, 45, 48-94, 104, 112, 186.

Hatcher, Harlan, *Lake Erie* (New York, 1945), 45.

Howe, Henry, *Historical Collections of Ohio*, 2 vols. (Cincinnati, 1888), II, 426.

Kinietz, W. Vernon, *Indians of Western Great Lakes*, 3, 164.

Livingston, William, *Review of the Military Operations of North America* (New York, 1757), 25-27, 37-39.

Lydecker, John W., *The Faithful Mohawks*, 56-57.

Morison, Samuel Eliot, *The Parkman Reader*, 391-433.

*New York General Assembly (Colony) Journal*, n.e., 2 vols. (New York, 1766), II, 79-80, 124, 125, 130, 540.

*New York Journal*, November 24, 1746.

Parkman, Francis, *Montcalm and Wolfe*, I, 21, 37, 43, 53-54.

Peckham, Howard A., *Pontiac*, 32-37, 152.

*Pennsylvania Archives*, 1st series, 5 vols. (Philadelphia, 1852-1853), I, 751.

*Pennsylvania Colonial Records*, 10 vols. (Philadelphia, 1851-1852), V. 7-26.

Smith, William, *Province of New York*, II, 83, 100-101, 191.

*Sir William Johnson Papers*, I, 29-30, 40-43, 49, 52-54, 60-66, 73-74, 81-84, 93-96, 100-109, 111-119, 146-150, 161-165, 172, 177, 199-200, 898; II, 899; III, 483, 825, 993; IV, 166, 468; IX, 4-6, 8-31, 148.

Stone, William L., Jr., *Johnson*, I, 162-172; II, 481-484.

Stone, William L., Sr., *Life of Joseph Brant*, 2 vols. (New York, 1938), II, 354.

Wallace, Paul A. W., *Conrad Weiser* (Philadelphia, 1945), 226-228, 238.

## CHAPTER III

Andrews, Matthew Page, *Virginia*, 187, 208, 212f., 234.

Cotterill, R. S., *The Southern Indians*, 4.

*Documents Relative . . .* , VI, 532, 594; VII, 267.

Flexner, James Thomas, *Mohawk Baronet*, 25-26, 89-99, 99f., 100-107.

Galloway, William Albert, *Old Chillicothe* (Xenia, O., 1934), 202.

Howe, Henry, *Collections of Ohio*, II, 557-558, 597-599.

Kinietz, W. Vernon, *Indians of Great Lakes*, 3-4.

*Magazine of American History*, March, 1878, 57.

Parkman, Francis, *Frontenac and New France under Louis XIV* (Boston, 1894), 376.

Peckham, Howard A., *Pontiac*, 36-37.

*Pennsylvania Colonial Records*, V, 425, 482, 515-518, 522-523, 527-530, 547, 551-554.

Schweinitz, Edgar, *Life of David Zeisberger* (New York, 1891), 112f.

Wood, Norman B., *Lives of Famous Indian Chiefs* (Aurora, 1906), 122-123.


## CHAPTER IV


Andrews, Matthew Page, *Virginia*, 234.

Bigelow, John, *Works of Benjamin Franklin*, 5 vols. (New York, 1904), IV, 41f., 81.

Campbell, John W., *Biographical Sketches* (Columbus, O., 1838), 147.

Coogan, John E., "Eloquence of American Indians," 81.

*Documentary History . . .* , II, 621; II, 1039.

*Documents Relative . . .* , I, 463; VI, 490-491, 506, 515-517, 534, 777-778, 780; X, 186-188, 201-204, 246, 479.

Flexner, James Thomas, *Mohawk Baronet*, 108-114.

Hatcher, Harlan, *The Great Lakes*, 127.

Henry, Alexander, *Travels in Canada*, 80.

Howe, Henry, *Collections of Ohio*, II, 253, 593, 600-601.

*Magazine of American History*, XV, 256-257.

Parkman, Francis, *Montcalm and Wolfe*, I, 65-77, 61-85, 100, 110-111, 133-133f.

Peckham, Howard A., *Pontiac*, 37-38.

*Pennsylvania Archives . . .* , II, 14-24.

*Pennsylvania Colonial Records . . .* , V, 508-509, 598-599.

Piquet, François, *Mémoire sur le Canada 1749-1760* (Paris, 1771), 27-49, 52-58, 67-113.

Pouchot, Pierre, *Mémoire sur la dernière Guerre de l'Amérique septentrionale*, 2 vols. (Paris, 1781), I, 7-9; II, 143-144.

Roosevelt, Theodore, *The Winning of the West* (New York, 1902), I, 96.

*Royal Magazine*, 1759, I, 167.

*Sir William Johnson Papers*, I, 89, 197, 209, 220-223, 230-238, 253-254, 260-264, 266-268; IX, 81-85.

Tracy, William, *Indian Eloquence* (Madison, 1899), 456.


## CHAPTER V


Adams, R. G., *The Journal of Major George Washington* (New York, 1940), 25-28.

Andrews, Matthew Page, *Virginia*, 211-216.

Brooks, Edward Howard, "George Washington and the Fort Necessity Campaign" (unpublished thesis, June, 1947, Stanford University Library Collection), 31, 38-43, 45-56, 86-87, 90-92.

Claus, Daniel, *Narrative of His Relations with Sir William Johnson,* (New York, 1902), 3-7.

Darlington, W. McC., *Christopher Gist's Journals* (Pittsburgh, 1893), 82.

*Documentary History . . . ,* VI, 780, 806; X, 255, 273, 814, 835.

*Documents Relative . . . ,* VI, 521-526, 541-549, 559-560, 589-591, 604, 608-611, 715-726, 739, 778-779, 781-782, 797, 808-815, 853-899; VII, 840.

Dussieux, P., *Le Canada sous la Domination Française* (Paris, n.d.), 118.

Fitzpatrick, J. C., *The Diaries of George Washington, 1748-1799* (New York, 1925), I, 43-48, 55-59, 61, 65-67, 75, 84, 91-93.

Gipson, Lawrence Henry, *British Empire,* 53.

Hatcher, Harlan, *Lake Erie,* 126-127.

Headley, J. T., *Washington and His Generals,* 2 vols. (New York, n.d.), I, 5-6.

Hughes, Rupert, *George Washington* (New York, 1927), I, 52-56, 69-82, 97-99, 102.

Lumina, Poulin de, *Histoire de la Guerre contre les Anglais* (Paris, 1781), 15.

*Maryland Gazette,* March 7, July 25, and August 29, 1754.

Moreau, J. N., *Mémoire Contenant le Précis des Faits avec leurs Pièces Justificatives, pour Servir de Réponse aux Observations Envoyées par les Ministres d'Angleterre dans les Cours de l'Europe* (Paris, 1756), 110, 115-117.

Pargellis, S. McC., *Lord Loudoun in North America* (New Haven, 1933), 109.

Parkman, Francis, *Montcalm and Wolfe,* I, 87-89, 113, 128-133, 133f., 134-138, 143-150-150f., 151-151f., 152-155, 155f., 156-161, 171-172.

Peckham, Howard A., *Pontiac,* 38-39.

*Pennsylvania Colonial Records,* V, 607, 625-626; VI, 50, 150-152.

Pouchot, Pierre, *Mémoire,* I, 8.

*Sir William Johnson Papers,* I, 40-41, 179, 197-199, 205, 210, 242-245, 249, 257, 260-261, 270, 273-274, 276-282, 288-289, 295-296, 302-303, 306-307, 314-319, 324-327, 329, 333-334, 339-344, 381, 396-401, 405, 409-410, 426-427, 431, 433, 454-456, 616, 923-927, 931; IX, 57-58, 78-79, 123, 131-134, 142-145, 150-160.

Stephen, Captain Adam, *The History of an Expedition Against Fort Duquesne in 1755* (Philadelphia, 1855), 42-46, 46f., 47-60.

Stone, William L., Jr., *Johnson,* I, 393-394.

Toner, J. M., *Journal of Colonel George Washington* (Albany, 1893), 5f., 16-17, 17f.

Van Doren, Carl, *Benjamin Franklin* (New York, 1938), 209.

*Virginia Magazine of History and Biography,* January, 1894, vol. I, no. 3, 278-284.

Wallace, Paul A. W., *Conrad Weiser,* 304, 307-308, 323-331, 346, 351, 359, 373, 375-377.

## CHAPTER VI

Andrews, Matthew Page, *Virginia,* 222-224, 236.
Cuneo, John R., *Robert Rogers,* 17-18.
*Documents Relative . . . ,* VI, *passim,* 15, 141, 161, 368, 404, 480-482.
Drimmer, Frederick, *Scalps and Tomahawks* (New York, 1957), 372.
Fitzpatrick, J. C., *Diaries of Geo. Washington,* II, 68-93.
Flexner, James Thomas, *Mohawk Baronet,* 124-133.
*Gentleman's Magazine,* August 1755, 378, 462.
Grant, Anne, *Memoirs,* ch. VI.
Hamilton, Edward P., *Adventure in the Wilderness: The American Journals of Louis Antoine de Bougainville 1756-1760* (Norman, Okla., 1964), 7.
Hatcher, Harlan, *The Great Lakes,* 127-130.
Henry, Alexander, *Travels in Canada,* 80.
Howe, Henry, *Collections of Ohio,* I, 291, 299.
Moreau, J. N., *Mémoire . . . ,* 168, 267-269.
Pargellis, S. McC., *Lord Loudoun,* 253.
Parkman, Francis, *Montcalm and Wolfe,* I, 21, 181-183, 187, 191-201, 203-232, 234-284, 286-288, 320, 321-323, 366.
Peckham, Howard A., *Pontiac,* 40-46, 76.
*Pennsylvania Archives,* II, 294.
*Pennsylvania Colonial Records,* VI, *passim,* 15, 141, 161, 368, 404, 480-482.
Pouchot, Pierre, *Mémoire,* 25-37, 168.

## CHAPTER VII

*A Brief State of the Province of Pennsylvania* (London, 1755).
*A Brief View of the Conduct of Pennsylvania for the Year 1755* (London, 1756).
*A Prospective Plan of the Battle near Lake George, with an Explantation thereof, containing a Full, though Short, History of that Important affair, by Samuel Blodgett, occasionally at the Camp when the Battle was Fought* (London, 1757).
*A True and Impartial State of the Province of Pennsylvania* (Philadelphia, 1759).
*An Answer to an Invidious Pamphlet Entitled "A Brief State of the Province of Pennsylvania"* (London, 1755).
Andrews, Matthew Page, *Virginia,* 233.
Butterfield, Consul Willshire, *History of the Girtys* (Cincinnati, 1890), 6.
*Conduct of Major General Shirley, briefly Stated* (London, 1758).
Cuneo, John R., *Robert Rogers,* 19-32.
Flexner, James Thomas, *Mohawk Baronet,* 1, 134-152, 156-160.

Parkman, Francis, *The Conspiracy of Pontiac*, 2 vols. (Boston, 1894), II, 143, 152.

———, *Montcalm*, I, 228-230, 233, 284, 288, 293-299, 301-316, 320-326, 328-335, 378-391.

Peckham, Howard A., *Pontiac*, 46, 51.

*Pennsylvania Archives*, II, 485-487.

*Pennsylvania Colonial Records*, VI, 480, 584, 631-632, 682, 684, 692, 712-714, 734.

## CHAPTER VIII

*Account of Conferences Held and Treaties Made between Sir William Johnson, Bart., and the Indian Nations of North America* (London, 1756).

Andrews, Matthew Page, *Virginia*, 226-228.

*Boston Evening Post*, May 16, 1757.

Butterfield, Consul Willshire, *Girtys*, 7-15.

Claus, Daniel, *Johnson*, 20-21.

Cuneo, John R., *Robert Rogers*, 31-36, 40-45.

*Documentary History* . . . , I, 482; X, 700-703, 733-736.

*Documents Relative* . . . , VI, 44-74, 126, 134-150, 152-160; VII, 18, 54-71, 82-85, 94-107, 109-120, 130-161, 208-215; X, 421, 434, 445-453, 467, 477, 480-483, 680.

Flexner, James Thomas, *Mohawk Baronet*, 125-126, 161-164, 164f., 165-167, 171-172, 174-175.

Hamilton, Edward P., *Journals of Bougainville*, 8-9, 12-17, 24-29, 33-44, 50-51, 59-60.

Hatcher, Harlan, *Lake Erie*, 130-131.

*London Times*, October 28, 1865.

Lossing, Frederic, *Life of Schuyler*, 2 vols. (Albany, 1860), I, 131.

Morison, Samuel Eliot, *Parkman Reader*, 60.

*New York Gazette*, July 19, 1756.

*New York Mercury*, May 10, 1756.

Parkman, Francis, *Montcalm and Wolfe*, I, 330-332, 352, 360-380, 383-384, 388, 391-399, 405-414, 414f., 415-416, 420-430, 437-440, 459-463, 466-467.

———, *Pioneers of France in the New World* (Cambridge, 1865), 315.

Peckham, Howard A., *Pontiac*, 46, 201.

*Pennsylvania Archives*, II, 144, 744, 770, 775.

*Pennsylvania Colonial Records*, VII, 75-76, 88, 194, 232, 242, 257, 358-380.

Pouchot, Pierre, *Mémoire*, I, 67-81.

Putnam, Israel, "Report of a Scout to Ticonderoga in October, 1756," *Magazine of American History*, March 1882, XV, 257.

*Sir William Johnson Papers*, I, 266-268, 343-350, 388, 447, 468, 469, 486-488, 506-514, 537-538; IX, 404-416, 424-425, 430, 449-450, 491-492, 496-497, 548-555, 558, 574-581.

Smith, William, *New York*, Part II, 242.

Stone, William L., Jr., *Johnson*, II, 24, 24f.
Wallace, Paul A. W., *Conrad Weiser*, 450.

## CHAPTER IX

Atkin, Edmond, *Indians of the Southern Colonial Frontier*, 2 vols. (Columbia, S.C., 1954), I, xxxiv; II, 485.
*Boston Gazette*, August 15, 1757.
Cuneo, John R., *Robert Rogers*, 43-54.
*Documentary History* . . . , II, 737.
*Documents Relative* . . . , VII, 208-215, 222, 245, 254, 266, 276-279, 341; X, 672.
Flexner, James Thomas, *Mohawk Baronet*, 71-89, 177-183.
Gipson, Lawrence Henry, *British Empire*, VII, 65, 149.
Hamilton, Edward P., *Journals of Bougainville*, 146-175, 190-191, 332-334.
*Harper's New Monthly Magazine*, XCV, 1897, 51.
Lévis, François Gaston duc de, *Collection des Manuscrits du Maréchal de Lévis*, 12 vols. (Montreal, 1889), VII, 301; XI, 110-111.
*London Magazine*, 1757, 457.
Moreau, J. N., *Mémoire*, 71-89.
Parkman, Francis, *Montcalm and Wolfe*, I, 355, 440-451, 453-457, 477-489, 492-494, 496-503, 513, 515-575; II, 1-11, 429-431.
*Sir William Johnson Papers*, I, 81; II, 684-685, 719-725, 730-741, 748-761, 769; VI, 30-31; V, 760; IX, 640, 664-681, 684-688, 711, 796-799, 809-812, 815, 827-828, 839, 852-863; X, 672-674.
Smith, William, *New York*, II, 254.

## CHAPTER X

Andrews, Matthew Page, *Virginia*, 230-231, 231f.
Butterfield, Consul Willshire, *Girtys*, 17.
Cuneo, John R., *Robert Rogers*, 55-59, 79-80.
*Documents Relative* . . . , X, 708, 739-741, 787, 822-823, 893.
Flexner, James Thomas, *Mohawk Baronet*, 187-199.
Grant, Anne, *Memoirs*, 226-235.
Hamilton, Edward P., *Adventure*, 200-202, 204-205, 215-242, 260-261, 284-290.
Hatcher, Harlan, *Lake Erie*, 133-135.
Jones, Thomas, *New York*, II, 374-375.
Knox, John, *Historical Journal of the Campaigns in North America for the Years, 1757, 1758, and 1760* (Toronto, 1914), O, 148.
Lévis, François Gaston duc de, *Collection de Lévis*, II, 153; VII, 322-328.
*London Magazine*, 1758, 216.

Parkman, Francis, *Montcalm and Wolfe*, II, 52-82, 86-113, 121, 173.

Peckham, Howard A., *Pontiac*, 49-50.

*Pennsylvania Archives*, III, 474.

Pouchot, Pierre, *Mémoire*, I, 137, 145, 153-162.

*Sir William Johnson Papers*, II, 778, 791, 821-824, 840-844, 851-854, 858, 875, 889-890; III, 171-173; IV, 888-890; VIII, 130-131, IX, 21-25 874-875, 879-884, 894, 901-904, 937-941, 952-953; X, 43-48, 51-67.

Stone, William L., Jr., *Johnson*, I, 387f.

Volweiler, Albert T., *George Croghan and the Westward Movement* (Cleveland, 1926), 139, 210.

Wallace, Paul A. W., *Conrad Weiser*, 532-552.

## CHAPTER XI AND EPILOGUE

Amherst, Jeffrey, *Journal* (Chicago, 1931), 105-110, 147.

*Boston Post Boy*, December 3, 1759.

Butterfield, Consul Willshire, *Girtys*, 16-19.

*Documents Relative . . .*, VII, 378-395, 399, 402-403, 432; VIII, 479, 485; X, 990-992.

Drimmer, Frederick, *Scalps and Tomahawks*, 372.

Flexner, James Thomas, *Mohawk Baronet*, 198-199, 201-210, 346-347.

Galloway, William Albert, *Old Chillicothe*, 212-216.

Gipson, Lawrence Henry, *British Empire*, VII, 341-354.

Henry, Alexander, *Travels in Canada*, 3, 80.

Howe, Henry, *Ohio*, I, 910.

Jones, Thomas, *New York*, II, 373.

Knox, John, *Campaigns in North America*, I, 354; II, 32, 61-67, 151, 182-191; III, 21.

Lee, Charles, *Papers*, 3 vols. (New York, 1872), I, 21.

Long, John Cuthbert, *Lord Jeffrey Amherst* (New York, 1933), 71.

Mante, Thomas, *History of the Late War in North America* (London, 1772), 244.

"Memoirs of the Siege of Quebec," by Sergeant John Johnson of the Fifty-eighth Regiment; unpublished manuscript in New York State Library Collection, Albany.

Moreau, J. N., *Mémoire, 1749 jusqu' à 1760*.

*New York Weekly Mercury*, August 20, 1759.

Parkman, Francis, *Montcalm and Wolfe*, II, 21-37, 167-169, 174-180, 196-233, 238-239, 242-249, 296-310.

Peckham, Howard, *Pontiac*, 49-52.

Pouchot, Pierre, *Mémoire*, I, 8; II, 46-52, 58-59, 94, 105-106, 130, 161f., 171-191, 201-205.

*Sir William Johnson Papers*, II, 44-46, 182-191, 212; III, 19, 27-31, 38-46, 62-90, 106-113, 116, 128, 174, 271-272; VIII, 827.

Smith, R. B., *History of Canada* (Quebec, 1815), 88-143.
Stone, William L., Jr., *Johnson*, II, 374-378, 394-429.
Wood, Norman B., *Indian Chiefs*, 121-122.

# CHAPTER NOTES

These chapter notes have been placed at the rear of the book in order not to detract from the narrative flow, as so often occurs with footnotes. Though the reader may enjoy doing so, it is not *necessary* that he refer to this note section each time a supernumeral is given in the text. These are merely amplification notes and they are primarily intended for added interest; the narrative is not dependent upon them.

As much as possible, these amplification notes have been held to a minimum. In many cases they merely transpose the sixteenth-century locales of *Wilderness Empire* to modern-day landmarks, thus enabling the reader to acquire a better mental image of where the activity in question is occurring. However, there is also a certain amount of information included which, while it may not be directly germane to the narrative itself, is of such pertinence and interest tangentially that it should not be altogether omitted.

\* \* \*

## PROLOGUE AND CHAPTER I

1. Michilimackinac is pronounced Mish-ill-lah-mack-in-naw. It was located on the site of what is now Mackinaw City, Michigan.
2. The St. Ignace Jesuit mission was located on the site of present St. Ignace, Michigan.
3. Fort St. Joseph was located near the site of present Niles, Michigan.
4. The governor's correct full name and title of nobility was Louis de Buade, Comte de Frontenac et Palluau.
5. Chippewa and Ojibwa (or Ojibway) are names which signify the same tribe.
6. Pinpointed to present-day locations, these French forts were located as follows: Fort Miamis at the site of present Fort

Wayne, Indiana; Fort St. Louis near present North Utica, Illinois; Fort La Baye at the site of present Green Bay, Wisconsin; Fort La Pointe at the site of present La Point, Wisconsin, on Madeline Island; Fort Ouiatenon (pronounced Wee-ah-ten-on) near the site of present Lafayette, Indiana; and Fort de Chartres near the site of present Prairie du Rocher, Illinois.

7. There is a great deal of dispute regarding the year, place, and parentage of Pontiac's birth. Where year is concerned, 1720 is admittedly no more than a well-calculated estimate. He was a powerful chief considerably before his peak of prominence in 1763. At that time he was obviously a mature individual, yet still an active warrior in his prime. In his own words, he was actively engaging in warfare in 1746. Francis Parkman thought him to be about fifty years old at the siege of Detroit in 1763, but this is doubtful because comments of individuals during that siege indicate that he was a healthy, powerful man in his prime and probably in his early forties. Benson J. Lossing has stated unequivocally that he was born in 1720, and this was also the year stated by Dr. Cyrus Thomas in his sketch of Pontiac for the Smithsonian Institution's *Handbook of Indians North of Mexico*. Dr. Howard Peckham, director of the Clements Library at Ann Arbor, Michigan, and an esteemed historian, states in his book *Pontiac and the Indian Uprising* (p. 18), that "Certainly the year 1720 is more probable than 1713, and indeed Pontiac may have been born as late as 1725." Where place of birth is concerned, opinion is highly divergent. *Encyclopaedia Britannica* gives his birthplace as being on the Maumee River in what is now Ohio. A half-breed Miami chief called Peshewah (Wildcat), but known among whites as Jean Baptiste Richardville (1761-1841), reportedly knew Indians who had been associated with Pontiac. He claimed Pontiac was born on the Maumee River at the mouth of the Auglaize on the site of present Defiance, Ohio. But there is no evidence, documentary or archaeological, to show that any Ottawa band had settled on the Maumee until 1748, and Richardville (who also incorrectly claims that Pontiac's mother was a Miami Indian) may merely have desired to claim relationship with the famous chief; or he may simply have been mistaken, since it is quite true that Pontiac did live on the Maumee later on. Lossing claims Pontiac's birth to have been on the Ottawa River, but not only provides no authority for such claim, but does not clarify *which* Ottawa River: the Auglaize River in Ohio once went by that name and even today has a tributary called the Ottawa River. Perhaps Lossing meant the huge Ottawa River which is the boundary of Ontario and Quebec, but again there is question whether any Ottawas had settled along it before 1750. The most probably correct location of the birthplace was that given by Peckham, who says

(p. 16), after careful analysis of all known sources, "the great chief was probably born in the Ottawa Village which in 1718 was still on the north side of the Detroit River, but which before 1732 was moved across to the site of modern Walkerville, Ontario." Where parentage is concerned, the names of neither of Pontiac's parents has ever been found recorded and even their tribal affiliation is not terribly clear. Present Ottawa tradition gives his father as Chippewa and mother as Ottawa. A U.S. Indian interpreter, Henry Conner, stated that Pontiac's mother was Chippewa. The Indian Agent, Henry Schoolcraft, stated flatly, "Pontiac was an Ottawa by a Chippewa mother." Richardville, as mentioned, claimed she was a Miami. New York's Chief Justice William Smith in 1763, with no foundation for it, claimed that Pontiac was a Catawba captive of the Ottawas who subsequently became their chief, which is hardly likely. Pierre Chouteau (1758-1849) of St. Louis believed Pontiac to be a Nipissing. Francis Baby (son of Jacques Duperon Baby, who personally knew Pontiac very well at Detroit) told Francis Parkman (Parkman Papers, 27d p. 171) that he understood Pontiac belonged to a western tribe and had been adopted by the Ottawas. All these claims are no more than hearsay and may deliberately have been bandied about by the Ottawas themselves in a later effort to disown Pontiac. No person—with the single exception of Jacques Baby—who ever knew Pontiac personally, ever referred to him as anything except an Ottawa by birth. Since, among intertribal marriages of upper Great Lakes Indians, it was more the rule for the woman to go live with her husband's tribe than vice versa, and since Pontiac did indeed rise to leadership of the Ottawas while still enjoying considerable influence over the Chippewas, then the belief that Pontiac's father and mother were Ottawa and Chippewa respectively is probably correct.

8. Fort Oswego was built on the site of present Oswego, N.Y.
9. Originally established some two hundred years before, the Iroquois League had always been known as the Five Nations and was by far the most solidly based Indian confederacy in recorded North American history. When, in 1711, the Tuscaroras of the Carolinas embarked on a war against the whites to halt their encroachment, they were defeated and so decimated that extinction was a palpable threat. They appealed to the Iroquois League, through the Oneidas, for admittance to the League. After considerable counciling on the matter, the Iroquois permitted them to join the League in 1715 and establish their villages in northern Pennsylvania and adjacent New York. They were termed the adopted children or "nephews" of the Oneidas and, though given full membership, were not given the right to vote in League Councils. While many people still referred to the Iroquois as the Five Nations for a long time after this occasion, the cor-

rect term after 1715 (and the term that the Iroquois themselves used) is the Six Nations. Since this book deals with post-1715 events, the Six Nations is the term which will be used.

10. Fort Hunter was located at the site of present Fort Hunter, N.Y.

11. Pronounced Tee-ahn-tahn-tah-low-go. This village, located originally on the south bank of the Mohawk at the mouth of Schoharie Creek, was later moved directly across the river to the north bank, in order to be free of the too-close influence of Fort Hunter and to be better able to take advantage of the protection of William Johnson.

12. Onondaga was on the site of present Syracuse, New York.

13. The "Wyoming or Shamokin" referred to by Canassatego were the Wyoming Valley and the Shamokin Valley; the first being located at present Wyoming, Pennsylvania, between Scranton and Wilkes-Barre; the second being located along Pennsylvania's Shamokin River from the present city of Shamokin to the river's mouth on the Susquehanna River at present Sunbury, county seat of Northumberland County, Pennsylvania.

14. These sites were: Muskegon River, at the site of present Muskegon, Michigan; Grand River, at the site of present Grand Haven, Michigan; Grand Traverse, at the site of present Traverse City, Michigan; and L'Arbre Croche (meaning "crooked tree") near present Waugoshance Point, Michigan. In respect to this last location, see also Note 16, below.

15. The Hurons established their village on the site of present Sandusky, Ohio.

16. Milo Milton Quaife, in his edition of *Alexander Henry's Travels and Adventures in the Years 1760–1776*, states in a footnote on page 47 that L'Arbre Croche was located at the site of present Harbor Springs, Michigan, on the north shore of Little Traverse Bay. This is approximately thirty-two miles south by southwest of where Fort Michilimackinac stood. Yet, Alexander Henry consistently says they had to go west to get to L'Arbre Croche (though there were trails going both south and southwest from the fort) and that it was a one-day journey. Harbor Springs, no less than forty water miles (and one land portage) away from the fort, was at least a two-day journey. Quaife also calls Waugoshance by the name of Fox Point, yet present maps identify this point as still being called Waugoshance Point. L'Arbre Croche could not have been far from this point. Peckham states that L'Arbre Croche is present Cross Village, Michigan. Indeed, historical markers in that area claim the same. While this is more apt to be correct than Quaife's assertion, yet there is still a distinct likelihood that L'Arbre Croche was at neither of these locations but, instead, within just two miles of Waugoshance Point. Henry definitely states (pp. 95–96) that

the Ottawa village of L'Arbre Croche lay "about 20 miles to the westward of Michilimackinac on the opposite side of the tongue of land on which the fort is built." Henry also describes (p. 96) Waugoshance as being "distant 18 miles from Michilimackinac" and therefore within two miles of L'Arbre Croche. It is the author's firm conviction that L'Arbre Croche was located on the mouth of the stream which empties Neil Lake into Lake Michigan, the mouth of this stream being only two or three miles south of Waugoshance Point.

17. This route was roughly the same course to be followed later by the Erie Canal which was to help make New York the greatest city in America. The Onondaga River referred to here has since had its name changed to Oswego River.

18. The Reverend Henry Barclay in later years became the rector of New York's Trinity Church.

19. Later the tribes spread out considerably; but when the League was formed they were, indeed, in a relatively straight line, beginning with the Mohawks between present Utica and Albany, and ending with the Senecas, west of Seneca Lake and as far as Niagara Falls and the upper Allegheny River.

20. The wampum belts were not money, but rather a form of record-keeping; they were used for recording treaties, speeches, war declarations, etc. They were as such highly valued, but not in a monetary sense.

21. The whites who were versed in politics and government at this time had every reason to marvel at this form of Indian government which recognized the individual tribes as independent entities, yet united for mutual offense and defense. Actually, so admirable was the League's democratic form of government, that it is said, with some authority, that in 1744 when Connecticut and Pennsylvania were negotiating with the Indians to adjust land claims, an Oneida chief suggested to the colonial delegates that since the League had worked so well with the Iroquois, something similar might be established to govern the relations of the Colonies. A similar suggestion was made in Albany in 1755. Knowledge of the League's success, it is believed, strongly influenced the Colonies in their own initial efforts to form a union and later to write a constitution.

22. Pronounced War-rah-hee-yay-gie.

## CHAPTER II

1. Balcony Falls was located in present Rockbridge County, Va.
2. The Saratoga described here was on the site of present Schuylerville, New York, on the west bank of the Hudson River some eleven miles east of present Saratoga Springs.
3. The English population at this time, from Georgia to Maine,

was 1,160,000. The total French population in the rest of French-inhabited North America was only 55,000.

4. Shikellimus was the father of Tay-gah-yee-tah, the Indian who was to become known and revered by both Indians and whites as Chief Logan.

5. The Mohawks had orginally equalled the Seneca tribe as the most populous in the Iroquois League. But, since the Dutch first came to New York, followed by the English, the Mohawks were in closest contact with the whites. As a result, they were sooner and better armed than the other members of the League. For this they undertook the brunt of the League's fighting and, while the respect and glory they earned as warriors soared, they also wound up sacrificing the most men in battle. At this time their population hardly equalled that of the Tuscaroras.

6. Walter Butler, Jr., was the son of the late commandant of Fort Hunter who, in cahoots with Governor Crosby, had feloniously bought the Warrensburg tract from the Teantontalogo Mohawks.

7. Present Lake George, New York.

8. By this he meant the flight of the residents of Saratoga without putting up any defense whatever against the oncoming enemy.

9. The principal chief of the Miami tribe, Unemakemi's name was actually Unemakemi Quilehtse, which translated to Thunder Bug or Thunder Fly, meaning Dragonfly—the name derived from the rattle (or "thunder") of that insect's wings in flight. The French translated this to Demoiselle, also meaning Dragonfly, and it is as Chief Demoiselle that he is most often referred to in historical accounts. Later, as will be seen, the English named him "Old Britain" to honor him for his stand against the French.

10. Chief Aroghyidecker was known also, especially to his own people, as Nichus and, to the English, as Nichus Brant. He was the son of Sagayeanquarashtow, also known as Brant, who, like Tiyanoga, was one of the four Indian "kings" who had been taken to visit Queen Anne in London. Nichus was also father of Degonwadonti, also known as Molly Brant, who ultimately became the wife of William Johnson; and Nichus was also father of, at this time, a six-year-old son known by his father's name of Aroghyidecker as well as by his more comon Indian name of Thayendanegea—who grew up to become famous as Chief Joseph Brant.

11. Rumor was to circulate in years to come that William Johnson had sired no less than seven hundred children and perhaps as many as a thousand. Governor Clinton felt this to be somewhat of an exaggeration and personally declared that the real figure, though quite large, was probably not much over three hundred!

12. The company was incorporated by Lawrence Washington,

elder brother of George Washington. Governor Dinwiddie was a member, as were Philip Ludwell Lee and Thomas Ludwell Lee (both sons of the company's first president). Other members were Robert Carter II, Gawin Corbin, John Taylor and George Fairfax.

13. The present Loramie Creek.
14. Michikiniqua, who took principal leadership of the Miamis on the death of Unemakemi, was later to become famous as a great warrior who fought so well for the British against the Americans that he was given the rank of brigadier general in the British army. He was well known under the name the English had given him—Chief Little Turtle.
15. Near the site of present Piqua, Ohio.

## CHAPTER III

1. Actually, this place was first known as Taranto, but by 1749 the name had been corrupted to Toronto.
2. The site of present Ogdensburg, N.Y.
3. The site of present Kingston, Ontario.
4. At the site of present Buffalo, New York.
5. The present town of Portage, N.Y., about ten miles southwest of Dunkirk, N.Y.
6. Present Chautauqua Lake.
7. Site of present Celoron, New York.
8. Cassadaga Creek bears the same name today. Kanaouagon Creek is presently known as Conewango Creek.
9. Although he called the river in question La Belle Rivière, "the Beautiful River," which was the French name for the Ohio River, actually this stream was the Allegheny River, which, downriver about a hundred miles from here, joins the Monongahela to form the Ohio River at present Pittsburgh, Pennsylvania. The Allegheny River here was encountered by the party at the mouth of Conewango Creek, the site of present Warren, Pennsylvania.
10. California at this time was thought by the English and French to be an island.
11. The story that this Mohawk squaw was Caroline, Tiyanoga's niece, and that she also had two daughters by William Johnson, cannot be authenticated and is more than likely no more than an example of the gossip which constantly swirled about Johnson in regard to everything he did. In Johnson's will, this boy, known locally as "William of Canajoharie," was named as "young Brant, alias Keghneghtaga," and commonly known as Brant Johnson in later life. Although he was very probably some relation to Molly Brant, who was to be Johnson's greatest love, Molly was not Tagchuento's mother, since she herself was only a child when Brant Johnson was born.
12. Site of present Franklin, Pennsylvania.

13. Present East Sandy Creek.

14. Site of present Kittanning, Pennsylvania.

15. This Chiningué is not to be confused with another village of the same name, called Shenango by the English, located on the Allegheny.

16. Site of present Wheeling, West Virginia.

17. Site of present Marietta, Ohio. Here, forty-nine years later, on August 2, 1798, two boys discovered the plate while swimming in the river. It had been partially exposed by rainstorms which had worn away the bank. They knocked it down with a long stick, melted half of it into bullets and then gave what remained to a neighbor from Marietta who, having heard about the mysterious relic engraved in a foreign tongue, came to rescue it. It is now in the possession of the American Antiquarian Society.

18. Now known as the Great Kanawha River, which empties into the Ohio River at Point Pleasant, West Virginia.

19. Site of present Portsmouth, Ohio.

20. The mouth of this river is near the site of present Cincinnati, Ohio. A hill overlooking it at the point is now a public park called Shawnee Lookout.

21. The Stillwater River, the Mad River and Wolf Creek. The site of these junctions is presently within the city limits of Dayton, Ohio.

22. Near the site of present Fort Loramie, Ohio.

23. The site of present Toledo, Ohio.

24. Actually, Bonnecamp's figure was remarkably accurate under the circumstances, as the distance actually traveled was approximately 2,400 miles.

25. Site of present Louisville, Kentucky.

26. Site of present Big Bone, Kentucky, where abundant fossilized remains of mastodons and other prehistoric creatures have been found.

27. This tract took in the site of present Syracuse, New York.


## CHAPTER IV


1. Site of present Franklin, Pennsylvania.

2. This island is now known as Wolfe Island.

3. The tribe he speaks of as Mississaugas were actually Mississaugis, an offshoot of the Chippewas, who were often referred to as the Mississaugi Chippewas.

4. Site of present Rochester, New York.

5. Site of present Sodus Bay, New York, about halfway between Rochester and Oswego.

6. The Flatheads referred to were actually Choctaws.

7. The Dog Tribe was another name for the Cherokees.

8. The site is five miles above the present capital city of Pennsylvania, Harrisburg.

9. The site of present Fort Hunter, Pennsylvania.

10. It is erroneously stated by Theodore Roosevelt in *The Winning of the West,* Vol. I, p. 96, that Simon Girty, Sr., was tortured at the stake and finally tomahawked to death by an Indian infant held up by his father for this purpose. This death is evidently confused with the subsequent death of John Turner at the hands of the Delaware Indians.

11. The governor of Canada, the Marquis de la Jonquière, died on March 6, 1752, as officially noted by Intendant Bigot in his letter to the colonial minister dated May 6, 1752, rather than on May 17, as is recorded in *Mémoires sur le Canada, 1749–1760.*

12. Miami-of-the-Lake was another name for the Maumee River; a literal translation of the Indian name for the stream, which was Omee Wi-theepi.

13. Greenville Creek and the Stillwater River in Miami County, Ohio, near the site of the present town of Covington.

14. A ceremonial peace pipe carved of a red clay which is quite malleable when first removed from the earth but dries to stone hardness.

15. The Oneidas referred to themselves as the Onioto-people. The Rising Sun people signified the Mohawks, who were the farthest east of the Six Nations, in the direction of the rising sun; just as the Senecas, being the farthest west of the Iroquois League tribes, were called the Setting Sun people.

16. All dates after this day are given in the new style. All dates prior to this date are old-style dates. In other words, though our modern calendars show George Washington as having been born on February 22, he was actually born on February 11.

17. Presently called Charlotte Creek.

18. Site of present Johnstown and Gloversville, New York.

## CHAPTER V

1. Site of present Erie, Pennsylvania.

2. Present French Creek.

3. Conrad Weiser, Pennsylvania's Indian Supervisor, later insisted that this was a rigged affair between Tiyanoga and Johnson and that the argument, the threats, and the walk-out were all part of an elaborate plan to force colony officials to fall back on Johnson for help and thus, in effect, admit that he was the only person who could help them. And there is good evidence to back up this contention. It would not be the first time Johnson and Tiyanoga had engaged in such games.

4. The Erighs—or Eries—were a tribe which orginally inhabited northwesternmost Pennsylvania. For harboring an enemy of the Iroquois, the Six Nations annihilated them—every man, woman, and child being slain, the tribe was wiped out of existence. Lake of the Erighs is, of course, Lake Erie.

5. The name of the fort was taken from the name of the stream, which was called Le Boeuf Rivière (present French Creek). It meant Fort of the Cattle or Beef and undoubtedly the river had been named Beef River because of the herds of buffalo—"forest beef" as they were called—which moved through the area.

6. Actually, the Allegheny River is meant.

7. Present Beaver River.

8. Much to-do has been made by many historians over the fact that although it was Washington who fell into the icy water, it was Gist who wound up with frozen hands and feet; the implication being that Washington was hardier than the seasoned frontiersman Gist, and that this was some sort of comeuppance for frontiersmen in general. This, of course, is patently unfair. Had not Gist, at the expense of getting so frozen, taken care of Washington as he did, the latter would almost certainly have died of exposure—a fact that George Washington himself later admitted.

9. Near the site of present Uniontown, Pennsylvania.

10. There is considerable disparity between English and French accounts of this engagement (and others). The French contend that Jumonville's mission was a peaceable one and that he was merely trying to deliver the order for Washington's army to get out of the country. Yet, Contrecoeur had given specific orders for Jumonville to send him two men as soon as the strengths and weaknesses of Washington's force had been determined. As Francis Parkman declares in *Montcalm and Wolfe,* Vol. I, pp. 148–149, "It is difficult to imagine any object for such an order except that of enabling Contrecoeur to send to the spot whatever force might be needed to attack the English on their refusal to withdraw." Jumonville had sent the couriers, and had hidden himself, apparently to await the result. He lurked nearly two days within five miles of Washington's camp, sent out scouts to reconnoiter it, but gave no notice of his presence; played to perfection the part of a spy, and brought destruction on himself by conduct which can only be ascribed to either a very sinister motive or else gross folly. French deserters told Washington that the party had, in fact, come as spies, and were to show the summons from Contrecoeur only if threatened by a superior force. This last assertion is confirmed by the French officer, Pierre Pouchot, who says that Jumonville, seeing himself the weaker party, tried to show the letter he had brought. French writers say that, on first seeing the English, Jumonville's interpreter called out that he had something to say to them; but Washington, who was at the head of his men, brands this to be absolutely false. The French say further that Jumonville was killed in the act of reading the summons. This is also denied by Washington, and rests only on the assertion of the Canadian who ran off at the

outset, and on the alleged assertion of Indians (with the French party) who, if present at all (which is unlikely, or Monakaduto would have known of it) escaped before the affray even began. Druillon, an officer with Jumonville, wrote two letters to Dinwiddie after his capture, to claim the privileges of the bearer of a summons; but while bringing forward every other circumstance in favor of the claim, he does not pretend that the summons was read or shown either before or during the action. The further assertion of Abbé de l'Isle-Dieux, that Jumonville showed a flag of truce is entirely unsupported and no other reporter of the event ever made any such claim. In 1755, the widow of Jumonville received a pension of one hundred and fifty francs and, twenty years later, Jumonville's daughter, Charlotte Aimable, wishing to become a nun, was given by the King six hundred francs for her trousseau upon entering the convent.

11. The term Onontio (sometimes Onioto) was the designation given by the Indians to the King of France.

12. This information appeared in the original *Journal de Villiers*, but was omitted in the copy of this journal as printed by the French government. Another short and very inaccurate abstract of this journal can be found in *Documents Relative to the Colonial History of the State of New York*, Vol. X.

## CHAPTER VI

1. Pucksinwah, chief of the Kispokotha Sept of the Shawnee tribe, was chief of the village of Kispoko on the Scioto River of Ohio, and war chief of the entire tribe. He was also, in thirteen more years, to become the father of a boy who would become one of the most memorable Indian chiefs in history, Tecumseh. Catahecassa—called Black Hoof by the English—was third principal chief of the Shawnees, under Hokolesqua and Black Fish. White Eyes was a sept chief and the war chief of the Delawares.

2. Mingo was not actually a tribe. Rather, it was the designation of a loose confederacy of Indians—Delawares and Senecas first, but later joined by Cayugas and Shawnees—who continued to live in the Fort Duquesne area.

3. Dumas, however, claims the plan as his own, and declares that Beaujeu adopted the plan at his suggestion. (*Dumas au Ministre, 24 Juillet 1756.*)

4. Tumbrils were high, two-wheeled supply carts, generally drawn by only one horse. Coehorns (or, more modernly, cohorns) were small bronze mortars capable of lobbing rather light explosive shells a fair distance. They were mounted on a block of wood with handles on each side for carrying. The weapon was invented in 1704 by the Dutchman, Baron Menno van Coehoorn.

5. There is considerable question as to whether or not this was

what Braddock had actually ordered Dunbar to do. The character of the dying man was such that it is almost inconceivable to consider him giving anything more than an order to get the supplies loaded and fall back to Fort Cumberland to make a stand there. There were unsupported rumors that later Dunbar privately admitted that such was the case, but no real documentary proof of the claim has ever come to light.

## CHAPTER VII

1. Site of present Rome, N.Y.
2. As mentioned earlier, the Onondaga River is now the Oswego River.
3. This school was founded and became the present Williams College.
4. Site of present Fort Edward, N.Y.
5. The remainder, some of whom had gotten lost, straggled in during the next two weeks.
6. Not the same as the Wood Creek at the Great Carrying Place on the upper Mohawk River portage toward Oswego.
7. Not on the site of the present city of Crown Point, N.Y., but rather some six miles to the north of there, on the northward-jutting Crown Point peninsula where the upper portion of Lake Champlain meets the main portion and where the lake is its narrowest, directly opposite Chimney Point, Vt.
8. Although the French continued to call that body of water Lac St. Sacrement, to avoid the confusion of two names for the same body of water the name Lake George is hereafter used.
9. This little body of water is now called Bloody Pool.
10. These figures were early ones, and though no positive loss figure is known, Parkman sets the accepted figure at two hundred sixty-two killed, wounded, and missing.
11. The French in their own accounts set their loss at two hundred twenty-eight.
12. This creek retains the same name today; the forted house was located on the site of present Millersburg, Pennsylvania.
13. Though John Turner had continued living with the Girty family after Simon Girty, Sr. was killed, it was not until fourteen months after Girty's death that Turner married Girty's widow, Mary. Turner thereupon became step-father to the Girty brothers, Thomas, Simon, James and George. John and Mary Turner had one child of their union, named John, and born about a year after they were married.
14. Near the site of present Loyalton, Pennsylvania.
15. John Harris, initially a trader, settled on the east bank of the Susquehanna at a fording place in 1726. In 1753, his son began operating a ferry here and the settlement which grew as a result of it became known as Harris's Ferry. In

1785 the younger Harris laid out a town which was known as—and still is—Harrisburg. It became the capital of Pennsylvania in 1812.

16. The Quakers were not, however, too consistent in their assertions of peacefulness. When they felt their own interests threatened, they were not against arming themselves with rifles and preparing to do battle, as was the case a few years after this when, heated with party passion and excited by reports of the forceable entry of angered Presbyterian border people, the Quakers donned their black broad-brimmed hats, shouldered their muskets and marched through the streets of Philadelphia.

## CHAPTER VIII

1. Site of present Rome, New York.
2. French accounts place the English dead in this attack at sixty to eighty. Most English claims say twenty-nine, neglecting to count the twelve wagon soldiers who were slain. At this time, too, there was a mass desertion of twenty-seven private soldiers from nearby Fort Williams, none of whom was ever apprehended or ever seen again, and it is a good possibility that they were destroyed by Léry's force, which would account for the larger claim by the French. Suffice to say that in addition to perhaps twenty-five scalps retained by the Oswegatchie Indians, the Canadians brought back to Montreal with them a total of thirty-nine scalps. Some historians have claimed that the scalps were divided—that is, cut in half to make two scalps out of one (a practice in which the Indians sometimes engaged to make those at home think their victory even greater) but, all things taken into consideration, the author does not believe such was the case on this occasion. There were probably a total of sixty-eight killed.
3. Villiers got his orders from Vaudreuil on May 28, 1756.
4. This skirmish marks one of those occasions where both sides claimed victory. Exaggerations are great on either side and it is difficult to determine who "won," if anyone did. Certainly the French aim to cut communications with Fort Oswego was not successful. Equally, the English loss was probably greater than the French. Estimates of the size of Villier's attacking force have been given as 400, 500, 600 and 800. The English loss is given as 800, 900, 400, 500, 300, and 60 to 70. The last figure is the most nearly correct. The loss on the side of the Canadians and Indians is impossible to determine, but was probably somewhere between 20 and 40.
5. The stream entering Lake Champlain at Vergennes, Vt.
6. Bougainville makes the common error of the time of calling the Iroquois the Five Nations. To avoid confusion, this has been changed to Six Nations where called for.

7. Twelve arpents is equivalent to 10.2 acres.
8. A minot is slightly over a bushel.
9. The brother of Neyon de Villiers, whose name is Coulon de Villiers, is at this same time commandant of Fort Frontenac. Confusion often results between the two in historical records.
10. Kittanning is the present name of the city at this location.
11. Present Sackett's Harbor, New York.
12. Present Wolfe Island.
13. A fascine was a long cylndrical bundle of sticks used for filling ditches so they could more easily be crossed, or they were sometimes used for strengthening ramparts. A gabion was a hollow, basketlike, bottomless, wickerwork cylinder which was carried to wherever men would be exposed to rifle fire. Here it would be stood on end and filled with earth to form a shelter from behind which a soldier might fire in relative protection. An abatis was a defensive obstacle very difficult to surmount. It was formed by felling trees and securing the trunk ends toward the place to be defended and the branch ends pointing toward the enemy. Most often these branch ends were then trimmed to sharp points. The abatis was, in effect, the forerunner of barbed-wire coils on modern battlefields.
14. On June 27, 1756, the sloop *Ontario* had been captured by French vessels out of Fort Frontenac.
15. There is considerable disparity in most historical accounts regarding the numbers of the English garrisoning the forts of Oswego, Ontario and George immediately prior to the battle. The figure given of seven hundred effective men and seven hundred made ineffective because of disease has been arrived at only after careful study of a multitude of documents. In his Journal, Bougainville says ". . . about 1,700 prisoners. About 80 English killed and about 30 of ours." However, neither he nor Montcalm mentions the following massacre by the Indians and Canadians which, according to best available reports, resulted in the deaths of between 80 and 100 individuals. Nor were the 100 women on hand figured in either French or English accounts, unless Bougainville lumped them with his total of 1,700 prisoners. Whether or not the crews of the vessels under Captain Broadley were included is a moot point. Governor Vaudreuil claimed the surrender of 1,600 English, "which included sailors, laborers and women" and this has the earmarks of being a very accurate figure. Some English accounts, otherwise trustworthy, claim the English loss in dead was less than 50. Shirley said the garrison, exclusive of civilians, did not exceed at the utmost, 1,400. And in the published *Conduct of Major-General Shirley Briefly Stated*, the number is set at 1,050. There are also a number of separate reports which corroborate the fact that in order to stop the massacre, Montcalm was forced to give up to the Indians some fifteen or twenty

English privates who would supposedly be adopted to replace warriors recently killed, but since these were never heard of again, it is safe to assume (if it is true that they were given to the Indians) that they were killed as soon as they were away from the influence of Montcalm.

16. These signs were written and placed by Captain Bougainville.

17. Bougainville, in his Journal, sometimes refers to this lake as Lake George, other times by its previous name, Lac St. Sacrement. The name Lake George has been used throughout to avoid confusion.

18. A redoubt is a separate, enclosed defensive construction, usually of a temporary nature.

19. The Falls of Lake George are in the Ticonderoga Narrows.

20. One of his officers was Captain Hugh Mercer (later Colonel) who was no relation to the recently killed Colonel Hugh Mercer of Fort Oswego.

21. Near the present junction of Cattaraugus Creek and South Branch, about three miles southeast of present Gowanda, N.Y.

22. Near the site of present Chillicothe, Ohio.

23. Pronounced Go-shock-gunk. On the site of present Coshocton, Ohio, a corruption of the Delaware name for the original village.

24. Meaning: "When you are fortunate, you will have many friends. If conditions are gloomy, you will be alone."

25. Near present Williamsport, Washington County.

26. German Flats was located on the site of the present Herkimer, New York.

27. Musquetoons were large mounted blunderbusses. Patereroes were very small cannon.

28. In England, William Shirley very nearly got court-martialed for treason. He was subsequently exonerated and given the appointment of governor of the Bahamas. He finally returned to America and died at Roxbury, Massachusetts, on March 24, 1771.

## CHAPTER IX

1. When or where William Johnson became infected with syphilis is not known. It could have been any one of a thousand or more women, Indians and whites, with whom he engaged in sexual intercourse. He wrote to his friend and former aide, Peter Wraxall, about this time of his illness—not only the fever and cough, but equally the syphilis. Wraxall replied: "I thank God the pain in your breast is removed. I hope your cough will soon follow. As to the rest, you deserve the scourge, and I won't say I pity you." (*Sir William Johnson Papers*, I, 472–473.)

2. Present Five Mile Point.

3. Thomas Brown survived his wounds and was subsequently liberated and wrote an accurate journal of his experiences, entitled: *A Plain Narrative of the Uncommon Sufferings . . . of Thomas Brown*.

4. Both Rogers in his *Journal* and Francis Parkman in *Montcalm and Wolfe*—along with Abercromby in his correspondence—refer to Captain Thomas Speakman as Captain Thomas Spikeman. Military records and his personal correspondence, however, indicate that Speakman is the correct spelling. In this fight, as usual, there is much divergence between French and English estimates as to the number which took part on both sides in the battle and the number killed, wounded or captured. Vaudreuil claimed that his forces were composed of 89 regulars and 90 Canadians and Indians, and that 40 English were left dead on the field of battle, while only three reached Fort William Henry alive. This latter comment undoubtedly arises from the fact that Stark and two men arrived back at the fort first for help to go after Rogers and the others. Private Brown in his narrative says of the French losses: "as I learnt after I was taken, we Killed more of the Enemy than we were in Number." This would set the French-Canadian-Indian loss at higher than 74. Vaudreuil admits to 37 of his men being killed or wounded. In light of all the original reports—Vaudreuil's, Rogers's Bougainville's, Brown's, Abercromby's, Montcalm's, Stark's, Malartic's, Eyre's, Montreuil's—plus those of Parkman and later historians, I have selected the figure of "close to fifty" in addition to the seven slain prisoners as being a reasonable estimate.

5. "His own liking leads each on" — Vergil.

6. Principal chief of the Nipissings.

7. Principal chief of the Algonkins.

8. The impression is given in practically all accounts that the Iroquois League had now become allied to the French. This is not true. A certain number of small Iroquois parties and individual villages did lend themselves to active French support, but most of these Iroquois on hand now were actually Caughnawagas and divergent Senecas and Onondagas who had gathered at Abbé Piquet's La Présentation mission at the mouth of the Oswegatchie. The official stand of the Iroquois League was still one of neutrality, with support of neither English nor French.

9. Since the French flag was white, a red flag was used as a truce symbol so there could be no possibility of confusion.

10. The glacis, a standard defensive works, was an artificial earthwork which sloped downward toward the fort from some distance out so as to expose any attackers who might try to

approach to the downward fire of the defenders on the ramparts.

11. Montcalm's camp was located some distance to the north and west of the fort, while the encampment was south and east of it. The two camps were the better part of a mile in separation.

12. Now Old Town, Maine.

13. It is stated in a dubious source that two French grenadiers were wounded and one killed in this incident, but no other report has ever claimed such to be the case.

14. A Connecticut soldier who was present stated that Frye killed one Indian who barred his way, but Frye himself makes no mention of it in his report.

15. "Ah! Flee the cruel lands, flee the cruel shore."—Vergil.

## CHAPTER X

1. No definite identification of the disease which afflicted General Forbes has ever been recorded, but signs seem to point to some form of intestinal malignancy.

2. Present Bedford, Pennsylvania.

3. Since then named Rogers Rock.

4. Now called Mount Defiance.

5. Again there is much difference between the French and English reports in regard to dead, wounded, and missing. The French consistently exaggerate the total strength of the English and the English battle losses. The French claim here for the English a total strength from as few as 20,000 to as many as 31,000, and they claimed the English dead to be in the neighborhood of 4,000, although the reports vary in the number of dead lying before the abatis from a low of 800 to a high of 3,000. The total figure given by Abercromby to Pitt in his report of July 12 gives the following breakdown:

    464 dead—regular officers and men
     87 dead—provincial officers and men
     29 missing—regular forces
      8 missing—provincial forces
  1,117 wounded—regular officers and men
   239 wounded—provincial officers and men
  ―――――
  1,944 total in English dead, wounded and missing.

6. "Nabby" was at this time the nickname for Abigail, and hence a most derogative term when applied to Abercromby.

7. Built on the site of present Rome, N.Y.

8. Putnam, who was to become a famed major general in the Continental Army, was badly mistreated by the Indians, but was finally surrendered to Montcalm at Fort Carillon and later included in an exchange of prisoners.

9. Presently called Beaver River.

10. This post was established on the site which subsequently became Fort Ligonier and, finally, present Ligonier, Pennsylvania.

11. Present Grant's Hill in Pittsburgh, Pennsylvania.

12. "Poor King, Poor France, dear country!"

13. Forbes lived to reach Philadelphia in January and managed to hang on to life until March, when he died and was buried in the chancel of Christ Church, with military honors.

## CHAPTER XI AND EPILOGUE

1. Kispoko Town was located just across the Scioto River from the Pickaway Plains, about midway between present Circleville and Chillicothe, Ohio.

2. Chief Old Belt was apparently referring to the sea mink, a large minklike animal of the eastern seaboard which became extinct before Europeans came to North America.

3. This was a threat the Iroquois frequently used to intimidate tribes or individuals who would oppose them—all of whom knew well through tales handed down from generation how the Erighs were exterminated by the Iroquois for sheltering the Hurons, with whom the Iroquois were at war.

4. If Montcalm actually did leave such documents in the hands of Father Roubaud, it was an unfortunate choice of men by Montcalm. Roubaud soon proved himself to be a man with little honor. The papers in question were not relayed to France, and Roubaud himself renounced the Jesuit order and his own Catholic faith, deserted his country and took asylum with the English. When later he was questioned at intervals about the existence of the papers Montcalm had allegedly given him, he gave a variety of inconsistent and considerably contradictory replies. At one questioning he asserted that his enemies and the enemies of Montcalm had discovered the papers among his—Roubaud's—effects at the mission of St. Francis and burned them to keep them from falling into French governmental hands. Later he asserted that he had given the King of England certain letters of Montcalm's. At still another time he gave the impression that the story of the letters was a figment of the imagination and that in truth they never existed. Whatever the case, the alleged letters or documents have never been found. Nevertheless, Bigot, Vaudreuil, Cadet, Péan and others—many others—involved in the corruption which ultimately resulted in the loss of Canada, were brought to trial in France. With

the single exception of Vaudreuil—who was freed for lack of evidence—all were given severe sentences and imprisoned in the Bastille.

5. Near present Cleveland, Ohio.

# LIST OF INDIAN CHARACTERS

In the following identification key, the Indian characters in *Wilderness Empire* are listed alphabetically by tribe, with the meaning of the tribal name given, if known. Also included are other names the individual was known by, his tribal rank and his family relationship where pertinent. In cases where the Indian name may be difficult to pronounce, a phonetic pronunciation is given.

## THE ABNAKI TRIBE

(The name of this tribe, which was formerly Wabanaki, means "People-Living-in-the-East" or, simply, "Easterners.")

PANAOUSKA [Pah-nah-OOS-kah]. War chief of the Abnakis; village chief of Penobscot.

## THE ALGONKIN TRIBE

(The name of this tribe means "One Who-Spears-Fish-[or Eels]-from-the-Bow-of-a-Canoe.")

AOUSSIK [OW-sik]. Principal chief of tribe; chief of the village at Two Mountains Lake on the Ottawa River.

KANECTAGON [Kah-NEK-tuh-gahn]. War chief of the Algonkin Tribe.

## THE CATAWBA TRIBE

(Significance of tribal name is unknown.)

CHIK-O-GEE. A chief of the tribe.

COLONEL BULL. Another name for Chik-o-gee, given to him by the English.

## THE CAUGHNAWAGA TRIBE

(Significance of tribal name unknown, but may have been adopted from the name of the river upon which they settled after separating from their parent tribe, the Mohawks.)

IPTOWEE [Ip-TOW-ee]. Principal chief of the tribe; village chief of Caughnawaga town.

## THE CAYUGA TRIBE

(Significance of name unknown. One of the six tribes of the Iroquois League.)

LOGAN. English name for Tal-gah-yee-tah.

SACANGHTRADEYA [Suh-KAHN-trah-DAY-ah]. A chief of the tribe.

SHIKELLIMUS [Sheh-KELL-ee-muss]. Principal chief of the tribe; father of Tal-gah-yee-tah.

TAL-GAH-YEE-TAH. Chief of Cayuga faction which joins Mingo confederation; called Logan by the English; son of Shikellimus.

## THE CHIPPEWA TRIBE

(The name of this tribe means "People-Who-Roast-Until-Puckered," referring to the tribal practice of heating newly made moccasins over a fire to cause the seams to pucker. This tribe also known as the Ojibwa Tribe.)

LE GRAND SAULTEUR. French name for Minivavana.

MINIVAVANA [Min-ah-vah-VAN-ah]. Principal chief of the tribe.

## THE DELAWARE TRIBE

(The name of this tribe is derived from the Delaware River, in turn derived from Lord Delaware, early Virginia governor. The tribe referred to itself as the Lenni Lenape, which means "True Men.")

BEAVER. A village chief.

CAPTAIN JACOBS. English name for Tewea.

CAPTAIN PETER. English name for Tollema.

CAPTAIN PIERRE. French name for Tollema.

DELAWARE GEORGE. English name for a Delaware village chief. Indian name unrecorded.

EAGLE CLAW. English name for Delaware warrior. Indian name unrecorded.

EI-SAKS-TEHL [I-sax-TELL]. A subchief of the tribe.

(THE) FISH. English name for No-me-tha.

ISAAC STILL. English corruption of the name of the subchief Ei-saks-tehl.

NEMACOLIN [NEE-muh-COH-lin]. A chief of the tribe.

NO-ME-THA. Warrior from village of Kittanning; brother of Chief Tewea.

PIMOACAN. [Pi-MO-AH-can]. A chief of the tribe.

PIPE. English name for a chief of the tribe. Indian name unrecorded.

RED MINK. English name for Tollema.

SHINGAS. [SHIN-gess]. A Delaware village chief.

TEEDYSCUNG [TEE-dee-skung]. Self-proclaimed Delaware prophet, without official tribal standing.

TEWEA [Tuh-WEE-ah]. Chief of the village of Kittanning; brother of the warrior No-me-tha.

TOLLEMA [Toe-LEE-muh]. A chief of the tribe.

WHITE EYES. War chief of the Delawares; chief of a Delaware sept.


# THE HURON TRIBE

(The name of the tribe is derived from the French *hure,* meaning "rough." The tribe split almost in half and the new segment formed became known as the Wyandot tribe, with the name Wyandot— or Guyandot—meaning "Dwellers-on-the-Island" or "Peninsula-Dwellers.")

ATHANASE [ATH-uh-NACE]. Chief of the village of Catholic-converted Hurons at Lorette, northwest of Quebec.

NICOLAS. French name for Orontony.

ORONTONY [Oh-RON-tun-nee]. Chief of a Huron village.


# THE MIAMI TRIBE

(The name of this tribe means "People-of-the-Pigeons," referring to the great flocks of passenger pigeons which nested near their villages.)

COLD FOOT. English name for a village chief. Indian name not recorded.

DEMOISELLE. French name for Unemakemi.

LITTLE TURTLE. English name for Michikiniqua.

MICHIKINIQUA [Mish-ee-KIN-ee-kwah]. Principal chief of the tribe; successor of Unemakemi.

OLD BRITAIN. English name for Unemakemi.

UNEMAKEMI [U-nuh-MOCK-uh-me]. Principal chief of the tribe. Predecessor of Michikiniqua.


# THE MISSISSAUGI TRIBE

(Actually a subtribe of the Chippewas, but with increasing autonomy as time passed until it became virtually a tribe of itself. Often called Mississaugi Chippewas. Meaning of Mississaugi not certain, but thought to mean "Snake-People.")

COOH [COO]. A chief of the tribe.

KAIWAHNEE [Kay-WAH-nee]. A chief of the tribe.

NOKALOKIS [NO-kah-LOW-kiss]. Squaw; mother of Cooh.

# THE MOHAWK TRIBE

(Significance of tribal name uncertain, but probably meaning "Wolf-People." Member of the Iroquois League.)

ABRAHAM. English name for Steyawa.

AROGHYIDECKER [Air-ROW-gee-HI-ih-deker]. Another Iroquois name for Nichus.

BRANT. English name for Sagayeanquarashtow.

DEGONWADONTI. [De-GON-wuh-DON-tee]. Indian wife of Sir William Johnson: Sister of Thayendanegea; daughter of Nichus; granddaughter of Sagayeanquarashtow.

GINGEGO [Jin-JEE-go]. Warrior of the village of Canajoharie.

HENDRIK. Dutch and English name for Tiyanoga.

JOSEPH BRANT. English name for Thayendanegea.

MOLLY BRANT. English name for Degonwadonti.

NICHUS [NICK-us]. A chief of the tribe; son of Sagayeanquarashtow; father of Degonwadonti and Thayendanegea.

NICHUS BRANT. Combined Indian-English name for Nichus.

SAGAYEANQUARASHTOW [Say-guh-YEE-an-kwah-RASH-tow]. A chief of the tribe; father of Sarghyidaugh and Nichus; grandfather of Degonwadonti and Thayendanegea.

SARGHYIDAUGH [Sar-gee-HY-ih-daw]. A subchief of the tribe; son of Sagayeanquarashtow; brother of Nichus; uncle of Degonwadonti and Thayendanegea.

SCARROYADDY [Scare-oh-YAD-dee]. A subchief of the tribe.

STEYAWA [Stay-YAH-wah]. A subchief of the tribe; brother of Tiyanoga.

TAGCHUENTO [Tag-chew-EN-tow]. Halfbreed son of Sir William Johnson.

THAYENDANEGEA [Thay-en-DAN-eh-JEE-ah]. A major chief of the tribe; founder of a confederacy; brother of Degonwadonti; son of Nichus; grandson of Sagayeanquarashtow.

TIYANOGA [Tie-an-NO-gah]. Principal chief of the tribe; predecessor of Wascaugh; brother of Steyawa.

TOOLAH. Warrior.

WASCAUGH [Waz-CAW]. Village chief of Teantontalogo; successor of Tiyanoga as principal chief of the tribe.

WILLIAM OF CANAJOHARIE. English nickname for Tagchuento.

# THE MOHEGAN TRIBE

(The name of this tribe means "Wolf.")

AIRE [AIR-ee]. Warrior.

# THE NIPISSING TRIBE

(The meaning of the name of this tribe is not known.)

KISENSIK [Kee-SEN-sik]. Principal chief of the tribe.

KONNIK [KAHN-nick]. Second principal chief of the tribe.

# THE ONEIDA TRIBE

(Meaning of the name of this tribe unknown. Member of the Iroquois League.)

COH-EGA [Co-EE-gah]. A chief of the tribe.

PLATTKOPF. Dutch name for Sconondoa.

SCONONDOA [Sko-non-DOUGH-AH]. Ancient chief of the tribe.

STOKKA [STOKE-ah]. A chief of the tribe.

TORACH [Tuh-ROSH]. A chief of the tribe.

# THE ONONDAGA TRIBE

(Meaning of the name of this tribe unknown. Member of the Iroquois League.)

ARAGHI [Uh-RAH-gee]. A subchief of the tribe.

ATOTARHO [Ah-tow-TAR-ho]. Powerful spirit-chief; founder of the Iroquois League.

CANASSATEGO [CAN-nuh-sah-TEE-go]. A village chief; principal speaker of the Iroquois League.

HIAWATHA. Powerful chief who helped to form the Iroquois League.

ONOKIO [Oh-NOKE-ee-oh]. A subchief of the tribe.

RED HEAD. English name for the principal chief of the Onondagas, whose Indian name is unrecorded; predecessor of Rozinogh-yata.

ROZINOGHYATA [RAHZ-in-oh-gee-YAH-tah]. Principal chief of the tribe; successor of Red Head.

TAOUNYAWATHA [TAY-yun-yuh-WAH-tha]. Another Indian name for Hiawatha.

# THE OTTAWA TRIBE

(The name of this tribe means "People-Who-Trade." Also frequently called Tawas.)

DIYAG [Tee-yag]. Great-grandfather of Pontiac.

MACKINAC [MACK-in-naw]. Principal chief of the tribe.

OOLATHA [Oh-oh-LATH-ah]. Squaw; wife of Charles Langlade.

PENNAHOUEL [Pen-nuh-WHO-ell]. Ancient chief.

PONTIAC. Village chief; successor of Winniwok as tribal war chief; chief of loose confederation of tribes.

WINNIWOK [Win-nee-wahk]. Village chief; tribal war chief; predecessor of Pontiac.

# THE SENECA TRIBE

(Meaning of the tribal name is unknown. Member of the Iroquois League).

ALEQUIPPA [Al-ee-kwip-puh]. Squaw chief of village.

FRON-GOTH. Village chief of Venango.

GROTA YOUNGA [GROW-tuh Yung-ah]. A chief of the tribe.

HALF KING. English name for Monakaduto.

HANGING BELT. A chief of the tribe; Indian name not recorded.

KAENDAE [CANE-die]. A chief of the tribe.

KENEGHTAUGH [Ken-NEG-taw]. Chief of the village of La Paille Coupée.

MONAKADUTO. Village chief.

OLD BELT. English name of a chief of the tribe; Indian name unrecorded.

QUEEN ALEQUIPPA. English term for Alequippa.

SEQUAHE [See-KWAH-hee]. Warrior.

YELLOW EYES. English name of subchief of the village of La Paille Coupée.


## THE SHAWNEE TRIBE

(The name of the tribe means "People-of-the-South.")

BLACK FISH. English name for She-me-ne-to.

BLACK HOOF. English name for Catahecassa.

CATAHECASSA [CAT-ah-hee-CASS-suh]. Third principal chief of the tribe.

CORNSTALK. English name for Hokolesqua.

GRENADIER SQUAW. English term for Non-hel-e-ma.

HOKOLESQUA [HOKE-oh-les-kwah]. Principal chief of the tribe; brother of Silverheels and Non-hel-e-ma.

KI-KUSGOW-LOWA [KEE-KUSS-go-LOW-wah]. Village chief; chief of the Thawegila sept.

MOLUNTHA [Mo-LUN-tha]. Village chief; chief of the Maykujay sept.

NON-HEL-E-MA. Village squaw-chief; sister of Hokolesqua and Silverheels.

PUCKSINWAH [Puck-SIN-wah]. Village chief of Kispoko Town; chief of Kispokotha sept; tribal war chief; father of Tecumseh.

RED HAWK. Second village chief of Sinioto. Indian name unrecorded.

SHE-ME-NE-TO. Second village chief of Kispoko Town; second chief of Kispokotha sept; second tribal war chief.

SILVERHEELS. English name of subchief of tribe; brother of Hokolesqua and Non-hel-e-ma.

# INDEX

739

742

746

748

Vitry, Catiche, 90
Vitry, Catrine, 90

Wabash River, 8, 10, 21, 35, 36, 44, 106, 120, 197, 206
Waggoner, Capt. Phineas, 335-36
Walhonding River, 20
Walhonding Valley, 120
Walker, Pvt. Peter, 462
Wamsutta (Alexander), x
Ward, Capt. Edward, 266, 459-61
Warner, Pvt. Edgar, 395
Warraghiyagey. See Johnson, William
Warren, Adm. Peter, 25, 30-33, 63, 67, 696
Warren, Susannah Delancey, 25
Warrensburg, N.Y., 32-33, 38-39, 49, 50
Wascaugh, Chief, 65, 75, 76-77, 80, 150-53, 227, 355, 400, 411, 414, 445-49, 451-53
Washington, John Augustine, 355
Washington, George, 380, 395, 633, 634; leads protest expedition to French, 240-41, 245, 248-59; popularity and promotion, 259-61; appointed to construct Ohio fort, 260-61, 263-64; protests pay, 264; ambushes French spying party, 267-68, 269-71, 273; poor position, 274-77; commands army, 278; foolhardy march, 279-80; builds Ft. Necessity, 280, 282-83; defeat at Ft. Necessity, 282-87; effect of defeat, 290-91; exasperated by public apathy, 308; conflict with Braddock, 309-11; irritated by slow march to Duquesne, 325-27; at ambush of Braddock's army 331-32, 337, 339; retreats, 347-48; reports on action, 354; demands assistance against frontier raids, 402-403; desire to retaliate for raids, 417; advances to Duquesne, 634
Washington, Lawrence, 240
Waugoshance, 43
Webb, Gen. Daniel, 419, 432-34,
467, 470-72, 489-90, 516-18, 526-35, 542-44
Weisenberg, Ann, 50, 93, 135
Weisenberg, Catherine (Catty), 49-51, 64, 65, 66, 67, 88, 93, 135, 453
Weisenberg, John, 50, 93, 135
Weisenberg, Mary, 64, 93, 135
Weiser, Conrad, xi, 66, 82, 272, 289, 402
West, Capt. Benjamin, 635
Westover, Mass., 25
Wheeling Creek, 144
White Eyes, Chief, 313, 329, 334, 454
White River, 106
White Woman's Creek, 163
Whiting, Lt. Col. Richard, 382, 384
Whitworth, Miles, 538
Williams, Col. Ephraim, 364-65, 381-83, 386, 390, 394
Williams, Col. Israel, 364, 584
Williams, Josiah, 394
Williams, Col. Stephen, 365, 375-76
Williams, Dr. Thomas, 390-94
Williams, Col. William, 584
Williamsburg, Va., 115, 135, 260, 269
Will's Creek Station, 248, 256, 259, 261-64 passim, 266, 277, 279, 287, 300, 308
Winchester, Va., 248, 262
Winniwok, Chief, 68
Winslow, 321
Wisconisco Creek, 396
Wolfe, Gen. James, 555, 560, 585, 648, 661, 679-87, 689
Wood Creek, 47, 73, 356, 366-67, 370, 373, 417-18, 433, 471-72, 588, 598, 654
Wraxall, Peter, 375, 390
Wyoming Valley, 29, 613

Yadkin River, 172
Yellow Eyes, Chief, 139-40
York Co., Pa., 309
Youghiogheny Valley, 46, 488
Young, Col., 526, 536